I'M KEITH HERNANDEZ

A Memoir

KEITH HERNANDEZ

LITTLE, BROWN AND COMPANY

LARGE PRINT EDITION

Little, Brown and Company
Hachette Book Group
1290 Avenue of the Americas, New York, NY 10104
littlebrown.com

First Edition: May 2018

Little, Brown and Company is a division of Hachette Book Group, Inc. The Little, Brown name and logo are trademarks of Hachette Book Group, Inc.

The publisher is not responsible for websites (or their content) that are not owned by the publisher.

The Hachette Speakers Bureau provides a wide range of authors for speaking events. To find out more, go to hachettespeakersbureau.com or call (866) 376-6591.

ISBN 978-0-316-39573-1 (hc) / 978-0-316-55243-1 (large print) / 978-0-316-41981-9 (signed edition) / 978-0-316-52686-9 (Barnes & Noble signed edition)
LCCN 2017963935

10 9 8 7 6 5 4 3 2 1

LSC-C

Book design by Marie Mundaca

Printed in the United States of America

This book is dedicated to my mother and father, my three daughters—Jessie, Melissa, and Mary—Kenny Boyer, Lou Brock, Jack Buck, Héctor Cruz, Bob Kennedy Sr., George Kissell, Joe "Ducky" Medwick, Tony Santora, A. Ray Smith, Carl Vallero, Bill Webb, and, most important, my loving brother, Gary

CONTENTS

I'M
KEITH
HERNANDEZ

INTRODUCTION

I LOVE BASEBALL.

But I find most books about baseball players boring. There seems to be a standard template for how you write them. Maybe it's because there are so many of these books out there, but it feels like they've become a paint-by-numbers exercise, dictating *what* you talk about and *how* you talk about it.

Forget that. I'm Keith Hernandez. I want to write this my way.

When I was a kid, my father would come home from his twenty-four-hour fireman shift and bring fresh San Francisco sourdough bread from the local bakery. If we were lucky, he also would have stopped by the Spanish market and picked up chorizo sausage. The bread would still be warm from the baker's oven, and Mom would spread some butter or jelly over it and give it to my brother and me. Soft on the inside with a crust that made your teeth work just the right amount. It was wonderful. I want to make this book something like that. Something that you set your teeth into and say, "Keith, that's pretty good. More, please."

So I'll need to keep things easy and moving along. I want you to feel the spontaneity I feel when I reflect.

And I have specific periods I want to focus on. (In the broadcast booth, I find that when you try to talk about everything, you wind up saying nothing. People just tune you out, and even if they don't, they can't possibly learn very much.) I want to talk about my development as a baseball player and how it got me to the major leagues; I want to talk about how I gained the confidence to thrive in the bigs despite a grueling haul; and, finally, I want to talk about how my development as a young player affects how I see the game today from my seat in the broadcast booth.

Because I've spent most of my life around baseball, I have good stories to tell. And I love sharing them with others.

Like the other night: I was sitting at a table at Harvest on Fort Pond in Montauk, New York, with my good friends Paul and Chantal Weinhold. The place was packed with folks enjoying the cozy environment and excellent food, and I had brought a couple of bottles from my wine cellar for the table. We were happy, and the talk was easy and fun. It's always that way with Paul and Chantal, a married couple I've known since my playing days with the Mets.*

Somewhere along the way, we started talking about baseball—specifically, this year's Mets team. Paul, who's a psychologist and finds the mental aspects of the game fascinating, asked about a Mets starting pitcher, a flamethrower who was successful at getting batters out but had a tough time holding them on base during the rare occasions they got on. The opposing team had made five swipes against him a few nights earlier.

"He's been doing it one way for years," Paul said, referring to the pitcher's delivery to home plate. "And now people expect him to change. Can he?"

"Why not?" I said. "Doc [Gooden] did it at the start of his major league career. He had the same issue."

"But how difficult is that sort of adjustment?"

---

* I met Paul, who's nickname is "The Mayor" because he can start a conversation with anybody, at the old Vertical Club, which was located on 60th Street, between First and Second Avenues, right by the 59th Street Bridge.

Chantal asked. "After all, like the rest of us, aren't baseball players creatures of habit?"

I said it would take time, and, yes, some players get stuck when opponents expose a weakness.

"It's more about mental toughness than the actual adjustment," I said, and I told them how Nolan Ryan would storm around in between pitches, strutting like John Wayne ready for a gunfight in the town square. "You got the feeling that, if he had to, Nolan could throw the ball with his other hand and still find a way to get batters out. For this guy on the Mets, he's got to tap into that sort of mentality: *This is my mound, and I will do anything to protect it.* After that, it just becomes a matter of decreasing his delivery time to home plate while not giving up any of his outstanding stuff. It's that simple."

Then I recalled a story I had been told years earlier. To me, it defines that territorial attitude a pitcher must have to be successful.

"Did I ever tell you what Don Sutton told me? About what he did when Tommy Lasorda tried to mess with his pregame routine?" I asked while topping off the glasses with a 2007 Insignia. Paul and Chantal shook their heads, and I could see they wanted me to go on. I mean, it's Tommy Lasorda and Don Sutton, two Hall of Famers, so it was not a hard sell.

The Dodgers were in Pittsburgh for a series. They lost the first game, and Tommy Lasorda, the Dodgers' then-manager, was bent out of shape because the Pirates had stolen, like, five bases during the game. This was 1979 or 1980—Lasorda's third or fourth year as their manager. So Lasorda, who liked to cuss, came into the visitors' clubhouse after the game and began screaming at his pitchers. All of them. He yelled "You motherf—ers" this and "You c—suckers" that, and he told them that they all were coming out the next day, before the game, to practice holding runners on base.

Don Sutton, a veteran who was having another stellar season, raised his hand and said, "Hey, I'm pitching tomorrow. You still want me to come in at three?"

"You're goddamn right!" yelled Lasorda.

"Okay, I'll come in at three," Don said.

The next day Sutton and the rest of the starting staff showed up. It was the middle of the afternoon and on lousy Astroturf, so it was, like, 100 degrees. Lasorda had them all out there in the heat for about forty minutes, working on holding runners on base.

The game started and Sutton took the mound in the bottom of the first. Omar Moreno, the speedy base-stealing center fielder, led off for the Pirates, and Sutton gave up an immediate single. *On purpose.*

"I just threw a BP fastball down the middle" is what Don told me later. Sutton had great control and command of all five of his exceptional pitches: In the sixty-four times I faced him over my career, he walked me *twice*. That's 1 per 32 at-bats, and I averaged 1 walk per 6 at-bats over my career against the rest of the league. So if Don Sutton wanted to give you something you could slap, he could do it. The question was, why?

Now Sutton had Moreno on first—the exact situation Lasorda had him and the other pitchers working on before the game—and Sutton looked for his sign from the catcher, went into his stretch, and balked! On purpose!

"Lasorda never messed with me again," Sutton said.

Even though they're not ballplayers, Paul and Chantal understood the psychological significance of this story. Sutton was saying, *Okay, Lasorda, this is my day to pitch and my mound. I'm in control! Don't you dare screw with that again.* And a pitcher who's got that sort of cojones—giving a batter a free pass to second base just to make a point to his manager—will also have the guts and the grit to figure out how to keep winning ball games. He will make adjustments.*

"Now," I said to Chantal and Paul, "all quality major leaguers—pitchers and hitters—have that sort of moxie. Sutton had it in spades, of course, but everyone's got to have at least a little bit. Because a baseball career is really just a series of adjustments. Those who adjust get to continue, while those who don't need to find another line of work. So if this kid from the Mets is going to be around awhile, and I think he will be, he'll make the necessary adjustments and get over this speed bump, because it's his mound and nobody's going to take it away from him. He'll do what needs to be done, period. And the longer he can do that, the longer he'll be in the league."

Then I couldn't help myself—here we were talking baseball, and it brought me to another place. *Another time.* So I told my captive audience that I had one more story for them:

---

* It also shows a certain tenacity and stubbornness that is required in an athlete. But I wouldn't recommend this approach if you're a marginal, struggling, or striving young player. You're talking about a future Hall of Famer and a 300-plus-game winner in the prime of his career!

It was 1978, the year after my first breakout season with the Cardinals. The Reds were in town, and they had Tom Seaver going on the mound. Tom, of course, pitched a brilliant complete game and beat us 2–1 with vintage Seaver stuff. *Hard, off-the-table breaking ball, blazing fastball, painting the corners like a Dutch master.* And I remember coming back to the bench on that hot and humid night in St. Louis, after my second or third futile at-bat, and blurting out, "Goddamn, he's throwing hard!" And sitting next to me was Lou Brock, who simply said in his very soft and understated manner, "You should have seen him in '69."

Eleven days later, we were in Cincinnati and, lo and behold, Seaver was back on the mound, and I went up to the plate and dug in with my back foot *extra* deep to get ready for the heater. But to my surprise, I saw that Tom had nothing on his fastball. He couldn't break a pane of glass, as we say. *Is he playing with me?* So in my second at-bat I was suspicious and got ready for the gas. But it was the same thing—*no fastball!* This wasn't the Tom Seaver from eleven days ago—it was some "cunny thumber," throwing big, sweeping, slow curveballs and sinking changeups

10

over the outside corner, spotting fastballs, and throwing sliders inside just enough to keep me honest. He was *tossing salad up there*! But he made the most of what he had, and he never missed over the plate—if he missed, he missed out of the strike zone. All of this showed the intelligence, *and confidence,* of the man—he must have known in that first inning or warm-up session that he had zero and adapted accordingly.

"And what was the result?" I asked the table.

"A no-hitter," said Paul.

"That's right!" I said. "The only no-hitter of Tom's career. Imagine that! There had to have been a bit of satisfaction knowing that he'd achieved it without anything close to his usual dominant power stuff."*

"Had you ever seen an adjustment that stark by a player?" asked Chantal.

"Never," I said. "Before or since. One night he was Dr. Jekyll, the next, Mr. Hyde. It was amazing. But, again, Tom just understood what had to be done and made it happen."

From there, the conversation at the table

---

* Whenever I see Tom, we laugh about his magnificent start. I tell him he had nothing, and he agrees.

moved away from baseball, but the theme of performance and mindset hung around, a steady driver for the rest of the evening's talk. And that's the beauty of a good baseball story. It not only slides well into conversation but also feeds conversation. That's why it's the national pastime: it fits in with our own stories, ballplayers or not. Baseball is additive rather than disruptive or merely benign.

So how do I start *my* baseball story? How about this:

> *Hi. I'm Keith Hernandez—former St. Louis Cardinals and New York Mets first baseman turned broadcaster. If you didn't follow the game in the 1980s (or catch today's telecast), you may think we've never crossed paths. But you have seen* Seinfeld, *right?* Oh, that Keith Hernandez. *Yup, that's me.*

I guess that could work, but I'd really just be selling us both short. Because when you're fortunate enough to be around the game and in the public eye as much as I've been, you develop standard responses whenever people want to know something about you. Even if you're good at "being yourself," you still have your go-to's. And that sort of a beginning would send me on a path of a lot of go-to's.

Throw it on the boring pile . . .

I want to go deeper. I want to strip everything else away to reveal something about myself you can't "discover" in a Google search. *I want to get to the core of my baseball story.*

I should note that my original intention was to slog through my life, dragging you, the reader, along with me in this slow, chronological procession. Like a death march (and standard operating procedure for a sports memoir). Interestingly, I think my brief time on the *Seinfeld* set those many years ago has helped inspire me to do otherwise. Because it was there, seeing Jerry and company at work, that I first caught a glimpse of storytelling's creative process. Going into the week of shooting "The Boyfriend" episodes, I had thought that we would simply stick with the script. But once I was on set, I saw that the script—the original idea—was really just a starting place. There were three writers in addition to the show's creators—Larry David and Jerry—and then, of course, the incredibly talented principal actors. All of them had input into each scene. It was very experimental—*Let's try this; how about this?*—and I was fascinated by just how much the original scene could change once the ensemble's creative juices were flowing. And when you think about it, that inventiveness and spontaneity is actually a lot like playing in a baseball game, where you're forced to improvise almost constantly. Well, then, that's the way I wanted to go about this endeavor: loose and ready for anything.

Then it hit me one day in the grocery store:

That plane ride to Florida...1972...My first spring training...

That's where I want to start the book! So I thought for a while until I hit on another plane ride:

The year 1979...My manager told me, "You'll be in the lineup every day, even if it costs me my job."...My season turned around...

And those became my goalposts: Every time I tried to move beyond '79, I came back to that span of years—particularly to '74, '75, and '76. Those were the hardest yet most instructive years.

Talk to any player who was able to achieve a sustained career in the major leagues and ask him what the most important years in his career were. He'll say, "The hard ones." Because it's in those struggles, when you're fighting to survive, that you're actually learning how to *thrive* in baseball. (Though you may not realize it at the time, it's happening.) But first, the game will have its pound of flesh. And for some of us, like me, it was more like two pounds. You have to keep fighting. You have to bare your teeth and growl and claw and scratch until one day, still hanging on, you realize, *Hey, I'm a bona fide big leaguer and a damned good one!*

So that's what I want this book to be. A story about a promising talent who became a professional ballplayer with a lot of expectations but not necessarily with the moxie to "own it"—to get in the box against guys like Tom Seaver, Don Sutton, and Nolan Ryan and say, "Okay, I'm gonna go toe-to-toe with you, and I'm gonna win."

That sort of confidence came, but it took a while, and *that* journey—*the making of a player like Keith Hernandez*—feels like something worth sharing.

Something to chew on.

I realize that if you're an '86 Mets fan or you're looking for the story behind Whitey Herzog's '82 world-champ Cardinals, this book is a prequel to the movie. The in-depth stories about those teams are terrific but have also been exhaustively celebrated in magazines, films, and, of course, books (I've written a couple of them). My hope is that after reading this, you will better appreciate my role in and contribution to both of those storied teams and franchises.

I don't want to gloss over my "hard" years. They're too important to me—to my love of baseball. Because after withstanding them, I could withstand anything.

Okay. Let's begin our journey.

Part I
BRICKS AND MORTAR

CHAPTER 1

I'M IN A GROCERY store in South Florida, buying eggs.

But anybody looking at me standing here would say I'm staring at the eggs. There are rows and rows of them—dozens of raw eggs in delicate shells tucked away in soft packaging. One misstep by any of their handlers—human or domesticated fowl—en route to this shelf and *splat*, there goes the chance to become somebody's omelet.

I chuckle at this notion. *Kind of like the perilous route from Little League to the majors.*

And now I'm looking past the eggs—I'm a hundred miles away. I'm thinking. No, wait, I'm dreaming. I'm lost in something that happened years ago.

The phone buzzes in my pocket. It brings me back.

"Hello?"

It's my book agent.

"I was just thinking of a good place to start the book," I say.

The book agent gets excited, but I cut him off.

"I gotta buy some eggs. Can I call you back in twenty?"

He says okay, and I hang up and grab a dozen eggs. I go for the organic because that's what my present company at the condo wants. She's famished.

Publix Super Markets are king in South Florida. Every region of the country has their mega chains, and in the lovely Sunshine State, it's Publix. They got one on every corner. And you never know who you might run into. A bunch of former players live down here. I sometimes hang with Rusty Staub, Jim Kaat, Jim Palmer, and Mike Schmidt, to name a few. It's kind of like Disneyland—all these characters from the sport's yesteryear walking around. And they all shop at Publix. But I don't run into anyone today—it's just me and the eggs.

I drive home and park the 2006 Mercedes-Benz C55 AMG next to the 2015 BMW 650i. The Benz is great—the best car I've ever owned. *Zoom!* But the BMW has a convertible top, and that sure is delightful in the warm Florida winters. Such decadence. But you know what? I've worked hard my entire life to get where I am, and as with my poultry companions in the passenger seat, it wasn't a smooth ride by any stretch. More than once, I ended up with egg on my face.

I get home, and Hadji, my fifteen-year-old Bengal cat, greets me at the door. My Sancho Panza. I put the eggs in the fridge, step outside onto the balcony, and call my book agent back.

I'm standing out on the balcony, looking over the Intracoastal Waterway. It's a beautiful day, and there are a lot of boats on the water. A bunch of teenagers are on one; they're listening to music and the girls are sunbathing. My agent picks up and wants to know more about my idea for the book's opening. So I tell him the story I was thinking about back in the grocery store.

1972. I was getting ready to go to my first spring training. My dad, who was this tough Depression-era guy and hated blue jeans because they reminded him of his adolescent poverty, said he was going to help me pick out my wardrobe for the plane ride east.

"C'mon, Dad," I said. I was a kid of the '60s, so jeans were cool.

But he just shook his head, and we went out shopping. We came back with a long-sleeved solid purple shirt, a pair of black knit slacks with cheesy patterns stitched into them, and white patent-leather shoes.* *Ouch.* When my summer league baseball coach, Tony Santora, stopped by the house to say goodbye and wish me luck, he saw my outfit and said, "Keith, you look like the Cuban flag!"

"Thanks, Tony."

I hugged my parents goodbye at San Francisco International and flew east with this other kid, Marty DeMerritt, a big redheaded pitcher from South San Francisco who the St. Louis Cardinals had drafted twenty rounds before me. Marty wore an outfit that was somehow worse than mine—red on red. He looked like Bozo the Clown.

We'd faced each other in high school and summer leagues, so I knew Marty competitively, which is why we both acted like it was no big deal when the plane flew into a giant thunderstorm over the Gulf of Mexico. But I'm sure, deep down, Marty was terrified and, like me, thought we were going to die. I had never flown before, and there was all this lightning and the plane was bouncing up and down. Having been on a lot of airplane rides since, I can easily say that approach

---

* Patent-leather shoes, believe it or not, were "in" back then and worn by most of the big leaguers.

into Tampa is number one on the chart of check-your-lunch flights.

Safely landed in the Sunshine State, I was still scared to death—I was eighteen years old and suddenly on my own.

We collected our bags, and a Cardinals representative escorted us to a waiting van for transport to St. Petersburg, a small city less than thirty miles from central Tampa and home to the Cardinals' spring training complex. As we headed out, I felt like I was in a foreign country. Gone were the Northern California redwoods and sequoias, the coastal mountain ranges; instead there was a flat landscape dotted with palm trees and prehistoric-looking birds called pelicans.

Strange.

We came up to a series of cheap roadside motels scattered on both sides of the highway. Marty and I had been told our motel assignments in advance, and I was dropped off first. I stepped out of the van into the hot, sticky air, said goodbye to Marty, and headed to the motel's little office to check in. I can't remember the name of the motel, but it certainly wasn't the Ritz—just two twin beds, a shower, a black-and-white television, and one of those electric AC units hanging out a window.

As with the other five hundred players in

camp, this would be my home throughout spring training.*

I settled in quickly—I didn't have much stuff—and went to my suitcase for my Strat-O-Matic, a board game popular at the time and sort of the precursor to fantasy baseball. There were pitcher and player cards, and you'd roll three dice for the outcomes: hit, strikeout, walk, out, error. I'd invested months in the game over the winter, playing the entire National League 1971 season, managing all the teams, playing both sides. And I'd gotten through 127 games of the 162-game schedule.

That's 762 games.

Multiply that by the half hour it took to play one game, and I'd spent over two weeks of my life dedicated to the 1971 Strat-O-Matic season. I'd stashed the game, along with the fat spooled notebook where I kept extensive statistics game by game, month by month, at the bottom of my suitcase beneath my clothes. But the Strat-O-Matic wasn't there. It was gone!

Instantly, I knew why.

---

* Also taking up residence were more than a few giant cock-roaches. Floridians call them palmetto bugs. I didn't care what they were called; I had never laid eyes on a bug that large and they terrified me. *Where the hell am I?*

"Dad, where's my Strat-O-Matic?" I frantically yelled into the receiver of the motel phone. My parents had said I could call home, collect, once a week.

"You gotta concentrate on real baseball, Keith," my dad said. "No Strat-O-Matic."

Oh, the horror. Dad had been one step ahead of me—he'd figured it out and taken the game from my bag before I left. I telephoned my brother, who was on the road somewhere with the University of California Golden Bears baseball team—Gary was their starting first baseman—but he was little help. He just laughed and laughed. But I was crushed. I would never know who won the pennant that 1971 Strat-O-Matic season.*

There was no escape now—I was a professional baseball player, and no roll of the dice was going to help me get through.

---

* I never did finish that Strat-O-Matic season. When I went home after the season, I never took it back out. I guess that's what a year of professional ball does to a person: he craves the real thing.

CHAPTER 2

I VISIT MY OLDER brother and only sibling, Gary, in San Francisco, and we take the eighteen-mile drive south down the Cabrillo Highway to Pacifica.

There are easier, more direct routes, but we're taking it for old times' sake. Back in the '50s and early '60s, this was the only way to get to Pacifica from the city. We make our descent from the coastal hills of Daly City into the beach communities of Edgemont, Sharp Park, and Vallemar, and continue south over the small mountain crest just past Rockaway Beach, down into Linda Mar Valley.

Gary makes the left turn onto Linda Mar Boulevard, and a half mile inland we turn right onto Hermosa Avenue. "My God," I say to Gary, who's probably thinking the same thing. "It's so small." When we were kids, the street seemed about a mile long. But now I see it's only a bit more than a hundred yards. And I wonder how many times we walked and rode our bikes on this block—to school, to workouts—in rain, fog, wind, and sun.

We pull into the cul-de-sac in front of our old house. There is now a second story, and the small front yard has been replaced by a concrete walkway, but the brick facade and wishing well are still there. As little kids, Gary and I got a few days off from school to help Dad brick the wishing well. He loved using bricks to dress up the house. When Mom wanted a flower bed, he installed one across the front of the house with bricks.

That's still here, too.

But the fence he made—a ranch-style fence with wooden rails and, of course, brick pilings—is gone.

We get out of the car and stand in the cul-de-sac that was our first baseball diamond, and I wonder if there are any kids in the neighborhood still breaking windows with line drives. We must have broken the Barretts' window five times, and Dad would always immediately go over and clean up the glass and get a glazier over to replace the window. The Barretts never complained. It was just kids playing.

Gary and I stand in the street for another minute and take a last look at the house. There were four of us living here, plus a dog, Tex, then after Tex died, a Persian tomcat, Sinbad—1,100 square feet purchased with $12,000 and some help from Dad's GI Bill.

More than half a century ago.

I peek down the side of the house to the backyard. When we were boys it was just a quick scale over the backyard fence to the large artichoke farm, where we'd play hide-and-go-seek and sometimes cut through to get to school. And along the farm's southern edge was San Pedro Creek. The creek begins somewhere up in the surrounding coastal mountains, and as a kid I tried a few times to follow it to its source, but it just kept crawling around, up through the hills. So I never did find it. Mom didn't like us going down to the creek, but we'd sneak off anyway, playing cowboys and Indians with the other neighborhood kids. But between the dirt on our clothes and the painful poison-oak rashes, she'd usually find out. Eventually, she gave up—*boys will be boys*—and sometimes we'd head down to catch rainbow trout in one of the stream's deeper pools, and Mom would cook them on the stove for our lunch.

We're back in the car. Gary takes a right out of the neighborhood, back onto Linda Mar Boulevard, and I catch a glimpse of the old drainage ditch that trickles into the creek. We pass a mini mall with a pizza shop, where Ed and Jim's Union 76 used to be. The gas station sponsored our Little League teams. Ed was the old man and Jim was the son, maybe early forties, and they'd come over to watch our night games after they'd closed up for the evening. I remember Dad sketched out the design of the uniforms on a piece of paper—not only the shirts but also the pants, socks, and hats—and Ed and Jim paid to have them made. Mom cut out the letters and ironed them on the hats for all the kids on our team. *A family affair.*

The baseball fields aren't much farther—close enough that when we were kids we'd ride our bikes or walk—but they're gone, too. A private Christian school now stands where my friends and I played five years of Little League and Pony League ball, where Dad taught us everything, from baserunning and cutoffs to double plays and rundowns.

Gary and I talk about Mr. Otenello, another coach who helped Dad build the fields. He brought an earthmover from San Francisco to level the pasture, and we realize that he couldn't have driven one of those monstrous vehicles on the Pacific Coast Highway—he must have loaded it up on a flatbed and hauled it down.

And after they'd prepared the field, Dad would

head out in the early mornings to water the seeds so they would take root and grow strong.

Pacifica, 1959

I am five and I spend hours standing on our front lawn, throwing a tennis ball against the side wall of our garage about fifteen feet away.

The wall isn't smooth. Its facade is brick, with mortar inset between the brick. So if I throw the ball against the wall, it might hit a corner of the brick or an indentation within the brick itself and not come straight back.

It is unpredictable, just like a live batter.

That's what makes it fun. The ball might hit flush and bounce back straight; it might hit on a lower angle and come down hard; it might hit the upper part and speed through the air; and if it hit the side, it could go left or right. Sometimes I have to dive. Sometimes I have to charge. Sometimes it's a blooper and I have to leap. And as I get better, I move in closer and closer, which gives me much less time to react. All good for agility and quickness. Lord knows how many times Mom scrubbed the grass stains out of my jeans.

Pretending I am an All-Star shortstop like Pittsburgh's Dick Groat, I will play games against the wall: a clean fielding with a sharp throw is an out; a ball that gets by me up the middle is a single; down the line is a double. If the bases are loaded with less than two outs, I'll move in closer and play the hot corner over at third.

I love these imaginary games and will play them until Mom calls me in for dinner or the sun goes down. Sometimes Gary will join me—we'll be middle infielders working together. Otherwise, I'll be by myself, off in my own little world.

CHAPTER 3

MY ROOMMATE FOR 1972 spring training finally showed up around 9 p.m. Mets fans remember Mike Vail well because in 1975 he set a modern MLB rookie record with a twenty-three-game hitting streak, which not only began with his first MLB at-bat but also was the longest hitting streak in Mets franchise history.*

Imagine that, setting a franchise hit record right out of the gate...

But at that time, Mike was just another Bay Area kid, drafted out of De Anza College in Cupertino. A couple of doors down from us were Jerry Mumphrey and Larry Herndon, two African Americans who would have long careers in the big leagues. Jerry was from Tyler, Texas; Larry hailed from Sunflower, Mississippi.

---

* Both records have since been eclipsed.

I remember one hot, humid evening we were sitting around outside our rooms, and Larry and Mumph were eating something out of a big glass jar.

"You want one, Keith?" they asked.

"What the hell is it?"

"Pickled pigs' feet," they told me.

I declined, and they just laughed and said, "What's wrong with you?"

This was part of the beauty of coming into the world of Major League Baseball: it plucked me out of my little Northern California bubble and introduced me to a wide variety of people from across the country. And, of course, there were plenty of players from the Caribbean and Latin America. St. Petersburg of 1972 and every other town I played professional ball in after that was a heck of a place for a young person to meet folks from all over.

But besides baseball, there wasn't much for our eclectic bunch to do: St. Pete's small downtown was a long bus ride away (no one had a car) and seemed to be inhabited exclusively by retirees and octogenarians. The one thing that saved us from complete boredom was the ill-maintained shuffleboard court on the motel property.

Food, unfortunately, was just as scarce as the entertainment. Before workouts, we were given breakfast, which consisted of toast, bagels, and cold cereal along with coffee, milk, and juice. There was also a lunch of soup and crackers. It was hardly enough sustenance for a professional baseball player trying to make the cut. So after practice we would take the city bus down Fourth Street to Morrison's Cafeteria, an all-you-can-eat restaurant chain.

Thank God for Morrison's.

It was six dollars for dinner—a good thing because we weren't paid a salary during spring training, and our weekly allowance was just seventy-five dollars (ten dollars a day for food and five dollars for laundry). There would be around twenty of us scarfing down plate after plate, the grayheads at the rest of the tables watching in shock and awe.

It didn't really matter that there were more things to do on the moon than in St. Pete, because after a long day's practice and stuffing ourselves to the gills at Morrison's, we were exhausted: a few rounds of shuffleboard, then we'd hit the sack. Team busses started rolling to the complex at 8 a.m., and we were expected to be in uniform and ready to go by 10.

The practice regimen consisted of calisthenics, running, drills, fundamentals of all sorts, more running, and then actual live batting practice, shagging, and, for us infielders, lots of ground balls until the lunch break at noon. *Soup anyone?* Then we were back out on the field with more BP and "fundies" until everyone—all 500 of us—had hit. At around 4 p.m., the day was finished off with yet more running, then we'd shower and bus back to the motel, and it was off to Morrison's again.

Of the 500 players, only 175 would find a spot on one of the Cardinals' seven minor league teams. Competition was keen, and the workouts had to be well structured in order for each player to show his abilities to the minor league brass, managers, hitting instructors, and pitching coaches. They all would be scattered around the four fields, in the batting cages, and up in the observational tower located in the middle of the complex. As a player, you felt their eyes upon you at all times, and you tried *very, very* hard to impress them. That was the goal: *to make a good impression.*

So what was their first impression of me?

Well, have you ever seen the movie *The Natural*? It's one of my favorites. Robert Redford is perfect as Roy Hobbs, an immensely talented baseball player with a cryptic past who, after years of suffering, finally gets a second chance to play with a big-league team. In the film, there's this great scene where Hobbs takes his first BP session. It's in the big ballpark, and all the players and coaches are there, halfheartedly watching Hobbs, who's pushing forty, step into the batter's box. He takes his first cut and crushes the ball over the right-field fence, putting it way up into the seats. The next ten swings yield a similar result: Hobbs, the natural, hitting balls so pure and long that even the great Ted Williams would be envious. Only in Hollywood! (But Redford has a nice, athletic swing; and Randy Newman's music score is off the charts.)

Well, the circumstances surrounding *my* first professional BP session on that opening day of camp couldn't have been any more different, or less magnificent.

First, I was still a kid, just old enough to buy cigarettes and girlie magazines from the drugstore (hypothetically). Second, I wasn't a nobody; in fact, I was a "bonus baby," which meant the Cardinals had paid big money to sign me. I knew the Cardinals' brass and coaches as well as some informed players would be watching the $30K buy from the forty-second round of the draft. Third, and I'm not proud of this, I whiffed on my first swing.

I guess I thought everyone was going to be hurling 190-mile-per-hour fastballs, and, in retrospect,

I should've taken the first pitch. But I swung before the ball was even halfway home. Of course, there were tons of players and coaches around the batting cage to witness this whiff on 85-mile-per-hour cheese, and I heard a few chuckles coming from behind the cage.

The second pitch came in, and this time I murdered the ball...

Just joking. The pitcher jammed the crap out of me, and I sent a dribbler halfway to first base. So it wasn't exactly a Hollywood introduction. But by the fourth pitch or so, I got my bearings, worked back over the middle of the plate, and had a decent BP session. (As it turned out, I wasn't the only one nervous that day: my flight buddy, Marty DeMerritt, threw a curveball over the batting cage his first time out pitching. I'd never seen that before.)

So why was I a big-shot "bonus baby"? Again, I'd been picked in a distant galaxy otherwise known as the forty-second round of the June 1971 amateur draft; usually guys taken that late aren't even signed, let alone given big money. The short answer is that I should have been taken in the early rounds, but my high school coach was a bit of a jerk, so I didn't play baseball during my senior year. It wasn't until *after* the draft and I kicked butt in summer ball that the Cardinals said, "We really gotta sign this kid." Otherwise, I was off to college (I'd been heavily recruited by Stanford and Cal for both baseball and football, and I'd received congressional consent to the Air Force and Naval Academies).

So it all worked out. I had been a good student in high school, but I wasn't interested in anything other than playing professional baseball. If there had been any doubt about that, it went away after I signed with the Cardinals and Dad insisted I enroll in a semester's worth of classes at the junior college while I waited for spring training. *Screw that.* Instead, I'd head out of the house every morning, drive my parents' car to the San Fran airport, and park in the old high school lovers' lane to watch the planes take off until I went to sleep. I got incompletes across the board, and, of course, the report card was sent home.

"Keith, that's on your permanent scholastic record," my brother, who was a senior at Cal Berkeley, told me. "You should've just dropped out if you didn't want to go."

Well, I didn't know all that, and I didn't care. Dad was mad, but not as mad as I thought he'd be. Of course, it wasn't an adult conversation we had—Dad liked to fly off the handle and yell and scream—but he relented, and I sensed that he was impressed by my single-mindedness: *baseball superstar or bust*.

Back to camp.

Initial cuts were made, and those of us remaining were organized into groups corresponding to the respective minor league teams we would most likely be playing for that season. At the lowest level of the Cardinals' minor league food chain was the Gulf Coast League. They would play their season at the spring training facility with no fanfare and all day games. The next step up was A ball, and there the Cardinals placed three teams: Cedar Rapids, Iowa, was the lowest A ball classification in the Midwest League; St. Petersburg in the Florida State League was a tough midlevel A league; and Modesto, California, was the highest A ball classification in the California State League. Then came AA at Little Rock, Arkansas, in the Texas League, and finally AAA Tulsa, Oklahoma, in the American Association.

I was placed at St. Petersburg in the Florida State League under the command of chain-smoking hard-ass Roy Majtyka. I remember one day in early spring training, Roy was hitting me fungoes at first and I was flashing my future Gold Glove leather, making all the plays, catching everything to my right, then left, soft, then hard. After about twenty-five minutes of hitting grounders in the Florida heat, an exhausted Roy said, "Okay, that's enough." When I told him I wanted more, he just laughed. "Come see me in ten years—it'll be enough then." So I guess the manager expected that I'd be sticking around for a while.

Cuts were always made on a Sunday before Monday's new payday for the upcoming week. But I really didn't have to worry about being cut that first spring training because the organization had invested a lot of money in me as a prospect. It meant I had time to develop, which is comforting to a young person who's away from home for the first time and trying to get his bearings in a highly competitive field. Otherwise, it would have been a very stressful period—you could sense the tension building within most of the players as the numbers whittled down. I'm confident I would have made it—bonus baby or not—but baseball is about rhythm for me, and it would have been much harder to find that rhythm with the extra pressure of making the cut.

While I relaxed, Mike Vail, my roommate, was convinced that his head was on the chopping block. Poor Mike spent the whole night before final cuts pacing back and forth in our room.

"I'm toast," he'd woefully announce every five minutes.

"You're not toast. Go to sleep." I'd seen Mike hit. He had a nice swing, and besides, he was a fourth-round pick by the Cardinals.

"That's easy for you to say, Bonus Baby!"

"You're right. You're toast. Now please shut up and go to sleep."

Well, that approach didn't work either, so we both were awake most of the night. But Mike survived the cut, of course, and he and I finished camp with our dreams of one day playing in the major leagues intact.

One night during that final week of camp, some of us took the bus downtown to watch the major leaguers play. Our games usually coincided, but this was an exception. The lights were on at Al Lang Field, and the Cardinals were playing the Mets. The organization had given us tickets and put us in the peanut gallery. But spring training stadiums are really just minor league parks, and I was excited to see a big-league game this close up.

We sat down, and there they were—the mighty Cardinals—taking infield and dressed in their home "whites": Gibson, Brock, Wise, Matty Alou, Ted Simmons, and last year's batting champ and MVP, Joe Torre. It just made me want to be there on that team and in that uniform: the red birds perched on the yellow bat, my last name printed in an arc above my number on my back.

It was all so close, I could feel it.

And yet so far. Within a few days of breaking camp and starting the A ball season, I fractured the ulna in my right forearm. It had been just a routine putout play following a swinging bunt—something I'd done already a million times at camp—but the hard throw from the third baseman sank down toward the churning knees of the runner, who also happened to be about six inches inside the foul line. *Crack!* The doc put a cast on my arm, and I missed the first 48 games of St. Pete's 132-game schedule.

Good grief.

CHAPTER 4

Pacifica, 1960

MOM AND DAD THROW *Gary and me into the Mercury station wagon and, together, we head up the Pacific Coast Highway to San Francisco. We make this trip twice a month to pick up Dad's paycheck and then visit my grandparents. Dad drives and we listen to the radio, Mom dialing in Don Sherwood on KSFO. Gary and I laugh as Sherwood does his crooner impersonation between songs.*

On this particular trip, we pick up Dad's paycheck but don't go to my grandparents'. Instead, Dad steers along Taraval Street near the Fleishhacker Zoo to Flying Goose Sporting Goods. We aren't a rich family—Dad often has to make sure he deposits his fireman's paycheck on the first and fifteenth of each month to be able to cover the mortgage, utilities, and grocery bills—but the Flying Goose will become a regular destination in the future. Dad, a former professional baseball player, will make sure his boys always have the proper equipment.

Dad is a first-generation American. His parents emigrated from Spain via the Pacific, arriving in San Francisco in 1916. He is proud of his Spanish heritage, frequently gathering Gary and me together and asking, "Now, sons, who are you?"

"Spaniards, Father!" we say, trying to match his gusto.

"And where is Spain?" he asks.

We'll find the globe in Gary's room and point to the place Dad has already shown us a million times. "In Europe, Father!"

"Correct! Don't forget this!"

But Dad loves America. "In America," he says, "you can do anything you want so long as you put your mind to it and work hard enough." That "thing" for Dad, like for many San Francisco boys growing up during the teens and twenties of the twentieth century (including one named Joe DiMaggio), had been baseball. A standout at Mission High School, John Hernandez broke all kinds of school records, leading his team to a championship game at Seals Stadium, where he hit five doubles, was named MVP, and was christened by the city as the next big star to come out of the Bay Area.

But Dad's father, Pa, who spoke no English, never knew much about his son's baseball accomplishments. While his son played on the ball fields, Pa worked long hours for the Simmons mattress company as an upholsterer. Being European, he did not understand baseball and always chided his son to stop playing silly games and go to work. The only game he ever went to was his son's championship game at Seals Stadium, and only after seeing that his son was obviously very good and everyone in the crowd was talking about him as the next Joltin' Joe did Pa seem to care.

"He had no problem taking an interest then—after I'd done all the hard work," Dad will sometimes say.

So Dad had never gotten the support that he is now determined to give Gary and me, his two sons, and an hour after parking the station wagon, he leads us out of the sporting goods store carrying two brand-new wooden bats. On the way home, Dad switches off the radio and says, "Hitting lesson number one, boys: Always have a bat in your hands that you can handle. Never too heavy. Never too light. You should swing the bat, not let the bat swing you."

As usual, Dad parks the station wagon on the street in front of our house. There is a two-car garage, but Dad is always creating something in there. He loves working with his hands—woodworking, masonry, or artistic endeavors—so he needs the space for his saws, tools, and workbench. The washer and dryer are in there, too. It's *not a mess, but it's tight. He'll squeeze the car inside once he's finished working for the day.*

Gary and I shuffle out of the car and follow Dad into the garage. The bats are official Little League and much too long and heavy for us. Dad saws the barrel ends down, then secures the bats in a vise and sands them. Finally, he hands each of his two sons a custom-fitted bat.

Then he takes us outside, closes the garage door, and begins throwing batting practice against it. He throws tennis balls because they are soft and don't hurt if they hit us. We are so young—just learning this game—and he wants us to be at ease, without fear. He wants us to love baseball.

We'll take BP off Dad any day he's home from work—twice a day in the summertime. Dad works a twenty-four-hour shift at the fire station and then is home for forty-eight hours. He leaves in the morning and is back the next day for breakfast. After a nap, he's all ours for two days.

CHAPTER 5

THE FLORIDA STATE LEAGUE in 1972 was (and still is) a pitcher's league—the big ballparks and heavy summer air made it more difficult for the hitters to put up high averages or power numbers. Being a Northern California kid, I'd never experienced anything like that tropical swelter, and my uniform would be soaked before the end of the national anthem.

But I was eighteen and strong, and after missing the first 48 games because of my fractured forearm, I played the remaining 84, hitting .256 with 16 doubles, 5 triples, 5 home runs, and 41 RBI. To me, a guy who had hit well over .400 his entire baseball life, that .256 was a hard pill to swallow; but my teammate Mike Potter, who would play with my brother in Modesto, later told Gary that it was the "hardest hit" .256 he'd ever seen.

It's important to note that back then power numbers were not emphasized like in today's player development. If the coaches and brass felt there was power potential in a kid, they would let it come at its own pace. For me—a player who was not interested in hitting anything but line drives and a .300 batting average—this was extremely helpful. It meant that I could concentrate on my game and not worry about "lifting" the ball over the fences.

Part of the reason organizations could be so patient with their prospects was because they mainly drafted kids out of high school, and there wasn't any rush to bring them up. They loved to get a player at the tender age of eighteen and begin teaching him the proper way to play the game. The upside was if the kid progressed naturally, he could be in the bigs in his early twenties. So that gave me time to develop at the plate. As for defense, I was coming along just fine. Some execs, scouts, and coaches claimed that young Keith Hernandez was the best defensive first baseman—at any level—they'd come across in quite some time.

The biggest adjustment was just playing so much baseball. High school players practice two hours a day and play two games in a week. That all changes when you become a professional: 90 percent of your time is spent playing baseball or traveling for away games.

And it's not like the travel is five-star. For the closer Western Division games, we'd bus to the parks in uniform, play the game, and bus back for a shower at our clubhouse. Then we'd sleep in our own beds, report to the clubhouse the next afternoon, and bus back to the same ballpark for game two of the three-game series. For away games to the Eastern Division, we'd stay in "el cheapo" motels. Real fleabag places. One time in Daytona my teammate Mark Gasperino was bitten on the neck by a spider in the middle of the night and had to be rushed to an emergency room. Mark would be okay, but not before his throat swelled to a life-threatening softball size. I didn't sleep a wink the rest of our stay, but such was life in the minor leagues, where even the budget for such crucial items as baseball bats was tight.*

But all that was part of the charm of the minor leagues and Florida in the '70s: lots of baseball

---

* We were each asked at the beginning of the season what bat model we liked. "Henry Aaron R43 model, thirty-five inch, thirty-three ounce," I told them, and the bats came in. Then our owner, Ralph Miller, who couldn't have made much money on the team, relentlessly gathered all the broken bats over the course of the long season to trade them in to the Louisville Slugger and Adirondack bat companies for discounts on the next season's bats.

and sunshine with little pay and few amenities. Towns like West Palm Beach—now a bustling mass of suburbia—were only small seaside communities yet to be consumed by overcrowded roads, shopping malls, and golf courses. So I enjoyed the bouncing around. Unfortunately, due to my fractured forearm, I missed the southern swing, which included a series against the independent team in Key West—that sleepy little village at the tail end of the country and a remnant of old "Hemingway" Florida.*

Speaking of old-school, Early Wynn, a Hall of Fame pitcher from the '40s, '50s, and early '60s, was the manager of the Orlando Twins. I went up to him during BP before a game and introduced myself, a young starstruck kid. But Mr. Wynn very coolly shook my hand and walked away, a look of disdain on his face. Instantly, I understood the message: *Never talk to the opponent.* My father, a former minor league ballplayer, preached the same tough, Depression-era philosophy.

---

* I finally did make it to Key West in 2012. But by then it was overrun with tourists shuttling back and forth from countless cruise ships and rum bars all playing the same five or six Jimmy Buffett tunes. I was on my honeymoon with my second wife, and after a couple days, we'd had enough of "Margaritaville" and pulled anchor.

Oh well… at least I got to shake the hand of a three-hundred-game winner.

But I didn't always have such a tough skin that season. That was evident during one twi-night doubleheader when I experienced my first intense razzing. It came from about half a dozen college-aged kids seated a few rows back on the first base side and lasted throughout the first game. *Please, God,* I thought, *don't have them stay for the second game.* But when I walked out of the clubhouse to the field, there they were. Waiting. Stupidly, I challenged them to come over the fence: "I'll kick all your asses," I yelled, and of course that was all the encouragement they needed. It got the best of me, and I made two errors in the second game: a towering pop-up that I got in my glove only to drop, and an easy, long pickup at the bag.

Cue the jerk-offs!

After the game, manager Roy Majtyka called me into his office, closed the door, and went through his spiel about how razzing is just a part of the game and a player needs to let it roll off his back. I started to respond but instead broke down in tears. And Roy, cigarette in his mouth, leaned forward, put his hand on his forehead, and blurted, "Oh Jesus." But he calmed me down, and that was the end of it. I guess it's one of the downsides of dealing with kids right out of high school—they can be tenderfoots—and walking back to the motel, I felt like the world's biggest wuss.

I did need a pick-me-up every now and then during the long season, and at some point my high school sweetheart came for a visit. Around four days into her stay, Dad called me and was livid—someone in the organization had tipped him off.

"Get her on a plane, ASAP!" Dad boomed. "Suppose you get her pregnant! You don't need the added responsibility of being married at your age and at this stage of your career! I've seen careers ruined in the sheets! You need to be focused on making it to the big leagues! What the hell's wrong with you?"

But Dad was right—the relationship wasn't practical, and she eventually made it home. She would meet someone else later that summer, and that was the end of us. It hurt, but I got over it, and I suppose it had to happen.

Sometime after that, I hit my first professional batting slump, and I didn't handle it well. Fortunately, I had my brother to lean on. Gary, an all-American first baseman with Cal, had been drafted by the Cardinals in the seventeenth round of the June 1972 draft and sent to Sarasota's Gulf Coast League in the late summer. We talked on the phone weekly. When I hit my drought at the plate, Gary must have sensed I was down in the dumps, and a few hours after hanging up, when I was warming up in front of our dugout before our game in St. Pete, I heard, *"Hey, Keith!"*

"Gary?"

I couldn't believe it! My big brother, along with a couple of his teammates, was in the house. We chatted before the game, Gary pumping me full of confidence, and I broke out of the slump that night with a multi-hit/RBI game. Despite needing to return to his apartment and get a good night's sleep because they only played day games in the Gulf Coast League, he stayed the entire game and came into our clubhouse afterward. Only when he was satisfied that his positive vibes had done the trick did he drive the ninety minutes back to Sarasota.

Over the course of a long season, you inevitably run into two or three slumps. By slumps, I mean an 8 for 60. That's, like, fifteen games—or two weeks—of coming to the park and feeling like a monkey humping a football. It's as if you'd never had a baseball bat in your hands before. I'd call home and say to Dad, "I'm feeling crappy at the plate," and we'd talk through my at-bats. My father knew my swing better than anyone, and he could decipher what I was doing wrong based on just what I told him: "Sounds like you're shortening up"; "Keep your hands back"; "Step up in the box to catch that sinker before it breaks." But sometimes he'd just say, "It sounds like you're solid, son. Just keep swinging the bat."

But it's hard to be patient in a slump. In that first year, I tended to handle them with anger, and a bad temper only makes it worse. I never broke any watercoolers, but I did slam my share of helmets. What galled me most was when I smoked a BB right at someone for an out. That would send me through the roof. *How can I get out of this slump if every time I rip the ball it's right at the other team?* It really does feel like you're jinxed.

I remember one home game when I came up to the plate with the bases loaded. It was in the later innings of a tight game, and I hit a bullet at the third baseman. He caught it for the out, and I took a deep breath, seething inside, but Majtyka had been trying to get me to calm down in situations like this. So I walked back to our third base dugout, trying to keep my composure, and just before I reached the first step down into the sunken dugout, my teammate Pat McCray greeted me with a big "Hang in there, Keith." He meant well, of course, but I snapped—not at him, but at the situation—and I kicked the ground, and dirt splattered into Pat's face. I was mortified and apologized profusely to Pat, who spent the next few minutes getting the grit out of his eyes.

It was also unfortunate that some of the brass had witnessed the outburst. Joe Medwick, the Cards' minor league batting instructor, was in town, along with the general manager of the Los Angeles Dodgers, Al Campanis, who told Medwick how that sort of player would never get to wear a Dodgers uniform.

The next day, Medwick came up to me and related to me what Campanis had said. "I thought he was being a little hard on you, Keith," Medwick said. "I told him so, but you've gotta quit this tantrum business and remember that the good hitters hit more balls hard right at people than they hit bloopers or bleeders. It's just part of the game."

That was Joe Medwick: a hard-nosed guy who was very honest in his criticisms as well as his praises. He was also chock-full of great baseball stories, and when he was on the road with us, the other players and I would usually find him at the motel pool, soaking in the sun—drink in hand—and he'd start rattling them off.

Joe "Ducky" Medwick had been a member of

the famous 1934 Cardinals, aka the Gashouse Gang, and the last National Leaguer to win the Triple Crown (1937). The man was a legend. One of my favorite stories was when Medwick was famously taken out of the Cardinals' seventh-game-blowout World Series victory in 1934 in the bottom of the sixth for sliding hard into third base on an RBI triple that increased the Cardinals' lead to 8–0. The game was played at Detroit's Navin Field, and some Tigers fans thought the slide had been dirty, or at least unnecessary due to the Cardinals' big lead.

"They started throwing all sorts of things at me," Joe recalled. "Bottles, fruit, and whatever else they had on hand." It got so bad, he said, that the commissioner, Kenesaw Mountain Landis, removed him from the game for safety reasons. Joe was obviously from a generation that gave little quarter, but he made it out of Detroit in one piece and went on to celebrate the Cards' world championship unscathed.

Unfortunately, my first professional season ended in less fanfare: we finished 66–66, a distant fourteen games behind the Western Division champion, the Daytona Beach Dodgers.

But I was learning a lot about baseball to go along with that humbling .256 average, and even more about myself.

CHAPTER 6

Pacifica, 1961

I AM SEVEN; GARY *is nine. We're standing in the outfield grass along with the other boys trying out for Little League. Technically, I'm not old enough to play—I have to wait another year to join the ranks. But my dad, who organized the draft, lets me fart around in the outfield and shag balls with the older kids.*

I wait my turn in line. When it comes, Mr. Otenello—one of the league coaches—smacks a high popper in my general direction. I get under it, catch it, throw it back, and ready myself for his next swing. This time it's a line drive. I get a bead on the ball, chase it down, and catch it. I throw it back. I shag a few more balls and return to the line with the other kids to wait for the next round.

At some point during this repeated process Mr. Otenello calls my father over.

"Hey, John!" he yells. "You need to see this."

Mr. Otenello hits me a series of hot smashes—

line drives and fly balls. Each time, I scamper to my left or my right, behind me or out in front, and make the catch. Mr. Otenello glances at my father. Then he belts a series of soaring fly balls.

"I can't hit them any higher, John," he says to my father.

My dad will recount this story to me years later, saying, "You were camped under everything and catching on the run like you'd been playing the game for a decade. Some of the other kids could catch, too, but none of them made it look so easy."

CHAPTER 7

AFTER THE 1972 SEASON in St. Pete, I was itching to get back home to San Francisco.

I had been paid only $500 per month during the season—barely enough to subsist on, let alone save—so I didn't have many other options. Dad thankfully gave up the notion that I would take another semester at community college, and I planned to just putter around. But I wasn't home two days when the Cardinals' director of player development, Bob Kennedy Sr., called and said he wanted me to join the Tulsa Oilers, the organization's AAA team. Evidently, the team's first baseman, future Red Sox player Mike Fiore, had injured his hand and was out for the remaining twelve games of the AAA season.

I got off the kitchen phone and told Mom and Dad, who started jumping up and down. I said I didn't want to go and that I needed a break. Really, I was just nervous. But Dad lit into me: "I'll arrange a flight first thing tomorrow morning, and you will be on that plane! Start packing!"

So off I went, and as soon as I arrived at the stadium, I was called in to see the Oilers' manager, Jack Krol. "Keith," he said from behind his office desk, "this is a must-win series for us, so be ready, and welcome aboard."

After that, I met the team. There was Jim Bibby, Mick Kelleher, Bake McBride, Ken Reitz, Ray Bare, and Rich Folkers. These were good players— one step away from the bigs—and much older: the average age of the Oilers' roster was slightly younger than twenty-five.

I was nervous as hell.

The yard was packed with fans. We were playing the Wichita Aeros (Cubs), managed by former original 1962 Met Jim Marshall. Even though it was a dilapidated complex with bad lights—nothing compared to the major league spring training complexes I'd grown accustomed to in the Florida State League—I'd never played in front of a full stadium before, and the dimness of the lights added to the excitement of this first game against the division-leading Aeros.

I pinch-hit late in the game off submarining right-hander and former Chicago Cub Ron Tompkins. When I got up from the on-deck circle and my name was announced over the PA system, I not only heard the buzz from the fans; *I could feel it.* Tulsa is only about 1,300 miles southwest of St. Louis, and Oilers fans loved watching future Cardinals come up through this final rung on the ladder. Now they were getting their first look at one of the organization's top young prospects, and their excitement seemed to match mine. I don't remember the sequence of pitches or if I hit the first pitch, but I ripped a bullet up the middle that almost undressed Tompkins. Krol sent in a pinch runner for me, and the crowd gave me a rousing standing ovation as I glided back to the bench.

Following the series with Wichita, we were off to Colorado to face the Denver Bears. Here I was on a twelve-hour bus journey and the only person underage—not that anyone was carding. Beer on the bus, card games, smoking, laughing, joking, needling. It was a new experience, and I enjoyed every moment of it. Soon after we checked into the Holiday Inn, I wandered into a poker game going on in one of the rooms. There were fewer than a dozen players around the bed and some other folks just hanging out. One of them was a fairly attractive woman I assumed was with one of the players, though I didn't know which one. But third baseman Ken Reitz did, and during a break in the action, Reitzie got his hands on the player's room key and snuck away to cut about a dozen silver-dollar-sized holes in the player's bedroom curtains. Later, when the card game finished and the player left with his pretty companion, the rest of us waited around fifteen minutes and then quietly gathered outside their window. *Peep show, anyone?* Of course, it's impossible to contain the laughter and catcalls of more than half a baseball team watching their fellow player get lucky, so the performance was cut short, and a scattering chase quickly ensued.

Such juvenile behavior may seem off-putting, but I recommend these sorts of antics for any minor league ballplayers taking themselves a bit too seriously—something magical happens in such silly moments. I know it made me feel less like an intruder and more a part of a team.

I finished the season with the Oilers, playing in 11 games and hitting .241 in 29 at-bats with 1 double, an RBI, and 6 strikeouts. Not bad for an eighteen-year-old making his AAA debut, and I was home again in September, but not for long. The Florida Instructional League in St. Pete began in early October, and we reported a week early for a mini fall training in preparation for the thirty-plus-game season. This was a very prestigious league. There were fourteen teams from various organizations in our division, and only the top prospects from A, AA, and AAA were invited.

The occasional major leaguer, too.

When I reported to camp, to my surprise, Houston Astro Bob Watson was part of our squad. Bob was twenty-five and coming off his best year in what was his fifth full season in the bigs (.312 / 16 HRs / 86 RBI). He was on loan from the Astros to hone his skills behind the plate. Just being around Bob, a bona fide major leaguer, was instructive. He could play ball, of course, but he was also human: he put on his shoes the same way we minor leaguers did and even struck out on occasion. To witness that—to understand that one doesn't have to be perfect to achieve the next level—gives a player confidence.

The other outsider on the team was Phil Garner, a middle infielder on loan from the A's. Phil was a character. He rode a motorcycle to work, and that's sort of how he went about his day—free and easy, but tough, too. Appropriately nicknamed Scrap Iron, Phil was as solid as they come and would have a long career in the big leagues with the Pirates and the Astros—I just wish I could have played with him during one or two of those sixteen years.*

Despite the high caliber of players, our team

---

* Phil was a member of the 1986 Astros and thus a part of that incredible NLCS against the Mets.

got off to a horrendous start: 0–6 or something like that. It pissed off the Cardinals' brass, and they sent down George Kissell, baseball fundamentals guru, to whip us into shape. Kissell had spent most of his playing days as a so-so minor leaguer from 1940 to 1952,* and he had managed teams in the Cardinals chain from 1950 through 1968 before joining the St. Louis coaching staff as bench coach. In the words of former Cardinals catcher and Mets television announcer Tim McCarver, Kissell was "the father of the Cardinal Way." He literally wrote a complex book on fundamentals for every position and every conceivable game scenario. A true baseball "lifer," Kissell was wed to the game of baseball the way a priest is to the church, and he wasted no time exhorting "the word of baseball" to us.

"You guys are our finest minor leaguers, and you're here because we feel you're the best," he began, addressing us in the clubhouse the day he arrived. "And to play like you've been playing not only reflects poorly on yourselves; it's an embarrassment to the organization. Make no mistake, you will turn this thing around, because starting

---

* Kissell did not play baseball in 1943 through 1945 due to military service in World War II.

today we are going back to fundamentals, working hard, and doing things right."

That all may sound a bit corny, but if there was any doubt about Kissell's ability to lead and inspire the troops, it disappeared once he was on the field and in uniform. His love for the game was contagious; his knowledge of all things baseball, including its finer points—like baserunning, rundowns, and relays—was unquestionable. These weren't just different "aspects" of the game to Kissell, they were art forms, and his passion to instruct us in each of them was inspiring. I also enjoyed Kissell's militaristic approach to preparation. Everything from how we played to how we looked—socks lined up, shirt tucked in with letters showing—was important, he said. It fostered pride in and dedication to ourselves and the organization.

Things went so well after Kissell showed up that the brass sent down their big-league manager, Red Schoendienst, along with the great Lou Brock to help instruct the promising talent. *Can you imagine?* Being a recently turned nineteen-year-old kid walking into a clubhouse and there's Lou Brock, Cardinals starting left fielder and no-doubt future Hall of Famer, seeking you out to talk about baseball and shoot the breeze.

All that was like a magic potion, and we went

on to win twenty-six of our last thirty-two games and capture the league championship. It felt great—not just the championship but winning all those games en route to it. We were putting the competition away, day after day, despite the bad start. And that lesson in perseverance, stemming from Kissell's instruction on "what it takes to be a champion," was crucial in my early development.*

For the cherry on top, I hit .352 that winter league, winning my first professional batting title. I "wore it out," as we say—my achievements were even recognized in the back pages of the December 4, 1972, issue of *Sports Illustrated*.†

---

* Kissell, known as "the Professor" to later Cardinals generations, enjoyed one of the longest tenures of any coach or player with one team. Sadly, at the age of eighty-eight and still going with the Cardinals youngsters, George was killed in a car crash when a driver ran a red light. His wake, appropriately held at Al Lang Field in St. Pete, was a testament to the man: scores of players from various eras and levels of success attended the service, and we all told stories about Kissell and how instrumental his lessons were, not only in our careers but in our lives. Reverence doesn't begin to describe it.

† The article was titled "The Phenoms That Bloom in the Fall," and it featured half a dozen prospects who excelled in the fall leagues in both Florida and Arizona. And there, right below the headline, was a photo of me in uniform. In the article, I stated, "I believe I can get to the major leagues in two years. The Instructional League has helped me in every aspect of the game. Now the rest is up to me." *Really, Keith?* What

*　　*　　*

After the championship, I was home yet again, this time for a few months. And I remember my first Friday night back: after saying goodnight to my parents, I was on my way out the door to meet some buddies, and my dad said, "Have a nice time, son. Be home by midnight."

"What? Midnight?" I asked. "Dad, I'm nineteen years old, and I've been on my own all summer."

"If you don't like it, get a job and an apartment. As long as you're living under my roof, you'll do as I say."

Though I might have just won a batting title and been in a popular sports magazine, Dad was still the boss.

But my first year was in the bag, and things were looking up.

---

chutzpah! The funny thing is I don't remember being that confident, but there it is in black and white.

CHAPTER 8

Pacifica, 1961

GARY AND I SCARF *our second helpings of breakfast. Dad had bought chorizo and linguica sausage
from the Spanish market that morning on his way
home from work, and Mom had cooked the sausage
and then the eggs in the spicy, salty oils. Delicious.*

*Dad folds up the sports section and hands it over
to Gary. "The Senators lost again," Dad tells me.
"Too bad for Mr. Lavagetto."*

*Mr. Lavagetto is Cookie Lavagetto, manager of
the Washington Senators. I've seen his photograph
in Dad's scrapbooks from his playing days. Sometimes we'll take them out and Dad will show us all
the pictures and tell us the stories. Mr. Lavagetto
and Dad had been teammates on the navy's baseball
team during World War II. He had played infield
for the Brooklyn Dodgers and had been an All-Star
before shipping off to Pearl Harbor. Dad says that he
learned more about hitting from Cookie Lavagetto
than any other person.*

"Like a lot of great players," Dad says, "Cookie had his Major League Baseball career curtailed as a result of his military service."

I've heard this before, but I still listen. I, too, am falling in love with the game. Dad talks and like a sponge, I take it in. And when he mentions the famous men he played with and tells stories of the wartime games they played together, something strange happens: my father becomes almost godlike to me, like I'm living with a character out of Greek mythology, and I love being around this man who used to do all these wonderful things like the other gods I follow through morning-paper box scores.

Like the story about Ted Williams, who played for the Army Air Corps. Williams struck out one time, Dad said, and threw his bat as high as he could into the air. "People say he's temperamental," Dad explained, "but he's really just consistent in his pursuit of perfection. It's why he can hit .400."

Of course, only Dad knows this inside information, because he was on that field, playing first base. So while the other boys in the neighborhood have to rely on magazines for their information, Gary and I have Dad and know all about Williams and other things, like the Gashouse Gang with Dizzy Dean, the Yankees and DiMaggio, and Charlie Gehringer and Hank Greenberg in Detroit. He's told us about the Brooklyn Dodgers' Mickey Owen and his passed ball on a third strike with Tommy Henrich up at the plate in the 1941 World Series, giving a crucial extra out to the Yankees, who would go on to win the game and eventually take the Series, and about Cardinal Enos Slaughter's "mad dash" around the bases to score the deciding run in Game Seven of the 1946 World Series. Dad knows all of that—so his boys do, too.

And it's not just Gary and me who like it when Dad talks baseball. It's Dad's close friends, too. Carl Vallero, a former minor league catcher, and Joe Ortega, a fellow Spaniard who never played but loves the game, will come over with their families or we'll go over to one of their houses for evening barbecues. After the sun goes down, we kids will traipse into the dining room, sweaty from our neighborhood games of baseball, hide-and-go-seek, and tag, and settle down on the rug to listen to the fathers talking baseball over coffee and dessert.* And it's mostly Dad talking—the other men are as captivated as us kids.

"The two most important things Mr. Lavagetto

---

* Looking back, it was very tribal, as in Thomas Berger's classic novel *Little Big Man*: all the young Cheyenne boys sitting around the campfire as the elders and Old Lodge Skins passed down from generation to generation the history of their people.

ever told me," Dad now says at the breakfast table, "were 'Drive the ball from gap to gap' and 'Know your strike zone.'" And with that, Dad stands up and walks over to Mom. He's tired after a night-watch shift at the firehouse.* He gives her a kiss and heads into their bedroom.

On the breakfast table, Dad's left unopened packs of baseball cards—ten cards and a stick of gum per pack. They're the second treat this morning, after the chorizo. Mom says we can skip our chores, but we clear our dishes and wash our hands to get off the grease. Then we're back at the table, opening up the packs of cards, praying for a Mickey Mantle or Willie Mays, but they're not there—the superstars never are. We count our cards, put our favorites into our pockets along with an extra stick of gum, and Mom tells us to go outside and play so Dad can rest. Gary and I know the drill by now and are thankful that those night watches are only once a month. We head out the front door to see what the rest of the neighborhood is up to.

---

* Back in those days a lone fireman had to stay up all night as the rest of the guys slept, standing sentinel over the ticker tape, on the alert for any alarms that may sound in the middle of the night.

CHAPTER 9

AFTER SPRING TRAINING IN 1973, I was tapped for AA Little Rock in the Texas League, skipping high-A Modesto in California. This was a fairly big jump, and one that I didn't handle well.

But there were some bright spots. First, I beat out my competition at first base, a player named Ed Kurpiel. The overall eighth pick in the June 1971 amateur draft, Ed was a proverbial brick shit-house at 6'3", 220 pounds and towered over my then 5'11", 175-pound frame.* After a full season in Modesto, Ed, like me, was sent to Little Rock but was transitioned to the outfield while I continued to start at first base.

---

* The left-hand hitting and throwing first baseman was drafted out of Archbishop Molloy High School in Queens, New York, where in his senior year he set a New York City high school record for home runs. Ed and I would get off to a bad start in 1973 because of the intense competition, but as time moved on, we became good friends and teammates.

Second—and this is one of my favorite things about all of my minor league years—I loved the fans. Little Rock had some real characters. First, there were "Big Beulah" and "Dirty Judy"—at least that's what we called them. They'd been coming to the games for years, never missing a Sunday doubleheader. In her midforties, Beulah was a head turner: she wore big black sunglasses, and her hair was jet-black and set in beehive fashion; the jewelry was always noticeable above her low-cut neckline, which left nothing to the imagination; and she always had on a tight-fitting black dress with the hemline cut just below the knees. Also well endowed financially, Beulah carried herself with perfect posture and sophistication but wasn't above courting a professional wrestler whenever the circuit came to town. Hilarious.

Beulah's cohort, Dirty Judy, was in her early to midthirties, blond, and a real looker. She'd show up at those hot Sunday games in a bikini. Nothing doctored there, folks—Judy was an all-natural brick house. I should know because she and Beulah sat in the front row, just down the first base line. They would come an hour before the game, and Beulah would talk to the players, including me, in her smooth yet playful Southern drawl. A total flirt. Judy was quieter but equally intimidating to a nineteen-year-old kid—both women just oozed sensuality.*

Then there was the state mental institution over the left-field fence. On Sundays, about a hundred of the in-therapy patients would take in the doubleheader, and they'd come marching in together, under supervision, of course. Brad was one of my favorites. He would somehow find his way to the front row behind home plate during BP and shout, "Brad! Brad! The best friend you ever had!" over and over again, continually throughout the game from his seat down the left-field line. Then there was the elderly, silver-haired Willie. He'd dress up in a Cardinals uniform and run up and down the aisles at full speed, ending in a slide, then pop up and yell, "Safe!" both arms signaling the call like an umpire. Back and forth, inning by inning, game by game—*"Brad, Brad, the best friend you ever had!"* and *"Safe!"* ringing through the ballpark.

Unfortunately, the pitching of the Texas League nearly drove me into a straitjacket: six weeks into the season, I was hitting .190.

---

* In 1988, when *Bull Durham* hit theaters, the character Annie Savoy, played so beautifully by Susan Sarandon, reminded me of Big Beulah. In fact, the whole film captures life in the minors to a T. Definitely a big thumbs-up.

I just couldn't get it going. Maybe it was the heat. I know that sounds ridiculous, especially coming from the Florida State League. But that year's spring was one of endless rain for much of the Deep South, and there had been record flooding all up and down the Mississippi, thrusting the entire region into an endless summer of stagnant 100-degree days.

If not the heat, maybe it was the long bus rides. Again ridiculous, but ask anyone who's played in the Texas League about the road trips, and get ready to see that man cry. Because, my God, those were long journeys.

Traveling within our Eastern Division wasn't so bad. The Memphis Mets were only 128 miles to the east, and I liked all the barbecue joints. Next was the three-hour bus ride from Little Rock to Shreveport, a tough sailors' town along the Red River and home to the Brewers outfit. There wasn't much to do there, but just across the river was Bossier City, reportedly loaded with strip joints. *Now we're talkin'!* But our manager wisely thought a bunch of young guys might get into trouble there, so he instituted heavy fines on anyone who dared to venture over. Oh well, I was still too young to get into any bars, so what did I care?

After Shreveport, we'd continue our road trip south another three hours into the very heart of

Louisiana and Dixie to the town of Alexandria to take on the Padres. Boy, was I thankful I didn't have to play in that town for a full season. They had the worst ballpark in the minor leagues—old, bad lights, and just over the outfield fence was an endless swamp loaded with cottonmouths and copperheads. *Those are poisonous snakes, folks! No, thanks.* The opposing players told us that sometimes the reptiles would slither onto the field, and the poor grounds crew would go out armed with extra-long rakes and assume battle-line formation to beat them back into the swamp.

It was during one of these Alexandria games that I experienced my first racially tinged razzing from a fan. The man was sitting up close, between home plate and our on-deck circle. "Hey, Hernandez," he went, his tone a relaxed Southern drawl. "What's with your name? You some sort of Mexican? Are you a wetback, Hernandez?" It was like he was trying to engage in conversation—he never raised his voice—but I'd learned my lesson in St. Pete and didn't engage. I never even looked at him, though I did sorta chuckle, and I guess he got bored because he quit after my second at-bat.

I bring this up for another reason: this confusion as to my heritage was something I had to deal with a lot in the minor leagues. Not from the fans, but from the players—the Latin American players in particular. The conversation would go something like this:

"Hey, Keith, what's with the last name, *Hernandez*? Where are you from?"
"California."
"Well, what are you?"
"Half Spanish and half Scots-Irish. Spanish on my dad's—"
"You sure you're not a Mexican?"
"Hey, if I was Mexican, I'd say I was Mexican and be proud—"
"C'mon, man, you're a Mexican."

I would get that throughout the minor leagues, until finally I got tired of the conversation and just started saying, "Okay. I'm Mexican." And at some point people started to call me "Mex," which absolutely horrified my father, the proud Spaniard.*

Anyway, after the series in Alexandria, we'd hop onto the bus and drive the six hours back up to Little Rock for a home stand, and that was

---

* The nickname stuck throughout my career. All my teammates, they called me Mex. Some I still let—my real, real, real close teammates—but once I retired, I told all my friends, "Don't call me that anymore. I'm Keith."

as good as the road trips got, because we'd then head out to the Western Division in the Lone Star State. And as the old saying goes, "Everything's big in Texas."

The first swing was to the Giants' AA squad in Amarillo, then on to the Cubs' outfit in Midland-Odessa.

Ten hours due west of Little Rock, Amarillo was a cattle town right on Route 66 (Interstate 40) in the Texas Panhandle. The ballpark was pretty good, but over the left-field fence, where the wind blew from, was a major rail hub surrounded by enormous cattle stockyards and slaughterhouses. The smell from the stockyards was nauseating, and the giant horseflies, not content to feast upon just the cattle, took a liking to ballplayers. They were everywhere, buzzing around and biting the crap out of us during BP.

After a four-game series and being sucked dry in Amarillo, we'd load up onto the Greyhound and head four hours due south to Midland-Odessa, aka the middle of nowhere. It was just flat country with thousands of oil derricks pumping away 24/7. The ballpark, however, was brand-new with a nice field and clubhouse. Most important, it had terrific lights—mercury vapor lights, an innovation at the time, and they were being instituted in all the major league parks.

These lights "grabbed" the field, sharpening even the tricky dusk hour and allowing the hitter to see the ball very well. But we weren't the only ones entranced with these modern marvels; the region's vast tarantula population also found them appealing and would come scampering out onto the field, sometimes fifty at a time. Once again, just like in Alexandria, the grounds crew was prepared for battle: out came the long rakes and tight formations, sending the giant spiders into full, leaping retreat. Fortunately, there was no counterattack during our four-game series in Midland, and we headed back safely to Little Rock, some 700 miles away.

The other swing was to the Angels' AA club in El Paso, 1,000 miles—or sixteen hours—away, then 552 miles (nine hours) southeast to the Indians' affiliate in San Antonio. Then mercilessly back home to Little Rock, about 600 miles (ten hours) away. *No exaggerations!* As my friend former New York ABC Sports news anchor Warner Wolf would say, "You can look it up!" Just remember that we had fewer freeways and a bus that didn't exceed fifty-five miles per hour, the national maximum speed limit at the time. So we weren't breaking any land-speed records.

One road trip I really did almost go crazy.

It started in Memphis, where the owners capped

off the weekend series with a big promotional night game on Sunday, usually a getaway day.* It had rained all day and into the evening, so the start time was pushed back even further, and the overworked grounds crew poured gasoline on the infield dirt and lit it on fire to dry it after the owners, hell-bent on getting the game in for the sold-out crowd, had a helicopter hover over the field to blow the water away.

We eventually played the game and sometime after midnight got back on the bus to begin our 1,200-mile trek across two states to El Paso. (That's right: a game out east followed by a western swing!) We drove through the night and took turns sleeping on the luggage racks above the seats, like vampires in coffins, lying on our backs, arms folded across our chests, the ceiling of the bus just a few inches from our faces. We pretty much drank ourselves to sleep—we had to; otherwise, there was no escape. At dawn I woke up with the worst hangover and cotton mouth, and happened to look out the window: there, coming up on the right side of the bus, was a road sign: EL PASO 750 MILES. Something like that. And I went,

---

* Meaning you play a game in the afternoon rather than in the evening so the team(s) have enough time to travel, or "get away," to their next series.

"Oh my Lord," because we'd already been on that bus for an eternity.

In El Paso, we always seemed to have some interesting adventures.

Like one night a handful of us ventured across the Rio Grande into Ciudad Juárez, Mexico. Héctor Cruz, our all-league superstar and native Spanish speaker, served as our interpreter, and no sooner were we south of the border than a cabdriver approached us and asked Héctor if we wanted to see a donkey show. (For those of you unfamiliar with it, a donkey show isn't a carnival ride or circus act but a beastly sex show that's guaranteed to send any viewer straight to hell.) Of course, we all thought it was a great idea, climbed into the taxi—really just an unmarked van—and rode with this nice man about fifteen minutes to the outskirts of Juárez and a dumpy little cantina, where he took us upstairs.

At this point I took a keen interest in knowing where the exits were, and I saw four: one along each wall and covered by a curtain. A man collected our admission fee—I think ten or fifteen dollars a head—and an unattractive older woman dressed in skimpy lingerie came out from behind one of the curtains. She started dancing to some recorded music, and nothing else happened for, like, five minutes until Héctor complained on our behalf. *"¿Dónde está el burro?"* But instead of a donkey, six men armed with clubs stepped out from behind the curtains. They looked like they meant business—no translation required—so I whispered to Héctor, "Maybe tell them we would like to leave now." That seemed to defuse the situation: they kept the money, and we made it back to our stateside hotel safely.

The hotel was a real nice Holiday Inn with a very large pool, which was good because the weather was desert hot. I remember one time a group of television wrestlers was in town performing, and they were all buff poolside with their very large entourage, including several very buxom women lying out in bikinis, but we didn't dare try to jerk their sheets for obvious reasons of self-preservation.* Anyway, it was during either this trip or the one with the donkey show that our carnal interest was piqued. So one of my teammates hired two prostitutes to be in his hotel

---

* If memory serves me right, this pool was also where a bunch of us met twenty-two-year-old actor Kurt Russell. We were told that his father either owned the El Paso minor league team or had a piece of it. At any rate, Kurt had made only two movies at this point and was a part-time middle infielder with the team. We rapped for about thirty minutes, and I remember being very impressed because he could have been an asshole but he was a very nice, normal person.

room after a game and asked if anyone was interested. He'd negotiated a price of ten dollars per head. So we all lined up in the hallway just outside his room, and the girls conducted their business—one on each twin bed—and in quick order. Not our finest hour, and of all the things I was learning in my young adult life, this was one lesson I could have skipped.

Back to baseball.

Remember what I said? Baseball is rhythm. Well, try being in rhythm after strapping into a diesel-fumed tin can and driving fifteen hours through the middle of nowhere. *Impossible.* Except some of my teammates, especially Héctor Cruz, were handling the Texas League just fine. Héctor—who always had a smile on his face and a good joke to tell—never seemed to get down. We were all young and playing baseball, so who cared about long bus trips?

Just enjoy the adventure, Keith.

Héctor was also the funniest person I'd ever met. I remember someone playing a radio on the bus, and when a good dance song came on, Héctor took all his clothes off—he was stark naked—and started dancing down the aisle. "I'm just a good-looking Puerto Rican boy," he boasted with a big smile on his face, and we started catcalling and saying, "Oh no, here he goes again!" because he'd done it before. One time he made a catch crashing into the wall in the outfield. His foot went in between the baseboard and the fence, and he got stuck. He couldn't move. He just lay there, and we had to call a time-out to get his foot out. After that, whenever Héctor did his naked prancing routine or some other antic, someone would always yell, "Why don't you go get your foot stuck in that fence again?"

Héctor could also hit. *Really hit.* That year in Little Rock he batted .328 with 30 homers and 105 runs batted in. And he did all that in only 405 at-bats, because the Cardinals came calling and Héctor went up to the majors—skipping AAA—for the final month of the season.

I envied Héctor. Not for his stats, but for the way he was. I'd look at him, see that big grin on his face, and wonder, *How is he able to stay so loose?* Because I was stuck, still adjusting to the demands of professional baseball. Again, you're not going to hit .400 like you did in high school, and you're not going to have time to regroup and catch your breath. You've got to be okay with both of those things and just weather the ups and downs in a long season against better competition. Guys like Héctor seemed to adapt right away, but it was taking longer for me. I was always on edge, my mood dictated by my most recent performance.

And I didn't have an outlet to just forget about baseball when I went home at night. I still couldn't get into bars, and a lot of the players were older and some were married with kids. I'd also made the big mistake of living on my own, because the previous season my roomie's extracurricular activities with his future wife had kept me on the living room couch watching far too much Johnny Carson and late-night TV. I had wanted my own bed and a good night's sleep, and with the $250 more per month I was making that season, I could afford it. But I just wound up isolating myself from everyone else, and I was lonely as hell.

One day in mid-July, about two-thirds through the season, we played a Sunday doubleheader in 100-plus degrees, and I went 6 for 8, finally kicking my average above .300. It had been a long six-week climb from .190, and I was emotionally exhausted.

Beyond exhausted . . . I was toast.

So I went back to my place after the game, took a piping-hot bath, and fell asleep in the tub. When I awoke, I had the sensation that my spirit was somehow exiting my body through the top of my head, down to the soles of my feet, moving up toward heaven. I lunged out of the water and frantically pulled what I swear was my soul back in. No joke—had anyone seen this they would have had me committed. I fell back in the tub, trying to catch my breath, convinced that I'd nearly lost everything. It was an indication of how strung out I was, and in three weeks my average plummeted back down to .260.

So, yeah, things weren't good in Little Rock.

CHAPTER 10

Pacifica, 1961

DAD PLACES THE STEPLADDER *in the middle of the garage.*

He's called Gary and me away from our Saturday morning cartoon routine, which stretches past noon. We stand beneath the opened garage door, watching him climb the ladder, a long, thick rope in his hand. There's no Sheetrock on the ceiling, and he swings one end of the rope up and over the exposed center beam. He ties a knot in the rope and doubles it. Satisfied, he climbs down the ladder and walks over to the bucket of tennis balls sitting next to our custom bats. He reaches down into the bucket and pulls out a tennis ball.

To connect the tennis ball to the rope, Dad uses two thick white athletic socks: he stuffs the ball inside the first sock, pushes it down to the bottom, and doubles this covering with the second sock. Finally, he ties the socks to the rope, and it's finished: a tennis ball swings suspended from the ceiling, hovering a foot above the floor.

"Grab your bats," Dad tells us, and Gary and I argue over who gets to go first. Dad has just built us our own batting cage.

The idea is that you get the ball swinging on the rope, like a pendulum, and the ball will come in and you'll hit it, sending it away and upward until it smacks against the underside of the storage loft and comes swinging back to you, ready to be hit again. The ball hangs at my knees for a low strike. To raise it for a higher pitch in the strike zone, all I have to do is throw the ball up and over the beam—two times around for a letter-high strike.

"Focus on the top half of the ball and drive it," Dad says.

I swing the bat and it connects with the ball. Pop...I look up at my father, who's smiling at me and his wonderful new invention. I let it swing back once, and on the second pass, I'm in my stance and ready to strike. Pop...

I take to this game the same way I took to the throwing of tennis balls against the outside brick wall, and I play every day, constructing nine-inning games by scoring each contact as a single, double, triple, fly ball, etc., depending on where it strikes the underside of the storage loft. In the beginning, Dad will watch and instruct, making sure we move our hands directly back without hitching, our swing is level, our stride is perfect, and our bat is moving directly to the ball. But as time goes on and we know what a proper swing feels like, he'll watch less and let us have our fun.

Pop . . . pop . . . pop . . .

Eventually, I get so good that I can maintain a level swing and "tip" the very underside of the ball—like a golfer's chip shot—off the top of the bat, sending it up and into the storage shed for a "home run." This little trick doesn't exactly meet the Cookie Lavagetto principle of driving the ball, but it does make me more acute, like a marksman, as I'm able to pick out portions of the ball as it approaches.

Pop . . . pop . . . pop . . . *All day long. Hundreds if not thousands of swings.* Pop . . . pop . . . pop.

CHAPTER 11

I CAN SEE THE HEADLINE NOW: NASA LOSES SPACE RACE TO BASEBALL.

If a young player struggles in the minor leagues, like I did in 1973, he's typically sent down to the next-lowest rung or released. In today's baseball world, that process goes something like this: Some computer whiz kid, who either has or hasn't thrown a baseball in his life but has a job in the general manager's office of a Major League Baseball team, gets a notification on his computer that one of the organization's prospects is tanking. Said whiz kid, who is perhaps thousands of miles away from said prospect and has not seen the prospect play, plugs the statistical drop-off into the all-knowing algorithm developed the previous year at MIT and makes a call upstairs to the GM. Said GM uses more whiz kids with more computers utilizing more algorithms to arrive at a decision of what to do with said prospect. The decision is made, and the GM's office calls the minor league team manager. Said team manager, a former professional baseball player who's dedicated his life to understanding the game and may disagree with the analysis, is told the following: drop said prospect from the sixth spot to the eighth spot on tonight's lineup card, keep him there until further instructions, and remember, Big Brother Is Watching. Said prospect understands he is under a microscope, goes into panic mode, and spirals in an 0-for-18 stretch. Said prospect is on the bus to A ball, where he plays sporadically the rest of the season and is placed on waivers thereafter.

Eat your heart out, UPS and FedEx: when it comes to logistics and moving assets around, MLB destroys you. And you guys, Walmart and Target, you thought you were fast pulling product from the shelves. It's no wonder, NASA, your space program is stalled: all the smart kids went into baseball management.*

Okay, so I'm being overly simplistic, facetious, and divisive here, but to a large degree, such is baseball now, with its heavy dependence on data and algorithms to forecast player performance

---

* Astros GM Jeff Luhnow actually hired a guy from NASA to lord over his analytics division.

and construct rosters. I'm not saying this is the right or wrong way to go about the game. A big part of me dislikes it in the way a master carpenter must dislike IKEA, but whatever—I can roll with change, even if at times it feels like it's eroding our culture and making us all robots. But thank you, God, for holding off on making baseball a computer programmer's joyride until after my time. Otherwise, I'd be going on forty-five years in some business other than baseball.

Fortunately for me, the game in 1973 was still one that took place on the field and was strategized and analyzed by men who knew baseball. For the Cardinals' farm system, that man was the farm system director, Bob Kennedy Sr. He was typical of that era: a baseball executive who had started out as a major league player, became a scout, then a coach, and, in Kennedy's case, a big-league manager for four years. All told, Kennedy was involved in Major League Baseball for thirty-five years before running into the question "What do we do with a struggling Keith Hernandez?" And what all those years in baseball gave him as an answer was "Promote Hernandez to AAA."

Wait. What? Promote?

Why would Kennedy do this? Statistically, I had no business being in AAA. My numbers in AA were atrocious. If anything, I should have been left to shrivel up in that miserable Texas League or sent down to single A. A few years later, after I became a star, I got the chance to ask Kennedy, who was then general manager of the Cubs.

"Bob," I said, "why did you call me up instead of sending me down?"

Kennedy looked at me with a serious gaze—Bob was a man who seldom laughed while in uniform—and said, "Keith, I knew if I left you in Little Rock, you might have hit .230 and been done. If I sent you down, it could have destroyed your confidence and you would have been done. So I took a chance because I knew you had the talent."

Well, I'm grateful to Bob, and I doubt it could happen in today's game. Because Kennedy would be forced to quantify his hunch about me—to flesh it out with complicated statistics—and my numbers lacked the ammunition to make that case. Kennedy thought any problem with me was mental or emotional or both—not physical. He knew that I put too much pressure on myself and had not learned how to play every day. To get me over the hump, he thought that I needed something positive to know the organization believed in me.

I've since discovered that Kennedy's faith in my ability was well known by the St. Louis press. After that first year in St. Pete, he told the *Post-Dispatch* that I was "ready to play defense in the major leagues" and that I was the only young player he'd ever seen who he felt "could make it to the Hall of Fame." And that was after I hit .256!

But I didn't know any of that at the time I was struggling in Little Rock—I didn't read the St. Louis papers. And it's not like we had the Internet. So when my AA manager, Tom Burgess, called me into his office, I thought I was getting sent back to St. Pete or Modesto. But instead he told me I'd been called up.

"Good luck, and show them that you got *a little hair on your bump*," Tom said, employing one of his favorite expressions.

I was flabbergasted, still wondering how it all had come to be as I set out in my little Saab Sonett III the next morning for Oklahoma.

I'd had no idea that northern Arkansas was so hilly and soon realized that I was passing through the country's oldest mountain range, the Ozarks. Scooting around those bald-headed domes, depleted from eons of wind, rain, and snow, in that tiny sports car, which I'd stuffed with all my crap—the stereo system and boxes of LPs taking up most of the space—I had the radio on and the driver's side window open to let in the cool, refreshing air. I was out of that hot and humid Little Rock sweatbox, and any uneasiness I had about the future had been pushed far away. After a day of hard driving and clearing my head, I made it to Tulsa.

I flew out the next morning to join the Oilers for a three-game series in Wichita. Once again, I reported to Jack Krol, the same manager who'd welcomed me to the Oilers the previous season, when I'd been assigned to the team for their final ten days. But this time the Oilers were ten games under .500 and, according to Krol, "out of the hunt."

"You will play every day the rest of the way," Jack said. "There's no pressure, so just relax, play this game you love, and have fun."

Jack must have heard from Bob Kennedy Sr. how tight I'd been in Little Rock. He had an easygoing manner and was a bit of a wiseass, with this infectious, shit-eating grin on his face. I liked him very much. But sitting in that office the first afternoon, I was very uncomfortable and kept shifting in my seat.

"What's wrong?" Krol finally asked.

"I'm sorry," I said, pulling at my pants, "but I think I got the clap."

Jack just stared at me, not saying anything, and I explained that earlier that week a pretty girl had been hanging around my Little Rock apartment building. I'd never seen her before, but she was dressed in nurse's whites, and I don't know if she was stalking ballplayers or what, but five minutes after she came and said hello, we were in the bedroom.

"Oh, Keith," he said, then took a long drag from his cigarette. "Okay, not to worry. I'll get their team doctor over here, but you're playing tonight."

Well, stupid me, and just one more reason I was glad to be out of Little Rock. The doctor injected me with two doses of penicillin—one in each butt cheek—and, boy, did that hurt. But playing for the Oilers turned out to be exactly the medicine I needed, because I tore up the league, hitting .333 in 31 games with 20 runs, 6 doubles, 1 triple, 5 home runs, and 25 RBI. A hefty .525 slugging percentage and .919 OPS (on-base plus slugging) along with a smashing .394 OBP (on-base percentage). As for the Oilers, ten games out of first place when I came aboard, we went 19–10 down the stretch and made a run for the division.

It came down to the last two games of the season, a makeup doubleheader against Oklahoma City. We were a half game behind the Wichita Aeros, and during the early innings of the first game, it came over the PA system that the Aeros had lost their final game. Our home crowd went wild. Now if we took both games, we were divisional champs. And that's exactly what we did, beating Lowell Palmer and Jim Rittwage—two ex–major league pitchers—in the process. Euphoria in the clubhouse. Champagne popping. Hugs and laughter.

But we weren't finished.

Next up were the Eastern Division champs, the Iowa Oaks (White Sox), who were the league powerhouse with a record of 83–53, running away with their division by nine games. We faced off in a seven-game series for the American Association Championship, and for some reason the series opened up in Tulsa. I don't remember much about the series, but I recall that first game.

We were down a run, bottom of the ninth. I was up to bat with two outs and a runner on base. On the hill was Dave Lemonds, a lefty reliever who'd pitched in the big leagues earlier in the season. Full count. He threw a hanging slider, middle of the plate and down. *Crack!* The ball went over the right-center-field wall, and I sprinted around the bases like Bill Mazeroski in the 1960 World Series. I leapt onto home plate as my teammates pounded my helmet, jumping all around me, because we'd just won game one. A walk-off, two-run homer.

It was exactly what I'd dreamed all those years ago in my imaginary games in the garage. *Two outs, bottom of the ninth, down a run, and Hernandez steps up to the plate...* Every kid's baseball fantasy, and I got to experience it. Amazing. The next day the pitcher, Lemonds, came up to me during BP before game two and asked me why I'd gone around the bases with all that emotion. He was more curious than angry. I said I had never done that before—won a big game in the ninth, let alone been in a championship series—and I just got caught up in it. He looked at me and said, "Okay." And that was that. I had no intention of showing him up—Dad had taught us never to do that. "Let the bat do the talking," he'd said, "and get your butt around those bases."

We won the series in five games. Oilers owner A. Ray Smith bought up the entire top floor of the Hotel Fort Des Moines for the night, and we partied into the wee hours of the morning. I drank tequila for the first time in my life. Shooters all night. *¡Borracho con cojones!* I remember the Tulsa Oilers Wildcat Band partied with us. They played at every home game during the season: bunch of old guys playing Dixieland music in barbershop outfits and white panama hats. Late in the night, I got my hands on their big bass drum—its rightful owner probably passed out by then—and I strapped it around my shoulders and beat the heck out of that drum. *Boom, boom, boom,* marching all over the penthouse level of the hotel. I woke up in the morning, hungover as hell, with a blister the size of a silver dollar on one of my palms.

But it didn't matter—we'd won the championship.*

Now that the season was over, my monthly salary of $750 was terminated, and I hadn't saved a single dime. So I was headed back to San Francisco to stay with my parents over the winter, and I looked forward to the drive, my first cross-country trip. Having experienced a taste of Denver and the Rocky Mountains, I planned to drive due west, through those mountains, the Sierra Nevada, and beyond.

I called home and announced my plans. Big mistake.

"No, son," Dad began, "you're not driving home alone. You're not old enough yet."

---

* A. Ray put together a Junior World Series with the champions of the Eastern League, the Pawtucket Red Sox. A lot of those players would be part of the Red Sox squads that were so good in the mid-1970s, and they kicked our proverbial asses in a four-game sweep. They were better than us by a long shot.

"Give me a break," I said. "This is my second year on my own—I can handle this."

So Dad raised the volume. *"I'm flying out tomorrow morning, and we're driving home together."*

I told him he could fly out, but I wouldn't be there to pick him up. "I'll be six hours on the road by then," I said.

"Son," he said, *"you be at the airport tomorrow or there'll be hell to pay."*

He held all the cards: I didn't have time to get a job, and even if I did, I didn't want to. I'd been playing baseball for eighteen months straight. So I hung up, went to bed, and drove to the airport the next morning. He arrived, and after a lovely dinner at teammate Byron Browne's apartment with Byron, his wife, Chiquita, and their two young children, we went back to my place and I finished packing. Then I went over the route home with Dad.

"No, son," he said. "Not through the mountains. It's late September, and we could get caught in a snowstorm or a blizzard. We're driving Route 66 through New Mexico, Arizona, and Southern California."

Snowstorm my ass—Dad just liked the desert almost as much as he liked giving orders. Again I relented, and side by side—crammed in my little Saab Sonett—we headed out: three long days on the road through endless desert with Dad giving constant orders, telling me how to drive, when to eat, when to piss, where to get gas, when to sleep. *Ughhhhh*... It was like I was fifteen years old all over again.

Finally, we began our climb through the eastern mountains of the Bay Area. It was dark—we'd been driving all day—and San Francisco was just over the next rise when the car blew a water hose. But it was I who exploded: I started shouting at Dad at the top of my lungs, screaming that he had ruined my trip. Up and down, I berated him until the tow truck arrived. I couldn't help it—every ounce of frustration that had been simmering during the previous three days just boiled over. And he didn't say a word, which surprised me. We got home well after midnight, and I didn't talk to Dad for two days. We just ignored each other in that little house.

But it was good to see Mom; and sad, too. Rheumatoid arthritis had struck her when I was in the seventh grade. She just woke up one morning and wham: This thirty-eight-year-old, beautiful, feisty woman, who used to get us up for school chiming, "Rise and shine!" was suddenly robbed of her strength and vitality. And you knew it had to be agony, because Mom, who came from tough Texas stock, was never a complainer.

As kids, Gary and I hadn't known what to do. It had been too heartrending to acknowledge: our dear mother being slowly crushed and twisted bone by bone, joint by joint. And then there were all the medications, each with various side effects: cortisone and prednisone—steroids that blew her up like a balloon—experimental drugs, including injections called gold shots, which had been developed in England and were particularly brutal. So I had slowly become inured to her affliction because, as Gary said, if we didn't insulate ourselves it would kill us.

But once I turned professional, each time I came home, I could see the toll the disease was taking. Bit by bit. I would try to prepare myself before walking in the door, but it would hit me, and I'd have to fight it back.

CHAPTER 12

Pacifica, 1962

MOM JOINS US FOR today's round of BP. She has a home movie camera in her hands and is positioned near the third base on-deck circle but behind the protective cyclone fence. This is the angle Dad wants—into the body—so we can study our swings once the film is developed.

More and more, Dad is taking Gary and me to the baseball field for batting practice. He throws hard baseballs now instead of tennis balls because we're comfortable staying "in the box," keeping our front shoulder tucked and striding and driving "toward the pitcher." After each pitch, Dad will tell us where the pitch was: "That's a strike on the outside corner," "That's a couple of inches inside," "That's a bit high," "Right down the pipe."

"Learning the strike zone," he says, "is just as important as learning the proper swing."

Dad throws us round after round of BP, and Gary and I love every moment of it. We bounce back and forth between the batter's box and shagging balls in the outfield while Mom masquerades as the great Alfred Hitchcock with the camera.

"What a team," she and Dad will say after we've finished.

A week later, Gary and I come home from school and see the film projector and retractable screen set up in the living room. Dad must have picked up the BP footage from the developer. Mom says we will watch after dinner, "so get your homework done." Gary and I don't bother to protest—Mom's a stickler when it comes to homework. She makes us a snack and joins us at the kitchen table. (There's no fooling Mom: she loves "pop" quizzes, and if it's math or vocabulary, she'll drill us with flash cards until we're "all square.")

That evening, we watch the footage in the living room, now a darkened classroom. Dad stands behind the projector, dissecting each swing, from the "take back" to the "follow-through." He wants us to be smooth with a "quiet" bat. He doesn't like a lot of extra movement; nor does he like a hitch in the swing (something he says he did when he played).

"It can lead to bad timing," he'll tell us, "and you'll start lunging at the ball."

Gary and I pay attention to Dad—"our professor," as Mom lovingly calls him. After a year and countless repetitions with the tennis ball in the garage *and BP with Dad, our swings are developing. So when the professor says things like "Eye on the ball," "Hands back and away from the body," "Front shoulder tucked in," "Stride toward the pitcher," "Butt in," "Don't drop the back shoulder," "Level swing," "Up the middle," "Focus on the top half of the ball," we know exactly what he's talking about.*

Dad wants us to be line-drive hitters, and it's becoming second nature.

CHAPTER 13

I'M IN SOUTH FLORIDA, where I spend the off-season, sitting at the dining room table with Hadji, my cat, and we're working on the book. There's a laptop for writing, an iPad for research, and an iPhone for interviews. Yes, I'm starting to feel like a real techie—won't my daughters be proud.

The iPad buzzes, and I see my brother has sent me an email. He's been reading through the book and offers a note regarding Bob Kennedy Sr. Remember, Gary was a minor league player in the Cardinals organization, so he knows the farm system. Here's his note:

> Just saw your bit on Kennedy. Pretty much sums it up—my gosh, they really have turned the game into a giant spreadsheet. No fun. Regarding your promotion to Tulsa, Kennedy did the same thing with eighteen-year-old

Garry Templeton [a number one draftee with immense natural talent]. He was doing well on our 1975 FSL Championship team in St. Pete, but as the season wore on, he started to lose focus and his performance began to suffer. (Where your problem was confidence, Tempy's was perhaps boredom.) Our manager sensed it and talked to me and the other veterans about how to best re-engage Templeton. We tried, but it didn't work. So Kennedy pushed him *up* to AA Little Rock, with the same results you had going to Tulsa: he tore it up. Most guys would have been sent *down,* but that was Bob Kennedy Sr. again. The man knew his players.

So there—my older brother agrees that Kennedy was the man. Anyway, Gary's email is super helpful, and I put it in a special Gmail folder titled "Book."

The only problem is that each of these devices—the iPad, the iPhone, the computer—is also a source of distraction. Between the texts, emails, Facebook, FaceTime, low batteries, and all the other things that make for lots of buzzing and beeping, dinging and ringing, I'm starting to think that a few legal pads, a rotary telephone, and a library card would save time.

I find the various mute buttons and get back to business, when there's a knock on the front door.

Now, who in the hell is that? I wonder.

It's the building manager. She's come to see if I'm satisfied with some recent repair work. I point out a couple of things that need to be corrected and tell her that I'll be gone at the end of the week for the Mets' upcoming baseball season and they can finish the work after that.

"And will he be staying?" she asks, pointing to the cat. I guess she's concerned he may go hungry over the next six months.

"Oh no. He comes with me. We're flying up to New York together. I have a carrier for him."

She pets Hadji and talks sweet nothings to him. I guess she's a cat lover. I glance over at the waiting computer, now in sleep mode, and she asks if there's anything else she can do.

Then I remember that there actually is something. "I talked to my AC guy," I say, "and the filters are twenty-one by twenty-one by one, and I couldn't find them at Home Depot. They had different sizes."

"You have to order them online," she says.

"Ah."

She says goodbye, and I get in touch with the AC guy, who says he'll get me the filters. Then I leave a message with Cookie Knuth, my friend and neighbor who keeps an eye on the apartment when I'm gone, to be on the lookout for the AC guy and the repairmen. Finally, I turn my phone off mute in case Cookie calls me back.

I'm tired now, so I sit on the couch and watch the news. After Cookie calls, I go into the bedroom to take a nap.

I lie in bed and think of my brother's email and how I've always depended on his advice and encouragement. The older, wiser Gary helping the younger, impatient me. And it strikes me that Bob Kennedy Sr., who knew my brother and how our father had brought us up on baseball, would have understood my need for strong mentorship. I mean, who doesn't need a point in the right direction when you're approaching your twentieth birthday? It probably was another reason he sent me up to Tulsa.

Kennedy understood that AAA players are not like A or even AA players; by definition, they are a more select group with more experience and better skills, and nearly all of them had spent time in the major leagues or soon would. Guys like Dick Selma, a right-hander who broke in with the Mets in '65; Dan McGinn, a left-hander by way of the Expos; and Byron Browne, an ex-Phillie and thirty-one years of age. They were all terrific, helpful guys.

Especially Dick Selma. A complete whack job—and I mean that in a good way—Dick was a hard thrower for a little guy and played with the Mets through '68. He was traded in '69, first to San Diego, then to Chicago, where he was a member of that ill-fated Cubs team that was overtaken by the '69 Miracle Mets. Dick was legendary in Chicago for leading the Cubs fans in cheers from the bullpen down the left-field line during the seventh-inning stretch.

By the time we crossed paths in Tulsa, Dick had lost a few miles per hour on his fastball, so he'd resorted to throwing a "grease ball" and seemed to be covered head to toe with lubricants—Vaseline in his hair, Crisco under his hat, K-Y beneath his jersey. One day I asked Dick to show me how to throw the illegal pitch, and I finally got it while warming up before BP. The problem was controlling it—that was the art—but it sure did sink at the last moment.*

---

* The grip and, of course, the lubricant on the index and middle fingers were key. A player would grip the ball like he was throwing a fastball, but instead of having those two fingers over the seams of the baseball, he placed them over the white leather of the ball. And instead of having his entire two fingers in contact with the ball, he slightly elevated those two fingers by bending at the end joints so the pads of the fingertips were in contact with the ball. Then he would just throw

Dick also taught me a lot about the game. I remember one time we were playing in Denver and I was just mashing the ball. I went into the dugout after scoring, and Selma sat down next to me on the bench.

"Keith, what are you thinking when you get up to the plate?" he asked. "Do you have a plan?"

"Dick, I don't know," I said. "I just go up there, look fastball, see the ball, and hit it."

"Okay," he said, "but you do know that the pitchers have a plan, and they are trying to use it to get you out. You are aware of this fact? Right?"

I just shrugged my shoulders like the dumbass nineteen-year-old that I was.

"Well, they are," he said, "and they're always figuring out new ways to get you out. So pay attention to how they're pitching you and your fellow left-handed hitters. See if you can discover a pattern. That way, the next time you face them,

---

it like a fastball. The force of the throw would allow the ball to slip off the fingertips, thus the ball exited the hand in a rapidly tumbling, vertical orbit. It could be thrown as hard as a fastball or as slow as a changeup. It would approach home plate as if it were a fastball, but at the last moment, the bottom would drop out and the ball would dive about six inches or more. The fact that a hitter could not recognize this pitch (it looked like a fastball) made it doubly tough. Later the split-finger would make its debut, with the same results.

you've got an idea of what might be coming down the pike."

As ridiculous as it sounds, Selma was the first guy to tell me that. Previously, I had worried only about my mechanics and never really given the pitcher's strategy the slightest thought. But Selma turned on the light bulb in my brain. It got me thinking before I went up to the plate: *What is this man's plan of attack? Is there a pattern?* It would take me years to get really good at answering these questions, and I never stopped looking fastball 90 percent of the time throughout my career, but I could also play a hunch—sometimes it was correct; sometimes it wasn't. Though my rate of success improved with the more attention I paid.

Selma was the first among many older players who passed along such golden nuggets of advice, and I consider that conversation and the realization of *Oh my God, this game requires that I actually use my brain* as a big moment in my development. Heeding Selma's advice—to pay attention—would make all the difference in the years to come, because if you think about it, the long season was now an advantage. It meant that I would see each pitcher, particularly in our division, maybe 15 to 25 times per season. And with that big sample, I could get a decent read on their arsenal of pitches and how they might deploy them.*

This wasn't the only advice Dick would give me on how to handle a long season. Somewhere in the Midwest, Selma pulled me aside before BP and asked with a dead-serious look on his face, "Keith, what do you like to drink?"

"Beer," I said. "Michelob or Coors."

"No, I mean hard liquor," he pressed.

"Oh. I don't drink that much booze, but when I do, I like Canadian Club."

"You need to start drinking scotch whiskey," Selma instructed. "At first you won't like it. It's an acquired taste. But the one thing good about scotch is you're having it with either water or club soda. You're hydrating [though I'm positive he didn't use that term], and scotch has no smell of alcohol on your breath, so management will never know if you run into one of them after a game."

Was there truth in this or was it just an old wives' tale? I kind of thought the latter, but I nodded at Dick and he walked away, and from that point on, whenever I had a drink of the

---

* Remember, there were no computers, printouts, or videos back in those days. You had to really pay attention, catalog and archive each experience, and then store the information in the recesses of your mind.

hard stuff, it was scotch and water. The rest of my career. So you just had to love Selma—he probably had to see something special in me as a young player and took an interest. He didn't have to do that. After all, he was just trying to get back into the big leagues, so it would have been easy to ignore me. But he and the other guys were just so relaxed within their professionalism that taking time for me was okay, and that in itself—witnessing their easygoing manner while they got things done—helped me understand how to carry and pace myself during the long season.

But I wasn't a veteran. For one thing, I didn't have their balls: they didn't seem to give a shit about the brass or management. I remember when Bing Devine, the Cardinals' GM, got wind of our new team bus and requested we stop in St. Louis on our way to God knows where because he wanted to see it. The detour added a couple of hours to the trip and the veterans were not happy.

It was an amazing bus. It had a small kitchen with a refrigerator, oven, and range, and it could sleep the whole team comfortably: beds came down from the top and the seats would slide into new configurations—like a kid's Transformer—so there would be three levels of bunks and everybody could crash. No more sleeping like vampires up on the luggage racks. The Oilers' owner, A. Ray Smith, who loved his players and took good care of them, had bought and customized the bus at a cost of $100,000 to himself (though I'm sure it was a business write-off). We traveled all over the American Association in A. Ray's wonderful bus, a total luxury. To me, it was a gift from the gods, so when Bing said he wanted to see it, I offered it up.*

Not so with the veterans, who were bitching the whole way northeast through the Show Me State. This was pure trespass to them, and when we pulled up in front of Busch Stadium in downtown St. Louis, it was close to midnight, and most of the guys were drinking, playing cards, and pissed. All the lights came on, and Bing climbed aboard,

---

* Oklahoma City, just two hours southwest down the interstate, was the shortest trip. Wichita, Kansas, was also pretty close, about three hours (176 miles). The rest of the towns were marathons: Denver, twelve hours west (700 miles). The Eastern Division had longer bus rides. Omaha, Nebraska, was 386 miles away (six hours), followed by Des Moines, Iowa, which was another 135 miles (two hours) farther northeast, and back home to Tulsa, 463 miles away (eight hours). The other eastern swing was to Evansville, Indiana, about 559 miles (eight and a half hours), then to Indianapolis, Indiana, a further 169 miles (two and a half hours) east. Then the long trek back home to Tulsa, a cool 640 miles (ten hours).

inspecting the bus. Well, they let him have it. "Fuck this bus, Bing!" "We went out of our way just so you can take a look?" "You like this bus so much, you ride in it, Bing!"

Most of the venom came from the players that had never made it to the bigs. Minor league lifers like Alan Putz. The players that played in the big leagues and were trying to make it back were less angry. I just sat there, incredulous but grinning from ear to ear. *They're berating the GM—I could never do that!*

But I had it easy: I was on the way up.

I played with a lot of twenty-five-to-thirty-year-olds who had been around for more than a while, some already traded once, twice, maybe three times. Some were on the bubble; others were on the way out. Triple A is scattered throughout with those sorts of Crash Davis players—not willing to give up the dream. They knew their chances were zilch or dwindling fast. They'd been around, so they had to know. But if you're a professional baseball man, you'll take the crappy parts if it means more time doing what you love.

For some of the guys, I imagine, it was a bit unsettling to consider life after baseball. *I've got a family to feed. What will I do for work? Will I survive being home year-round?* All those springs, saying goodbye to their families, and now they were strapping together one last season or two before the inevitable. So Bing was doomed the second he stepped onto that bus. But I'm sure he knew that—he ignored the lambasting and snooped around A. Ray's wonderful hundred-thousand-dollar vehicle. Curiosity sated, he departed and we cast off from Busch Stadium. *How many more hours? Who's counting?* It was late and I was tired, so I pulled down one of those marvelous bunks that snapped free from the ceiling and went to sleep.

What a great time I had those six weeks in Tulsa. I realized it could be fun just trying to get to the big leagues.

Another contributor to my more relaxed mind-set? I started smoking marijuana shortly after my call-up to Tulsa. I was living in a motel owned by an ex–minor leaguer. About a week later, a former teammate was called up from Little Rock. I asked him if he wanted to move in with me and split the ten-dollar-a-day rent. So he moved in and un-packed his stuff, including a rectangular package wrapped in newspaper and tied with twine. He cut the twine and carefully began to unwrap the package.

"What's that?" I asked.

"You'll see," he said.

Well, it was marijuana, a big block of it, and

I thought, *Oh man, what did I do?* and maybe I should have just paid the ten dollars a night and not had the roomie. I asked him how much was there, and he said it was a pound. *Geez. A pound?* I had never seen more than an ounce before and had smoked the stuff only once, back in high school.

After he lit up, he offered me a toke. After about three or four hits, I was flying. My stereo system was hooked up, and we turned out the lights and I put the needle on side one of *The Dark Side of the Moon,* which had come out the same year. Lying on my back, eyes shut, arms spread out like the Southern Cross, with Pink Floyd aiding and abetting, I began to feel as if I were free-falling in space. That first tumble scared the crap out of me, and I opened my eyes and immediately came back down to earth, but I could not resist going back up there, turning and slowly tumbling, head over heels as if I were a big space station just drifting in the black void.

So I started smoking, and I've got to believe that it helped me relax. Because I wasn't like Héctor Cruz or the other guys who seemed like they could just push the game away and keep it at a distance. It was always on me, like a fever.

But now I had an escape, and I wouldn't take the game home with me. I would just head back to that motel room, roll a joint—all you needed was a few puffs—and go someplace very far from baseball. My roommate wound up meeting a girl he liked (another nurse), and they were always screwing around in the double bed next to me—just like in A ball—but I didn't care now. I was gone, stoned out of my gourd, floating through that pitch-black darkness until I had to get up and turn the LP over. "Excuse me. Sorry." And then I was gone again, because, my God, that pot had to have been laced with some sort of hallucinogenic. I don't know.* But I hit the crap out of the ball during those six weeks. It was going great, everything my way, and they couldn't get me out.

I'm still not asleep.

This happens a lot now that I've started the book. I'll just stare at the ceiling remembering things for a bit before drifting off. I start to laugh because I remember the bizarre meeting I wound up having with Roger Waters, the co–lead singer and visionary genius behind Pink Floyd. It was years after my *Dark Side of the*

---

* Nothing I would smoke after this came remotely close to having that kind of effect on me. Not even Colombian or Panama Red, or hashish, for that matter.

Moon smoking routine and sometime after my divorce from my second wife in 2011. I was just bouncing around New York City when I got a call one night from a gal I'd met about a month earlier, and she said, "Keith, it's Evelyn. I'm over at Roger Waters's town house in Midtown, and why don't you come by?"

Uh, yeah... So I grabbed a cab and went over.

At first, I thought maybe I had the wrong address, because the man who answered the front door (who wasn't Waters) looked like he'd come straight from a country club. Pressed trousers and shirt, V-neck sweater, navy blazer, and perfectly parted hair. I'd expected a houseful of British rockers, not Oxford and Cambridge. In a crisp British accent, he said he knew who I was, and didn't seem to give a rat's ass one way or the other.

There was a small, eclectic gathering of about fifteen people inside, and Evelyn greeted me and started introducing me around, including to Waters's wife, who was a Long Island girl and a big Mets fan. Everyone else kind of warmed up to me after that, though I felt a bit out of place. I mean, here I come knocking on the door, a perfect stranger in Roger Waters's home, and if I'm Waters, a man of fame, fortune, wealth, and celebrity, I wouldn't want any Tom, Dick, or

Harry walking around my home without my per-mission, and I wasn't sure Evelyn had asked.

But I said hello to Waters, who was shorter than I had expected and not particularly warm to me. *Suspicion confirmed.* He was fairly into his cups, chatting with everyone else and drinking from a wineglass, which never went empty because a young woman, who I guessed was under his em-ploy, kept following him around at a safe distance, and when his glass was close to empty, she re-filled it to the brim. All night long, around the room they went: Waters, girl, bottle.

Yap, yap, yap; glug, glug, glug; fill, fill, fill.

Eventually, a group of five or six people led by Waters got into the house elevator because he wanted to show them the music studio. It was on the top (fifth floor), and my friend wanted me to go along. But I wasn't sure Waters wanted me to—Evelyn was very pretty, and now I was there and maybe getting in the way. So I said I wasn't going to get on the elevator, which was tiny, but she said, "Come on. If you don't come, I'm not going up."

So I squeezed in, not realizing I was blocking all of the buttons, and Waters, who didn't share his elitist butler's refined Roger Moore accent (his was more a Michael Caine Cockney), asked me to press five. Well, I didn't know he was talking to me, and I guess he got pissed, because he got right under my chin and looked up at me with a nasty scowl. "Press fucking five! Goddammit!" I said, "Oh, excuse me," pressed five, and up we went.

We were getting a private mix session with the one and only Roger Waters, his genius on full display. If he seemed inebriated before, he was sober now. Totally in control. He was at the massive recording console, working the sliders, and the music went to a video that was being projected on three very large, connected flat-screen TVs set on the wall in front. He was really pushing up the faders, blasting the stuff, and the sound system was amazing. The corresponding video showed Waters in a poverty-stricken village somewhere in Latin America, and he was surrounded by at least two dozen smiling children. They were all following him around the village as if he were the Pied Piper, and he was teaching them how to play a variety of musical instruments.

It was amazing, but after about twenty minutes of it, my ears were ringing, so I decided to explore the rest of the very large rectangular room. I noticed a billiards table and a bookshelf at the far end.

If I'm a guest in someone's home, I don't snoop, but I do check out their library.

Well, I forget what books Waters had, but I do remember his gallery of artwork, which hung down the length of the room. A collection of Andy Warhol original works, all portraits of famous people. Actually, it was more like a rogues' gallery of twentieth-century Communist leaders. Lenin, Trotsky, Che, Mao, Castro—they were all there, these "men of the people" with a penchant for totalitarianism and mass murder, looking out over that man's billiards table and recording studio, perched atop his multimillion-dollar, five-floor town house.

It was getting very late, so we went back down, thanked our hostess, and departed. The next morning, I watched the news, and there was a report that Waters had been rushed to the hospital. Evidently, he had fallen and cracked his head open sometime after we left and had ended up in the emergency room. I remember thinking, *Well, no surprise there*. But I guessed he was okay, and it had been fun meeting Waters, though I would have liked the chance to tell him how much his music meant to me at a very critical period in my career. Maybe another time.

Only in New York.

CHAPTER 14

I WAS BACK PLAYING for the Tulsa Oilers in 1974, only now for a new manager. Ken Boyer, former Cardinals third baseman and 1964 NL MVP, had taken over the reins, and all us players were crazy about him.

Kenny was young—in his early forties—and just five years out of the big leagues. He knew and had played with or against a lot of the Oiler veterans, and after our games, in the various towns, they would throw parties on A. Ray's hundred-thousand-dollar bus. There would be a few girls and booze, and they'd live it up a little. Not me, of course, as my partying skills were still pretty much nonexistent; I was just smoking grass, listening to music, sneaking into the occasional bar that didn't card me, and playing ball. Still, I loved playing for Kenny. Like those wily veterans, here was another guy to set me at ease over the course of a long season.

I also had a little more money to spend; my salary had kicked up to $1,100 a month. I wasn't rich, but it was the first time I didn't have to watch every dollar I spent. The year before, sometimes the $750 a month had been hard to stretch. Like the time I got thrown out of a game in El Paso in the Texas League. I was fined $100, and one-seventh of my paycheck just went *poof.* Here's what happened:

> The umpire called me out on a pitch that was a mile outside. He'd been missing calls all night. I got pissed off and argued with him. He got in my face, and his breath reeked of hard liquor—not beer, hard liquor. He was drunk, this old umpire, and I was stunned. I mean, I'd never encountered a drunk umpire before. Finally, I said, "You're drunk!" right to his face, and he tossed me out of the game. Then he kind of bumped me, and I bumped him back, *hard*. My manager ran out and got between us.
>
> Well, Bobby Bragan was the president of the league. He was the former manager of the Milwaukee Braves back when Aaron and Eddie Mathews were there. Bragan didn't suspend me for bumping the umpire, because he knew the umpire had been drunk. But he

fined me one hundred bucks, and I wrote a check to the league and sent it off.

A few days later, the GM of the Little Rock Travelers and former Cardinals major leaguer Carl Sawatski came up to me at my locker and said, "Keith, your check bounced."

And I was like, "Oh my God. I'm terribly sorry. I must've miscalculated."

Someone told me later that Bobby Bragan had had a big laugh about it. He'd just chuckled. It embarrassed me, though—not particularly professional on my part. Anyway, I wrote another check that night and mailed it ASAP.

But in '74, I had more dough, and I splurged on a studio apartment rather than the usual motel efficiency. It was a decent space, and I settled into a nice daily routine in Tulsa.

First, I slept in. I had to, because we played mostly night games. During spring training, we had been on a day schedule: I got up around 7:30 a.m. to be on the field at 10 a.m.; I would be tired at the end of the day, so I'd have a nice dinner and go to bed. But when the regular season began and we started playing night games, I wound up sleeping later and later and later. So I would wake up in my blacked-out room at noon and have a shower.* Then, at around 2:30, I was off to Denny's, which I considered an upgrade from Burger King and McDonald's. I ate there all year long, a steady diet of patty melts, cheese-burgers, fries, salads, iced tea, and the occasional dessert. If we had a day game, it would be a steak, medium rare, two eggs over easy, hash browns, buttered toast with jelly smeared on top, and a glass of whole milk. Throw in a short stack if it was a doubleheader. I just needed a meal that would stick to my ribs, however many innings were slated that day.

We had to be dressed and ready to go at the ballpark by 5 p.m., but I preferred to get there early. Nobody wants to be in a rush. The routine was no different than it is in the big leagues: home team hits two and a half hours before game time. So for a 7:30 game, we hit at 5; the visiting team hit from 6 to 7.

I always enjoyed that hour when we'd hit. It was also when I'd get my fifteen minutes of ground balls, working on different situations: I'd work

---

* To this day, I keep my bedroom very dark in the mornings. When I'm on the road with the Mets broadcast and go to a hotel, I'll close the curtains, and if there's a crack anywhere, I'll use pillows, cushions—whatever—to make that room completely dark. I need my cave.

on double plays, focusing on the accuracy of my throws to second; I'd play back, as if runners were on first and second or the bases loaded; I'd play up, on the infield grass, as if I was holding a runner on, and I'd throw to the shortstop; then I'd take throws from each individual infielder. We'd all get our ground balls—there was no direct order. We kept things loose, and I needed only fifteen minutes. It's a long season, so you've got to pace yourself, but I always took that time *very* seriously. As my dad always preached: "Don't ever half-ass preparation; you'll form bad habits. Only *proper* practice makes perfect."

While the starting infield took ground balls, the bench players—usually five, six, or seven guys—hit. Then the lineup, including the starting pitcher, had the remaining forty-five minutes to hit. We broke into three groups, according to the batting order: 1-2-3, 4-5-6, 7-8-9. But the pitcher might hit in the first group so he'd have more time to go through his pregame routine. Then we were off the field and into the clubhouse. We changed our shirts because we were soaked, and we had an hour to kill before infield.

Then the home team took infield at 7, after which we had another twenty to twenty-five minutes to kill and get out of yet another soaked tee shirt—it was always hot in Tulsa, and there was no AC in the clubhouse. Ten minutes before the playing of the national anthem, we'd head out of that sweatbox, run a few sprints, and stretch on the outfield grass. Then it was time to go get 'em.

That was the routine—the rhythm of my day.

When the St. Louis Cardinals—the big club— came to Tulsa to play the annual exhibition game on June 13, 1974, I was heating up at the plate and sticking to that routine. *Bring on the patty melts!* Baseball players can be a superstitious lot, and a player might use the same dirty socks for a month if he thinks they're bringing good luck. The problem is that he never quite knows which part of the routine is helping him along. So he sticks to *all* of it, much to the chagrin of clubhouse managers, spouses, and/or girlfriends.

But it was a big deal for these minor league towns to get the chance to see the big leaguers play. For Tulsa, that meant Lou Brock, Bob Gibson, and Joe Torre, just to name a few. And some of the players—like Ted Simmons, José Cruz,* and Bob Forsch—had played in Tulsa when they

---

* Héctor's oldest brother.

were coming up the chain. So the town was pumped.

Remember, the Cardinals' fan nation extended well beyond Missouri's borders. For a long time, St. Louis was the farthest city west and the farthest city south with Major League Baseball. Before there were California or Texas teams, Atlanta, Arizona, Colorado, Seattle, or Kansas City, there was only the Cardinals. And there was radio station KMOX in St. Louis—one of the strongest signals in the country—broadcasting the games. You could be up in Wyoming, and Harry Caray—later Jack Buck—would be coming through the ham.

Even with those newer franchises coming on board, Missouri is the only state in the union that borders eight states, and the Cardinals drew from each of them: Arkansas, Oklahoma, Kentucky, Tennessee, Illinois, Iowa, Nebraska, and Kansas. So in Tulsa—and it was much the same in St. Pete and Little Rock—this was not only their minor league team but also their big-league franchise, and when the mighty Cardinals rolled into town, folks would get off work early so they could tailgate with their friends and family. If you were a kid, it meant a chance to stay up late and watch your favorite players—not on television, but in person. It was Major League Baseball comes to Main Street.

Of course, like Little Rock, there were also some great regulars in the Tulsa stands. Like the two women who sat in the fifth row, just behind our on-deck circle. I was attracted to one of them, but our clubhouse man informed me at some point in the season that they were a gay couple. So that never happened, but they were sweet gals, both schoolteachers. They always kept a scorebook and seemed to know the game well. Then there was this super-successful wealthy guy who sat with his family in the front row, behind the visitors' on-deck circle. He had a big, loud, booming voice, and he'd get on the players, even the Tulsa players: "What the hell are you swinging at? Oh, you're in trouble now, fourteen." Stuff like that. It was sometimes more mean-spirited, but he was harmless, and what better training to block out hecklers than to have one behind you every night?

Then there was this dude in his late twenties who had straight, long blond hair halfway down his back and a full beard. He'd always sit to the first base side of home plate in the front row. He wore a cowboy hat and dark sunglasses. And I was like, *Who's this guy?* Because he always had these two great-looking girls with him, and I finally went up to him before a game and introduced myself. His name was Don Preston, the lead guitarist for Leon Russell's *Mad Dogs and Englishmen* concert tour. Russell was an Oklahoma native and had formed Shelter Records in Tulsa in 1969, signing such artists as J. J. Cale, Freddie King, and Tom Petty and the Heartbreakers. A big-time record label.

And there was the great baseball legend Satchel Paige, who lived in Tulsa. He was an old man then, and of course we all knew who he was. They put a rocking chair in the bullpen for him, and he sat, rocking away, talking to the guys and watching the games. He never missed a home game, and it made Tulsa almost a baseball Mecca or a shrine for players and fans to visit. "See that man, kids? That's Satchel Paige, one of the best pitchers who ever lived." All this with the Tulsa Oilers Wildcat Band, those old guys tooting and blasting and drinking every night.

And when the big-league Cardinals came out in their road gray uniforms for that exhibition game, the packed house went nuts, and I had butterflies in my stomach. Okay, so maybe it wasn't exactly a routine day. I'd been to big-league spring training that year as a non-roster invitee,* but I hadn't played in a game, so this was my first compe-

---

* The only other non-roster players invited to camp were catchers.

tition against major leaguers. I remember them walking onto the field out of the clubhouse: Ted Sizemore, second baseman and National League Rookie of the Year in 1969, and, of course, Gibson, Brock, and Torre. So on the one hand, I was playing against guys I'd met and shared a clubhouse with, but on the other, they were still like Greek gods to me. Future Hall of Famers, former MVPs, and Cy Young winners. And here they were, running out onto the field, dressed in that wonderful uniform I'd worshipped since I was a kid, ready to face off. *Somebody pinch me!*

But for the major leaguers, an exhibition game in Tulsa during the middle of the season was a huge pain in the ass. They were just coming off a ten-day West Coast swing—playing the Giants, the Padres, and the Dodgers—and on their way to Atlanta to play the Braves. But first they had to land in Tulsa, bus to the stadium, and put on a show for the local folks, then head straight back to the airport.

Some off day!

And while we minor leaguers thought the Tulsa complex charming, it wasn't exactly Wrigley. Once you took the fans away, the stadium was really just a dump—straight out of *Bull Durham*, except we had the Otasco Man sign instead of a bull. The lights were terrible; the visitors' clubhouse was somehow hotter and smaller than ours, which was way down the left-field line and hardly convenient if you needed to take a leak during a game; and just beyond the right-field fence was an auto racetrack, and it was loud as hell. *Brrrrrrr! Wham! Crash!* It wasn't like pedigree stock car or Indy; it was a low-rent, beefed-up-engine type of thing, and every weekend there'd be that roaring cacophony going on during our games.*

So all the Cardinals regulars would give the sold-out crowd what they paid for with one, maybe two at-bats and get the hell out. Then the bench players would do most of the work. They needed the at-bats anyway. And it's not like they were going to put Bob Gibson on the mound; instead, they threw Mike Thompson, who had been our ace in Tulsa when we won the league the year before. Mike made the big club as their "swing-man," the guy who comes out of the bullpen in long relief or starts the second game of a double-header.

Bob Gibson or no, we were facing off against the St. Louis Cardinals—*the second-place team*

---

* In 1977, two years after I was gone and a year after A. Ray had moved the club to New Orleans, part of the grandstands collapsed and hurt some fans. A new stadium replaced it in 1980.

in the National League East—and though the big leaguers might not have given a rat's ass about the game, we Oilers wanted to win it. At 33–14, and already 11 games out in front in the American Association's Western Division, we were a tough team, and it's not like we didn't have any MLB experience on our side. We had eleven-year MLB veteran Jim Beauchamp (pronounced *bee-chum*), Hal Lanier (who had been the starting shortstop for the Giants when I was in high school), Bobby Heise, Dick Billings, and Jerry DaVanon. These were all guys with considerable time in the bigs, looking for another chance to go to the show.*

And where there were seasoned veterans, there were usually amphetamines. It was just part of the baseball culture back then. More than a few of my Tulsa teammates had possession of these pills, called "greenies" or "beans." One player had a large jar filled with about five different types of pills in different shapes and colors. There were two pharmaceutical types of amphetamines: one,

---

* Heck, early in the season ex–Baltimore Oriole and twenty-game winner (1963) Steve Barber was a teammate at age thirty-six. Steve was with us for about three weeks until he was picked up by the San Francisco Giants for what would be his last stop in the bigs. He was thirty-six, overweight, and out of shape, smoked cigarettes, and could pound beer. But you bet I knew who he was, and he was great to me.

called an orange heart, had five milligrams of pure Dexedrine; the other was called a green heart, with five milligrams of pure Dexedrine plus a touch of a downer so you wouldn't get the shakes. Sprinkled in was the street stuff called white crosses: tiny, white, round pills with a cross embedded on one side of the tablet. They looked like baby aspirin. The pills weren't very potent, but they were effective. We used to call them the martini olive, a little additive to your boost. It would all be in and out of our system in about six hours, so we'd take them two hours before a game, and they would wear off at around midnight, so we could get a good night's sleep.

This was the first year I ever experimented with amphetamines while playing—never in A or AA ball. I did them very infrequently, though I must confess that I bummed an orange heart for this exhibition game with the Cardinals. I was flying high—on top of the world—totally focused and energized, which was good because according to the St. Louis press, we were going to be hard-pressed to put some runs up on the board and keep the Cardinals from scoring.*

---

* The reporters had a point: So far that season, we'd won our games mostly with good pitching and strong defense. The Cardinals, on the other hand, were loaded at the plate and

But that, ladies and gentlemen, is why they play the games, because, as reported by the *Post-Dispatch* the next day, "the Oilers trumped the parent St. Louis Cardinals with a 12-hit attack for a 6–3 triumph."* But wait—there's more! The article goes on to say that "first baseman Keith Hernandez unloaded the big blow of the night with a three-run homer in the fifth inning." *Okay, Keither! Going downtown!* I remember the pitch: fastball, outer half, down in the strike zone. I crushed it over the sixty-foot-high center-field fence. It had to be a four-hundred-foot-plus bomb. At least. And don't forget, this was all in front of the Cardinals' coaches, who were certainly making evaluations along with Cardinals general manager Bing Devine, also in attendance.

Now, a minor league player is delusional if he thinks that one big night in front of the top brass will earn him a call-up to the majors. Because if he's labeled within the organization as just a AAA player—which certainly happens—there's little

---

would finish the season above the league average in thirteen out of seventeen offensive categories. Cardinals stars Bake McBride, Reggie Smith, and Lou Brock would all finish in the top ten batting averages for the National League.
* The National League averaged eight hits per game against the Redbirds that year.

he can do short of a full body transplant to change the organization's mind. But I was a serious prospect, highly touted, and I knew they were looking at me. How much, I wasn't exactly sure, because, again, I didn't read the St. Louis press (the article I cited previously, along with nearly all the articles I cite, I uncovered during preparation for this book and therefore well after my career).

But the Tulsa papers had been saying it was really only a matter of time before I went up, and I'd heard from a few of those reporters how Bob Kennedy Sr. and some other executives were comparing me to Stan Musial, saying I was the best all-around player the organization had seen since Stan the Man. So I'd really wanted to have a great game in front of Devine, Red, the coaching staff, and the Cardinals' beat writers, who'd been milling about during BP asking questions of various teammates but mostly focusing their pregame attentions on me.

Remember, we're talking about a young Keith Hernandez here—cocky on the outside, insecure on the inside—and I was hitting only .279 coming into the game. Granted, the sample size was small: only 111 at-bats because I'd missed the first six weeks of the Tulsa season after yet another spring training injury—a slight cartilage tear in my right knee. So there was still room for doubt to do its thing. But with another year of experience under my belt, and learning how to deal with the ups and downs of a season from my ex–major league teammates, I was waiting for my first red-hot streak, which I knew was just around the corner. I felt solid at the plate, and before the Cardinals showed up in Tulsa, I'd begun to heat up, getting 9 hits in my last 21 at-bats.

But what did all that add up to? With the Cardinals contending and Joe Torre entrenched at first base, I knew I wasn't going to be inserted into the big-league lineup any time soon. And let's face it, I hadn't had a full season in AAA and I wasn't ready.* But I was gunning for a September call-up. All I needed was a great second half and to maybe catch a break.

My father always said, "Don't wait for a break; *make* your break." The exhibition game against the Cardinals had been a good start.

Here's a funny sidebar.

When you came into what was then called Oiler Park, the Otasco Man was usually the first thing to catch your eye. An advertisement for auto lubrication, it was a caricature of a man

---

* Prior to the knee injury, reporters from the St. Louis press had speculated that I would be a midsummer call-up.

whose shoulders came to the top of the left-center-field fence, and his head protruded high above it—maybe fifteen feet. A giant wooden cutout of a head. Again, he added to the whole minor league charm of the place. But within a month of that exhibition game, the Otasco Man suffered a fatal injury when he was decapitated by a tornado that ripped through the city. I felt sorry for the Otasco Man—I would miss his smiling face. But it was better he die in that wicked storm than I, and I've got to tell ya, it had been a close call.

We were informed early that morning that the evening's game was already canceled, something quite unusual in the minor leagues, where most cash-strapped owners wanted to get every game in—no two-for-the-price-of-one rainout double-headers. But Tulsa is smack-dab in the middle of a region called Tornado Alley, and the media outlets warned everyone to batten down the hatches: a big storm was coming. So we got the day off and spent the afternoon preparing for the worst by drinking beer and playing volleyball in the apartment complex's pool. We were just splashing around, escaping the 100-degree swelter with a bunch of other young people living in the complex, most of them in bikinis, and I remember in the late afternoon looking to the southwest and seeing a thick wall of clouds low on the horizon. You couldn't have cut a finer line with a scalpel, and they were the green color of pea soup. Everybody in the pool went, "Oh crap," and ran inside. It was moving so rapidly that within ten minutes the clouds were over us, light turned to dark, and the streetlamps came on.

I sat in my apartment and waited for whatever came next. I had never been in a tornado before, and I left the windows cracked because I'd heard that the drop in barometric pressure could blow the glass out. But then I also remembered reading something about apartment complexes being put together like matchsticks, and I suddenly had visions of me getting sucked up like a hay bale with Dorothy and Toto.

Adorned in only my bathing suit, I ran out of my apartment, through the parking lot, and into a rain gully that was about ten feet deep. I stood in the ditch for about five minutes until a total stillness hovered over me—like the world had stopped. No wind, no sound—just hot, heavy, oppressive air. All at once, a hard, howling, and freezing wind came blowing, along with a deluge of sideways-driven rain. I went from sweating bullets to shivering as the water collected in the ditch almost up to my waist within about five minutes. Then I heard that dreadful sound—the sound of a freight train bearing down upon you. It was earsplitting, and I would've sworn that the funnel was on top of me. I looked to the sky, but it was completely dark, and the water was peppering my eyes. The only thing I could make out were the dark silhouettes of the thrashing trees all around and above me, and I thought one of them could uproot and fall on me.

Brilliant, Keith—now you're gonna drown!

So I clambered out of the gulley and raced across the parking lot to a teammate's apartment. I burst through the door and called for him but got no response, so I went into his bedroom, and there he was, buns up, on top of this girl, and they were going at it. *Okay,* I thought. *Guess this storm doesn't bother them. I'll just go back to my apartment now.*

So that's what I did, and I waited out the worst of the storm alone. Then I got a knock on my door; it was a recently divorced thirty-year-old woman every guy in the complex had been gunning for. She was scared, she said, and asked if she could come stay until the storm moved off. Obviously, my luck was changing. Being a gentleman, I said, "Sure," and we settled on the couch, and soon things went—well, let's just say that survival mode kicks up the hormones a notch.

The next morning the sun was out, but much

of the town was a mess—that freight train I'd heard had actually been a mile and a half away, cutting a swath thirty yards wide and taking off all the rooftops along one of Tulsa's most affluent streets. Fortunately, it didn't completely touch down or it would have destroyed everything and probably killed some people.

We got another day off—maybe in memoriam of the guillotined Otasco Man—and bussed the next day to begin a series against the Omaha Royals. Usually, the bus ride to Omaha wasn't bad, just a bit more than two hours. But that's when I started itching all over, and somebody on the bus said, "Keith, you're all red!" *Uh-oh*. I was covered head to toe in a poison-ivy rash. The gully I'd sought refuge in during the storm must have been loaded with it.

We got to Omaha, and my body was on fire. *Smoking*. The Royals' team doctor gave me a massive cortisone injection, which went to work immediately but didn't eradicate the rash for two or three days. Still, I played that whole weekend series in oppressive heat, itching like a dog with mange. *Good for you, Keith*. More important, the poison ivy didn't deter my red-hot bat, and I picked up where I left off.

CHAPTER 15

Pacifica, 1963

CHUCKIE REYNOLDS WATCHES PRACTICE *from the first base dugout. I'd seen him riding up on his bike during the middle of midweek practice. Chuckie is my third-grade classmate and a pal, but in a couple of days we'll be facing off for the Little League minors championship. Like kids playing army soldiers, Chuckie's just here to scout the enemy.*

Dad halts practice and calls the team onto the infield to give us a pep talk for the upcoming game. "I want you to play hard," he says, "and I want you to play fairly." Then Dad turns and points his finger right at Chuckie, still spying from the dugout. "And if Chuckie Reynolds slides into second base with his spikes high again, I will handle it, and Chuckie's father will have his hands full." Dad says this in his controlled yet stern voice, and Chuckie hears every word.

We're 11–0, Chuckie's team is 10–1, their only loss coming when they faced us midseason. During that game Chuckie slid into second base stiff legged and spikes high, and plowed into our fielder. No one was hurt and Dad let it go, but when we got home, he was fuming. "Where does a nine-year-old learn to slide 'spikes high'?" Evidently, Dad felt it was intentional and ordered by Chuckie's father, their team's manager.

So Dad says this to all of us gathered on the infield, and nobody says anything. Our eyes just go from Dad to one another and then to Chuckie, who is already on his bike, pedaling home to tell his father what Mr. Hernandez said.

The game arrives and it's played under the lights. I'm pitching, and I'm nervous. Both bleachers behind the dugouts are full, parents and kids spilling down the first and third base lines. Wow! Standing room only! Mom says I've always got ants in my pants, and sometimes, when I'm really bouncing or just excited, I stutter my words, and she and Dad will gently tell me to slow down. "Your mind is going faster than your lips, son. Just relax and take your time. Slow down." So that's what I tell myself now, walking out to the mound for the first inning. Slow down and throw like Dad taught you:

Front shoulder tucked, not flying open, the arm motion reaching down and back, the delivery coming over the top, almost like a windmill—

not sidearm or three-quarters or from the ear like a catcher. And, most important, don't rush the delivery or the arm action. Slow and relaxed.

But I know all this, and my body knows all this, because it's been drilled into me. Before Gary and I were old enough for organized ball, we'd head out to White Field, and Dad would conduct throwing and fielding workouts for us. The two things Dad always stressed with throwing were sound mechanics and a strong arm. The first drill was to warm up properly, then he would separate himself from us, according to our arm strength, increasing the distance little by little as our arms became stronger. We threw with 100 percent effort, in a straight line, without an arc, like an outfielder hitting the cutoff man. This is how I developed the strong arm I carried through-out my baseball career. So as I take the mound in this game, the butterflies in my stomach are there, but I'm also confident because I'm undefeated this season, sporting a dominant 5–0 record. I tell my-self to stay within myself and not to rush, just like in practice. And as Dad always says, "Proper prac-tice makes perfect."

I go through my warm-up pitches, and the catcher throws down to second. Here we go. I look beyond the left-field line and notice Dad arriving from *work just in time. He's in full San Francisco fire-man uniform, looking militarily prim and proper with his badge on his left breast, shirt tucked in. He does not have a belly like some of the other fathers, and his shoulders are square. My teammates sometimes ask Gary and me how strong Dad is, because he's very fit and has enormous forearms that flex whenever he demonstrates things like how to hold a bat properly. He smiles and nods at me. It has a soothing effect—ever since he'd called out Chuckie's dad at practice, the game's prospect had been full of tension for me. But now, with Dad there, I strike out the leadoff hitter and those trepidations wash away.*

It's a blowout. We're up 10–0 early, and by the sixth, I'm on my way to double-digit strikeouts. Dad heads back to work because another fireman has been covering for him, and Dad knows the championship is in hand. I strike out the last batter in the sixth to preserve the shutout.

I'm about to start jumping up and down with my teammates when Mr. Reynolds runs out of the opposing dugout to home plate. He's joined by his brother, Dave Reynolds, and both men start screaming at the umpire, Mr. Steiner, accusing him of favoritism toward our team. Mr. Reynolds then grabs Mr. Steiner by the throat and starts choking him. He's got Mr. Steiner up against the backstop, his hands wrapped around his neck, and the other parents from both foul lines are sprinting toward home plate to break it up. I can't see if there are any punches being thrown because more and more parents are crowding around the three men.

Meanwhile, joining me on the mound is Chuckie, and we just sort of sheepishly smile at each other, shrug, and return our gaze to Chuckie's dad and uncle attacking the umpire, with more than a dozen grown men trying to pry them apart. When they finally succeed, poor Mr. Steiner is left there, just sitting in the dirt, the dust still wafting around him while he's propped against the backstop with his hair matted and sweaty against his pale face and his hands on his throat, trying to catch his breath.

Dad gets home the next morning and is furious. I could sense, after the first game midseason, that he was on a slow burn with Mr. Reynolds. But now Dad is irate at the man, and he'll begin the successful proceedings of having Chuck Sr. and Dave Reynolds expelled from any further Little League activities.

But Chuckie and I will never talk about it. We'll just go on with our lives as before—classmates, friends, and competitors. All this other stuff has nothing to do with us.

CHAPTER 16

THE CHANCE OF BEING killed by a tornado is supposedly one in sixty thousand. According to the
Bleacher Report, the chance of making it to the
major leagues as a twentieth-round-or-later draft
pick is less than 7 percent. So it was something
like four thousand times more likely that I would
make it to the major leagues than be sucked up
by a giant funnel cloud. *Wonderful!*

Those odds were improving, too, because two
months after the exhibition game with the Cardinals, I was leading the American Association in
hitting, batting .351 with 63 RBI in 353 at-bats,
and helping the Oilers to extend their first-place
margin. I was so hot at the plate—and, more important, confident—that I even flew my dad out
to Denver to meet the team for a weekend series
against the Denver Bears.

It was a rare occasion that my father got to see
me play since I'd turned pro, and much of that

was purposeful. In fact, Bob Kennedy Sr. later told me that he had sent me to single-A ball in Florida rather than the California State League for my rookie year because he had wanted me to establish some distance from Dad and gain a little independence.*

My dad had brought me into baseball, holding my hand as a little boy and introducing me not only to the game's fundamentals but also to its beauty. He did that for all the kids in the neighborhood. To this day, my brother and I can't go anywhere around Pacifica without running into someone who remembers the countless "World Series" games Dad would host on the neighborhood diamond.

There would be two teams, and Dad would pitch. He showed us how to play the game, including its finer points, like how to turn two, baserunning, relays, rundowns, etc. We were all

---

* Probably what had happened was the Bay Area "bird dog" who had scouted me all that summer—a wonderful man named Jim Johnston—became aware of my father's controlling nature and, despite his high regard for my dad, passed the information along to Kennedy and the powers above. Gary, on the other hand, played for the Modesto outfit, and Dad headed out to watch a lot of his games. But as a college graduate, Gary was older and more mature, so Kennedy was probably less concerned about Dad's influence.

just seven, eight, nine, or ten years old, but we knew who the cutoff man was on a ball hit to left center with a play at the plate (the shortstop and first baseman), and we knew to hit that cutoff man to his glove side on a line. Dad taught us everything, and there wasn't a single kid or parent involved with those teams who wasn't grateful. He was all about the kids and teaching them the game he loved.

But Dad had a *tough* time letting go, and as I got older, his grip went from holding my hand to a suffocating chokehold. And it wasn't just with baseball: Dad could be heard screaming at me over the cheers in the gymnasium during basketball, or from the stands well behind the sidelines during a football game. And every night I came home from practice or a game, there was the serious threat of a chewing-out session.

It had started when I was in the sixth grade, playing basketball. At first, Dad was great. When he discovered that his boys were interested in the sport, he called up his brother Uncle Ralph, who worked in construction, and the two of them built a concrete half-court in the backyard with a top-of-the-line backboard and rim. Dad knew nothing about the game, so he went out and got books and began to instruct us in the proper fundamentals, like how to shoot a jump shot: elbow bent at ninety degrees and tucked into the body, moving up toward the basket, the wrist snaps over for the finish, and the ball rolls off the fingertips.* Dad would rebound the shots and feed us bounce passes as we made our way around the perimeter, baseline to baseline, working farther and farther away from the hoop, but not so far that we were dropping down to shoot from the hip. We'd run drills until the sun went down—Gary and I couldn't get enough.

But when I began playing pickup games with Gary and the older kids in the school yard, Dad began hovering. I'd see his blue Mustang creeping up the street, and he'd go past us, make a U-turn, come back around, and park along the school-yard fence. Same grand entrance every day he wasn't at the firehouse, which meant two days out of three. And he would stay there all day and watch us play. *All damn day.* When the games finished, Dad would finally leave, and I'd walk home with the basketball, dribbling with my non-dominant hand, eyes up—just like it said to do in Dad's copy of Oscar Robertson's book. *Bong…bong…bong…* Down Adobe Road to Linda Mar Boulevard, left on Hermosa Avenue,

---

* His go-to was Bill Sharman's *Sharman on Basketball Shooting*. Dad didn't mess around.

and the final 150 yards to the bottom of the cul-de-sac. *I could do that walk in my sleep.* Then I'd sneak around the side of the house into the backyard and up to the kitchen window. I'd peer in and see Mom at the kitchen sink, and I'd tap on the glass. Mom knew exactly what I was asking—*Is Dad mad?*—and she'd either smile or roll her eyes, like, *Well, you know your father.*

When I got to high school and Dad stepped up his surveillance with football and baseball practice—"Here comes Hernandez's old man in that Mustang again"—I'd get home and wouldn't want to go inside the house. I'd just sit out front for around five minutes, collecting myself, and then I'd open that door and there he'd be. Waiting for me by the foyer steps.

"You're not hustling out there, Keith!" he'd start in. I never understood Dad's definition of "hustle" because I was always busting my ass. To this day, it's one of the great mysteries—I wish he'd lived longer so I could find out what the hell he meant. But the man would be in my face, often *screaming* that I didn't do this and I didn't do that.

The worst part was that it wasn't 100 percent of the time. Otherwise I would have eventually tuned him out the way a soldier might tune out a drill sergeant who had only one volume. But Dad kept me on the line because sometimes I'd come home, take a deep breath, and he'd have a big grin, maybe give me a hug, and tell me how great I played that day. With Dad, you just flipped a coin.

I remember the final basketball game of my high school career. We were playing undefeated Hillsdale, and I needed 24 points to break the school's all-time scoring record, which everyone knew going in. After we blew them out the first half, they came into the second half with a full-court press and tried to slow us down. As the point guard, I destroyed the press—dribbling, passing, running the floor like a field commander in a crack brigade—and we handily won the game. I scored only 14 points and missed the school record, but so what?

We just beat the conference champs!

After celebrating with my teammates at the local pizza place, I came home and walked into the living room expecting cheers. Instead, Dad started berating me for not shooting the ball more and breaking the record. I was so embarrassed and humiliated because Aunt Florence and Dad's oldest brother, Uncle Henry, were there. I began crying, and all the good feelings that I'd had coming through the door from the game rushed out of my body. I mean here's Dad with all his talk about team play, the stuff he'd drilled into us when we were kids, but now he could give two shits that we'd won the game. All he cared about was his son breaking a meaningless record. Well, by then I was seventeen, and it wasn't the first time I had thought Dad actually wasn't so different from his own father, Pa, who he said could not have cared less about Dad's dedication to something larger than himself. All Pa had cared about was that his son was doing well by the family name because he was a star in some sport that all the others in the crowd seemed to admire. Well, Dad showed the same fault. The same stupid *Spanish pride*. Because it wasn't about the team. It wasn't even about me. It was about Dad and that *he* had raised a son who was a star.

And when he missed the chance to bask in that glory, he was unable to control himself.

At least Gary, God bless him, was there and told Dad off. "You don't know what a great game your son just played," Gary said after I'd gone to my room. "You don't know anything about basketball. Keith played an unbelievable game." But Dad couldn't see it that way.

Yet it was because of Dad and all his instruction and passion for baseball that I was now a professional baseball player and, in large part, doing so well in the minor leagues. I was implementing all the things he had taught me over the years. Ever since those early BP sessions in front of the garage door, whenever Dad pitched the ball, he told Gary and me where the ball was in relationship to the strike zone: *a couple of inches outside, low and inside, just missed down and in, about an inch down.*

As a result, I knew the strike zone like the back of my hand, and later, in my major league career, most umpires would give me the benefit of the doubt on a close pitch. So while I may have been the one stepping up to the plate, it's my father's tutelage that got me there.

And heading to Denver for a weekend series in the middle of an incredible 1974 season in which I felt I'd turned the corner as a professional, I wanted Dad to see it. So I flew him in and had an awesome series, displaying my wares to my mentor, who was pleased and full of praise and pride.

I'd done good.

CHAPTER 17

Candlestick Park, 1963

IT'S SUMMERTIME AND I'M *nine years old. Dad feels like I'm now old enough to go to the ballpark.*

Until this moment, my view into the magical world of Major League Baseball has been limited to NBC's Game of the Week, *the nine Giants-Dodgers telecasts from Dodger Stadium each season, and a healthy dose of imagination fostered by radio waves and morning-paper box scores. Like many kids across America at that time, my heroes—Mantle and Mays—lived mostly inside my head.*

The Cardinals are in town. Even though I was born and raised in and around San Francisco, the Redbirds are my favorite team. Stan Musial, the team's outfielder and first baseman, is one of the best hitters of all time. He and my dad are former teammates. They played together on the US Navy Ship Repair Unit's baseball team at Pearl Harbor during

World War II, where my father had led the league in homers.*

Riding up the escalator from the parking lot steps into the stadium, Gary and I are full of anticipation. I can't see the field yet, but I can smell it—green grass—and I feel the hair on the back of my neck stand up. My heart is pounding. It's pumping my little-boy legs in a rush to get my first peek at a major league stadium. Dad has to pull the reins on us like two wild mustangs in need of breaking.

The Giants have a very good team, but the thought of seeing Willie Mays, Willie McCovey, Orlando Cepeda, Juan Marichal, and Felipe Alou isn't what's had me smiling for the past week. Well, maybe a little bit, but they're not the prize waiting in the Cracker Jack box. That would be the Cardinals, who are just a so-so team in the standings. Mr. Musial, whose picture I've seen countless times in Dad's scrapbooks at home, left us the tickets. Each morning, I check the Cardinals' box score listed in the paper. Next to Mickey Mantle, my childhood hero, they're my first priority. Of all things baseball that I love—including Mantle—the Cardinals, aka the Redbirds, are my favorite.

---

* My dad was at Pearl Harbor for the entirety of the war after it was attacked, but Stan served only in 1945, the last year of the war with Japan.

And now we're coming into the park, and the sky is getting bigger and bigger, and I see the grandstands in right-center field, then a bit of the outfield grass, and finally I'm at the top of the steps leading down to our box seats, the entire field sprawled out before me for the first time. I look out to right-center field, the sunlight glistening off that wonderful green grass I'd just smelled, and I see, beyond the outfield fence, San Francisco Bay and the tons of ships, sliding this way and that across the water, the US Navy's Pacific Fleet at anchor in the distance. My father leads us to Mr. Musial's seats behind the Cardinals' dugout, five or six rows back and only a soft toss away from the field.

I sit down, and my eyes come to rest on a player right in front of the dugout. He's playing catch—just tossing the ball.

But he's not wearing his hat.

He's as bald as a cucumber, *I say to myself.*

I stare. I keep staring. I just can't wrap my nine-year-old brain around it. I lean over to my dad, sitting next to me. "Dad? Who's that?"

I ask this question because I am confused. Something doesn't make sense, and my father is good at making sense of things. How could this athlete, this professional baseball player, be bald? As a kid, I know that isn't possible. Yet there he is, right in front of me.

"That's Dick Groat. He's a great player. You know that," my dad says.

That's Dick Groat? The Dick Groat?

Of course I know who Dick Groat is. I've been following the amazing Dick Groat every morning at the breakfast table ever since he hit .325 for Pittsburgh in 1960 and won the batting title and league MVP. As a shortstop! Dick Groat's been turning double plays inside my head for years. I have tons of his baseball cards in the garage chest of drawers back home.

But he was never bald! Then it dawns on me that he always had his cap on in all those baseball card photos.

Many years later—when I'm in my sixties and my brain will do what sixty-year-old brains do, which is forget stuff—I won't remember much of this game. Nothing that Mays or any of the Giants do this day will carve a lasting impression. But I'll remember coming into the stadium and seeing that field and the ships behind it. I'll remember seeing Mr. Musial up at the plate and the peculiar stance he takes—so different from the stance Dad taught me.

And I'll remember Dick Groat's bald head, glistening in the California sun.

There's one more piece that will stay with me. It's such a fateful moment that even if I live to be a hundred and my brain is the consistency of dry toast, I'll remember it. Mr. Musial has instructed Dad to come after the game around the right-field line to the vistors' clubhouse area. Our names are on the list for entry.

Stan greets us at the door and leads us to his locker. The clubhouse is bustling with activity because it's getaway day: players everywhere, showering, getting dressed, packing their equipment bags; sportswriters huddled around certain players; equipment managers and visiting clubhouse kids gathering up dirty uniforms.

All this excitement, and I'm sitting on a stool next to Mr. Musial when I see Ken Boyer, the Cardinals' star third baseman and my future manager, both in the minor leagues and later with the Cardinals. He, more than any other manager, will help me find my way. Of course, I don't know any of that last bit and neither does he. I'm just a kid whose legs barely reach the floor, sitting on that stool. And he's just a young, famous baseball player, one year away from an MVP season, who probably thinks he will play this game forever.

His locker is two down from Mr. Musial's. He's got a towel wrapped around his waist, and he looks at me and says, "Hi," and I say, "Hi," and he tousles my hair.

Yeah, I'll never forget that.

CHAPTER 18

AFTER DENVER AND MY awesome series in front of Dad, September call-ups were only a few weeks away. But as fate would have it, I would become a major leaguer sooner than that, because on August 28, 1974, the Cardinals' Joe Torre sprained his thumb sliding back into second base.

Well, Torre was the first baseman for the Cardinals, who were only a game and a half out of first place. He was supposed to miss less than a week, but a few games can make all the difference in a tight divisional race, so they called up their red-hot, matinee-idol AAA first baseman, who was busy crushing balls in Tulsa, to fill in.

Me!

We were in Oklahoma City when the news arrived. I was shocked. Sure, I'd been expecting a September call-up, but the organization was now making me an official rookie, and I'd be a Cardinal for the rest of the season, including the postseason if they made it that far. The organization also called up my Tulsa teammate catcher Marc Hill. The best defensive catcher in the organization, Marc was my roommate in St. Pete, sharing an efficiency apartment with me at the luxurious Edgewater Beach Motel, so it was fitting that we were called up together. In fact, I'd like to give a shout-out to *all* my minor league roommates: without them (and their gals) I might never have discovered psychedelic music, grass, late-night sloth routines, and my distinct ability to ignore sexual intercourse occurring just a few yards away. *Thanks, guys! To be sure, none of this came in handy during my pending life in the major leagues...*

Anyway, Marc Hill and I just stood there in the visiting manager's office in Oklahoma City with these big, stupid grins on our faces as our manager, one Ken Boyer, gave us the news.

"You're on the first flight to San Francisco," Boyer informed us.

Now, in case you missed it, this is nothing short of a "Holy shit, Batman" moment in my life.

First, I was being sent to the big leagues as a St. Louis Cardinal—my childhood dream to wear the same uniform as Stan Musial one day had come true. *Wow!* Second, I was headed to my hometown for my major league debut, where the Cardinals would begin a three-game series against the Giants the following day. *Okay, not optimal, but...cool!* Third, the guy who was giving me this wonderful news—*You're going up, kid!*—was none other than Ken Boyer, the very same Ken Boyer who eleven years earlier, almost to the day, had tousled my hair and said hello to me sitting next to Stan Musial. *Okay, the hair on my arms is starting to stand up now...* And fourth, that had all happened in the very same place where I was now headed: the visitors' locker room in Candlestick Park.

Call it fate, karma, coincidence (I choose the first), but whatever the reason, I was about to come through those clubhouse doors again, only this time as a major leaguer. "Yes, Robin." Or in the immortal words of Group Captain Lionel Mandrake, played superbly by Peter Sellers in *Dr. Strangelove,* "Holy Colonel Bat Guano!"

Unfortunately, my "costume" walking through those doors was going to be as bad as the one I had worn in '72, flying in for my first spring training. Actually, it was worse. Let me explain.

When we got the call, we were on the road in

Oklahoma City, and Boyer didn't have any sort of dress code. All Marc and I had in our suitcases were faded jeans and Ban-Lon shirts—not exactly the proper attire to travel with the big club. With only a couple of hours before our flight to San Fran, we said goodbye to Boyer and sprinted to a nearby clothing store.

Remember that great exchange between Dan Aykroyd and the saloon waitress in *The Blues Brothers?*

> ***Aykroyd:*** Uhh, what kind of music do you usually have here?
>
> ***Waitress:*** Oh, we got both kinds! We got country *and* western!

Well that pretty much sums up men's fashion options in Oklahoma City in 1974. Not exactly sport coats and suit pants. This was a cowboy town. I remember we always stayed at the Holiday Inn, and they had a big bar that was straight out of the movie *Urban Cowboy.* It had a mechanical bull, and there were drugstore cowboys in ten-gallon hats and boots, and lots of pretty girls, who were quite friendly, but you had to be careful. I certainly didn't need some hard-ass cowboy with Lord knows how much liquor or crystal meth in his system looking to plant his pointy boot between my legs because his girlfriend was flirting with me.*

So Marc and I were forced to shop where those dudes shopped, and it was what you'd expect: boots, leather vests, and six-shooters. Even Marc, who was from Elsberry, Missouri—a very small town with maybe 1,500 people in it—was like "What the hell?" The closest things they had to acceptable were polyester cowboy outfits with snaps instead of buttons on the jackets, and more snaps on the shirts' breast pockets. Of course, only two colors were available, so we drew straws: Marc got the navy blue, and I got the other, banana yellow. Another Cuban flag.

We hustled to the airport and flew out to San Francisco wearing our normal clothes, saving our *Bonanza* outfits for the next day, when we'd meet the team at the park. *Won't* this *make a good first impression with the veterans.*

My dad picked me up from the airport, and I

---

* My brother once told me never to get into a fight in a bar over a woman. He said there would be gals who would flirt with me just to get their boyfriends jealous, and the last thing I needed was a drunk and angry BF looking for a fight. "Just say, 'I'm so sorry. I didn't know this was your girlfriend. Please forgive me.' Then *exit stage right.*" Sage advice, and doubly true in a town like Oklahoma City.

was very much on edge. Of all places to make your debut: in front of Mom and Dad and family and about fifty hometown friends. Just arranging all their tickets was stressful. Gary would be my rock, of course, but he didn't arrive until the second game of the series, flying in from Sarasota immediately after his season ended, so I had to withstand all the pressure alone. That's a word I hate: "pressure." Pressure is what people make of an otherwise opportune moment.

Pressure is a challenge.

But in this situation, there is no better word to describe what stirred in my gut. Because everything I'd put into baseball seemed so close to paying off. The hard work, the disappointments, the setbacks. It was all worth it if I could just make this work. It was like making camp on Mt. Everest before the final climb. *I've made it this far, but can I make it to the top?* And to begin that final leg of the ascent in my hometown was beyond nerve-racking.

I stayed in Gary's vacated bedroom with the double bed, and I got a good night's sleep under the same roof where I used to dream of making it to the major leagues. (If only I'd left some clothes in the closet, I could have spared myself the banana suit, but at least when I drove myself to Candlestick Park the next morning I was appropriately dressed for my first gunfight against major league pitching.)

To make room on the roster for Marc Hill and me, the organization waived backup catcher—and fan favorite—Tim McCarver.* McCarver, who was on his second run with the club, was a force behind the plate with the Cardinals' championship teams of the '60s. So one special St. Louis career came to an end while two others were hopefully beginning. Such is life in baseball. As my good friend and former teammate Ted Simmons says, "It's a logical progression." How true. But as Teddy—who ironically had taken McCarver's starting job as catcher three seasons prior, in 1971—knows, that doesn't make it any easier for the other veterans, who now have to manage the loss of not only a teammate but a friend. I mean, how many games did McCarver catch Bob Gibson over that glorious decade of the '60s? But now, in that friend's place, is a rookie who by definition doesn't know squat about major league baseball.

So here I was, first day, with a veteran team, feeling out of place, dressed in a ridiculous outfit.

I walked into that clubhouse, and it looked the

---

* The organization also sent reserve infielder Jerry DaVanon down to the minors.

same as it did in 1963. I immediately peered over at those three lockers and stools where I had sat between Musial and Boyer. *Holy cow.* Then I looked at the lineup card and saw that I was starting at first base and hitting seventh. *Holy crap!* You have to remember, this was not planned. It was not like the team had been grooming me and brought me up on purpose in front of my hometown. This was all a chain reaction beginning with Joe Torre diving into second base—something he'd done a million times before, just a bit differently on the million and first. And while he was out of commission for hopefully less than a week, the team still needed production at first base, and the Cardinals' brass was hoping I could fill the gap. There was a lot at stake for everybody, and, again, it was all on display for the folks at home.

Left-hander Mike Caldwell was on the hill for the Giants. At 12–3 with an ERA of 2.97, he was having a superb year and retired the first six batters. I drew a walk on five pitches—all sliders—to lead off the third. Taking all the way until I got my first strike, I never swung the bat: the first pitch was a ball; the second pitch was a strike, which I took, and the count was even at 1–1; and then he threw three straight balls that I didn't chase. In my second at-bat, I led off the bottom of the fifth, but Caldwell struck me out.

It's all about getting that first base hit. I knew that once Torre was back I wasn't going to get much playing time. So I needed to get things going. Plus, here I was playing with guys like Reggie Smith, Lou Brock, and Ted Sizemore. The Giants had Gary Matthews, Dave Kingman, Bobby Bonds, and Tito Fuentes, a guy I had grown up watching. I was twenty years old, three years removed from high school. *Are my insecurities on full display?* It was like I was a sapling next to mighty oaks. It was very daunting—it was the major leagues. Then there was my dad in the stands, and I knew how much this meant to him. And sitting next to him was "Constant Mom," wrapped in a blanket to protect her from the wind and chill that were synonymous with Candlestick Park.

Man alive, a base hit sure would be helpful.

It came in the ninth inning: with Bake McBride in scoring position, I singled to right field for my first major league hit and my first major league RBI. Plus, it sent Caldwell to the showers. The Giants won 8–2, so it's hardly like my effort improved the team's lot. But they were my firsts, and the next day, the *Post-Dispatch* read:

"Sure, I was nervous at bat," said 20-year-old Hernandez. "That Caldwell was throwing

170

some sliders on the corners [of the plate] that I had never seen before. I did get some fastballs that I should have ripped, but I fouled them off. But it was great getting that first hit up there."

Welcome to the major leagues, Mr. Hernandez.

Part II
GET TO WORK

CHAPTER 19

Long Island, New York

THE COUNTDOWN BEGINS WHEN my alarm buzzes at 8 a.m. The Mets have a 1:10 game today, a rarity on a weekday, and I'm working the broadcast. So I get up, feed Hadji and eat breakfast, take a shower, and get dressed. Just before 9 and on schedule, I'm ready to head out the door when a hornet dive-bombs me in the living room.

Uh, Houston, we have a problem.

Whatever the phobia is for bees and such, I have it, so I don't react particularly well when confronted by one. Once, when I was at the plate in Wrigley Field, a yellow jacket landed on my nose. *"Whoa!"* I pulled the ejector button and flew out of the box. Thankfully, the pitcher was still in his windup, and the umpire immediately called time to ask if I was okay. "Damn bee," I explained, and after a few chuckles, we proceeded without further interruption.

Another time, in the early '80s when I was

married to my first wife and we were living in Chesterfield, Missouri, I was driving the family van with the driver's side window halfway down, and a wasp flew into my side mirror, got sucked into the van, and landed in my lap. It was either dead or stunned, but of course I freaked—I was, after all, wearing shorts—and we went off the road, and I took out around thirty feet of my neighbor's fence. All my kids were on board, so it could've been a disaster. But thanks to my expert emergency driving skills, the vehicle stayed upright and no one was injured.

So with great trepidation and care, I finally coax this hornet out the now wide-open sliding door.

Recommencing countdown. My house is about seven miles west of Sag Harbor, and the ride from my doorstep to Citi Field is eighty-six miles, usually taking ninety minutes. But all it takes is one accident or stall and you're in deep trouble. It's times like these—when I'm in a rush—that I miss living in the city, where there are no yards or hornet's nests to tend to and everything's just a cab ride away.

So how did a kid from San Francisco who played ball for the Cardinals wind up living most of each year in New York? Well, the impetus was being traded by the Cardinals to the New York Mets in 1983. The next season, I moved into an apartment on the East Side, Midtown, and tried on "city life." As a ballplayer carousing around with his new teammates, it wasn't hard to get used to.

In those early days, our favorite place was Rusty's, owned by my teammate Rusty Staub. But if someone, usually pitcher Ed Lynch, said, "Hey, let's grab some sushi," then we'd head to Tokubei 86, a Japanese restaurant on 86th and Second Avenue (it's not there anymore). It'd be Ed, Rusty, and myself, and sometimes Ron Darling, who lived downtown. (We'd drop Danny Heep and his wife, Jane, off at the Mad Hatter, their favorite post-game establishment on the Upper East Side.) We'd all go and eat and drink. All the restaurateurs loved having us because the Mets, previous doormat of the NL East, were turning things around.

I remember one night we were a little rowdy—there was more sake and Sapporo going around than sushi—and the conversation somehow got on who would be the best lion tamer of the group. *Seems normal, right?* So someone (probably Lynchie) stood up, grabbed a chair in one hand, pointed the four legs at the rest of us, and with an imaginary whip in the other hand, imitated a lion tamer in his best ringmaster voice: "Stand back, everyone. I'll keep you safe from these terrible beasts!" Everybody in the restaurant seemed to enjoy our antics. But the owner came out, pleading with Rusty, the only mature one of us, "Oh, Mr. Rusty, not the chair! Not the chair!"

We were ballplayers—of course we could be obnoxious. Nights after a day game were especially fun: table for ten, dinner at a normal hour, and with Rusty in attendance, fine wine flowing. I remember one night we got loud, and Lynchie left the table to use the restroom. When he returned, he walked by an older couple, and the wife was angrily telling her husband, "I don't care if that is Keith Hernandez. I don't have to listen to that kind of language!"

Oops! (Never got to apologize for that one.)

New York just afforded more opportunities for shenanigans since nothing seemed too far or to ever close down for the night. And as ballplayers on a night schedule, Manhattan was the perfect fix; it was sort of like we were in college, only we used hot new clubs and fine restaurants as our fraternity houses.

I slowed down a bit after I retired from the game in 1991, trading the nightclubs and bars for the next generation, and I enjoyed everything Manhattan had to offer an older, possibly maturing Keith Hernandez. Then, in the spring of 2002, I met my second wife, bought the house out in the Hamptons later that same year, and moved there permanently in 2006 with our dog and three cats. I was doing only around thirty Mets games on the MSG network at the time, and I didn't think my role as television analyst would become anything more than part-time. We settled in, and my summer became those thirty games, barbecuing by the pool, tending my extensive rose garden, and enjoying the bucolic outdoors beneath the embrace of mature oak trees.

Well, that marriage fizzled, too, and now I do about 120 games a season, but I still have the house and its backyard retreat.

So I'm staying.

But there's no way around this commute to the ballpark. I've missed the morning rush-hour traffic, but as I get closer to Manhattan, stragglers are aplenty, and things always begin to back up around exit 39, where drivers can leave the Northern State Parkway and merge onto the Long Island Expressway.

The way home will be *far* worse. The game will finish sometime around 4:30, and it'll be about a ten-minute walk from the booth, through the bowels of Citi Field, past the visitors' clubhouse to the parking lot, saying my goodbyes and see-you-tomorrows to the ushers and vendors along the way. By the time I'm on the highway, it'll be after 5, and I'll be smack-dab in the middle of evening rush hour, everyone going east after a long workday in the city. I'll be anxious to get home, but just like when I stepped up to the plate in the big leagues, I'll have to take a deep breath, count to ten, and tell myself, *No, Keith, the HOV lane is not for you. Just go with the flow and don't weave in and out of traffic just to gain on maybe a car or two.* Finally, after about two and a half hours in the car, I'll be home.

It will go faster if today's game is like last night's broadcast: a nice and tidy two-hour-and-twenty-minute affair. That was awesome. I got home before midnight and had a good sleep despite the quick turnaround for today's day game. I wish all the games could move so quickly, but with so many pitching changes these days and manager challenges, even a low-scoring, well-played nine innings usually takes three hours and change.

Ughhhh...

Three hours for an average game is not good for baseball. The only thing it serves is more concession sales and television advertising revenues. The game was meant to be played at a faster clip, and if it is allowed to slow down further, I fear baseball will become a bore: a tedious exercise of managers and general managers trying to micromanage every second of the game. Why do they do it? Because the game, like everything else, has gotten so hyper-analyzed that those in charge—from general managers to managers to the umpires to the commissioner's office—mitigate risk at the expense of the game's pace: e.g., a constant flux in pitchers and "instant" replay.

People—sports television critics mainly—get on me sometimes when I complain during a broadcast about long games; they think my complaining reflects a less-than-enthusiastic tone about baseball. Well, I still love baseball, but if we keep up with these long games, they might be proven correct. Because while baseball was never meant to be played at a frenetic pace, there is, again, a rhythm to it, and with all the stopping and starting—from the batters stepping out of the box for days on end; to pitchers, particularly relievers, who take an eternity between pitches; to 3–2 counts ad nauseam; to an abundance of base on balls; to instant replay every five seconds; to countless pitching changes; to commercial breaks—that rhythm is under siege.

The commissioner's office is trying to crack down, but we've really just seen Band-Aids so far. I mean do they really expect to shorten the time of the game with a silly thirty-second limit for

the pitching coach or manager to come out to the mound? Besides, mound visits have always been part of baseball, as have older managers, who might not be able to make it that far in a sprint.*
So the league has tried to heal a broken part of the game by breaking another. To make it worse, while the league enforces such sacrilege, they promote all the replay, which just adds minutes upon minutes of gobbledygook to the running time.

Instant replay was instituted on August 28, 2008. It applied to home-run calls in only three situations: to determine if the ball was fair or foul, if in fact the ball had cleared the fence, and if the ball had been subject to fan interference. Now look where it has taken us: "Manager challenges," which were enacted in 2014, initially gave both managers one challenge at the start of the game and no more than two per game if their first challenge was successful. Then, in addition, a much wider range of calls, beyond the initial scope, were made subject to review. But the commissioner's office wasn't finished. In 2015 and

---

* Harvey Kuenn, manager of the 1975 and 1982–83 Brewers, was an amputee after suffering a blood clot in his leg in 1980. Will the league start making exceptions for exceptional people like Harvey?

2016, they made further modifications, allowing a manager to retain his challenge if a play was successfully overturned, and allowing the manager to no longer have to challenge on the field but instead from the dugout. This last bit was done for the sake of saving time.

Saving time? What a joke!

So the league has failed to address the real need: to rein in the beyond-excessive management and umpiring of the game. And it's not like managers or general managers are going to curtail their strategies. They're just trying to win ball games (though I do question the effectiveness of some of these micromanagement strategies—the constant changing of pitchers in particular). Those guys have jobs on the line, so it's not like they're going to say, "Hey, this is taking too long. Let's just keep our starter out there," just as the umpires aren't going to say, "Hey, let's skip the replay because I *think* it was a fair ball." It's the league's job to step in here, and so far their measures are inadequate. They have to decide if we're playing a baseball game or conducting a computer simulation. Because people make mistakes—it's part of human nature—and last time I checked, the game was still being played, managed, and umpired by humans.

But if we're going to allow folks to increasingly

micromanage every aspect of the game in an attempt to control each and every outcome, then a computer simulation is exactly what we're getting.

I want to add that this isn't an easy issue to solve. Times change; technology increases, as does our understanding of the game; and it would be impossible for baseball to be immune to these forces. When I played, the average game was well under two hours and forty-five minutes, which, according to George Will's *Men at Work,* was still a whopping forty-five minutes longer than games were at the turn of the twentieth century. That's an increase of 38 percent, or, in baseball talk, it's like stretching a normal nine-inning game to twelve and a half innings. I can only imagine a circa 1900 baseball fan watching a modern game. Beyond the strange gloves and testicle-stretching pants, he'd probably think he died and went to eternal hell because the game is taking forever. Interestingly, Will, who published *Men at Work* the same year I retired from baseball, cited that part of the reason for the longer games was batters were becoming more selective with their pitches and willing to go deeper into counts than their predecessors, and "because batters are going deeper into the count, there are more walks and strikeouts, both of which take time."* So I understand the idea that as the game evolves, more time may be required. That said, I would challenge some of our recent game "enhancements" on the grounds that their bad qualities outweigh their good ones, and that they are too disruptive to what is at the very core of baseball: *time* and *rhythm*.

Speaking of time, traffic is moving along nicely. I won't have to call ahead to let my producer know I'm running late. Instead, I want to call my youngest daughter, Mary, to go over the details for a Mets reunion. The franchise is hosting a weekend hubbub at the end of the month at Citi Field. Most of the '86 team will be there, and there will be lots of functions and parties, including a big televised event at the field. My family is coming in—my three daughters with husbands and grandkids, and my brother, Gary, and his wife, Marion. They know all the guys, so it should be a great time. Mary is coordinating everyone in the

---

* George F. Will, *Men at Work* (New York: HarperCollins, 2010). Pitchers today, versus those from the late '80s, seem reluctant to put a hitter away when they have the decided advantage of an 0–2 count. This careful pitching (to put it nicely) only adds to pitch counts (0–2 quickly becomes 3–2) and elapsed time.

family, and she really doesn't need my help. I'm just curious, so I give her a buzz.

My girls—Jessie, Melissa, and Mary—are wonderful. They continue to put up with a lot from a father who's had a knack for putting baseball ahead of everything, including them. But we're working on it and have been for a while.

CHAPTER 20

I WAS IN THE big leagues! Even when Joe Torre came back from his thumb injury on September 2, 1974, and I was relegated to the bench, I was like a kid in a candy store.* How could I be otherwise? Every day I got into uniform that September, it was in a new major league city, in a new major league stadium, dugouts filled with players I had grown up following. Remember, I had been familiar with every team's lineup since childhood. As a boy, I had picked up the sports pages and perused the daily box scores, and later I had played Strat-O-Matic baseball, which made me savvier than most fans. My knowledge about the players went much deeper than just the stars; I knew almost *everyone*, their careers, what teams they had played for,

---

* In the three games Torre missed, I went 3 for 10 with 3 walks.

and many of their stats and accomplishments. Couple that with the extensive baseball history my dad had taught me, and I understood I was in the presence of not just major leaguers but serious big-league lineage.

For example, after we left San Francisco, my first home stand was in Busch Stadium against the Expos. Playing first base for Montreal? Thirty-five-year-old Ron Fairly. *Who is Ron Fairly?* Well, of course I recalled that he had started his major league career as a member of the Dodgers teams of the '60s, which I had grown up watching on TV. Pretty much every year those transplanted Flatbush bums had stood in the way of the Giants in their quest for the National League flag, giving the Mays-led Giants the label "The Bridesmaids of the NL." And Fairly was a good, solid player—a .265 hitter averaging 10 home runs and 70 RBI a year with a very, very good glove at first base—but he wasn't a perennial All-Star. In fact, the previous year, 1973, had been his only year as an All-Star.*

Yet here I was, a rookie riding pine, thinking, *Holy cow, there's Ron Fairly!* Why? Because I also knew that he had played with Brooklyn

---

* Fairly would also make the All-Star team in 1978, though this time representing Toronto in the American League.

shortstop and Hall of Famer Pee Wee Reese.*
Reese, of course, had been a part of all those
great Brooklyn Dodgers teams to face the New
York Yankees in *seven* World Series between
1941 and 1956. So he had gone up against
Mantle and Berra in '52, '53, '55, and '56,
DiMaggio and Berra in '47 and '49, and DiMaggio and Bill Dickey in '41, which had been
Reese's first year in the bigs and Bill Dickey's
last. Bill Dickey had broken into the league
way back in 1921—a late-season call-up—and
with *his* keister parked on the bench, he got to
watch Lou Gehrig and Babe Ruth lead the Yankees to a World Series title over—you guessed
it—the St. Louis Cardinals.

How's *that* for lineage? So, yeah, I was seeing
all these big leaguers, and as I said before, most
of the time I felt like a sapling in a forest of
mighty oaks. But however small, I was now a part
of baseball history because I played against a guy
who played with a guy who played against a guy
who had been a teammate of Babe Ruth, the
mightiest oak of them all. And with chronologies

---

* I knew Mr. Reese from my minor league days when he
was representing the Louisville Slugger bat company. In
fact, he signed me to my first bat contract with Louisville
in 1973. I would stay with that company my entire career.

like that playing through the back of my mind, riding pine never felt so good.

And then, of course, there were the superstars. Tom Seaver, for one. We faced Seaver and the Mets on September 8 in what looked to be my sixth game in a row of never leaving the dugout. But so what? I was going to watch the reigning NL Cy Young winner, Tom Seaver, go against our ace, Lynn McGlothen. Talk about a show!

I'd faced McGlothen in the minors back in Tulsa when we'd battled Pawtucket in the 1973 Junior World Series. He'd made me look foolish in game one of that series—I'd never seen a hard, snapping curve like that before. Now McGlothen, 16–8, was throwing in his first full big-league season with a chance to be a twenty-game winner for the St. Louis Cardinals. But first he needed to get by Seaver and the defending NL champion Mets, who may have been 64–73 on the season, just beginning what would be another long stretch of disappointing, if not terrible, seasons for Mets fans to endure. But the names were still there: Bud Harrelson, Félix Millán, Ed Kranepool, Wayne Garrett, Rusty Staub, Jerry Koosman, Jon Matlack, and Cleon Jones. So McGlothen had his work cut out for him, while I had plenty of stargazing to keep me entertained.

Yogi Berra is the Mets' manager, for crying out loud! But, as it turned out, I would be a bystander for only *most* of the afternoon.

We were going for a three-game sweep after Bob Forsch shut out Koosman and the Mets in the opener, 2–0, and Bob Gibson outdueled Jon Matlack 2–1 in the second game. This was the Sunday finale, and we were a game and a half behind the Pirates with twenty-three games left in the season—a real stretch run.

We were losing 5–3 in the ninth when our manager, Red Schoendienst, walked down the dugout toward me and said, "Hernandez, be ready. I may pinch-hit you this inning." I raced to the bat rack, grabbed my bat and helmet, and retreated up the runway a few yards to begin stretching and mentally preparing.

Sure enough, with two outs and nobody on, Red signaled me to hit for Mike Tyson in the eighth hole. Deep breath. The scoreboard in left field had already posted a Pirates victory against the Expos, and I was the last chance for us to keep pace in the NL East.

I strode to the on-deck circle and rubbed some pine tar and resin onto my bat, making sure my hands adhered to it. I then slipped the weighted donut onto the bat and took a few swings to loosen up. During this on-deck circle ritual I heard my name being announced over the stadium PA system, and the crowd of slightly more than 34,000 fans, anxious to see this rookie who'd been in the papers of late, came to their feet in anticipation. I stepped into the box, looked up, and lo and behold, there stood Tom Terrific. A few more deep breaths, and I counted to ten... *I guess I'm ready*.

Not many people in life get a chance to face a Hall of Fame Cy Young winner's fastball, much less one from Tom Seaver. I don't remember the count, but I do know that he threw me a vintage Seaver up-and-in fastball, alive and "rising" with extreme velocity, zinging as if traveling along a telephone wire. And don't ask me how, because I thought the ball was by me, but I just reacted.

Whack! Boom!

I drilled a laser beam to right-center field in old Busch Stadium, where it was 386 to the wall in both gaps. That's a long, *long* way. Had we been dueling in Shea Stadium, that shot would have been a home run. As it was, it smacked above the protective padding off the concrete wall, a foot from a home run, and came bouncing back into the outfield. I dashed around the bases—the roar of the crowd only slightly audible above the pounding inside my chest—and I found myself standing on third base, thinking, *Man, I just got a pinch-hit triple off Tom Seaver.*

Seaver retired the next batter, Richie Scheinblum, on a pop-up, and the game ended. I was bummed, of course, because I wanted to be a part of a big comeback against the one-and-only Tom Seaver. But Tom would have none of it, and we fell two and a half games behind the Pirates with twenty-two to play.

The Phillies came to town the next night, and Red called on me to pinch-hit again—this time against Jim Lonborg, the 1967 AL Cy Young winner for the Boston Red Sox. A freshman in high school during that season, I remember tuning in to the 1967 World Series and watching Lonborg pitch three games against the Cardinals, winning Game Two and Game Five, but losing Game Seven to Bob Gibson on two days' rest. Shortly after that series, Lonborg blew out his knee while snow skiing in Aspen, and the veterans said he was never the same.* But I, for the second night in a row, was coming in cold off the bench to face

---

* The handsome Stanford graduate Lonborg was hitting the slopes with actress and super fox Jill St. John when he tore up his knee. From then on, all player contracts would include what is known as the "Lonborg clause," which voids the contract if the player gets hurt while snow skiing.

a Cy Young winner whom I'd never faced. *Advantage Hernandez?* I think not! I drew a walk—not exactly a stand-up triple, but I took it. Lonborg got through the inning unscathed, however, on his way to a complete-game shutout and his fifteenth win.

The next night, behind the complete-game pitching of Dick Ruthven, the Phillies beat us badly. I pinch-hit for another walk in the sixth, but it didn't mean much; they'd already put the game away. The much bigger deal was getting to see a huge piece of history being made when my thirty-five-year-old teammate Lou Brock broke Major League Baseball's single-season stolen-base record. He tied Maury Wills's modern-era mark of 104 when he stole second in the first inning, and he nabbed sole possession of the record with another swipe in the seventh.*

And this man was how old? Unbelievable. I remember they stopped play on the field after Lou set the record. Second base umpire John McSherry and Phillies middle infielders Larry Bowa

---

* Wills had set the record in 1962. Brock would finish the season with 118, a record that still stands today in the National League, although Rickey Henderson stole 130 in 1982 to set the current American League and overall mark. Henderson was twenty-three years old when he set the new mark.

and Dave Cash all shook his hand. I could see that Lou, besides being one of the greats, was well respected and liked by players, teammates, and competitors. We all charged the field and swarmed Lou with congratulations, and then stepped aside to let him soak in the glory. The class act that he is, Brock simply tipped his cap to the 27,000 fans who had sat through the blowout in hopes of seeing the record broken, and I believe it was important to Lou, a St. Louis favorite ever since he'd been acquired by trade from the Cubs in 1964, to break the record in front of the home crowd.*

But not everyone was thrilled with Lou when the game ended. Bob Boone, the Gold Glove catcher for the Phillies at the time, was one of the best throwers in the game and *very* difficult to steal on.† Well, he got pissed as hell at Brock in the ninth inning after Lou attempted yet another swipe. I remember I was standing in the dugout, about five feet back from the steps, and after the out was registered on a perfect throw

---

* The Cubs traded Brock a third of the way through the 1964 season, and he went on to hit .348 for the Cards for the rest of that season, helping them to a World Series title.

† He was also the son of former Cleveland Indians outfielder Ray Boone, who had been a minor league teammate of my father's at Oklahoma City in 1947. Talk about lineage.

by Boone, I saw him clench his fist while bending over to grab his mask and curse Lou in no uncertain terms. He was probably already upset that Lou had swiped two off him earlier to tie and break the record—a distinction no catcher would want—and now thought Lou was showing him up.*

This little incident, which was probably missed by most, seriously whet my appetite, and I remember saying to myself, *Of all the places in this world, this is where I want to be—amid all this kind of* competitiveness. *I want to stay here and do this on a par and as a peer with these guys.*

So I was seeing and learning quite a bit in a short amount of time. But despite the stargazing, I still very much wanted to play and was happy knowing my plate appearances weren't meaningless. I'd been hitting .350 in AAA, and thought I could really help the Cardinals. But it had been almost two weeks since my last start. *How in hell was I going to get into a rhythm with just pinch hits?* The triple off Seaver probably raised

---

* In Bob's defense, he felt Lou was breaking one of the unwritten rules in baseball: neither pour it on late in a game nor, in this case, pad your stats when you're down. After the game, Lou told reporters he was just trying to jump-start a rally.

some eyebrows, and the walk from Ruthven was my sixth in seventeen plate appearances. But the team was focused on beating the Pirates for the division, not on developing young talent, and they had a former MVP and batting champ in Joe Torre anchoring first base. I would just have to be patient.

We flew to New York to face the Mets in the first series of a crucial road trip: two in New York, three in Philly, and three in Pittsburgh. We landed at LaGuardia Airport sometime after 2 a.m., and as we were bussing into the city, I got my very first look at the Manhattan skyline. It was a beautiful, clear night, and I couldn't get over all those buildings, my eyes, of course, scanning for the Empire State Building. Lou Brock, who must have sensed my wonder at the whole thing, reached over to me and said, "Keith, there's a million stories in that city. And guess what? Now you're one of them."

But Lou's inspiring words were quickly tempered when we arrived at the New York Sheraton and George Kissell, Red's bench coach, had me follow him outside the hotel lobby to the street.

"New York City is a dangerous place, Keith," he began. It was past three in the morning, and I couldn't get over the number of taxis still out and about. "It's on the verge of bankruptcy, and there is a major criminal element walking these streets. You can wind up in a bad area and find yourself in trouble."

"Okay," I said.

George then pointed up Sixth Avenue. "That's Central Park," he said. *"Don't go there."*

I nodded.

Then he pointed west. "That's Hell's Kitchen," he continued. *"Don't go there."*

Another nod.

Then he pointed down the avenue. "That's Times Square. *Don't go there.*"

And I was thinking, *Where the hell am I? A war zone?*

Finally, George pointed east. "That's the Upper East Side. If you have to go somewhere in this city, *go there.*"

George then took me back inside the hotel, escorting me to the elevator, which I took in the only direction left: *up,* and to the safety of my room and bed. Such was my introduction to the city of New York, the place of a million stories and, according to George Kissell, a million ways to die.

Well, I *almost* was the story of the game the next night because I pinch-hit off Harry Parker, a right-hander, in the top of the twelfth and hit a rope to right field.* But the right fielder, Dave Schneck—all five feet nine inches of him—leapt up, crashing into the wall at full speed, and robbed me of a home run. So I was back on the bench, and the game stayed tied—until the *twenty-fifth inning! Damn you, Dave Schneck!*

As it turned out, the real "player of the game" was Claude Osteen, who entered in the fourteenth inning and threw 9⅓ innings of shutout relief for us during the marathon, keeping us in the game until we won it on a Hank Webb wild throw attempting to pick off Bake McBride at first. Osteen was another one of those baseball players I knew well because he had played for the Dodgers in my formative years, from 1965 to 1973, winning twenty games twice for manager Walter Alston, in 1969 and 1972. Claude was a super-nice guy and was wonderful to me that September. He was also a dead ringer for Jim Nabors, the actor who played Gomer Pyle on *The Andy Griffith Show;* I started calling him Gomer after a few of the veterans told me it was his nickname. Well, stupid me for falling for that, because Claude pulled me aside in BP one day.

---

* Near Shea's old bullpen gate.

"You know, Keith," he said, "I *hate* being called Gomer."

"Oh, Claude," I said, "I'm so sorry. I'll never say that again." Nor did I take any more of the veterans' advice when it came to nicknames.

Well, that marathon game against the Mets lasted seven hours and four minutes, forcing Red to use nineteen players and seven pitchers over the course of the game. By the time it ended—at approximately 3 a.m.—there was no food and just a smattering of beer left in the clubhouse for the guys who'd played the entire game. Were they pissed...*But, hey! We won, and the Pirates lost!*

The next night, we were back at Shea for game two. Down 4–3 with two outs and the bases loaded in the sixth, Red pinch-hit me, and I ripped a line drive to right center. This time Schneck muffed it, and the tying run and two go-ahead runs scored. We were now only a game and a half behind the Pirates. Good things happen, including errors, when you hit the ball hard, and some of the veteran players shook my hand in the energetic clubhouse after the game. I can't tell you how awesome it made me feel that I was gaining their respect, my contributions slowly bringing me into the fold.

After showering up, we were off to Philadelphia on a late-night, two-hour bus jaunt down the New Jersey Turnpike. A mixture of veterans and new players, the Phillies were on the verge of NL East dominance. We're talking Dave Cash, Larry Bowa, Greg Luzinski, Willie Montañez, and, of course, future Hall of Famers Mike Schmidt and Steve Carlton. On a five-game winning streak—including a two-game sweep of the division-leading Pirates—the Phillies were now 4.5 back in the standings, and our pending three-game set was crucial for both teams.

So imagine my surprise when I arrived at Veterans Stadium the following afternoon and discovered I was starting the game. *What?!* No one had said to me the night before or that morning, "Hey, Keith, you're gonna be in the lineup." But there it was when I entered the clubhouse, written on the chalkboard: HERNANDEZ, FIRST BASE. Not only that, I was batting fifth—an RBI spot in the lineup—behind Simmons and in front of McBride.

Jim Lonborg was on the hill for the Phillies, and, once again, Jim pitched a brilliant game. He may not have been the power pitcher he was back in '67, but he was smarter than most and could throw a breaking ball for a strike when he was behind in the count.* As a young hitter itching to hit a fastball, that was very, *very* frustrating. I'd be up in the count, say two balls and no strikes, but here would come this big 11-to-5 hard curve. On the black, outside corner, at the knees. *Strike!* Even if I'd been looking for it, which I wasn't at this early stage in my career, I just wasn't used to seeing this kind of quality curveball in triple A.† So Jim, who never seemed to leave anything out over the plate, gave me fits, and I was an insignificant 1 for 4 when he left the game after the eighth.

Fortunately, our starter, Lynn McGlothen, was dealing, and the game went into extra innings, tied 2–2. We eventually won 7–3, putting up 5 runs in the seventeenth inning. This after our twenty-five-inning marathon two days earlier.

---

* Jim had the intellect to reinvent himself after the knee injury. But that sort of thing takes time. He hung around, compiling a 27–30 record over 70 starts with the Red Sox, before being traded to the Milwaukee Brewers after the 1971 season. He started turning the corner in 1972, winning fourteen games, then was traded again after that season to the Phillies, where he would play six-plus years, winning 17 games in 1974 and 18 in 1976.

† Even as a veteran, ahead in the count like this, I wouldn't have swung at this "pitcher's pitch"—a quality breaking ball, painted perfectly down and away.

Imagine our bullpen! I went 2 for 3 in the extra innings, taking part in the winning rally: Ted Simmons led off with a single to left; I followed with a single to left; and McBride singled behind me, scoring Simmons and pushing me to third.

Boy, did it feel good to be a part of another big win, especially after not starting for twelve days.

I was back on the chalkboard the next day and went 1 for 5, taking part in a big fifth inning with an RBI triple and a run scored. The 9–2 victory was our fourth in a row and, coupled with a Pirates loss at Montreal earlier that day, propelled us into a half-game lead over the Pirates with sixteen games to play. After the win, my head was spinning, like *Holy cow, this is amazing.* Here I was with the Cardinals, not only in the middle of a neck-and-neck divisional race but in first place! *I could be in postseason play and a World Series, and I'm contributing!*

Back at the hotel and feeling pretty good, I decided to go out on a limb and make my way downstairs to the hotel bar with my buddy Marc Hill.* I remember being slightly skittish walking

---

* The soon-to-be infamous Bellevue-Stratford, an old and historic hotel on Broad Street, gained worldwide notoriety in July of 1976 when several American Legionnaires on convention were stricken by an unknown disease, later called

in because Bob Gibson, who didn't seem to have the most patience with rookies, was up at the bar along with Reggie Smith, Joe Torre, and Ted Sizemore. Big dogs. But Ted was always great to me, going out of his way to make me feel at home since I'd walked in the door in San Francisco.

So as casually as we could, Marc and I strode up to the bar to hang near—if not with—these baseball giants, and Reggie Smith, who was a little in his cups, immediately started laying the rookie stuff on me. It was just a typical razzing, nothing mean-spirited, that basically culminated in Reggie saying, "Go someplace else, rook." So I left the bar with my tail between my legs and tried not to take it personally. *What was I thinking, anyway?* I mean, we're talking about Reggie Smith here—a guy who nine days prior to my fourteenth birthday was helping Boston get to Game Seven in the 1967 World Series against the Cardinals with a 2-hit, 2-RBI performance. And now, as a Cardinal, Reggie was on his way to slugging .528 for the season! So big deal if he'd razzed

---

Legionnaires' disease. Evidently the bacteria thrived in hot, damp places—in this case, the water of the cooling towers for the air-conditioning system—and spread throughout the hotel via the air ducts, killing 29 people and sickening 182 others, none of them major leaguers. The hotel closed later in November of that year.

me a little bit. He'd earned the right. As for me, I was just some young pup, technically not old enough to be in the bar in the first place.

Oh well. Lesson learned.

I didn't play the next day, but we finished the series Sunday afternoon with a 3–1 victory to sweep the Phillies, defeating Steve Carlton, a feat in itself.* Rookie Bob Forsch outdueled Carlton, and with another Pirates loss in Montreal, we extended our lead to one and a half games. We boarded our little Ozark Air Lines "Green Goblin" aircraft and took off for Pittsburgh. The first-place, red-hot Cardinals were on a five-game road winning streak with fifteen games remaining and flying high!

It was a huge three-game series against a Pittsburgh lineup that boasted many of the same players as the 1971 World Series bunch: Al Oliver (best left-handed number-three hitter I ever saw), Willie Stargell (team leader, ferocious cleanup hitter), Bob Robertson, Richie Hebner, Manny Sanguillén, Dock Ellis, Bruce Kison, and Dave

---

* After the Cardinals traded Carlton—over a contract dispute—to Philadelphia eight days before opening day on March 25, 1972, Steve exacted revenge by dominating his former team. There is an old saying in baseball about a player's dominance: "He could've gone out there without a glove and thrown a shutout." Well, not so this day.

Giusti. Missing were '71 World Series hero Steve Blass (inexplicable wildness), Dave Cash (traded to Philly), Bob Moose (on the DL), and, of course, the late, great Roberto Clemente. The new offensive additions to this squad were Rennie Stennett, Richie Zisk (.313 / 17 HRs / 100 RBI), and a young Dave Parker (future MVP, two-time batting champ).

All mashers.

Newcomers to their pitching staff were starters, beginning with control master and Cardinal killer Jim Rooker (15–11 / 2.78 ERA), hard-throwing Ken Brett (13–9 / 3.30 ERA), and another hard thrower, Jerry Reuss (16–11 / 3.50 ERA). All lefties.

The first game matched Bob Gibson against Jerry Reuss. It was Gibby's fourth September start, and he was brilliant, going nine innings, allowing five hits, one run, and one walk, and striking out one.* *Dealing!* I didn't play because

---

* In July, before my call-up, Gibson became the first pitcher since Walter Johnson in 1923 to reach three thousand career strikeouts, although it had been a subpar season for Gibson, who by the end of August had a record of 7–11 with an ERA of 4.19. But Gibson, the old warrior, soon to be thirty-nine years of age, had now turned it on and would continue to dominate down the stretch, posting a 4–1 record with a 2.55 ERA in a whopping fifty-three innings pitched in September.

of the lefty Reuss, who remarkably went thirteen innings in this extra-inning affair and surrendered only one run in the first twelve frames, when Torre tied the game in the seventh with an RBI double. In the tenth, Red went to the whip with Al Hrabosky, aka the Mad Hungarian, who twirled *four* hitless innings in stellar relief for the win, striking out six, including Richie Hebner, aka the Gravedigger, to end the game with runners on first and second.

Our winning formula in the thirteenth? Something I would get used to in the next two years: a leadoff single by Brock, who then stole second; Sizemore bunted him to third; an intentional walk to Smith; followed by a sac fly by Simmons. That three-four of Smith and Simmons was the best switch-hitting combo I ever saw. And Pirates manager Danny Murtaugh had to pick his poison. Either way spelled death. In this case, he chose to walk Smith over the slow-footed Simmons in hopes of an inning-ending double play. But it didn't happen. Simmons came through, and we Cardinals had a two-and-a-half-game lead with fourteen to play.

After the game, the veterans were pumped up, and I could feel that we had the momentum, like *Hey, we're going to win this division*. I was just a kid, so what did I know? But I loved being a witness to all the energy in that clubhouse. *Could it happen?*

Not if Jim Rooker had anything to say about it. He bested us the next game, giving the Pirates a critical win to end their six-game losing streak. *Typical.* Jim was a left-hander who would continue to stick it up our asses for the next six years.* He threw a complete game, allowing a single run and beating our ace, McGlothen, who now wouldn't get to twenty wins on the season.† Talk about a big swing—if we'd won that game, it would have increased our lead to three and a half with thirteen to play.

I started the next game, the rubber match. *Can you believe it?* Red put me in the lineup *in Pittsburgh!* I went 1 for 3 with a single off Bruce Kison, and then Torre pinch-hit for me when Murtaugh brought in Ramón Hernández, a real tough veteran side-arming left-hander. Torre went 1 for 2 with a single, but we lost the game when their closer, Dave Giusti, struck out the side against the meat of our order to end the

---

* Over his NL career, Rooker started 29 games against the Cardinals. In those starts, he was 18–9 for a .667 winning percentage and an ERA of 2.46.

† McGlothen finished the 1974 season at 16–12 with a 2.69 ERA.

game, and the Pirates climbed back to within half a game.

A disappointing end to an eight-game road trip. We'd had our chance to further damage the Pirates. But to their credit, they bounced back from an opening series loss and a six-game losing streak to take the series and close to a half game. From our standpoint, we had opened the road trip two and a half games behind and returned home a half game in front. We'd played and won three extra-inning games (twenty-eight total extra innings) and come from behind late in another. Quite an exhilarating road trip, and we had to feel good about returning home for six games—three with the Cubs, then another three-game set against the Pirates.

The next night at Busch Stadium, I got my first taste of the famed Cubs-Cardinals rivalry: a sea of red with a smaller sea of blue, and by the sixth inning, brawls had begun in the stands. You just don't see that in the minor leagues.

Speaking of the minor leagues, my buddy from AAA, Pete LaCock, who had been called up about ten days before me, was starting in right field for the Cubs. Pete had played for the Wichita Aeros, and a bunch of those guys had become friendly with us during the minor league season. Pete was hilarious. The twentieth overall pick of the 1970 draft, he had spent most of his bonus-baby money on a yellow supercharged Porsche, and he'd go 110 miles per hour on Wichita's back roads, which were all S turns, and I'd be going, "Oh man," totally helpless in the passenger seat.

Pete would also get me into bars—he knew everybody. We were in a dry county, so it was bring-your-own-booze in these establishments. We'd walk in with a half-pint of something, and they'd take the bottle and ask, "What's your name?" I'd say, "Keith," and they'd put my name on my bottle and set it up on the bar. All they had was tonic water and club soda and other mixers, so I'd go up to the bar and say, "I'll have a Keith and tonic," and they'd have all the bottles in alphabetical name order and pour my drink.

Anyway, seeing Pete now brought the minors back to me. It had been only a few weeks, but it suddenly felt like ages since I'd left the Oilers.

We won the first game against the Cubs, 5–2, with Bob Forsch throwing another good game for the win. I started the second game, and we got crushed, 19–4. I went 0 for 4 with 2 strikeouts. The next day was a Sunday afternoon game with 43,267 Cardinals and Cubs fans in the seats to watch Bob Gibson match up against future American League Cy Young Award winner Steve

Stone. Spotted 4 early runs, Gibby pitched six strong innings until the Cubs tagged him for 4 (3 earned) in the seventh. I went in for defense late, and Ted Simmons won the game with an RBI single in the bottom of the ninth for a 6–5 win. Another thriller, coupled with a Pirates loss, and we pushed our lead back to a game and a half. Bring on the Pirates!

The Pirates took the first game 1–0 in ten innings, behind Rooker's nine shutout innings and a tenth-inning run off McGlothen. Our lead back to half a game, I started the second game, going 1 for 2 with a walk and getting pinch-hit for when the Pirates brought in a left-hander. The Pirates scored 4 in the sixth and 3 in the seventh, and we lost. We won the final game of the series 13–12 in eleven innings, our fifth extra-inning affair going back fourteen games to that marathon in New York. Down 3 runs, we scored 4 to win, not only avoiding a sweep but thrusting us back into first by a half game.

It was just a total slugfest: 25 runs scored between the two teams, and neither team would quit. As for me, I wouldn't play again for the remainder of the season. Red would rightly start Torre the rest of the way. Joe had begun to heat up and drive in runs on the last road trip, and even if he hadn't, you had to go to your seasoned veterans in a race this late and close.

With an off day on Thursday, we traveled to Chicago, taking two out of the three games at Wrigley, but the Pirates won three of four games against the Mets. So it was all tied up with one three-game series to play for both teams. Nail-biting. The Pirates headed home to face the Cubs, and we headed to Montreal to battle the Expos on the frozen tundra of Parc Jarry, perhaps the worst major league ballpark in history, especially in the waning days of the season. Besides the fact that it really was just a minor league park, it was frigid. The wind would blow directly out to right in a gale, and there was nothing in its way to stop it. Put a ball in that jet stream, even a routine fly ball to the right fielder, and it might clear the ridiculously short and low fence.

Well, we won the first game, and so did the Pirates. *Still even.*

Gibson pitched the second game, and we were up 2–1 with two outs in the eighth. Willie Davis, former longtime Dodger, got a single to put the winning run at the plate for Montreal. The batter was left-hand hitter Mike Jorgensen. Red went out to talk to Gibson on the mound. With Hrabosky ready in the bullpen, Red had a decision to make: leave Gibson out there or bring in Hrabosky, who was his dominant left-handed closer. But could he take Bob Gibson out of a 2–1 ball game that might decide the season? *He's Bob Gibson!* So Red left him out there, and Jorgensen, who was 1 for 2 with a walk, hit a humpback line drive, and the lousy Canadian wind kept pushing the ball farther and farther out to right field. Reggie Smith went back to the fence—that stupid, short, five-foot cyclone fence with padding on the top—and he had it in his glove but hit the wall at the same time, and the ball popped out of his glove and over the fence for a two-run home run. We lost 3–2 and were then a game behind the Pirates. The only game Gibson lost down the stretch.*

On the final day of the season, we needed to win, and the Pirates to lose. But it was snowing in Montreal—go figure—and our game was postponed until the next day. So we settled into the Queen Elizabeth Hotel, gathering in the hotel bar for some drinks while radio updates on the Pittsburgh-Chicago game trickled in, inning by inning. The Cubs were up 4–0 in the first, and

---

* From September 1 through the end of the 1974 season, Gibson, who would turn thirty-nine that November, went 4–1 with 3 complete games and 53 innings pitched, posting an ERA of 2.55. *And this man was how old?*

everyone breathed a little bit easier. They were still up 4–2 going into the ninth inning, but then a report came in: the Cubbies had blown it. They had allowed a leadoff walk, followed by another, and Ed Kirkpatrick had bunted both men over. Dave Parker grounded to second base to score one and move the tying run to third with two outs. Then Bob Robertson, who had hit a home run the day before to give the Pirates the win, swung and missed on strike three, but the would-be winning pitch got by catcher Steve Swisher, and the runner scored to tie the game.

The Pirates went on to win in extra innings and take the division.* Our season was over, ending right then and there in that Canadian hotel, the makeup game with Montreal now unnecessary.

Of course, I was bummed for the team—for the veteran guys like Lou and Gibson and Size-more it had to be tremendously disappointing—but it wasn't really my team. I was just along for the ride, and what a ride it had been.

I was also a bit naive, not fully understanding just how difficult it is to make the playoffs; the Cardinals and I wouldn't sniff the postseason for another eight years.

---

* The Pirates would lose to the Dodgers, 3–1, in the NLCS.

KH BATTING

Year	Games (G)	At-Bats (AB)	Batting Average (BA)	On-Base Percentage (OBP)	Slugging Percentage (SLG)
1974	14	34	.294	.415	.441

On the plane back to St. Louis, Anheuser-Busch products were aplenty as well as hard liquor. Most of the guys opted for the latter. So we were "opening the cups," and most everyone was getting a bit "boxed." Especially Reitzie, who was ranting that Cubs catcher Steve Swisher had let the ball get by him on purpose. He just kept getting madder and madder, saying that he was going to go after Swisher the first time the Cardinals and Cubs met next April. The guys just let Kenny vent. April was six months away, enough time for even a tough kid like Reitzie to cool down.* In the meantime, they figured alcohol would do the trick.

---

* Reitzie, who was also from the Bay Area, had attended rough-and-tumble Jefferson High School in Daly City. So he knew how to handle himself in a fight.

Sonny Siebert, a veteran right-handed pitcher and a really good guy, sat next to me on the plane, and he said to me, "You know, Keith, I'm getting sick and tired of those tired-ass jeans you always got on." It was true. I'd pretty much been wearing them every day since my call-up and God knows how long before that. Well, Sonny grabbed hold of one pant leg and just ripped it, from the crotch down to the floor, and then he got the other one and ripped that, too.

We landed in St. Louis at about 11 p.m. Two trucks were waiting on the tarmac to pick up all the equipment, like bats, balls, players' duffel bags, dirty uniforms, etc., but back in those days players' personal luggage came up in baggage claim.* So we went through the terminal and toward the baggage claim area, where all the players' wives, kids, and girl-friends, along with a multitude of distraught, commiserating, and well-wishing Cardinals fans, awaited our arrival. As my future friend Howard Cosell would have said, we were "a sight to behold."

---

* Today, there would be two luxury busses waiting on the tarmac to take everyone and their luggage to Busch Stadium. No mingling with the general public necessary.

And now, ladies and gentlemen, under the cheers of the consoling crowd, here come those mighty Cardinals, stumbling into the waiting arms of loved ones while their passed-out third baseman, Ken Reitz, is being carted through the terminal like a wounded soldier—feet dragging, head down, body limp. The man seems completely gone. And look, there's Keith Hernandez, the youngster, his jeans shredded beyond recognition, their underside completely ripped away, providing no more coverage than an American Indian's breechcloth, the promising rookie's season now over.

CHAPTER 21

Citi Field, Flushing, New York

I LEAVE THE CAR in my parking space and begin
the walk toward the second security checkpoint
to enter the "safety" of the stadium confines—
here only personnel, players, and press can roam.
If that sounds more like a diplomatic compound
than a gathering place for America's pastime,
you'd be right. Unfortunately, baseball, like every
other good thing in America, had to adjust to this
"new normal" after 9/11.

"Mr. Hernandez?"

It's some guy decked out in Mets gear. He's
caught me before I can get inside, and he has a
baseball card he wants me to sign. Some ballplayers
may get pissed: *I'm just trying to get to work here,
buddy.* But this guy's all right, and there's plenty of
time before the 1:10 p.m. start, so I take the pen.*

---

* Of course, you get the occasional bonehead. What ticks me off
is the fan who asks for a quick picture and then winds up shoot-

"You think the weather's gonna hold off?" the fan asks while I'm signing.

Why is it that people feel the need to fill in the three seconds it takes to sign an autograph with idle chitchat? I'm not complaining; it's just an observation, and I think it's hilarious. Maybe they just want to smooth over any annoyance they may have caused. I mean a grown man did just ask if another grown man could sign his baseball card.

"They'll get the game in if they can," I answer, and in fairness to his question, there is a cold front moving in, and it's been drizzling all morning. I hand the man the signed card and the pen.

"Thanks, Keith! Good luck today," the guy says.

Good luck for what? I'm just a spectator in a broadcast booth. It's not like I have to get up there in the bottom of the ninth with the game on the line anymore.

But I say, "Thanks" and "Go Mets!" and make my way through the stadium's "Checkpoint Charlie," then head for the elevators.

The card I just signed was a 1985 Topps Keith Hernandez Record Breaker card. Most cards don't grab my attention, but that one actually does. First of all, it reflects the 1984 season,

---

ing video: *Look everyone, I'm here with Keith Hernandez!* That's a no-no.

which was my first full season with the Mets after being traded from the Cardinals in 1983. Second, it's not my favorite card—the picture on it is ridiculous because I'm swinging and my helmet is coming off my head.* And while the image captured on the card reveals a nice follow-through—beautifully balanced and staying on the ball—I can tell from the disappointed expression on my face that I've grounded to the right side of the infield for a probable out. All that aside, I have mixed emotions about the "record" I broke that year. It's for "game-winning RBI," a statistic that came into existence just five years prior and was retired in just a few more.

Why was the stat retired? Well, "game-winning RBI" was well-intentioned—it was supposed to indicate a player's performance in the clutch, like a base hit or sacrifice fly in the bottom of the ninth to win the game. *Okay, that's worthwhile.* But the problem was it was too inclusive; *any* game winner—no matter when it occurred—counted. A player could drive in the first run in the first inning in an 8–0 game and get a game-

---

* I'd just gotten a shorter-than-usual haircut and my helmet wouldn't stay on, which was really annoying. But clubhouse manager Charlie Samuels got me a smaller size by the third game of the season, and all was well again.

winning RBI. Well, that's not right—that doesn't have the same weight as a deciding RBI when the game is late and close and the batter is feeling the pressure. So the stat was flawed, and baseball was right to throw it out, because it should have included only game-winning RBI from the seventh inning on.*

For my own sense of accomplishment, I appreciate the game-winning RBI stat. I know that a lot of my game winners *were* in late and close situations, and that makes me feel good. So I don't totally dismiss it. But another problem with that Record Breaker card has to do with the *other* Record Breaker cards from the 1984 season. There are two in particular. The first is Dwight Gooden's youngest-player-ever-to-win-twenty-games, breaking "Bullet" Bob Feller's record *set in 1939* by one month. That's a record that stood for forty-five years! Gooden was my teammate, and I consider the fact that I got to watch "Doc" throw every pitch of that amazing year one of the highest honors and spectacles of my career. It was nothing short of incredible—godlike stuff. The second was Pete Rose breaking perhaps the most legitimate and

---

* This improved statistic would much later be instituted in the sabermetrics era under the title *Late and Close*, a stat that I love and one I employ on my scorecard before a broadcast.

one of the longest-standing records in baseball history: Ty Cobb's all-time hits record of 4,189 set in 1928 when Cobb retired. So although my card is a nice feather in my cap, and it proves that I helped the 1984 Mets win some ball games, it's rather absurd for it to have the same heading, "Record Breaker," as Doc's or Pete's: their records are of *absolute* importance, whereas mine is just of *obsolete* importance.*

Baseball stats are more than just numbers; they're records of performance. They're benchmarks by which players, management, agents, arbitrators, and fans can compare those performances. *But they are also just numbers and don't tell the whole story.* Sometimes, like with game-winning RBI, they also tell a *misleading* story. I say all this because we are in a new era of baseball, one that is increasingly defined by statistics. And with the new sabermetrics evaluations coming into play, I urge caution, because not all of the worthwhile performances we see every day can be accurately quantified with numbers.

How, for example, can you quantify defense? Errors and fielding percentage were historically

---

* Still, I'll take it, and I guess the silver lining for me is that since the stat has been retired, it can therefore never be broken.

the two most often cited fielding performance metrics, but few baseball men put stock in them. My father, for example, was always suspicious of players with few errors because it could simply indicate poor range. Well, that makes sense—the player with great range is going to have more chances to make errors, but he'll also save more runs. So rather than using these somewhat blunt stats to determine a player's defensive value, any baseball man worth his salt would make his evaluations by simply *watching* the player play.

But such *subjective* analysis seems to be increasingly dismissed in today's game—"hard data" yielded by more and sharper metrics is what GM offices want to tell the story of performance. Okay, fine. Show me a stat that accurately reflects a player's range, and I'm sold. Show me a stat that measures a player's savviness and grit and intelligence, like Jeter's "flip play" in the 2002 ALDS against Oakland when he streaked across the infield, picked up the errant throw bouncing in from right field, and backhand-flipped it to the catcher for the crucial tag at home plate. How is that defensive contribution quantified? As "one assist, save one run"? *That single play was worth a thousand assists and a thousand saved runs!*

Again, show me that stat, and I'll say, "Great, let's use it!" Until then, let's temper our enthusiasm on every new stat coming down the pike, and put the scouts and coaches back into the decision-making process.

And think about this: Jeter had no business being involved in that play. But he surveyed what was going on as it unfolded and anticipated the remote possibility that he'd be needed.* Well, that didn't just happen. Derek was in that spot—on that field, with that team—precisely because he was that sort of heads-up player. He'd been pushed through an appraisal system, which at the time was still very much run by scouts and coaches, and rewarded accordingly. And there's no way those decisions could have been made based on stats alone. Why? Because the metric didn't and *still* doesn't exist. Instead, people just kept saying, "This kid's got *it*." Well, in today's game, that phrase is becoming less and less acceptable to the powers that be.

But I understand why. Human judgment is far from foolproof, and the story of professional baseball is in large part a story of big-time "busts"—supposed "superstars of the future"

---

* As good a fielder and heady player as I was, I don't know if I would've anticipated and made that play. When I saw that play live on television, I about jumped out of my seat with excitement and incredulity.

who just never panned out despite all the coaches and scouts claiming, again, "This kid can't miss." Quantitative analysis can hedge this perspective, particularly in evaluations at the plate, where quantitative metrics are more useful. *On-base percentage. Slugging percentage. Strikeout-to-walk ratio.*

You also have to take into consideration the successes of more than a few, if not all, general managers who rely heavily on these and other metrics. Jeff Luhnow of the Astros, Billy Beane of the A's, the Mets' Sandy Alderson, and, most notably, Theo Epstein, currently with the Cubs. What Theo has accomplished, bringing World Series titles to both the Red Sox and the Cubs, is unprecedented and historic—perhaps no GM will ever surpass those two feats. These examples—along with a willingness to learn new tricks—have gradually swayed my "old-school" opinions about "new stats."

However, I still think even the most practical, quantitative statistics, like on-base percentage, should be put in context with what's happening on the field: i.e., *What's the situation?* Like when a batter comes to the plate with a runner on third and less than two outs. Depending on the score and the inning, getting the runner home from third may be more or less important than getting on base. Or what if a team is down three or four runs late in a game and the batter comes up with runners on? Again, what the batter should be trying to do depends on the context. *Does the batter represent the tying or winning run, or is the tying run in the on-deck circle? Are the runners in scoring position? Is there a force play? Where is the hitter in the lineup, and who is on deck? Is the infield playing in, at double-play depth, or back? What type of hitter is at the plate?* What the hitter should be trying to do will depend in part on the answers to these types of questions.

Again: *What's the situation?*

Even more important, quantitative statistics cannot capture whether the hitter *knows* what he is supposed to be doing on any particular play or at-bat to give his team the best chance to win the game. Or whether the player is fully committed to that course of action, even if it does not reflect as well on him personally in the box score. *Is the player knowledgeable, committed, and talented enough to understand and achieve a successful outcome or at-bat for the team in each situation?* If so, how can you possibly measure that baseball IQ with a quantitative metric?

And this is my biggest concern with baseball's growing obsession with sabermetrics: it discounts those parts of the game that are not easily captured by such quantitative evaluations.

If, for example, a quantitative approach clearly measures home runs, on-base percentage, strikeouts, and walks, but does not clearly measure situational hitting, defensive positioning, or range, then the latter (situational hitting, defensive positioning, and range) will become less valuable in the eyes of decision makers (GMs) adopting a quantitative approach to the game. And as such attributes are discounted, the game begins to change: players with fewer home runs or a lower on-base percentage but with excellent situational hitting skills are passed over in favor of those with more home runs or a higher on-base percentage. And at some point those players with excellent yet unquantifiable skills begin to disappear from the game. If that happens, baseball loses much of its subtlety and beauty.

Bottom line: While sabermetrics will continue to improve, plain old human evaluations will always be an important part of the game. Only they can account for a player's intangibles—from leadership and grit to aspects of defense and situational hitting.

I take the fancy elevator up to the fancy broadcasting booths and press-box area wrapped in the fancy new stadium, Citi Field. I sort of miss the Mets' old stadium, good ol' Shea, which they tore down after the 2008 season, but it's hard to complain about this new one. Like the original "new" ballparks—Camden Yards in Baltimore and The Jake in Cleveland—Citi Field is a true baseball park. The brick-and-steel facade harkens back to an era when baseball, not football or soccer or rock concerts, was the one and only pastime worthy of a complex that could hold thirty thousand fans eighty-plus times per year in such a way that made the crowd feel like they were entering something special, something sacred.

Now, don't get me wrong. When I played for the Mets, I grew to love Shea, once we started winning and the fans came out, bringing with them the most electric energy I've ever felt in a baseball stadium. And I'd rather play in front of great fans than in a great stadium any day. But Shea itself was just an old park, and not in a good way like the really old parks, like Wrigley or Fenway. Its clubhouse was just so-so, and the field lacked the charm and character of its postmodern contemporaries, like Dodger Stadium or Jack Murphy Stadium (before they boxed it in for more Super Bowl seats). One of Shea's saving graces was that it was an open-air stadium, not a coliseum like Three Rivers or Veterans Stadium. And it had a natural grass surface—there is something about the smell of grass, the feel of grass under your feet, as opposed to the sterile, odorless, synthetic crust of Astroturf.

Anyway, there wasn't much about the building itself that made a player say, "Let's play some baseball!," particularly during those down years after the Seaver trade, when the Mets were a perennial last-place team and couldn't fill up 15 to 20 percent of the stadium. But they've got that in spades at this new park.

Sometimes when I'm in the booth, looking down at that perfectly manicured grass, I say to myself, "Gee, wouldn't it be great if..." *Yeah, right, Keith!*

CHAPTER 22

IN 1975, I BEGAN my second year in big-league camp. Only this time the expectations were higher, because during the off-season, the Cardinals had traded Joe Torre to the Mets. And at twenty-one years old, I was clearly the heir apparent to take over at first base.

That first day in the Sunshine State, I waited all afternoon to see who my roommate was going to be. Lo and behold, the one and only Ron Hunt walked in the door. The man who broke in with the fledgling New York Mets as a second baseman in 1963 before being voted a two-time All-Star, representing the Mets in 1964 and 1966, and then played for the San Francisco Giants during my freshman through junior years in high school (1968–70). You can bet your sweet bippy I was tickled to death. I'd sorta figured I would be paired with someone my age—i.e., a non-roster or minor league player—but the organization must have thought me hanging with a twelve-year veteran was a good idea.

Learn from one of the ancient masters, young one. Zen.

Lesson number one? How to stock a spring training fridge. After introductions, Ron immediately got on the hotel phone and requested a small refrigerator for the room. *Good idea,* I thought. *Perfect for beer, soda, water, and such. Ha-ha, silly Keith. Watch and learn.* Ron went out to the store and came back with a shopping bag filled with vodka, Kahlúa, and cream—the ingredients for a White Russian. He would fix one every night before bed the entire spring. *Not too bad,* I thought, tasting my first nightcap. Later in the spring, however, we got smashed together on those White Russians, and I was throwing up in the bathroom, pleading, "Ron!"

"I'm not your daddy! You figure it out," he suggested. So I wised up, never touching a drop of Kahlúa again.

Fortunately, lesson number two was more easily digested. Here's what Ron, a man who led the National League in "hit-by-pitches" for *seven* consecutive years,* told me:

---

* From 1968 to 1974, including fifty times in 1971, which is second all-time to Hughie Jennings's fifty-one times in 1896.

When you sustain a playing injury to a joint, elbow, wrist, or finger either by a pitched ball or a bad hop, or a sprain of any sort, twenty-four hours of icing is the magic potion. Go home that night with an ice bag and an elastic bandage, wrap the ice bag on the injury, and keep it elevated. You'll wake up around three or four in the morning, throbbing. That's because the ice has melted. Get out of bed, reload the ice bag, and continue the process. This is critical. When you wake up in the morning, continue to ice until you leave for the park. I guarantee you that there will be minimal if any swelling, depending on the severity of the injury, and you will be able to play that night.

It may sound trivial, but over the course of a 162-game season, playing six to seven nights a week, this was vital information. I mean, try playing first base the night after catching a fastball on the elbow or wrist. Ron knew all about bumps and bruises. He used to choke up on the bat about four inches, crowd the plate, and wear body padding beneath his uniform top for protection. He was the first guy I'd ever heard of doing that sort of thing. He would lean into a pitch on purpose, infuriating pitchers.

Steve Carlton and Bob Gibson both told the same story about facing Ron. They would be ahead by more than a few runs, and they knew Ron was going to foul off pitch after pitch, so instead of wasting precious bullets, they'd just hit him on the first pitch. *Go ahead! Take first. I can afford a base runner with my stuff and this lead.* Hilarious, so from that spring on, I adopted Ron's mantra whenever I suffered an injury, no doubt sparing me missed games or trips to the disabled list.*

Still, you can't be an everyday player if you can't hit left-handers, and the first thing I recall about the start of the 1975 regular season—besides being the new first baseman for the St. Louis Cardinals—was facing *a lot* of left-handers. That was a bitch. *Nice rookie debut, Keith—try these lefties on for size!*

Left-hander Dave McNally started for Montreal in the season-opening series, and I went hitless; the next day, I notched two singles and an intentional walk late in the game off righty Steve Rogers.† On the following day, in the fourth, I hit

---

* In fact, I was able to avoid the DL until 1988, my *fifteenth* season in the bigs.

† That's right, an intentional pass ordered by Montreal skipper Gene Mauch!

233

a two-out triple with 2 RBI that tied the game off another lefty, Woodie Fryman. Rogers was a tough pitcher, and Fryman was a thirty-four-year-old flamethrower. I went 3 for 11 in the series, and we took two of three. So far, so good, but we were just getting started with all these lefties...

Up next were three games in Philadelphia, featuring Steve Carlton and Tom Underwood, both lefties. I went 1 for 3 with 2 walks and an RBI against Carlton, and I eked out an infield hit (1 for 4) off Underwood, who shut us out. But we took another series, and back home we went for a two-game series against the New York Mets, who ran Jon Matlack and Jerry Koosman at us—two more lefties, and nasty. Matlack struck me out looking with a vicious 3–2 slider in the second, and after I returned to the dugout and took a seat, I remember Gibson saying to me with a chuckle, "I bet you didn't see sliders like that in Tulsa." I was inclined to agree and said as much. I went 0 for 6 with 2 walks.

Then it was Pittsburgh with Cardinals killer Jim Rooker and hard-throwing Ken Brett, both lefties. *Where did they find these guys?* Eleven games into the season and *eight* left-handed starters, with more southpaws streaming out of the bullpen, like the Pirates' Ramón Hernández, six-time All-Star Sam McDowell, and Tug McGraw of the

Mets. By the end of April, we'd played seventeen games, I'd faced eleven left-handed starters, and I was batting .188. *Ugh.*

Why were lefties a problem?

First, I'm a left-handed hitter—so a lefty's breaking ball starts at my head and moves down and *away* from me. That's a lot of plate to cover *and* still be able to turn on the inside fastball whether straight or sinking.* It's the same thing for a right-handed hitter against a right-handed pitcher, and it's a big reason why managers will often platoon players to get the matchups they want—lefties against righties, and vice versa. Second, something like 90 percent of the world's population is right-handed, so like everyone else, it wasn't until I got to professional ball—with rosters full of lefties—that I started to see them with more regularity. Even for right-handed hitters, that requires an adjustment. Third, as with every step up the baseball ladder, the lefties were that much better: better location, better movement, better command, better stuff, and all with the same "backward" delivery and pitch action.

---

* McNally, Hernandez, and Koosman had hard sinkers. Matlack, Rooker, Tug, and Brett were straight, with varying degrees of velocity. Fryman and McDowell were hard throwers with fastballs that ran in on your hands.

With only eight of my forty-one plate appearances in '74 coming against lefties, I was having a hard time against them in the opening weeks of '75. And by the end of April, Red had started to bench me against lefties. I just needed to have more at-bats against major league left-handers to be successful, and it looked like I wasn't going to be getting them any time soon.

By May, I was having trouble against the righties, too. They were bringing slider after slider in on my hands, and my confidence—along with my batting average—dropped with every strike-out or fisted ball. I remember standing in the on-deck circle during one game in St. Louis and a fan yelled, "Stan Musial my ass!" It was just one fan in a sea of others, but at the time, it really bothered me. As a young player, you're just trying to get your feet wet, and coupled with all the high expectations, getting booed at home wasn't cool. (Just ask my future teammate George Foster.) So I started to do what a lot of young players do: I started to *press.*

After an 0-for-9 series against the Dodgers at home ending on May 14, my average was an abysmal .203, and I flew with the team to San Francisco to begin a West Coast swing. I crashed at my parents' house, sleeping in Gary's bed, and the next day, Dad insisted he throw me BP before

I headed to Candlestick. Dad, the only person who possibly worried more about my swing than I did, would get a sense of urgency—more than usual—whenever I wasn't hitting well. That could create friction between us, but this time I didn't protest. Red was benching me more and more, so I would take all the extra BP I could get.

We headed out to the local high school at about noon, and Dad threw BP. At the age of fifty-two, the man could still throw good BP, and from the pitcher's mound, the full distance, not halfway in front like all the major league coaches do today. He didn't even use a protective screen, while a major leaguer stood sixty feet six inches away, hitting line drives back at him. When I wasn't fighting Dad—when he had my undivided attention—he would be instructive and positive, and though I don't recall what he said during this session, he probably kept the coaching to a minimum, emphasizing the basics.

We'd been working together since I was five, so, like two jazz musicians, a little nod here or a gesture there was all that was required to communicate without breaking rhythm. I went 1 for 3 in that night's game, scoring a run and drawing 2 walks against John Montefusco, the Giants' right-hander, who had a great slider. So Dad's groove session had helped, but it really was just a Band-

Aid that didn't address the larger issue: my confidence. For Dad, it was always about mechanics, like Vince Lombardi in front of a chalkboard with all those x's and o's, describing the famed Packers power sweep. But if you don't believe in yourself, then no physical adjustment or tip is going to do the trick. (Dad could never figure out this part of the game. Maybe he was blinded because it was his son. He always felt he could fix things with mechanics, like tinkering with an automobile engine. He had forgotten the mental aspects, the psyche of an athlete.)

So the rhythm didn't last.

I sat game two and faced Jim Barr, a former USC all-American, the next day. I knew Jim from the off-season—we'd played intramural basketball together in San Francisco along with a few other Giants players. An affable guy playing hoops, Jim was a mean bastard up on the hill, and he "flipped" me on the first pitch, sending a fastball up under my chin. I hit the deck. The fastball may have missed me, but its message was clear: *Sure, we played hoops together, but uh-uh. Not here.* That's the big leagues for you—*Good to see ya. Try this one on for size*—and I went 0 for 3 against Jim.

We made it back to St. Louis, where things went from bad to worse, because that's when

Harry Walker, aka Harry the Hat, started messing with my mechanics. Not good. Harry had an eleven-year career as a player (1940–51), and a seven-year career as a manager for the Pirates and the Colt .45s/Astros (1965–72). He claimed a career .296 BA and a batting title (.363) in 1947. But with only 10 career home runs, he was an inside-out singles hitter, or "ping" hitter.* Then, in 1966, when Harry was manager of the Pirates, he helped the recently acquired Matty Alou win a batting title his first year in Pittsburgh (.342) by getting him to "slap" the ball the other way, much like he had done. Alou, all 5'9", 165 pounds of him, was a perfect pupil for Harry: a singles hitter with no power and good speed—the perfect lead-off man. It worked for Alou, who would go on to hit .300 for seven years.

But now Harry, who served as special assistant to General Manager Bing Devine, came down

---

* I do not want to disparage Harry. He won a batting crown and played on those world champion Musial-led Cardinals teams of 1942, 1944, and, most famously, 1946. In the seventh game of that World Series against the Boston Red Sox, Harry most famously drove in the deciding run in the eighth inning. With the score tied at 3–3, his hit-and-run, line-drive double scored the ever-hustling Enos Slaughter. Slaughter's "mad dash" caught cutoff man Johnny Pesky off guard, and the rest is World Series history. Harry also hit .412 with 6 RBI in that Series.

from the front office and started preaching his ping hitting philosophy to me. He meant well, of course, but what he was offering—for me to deal with my struggles by swinging inside out and becoming a banjo or Judy opposite-field hitter—wasn't helpful. He was trying to turn a V8 engine into a V6. Now that can be a good strategy when you're behind in the count with two strikes off a tough twirler, and one I could execute when necessary later in my career, when I was able to foul off pitches and stay in the at-bat until the pitcher made a mistake. I called it my "emergency swing."

But I was first and foremost a line-drive hitter. A gap-to-gap hitter. That's what my dad had preached to me since I was kid. Yes, I was having trouble with the inside pitch, but I'd had only 200 at-bats in the big leagues. I just needed time—*not* a change to my swing. In fact, the year before, Harry himself had told the papers, "Hernandez has the type of swing that you just don't touch."

Well, I guess Harry had forgotten about that, because every day during this crucial period he had me come to the stadium early for extra BP, telling me to hit everything to the opposite field. Even the inside pitch. That was the last thing I needed to do! But what are you going to do when you're a twenty-one-year-old kid? Are you going to say "No, thank you" to Harry the Hat when, with every swing, he keeps saying, "Yes, yes, yes—that's the way to do it. Everything to the opposite field," and if you resist or refuse to go along, he might spread it around that you are uncoachable and a malcontent? No way. So these BP sessions set me back. They not only created a bad habit in my swing but also overloaded my brain with too much advice. Paralysis by analysis. My confidence was evaporating with each passing game.

As crazy is it sounds, my manager, Red, had no idea about Harry's meddling. I mentioned it to Red a few years later, and he just shook his head in disgust, saying he would have put a stop to it had he known. It wasn't the first time Red had heard about Harry's messing with players, because he told me that Harry had tried to get a young Willie Stargell to go the other way. *Can you imagine?* Big old burly Willie "Pops" Stargell, the man who would go on to hit more than 500 home runs, slapping it to the opposite field! Fortunately, Willie sought a second opinion, asking Red for his advice when the Pirates were in St. Louis and they met before batting practice.*

---

* This is *highly* unusual—Red was the opposing team's manager—but Red was willing to talk.

"Harry Walker is trying to get me to hit the ball to left field," Stargell told Red. "And I don't think I should do it. What do you think?"

And Red said, "Willie, you're a big guy. If I were you, I would keep doing what you're doing and pull the ball."

There was Willie, thinking for himself and knowing better than to trust what Harry was telling him. But I wasn't Willie. I wasn't that confident. And I can't blame Red for not knowing what was going on. Managers and coaches didn't show up at the park at noon for a night game like they do today. They were less hands-on and didn't talk that much to players, especially the young ones. They weren't big communicators. At least, for the Cardinals and Red they weren't.

That might be hard to understand, looking at today's game, when it seems that most managers and coaches want to be a player's friend, giving him a slap on the backside for something as benign as a check-swing single. But when I came up, Red and most of the Cardinals coaches weren't so gregarious.* Remember that stand-up

---

* Barney Schultz, Red's pitching coach, and George Kissell, Red's bench coach, were the only exceptions. In George's case, I think the Cardinals organization was just letting him get his four years in so he could be eligible for a major league

triple I got off Seaver for my first hit at Busch Stadium? That bullet off the top of the wall? Well, by today's standards, such a laser beam would have earned me some major kudos from a third base coach. But Red's third base coach, Vern Benson, just came up to me and said, very matter-of-fact, "Two outs. You're the tying run. Get a good lead with the pitch, and be ready to score on a passed ball or wild pitch." *Yes, sir, with a salute!* Vern was an old-school Carolinian with a Southern accent, one of Red's cronies, and that's just the way the old-school went about things—players were expected to take care of their game without the coaches blowin' smoke up their wazoo.

On May 21, 1975, the Padres swept us, but not before I went 0 for 4 in the series finale. Another *oh-fer*—I was like a sputtering engine (not even a V6). We went to L.A. and took on the Dodgers, and I started against a lefty. Why, I have no idea at this point. But it was Al Downing—the old Yankee. Here I was, little Keithie Hernandez, hitting off Al Downing! I mean I was seven years old, shagging balls at my brother's Little League tryouts—too young to play myself—when

---

pension. That was their way of saying thanks for all his service to the Cardinals. Again, George's passion was teaching in the minors.

Downing made his MLB debut. I went 1 for 4, getting a single off Downing in the fifth. The next day, Red had me in the lineup again against another lefty, Doug Rau, and I hit my first MLB home run: a two-run bomb off Rau in the seventh to put us up for good, 3–1. It was a fastball up and in—the same thing that Seaver had thrown in 1974—and I don't know how I hit it. I just reacted, which was probably why I hit it, and I cracked the ball to right-center field, way back into the bleachers of Dodger Stadium.

Of course, I called home all excited after the game. Back in those days, we called it "black cord fever," when you had a big game, whether it was a home run or a game-winning RBI, and called the folks back home. Next, I called Randy Moffitt, another good friend from the Giants. He was home in bed and out like a light when I called. "Randy," I said, "I hit my first major league home run!" Then I apologized for waking him up and hung up. The next day I was in the lineup again, and I went 2 for 3 off Don Sutton with a double and a run scored in the seventh. I hit .296 on that road trip with a home run and 4 RBI in 8 games, raising my average to .226 for the year.

But the team was struggling: Don Sutton beat us 7–3 to end a dismal 3–6 road trip, and we headed back to St. Louis. We were 16–22 overall, in fifth place in the East, but only five games behind the pretending first-place Cubs.

I say it on the air all the time now: when you've got a team that's losing and sluggish at the plate, it's tougher on the youngsters than it is on the veterans. Because a bad April for a veteran is "a slow start," and a bad June for a veteran is "a slump." But for a young player, there's no such luxury, because there's no prior body of work to compare it with. Management starts thinking, *He's not ready. Maybe he needs more seasoning.* And remember, like the players, the general manager and manager are paid to win. Their job security is in jeopardy, too, and both Bing and Red probably felt the heat coming down from the owner, August Anheuser "Gussie" Busch Jr.,* that cantankerous, gravel-voiced man who, at age seventy-six, was probably feeling his mortality and wanted another winner before he headed to that great Oktoberfest in the sky, and he made this sentiment known publicly in the newspapers.

---

* Gussie took over the brewery upon the death of his older brother, Adolphus Busch III, in 1946. By 1957 he had turned Anheuser-Busch Company into the largest brewery in the world. A modern-day robber-baron-type character, he purchased the St. Louis Cardinals in 1953, ironically the year of my birth.

We opened up a nine-game home stand against the Padres, the Reds, and the Braves. For yours truly, it was like Custer's Last Stand, going 2 for 11 against the Pads, then 0 for 10 against the Big Red Machine, which featured hard-throwing right-hander Clay Kirby, super-hard-throwing lefty Don Gullett, and then sinker-balling right-hander Jack Billingham. The part that sticks out in my memory was my second at-bat in the fourth off Gullett, who was pure upstairs, country hard-ball.* He struck me out swinging on three high hard ones, and you just don't forget an ass-kicking like that. He completely overmatched me, and the embarrassing plate appearance took all the starch out of me. The next day, totally defeated, I was 0 for 4 against Billingham.

Management had bet on me, trading away Joe Torre in the off-season, but by the beginning of June, their optimism, along with my confidence, was exhausted, and after that Cincinnati series, it was obvious to everyone in the organization that I was overmatched. I pinch-hit two days later against the Braves and got the call into Red's of-

---

* Gullett would eventually ruin his shoulder with the Yankees after being the ace of the Big Red Machine, cutting short a Hall of Fame–paced career. What a shame. But, boy, what an arm he had.

fice after the game. I was demoted to AAA. I don't recall if Bing Devine talked with me or not.

Cry all you want (and, believe me, I went home and cried my eyes out)—you can't blame management. I'd had my opportunity, and I'd failed. I packed my clothes, jammed them along with my stereo equipment and three hundred LPs, safely stowed in cardboard boxes from Tower Records, into my brand-new 1975 burgundy Monte Carlo, which I'd bought in the off-season, and proceeded to drive the 396 miles (five hours and forty-one minutes) southwest down Interstate 44 back to the great city of Tulsa, Oklahoma.

CHAPTER 23

Citi Field

IT'S THREE AND A HALF hours before game time, but there's already action in the Mets' broadcast booth. Fox local news is taping a promotional interview for a Mets trivia contest that will air mid-season. The cameras and lights are rolling while a reporter tries to stump the formidable team of Gary Cohen and Howie Rose, the Mets' play-by-play announcers for TV and radio, respectively.

"What shampoo did Mike Piazza endorse?" the reporter asks.

Who gives a rat's ass? I want to say. *Ask something about baseball!* But instead I say hello to our stage manager, Cari Loberfeld. Per usual, she greets me with an enthusiastic smile.

"How ya doin', Keithy?" she whispers in her wonderful New York accent, handing me a coffee.

The booth, which is deep enough that you can be off-camera and carry on a quiet conversation,

Buff Stadium, Houston, Texas, 1947: Mom and Dad married at home plate before the last game of the regular season. Dad went on to play two more seasons in the minor leagues before retiring and becoming a San Francisco fireman. (Collection of the author)

Linda Mar, California, 1962: First year in Little League with Pacifica Lumber at eight years old. I pitched a shutout in the championship game. Dad is on the far right. That's me, chewing gum with an oversize first baseman's mitt, next to Mr. Otenello (far left). Look at my "Bucky Beavers"! (Collection of the author)

Linda Mar, California, 1964: Another championship season. Dad is at center with the sunglasses, and the wonderful Mr. Valero is to his right with the baseball cap. I'm the third face from the left. (Collection of the author)

Linda Mar, California, 1965: With Ed and Jim's Union 76. We're looking good in Dad's uniforms, and we're on our way to another undefeated season. (Collection of the author)

Oiler Park, Tulsa, Oklahoma, 1974: On my way to my second batting championship (if you're counting the 1972 Florida Instructional League...I am). Note the box seats in the background. Just to the right was where guitarist Don Preston sat with a couple of beautiful women on most nights. (Collection of the author)

Oiler Park, June 1975: First day back in Tulsa after being sent down from the majors. The humiliation and embarrassment were instantly mollified by my roommate and dear friend, Héctor Cruz. (Collection of the author)

Busch Stadium, 1977: Still figuring things out in the big leagues. Umpire David Davidson gets a close look at my nosedive into the plate for the only inside-the-park home run of my career. (AP Photo)

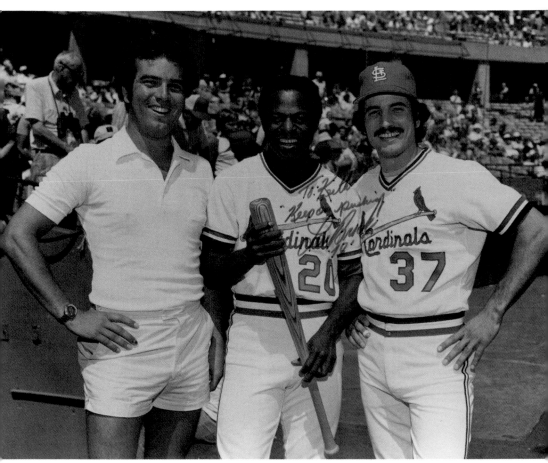

Busch Stadium, 1978: My beloved brother, Gary, and my second father, Lou Brock. One of my favorite photos. Note Lou's inscription: "Keep on pushing." (Jim Herren)

June 9, 1979: Great friend and former Cardinals pitcher Eric Rasmussen sent me this thank-you note after receiving one of my line drives in the leg in a game against the Padres. (Peter Koeleman)

Veterans Stadium, 1979: I look on as the Phillies' Pete Rose tips his hat after striking his two hundredth hit of the season on September 24, 1979, in Philadelphia. Pete was relentless at the plate that September. (AP Photo / Gene Puskar)

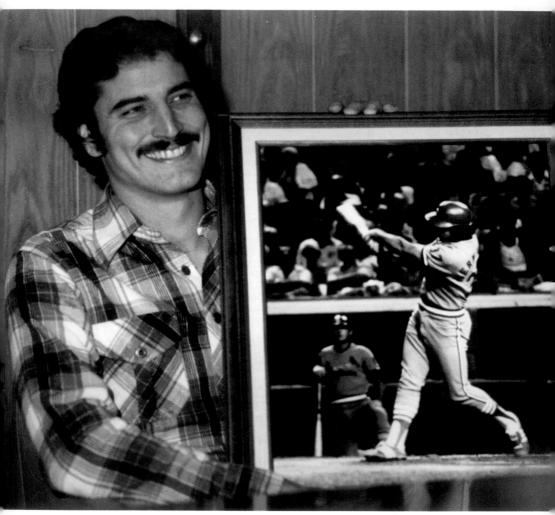

Busch Stadium, November 1979: Press conference announcing that I had won the 1979 NL MVP along with Willie Stargell. Since I hadn't received my award yet, I posed with my 1979 NL Player of the Month Award for August. (Lynn T. Spence / *St. Louis Post-Dispatch* / Polaris)

St. Louis, winter 1980: Making the dinner rounds after the 1979 season. With Stan Musial (left) and St. Louis Cardinals quarterback Jim Hart (right), as well as local television sports anchor and Cardinals television play-by-play announcer Jay Randolph (behind me). (J. B. Forbes / *St. Louis Post-Dispatch* / Polaris)

Cardinals locker room, 1980: Gearing up after the MVP season. I would stay with the Cardinals until 1983, when I was traded midseason to the New York Mets. (AP Photo / David Durochik)

With the Mets at Dodger Stadium, 1984: New colors, same swing. (Icon Sportswire via AP Images)

St. Louis, 1985: Ah…with the kids, Mary, Melissa, and Jessie, at the base of the Gateway Arch posing for an article in *Sports Illustrated*. (Tony Tomsic / Getty Images)

From my condo balcony in Manhattan, 1986: Posing for *Sports Illustrated* prior to the 1986 postseason. Besides helping the Mets win ball games, I was also discovering that "baseball for art" was a good quid pro quo in New York. (Tony Tomsic / Getty Images)

Citi Field: In the booth with former teammate and fellow analyst Ron Darling (left) and play-by-play man Gary Cohen (center). *Play ball!* (SNY Network)

is the stage manager's domain. They're the eyes and ears for the producers out in the production truck and make sure we announcers have what we need for a successful broadcast: stat sheets, advertising copy, water, coffee, soda, popcorn, Cracker Jack, cookies, pretzels, Tootsie Pops, Kleenex, napkins, aspirin, eye drops, and, most important, a tidy work space so nobody trips on a sprint to the john between innings.

"Oh, traffic was a breeze," I say.

"Wait till it warms up and everyone's going back and forth to the beach," says Richie Rahner, our A2 audio engineer. He's our "fixer"—any audio or video issues, and he's got it covered. Every December Richie sends me a Christmas card with pictures of his kids.

"The network promises to get me a helicopter," I joke.

"You and me both," says Cari, chuckling.

So how did I, a former ballplayer, get into this TV business in the first place? Well, I retired as a player after the 1990 season (sooner than I'd hoped), and I divorced myself from the game. I just needed to experience life without baseball for a while. I bounced around the city when I wasn't traveling. I never even considered a new career, because there was nothing I wanted to do: I had no inclination for business, Wall Street was out of the question, and I didn't want to sell real estate. Nothing motivated me. I was put on this earth to hit, catch, and field a baseball. That was my purpose in life, or at least I'd made it that. There was nothing else I wanted to do.

Then one night, about four or five years into my sabbatical from the game, I was sitting at a table at Elaine's, a restaurant in New York City, opened in the 1960s, that attracted a lot of interesting people, especially actors and writers. I was hanging out there—like I always was back then—doing nothing, drinking lots of wine, and Elaine, the owner, who was the real reason anyone worth his salt went there, roamed into the restaurant. She came over and gave me a backhand on the shoulder and said, "What the f— are you doing with yourself? What are you doing with your life?"

I said, "What do you mean?" She sat down—Elaine would always come over and sit with her special customers—and said, "You're too smart to do nothing. You should go be a GM or manager." I said, "Elaine, I don't want to do that. I have no desire. I don't want to get involved in baseball." And she said, "Well, you can't just sit on your ass! Find something! You got too much going for you!" Then she got up and walked away.

It was like a mother talking to her son.

Well, sometime shortly after that I met David Katz, who would become my first media agent. David came up to me at Elaine's, introduced himself, and asked if I'd ever consider doing sports broadcasting. I told him I wasn't interested, so he asked me if we could exchange phone numbers and if he could call every month or two to see if I'd change my mind. He called me once every three months for I don't know how long—it was more than a couple of years—and finally he called one day and I said I'd give it a shot. David took it to the Mets. I started doing thirty games a year, and it moved on from there.

So I owe a debt of gratitude to David, and to Elaine, who died in 2011. She woke me up out of my slumber.

And I do enjoy being back in the game. Working on a broadcast team is, in many ways, like working on a baseball team: you're relying on the person next to you to do their job and do it well. So it's fabulous working with people like Cari and Richie.* They keep me out of trouble, because

---

* Dominick Tringali, Cari Loberfeld, and Russ Relkin are our three stage managers for home games. Boots Mehrmann, Dave Ornstein, and Richie Rahner are our three A2s. All are fantastic people. They alternate—there's only one stage manager and A2 at each game—and on this particular day it's Carrie and Richie.

I'm not a trained professional broadcaster, and there are lots of things on the production side that I don't know. It took me five years just to understand what the heck B-roll meant.*

If you were following the broadcast back in 2010, there's a good chance you saw Cari. She was the one waking me up when I fell asleep "on the air" during an extra-inning game against the Giants. I was exhausted—I'd been doing a two-day appearance out in New Jersey for Habitat for Humanity, swinging a hammer and carrying sheets of plywood and drywall all over the place from 8 a.m. to 3 p.m. Plus, I was in the middle of my second divorce and an emotional wreck. So we went to commercial break, and I told Cari that I was going to shut my eyes and asked her to please wake me up before we came back from commercial because I might fall asleep. Well, I did fall asleep, and Cari woke me up as planned. But the guys out in the truck thought it was hilarious, so they taped the whole bit with the booth camera and aired it when we came back to the

---

* B-roll: "supplemental footage inserted as a cutaway to help tell the story. B-roll includes the shots that are shown to introduce a segment and/or in between the live or taped interviews" (sites.google.com/a/queensburyschool.org/media-production/home/news-package).

broadcast. Oh boy, did that go crazy over social media, and all the networks had a field day: *Look, everyone, Keith Hernandez falls asleep on the job! Ha-ha-ha!* I caught some flak from some of the local sports media critics and late-night talk-show hosts.* I guess they didn't understand that the actual event took place between innings. *It was B-roll, guys! Duh...*

When we're on the road, the production team changes: there's a new stage manager and engineer, new cameramen and roadies to help load and unload all the gear. That's also fun, because the personalities from city to city are so different—like in Pittsburgh, they're hard-ass, rust-belt guys with lots of tattoos and Harley-Davidson shirts who look like they can punish a case of beer in an hour. I love working with different types of people from across the country, a real slice of working-class America. Having grown up in a blue-collar household, living paycheck to paycheck, I feel comfortable around this group,

---

* David Letterman had a particularly good time with this one. He exclaimed how much fun Yankees games were and showed Yankees radio voice John Sterling doing his routine after every Yankees win, with both arms pumping: "The Yankees win! The-e-e Yankees win!" Then Letterman said, "Unlike the Mets games," and showed the video of me asleep in the booth.

regardless of where they're from or what they look like. That helps me, because it's important for the "talent" to connect with the crew. Not only are they usually wonderful people; if they thought I was just some New York media schmuck thinking he was the cat's pajamas, they could also make my life a living hell. *Screw you and your big city attitude, Hernandez!* So I may not understand all the nuts and bolts of the operation, but I do know it takes an army, and I try to go out of my way to develop a rapport with everyone.

People ask me if I get nervous about being on TV. "No," I tell them. I'm comfortable in front of the camera. But it wasn't always that way. I remember being very nervous when I was interviewed on a St. Louis TV channel soon after my first call-up. I stuttered—something I did as a kid—through the entire interview. But I just told myself the same thing my folks told me as a child: "Slow down. Don't let your mind race ahead." As I got older and more confident in my career and myself, a more casual yet deliberate cadence became second nature to me (though sometimes, even now, I will "get stuck" on a word or two, particularly if I'm excited and talking fast), and after a million interviews on national TV since the late '70s, appearing with Dick Cavett, Robert Klein, Charlie Rose, Roger Ailes, and on numerous morning shows, I'm not the least bit anxious. It's actually kind of fun. Plus, I'm talking about baseball, so it's easy.

That said, America's pastime isn't immune from the larger social and political discussions going on around the country. And that part of the broadcasting job can be stressful. As a member of an older generation with somewhat conservative political and social views that aren't radical but perhaps not mainstream either, I have to watch my step when those sorts of topics make their way into our broadcast. I have, on occasion, gotten myself into a bit of trouble.

For example, I sort of flipped out on the air back in 2006 when the camera showed a woman in uniform in the Padres' dugout. It was during a game, and she was high-fiving Mike Piazza after he'd hit a home run against the Mets. It was the first time I'd ever seen a woman in uniform in the dugout during a major league game.

"Who's the girl in the dugout with the long hair?" I exclaimed. "What's going on here? You have got to be kidding me. Only player personnel in the dugout."

The inning ended and we went to commercial break, realizing we had a problem. The issue was discussed in depth with director Bill Webb, coordinating producer Gregg Picker, and play-by-play partner Gary Cohen. There was disagreement on how to handle the situation. We finally decided to address the issue when we came back on the air. During my mea culpa, I blurted, "I won't say that women belong in the kitchen, but they don't belong in the dugout." I then laughed and said, "You know I am only teasing. I love you gals out there—always have."

How much further could I put my foot in my mouth? In an effort to qualify my comment, I only made it more objectionable. The network formally reprimanded me, I apologized the next day on the air, and we moved on with the rest of the season in hopes that it would soon be forgotten and I would survive the pending firestorm (obviously, I did).

But none of that really answered the fundamental question: Why would Keith Hernandez, a father of three girls, whom he's always told they can achieve anything in life, say such a thing? Right or wrong, I had my reasons, but when you're on live TV, you don't have much time for nuance, especially after a knee-jerk reaction when you need time to collect your thoughts. Now that I have the opportunity, here are my measured thoughts:

I used to get pimples on my ass. Mom thought it was because of the enzymes in the detergent she was using at the time. To this day, I have to shower every morning to make sure I don't break out. But I still have the scars, and anywhere I walk in the buff, there follow two butt cheeks pockmarked in true moon fashion.

It never really bothered me, even as a young player in the Cardinals' clubhouse, where I'd go to and from the showers without ever covering up. But in 1978, after a New York federal judge ruled that the MLB policy banning women reporters from the clubhouse was unconstitutional, I suddenly had to reconsider my level of comfort exposing myself in the locker room.

In his decision, the judge cited that Major League Baseball's policy gave an "unfair advantage" to male reporters and "violated the Equal Protection Clause of the Fourteenth Amendment."[*] As someone who grew up in the 1960s and was proud of baseball's integration as a precursor to the civil rights movement, that sounded like good reasoning to me. Plus, I'd spoken to female sports reporters in the past—not in the clubhouse,

---

[*] Maxwell Strachan, *Huffington Post*, September 25, 2015.

but on the field and such—and I thought their questions and angles were great. It sometimes brought a new perspective to the game, and beyond that, it made sense, given the fact that women made up a growing portion of the game's fan base.

But I still had boil scars on my rear end, and I wasn't super comfortable showing them off to strangers of the opposite sex. Well, the Cardinals, old-school themselves, figured out a solution: put curtains in front of the players' lockers, have the players change in there, and give them towels, secured with Velcro, to go back and forth to the showers. Well, when you put it that way—forgo the expanse of the locker room for a few miserable square feet after I'd just played my seventh game in five days—I guess I'd be okay changing in front of the ladies. So that's what I did. I didn't bother with the curtain, nor did I cover up to and from the shower. I wasn't celebrating anything or trying to make a point, but the judge's decision to open up our locker room to women forced me to make a choice: exposure or freedom of the workplace.* (Out of respect and

---

* I did make a bit of a demonstration one night in New York after the federal judge's decision. The visitors' locker room,

courtesy to these professional women, I no longer gave postgame interviews in my birthday suit.)

Thirty years later, I witnessed a new frontier: women in the dugout. My instant reaction to that was hostile because once again I saw players having to make a choice: expose your standard behavior—including any bad language, farts, snot rockets, and competitive posturing to the other team—in the presence of a woman or give up that freedom of expression in the workplace. Only now, unlike the clubhouse-interview scenario, players were being asked to do this *during* the game. For me, that went too far, and as a player, I would not have appreciated being put in that position. Because in the heat of battle, I often communicated with my teammates, coaches, and especially the opposing team in a way I

---

which wasn't big to begin with, was crammed with reporters after the game, many of whom were women who didn't seem to be there for anything other than the spectacle of the men's locker room. I wasn't pissed, but I decided to add to the circus and proceeded to walk buck naked, on my hands, across the locker room. Silly boy. But I did that only once. Eventually those women who seemed to be showing up in the clubhouses for the novelty stopped coming in, and the ones who remained were the professionals.

never would in front of a woman. Again, call me old-fashioned, and if today's players can handle that situation without feeling compromised, all the more power to them.

Obviously, live TV is not the proper venue for such thoughts, and after twenty years in front of the camera, I'm getting better at controlling my knee-jerk reactions. As our SNY executive producer, Curt Gowdy Jr., reminds me on a regular basis, I can always go home, sleep on it, and, if I still have something to say the next day, fire away. But I'm usually glad by the following broadcast that I've kept my mouth shut. *Play ball!*

Anyway, I'm starving. There's a cafeteria next door to the booth, so I'm going to grab an omelet. I can't start my prep work until the news team clears out anyway. Before I go, I catch another trivia question from a reporter.

"There have been only two players in baseball history," he begins, "to record two hundred hits, fifty steals, and twenty triples in a single season. One is a former Met and one is Ty Cobb."

I can see the boys are struggling on this one. "Come on! White Sox," I shout, because the player in question spent eight years in Chicago before signing with the Mets.

"Lance Johnson," Gary Cohen says, picking up on my reference. "Thanks, Keith!"

"Keith Hernandez popping in with a little help," shouts the reporter, and the cameraman turns to me. "He is clutch!"

CHAPTER 24

ACCORDING TO THE LABOR laws of baseball in 1975, a player had seventy-two hours to report to his new team. Needing to clear my head after being demoted because of two lackluster months in the bigs, I took all three days to get to Tulsa. When I arrived, manager Ken Boyer called me into his office, sat me down, and asked one simple question: "What happened?" I told him about not getting enough at-bats against the lefties and how the hard slider in on my hands from right-handers was giving me fits. Then I told him about Harry Walker's BP sessions.

"Goddamned Harry!" Boyer said. It seemed Harry's penchant for trying to turn struggling hitters into happy slappers was well known around the organization.* "You're gonna come out every

---

* In fact, I've recently uncovered a letter from roving minor league hitting instructor Joe Medwick to my father express-

day at three p.m. for extra batting practice," Boyer declared. "I'll throw to you myself, and you're gonna pull *everything*. I don't care if it's on the outside corner, you're pulling it. We're bringing you back."

Two days into those sessions, Boyer made a suggestion. "I've noticed that you stand very close to the plate," he said. "If the slider from righties is giving you trouble, move off a bit."

"How much?" I asked.

"As far off as you can, but still cover the outside corner confidently," he said.

What Boyer was suggesting—changing only where I *stood* in the box—simplified things. He wasn't messing with my mechanics: telling me to open up my stance, widen my feet, hold my hands higher, or level my bat. He actually wanted me to go back to what I'd been doing all along, only give myself a little more room to do it.

So I tinkered around until I discovered that six or seven inches off the plate was as far as I could move away and still cover the outside corner confidently. But it also meant that I had a new strike zone to perfect—the inside

---

ing his concern about Harry the Hat and his potential for meddling.

corner in particular.* After all, I was battling perceptions and reflexes that had taken years to develop, and recalibrating that decision-making process takes time. But I kept at it, disciplining myself in batting practice with Boyer, and once I made the adjustment, I was somewhat liberated from that pitch in on the hands and could better handle the slider and the hard cutter inside.†

My first game back in Tulsa, I was embarrassed because of my demotion. I remember being in the on-deck circle, awaiting my first at-bat and wishing I could dig a deep hole to hide, but I got a very nice standing ovation from the home fans. I then proceeded to hit a little bleeder down the third base line for an infield hit. *So much for pulling everything*...But it got me going. Now I just needed to continue perfecting my new strike

---

* What was on or off the outside corner wasn't an issue, but the inside corner, where you have to be quick with the bat, required an adjustment, because that tough inside pitch on my hands was now six to seven inches inside and I could lay off. But try putting that into effect when you've got less than half a second to pull the trigger...

† The key was, I had to learn not to swing at the cutter or slider that was a strike before I had moved off the plate. Now that pitch was a ball. That was hard work in the cage and on the field in BP. Day after hot day K.B. would throw to me until I was back on track.

zone, rid myself of that inside-out crap, get hot at the plate, and make my way back to the big leagues. Piece of cake!

To make things easier, I was surrounded by players I knew well and were my own age. The psychological support that gave me—feeling like one of the guys—had been missing in the St. Louis clubhouse, where the average age on the team was pushing thirty. The older players had been great to me—Ted Sizemore, Al Hrabosky, and Lou Brock in particular. Still, they had all seemed like big brothers, even fathers, to me, and it had been hard not to feel like the little kid on the block.

Bob Gibson had been especially intimidating. I remember one incident in the trainer's room. It was early in the 1975 season, and I'd developed a small blister on my finger. I was taping the blister when Gibson walked in and saw me. "What in the f— are you doing in the trainer's room?" he shouted. "Get your ass out of here, and if I catch you in here again, I'm gonna kick your ass, rook!" Evidently, kids with fresh legs weren't allowed to receive medical attention, at least not according to Gibson, whose aged knees had begun to deteriorate at that point. As quickly as possible, I grabbed a roll of tape, a box of Band-Aids, and an aerosol can of Tuf-Skin, and got the hell out of there, never to return to the trainer's room that season.

Even without the reprimanding, Gibby could set a young rookie straight. Around the same time as the trainer's room incident, Reggie Smith and his wife threw a party at their apartment, and the music selection was mostly jazz and R & B. I got into a conversation with a gal who suggested I bring over some of my LPs for a change of pace. *Say no more!* I dashed over to my nearby apartment, grabbed about twenty records, and headed back to the party to crank some rock 'n' roll on Smith's massive speakers.

Let's stick it to the man, everybody!

Well, Gibson noticed me and my stack of LPs as I came through the door, and gave me a look that said, *Looks like you're crowding the plate, young man.* Ask any National League batter who played between 1959 and 1975 and they will tell you that is *not* a good thing. So, very gently, I laid the albums by the front door, vowing never again to attempt to hijack the music at someone else's shindig.

Much later in the evening, I was just sitting on the floor, minding my own business, and Gibson's wife-to-be walked across the room and asked me to dance. *Please, God, no,* I thought. But she said, "C'mon, Keith," and pulled me up off the floor.

So there I was, sweating bullets—the most uncomfortable I have ever been in my life—dancing
with this beautiful woman while her fiancé, one
Bob Gibson, looked on from across the room.
Not good. Can't she just choose someone else? That
song seemed to go on forever, and when it finally
ended, I thanked her and quickly resumed my
seated position on the floor and as far away from
Gibson as possible.

Sit, Booboo, sit. Good dog.

But I can't say that I didn't have any buddies
while I was in St. Louis. Ken Reitz, the starting
third baseman, was a pal, as was Ted Simmons,
who despite being only twenty-five was already
a three-time-consecutive All-Star. But neither of
those guys was particularly helpful in my adjusting to the major leagues: Kenny was in his third
year in the bigs, newly married, and coming off
a .271 season the year prior, and it seemed that
Simmons, who was very intimidating in his own
right and more than a bit moody, was still figuring
out his role in the clubhouse as one of the team's
top performers. It's rare for someone working
through that to walk up to a kid like me and say,
"Hey, rook, you stick with me, and I'll help you
along."

We were all just sort of thrown into it and left
to survive with old veterans and coaches who ex-

pected that if we were in the big leagues, we were mentally tough enough to handle it. And it's not like Red was saying to Simmons, "Hey, Ted, why don't you talk to Hernandez and see how he's doing?" Simmons, who'd grown up in Detroit, wasn't naturally inclined to walk up to some California kid and chum it up, because back when he was a rookie, the next-youngest guy on the team was twenty-five-year-old Steve Carlton, who hadn't made connecting with Simmons a priority. It was something cultural about the organization. Again, *old-school*.

Not appreciating this at the time, I put my foot in my mouth when I got sent down, telling a Tulsa reporter that the Cardinals players hadn't been welcoming. It got picked up by the St. Louis press, and a few of my former Cardinals teammates expressed their displeasure, Reitz in particular. *Gee, Keith, you're really making friends fast in the big leagues.* Well, it was a stupid thing for me to have said—I'd been feeling sorry for myself, making excuses. Like the records at Reggie's party, it was just bad form.

But now in Tulsa, I had a whole locker room full of support from guys I'd played with throughout my minor league career: Larry Herndon, Jerry Mumphrey, Leon Lee, Joe Lindsey, Eric (known then as Harry) Rasmussen, John Denny, Marc

Hill, and, most notably, Héctor "Heity" (pro-nounced *high-tee*) Cruz, or "Cruzi Baby." Looking back, I think Héctor was as important to me that year as Bob Kennedy Sr. had been in '73: where Kennedy instilled confidence at a crucial time, Héctor now reminded me how to relax and have fun, taking the sting out of my demotion.

With all those guys in my corner and Boyer giving me my swing back, it didn't take long before I turned 1975 around. In the 85 games I played in Tulsa, I hit .330 with 29 doubles, 48 RBI, and 70 runs scored. All this while my good friend Héctor was named Minor League Player of the Year, batting .306 with 30 doubles, 29 home runs, and 116 RBI. Add "loosening up Keith Hernandez" to that list of accomplishments, and, for me, Héctor Cruz was Player of the Decade.

I was also getting out more socially. Now twenty-one, I could get into bars and clubs after games, but I found the whole experience to be difficult. First, I just didn't know how to strike up a conversation with girls, so I would stand against the wall, listening to the music, hoping a girl would come up to me or give me the eye. Second, it was the drug era, and some of these people were just gone. I remember Don Preston was playing at a club called The Magician's Theater in downtown Tulsa, and I showed up—either it was an off day or I had hustled down after a game. I was high, having smoked a joint during the twenty-minute drive, and I spotted this girl at the bar. She was breathtakingly gorgeous, and after a few pops, I mustered enough courage to slowly shuffle up to her and strike up a nervous conversation. She just looked at me with these beautiful, glassy eyes, smiled, and tried to say something, but her words were garbled. She was totally boxed, and not just on alcohol. After a few more tries to communicate, I gave up and walked away. I never went back to the club again. It was alluring, for sure—A-list bands and beautiful girls—but I was also afraid of it. My whole life, growing up, my dad had warned Gary and me about the evils of hard drugs.

I also went to more than a handful of cockfights in the Tulsa area in '75. Talk about bizarre. It'd be in some old barn out in the sticks with about three dozen farmers in their OshKosh B'gosh overalls with big wads of cash in their hands, making high-stakes wagers. I never bet; I just watched. One of my good Tulsa buddies and wingman, Bob Ferris, who was older and a bit of a hell-raiser, had a rooster that never lost, until, of course, he did. And when they lose, they're dead. But it was an interesting experience—like

I'd somehow walked into a Faulkner or Twain novel.

After one particular cockfight, Bob took me to a party packed with pretty girls. They were dressed in the hippie fashion of the times—bell-bottom pants, tie-dye, beads, etc.—and at some point Bob called me aside and said he wanted to show me something. He led me to one of the back bedrooms, and a girl was in there, sitting in a chair. She was stunning. She had her blouse sleeve rolled up, and one of the other folks in the room wrapped a band tightly around her biceps. The guy standing in front of her had a syringe loaded with a clear liquid, and I asked Bob what it was. "Crystal meth," he said. Then the guy stuck in the needle, pushed the plunger, and within a split second, the girl shot out of her chair like a bat out of hell. It scared the crap out of me, which I guess was Bob's intention. He may have been a hell-raiser, but he was looking out for me. He told me after, "That girl's in deep shit. Never mainline, Keith. There's no more rapid sensation and reaction than to the needle. Once you try it, the odds are you'll never go back. Bad news."

So I just stuck with marijuana and the very occasional greenie, which would stay in my system for a while after a game, and I'd hit the bars and dance the night away, *going boldly where*

271

Keith rarely went before because the amphetamine would help me shed my shyness and inhibitions. But again, all that was rare; even if I'd known where to get my hands on amphetamines, I certainly couldn't have afforded them. How the other guys managed to get them, I didn't know, and they certainly weren't going to let me mooch too often and deplete their stash.

As for the harder stuff, I was terrified of it. I'd grown up hearing horror stories of kids lost to drugs, and now in Tulsa I had witnessed it. Like the girl at the nightclub and then the girl at the party, a lot of kids my age back then were checked out. Well, that stuff wasn't for me. I was invested, and I wasn't about to go jeopardizing my career by becoming a druggie.

In September, the organization called me back up to the big leagues—aka "the show." I'd figured they might leave me off the guest list because of my earlier comments in the paper about the Cardinals players not being too supportive. But I got the nod and headed back to St. Louis.

I remember, my first day back, walking through the tunnel that led to the field, when Jack Herman of the *St. Louis Globe-Democrat* stopped me for a few questions in our dugout. It was just past 5 p.m. and the gates weren't open yet, so I said sure, though technically I was a wee bit late since the pitchers were just beginning to hit. Within seconds of Jack's first question, I heard Gibson yelling from behind the batting cage: "There you are, Hernandez, always talking! Talk, talk, talk! Why don't you just shut up and get your rookie ass out here to shag some balls!" So Jack and I just looked at each other and I said, "Sorry, Jack, but I gotta go." Jack, of course, understood. He was an old beat writer who had been covering this Gibson-and-Brock-led team for years.

Gibson wasn't laying off, that was for sure. But if you read his 1968 memoir, *From Ghetto to Glory* (a terrific book), it makes sense why he was tough on younger players. He was raised in Omaha in the 1950s, when the odds of being black and successful were against him. Gibson's older brother recognized his sibling's potential and kept him on a tight leash, not allowing young Bob to get sidetracked or into trouble. Because of that tough love, Gibson says he was able to go on and succeed.

So Gibson was rough with rookies like me and some of the others because that's what his brother had done with him. And the more potential a young player had, the tougher he would be. It was a nurturing thing; at least, looking back, that's the way I take it. Years later, after we'd both retired, I saw Gibson at an All-Star Game, and I went up to him and said, "Bob, you know I just wish that…when I came up, that…" I was nervous, stumbling for words, and Bob, patient as ever, said, "Well, you just played like a damn twenty-year-old, that's all!" So, again, I think in his own way he was just helping a kid grow up.

While my Tulsa buddies were off winning the American Association Championship without me, I mostly rode pine those first two weeks back up with the Cardinals, getting only three pinch-hit plate appearances (1 for 2 with a walk). Because of the somewhat cool attitude toward me in the clubhouse, I had too much time to be alone with my thoughts, and I certainly did not want to stay at the airport motel again, so I accepted an invitation from the two visiting clubhouse managers, Jerry Risch and Buddy Bates, to move in for the remainder of the season. We'd become friends during spring trainings, Jerry turning me on to a lot of music that wasn't mainstream. Stuff like Seatrain, Jeff Beck, and Leo Kottke.*

---

* The album that Jerry had was Leo Kottke's second album, *6- and 12-String Guitar,* which was released in 1969. I remember the album because I went out immediately and bought it. I also loved the cover artwork, with an armadillo in the middle on a black background, like a charcoal painting. A few years ago, Leo was playing in Amagansett, New York, at

Before I was sent down, the three of us had gone to see Jeff Beck, who was showcasing his new album, *Blow by Blow,* at the old Ambassador Theatre in downtown St. Louis. It was my second concert ever, Dad never letting Gary and me go in high school. With songs like "Freeway Jam," "Scatterbrain," "She's a Woman," and "Cause We've Ended as Lovers," Mr. Beck put a spell over the crowd, each guitar lick and phrase softening and bending our senses. Of course, the rolled marijuana joints being passed throughout the theater helped, and I remember one of those joints had a much different, distinct flavor and texture—like velvet slipping down my throat, caressing my lungs. I asked the guy who'd shared it, "What's the deal with this one?" and he said that he'd sprinkled a little bit of opium in it. *Wow.* I took a few more hits—the only time I would ever encounter the drug—passed it back, and let the sounds from Beck's guitar wash over me. Anyway, it was great of Jerry and Buddy to let me

---

the Stephen Talkhouse, a great little club that has live music all during the summer season in the Hamptons. I love the Talkhouse; the owner, Peter Honerkamp, and the bartenders know me well. So after the show, Peter brought me upstairs to meet Leo, and I was able to tell him how important his music, particularly that album, was for me at a very precarious time in my career. It put a big smile on both of our faces.

crash on the couch in their living room, where Jerry's record collection and stereo system helped me settle back into an otherwise turbulent life in the bigs.

But the biggest boost I got those first two weeks was a phone call from my brother. I was in Chicago, playing the Cubs, and Gary had just wrapped a season in St. Pete.

"I'm driving up for tomorrow's game," he said.

Wait, from Florida?

"Just leave two tickets for me at will-call."

Amazing. Gary and teammate Claude Crockett, born and raised in the Windy City, planned to drive through the night, and I told Gary, my good-luck charm, that he must have already been sending me positive vibes, because earlier in the day I'd hit a three-run shot off Steve Stone in the top of the fourth. Another pinch hit. Gary was pumped, enough to step on the gas a little harder, he said.

I was on the chalkboard the next day, *batting third.* Again, probably Gary's doing: my big brother's selflessness unfolding good things in the universe for me. I dressed and went out to the field, looking for Gary, but he wasn't there. *I hope he makes it,* I thought.

The first thing most players do when they walk out onto the field at Wrigley is look at the direction of the wind, gauging its ferocity. And this was a typical September afternoon in Chicago: a bit chilly with the wind blowing in from left field. So I focused on hitting line drives in BP. *No fly balls—all line drives.* Rick Reuschel was the Cubs' starter that afternoon. A hard sinker baller with a funky delivery, Reuschel released the ball almost underhanded, which gave the pitch a good sink but flattened out his slider. The sinker would jam the crap out of right-handers but could find the barrel of a lefty's bat. (Rick was always double trouble for right-handers.) Still, with that bread-and-butter hard sinker down and away, Reuschel was a tough mark. He got me to ground out to second in the first inning, but I got the best of him in the fourth: our team trailing 6–1, I hit a two-iron bullet line drive to left-center field. Too low for the wind to knock down, the ball cleared the ivy wall, and after days of limited pinch-hit duty, I had two home runs in back-to-back games.

We took the field after the inning, and halfway through the frame, I noticed my brother, maybe eight rows up by our dugout, standing and fist-pumping with that big grin. *Did he see the home run?* Only after the game could Gary tell me that they'd driven through the night and early morning and stopped off at Crockett's house, un-loaded luggage, and said hello to his mother before rushing to Wrigley. An hour late, they dashed into the stadium just as my name was announced over the loudspeaker—"Now batting, Keith Hernandez"—and Gary raced through the closest entryway to a view of the field just as the pitch was delivered. *Crack!* He saw the whole thing! Like Glenn Close standing among the seated crowd to rouse Roy Hobbs's sleeping bat in *The Natural*, there was Gary, my talisman, summoning my bat for not just the home run but two more hits that day, and a fantastic rest of the season, as I played in 22 games with 14 starts, hitting .350 (21 for 60). I was back on track.

Thanks, Gary!

KH BATTING PROGRESS (BY SEASON)

Year	Games (G)	At-Bats (AB)	Batting Average (BA)	On-Base Percentage (OBP)	Slugging Percentage (SLG)
1974	14	34	.294	.415	.441
1975	64	188	.250	.309	.362

CHAPTER 25

Citi Field

THE TV NEWS GUYS have cleared out of the booth, and I've had breakfast.

Now I'm preparing. There are stat sheets—pages and pages of stat sheets—to assist me. I flip through and circle the handful of categories, like clutch stats, I may reference during the game. The rest is mostly gobbledygook. I mean, do I really need a listing of who's currently got the lowest ERA in MLB for *night* games? *Can we just play the baseball game already?* As a former player who studied the intricacies of the game from the inside—while it was happening to and around me—I have little patience for the grossly abstract.

Play the game, and I'll react as it unfolds.

And that's precisely what I'm paid to do: lend my expertise as a former major leaguer who took enough pride in the game to know what the heck was going on and share that baseball IQ with an interested audience. It may have said exactly that in the job description.

A big reason I can be so loose with all these stat sheets and preparation is because Gary Cohen is one of the best play-by-play announcers in the business. Gary knows the game and stays current with the latest news across both leagues. So as I'm ripping through pages and tossing most of them into the trash can, Gary sits at the broadcast desk next to me, quietly absorbing the materials along with whatever extra research he brings. There's no shuffling papers, wildly circling things, or exasperated sighing in Gary's preparation—it's a much tidier, quieter exercise, like a monk studying scripture: elbows in tight, chin resting on hand.

It's really incredible, because whenever I have a question, I can just ask the encyclopedic brain next to me. *Screw the stat sheets!* Like now, I'm wondering what the win-loss record is of the pitcher starting for the Braves. I should probably know that. I flip back through the pages, but that's the problem with too much information: it's nearly impossible to find what you want. More sighs. *Oh, wait! I'll just ask Gary!*

Poor Gary. He's like the studious kid who got partnered with the dumb jock in some everlasting school project and has to carry most of the weight. But it's great working alongside him. Because if there ever was a human being built to announce Mets games, it's Gary. As a kid growing up in Queens, he went to nearly every home game throughout his childhood, and that was during some lean Mets years. So you know he's committed, and Mets lore is embedded in his DNA. Hopefully, I won't have to tax his innate knowledge too much today; it's the final game of the series, so we're all familiar with how both teams have been playing.*

The temperature is really dropping—so much for spring. But I'll be just fine if it's a well-played ball game, and, fortunately, we're seeing more and more of those in the league these days. After the dilution of talent that came with two rapid league expansions back in the 1990s, it's been a slow climb. You have to remember that when they expanded by four teams, that meant forty-

---

* I do have to pay more attention to the sheets when it's the first game of a series. That's always the most work. Of course, I know about the Mets and their players because I see them perform on a daily basis, but the visiting team is a whole different ball of wax. I need to research them thoroughly. Fortunately, we also have Dave Fried, statistician extraordinaire, to help us all out. And Dave knows the stats I really like to see and is always right there with an assist when we're preparing and executing the broadcast.

eight minor league pitchers were suddenly thrust into the majors. And three of the four teams—Arizona, Colorado, and Florida—were in the National League, so the NL hitters got to feast on thirty-six pitchers that didn't belong. That rate of expansion—three teams over six years—was too much. While it was maybe fun for the hitters, it dropped the level of play, from the major league level on down. Because baseball, like all sports, feeds on competition, and the better the competition, the better the level of play. Conversely, the softer the competition, the softer the level of play.*

Big deal, Keith! That was, like, twenty years ago.

Well, I'll say it again: *baseball feeds on competition.* And like any other meritocracy, if you suddenly ration its food supply, that leads to poor results. All you have to do is look at the interleague records of the NL versus the AL. Between 1997—the start of interleague play—and 2003,

---

* I remember a conversation we had with the very humble Hall of Famer Mike Piazza in the booth shortly after his retirement. He commented that he was very fortunate to have played during the '90s expansion—not only was the pitching diluted but in both Denver and Phoenix the ball really traveled. Well, Mike would have made it to the Hall in any generation, but his point is noted: those were really advantageous years for hitters.

the NL held its own, winning more than 50 percent of the games in three of those first five years. That even match makes sense because the stock in the league was overwhelmingly composed of players who had come up before the expansion. Their skills could go toe-to-toe with the AL. But as that stock depleted and was replaced by post-expansion players—players who had been raised on a diet of substandard competition—the NL teams started to get their asses handed to them.*

Finally those matchups are starting to even out again. I say this in hopes that the rumors about more expansion are untrue—the league has said so, but we'll see.† Otherwise, I may have to trade in my baseball affection for something like bull-

---

* According to the Bleacher Report, between 2003 and 2016, AL teams compiled a 1,765–1,465 record against their NL counterparts—good for a .546 winning percentage—and won interleague play by a grand total of 1,688 runs (from Neil Paine at FiveThirtyEight: https://fivethirtyeight.com/features/the-nl-is-finally-winning-interleague-play-for-now/). That's not winning, that's *dominating*.

† Baseball's new commissioner, Rob Manfred, has made known his distaste for interleague play and would like to scale it down. But to achieve this scheduling-wise, there would have to be two more teams added. *Good Golly, Miss Molly!* More diluted and minor league talent in the big leagues? I love the idea of getting rid of interleague play, but at the expense of fifty mediocre-to-marginal players and two El Stinkowski teams?

fighting, where the customs, traditions, and quality of the fight are more sacred than any resulting commerce (and I am, after all, 50 percent Castilian). Or maybe a card game like bridge—that pastime may be dying, but the old folks who play it sure know what the hell they're doing.

I glance out the open booth window, onto the field. A light fog has settled in and around the stadium. It reminds me of growing up and playing ball in Northern California on chilly, damp afternoons. But the memory is interrupted when suddenly techno music starts blaring throughout the stadium—*boom, boom, boom*—and an MC on a microphone starts shouting through the PA. He's on the edge of the field, calling out to the thousands of schoolkids bussed in from all over the city to enjoy a day off from school and a game on the house.

"Who's ready for some baseball?" he shouts, like he's working a WWF match rather than America's pastime, and the kids go berserk. They shout back in a roar, feeding the MC, who gets louder and louder with every turn while the incessant music pumps the frenzy.

Gary looks up, the nonsense outside breaking his concentration. "Why do we treat these kids like they're morons?" he asks.

Out on the field, some of the Mets players run

and stretch, and I wonder if the kids even notice that their big-league heroes are out on the field. Whatever attention they can give is being crushed to death by the thumping of some electronic bass drum set to go off precisely every half second for minutes on end, until it is replaced by another electronic bass drum set at some slightly altered but still incessant tempo.*

"That's right, kids," I shout out the window, into this beautiful ballpark that reminds me of a great big Ferris wheel—a throwback to yesteryear. "Let's get pumped up for some baseball! Let's all plug in and get juiced up!"

Gary chuckles—he appreciates the sarcasm—and we both head to the cafeteria for some more coffee and an escape from the noise.

---

* I just want to say that Vito Vitiello, who runs the command center that controls the scoreboard, music, advertisements, in-game recorded cheers—basically the whole shebang—is a fantastic fellow who is just doing his job when it comes to all these bells and whistles that sometimes get on my nerves. It's not his fault; he gets paid to respect today's tastes and play what ownership desires. And he still takes care of us oldies but goodies. Like during every Sunday day game, Vito always plays Bobby Darin's recording of "Sunday in New York," which just happens to be my favorite of all the songs written about Manhattan.

CHAPTER 26

AFTER THE 1975 SEASON—once again without a dime to spend*—I headed home to San Francisco, but this time without Dad and his damn desert. Instead, I'd asked my friend Jerry, the visiting clubhouse man, to take the trip. So off we went, westward toward the Rocky Mountains.

We stopped in Denver for a night and headed over to The Loft, an Oilers' favorite bar and a total meat market. Still shy around women, I was more comfortable in social scenes when I had a wingman and a few drinks in me, and after an hour or so at the bar, I started chatting up this very hippieish brunette from Boston. We were a perfect match—I'd let my hair grow fairly long that season and hadn't shaved in a couple of weeks. We went back to her place, a studio apartment that

---

* I had made only $18K in 1975.

was an absolute mess, I mean a pigsty. We rolled around in her already unmade bed for most of the night while her dog—this huge wolfhound or something—slept on some of the clothes strewn about the bedroom. We said our goodbyes the next morning, and Jerry and I hit the road again, heading west on I-70 with the radio blasting.

In the late afternoon, somewhere in western Colorado, I began to itch. All over. I got home, and Mom was horrified. "You look like something the cat *drug* in," she said. Dad thought I was turning into a hippie and reacted in his usual way. I told them about the itch, which sent them further into a tizzy, so I headed up to Kaiser Hospital in South San Francisco, where the doctor, this old guy, examined me. He looked at me and asked, "Where have you been living? A commune?"

"No," I said.

"Well, you've contracted scabies," he said, explaining that parasitic mites had taken up residence in my skin, a condition that people get from unsanitary environs.

A light bulb went off in my head: *that gal in Denver...her filthy apartment...the damn hound!*

The doc gave me a prescription for Kwell shampoo and hustled me out the door.

I'd asked my folks if Jerry could stay for a few days, and they said absolutely not. They were pissed off about the whole scabies thing. *It's not like it was Jerry's fault . . .* So I called Randy Moffitt, the closer for the Giants, to see if he could help. Randy's wife was a flight attendant, and she had a bunch of coworkers who were always in and out of town. Randy, who knew Jerry from the Cardinals' visiting clubhouse, was happy to help and found Jerry a place to crash with a bunch of the in-flight ladies. Lucky him.

As for me, I headed into my folks' bathroom, filled the tub, poured in the prescribed amount of Kwell, held my breath, and submerged myself. In an instant, little red bumps appeared all over my body. Those little microscopic bastards were fleeing their host in an attempt to save themselves. After soaking for about twenty minutes, they were vanquished. Mom was still pissed, of course. She had already washed my clothes with added bleach.

"You're no son of mine!" she kept saying.

I suppose I was going through my liberal and sympathetic stage of life. The longish hair, the mustache (which had made its first appearance that season), pot smoking, and rock 'n' roll. I was swept up in the way things were back in that period. So I felt a little cramped at my parents' house that off-season—Dad was just too much of a watchdog, and besides, having turned twenty-two that October, I was getting too old to still be crashing with my parents.

Come mid-February, I was back in the Monte Carlo, headed for Florida. Riding shotgun for the first leg of the journey was John D'Acquisto, the fireballing right-hander for the Giants, who was going to Phoenix for his spring training. We stopped in Las Vegas because John had a relative who was in a high position at Caesars Palace on the old strip.* His relation got us a beautiful suite, chips to gamble with, tickets to all the shows, and free meals. He also sent up two high-class call girls, both extraordinarily beautiful, but it wasn't much more fulfilling than the ten bucks a pop back in El Paso. Impersonal at best, it was my second and final dalliance with a woman of the night.

But my parents, along with any future inoculating doctors, had nothing to worry about. Despite my rebellious behavior, my MO was still very much "Baseball star or bust."

In fact, I was taking a gamble driving out east, because there was a good chance that all MLB players were going to be out of work for the foreseeable future. Trouble had been brewing on the

---

* I still prefer the old strip to the overcommercialized new one.

labor front ever since the Seitz arbitration ruling had come down against MLB in December 1975. A landmark decision that would forever change the face of baseball, the ruling eliminated the "reserve clause" in players' contracts, finally giving them a place at the negotiating table. The owners, who'd enjoyed nearly a century of cheap labor, were, predictably, flipping out and planned to lock out players until an appeals process had run its course. I was young and still trying to prove my worth, so I didn't bother to understand any of this union stuff—I just wanted to play ball.

But I was nearly broke, without enough dough to survive the protracted labor negotiations. For some reason, this hit me after that wild night in Las Vegas (who knows, maybe I was hoping to score at the tables). So from my Vegas hotel room, I called A. Ray Smith, my friend and the owner of the Tulsa Oilers, and explained my predicament. If the owners were bluffing—which was unlikely—I had to be in Florida when camp opened. If, however, they planned to lock us out, it was unknown for how long, and I didn't have the money to survive two weeks, let alone a month. So I asked A. Ray for a loan. Thankfully, he said yes.

I said so long to D'Acquisto, who headed off

to Phoenix and the Giants, and resumed the drive east along Route 66. Radio up, smoking doobies, riding high. I stopped in Tulsa and went to the bank with A. Ray, who cosigned on a $2,000 loan. Driving through Tennessee the next day, I wondered if the money would hold out. It did, though I'm not exactly sure how. The lockout pushed all the way to March 17—nearly a month after we were supposed to report—when a federal judge upheld the Seitz ruling and we went back to work.

Three weeks later, the regular season started, and I was, once again, the Cardinals' starting first baseman.

I had two roommates in St. Louis that season: Pete Falcone, a newly arrived pitcher from the Giants, and Héctor Cruz, who was replacing Kenny Reitz at third base.* I was sorry to see Reitzie go, but with Lou Brock, Bake McBride, and Reggie Smith in the outfield, third base was the only place left to put Héctor, 1975's Minor League Player of the Year.

With Héctor and Pete in my corner, and my strong finish the season before, I went into the

---

* Falcone came over in the same deal that shipped Reitz off to San Francisco.

1976 season a bit more confident. But I hit .147 without a run scored or an RBI through the first 9 games. Games eight and nine were particularly demoralizing. We were playing the Mets at home, and I went 0 for 7 in the first game, an extra-inning affair in which Tom Seaver struck me out *three times*. I followed with an 0 for 4 against Jon Matlack. That game turned into a knockdown match after the Mets hit *two* two-run bombs off our Lynn McGlothen in the first, and Lynn, who didn't care for that sort of treatment, responded in kind with a couple of knockdown pitches.

Do pitchers have a right to intentionally hit a batter? Yes and no. Officially—and this is at the umpire's and the league's discretion—a pitcher who purposely hits a batter should be ejected from the game and/or fined by the league. That's for good reason, as a ninety-mile-per-hour fastball can inflict serious damage. But I can tell you that a good pitcher won't take abuse lying down. He'll come after a guy if he feels intimidated or disrespected. Remember, baseball is a battle between a pitcher and a hitter—neither wants to give ground. So McGlothen drilled the Mets' Del Unser on the elbow in the third inning in retaliation for Unser's two-run blast in the first. Typically a line-drive doubles hitter, Unser *feasted* on McGlothen, taking him deep 4 times in 28 at-bats between '75 and '76.

"[McGlothen] was wild all night," Red told reporters after the game. "I'm surprised he hit anybody if he was trying."*

Of course, Red knew it had been on purpose, and as Unser made his way to first base, both teams started eyeing one another. What ensued was somewhat predictable. The Mets' starter, Matlack, retaliated by brushing back McGlothen during his at-bat in the bottom half of the inning; McGlothen then retaliated by drilling Matlack in the hip in the fourth, and a melee ensued.

Dave Kingman immediately charged McGlothen from the Mets' dugout but was, as reported the next day, "tackled" by yours truly before reaching the pitcher.

At six foot six, Dave "King Kong" Kingman was one of the strongest men in the league. When he'd shake your hand, if you didn't get a good grip first, he'd ring it like a rag. Before the offending pitch, I'd noticed him crouched on the top step of the third-base dugout, his eyes ablaze and fixed on McGlothen. He was like a raging bull, pawing the dirt, ready to rush the matador. McGlothen had to have seen him but drilled Matlock on the next pitch anyway.

---

* *St. Louis Post-Dispatch,* April 21, 1976.

293

Both benches immediately emptied, and Kingman led the charge. Ted Simmons, coming up the third base line from his position behind home plate, tried to intercept, leaving his feet and launching at Kingman in full cross-check style. But Kingman, who was as agile as he was strong, ducked Teddy and continued his pursuit. I looked to my right for reinforcements. *Maybe Reitzie from third base?* McGlothen had scurried to my rear, making me the last line of defense. It was like a freshman defensive back in high school taking on an all-state fullback.

Boom!

I barely had time to brace myself. I remember being lifted off the ground from the initial shock of the attack, crashing onto the turf on my backside, and desperately trying to hang on to the V-neck of Kong's jersey as he literally crab-walked over me to get to Lynn. But by then the cavalry arrived and held Kingman down, landing a few punches along the way.*

The next day, I showed up in the clubhouse

---

* McGlothen was ejected, along with Red and Mets shortstop Bud Harrelson. Following the game, McGlothen was fined $300 and suspended for five days. As for Del Unser, he continued to get the best of McGlothen, going deep on him once again that September.

with a serious red welt on my neck, and Lynn came up to me and patted me on the back with a huge smile. "Thanks, my man!" he said, or something like that, and then strode out the clubhouse door for BP. The rest of the gang was slightly less appreciative, laughing and shaking their heads—even the radio broadcasters were making light of it. Being young and a tad bit sensitive, I may have muttered something like "Well, I didn't see you guys doing anything to protect your pitcher." But whatever. I'm sure that deep down they were all just happy that fate hadn't placed *them* between Kingman and McGlothen. And to be fair, I'd been positively *steamrolled*.

Chivalry or not, I'd stunk it up at the plate, and Red sat me down in three of the next four games. Ron Fairly started in my place.* *Uh-oh, here we go again...*

A week later, we were in San Francisco for a three-game series versus the Giants. *Perfect timing.* I stayed with my parents, and Dad, predictably, was on edge and spouting advice every three seconds. Even during the game, there was no escaping the man.

---

* Ron had come over from the Phillies the year before and hit .301 for us—which was part of the reason I'd been sent down in 1975.

The final day, Mom, Dad, and Gary were in their usual fifth-row box seats behind our third base on-deck circle. I started the game and could see my family from my position at first base—I was facing them whether I wanted to or not. There was Dad, standing up, waving his arms at me, trying to get my attention. He was like a man on an aircraft carrier signaling the planes as they were lining up for takeoff. *Please, God, make him stop,* I thought, and I tried to wave him off.* But each time I did, he started demonstrating how I should hold my bat.

This happened for multiple innings—I was waving him off, but he just wouldn't stop. I went 0 for 3.

"What were you doing?" I shouted at Dad after the game. He, Gary, and Mom had been waiting for me just outside the clubhouse door. "For crying out loud, get a grip!"

"Ah, never mind that," he said, dismissing my frustration like I was some fifteen-year-old kid. "I know what you're doing wrong."

"Never mind?" I screamed. "Don't you ever do that to me again!" I kissed Mom, said goodbye to Gary, and stormed off to the team bus without saying anything else to Dad.

---

* Pete Falcone later told me he thought I was going crazy out in the field. He couldn't see Dad's antics from his dugout seat.

The team flew to L.A. that night, and the next day I went 0 for 3 against Don Sutton. I didn't start the rest of the four-game series—just two pinch-hitting appearances, both strikeouts. Ron Fairly started against the right-hander Rick Rhoden, and Red surprisingly put backup outfielder Mike Anderson at first against the left-hander.* I could read the tea leaves—Bing and Red were obviously looking into other alternatives.

After losing the afternoon finale, we flew all the way back east to Atlanta, where we played three games against the Braves. We arrived very early in the morning and thankfully had a day off. I was in my room, probably just waking up, when the phone in my hotel room rang. *Who the heck is calling me in Atlanta?*

"Hello?"

"Keith, it's Murph."

That was the nickname of my teammate Willie Crawford, whom we had acquired in the off-season from the Dodgers. The left-hand-hitting outfielder was a hard-nosed African American from the L.A. area. A no-nonsense guy who had played with the Dodgers from '64 to '75 until he was traded to us for Ted Sizemore in early March 1976.

---

* Mike had come over from the Phillies in the off-season and was off to a good start, though in limited play.

"Yeah, Murph?"

"I want you down in the lobby by two p.m. We're going out to the park for extra BP."

"Ah, c'mon Murph," I whined. "It's an off day."

"Get your butt down here by two or I'm coming up!" *Click.*

So I met Murph, as instructed. We got to the park, and I noticed most of the other bench players were there for the same purpose. It finally dawned on me: never a full-time starter in his career, Murph was used to being in a platoon role and knew what it took to stay in shape and be ready. In the past I'd taken extra BP only when I was in a slump. But now, playing sporadically, I needed the extra BP regardless.

Unfortunately, the extra swings had little effect on my immediate performance, and on May 14, the team announced a major change at first base: Ron Fairly would play against right-handers; outfielder Reggie Smith would play third base against right-handers and first base against left-handers; and Mike Anderson would take over in right field. I was officially benched. The move also meant that the team was platooning Héctor at third base, playing him only against left-handers. At the time Héctor was hitting only 3 points higher than me at .181.

The two stars from Tulsa were duds in St. Louis.

CHAPTER 27

Citi Field

"LAST NIGHT WAS A good broadcast," says Gregg
Picker, the coordinating producer for SNY. We're
seated at a table in the press cafeteria, drinking
coffee and killing time with Gary Cohen and a
few other radio and TV guys.

"I felt flat last night," I say. "I just didn't have
any energy."

"Well, the whole game was flat," Gary says. "It
wasn't you."

"The game was lousy, but you guys sounded
great," Gregg says. He wasn't working last
night—a rare day off—but tuned in to the broadcast anyway. I don't know how Gregg does it.
Every game is three hours plus. And regardless
of how the team is doing, he has to figure out a
way to keep things moving along and the viewers engaged. On top of that, he has to worry
about every word in the broadcast. So if I stumble
on a phrase or a word—let's say the word is

"boisterous"—there's Gregg, sensing my stumble and coming in loud and clear in my earpiece, "boisterous," without skipping a beat, and I continue on with my analysis.

Anyone who thinks TV producing is easy should hang out with Gregg Picker for an hour. They'll have a heart attack. Gregg worked years on the USTA circuit with USA Network and ESPN, and if I'm any good at my job as a color commentator, it's in large part because of him. From the very beginning of our collaboration at SNY in 2006, he's always encouraged me to be myself on the air.

"It's a great listen," he says. "It's almost like you guys aren't on TV but in my living room, sitting on the sofa, having a conversation about the game."

Gary laughs. "Well, Keith didn't think we were on TV either," he says, and explains to Gregg that the last thing SNY viewers heard from last night's broadcast wasn't Gary saying his usual "Goodnight," but me saying "Oh, are we still on?"

Everyone at the table laughs, me included. As with ballplayers, a coffee break among broadcasters usually includes a healthy dose of busting chops.

"Nice one, Keith," says Gregg, rolling his eyes before sipping his coffee.

I enjoy this pregame ritual with the guys. When I was a kid and would go with my dad to pick up his paycheck at the firehouse, the other firemen would always be at the table, drinking coffee, talking, or playing cards. Even as a young boy, I sensed that the firemen liked hanging out at the station together—they weren't just spinning their wheels, waiting for the alarm to ring. When I started playing professional baseball, I got something very similar to that. Because I spent *a lot* of time with teammates before and after games, and like the firemen, I enjoyed the hanging around. But when I retired, that part of my routine just went away.

Poof.

So when I came to broadcasting ten years later and was very unsure if a return to "baseball life" was what I wanted to do—the night games, late travel, hotels, road trips—one of the things that eased me back in was a work culture that provided plenty of time to talk shop or just shoot the breeze.

Anyway, it's nice to hear from Gregg that even when we're not on our A game, the broadcast is still conversational. That's something that we all want it to be.

"It's apparent you're never forcing things," Gregg now says. "And you know, the whole entertainment business is in an era where people feel like *I'm on the air so therefore I gotta be this type of personality all the time.* It's very forced and relentless."

Boy, do I agree with Gregg on this last point. At times when I watch sports on TV—anything from baseball to football, even golf—the volume is usually muted. Otherwise, the noise keeps me from why I turned on the tube in the first place: *the game.* It's just talk, talk, talk, while the network puts up all these crazy graphics and sound effects. Nothing ever shuts up. It's like that MC with the kids in the stands this morning—he thinks he needs to yell and scream all the time. And you just want to grab the guy and say, "Hey, buddy, how about a little peace and quiet while they take it all in?"

As usual, Yogi Berra said it best: "It was impossible to get a conversation going, everybody was talking too much." *There you go, Yogi!* I wonder what he and some of the other old-timers would say if they heard some of the broadcasters in the game today. Too many of them emphasize all these crazy stats, like "exit velocity," "trajectory angles," or, and this is my favorite, "percentage rate of someone making a catch." "His probability rate of making that play was sixty-seven percent!" Give me a break. Who cares how many miles per hour the ball traveled once it left the bat, or how high the ball traveled in degrees, or how many seconds it took to leave the ballpark.

When did baseball become NASCAR?

Why can't they just say "Wow, he hit that ball hard!" or "Geez, what a rope"? Did Harry Caray ever talk about exit velocity? Vin Scully? I doubt it. Is that even part of the game's vernacular? When a kid today is playing baseball out in the street with his buddies, does he exclaim "Did you see that monstrous *exit velocity*?" as the ball bounces down to the end of the block? Gosh, I hope not. Hopefully he just says, "I hit the dog outta that ball."

Am I dating myself? Am I a dinosaur? I guess to a degree I am, and I have been called such by a few newspaper critics. But for some reason a lot of commentators and networks think fans need all that extra stuff, *all* the time. Yes, it's the job of every broadcast to keep the viewers from turning the dial, but enough already. *Play ball!* Let the game provide the bulk of the entertainment.

Of course, times change and maybe more noise and chaos is what people want these days. I'm not sure. But that great adage "Less is more" is absolutely true in TV sports, where overindulgence in production prevents viewers from *seeing* the action. It's like we've combined the techniques of radio days—when producers had to sonically create the action and emotional landscape with constant narration and literal bells and whistles—with a now ultra-high-def visual experience. Well, that sensory *overload* makes zero sense, and I'm happy that the Mets owner-ship likes our broadcast as is.

Conversational.

"And I think we stay away from the clichéd boilerplate stuff that can kill a broadcast," says Gary as he gets up to head back to the booth. "I mean there's some—it's unavoidable—but we do a good job staying away."

Well, that's true, too. You don't need filler when you know what you're talking about, and, again, none of us is afraid of a bit of silence between talking points. No doubt, that ease starts with Gary's play-by-play. Like the conductor of an or-chestra, he's the one who sets the tempo of the broadcast. Ron Darling and I just follow his lead. And if the maestro isn't feeling the need to fill the space with cacophony or race to the next section of music, neither are we.

That's why I say Gary is one of the best in the business. Not only is his knowledge base substantial; he also has a feel for what's appro-priate and when. His sense of timing is terrific. He may never have played the game beyond Lit-tle League, but Gary *feels* baseball better than a lot of veterans I played with. And that makes Ronnie's and my job as color commentators in-finitely easier. We're just the brass and string sections taking our cues from the man with the baton.

And while I may have the most television experience covering the Mets of anyone in the booth, I am not, as further evidenced by last night's faux pas, a professional broadcaster. I'm just a former ballplayer who happens to know a good bit about the game and can concisely comment about what's going on in the field without getting too much in the way. And for that opportunity, I owe a lot to my predecessors, former players turned broadcasters who blazed a trail for the rest of us. Guys like Dizzy Dean, Tony Kubek, Joe Garagiola, Jim Palmer, and Tom Seaver, to name a few.

But the one I think deserves the most credit is Tim McCarver. He showed, better than anyone, how having a former player with a microphone in his hands can be an asset to a broadcast. Some say he talked too much—overanalyzed. I disagree. Considering the time when Tim came onto the broadcast scene—just when networks were starting to really revamp their broadcasts with more slow-motion instant replay and analytical statistics—McCarver met the demands of those changes with acute, confident observations while maintaining the easygoing manner that, to me, is most complementary to the game. That isn't a simple balancing act, and no one did it better than Tim.*

I check my phone for the time. "Oh my God," I say. "We still got fifty-five minutes to kill," and I head back to the cafeteria line to get another cup of coffee.

When I return to the table, I see Ron Darling has joined the fray. It's a pleasure to work with Ronnie—we've known each other a long time, since our playing days with the Mets, where we shared the field together for seven years. That's a good amount of time in baseball. Guys get traded, sent back down, or retire. They come and go. Most go. I remember when Ronnie was called up from the Tidewater Tides in September 1983, soon after I'd been traded to New York from St. Louis, and two things immediately jumped out about him in the five starts he made that final month of the season: one, he was well on his way to having one of the best pickoff moves I would ever see (he'd sometimes even catch me "leaning"); and, two, he had guts and wasn't afraid to go after batters inside. That's what I always looked for in pitchers, and I could see that Ronnie was a mentally tough kid to go along with

---

* Tim was inducted into the broadcasters' wing of the Baseball Hall of Fame in 2012.

that Yale intellect, a dangerous combination for a pitcher in the bigs and one that Ronnie would exploit over his career.

So it's great to still be working with him, and I think we're beneficial for the color side of the broadcast. There's no ego or authoritativeness—we're both confident the other guy knows his stuff, and we have a great time together in the booth.

I sit down. Ron and Gregg are talking about last night's starter, Matt Harvey, whose suddenly anemic fastball has cost him a few tough outings.

"Well," says Ronnie, "DeGrom [another Mets starting pitcher] isn't throwing his hardest either. But he's getting by. He's just figuring out a different way to do it until he gets his fastball back. But Harvey's whole persona is to blow you away, and when he's not doing it—when guys are catching up to his fastball—it throws him off. He looks stung out there."

Ron has hit the nail on the head. I said last night between innings that Harvey looked a bit lost out there. But "stung" is better.

"And I've been there before," says Ronnie. "It's tough to deal with that. You just stand on the mound, thinking, *You gotta be kidding me!*"

"That makes sense," says Gregg, who's seen enough professional athletes to know when one of them is mentally struggling. "A lot of today's pitchers want to be *the* strikeout guy. But as soon as the other team chips away and puts up a run or two, it erases the hope of pitching that great, ten-strikeout shutout."

"Well, that happens to everyone," says Ronnie. "You got five days between starts and you wanna kick ass, so you get deflated when things go badly early on."

"But that's the name of the game," I say. "It's all about being able to battle through adversity."

"It sucks, but it's true," Ron agrees.

"It's like that time you told me about," I say to Ronnie, recalling one of my favorite anecdotes about pitchers *learning* to be mentally tough. "You were getting blown out in Tidewater [AAA] and Davey [Johnson] paid you a visit on the mound and said, 'Hey, my bullpen is dead. You better figure out a way to get out of this.' And he left you out there to clean up your own mess."

Ronnie sits there across the cafeteria table, nodding his head the way we former ballplayers do after recalling some crucial moment in our careers. "A good lesson," he finally says. "And you know what? I got out of the mess!"

"Well, that's what Harvey needed last night," I say. "To stay out there and get out of his own mess. But that's not gonna happen with teams pulling these guys in the middle of innings because of pitch counts."

"When they should keep him out there and let him get his ass kicked," says Ronnie. "It's the only way to figure it out."

Unfortunately for the development of talented guys like Harvey, baseball has become, like anything else in which lots of money is involved, too conservative. One reason teams pull their pitchers early is because they're being fed all this data that suggests a high pitch count can ruin an arm, and they need to protect their investment. Well, it's true. You can ruin an arm. Some of the old-school teams and managers used to not give a shit. Why? Because the owners used to pay their players like indentured servants, so what was one arm to them? They could just toss it in the trash heap and find another. Well, I'm certainly not advocating that—everyone should have a chance to play a long, healthy career.

But high pitch counts also provide something useful: an opportunity to work on a pitcher's mental toughness when things aren't going his way. And it's being forgotten. Okay, you want to save the arms because you're paying these guys a lottery check every two weeks? Fine. But realize that your protectionism at every turn is costing them the vital lessons necessary to become a *resilient* pitcher. One that can adapt to adversity. Like Ron Darling in Game Seven of the 1986 World Series—that's the type of pitcher who wins big games. And in my opinion, a good arm isn't worth much if it's attached to a head that goes to Jell-O any time the opposing team lands a punch.*

Ronnie probably realizes that we're starting to sound like a bunch of old men, complaining that today's game isn't up to snuff, because he changes the subject. "You ready for your vacation, Keith?"

"You bet," I say. After the game this afternoon, the team will head out on a West Coast swing, but I'm staying home for a little R & R and to work on the book.

Eleven days off! Yes!

"You know," says Gregg, "we're gonna have to get you on the phone during one of the games." I think he's worried Mets fans might forget about me or something.

---

* There's nothing worse than a pitcher, particularly a starter, looking down toward the bullpen when things start to unravel. Those are the pitchers you don't want. But there were guys like that when I played, too, and I do feel that the great majority of today's pitchers, like Harvey, are pissed when they get yanked and would love to go nine or pitch their way out of a jam in the seventh instead of handing it over to a reliever and hitting the showers. As competitors, they relish the opportunity to battle back and get stronger.

"Sure," I say.

"Yeah, he loves free publicity," jokes Ronnie, who I can tell is just winding up. "Maybe get a camera on him at the bar at the American Hotel, sipping scotch and watching the game along with everyone else."

"Actually, that's not a bad idea," says Gregg, who is serious.

"Oh yeah, that'd be hilarious," says Ronnie. "Or at the barbecue making a steak. Feeding the cat."

Well, folks, I learned a long time ago that if you can't beat 'em, join 'em, so I suggest, "How about getting a shot of me and Hadji in the living room. Maybe have the TV in the background with some soft porn going? Just a little bit fuzzy and out of focus."

The whole table laughs, especially Ronnie. "Yeah, picture in picture with the game and the porn!" he says, somewhat above the cafeteria din. "It's perfect!"

Uh-oh. Looks like some of those old Mets players are getting loud and obnoxious again . . .

CHAPTER 28

I SAT IN FRONT of my locker in full uniform, staring off into space.

It was 1976, and I'd just been officially benched. It was hard not to feel sorry for myself. *Keith Hernandez, now twenty-two years old, is a major league* bust...Thankfully, I didn't have much time to sulk because our third base coach, Preston Gomez, came calling. "Come with me," he said, and with a fungo bat in his hand, he led me onto the field.*

---

* Preston was an outstanding third base coach. He had different signs for each of our fifteen position players. That's fifteen individual signs for bunts, hit-and-runs, steals, squeezes, and takes. So if there were two men on base and the bunt was on, Preston would have to give three separate signs. And he did this in extremely fast motion, like someone fluent in sign language. *Amazing!* I remember in late spring training, when all the cuts had been made and the team was set, he took all fifteen of us aside separately and gave us our codes for opening day. I don't know if everybody had the same "indicator" or "wipe off,"

Preston was the greatest fungo hitter I'd ever witnessed: any angle, any location, Preston knew the speed and spin it required. He would start nice and easy to warm me up, but as our session progressed, he would pick up the pace until it reached a crescendo, and I'd be drenched in a full sweat, breathing heavy. That afternoon he worked me doubly hard, and for a moment I forgot my troubles. When the session was over, he told me to come out early every day for ground balls until further notice. Like Murph's insistence on extra BP, Preston was looking out for me. Who knew how long the benching would last, but until things changed, Preston wasn't going to let me slack. *Far from it.*

Those extra sessions did more to increase my range than anything else in my professional career, and I think Preston enjoyed conducting them as much as I benefited from them. He would laugh and shake his head when I made a great play—even after seven weeks, I could still make him marvel a bit.* He went out of

---

but it didn't matter; I was focused on my signs. And it made us more alert. "Don't tell your teammates your signs," he instructed. "Players get traded."

* I would go the rest of my career searching in vain for a coach to challenge me with grounders like Preston could. He really made you work.

his way to praise me, probably because he could sense my need for it. Players, whether "screwbeanies" or superstars, desire praise, and at this point I required more than most. Unlike a lot of other coaches of his generation, Preston understood that.*

My teammates, too, helped me through. One day in Chicago, Pete Falcone encouraged me to run with him after our day game at Wrigley.

"Run? Run where?" I asked.

"Back to the hotel."

Why not? I've got energy to burn these days . . . We ran all the way to the Westin Hotel in downtown Chicago—a beautiful late afternoon through Lincoln Park, with more than a few ladies to look at as we jogged. It was a great way for me to clear my head and, most important, stay in shape, so I stuck with Pete's routine the rest of the benching. Even Ron Fairly, the man replacing me against lefties, was helpful. Ron had the disposition of an army officer, so he wasn't overly friendly, but he

---

* I lost track of Preston after 1976. Years into my retirement, I read in the paper that the almost-ninety-year-old Preston had been struck by an automobile and had survived. I got in touch and thanked Preston for his care in 1976. "Keith," he said, "you were like a young stallion penned up in a stable. You just needed space to gallop." I'm forever grateful that he felt that way. He helped change the course of my career.

took the time to show me how to better break in a first baseman's mitt and how to "cheat a little bit" on a close putout at first. "You're moving forward to get the ball with the glove," he explained, "extending your body, and your foot comes off the bag just before the ball arrives." Ron showed me how to do all of that smoothly. "Don't rush it," he said, "or the ump will catch you pulling your foot." I worked on it every day during infield until I had it, and took Ron's sly little move with me for the rest of my career.

Despite all this help, I could still sulk with the best of them. Besides the occasional pinch hit, I was all but forgotten by Red. I remember one night when I was down at the end of the bench, moping after a pinch-hit strikeout. *Wait. Really? We're in a close game, the Phillies jumping out in front of the division, and the twenty-two-year-old punk is off by himself sulking? Not gonna cut it.* So here came Lou Brock, taking a seat next to me, basically telling me to stop being such a prima donna. But it was Lou Brock, so he didn't put it that way. Instead, he very gently said:

What the hell are you poutin' about? No one's gonna feel sorry for you. You getting mad and feeling sorry for yourself? Who's making you mad? You see that guy on the mound? He's mak-

ing you mad. Get him. Take it out on him. He's the one who's gonna put you into a day job. You wanna go to work nine to five and have two weeks off a year? Then go ahead and do what you're doing. Or get mad at him. He's the one who's gonna take the job away from you.

Without another word, he got up and walked to the other end of the dugout. That was Lou's version of tough love. He wasn't "My way or the highway" like my dad, or intimidating like Bob Gibson, or all about the silent treatment like Red and most of the coaching staff. Lou engaged with a calm gentleness that was more stirring and powerful. He made you *want* to do better, like your favorite teacher in high school, only this was the great Lou Brock, who would hit .301 that season at the age of thirty-seven.

No more self-pity for this guy.

One thing I'll never forget was watching Lou calm down a seriously pissed-off Wayne Twitchell, a big, hard-throwing starting pitcher for the Phillies. We were in the clubhouse after a game in which we'd pretty much beaten the tar out of "Twitch," sending him to the showers early. He burst through the door—all six feet six inches of him—still in uniform, soaked in sweat. He hadn't even changed his shoes!

"Where's Hrabosky?" Twitchell demanded, referring to our animated closer, Al Hrabosky. Evidently, Al's antics on the mound, which had earned him the nickname the Mad Hungarian, had steamed Twitch.

While most of us just stared, thinking, *This man is gonna kill somebody,* there was Lou Brock, walking forward, quietly saying, "Now, Wayne, calm down." And he put his arm around the 220-pound Twitchell, whose eyes still glowed beneath his cap, and kept talking to him—like a parent soothing an upset child—while he slowly turned him around and walked him out the door. Such was the quiet yet persuasive power of the mighty Lou Brock.

Sometime around the beginning of June, Red called a meeting before a game. We were more than a dozen games back in the standings. He was angry and chewed us out, and ended the meeting by naming Ted Simmons and Reggie Smith co-captains. *Really?* Even I, the twenty-two-year-old, underachieving, emotionally soft, benched first baseman, knew this was a hare-brained idea. Sure, Reggie was a premier player—one of the best switch-hitters with power in the game, and a Gold Glove outfielder with a very accurate cannon for an arm—but he'd spent the last month, since being moved to the infield, sulking and brooding in the clubhouse. Everywhere he went, a dark cloud followed. That was not captain material. Besides, there was no doubt in anyone's mind—young players and veterans alike—that the real "captain" was Brock, the longest-tenured veteran of our team.*

After the meeting, I went back to my locker, four stalls away from Lou's. He was pissed and muttering under his breath—one of the few times I saw Lou "angry." I didn't blame him—management was taking him for granted just to appease the disgruntled Smith. But Lou, further proving his class and professionalism, never created a stir. Instead, he came to the park every day with the same work ethic and remained as helpful as ever.

As for Reggie Smith, the olive branch offered had zero effect on his gloom. So at the June 15 deadline, Bing traded Reggie to the Dodgers in exchange for catcher Joe Ferguson.† With Reggie

---

* Gibson had retired after the 1975 season at the age of thirty-nine.

† The Cardinals also got two minor leaguers: Bob Detherage and Freddie Tisdale. Neither was considered a big-time prospect. Detherage would make it to the majors in 1980 but only for a cup of coffee. Tisdale remained in the minor leagues and Mexican leagues his entire career.

gone, the team moved to yet another "plan B" at first base: they'd stick with forty-year-old Fairly against right-handers and, against lefties, move Ted Simmons to first, with Ferguson behind the plate. Where did that leave me? Same old place—bench city.

What does management do when they have a promising young player who just hasn't gotten over the hump? How long do they continue to ride out his struggles? For me, it wasn't very long—the Cardinals just didn't have a lot of patience. In the previous season, that had made sense, because the team was only five games out of first place by the end of May 1975. They weren't in a position to give me more starts, especially when Ron Fairly had gone about his business at first base, hitting above .300. But 1976 was a different story: the team was *fifteen* games behind the surging Phillies and out of contention at the June 15 trade deadline. It was apparent to all that we were going nowhere.

Is the team giving up on me?

Again, the annals of baseball are littered with "can't miss" talent that never panned out. Well, I was determined not to be in that classification. But the chances now were few and far between, because it seemed that everyone *but* me was getting a shot at first base. After the Ferguson trade, it became clear that I wasn't part of the organization's plans for the remainder of 1976. But this was my dream, or as Steve Martin would say, "my special purpose"!

I started the next day because Ferguson hadn't reported yet, and I had a big day: 3 for 4 with 2 RBI. But I sat the next five games. Finally, I snapped and stormed into Red's office. I didn't bother to close the door, and my teammates probably heard every word.

"What's going on here? Why aren't you playing me?" I shouted. Red, sitting behind his desk, responded that they had to give the Ferguson-for-Smith trade a chance to work. What were Red and Bing to do? Not play Ferguson, when they'd just traded away a superstar, Smith, for him?

But I would have none of that. *"You gotta be kidding me!"* I said. "You're just worried about your job!"

Well, Red got all flushed in the face and stood up from his chair. He walked around his desk toward me, and I thought, *Oh God, this old man's gonna take a swing at me!* Instead, he closed the door, reached into his office cooler, and grabbed a Budweiser. After a long sip, he came back to his desk and sat down.

"Keith, I understand. But we have to make this trade look good."

Now with tears streaming down my face, I said, "Red, we're out of the hunt, and you play a forty-year-old first baseman and a backup catcher?"

And Red goes, "Okay. Now, Keith, I want you to go home and calm down. We're not changing anything right away. But I'll call Bing, and I think he's gonna want to see you tomorrow."

Dad was in town, visiting for the home stand, and we drove home together. This time I was the semi-hysterical one; Dad stayed calm and helped me pull myself back together. He just said, "You did good, son. At times in life you have to stand up for yourself. I'm proud of you. Let's wait and see what Bing Devine has to say tomorrow."

The next day Red called me back into his office and said, "Bing's coming down to talk to you."

Bing basically repeated what Red had said the night before about making the Reggie Smith trade look good. "But I'll tell you what," he offered, "if we're still fifteen games behind at the All-Star break, then you'll play every day the second half of the season. If we get back in the hunt, then I'll do my best to try to trade you to a team you'd prefer—if not this year, then in the off-season."

I felt like saying, *Are you blind? We're already out of it!* But I agreed to the proposal and rode the pine without complaint, coming out early every day, taking extra BP, and fielding ground balls with Preston.

Having stood up for myself, there was nothing else I could do.

CHAPTER 29

Citi Field

THE METS ARE UP 6–0 in the bottom of the fifth.

As per usual, they've done it with home runs, sending three balls over the fence in their first fourteen plate appearances. The first Met to "go yard" was catcher René Rivera. *Good for him.* Drafted in 2002, Rivera has spent the majority of his professional seasons grinding it out in the minor leagues. That's a lot of bus trips, a lot of patty melts.

Leading off the inning for the Mets is Michael Conforto. The young left-handed hitter has one of the nicest swings I've seen in a while, but he's cooled off at the plate lately, going just 1 for his last 14.

"They have really been working him inside this whole series," says Gary, referring to the Braves' pitchers.

Correct. After the young slugger's terrific start, where he continued to demonstrate patience by not chasing pitches out of the strike zone, the pitchers have been probing for weak spots, and the Atlanta hurlers think they've found one. They're pitching him more aggressively—fastballs and hard breaking stuff inside—early in the count, then getting the young slugger to chase the softer, low-and-away stuff if they're behind in the count or once they're ahead. With the rest of the league looking on, it's a safe bet that Conforto will continue to see a steady diet of these pitches until he makes the necessary adjustment and stops swinging at the soft stuff out of the strike zone.

Such is a batter's career in the major leagues, which really can be seen as just a series of adjustments. Those who adjust get to continue; those who don't have to pack it up. Pitchers are always hunting for vulnerabilities, and when they find one, they exploit it. (And let's not forget all those advance scouts in the stands, watching and looking for a weakness.) Then it's the batter's turn to try new things—it could be something as simple as a plate adjustment. Moving closer to the plate or farther away. Maybe up in the box or back in the box.

And around and around we go. It's a game of constant adjustment and relentless tinkering. That's a rude awakening for young players, who are just trying to get used to the quality of the pitching, let alone its variability. Weathering all this is really the difficulty of becoming an everyday player at the highest level. There are starts and stops, two steps forward, one step back, two steps back, one step forward, and then a couple more. The knowledge—along with the patience—to survive the chaotic dance takes time to develop.

The change from facing AAA pitching to the majors is a huge adjustment. For me, it was night and day. Sure, some of the AAA pitchers I faced had been in the bigs, but they hadn't quite had the quality stuff to stick around or were trying to come back from arm injuries. Then there were others—like former White Sox hurler Joe Horlen and his great curveball—who'd enjoyed good years in the majors but were now in their thirties and trying to get back without their best stuff. Sprinkled in here and there were the up-and-comers: guys like Joaquín Andújar and Jim Kern, who were on their way to having All-Star careers. But in the big leagues, there were ten pitchers (today, it's twelve to thirteen) on every staff with above-average stuff. That's a huge upgrade. Plus, in AAA you aren't going to face any Steve Carltons, Tom Seavers, Jerry Koosmans, J. R. Richardses, or Don Suttons—guys with *exceptional* stuff.

No way. So the player has to adjust, if he can. And it's very seldom that someone like a Fred Lynn or a Ken Griffey Jr. or a Mike Trout comes into the league and says, "Okay, I'm a man-child, and I'll handle whatever you got from day one."

For most, it's not such smooth sailing.

"Strike three!" the umpire calls, and Conforto heads back to the dugout to figure things out. It's his second time striking out looking on the day. I don't mind strikeouts—they happen over the course of a season—but called third strikes, particularly on a fastball, are anathema to me. It tells me that the hitter is guessing. If you are an experienced veteran, okay—you know the pitcher and his tendencies, so maybe you take a chance and guess once in a while. But a youngster who hasn't been around long enough needs to stick to the basics, bear down, and go to hitting.

This reminds me of my first encounter with the legendary Ted Williams, when he grilled me on my hitting philosophy, *particularly* hitting with two strikes. It was January 1980, and I was working an endorsement gig at the largest sports trade show convention in the country at the McCormick Place Convention Center in Chicago. I'd just won the batting title and MVP in the '79 season, so there was a good crowd around my booth—folks looking for autographs—when all of the sudden I noticed a tall, confident man striding toward me. Any baseball fan worth his salt would have instantly recognized the Splendid Splinter, dressed in his typical corduroy sport jacket, turtleneck sweater, and slacks. *Gulp.* He quickly introduced himself, and before I could find the words to say "Hello, Mr. Williams," the interrogation began.

"What's your approach at the plate, Hernandez?" he asked. There was now a crowd gathered around to hear this conversation between baseball god and mere mortal, and I, the latter in that equation, was terrified I would say something stupid.

"Well," I sheepishly began, "I generally look fastball, going up the middle and adjusting to the secondary pitches. When I've got two strikes, I fight off the inside pitches and go the other way."

"Well, that's pussy hitting," Ted said, referring to my two-strike approach.

Silence. I could feel the hundred or so eyeballs upon me. *So much for not saying anything stupid...*

Fortunately, Ted, who I'm sure could read the room and see the panic in my eyes, said, "I'm sorry. I didn't mean to embarrass you," and quickly followed up with another question. "What's the easiest pitch location to hit?"

Stammering, I answered, "The pitch letter-high and away."

"Correct! Why?" There were no pauses between his words, like a teacher giving a sixty-second pop quiz.

"Because it's right there," I said, extending my right arm to indicate the location.

Ted then proceeded to demonstrate, as if he had a bat in his hands, taking a swing at a high pitch away, stopping the swing at "contact."

"Because it's the shortest distance for the bat to travel to the contact area," he said.

So I was 1 for 2 at the plate with Ted. *I'll take it!** But I went back to the hotel that evening kicking myself, because I hadn't been able to adequately explain my two-strike approach to Williams. I never became a "Judy hitter" (the less crude way of saying what Williams had said) when down in the count two strikes. I still looked to drive the ball as drilled by my father through-

---

* I had more opportunities to talk hitting with Ted, including the time when I referenced his book, *The Science of Hitting*. I told him it was the key to me overcoming swinging under a high pitch. Per the book's prescription, I got rid of the nasty habit of dropping my back shoulder on a high pitch by hanging a spare tire from my parents' oak tree in the backyard. I set the tire so that its central arc was at the letters and, as instructed, "chopped wood" all winter long. Ted loved that!

out my young years. But as I stated earlier, I had the ability to fight off a tough pitch in. My "emergency swing." I can't tell you how many times I must have frustrated pitchers who felt they made a great pitch but were thwarted by the quickness and adaptability of my hands.*

But it took the better part of four years in the bigs—nearly two thousand plate appearances—for me to perfect that two-strike approach.

Again, it just takes time.

So today's talented young players, like Michael Conforto, who is becoming a star precisely because he understands that nothing comes easily in this game, will have to continue to be patient and get better with each at-bat. *Two steps forward, one step back...*

Well, I'm glad I'm not in the lineup today. *It's cold out there, ladies and gentlemen*—49 degrees at start time. The electric heaters are going next to our feet, and I've got on more than a few layers beneath the network's blue parka. Fortunately for

---

* Despite being on record as saying that "good hitters have to guess," Ted, I think, would agree with me on this point about needing to "fight off" the inside pitch if you've "anticipated"—rather than "guessed"—wrong. Our semantics and explanations may differ, but I suspect our *intent* at the plate with two strikes would be somewhat similar.

Mets fans, current first baseman Lucas Duda has no problem staying warm. Two batters behind Conforto, Duda hits another home run, his second of the day and the team's fourth. *I swear this baseball is juiced.*

The Mets aren't the only team going deep to put runs on the board this season. In fact, the entire league is more reliant on the home run than ever before, including during the steroid era.* How is this possible? Are players once again doing things to their bodies that they shouldn't be doing? I don't think so. The league's drug testing has become extremely vigilant, and players today, though by and large in excellent shape, don't look as "blown up" as what we saw during the late 1990s and early 2000s.

But the league has to be thrilled with this increased dependency on the home run because the long ball helps them promote the game. We

---

* Back in 2014, one out of every three runs scored (33.4 percent) was off the home run. As Joe Sheehan of *Slate* pointed out, "That's a high figure historically, but not unreasonably so. In 1994, which of course seemed like a huge hitting year at the time, it was 33.5 percent. In 1961, an expansion year in which a notable home-run record was set, it was 33.7 percent" (*Slate*, September 1, 2017). Since 2014, however, that number has risen dramatically: 2015 saw a record set at 37.3 percent; in 2016, that record was broken, at 40.2 percent, and again in 2017, at 42.3 percent.

got talking about this before today's game, and Gary said the people at MLB don't seem to know how to promote the game any other way. It's just home runs and strikeouts, he said. I agree 100 percent. And for proof, you don't have to look any further than the sports-news highlights, where it seems every baseball play shown is either a home run or a fan putting a "K" sign up on a wall.

But what about a ten-pitch at-bat that taxes the pitcher and yields a base hit? Or a good sinker ball knee-high on the outside corner that the batter grounds into an inning-ending double play? Where are these elements of the game in America's daily updates? Or does America just not have enough bandwidth for such intricacies during their fast-paced, multitasking day?

Of course, our fascination with the home run is nothing new. Babe Ruth, after all, was the "Sultan of Swat." And what kid doesn't want to go to a ballpark and see his heroes hit bombs? It's spectacular stuff. It was one of the first things I looked for in the morning box scores: *Who hit a home run?*

But to keep up in a progressively more self-indulgent culture, is the league stoking our fascination with the long ball too much? Because not only do they continue to sell the home run; they've also actually gone ahead and *changed* some of the field parameters to encourage more of them, like making most of the new ballparks bandboxes and all but getting rid of the gaps, or power alleys, between fields with fences arranged in straight lines and right angles, rather than bowing arcs, from the corners to center field. Citizens Bank Park, Great American Ball Park, the new Yankee Stadium, anyone? *Please*...

Why would the league do this?

For the same reason they weren't quick to curtail steroids in the second half of the 1990s. They were giving the fans a lot of a good thing: home runs to fuel new records being set at a frenzied pace. On the heels of the disastrous 1994 strike, this boom was a godsend to baseball. And I'll admit it: Sammy Sosa and Mark McGwire's home-run-chase slugfest in 1998 brought *me* back to the game. Until then, I hadn't watched a baseball game since my official retirement in 1991. Not a regular season game, an All-Star Game, a playoff, or a World Series. Zip. Nada. I had no interest. But two guys crushing Maris's single-season record? Who wouldn't want to watch that? It electrified me just like it electrified everybody else.*

---

* It just didn't quite click about the steroids, McGwire and Sosa looking like two male models auditioning for a Michelin tire commercial. How did it not register in my brain? Seven years out of the league, and I was already a dinosaur.

So Duda hits the home run, and the kids go wild in the stands. *Yeah!* But I wonder if they know that five years ago they would have had to settle for a double. Because at that time, Citi Field's larger dimensions and taller wall—the Great Wall of Flushing, as we referred to it in the booth—would have kept Duda's hit well inside the park. But after the 2012 season, the Mets brought the fences in *twice* to give the fans and the hitters a little more offensive power during the games—i.e., more home runs.* So it's a home run for Duda, and *Let's go, Mets!*

This sort of tinkering with the game's parameters, like bringing in the fences in order to produce a certain result, worries me.

Let's suppose you were managing a baseball game. The goal, of course, is to put more runs on the board than the other team. How will you accomplish this? Like a general in charge of an army, you need to know your team's capabilities and the environment in which you'll be playing. If only two of the players in your lineup can

---

* I do agree that the original dimensions of Citi were as vast as the Russian steppes, on a par with the Astrodome and old Busch Stadium, where I played the majority of my career. They needed adjustment, but the second alteration was unnecessary.

hit the ball out of the park with any regularity, you have to do *other* things with the *other* seven players to score runs. Like hitting the other way, drawing walks, bunting, stealing, and—dare I say—hitting-and-running. But if all of the sudden the field of play is altered and now *most* of your players can hit it out of the park, you don't necessarily need to do those other things.

Well, this is precisely what is happening in today's game—the fences are in, and management has all the "bigger, stronger" players swinging for them. Suddenly, the low-percentage shot—like with the three-pointer in basketball—has become the layup. Hence the reason why things like on-base percentage in today's game are at an all-time low. You don't need to do all the little things if you can do the one big thing. And to win the day, you just need to bring bigger guns than the other team.

I'm sorry if I sound like an ex-ballplayer bitching and moaning about how the game isn't played the way it was played *in my day*. You're probably saying, *Shut up, old man!* Okay, I get it. I thought the older generation was often full of BS myself. But please understand: My intention is not to put baseball down but to raise it up for the wonderful game that it is. Or at least can be. And I have tremendous respect for today's players and their abilities—they're in far better shape and train more than we ever did. But when you have a culture that increasingly seems to have a shorter attention span and that attention span is purposely being overindulged with an emphasis on only the game's "spectacular" elements, then at some point the once-robust game of baseball will cease to exist. And that would be a shame—*not* because that's the way it was played "in my day," but because baseball has so many interesting other dynamics that to reduce it to one element—the home run—is like making a western omelet with just the melted cheese.

Where's the egg? Where's the ham? Where're the peppers and onions, for crying out loud?

Does finesse have no place in today's *power* game? I'm not convinced. How would a team with a lineup full of players who executed the little things fare against these long-ball lineups? I do wonder, but I'm afraid that's increasingly becoming a theoretical question, because we simply don't see that type of team in today's game.*

---

* The exception was the 2015 Royals, who won the World Series despite finishing last in the AL in home runs, with 147 (0.907 per game). How? With a big ballpark, solid defense, and pitchers that kept the ball in the park and the batters off the bases. *Imagine that!* They also were second in the league in stolen bases, with 121 swiped bags in the season. Rela-

Because on-base percentage is way down, teams don't steal, and I can't remember the last time I saw a hit-and-run in back-to-back games. To execute these things, players have to develop the skills at a young age and in the minor leagues. But from what I can tell, these skills aren't being taught there. Instead, most of the players—and their Statcast-era,* uppercut swings—seem to be geared toward one end: lifting the ball over that tantalizing fence. And who's to blame them? All they're doing is responding to the league's invitation to come to a perpetual home-run derby—no performance-enhancing drugs or doctored bats required.

---

tive to the rest of the cement-shoed league, they did the little things to score their adequate 4.17 runs per game (third to last in the league). But consider that 121 stolen base number compared to, say, the *314* swipes by the 1985 Cardinals, who despite hitting just 87 home runs that season (0.537 per game) were an offensive juggernaut that led the league in runs scored (4.611). So while the 2015 Royals seized an advantage over the otherwise home-run-bingeing league, there was still plenty more to be had.

* "In 2015 the league introduced Statcast, a 'state-of-the-art tracking technology capable of measuring previously unquantifiable aspects of the game,' giving teams, scouts and players access to detailed data which is used to make the physics of hitting a lot clearer. The biggest change brought about by the Statcast data is illustrating the importance of an uppercut swing that results more often in fly balls and line drives rather than groundballs" (*Washington Post,* June 1, 2017).

But the consequence is obvious: baseball is becoming one-dimensional.

I remember one game in Chicago a few years ago during which there were twenty-plus strikeouts and around seventeen walks between the two teams. *That's a lot of walks.* Jim Deshaies, the outstanding commentator for the Cubs, said, "You know, Keith, seventeen walks and [we'll say] twenty-one K's is thirty-eight at-bats where *nothing happened*. No action!" And I responded, "You know, I never thought of it that way." And we both agreed that it was a good way to put your fans to sleep. Because a game of home runs and strikeouts is boring.

So really, when you think about it, the decision to make fields smaller to "increase the drama" has had the reverse effect, and rather than bringing the fences in, teams should push them *out* and bring back the power alleys and the gaps. That would create a more dynamic game and force teams to diversify their personnel, putting more contact hitters with speed in the lineup. That's what Whitey Herzog did to the Cardinals when he took over in 1980. He took one look at the big dimensions and Astroturf of old Busch Stadium and told himself, *I need to build a team with speed, defense, and good pitching.*

What a concept!

And so by 1982, he had put together a team

that hit the fewest home runs in the National League but scored the fourth most runs and went on to be World Series champs by defeating, in seven games, the powerful Milwaukee Brewers. How? By stealing bases, hitting-and-running, always taking the extra base, good pitching (particularly our bullpen), great defense, and playing sound fundamental baseball. Back then and across the league, it was almost an automatic on a double in the gap, with a runner on first, that the third base coach would send the runner home. And a close play at the plate—now *that's* exciting baseball that fans can sink their teeth into: they see where the ball is, check the runner, the ball, the relay throw, where the runner is, where the catcher is... *Oh my gosh, it's going to be a close play at the plate...* Now we're talking baseball!

And please don't get me started on the hit-and-run. I know it's sacrilegious for sabermetrics folks because, as they say, it doesn't pay off. But with the right personnel—in any sized outfield—the hit-and-run can do a number of things for a team. And, again, if suddenly you're not going to be relying on the long ball to score, then you have to manufacture runs somehow, and hit-and-runs help set up a big inning and keep pressure on the defense. I personally loved to hit-and-run, and we made a living off it in St. Louis.

"Oh, but you were on Astroturf," people will say, "and the ball gets through the infield faster."

Sure, but look at the infields today, how manicured they are. There's no long grass anymore like Wrigley Field back in the '70s and '80s. Back then, the Cubs' philosophy was basically *Okay, we have a small and windy park, so let's stock our pitching staff with sinker-ball pitchers, in the hopes of keeping the ball out of the air, and grow the grass four inches long so the infield will eat up all those ground balls, turning them into outs.* And when Whitey's speedy Cardinals would come to Chicago, they would grow the grass an inch or two longer.* Still, we would hit-and-run and race all over Chicago.

Even with the bandbox stadiums, I wish the Mets would do it more often. It sure has to be enticing. I mean, all the infields in the league today are fast, like putting greens—perfect for ground balls to get through. And while there are plenty of terrific athletes, many of today's middle infielders have become big, offensive guys. They lack

---

* I remember batting champ Bill Buckner, who played for the Cubs from 1977 to 1984, cursing all the way down the baseline as one of what must have been a multitude of hard-hit grounders was gobbled up by that "lion's mane" (as we used to call it) of an infield. It was hard not to bust out laughing as Buck would shout in full gallop, *"Cut the motherf—ing grass!"*

the quickness to get to that hit-and-run ball in the hole. Despite these advantages, the Mets—like most of today's teams—don't hit-and-run. And on the rare occasion when some other team successfully executes it *against* them, I say under my breath, *Well, here you are, first and third with nobody out, and you've got a problem on your hands.*

Like with the hit-and-run, a lot of sabermetrics guys think stolen bases are to be avoided. Really? Those teams of my era and their heavier emphasis on speed would rampage in today's game, if for no other reason than to simply rattle the pitchers. Because pitchers now come up to the big leagues not knowing how to hold runners on. Why? No one steals anymore! Look at Noah Syndergaard in 2016. When other teams actually attempted to steal, *they stole him blind,* and it affected his pitching *enormously*. He was completely rattled. But that wasn't Noah's fault—no one had really worked with him in the minors. I guarantee you that if Noah, an extremely talented player, had come up in the '60s through the '80s, he would have been better prepared to deal with this stuff. So why don't teams take this approach with other pitchers? It's not like Syndergaard is the only one with a problem holding runners in check.

It's also not just the pitchers who feel anxiety when there's speed on the base paths. Fielders, too, feel the pressure. With speed on the bases, fielders are more inclined to rush the play or throw, thus making them more apt to commit an error. But, again, you need team speed to apply that pressure, and that quality just isn't a top priority for the GMs. In the process, the game has slowed, and baseball is becoming similar to the American League in the '50s and '60s. Boring, one-base-at-a-time, home-run baseball.*

Yuck.

---

* I tried playing Strat-O-Matic baseball's late-1950s American League season a couple of years ago. I didn't last through the first month of that season.

CHAPTER 30

THE 1976 ALL-STAR break was approaching, and I was still riding pine.

Looking back, I understand where Red and Bing were coming from—it's difficult for managers and general managers to endure a young player learning to play every day in the major leagues when it means you may lose a few more games. And between 1960 and 1975, the Cardinals had finished below .500 only twice, so losing wasn't part of the tradition, especially when there were deals to be made to bring in veterans instead of playing youngsters. But as the 1976 All-Star break approached, it was obvious that the organization had kicked the can down the road a bit too long: gone were the talents of Bob Gibson, Tim McCarver, Julián Javier, Curt Flood, and Nelson Briles, to name a few.*

---

* The bottom line is that athletes age. Look at the Phillies and their great run in the mid-2000s with Chase Utley, Ryan

Six games before the break, Red called me back into his office. We were now *nineteen* games back. "You'll be in the lineup every game, and it doesn't matter if you hit .190 or .400," he said. "You're in there, so don't worry about it." With all other plans exhausted, they were finally coming back to me.

I struggled a bit those first six games but went into the All-Star break with a home run off the Dodgers' Burt Hooton. Talk about the worst time for a rest! But I caught another guardian angel in Fred Koenig, now part of Red's coaching staff. A big beer-swilling guy with a Mr. Clean hairstyle, Fred was a cross between a marine drill sergeant and a barroom brawler. After the last game before the break, Fred walked up to me and offered to throw BP during the three days off. My eyes lit up. "Absolutely!" I responded.

These extra BP sessions didn't sit well with

Howard, Jimmy Rollins, Cole Hamels, Shane Victorino, etc. They all came up together and were dominant for half a decade. But the team held on to some too long, and rather than replenish from their minor league system, they traded their youth for quality veterans. This worked for a while with the likes of Roy Halladay, Roy Oswalt, and Cliff Lee as the Phils extended their post-season appearances another three years after their world championship in 2008 with yet another World Series appearance. But the inevitable came knocking, and the Phillies' last .500-plus season was in 2012.

clubhouse man Butch Yatkeman. Butch had been in the Cardinals organization since 1924, when at sixteen years of age he started out as one of the clubhouse kids who performed all the menial chores. He eventually worked his way up to head clubhouse man, and through his tenure he saw the Cardinals win thirteen NL pennants and nine World Series. He was around for Rogers Hornsby, Dizzy Dean, Johnny Mize, Bob Gibson, Lou Brock, and the greatest of all Cardinals, Stan Musial.* But Butch was set in his ways, always bitching and moaning about something, and he worked hard to let us know that today's players weren't up to yesteryear's snuff. Typical generation-gap stuff (like me in the previous chapter) but with Butch, it was more like three generations. He was downright cranky and a pain in the ass. We would eventually learn to like each other, but for now, Butchie didn't have much time for me, and there wasn't much love lost.

"You mean I gotta come to the ballpark and wash your clothes?" he whined after I gave him the news about the BP sessions.

"Butch," I said, "I'll take my clothes home and wash them myself."

---

* Butch would retire in 1982 after fifty-eight years of service.

"Well, I still gotta come to the park and open up the clubhouse."

"Butch, can't you have one of the front office people open the clubhouse for me?"

"I'm not letting anybody in my clubhouse without me present!"

Well, enough was enough. "Screw you, Butch!" I yelled, though maybe I used a different word. "It's my career on the line. So come to the *f—ing* clubhouse or have someone else *f—ing* do it. But I'm hitting tomorrow morning, and the *f—ing* clubhouse better be open!"

Lo and behold, the "f—ing" clubhouse was open the next day, and there was Butch, as pleasant as ever. I again offered to wash my clothes, but Butch, in full martyrdom, wouldn't have it. Oh well. My only regret is that I didn't offer to pay Fred Koenig a couple hundred dollars for his time and effort, or at least give him a case of Budweiser. Because that son of a gun was under no obligation to come to the yard those two blazing-hot and humid July afternoons and throw me BP. But he did, perhaps saving my Cardinals career.

Thank you, Fred! (You, too, Butchie.)

But I had good reason to ruin everyone's All-Star break—and not just because this was perhaps my last chance in a Cardinals uniform. I was making a major plate adjustment, this time against *left*-handers, who were giving me fits with the breaking ball away. It was Lou Brock, sensing that this was my moment, who'd made the suggestion.

"Why don't you move more on top of the plate [closer] against lefties," Lou said. "That's how Frank Robinson did it." Lou also told me to make this move obvious to all the opposing catchers and pitchers, by digging in *hard* so they couldn't help but see this drastic change. "You're going to go around the league for at least a month, they will see you on top of the plate, and they are going to throw you inside. Look for it and rip it! Pitchers can't relate to hitting. They don't know you're looking in there. It doesn't matter if you make an out or pull it foul, just hit it hard. Establish the inside pitch as *your* pitch. Each time you do this, they're going to say, 'Hey, that's my best fastball, and he hit the dog out of it. Maybe I *can't* get in there...' That's when you have them! Because then they're going to switch gears and throw right into your strength—the outside corner, with the barrel of your bat in full coverage."*

---

* Years later, I told Frank Robinson about Lou's suggestion, and he gave me a big smile. "Yes!" he exclaimed. "I learned to look in. They would always think they could jam me, but I had other ideas." I then relayed Frank's comments to former

So now I was off the plate against righties, per Ken Boyer's suggestion a year earlier, and closer in against lefties, per Brock's. By "closer," I mean *real* close—like six inches off the plate. While it's not a change in mechanics, it's yet another new strike zone. So lots of BP. It also requires nerve because you're giving major league pitchers—who aren't afraid to put one in your ribs—more reason to do it. Pitchers view the plate as *their* turf, and if you stand on top of the plate, that's a declaration of war.

Frank Robinson, Lou's example, stood on top of the plate from day one, and in his 1956 rookie season, he set a rookie record for hit-by-pitches with a whopping twenty. That led the league, and it didn't include all the brushbacks and dustings. Despite the assaults, Robinson hung tough and won Rookie of the Year that season.* Could

---

Cardinals teammate, 283-game winner, and lefty Jim Kaat, who had faced Frank many times when Frank was an Oriole and Jim a Twin. Jim's eyes lit up and he said, "Yeah, I remember seeing him on top of the dish when he first came into the league, and I said, 'I can get in there.' He *killed* me, and it took me a while to realize that was where he liked it. So I started throwing him my sinker away, and from that time on I had better success against him." A game of constant vigilance and adjustment.

* I remember Red Schoendienst telling the story that one time Robinson just killed the Cardinals in a series in Cincinnati,

I hang tough like that? Against ninety-five-mile-per-hour, up-and-in heat? Well, something had to give versus the lefties...

Again, *adjust or perish*.

Nerve aside, there was another, bigger challenge to working so close to the plate: I discovered that I could cover only three-fourths of the width of the strike zone at once. So when I looked *in,* I had to take the pitch on the *outer* quarter; conversely, when I looked *away,* I had to take the pitch on the *inner* quarter. Easier said than done. It required, first, *recognizing* the pitch's location out of the pitcher's hand, then deciding to pull the trigger or not, depending upon the location I was anticipating.

And *anticipating* is key here. You're not *guessing* what and where the pitcher's going to throw. Remember, I looked fastball 90 percent of the time throughout my career. You're just looking for a particular spot so you can jump on it *if* it comes. But there, too, I had to be careful, because some-

---

and the next week, when the Reds came to St. Louis, the Cardinals pitchers knocked him down as a sort of retribution. But it didn't matter—Frank still had a great game. And the next day, Red called a team meeting and said, "I'm calling this meeting to say leave Frank Robinson alone. Don't throw at the son of a bitch. You're just making him mad, and he's killing us."

times I pulled the trigger too quickly. Particularly when looking inside. That wasn't good because it created an inside-out swing. I'd fly open with my shoulder and, recognizing that I was early, drag my hands behind, producing mostly weak fly balls or bloops to center or left field. To counter this inclination, I remembered what my father had told me in my late-teenage years:

You have quick hands, Keith. Trust them. Don't rush. Let the ball come to you, then strike.

That's a tall order when we're talking about a pitch that seems to be on you in an instant, like an inside major league fastball. Could I make the adjustment?

We started the second half of the season on the road in San Diego. *God help us...another West Coast swing.* I came to the park expecting to see my name on the chalkboard. *Nope...* Brent Strom, a lefty, was starting that night for the Padres, so Ferguson caught and Simmons played first. The next day it was the same story: Simmons and Ferguson against another lefty, the crafty Randy Jones.* Had I been duped? Sus-

---

* I couldn't have been too disappointed missing out on Jones. Anyone who dismissed him as a "soft tosser" missed the

picious and brooding on the bench, I kept my mouth shut, and I kept coming to the park early for extra BP to stay sharp.

My brother drove me to the park on the final day of the San Diego series. Released by the Cardinals after the '75 season, Gary had recently taken a job in L.A. as a sales representative for Johnson & Johnson. We headed into the clubhouse together and saw my name up on the board. It felt like opening day. Trepidation galore. *Okay, Hernandez, this is it—time to put up or shut up.* And there was Gary: "You're going to have a great day, Keith. I can feel it." Once again, my selfless brother—my good-luck charm—was right: I went 3 for 5, with 1 run, a double, and 3 RBI in a 7–1 win over the Padres.

Then it was an hour-and-a-half flight up the California coast to San Fran with Dad waiting for me at the airport. *Don't I have enough on my shoulders? The last thing I need is to be talking baseball and hitting all night.* Thankfully, Dad was somewhat subdued and very positive. I guess

---

point: with a hard sinker and a wicked hard slider, much like Tommy John's, Randy threw his fastball hard enough to keep hitters off-balance. In 1975, he went 20–12 in 36 starts and finished second in the Cy Young balloting. This season, 1976, he came into the start with a 16–3 record, on his way to a 22–14 season in 40 starts and a Cy Young Award.

Gary had called him and given him a heads-up: *Let Keith breathe. Don't force any issues.*

After a good night's sleep in my old bed, I drove to the park for the noon doubleheader and the two right-handers slated for the Giants. I went 1 for 3 against Jim Barr—the same Barr who had knocked me down in '75—with a two-out, two-run single to center that tied the game at 4–4 in the sixth. *Take that, Jim!* But Red pinch-hit Ferguson for me in the ninth against one of the game's toughest lefty relievers, Gary Lavelle—a hard-throwing power pitcher with a power slider. The second game was another 1 for 3, and again Red pinch-hit for me against Lavelle. I started the series finale the next day, going 0 for 2 with 2 walks, and it was adios to Mom and Dad, who were all praise after the game. It was a double relief: Dad's words filled my sails like no others could while at the same time I was delighted to be escaping his scrutiny.

We wrapped up the road trip after two games in L.A., where I sat, of course, against lefty Doug Rau but hit a double off right-hander Don Sutton in the second game. On the whole, it was a good stretch: 5 games started, going 6 for 18 with 3 runs, 2 doubles, 2 walks, and an impressive 5 RBI. *But what about the lefties?* Red was keeping me from them. *Why?* If I was going to be an everyday player in the bigs—which was the goal—I had to face the southpaws.

We opened the home stand with a four-game series against the Cubs, who threw all right-handed starters. I went a whopping 6 for 11 with 2 doubles, 2 RBI, and 5 walks in the series.

One at-bat in game three was a turning point: I was facing Bill Bonham, a hard-sinker/slider-throwing right-hander. Bonham had me 1–2, and I just knew he was going to pound me inside. I knew it! So I anticipated the pitch and, sure enough, Bonham put a fastball right there—inside corner, on the black, just above the belt. *Patience. Front shoulder in...anticipate, coil, attack...* Whack! A BB up the middle for a single.

Perfect execution. No anxiety. Relaxed like a cold-blooded assassin.

But that's only half the story. The other piece is that I executed it without overcommitting. Instead, I had this assumption in the back of my mind—*I think this is what he's gonna throw*—but with two strikes, I still had to protect the plate; I couldn't commit 100 percent to the inside pitch. A lot of hitters are unable to do this, which is why the game has seen a multitude of "guess hitters" over the years. For them, guessing—or "selling out on the pitch"—is their way of responding to major league pitching. But in this at-bat against Bonham, I proved to myself that I could do it better and hedge my bets. Because as the ball shot up the middle, I understood that I'd still had enough time to adjust if the pitch had been somewhere else. That knowledge—*You have enough time, Keith*—was like being handed a trump card at a blackjack table: no matter what the pitcher dealt, I had an answer.

"From then on," as I later recounted to the *Post-Dispatch*, "I had it."

Like in Tulsa the previous two seasons, I was taking off. By the end of the month, I was 16 for 43 since my return to the starting lineup, hitting .372 with 9 runs scored, 6 extra-base hits, 9 RBI, and a slugging percentage of .558 in 13 starts. Moreover, I got on base an incredible 58 percent of the time with 9 walks and only 3 strikeouts. That meant I was getting the National League pitchers' respect—I was no longer "the easy out."*

On August 7, Red started me against lefty Jim Kaat. He did it again the next day against lefty Steve Carlton. *What's this? Two premier lefties and I'm starting?* That's when I realized I'd be playing every day. Righties and lefties.

---

* Or, to borrow a term from my esteemed colleague in the booth, Mr. Ron Darling, I was no longer "a lamb." (As a player, Ron would break the opposing lineup into two categories: those he wouldn't let beat him and the lambs.)

In retrospect, Red handled me beautifully against the lefties. Rather than just throwing me to the lions, he sat me down those first few weeks against the likes of Randy Jones, Doug Rau, Gary Lavelle, Tommy John, Woodie Fryman, John Candelaria, and Jim Rooker. All tough lefties— all lions. Then, as I got hot with the bat, he put me in the lineup against these guys.*

I had a solid August, hitting .315 in 21 starts with 16 RBI and a .365 OBP, and I put the pedal to the metal for the remaining 36 games of the season, batting .331 with 26 runs scored, 17 RBI, and 20 walks (a .420 OBP and a .515 SLG). The power line drives were coming now, too, yielding 8 doubles, 2 triples, and 4 home runs.

The home runs were especially gratifying, as 3 were off left-handers, including the Mets' Jon Matlack and Jerry Koosman.† Against Matlack, I led off the inning, which isn't my favorite thing to do because you have to run off the field, put your glove and cap down, get your bat and your helmet,

---

* I went through the second half of the season in chronological order, box score after box score, provided by that wonderful website Baseball-Reference.com, and I saw there was a method to Red's madness. Red sat me down later in August against Randy Jones and Don Gullett, but that was it.

† The third home run was off lefty Buddy Schultz, a September call-up for the Cubs.

get in the on-deck circle, and rush your warm-up ritual. *Thank God I didn't wear batting gloves.* I preferred time to get into the on-deck circle, prepare my bat with the proper amount of pine tar and resin, take a few swings with the weighted donut on the bat, and finally settle on one knee to watch the pitcher work the batter ahead of me. But Dad had always preached to me the importance of starting a rally, and my on-base percentage for leading off an inning was .409 that season. So I got up there, and Matlack threw me a nasty 3–2 slider—knees and black—and I crushed it to right-center field over the 386 sign at old Busch Stadium. Per Lou's advice, I was on top of the plate versus the lefty so the fat of my bat could cover the outside corner. Mike Phillips, a utility infielder with the Mets, later told me that Matlack came into the dugout all pissed off and shouted, "I'll knock him on his ass if he thinks he can lean over the plate like that again!" *Ahhhh, music to my ears, folks!* And after that home run, my batting average for the season stood at .290—exactly 100 points better than where it was at the All-Star break.

Four days later, I went deep off Koosman in the eighth inning at Shea. He was pitching for his twentieth win of the season, and "dealing." Protecting a 3–0 lead, he threw me an up-and-in fastball. *Bam*—a line drive into the Mets' bullpen in right. Jerry had never won twenty in his career, so he wasn't laying one in for me. *He wanted that shutout.* And I remember rounding the bases, thinking, *I've hit home runs off Matlack and Koosman! The cream of the crop!*

But the most satisfying home run that month was off Steve Dunning of the Expos.

I didn't care for Dunning. The right-hander was a former all-American from Stanford, and I'd played against him in AAA. He'd started one game in Denver and was crying at the umpire for most of the night. Bitching and moaning, and in my third at-bat I disgustedly said from the batter's box, "Quit your whining and throw the ball over the plate." He looked at me in absolute surprise and said, "What?" I motioned sweepingly with my left arm over home plate, inviting him to throw a strike, thinking for sure he'd put one in my ear. Instead, he threw me a changeup, and I grounded out to second base. *What a wuss.* Now in '76, we were going against each other again, and he threw me another lousy, straight, high change over the middle. I sent it over the scoreboard and into the swimming pool beyond. A very satisfying, monster two-iron off the tee at Parc Jarry.

Now, that's what I'm talking about! That's the Keith I know! Where the hell have you been hiding, for crying out loud?

So I *killed* it that September. Really, the whole second half was a romp: in 296 plate appearances, I hit .331 with 17 doubles, 3 triples, 7 home runs, 43 runs batted in, and 35 walks for an almost .500 slugging percentage. The only bummer was that the season was over, but I was also grateful. Luck had been on my side, because circumstances could have been very different. What if, like in 1975, the team had been in a divisional race? I don't think I would've made my way back into the lineup every day in the second half. What would've happened then?

KH BATTING PROGRESS (BY SEASON)

Year	Games (G)	At-Bats (AB)	Batting Average (BA)	On-Base Percentage (OBP)	Slugging Percentage (SLG)
1974	14	34	.294	.415	.441
1975	64	188	.250	.309	.362
1976	129	374	.289	.376	.428

While career saving for me, the second half of 1976 was the end of the road for our manager.

The season had been a disaster for the organization, finishing fifth in the NL East with a 72–90 record. It was the first time a Cardinals team had lost 90 games since 1916 (63–93), and the lowest finish in the standings since the advent of the two-division system in 1969. So after a twelve-year tenure,* which brought two pennants and a World Series title, Red was fired at the end of the season. I felt bad, of course. I liked Red, and my struggling the first half of the year hadn't made things easier for him. Despite that, he'd kept his word, inserting me into the lineup the second half of the season. He'd been yet another angel on my shoulder, and I was sorry to see him go.

For the first time, I didn't return home to my parents for the off-season. Instead, I remained in St. Louis for what turned out to be one of the coldest winters on record. The snow never melted; it just froze until the next storm came and covered it. To stay warm, I rolled joints and spun records, blues mostly—J. J. Cale's *Troubadour* and Roy Buchanan's *A Street Called Straight* were particular new favorites—and stayed in de-

---

* Tony La Russa's sixteen seasons managing the Cardinals, from 1996 to 2011, surpassed Red's for the longest tenure with the club.

cent shape because the Cardinals had instituted an off-season workout program. It was like *The Jack LaLanne Show* of the '50s and '60s: mostly calisthenics with a bit of running, stretching, and agility drills. Today's players would laugh at this regimen, but it was better than being a complete couch potato throughout the miserable winter.

I also hung out with a girl I'd met during the season, Sue. I'd spotted her in the stands one day while I was still riding pine in the first half of the season. Her father was in the lumber business, and once a year he'd get box seats behind the Cardinals' dugout for his big German-Catholic family. Four daughters, three sons. Sue was his eldest. I couldn't help but notice her. I gave one of the clubhouse kids a note asking for her phone number. I'd never done that before. She obliged, but of course I lost it.

A few months later, I was doing a promotional event at a bank, signing autographs, when she showed up with her sister. I recognized her immediately. She was twenty-one, a year younger than me. We didn't party—Sue had a two-year-old daughter, Jessie, from a previous, short-lived marriage. We just sort of hung out at my place or over at her folks', who were terrific people, and that was fine with me because I enjoyed being back around a family.

I was becoming more recognizable around town and didn't know how to handle all that came with being a local "celebrity." It's one thing to be noticed when you're surrounded by teammates but entirely another to be out there on your own in the off-season and have someone say, "Hey, aren't you Keith Hernandez?" Back then, I'd get nervous—sometimes even start stuttering—and would duck into a grocery store or a bank with sunglasses and a hat pulled down. Anything to avoid being recognized.

Hanging out with Sue let me skip a lot of that. Then winter was over and it was time to head to Florida again.

Play ball!

Part III
CONSISTENCY

CHAPTER 31

Long Island

AFTER YESTERDAY'S WIN AGAINST Atlanta, the broadcast crew flew out to the West Coast with the team, while I drove home for a nice dinner with friends and eleven days off to work on the book. *And relax.* This afternoon, I'm getting together with my friend Paton Miller. Paton is a fabulous and well-respected local artist. He sells to me at the "friendship price"—to date, I have seven of his paintings hanging on my walls.

I love to collect art.

Books, too. I started collecting Easton Press when I was twenty years old, and I have a soft spot for first editions if I can find a good deal online. I can't say I've read the entire collection, but it's here for anyone who wants to visit. Some players surround themselves with a lot of trophies and career mementos. Gary Carter, my former teammate and co-captain on the Mets, basically had a shrine to his career in his office. I haven't kept much—though sometimes I wish I had. As it is, all I've got on display is my MVP trophy and three Emmys for broadcasting. The rest is put away in closets or collecting dust in the basement.

When I was growing up, we had my father's artwork all over the house—paintings, wood-work, mosaics. I think Dad's artistic talent was the part of him that Mom loved the most, and his creations never ceased to amaze us. I have two of his mosaics, *The Corsican Sailor* and *The Three Wise Men*, hanging in my living room. They're made from stones we collected on Pebble Beach, a two-hour father-and-sons jaunt down the Northern California coast. Dad would hand Gary and me a couple of empty Folgers coffee cans, setting us loose on the beach to collect the various shapes of green, brown, white, and black stones.

I remember he instructed us to look for three tan elongated pebbles—a nose for each of the wise men—and I stumbled upon the perfect Ro-man nose. It was just lying on the beach among the millions of other stones. I rushed up to Dad and said, "Dad, I got a nose for you!" He took it and, holding it flat against the palm of his hand, inspected it, smiled, and said it was perfect. But it was Gary who had the find of the day: the lip of a 7Up soda bottle that had broken off and been smoothed over by the sea—the perfect jewel for the sailor's ring.

Dad was always taking bits of this and that for his creations. Like when he made a teepee for us in the backyard. A real Plains Indian tripod teepee. He used eucalyptus tree branches, whose limbs were long and strong—like poles—and Dad cut them down to size, about fifteen feet long. For the cover, Dad used pieces of fabric he'd gotten from Ed and Jim's Union 76, the same gas station that sponsored our Little League teams. They would occasionally have tire or service sales they'd advertise with signs made from big canvas sheets. When the sale was over, Dad would ask for the signs and take them home, usually for his oil paintings. But this time he stretched the material over the eucalyptus branches, like the American Indians must have done, using twine to combine the various pieces until the fabric completely enveloped the tripod. And using the pictures from our history books, Dad painted Indian symbols in oils on the outside of the teepee. Finished, he anchored the teepee in the ground and let us sleep outdoors during the rare hot summer nights in Linda Mar Valley.

Gary and I were so excited—*we were real Indians sleeping in our teepee out on the Great American Plains.*

Dad also painted two individual portraits of Gary and me in warbonnets (though we felt we didn't look very Indian-like because he had us smiling, and Indians were always portrayed as very stoic). We were in the center of the paintings, and on each side, flanking us, was an Indian on horseback: one was a medicine man dressed in a breechcloth and a buffalo hat with two horns; the other was in a full warbonnet and dressed in deerskin leggings, his spear and shield draped along the side of his Appaloosa. Below our group, off in the distance, a US cavalry troop was making its way through the hills, and the Indians were looking down at those men and pointing. It was fantastic. I still have mine, which I cut into sections. I framed each Indian, and they hang in my master bedroom in Sag Harbor. I wish I had kept the whole painting as one, but it was just too large to hang anywhere.

Though my brother got most of Dad's artistic talent, I love to draw. At least I used to before professional baseball. When I retire from announcing, I'll pick it up again.

One thing I've discovered is that lots of artistic people like baseball. Like at Elaine's. It was just a great place to hang out—the people were so interesting. The restaurant was up on 88th and Second Avenue. When Elaine started it in the

'60s, a literary crowd came in there. They were all aspiring guys—George Plimpton, Gay Talese, Norman Mailer, Kurt Vonnegut—and they were all broke. All these names. She let them eat, and they paid her when they could, so she developed this long-standing loyal following. The food was never the greatest, but nobody cared—it was all about the crowd. Established actors, screenwriters, choreographers, writers—you name it. It was their hangout, and it was phenomenal.

And I found that a lot of the "artists in residence" wanted to talk to me as much as I wanted to talk to them. So it was a good quid pro quo: baseball for art.

My good friend Bobby Zarem, the most famous publicist in New York, was responsible for introducing me around. Bobby knew everyone in the arts. I remember going with Bobby to a rescreening of *Lawrence of Arabia* at the old Ziegfeld Theatre. Peter O'Toole and David Lean, the film's director, were there, and we sat with them afterward at the party back at Elaine's. I asked Peter, "What did you think of the film?" And he goes, "You know, I've never watched the film." And I go, "No!" And he goes, "I don't watch my films. I must say, T. E. Lawrence was a very interesting character..." And I'm thinking, *You gotta be kiddin' me.*

So here I am, little Keith from Pacifica, California, sitting down at a table with David Lean and Peter O'Toole, and they're talking about making the film. Peter said, "I hated those fucking camels. It was so hard on my ass. I had to put about six inches of foam padding on it, on the top of the saddle."

And I sat with Elia Kazan one night. He occasionally came into Elaine's and one time he called me over. Huge baseball fan. He just started talking about all his films. James Dean, when they did *East of Eden*. Raymond Massey. It was incredible. I would sit there, just listening to these people go.

One of the most memorable times was meeting Plácido Domingo, after the one opera I've ever been to at the Met. Not exactly my favorite kind of music (I can't even remember which opera it was), but Bobby took me backstage after the show to meet Plácido. We walked in, and he was sitting on his chair like a king on a throne. He screamed across the room: "Keith! I am so sorry. I sang like a .230 hitter tonight. I have a cold. I promise you, next time I sing like you, a .300 hitter." So he was just a piece of work, and evidently a baseball fan.

My cell phone buzzes next to my computer.

It's Jo Craven McGinty from the *Wall Street*

Journal. We'd set up the morning call, but I'd sort of forgotten about it. She's writing a Behind the Numbers column about Joe DiMaggio's fifty-six-game hitting streak. It's the seventy-fifth anniversary of the streak, and she wants to know if I think the record will ever be broken.

"Well, if anybody could have done it, it would have been Pete Rose," I say. "Tenacious as he was." But Pete stopped at forty-four, and now I don't think anyone will do it. It's not an impossibility, I explain to McGinty, but I think Joe's record is safe. Rose got as far as he did despite what was, at the time, extensive media coverage—the TV networks rearranging their nightly programming so folks at home could follow Rose's at-bats. And who knows? Maybe the attention wore even him down.

Imagine what it would be like in today's game, where if a player makes it to just twenty-eight games—halfway there—the twenty-four-hour, can't-even-buy-gas-without-a-screen-in-your-face media kicks into high gear. Pete didn't have to deal with Twitter, Instagram, and Facebook. There wasn't even *SportsCenter*! It was the dark ages, comparatively, and I'm not sure any person could stay relaxed in today's bright spotlight for the two months it would take to break the record.

McGinty and I talk for about ten more minutes. She's wondering if any changes in the game over the past seventy-five years—specifically, the increases in travel and league size, the number of pitchers faced, and the types of pitches they throw—might also prevent the record from being broken. She's got a point on all of these, but there's also a flip side to consider with each one.

Regarding the increase in travel, what's the difference between today's six-hour flight to L.A. from New York and the 1930s six-hour train ride to Boston? And with the level of wealth and extravagance in today's game, you could make the argument that Joe DiMaggio's travel time was a more "roughing it" experience. I mean when I was coming up, the old-timers thought we were living in the lap of luxury, and compared to their day, I guess we were. Imagine what they would say about today's players with their concierge lifestyle, prescribed diets, million-dollar training rooms, huge clubhouses, and, in Atlanta's new SunTrust Park, a "quiet room" and a "sleep room" with bunk beds—*I would have loved that after staying out late on a Saturday night!*

But players didn't have three time zones to travel until 1958, when the California teams came on line. And the schedule for today's players, with seven teams out west and interleague play, is far more grueling than ever before. There's a lot of back-and-forth. In the days of two divisions, we made two trips to the West Coast a year, each trip stretching to ten days so we would acclimate to Pacific time. Now players may make four or five short coast-to-coast trips a year. Even for me, a guy who just picks his nose up in the booth, it's taxing.*

When you had two divisions, there was better continuity because the teams played each other more frequently and in quicker succession. And as a hitter, it was nice to see the same pitcher within a week or ten days because the previous encounter was fresh in your mind. But today, that continuity is gone: you can have the Dodgers' ace Clayton Kershaw throw a three-hit shutout in L.A. and then you don't play the Dodgers again for a month and a half. Well, that stinks. Without all this expansion and interleague play, you might see Kershaw just ten days later on a home stand.

---

* It's always easier to travel west and play, but coming back *is a bear*. Even if you get the much-needed off day after traveling, it takes two days to really recover. When I was playing for the Mets, I always felt sluggish that first game back after a trip out west. Former Angels third baseman Doug DeCinces told me that every time the Angels traveled east, they would open in Yankee Stadium. They would play a night game first, but the Yankees' owner, George Steinbrenner, would always schedule the second game during the day. Why? He knew the Angels would be on fumes, and the Yankees would kick their butts.

So, yes, all these new teams and expanded bullpens mean more pitchers faced, and there's less familiarity for hitters to know what's coming at them. I buy that 100 percent. I would rather face a good starter with his best stuff going that night in four at-bats than have to face four pitchers.*

The increase in the *types of pitches* thrown is perhaps the strongest argument for an untouchable fifty-six. Stan Musial, who faced a diet of fastballs, curveballs, and changeups through most of his career, was on his way out of the league when pitchers started throwing the slider, and he admitted that the pitch made it harder to succeed as a batter. I've said many times on the air that if there ever was a serious upset in the balance of power between pitchers and hitters in MLB, it was when the slider was introduced.

---

* But what's the quality of those relievers? Again, with the four-team expansion in the '90s came a long-term watering down of the talent pool, and with talks of future expansion always floating around, it's a consideration that probably isn't going away. So you could make the argument that while Joe DiMaggio (and, later, Pete Rose) faced fewer pitchers over the course of fifty-six games than a batter would face today, he was going against the cream of the crop more often. Not to beat a dead horse, but Rose and DiMaggio also weren't swinging for the fences every at-bat.

Why? Because it was the first time pitchers had a breaking ball that was close to the speed of their fastball, making it difficult for hitters to pick up. During my career, we were all adjusting to the split-finger fastball, which was introduced and perfected by Bruce Sutter, then a closer with the Chicago Cubs and a future Hall of Famer. That particular pitch enabled otherwise average pitchers, like the Giants' Mike LaCoss, to become much more formidable foes. It made the Astros' Mike Scott a Cy Young winner. In today's game, the *pitch du jour* is the "circle change," a five-finger pitch with the thumb and index finger forming a circle around the inside half of the ball, which can be lethal because it looks so much like a fastball coming out of the pitcher's hand. So it's true that each time pitchers put a new arrow in their quiver, hitters have their hands full.

But, again, hitters adjust. When I was with the Mets, I faced a left-hander for the Cardinals named Greg Mathews for the first time, and he threw me a high changeup inner half.

Wait, what's this? A lefty throwing a left-handed batter a changeup?

That strategy just wasn't around in my day. The pitch jammed me in on the hands and I hit a weak ground ball to the second baseman. As I ran to first base, I thought, *Okay, it's a new pitch.*

What did I do wrong, and what do I have to do to counter it the next time I face this guy? As a batter seeing something for the first time, that thought process instantly starts churning, and you begin to figure out how to combat it. I did the same thing with the split-finger, and Musial did the same thing with the slider.

Ted Williams, who, like Musial, left the game as the slider was coming in, was asked if he could have still hit .400 against pitchers armed with the slider, and he said, "I would've learned to hit it." And that's exactly what good hitters do. We adapt. Whether or not that means it's tougher now to hit in fifty-six consecutive games, I don't know. But I do know that hitters find their counterpunches: I mean it's not like after the introduction of the slider or the split-finger, hitters stopped hitting over .300, right?

The one disadvantage for today's hitters that the reporter failed to mention is the players being *bombarded* with too much statistical information to put together a fifty-six-game hitting streak. These hitting charts, bar graphs, and stat tables—it's all useful information, but as I mentioned before, there's that point when it reaches paralysis by analysis. I have to laugh every time there's a pitching change and I see the hitting coach bring out his big binder to show the batter what the new pitcher likes to throw and when. It's all this "He throws 30 percent breaking balls on a 2-and-0 count and 16 percent fastballs away on full counts." I feel this is overkill for these batters, who, the last time I checked, were baseball players, not engineers working for NASA with degrees from MIT.

The reason the batter's getting paid a lot of money isn't because he's got a genius IQ; it's because he has split-second reaction time that allows him to do what is almost theoretically impossible: hit a baseball slung by a man with a cannon for an arm who's just sixty feet six inches away and is motivated to not allow a hit. That's tough stuff, so "Don't think too much, stupid."

When I played, I was known as a thinking man's hitter, and it's true: I would go up there with a plan and could be fastidious in my approach. *But a player can overdo it,* and if I were a coach today, I'd throw half of that statistical stuff out and tell the players to rely more on these two sources of information: *their eyes and ears.*

It's amazing what we can pick up when we get our heads out of the data for a moment and *let our senses soak in the game* right before us. For example, the pitcher I faced the most during my career was Hall of Famer Steve Carlton. Against him, I hit .321 with 17 walks in 154 plate appearances.

The key to that success was my paying attention to *how Carlton faced my teammates*. Steve always tried to "extend the strike zone"—getting the hitter to swing at his nasty slider that, at first, looked like a strike but scooted well off the plate just before it arrived. Carlton would feed that slider in the same location the entire game as if it were spit out of a computer. That's the kind of command he had, and because it looked so enticing every time, a lot of very good hitters consistently took the bait. My Cardinals teammate Garry Templeton was a prime example. I would be in the on-deck circle and watch Carlton cast his spell on Tempy, who just couldn't lay off.

Well, if Tempy, who, along with Darryl Strawberry, was one of the most talented hitters I ever played with, couldn't lay off that pitch, I sure as heck better.* So I had to discipline myself not to swing—*Don't take the bait!*—forcing Carlton

---

* Like me, Templeton faced Carlton more than any other pitcher over his career (.261 in 111 at-bats). Interestingly, Tempy had more success against Steve after being traded to the Padres in 1982, where he saw Steve less frequently. As a Cardinal, Tempy hit just .205, striking out 15 percent of the time, in 78 at-bats against Carlton, but as a Padre, he hit an extremely impressive .394 in 33 at-bats and reduced his strikeout rate to 12 percent. So despite becoming less familiar with Carlton, Tempy obviously figured out how to lay off his nasty slider.

to grab more of the strike zone with his slider. (Easier said than done. Because Steve was also a *power* pitcher, who just happened to throw 90 percent sliders. That's kind of a paradox—most breaking-ball pitchers are not power pitchers.)

When it comes to gathering information, I would also tell hitters to talk more with other players—even players on other teams. *Ask* them questions and *listen* to what they have to say.

I remember Lou Brock told me once that when Steve Rogers came up pitching for Montreal in 1973, everyone in the league was trying to figure him out.* The right-handed Rogers had really good stuff—a great curveball, cutter, sinker, and a straight fastball—and he knew how and when to use all of them. Lou, *who hadn't faced Rogers yet,* started looking in the papers every time Rogers pitched and noticed that Rogers was throwing three-hitters, two-hitters, four-hitters, but *not* striking many batters out. The ball was being put in play, yet Rogers was walking away with shutouts.

Being the curious player Lou was, this piqued his interest, and he went to Billy Williams, the Hall of Fame left fielder for the Cubs, who'd

---

* Rogers was second in Rookie of the Year balloting in 1973, posting a 10–5 record with a 1.54 ERA.

faced Rogers. Like Lou, Billy was a left-handed hitter, and Billy told Lou that Rogers predominantly liked to go outside—that he could paint the outside corner with his outstanding curveball and nasty hard sinker. "He will pitch inside to keep you honest, but his bread and butter is the outside corner." Well, that explained the lack of strikeouts: Rogers wasn't overpowering guys, but he threw hard enough to keep them honest, and he knew how to pitch to contact. For lefties, that meant a lot of weak "rollover" ground balls to the right side of the infield.

So a few days later, Lou and the Cardinals finally faced Rogers, and when Lou got into the box, he crowded the plate, almost sitting on top of it. Why would he do this? To take the outside corner away from Rogers and make him pitch inside. Well, most pitchers don't like to pitch inside for a living—they get paranoid they're going to either hit the batter or leave one out over the middle of the plate—and Rogers was no exception. That adjustment on the fly gave Lou, who hit .358 in 67 career at-bats against Rogers, the upper hand against one of the game's more dominant pitchers.

Maybe a player like Brock, ever a student of the game, would have made the same deduction about Rogers with pie charts and graphs. But it's a lot of information to sift through in a very sterile, static learning environment, and despite all the headphones and video games in today's youth culture, we are all still social creatures. Our minds better process information when we're interactive—even if it's just watching our teammates from the on-deck circle, or through conversation with our hitting brethren around the batting cage.

Of course, any knowledge you bring into the batter's box—be it from experience or pie charts—isn't going to tell you nearly as much as what you'll learn once you've stepped in and seen a couple of pitches. That's why I took the first pitch in almost every first at-bat over my career.* I wanted to gauge in that first at-bat the quality of the pitcher's stuff on that particular day or night, in that particular inning. *How hard is he throwing? What kind of movement? How sharp is his breaking ball?* In a perfect world, the pitcher would miss on his first pitch, usually a fastball. *Okay, now I'm 1–0, and I can take another pitch in the hope that he'll throw a different pitch.* Then, if he missed with that one, I would be 2–0, a

---

* The only time I swung at a first pitch in my first at-bat was if I was red-hot and had runners in scoring position. But most of the time, even when I was red-hot, I took the first pitch.

hitter's count, and would have seen his fastball *and* breaking ball.

Ready to swing the bat.

Of course, that's the best-case scenario. Because if the pitcher threw a strike on his first pitch, I had to get to hitting. Maybe I hadn't seen his breaking ball, but at 0–1 I no longer had the luxury of taking another pitch. (Still, I was willing to go 0–2 in the count if necessary. Say the pitcher then came with a "bastard" pitch, catching a piece of the black that I couldn't handle. Then it's two-strike hitting, and I was a good two-strike hitter.*)

And hitters have to accept that sometimes they just won't have much information before pulling the trigger. Countless times I came up with the game on the line, with a reliever on the mound, and maybe I was familiar with him, maybe I wasn't, but I didn't have the luxury of taking a strike to gauge him. *I just have to go up there and see the ball and hit it.* If I'd made it more complicated than that, I would have frozen up. Instead, I trusted my eye at

---

* Albert Pujols once asked Stan Musial the definition of two-strike hitting. Stan's answer was "a great knowledge of the strike zone." *Absolutely!* Why? If a pitcher has you 0–2, you are in trouble. The hurler has pitches to waste, and most will attempt to get you to chase something out of the strike zone. *Don't fall for the bait!* If you have a good eye at the plate and don't chase those bad pitches, you can extend the count closer to your favor.

the plate and did what my dad had taught me as a kid: fall back on primordial instincts.

Dig in, growl, and hiss, recognizing the crisis of the situation, and say, "They're going to have to kill me if they want to get me out," and fight to the last breath.

In those sorts of do-or-die moments—and I'm sure both Rose and DiMaggio ran into many of them over the course of their respective streaks—there is no place for overcomplicated analysis.

Instead, rely on those multimillion-dollar reflexes, and see the ball, hit it.

It's like what Frank Robinson told me in his office when he was managing the Expos and I was just getting started in the booth: "They have got to throw it over the plate, Keith. I don't care what they got. Trick pitch? Illegal pitch? They've got to throw it over the plate."

Moments after Frank said that, a young intern from the GM's office entered Frank's office with about a *two-inch* stack of daily stat sheets. When the kid left, Frank picked out around fifteen pages and then turned to me and said, "Keith, here's what I think about the rest of this," and he threw the remainder in the garbage.

CHAPTER 32

Long Island

I'M OFF THE PHONE with the reporter, but I'm still thinking about DiMaggio and Rose. *What is it that allows a man to hit safely in fifty-six straight games, like Joe, or forty-four games, like Pete?*

A little luck, certainly, but it's no coincidence that those two men were also two of the most consistent players of all time.* Rose is the all-time leader with 4,256 hits (talk about a record that may never be broken), and DiMaggio's life-time average was .325, despite taking three

---

* A bleeder through the infield, or a bloop single off the end of the bat, and the streak stays alive. But the converse is also true. The day DiMaggio's streak was snapped, he hit the ball hard in every at-bat—but right at 'em. And the night Rose's streak ended, on national television with 31,000 Braves fans on their feet, the Atlanta hurlers pitched Pete as if it were the seventh game of the World Series, and Gene Garber, who ended Rose's streak (and the game) with a strikeout, celebrated as such when the game ended.

years "off" during World War II to serve in the army.* To accomplish these tremendous feats, each man just didn't have too many enduring slumps.

Streak or no streak, such fortitude is what we should marvel at: not only to have the ability and skill to do something difficult—like hit a baseball slung by a major league pitcher—but also to do it consistently over such a long period of time.

I can tell you firsthand that even approaching that sort of consistency is extremely difficult, and just because I'd made the necessary adjustments to major league pitching by the end of 1976, that didn't mean I would be able to succeed against it game by game, week by week, month by month, year by year. In 1977, my first season in the bigs as a full-time regular, I hit .291 with 91 RBI—a good season, but not .300. The following season, 1978, I fell apart after the All-Star break and finished the year at .255 with 64 RBI.

---

* More impressively, DiMaggio's career strikeouts (369) are almost identical to his career home runs (361). That nearly exact one-to-one ratio is the lowest in history of anyone with more than 300 home runs. Add his career doubles (389) and triples (181) to the mix, and the man was two and a half times more likely to get an extra-base hit than he was to strike out.

KH BATTING PROGRESS (BY SEASON)

Year	Games (G)	At-Bats (AB)	Batting Average (BA)	On-Base Percentage (OBP)	Slugging Percentage (SLG)
1974	14	34	.294	.415	.441
1975	64	188	.250	.309	.362
1976	129	374	.289	.376	.428
1977	161	560	.291	.379	.459
1978	159	542	.255	.351	.389

It made no sense!* I was young, healthy, and playing every day. So things should have gone smoother. Sure, sometimes pitchers would try new tactics, but nothing fooled me for long. I

---

* Maybe I pressed. I'm sure I did. As a team, with only twelve clubs in the NL, we ranked last in on-base percentage and on-base plus slugging, eleventh in runs per game (3.7), tenth in runs (600), ninth in batting average (.249) and home runs (79). Offensively, we stunk it up.

just wasn't able to play at a high level *consistently*.

Why? I don't have the answers. Maybe the second-half rut of 1978 was a sophomore jinx. (Dad said I was feeling for the ball. He was probably right, but I didn't want to hear that.) It was yet another shot at my confidence. Maybe players like Rose and DiMaggio didn't need help in that department, but evidently I still did. Where would I get it? Thankfully, fate stepped in and dealt me a good hand, and once again, it was Ken Boyer coming to the rescue.

And so I'm sitting at the kitchen table, about to leave to visit my friend Paton, and despite my best intentions to take the rest of the day away from the game, I'm lost in another one of its memories. Something that happened years ago, and, as time passed, would be the turning point in my career:

May 6, 1979

Airplane rides in the major leagues can be pretty fun. I'm on one now, traveling 600 miles an hour from St. Louis to Houston. The team is in good spirits. That afternoon we won the rubber match against the venerable Pirates, 4–2. With studs like reigning MVP and two-time batting champ Dave Parker, and seven-time All-Star Willie Stargell, the Pirates are the club to beat this year. After that good win and heading into a day off tomorrow, the guys are letting loose a bit. There's a lot of card games and bantering. And a lot of beer.

But I don't feel like cutting loose. I can't. Because I'm off to a bad start—another hole in April that I've dug for myself.

Are you kidding me? I'm twenty-four years old now—I can't afford this!

Back in '76, I got benched after a lousy April. Now, three years later, it's happening again. Today, against the Pirates, I had a good day at the plate. I went 3 for 4 with an RBI.

Great. My average jumped from a putrid .216 to a still-putrid .237. But beyond the numbers, there's something else: my swing feels off.

"I still don't feel comfortable yet," I told the reporters after the game. Because I am a perfectionist and a worrier (always have been and always will be). And I am obsessed with my swing. To be overcritical of your swing is like being overcritical of the very way you breathe. And when I question it, tinker with it, dream about it, pray about it, curse it, beg it...that one simple thing becomes a maze and chokes me off. That's what I'd meant when I told the reporter, "I still don't feel comfortable yet." I'm suffocating, dammit!

Years later, a manager of mine will understand

my torment and say that if Keith Hernandez didn't worry about his swing so much, he'd have a good chance to hit .400.

The plane levels out, and the flight attendant brings me a Michelob. I take a long sip. Half the beer is gone before I open my eyes again.

*My swing is off...It keeps repeating inside my head. My nemesis—I will only be satisfied with it when I'm red-hot. But that seems unlikely, because now we're heading to the Astrodome, where I'm just 8 for 52 in my career.** *

---

* I despised the Astrodome. Maybe I still had in the back of my mind those powerful San Francisco Giants teams of the mid-1960s and how many times their pennant hopes were dashed in September because of their inability to win there. The Giants hitters always complained how the Dome had a bad backdrop, which created what Mays and McCovey called a problem with "depth perception." Most stadiums have a black or dark-green wall over the center-field fence so the hitter can distinguish the white ball coming out of the pitcher's hand. The Dome had no such black wall. It was just this big, wide area that drifted deeper into nothingness toward a service entrance, some fifty yards behind the center-field fence. It was like some deep, dark, mysterious cavern that could have been a perfect prop for Gandalf and Frodo of *The Lord of the Rings* to enter at their own peril. Like the ancient Mines of Moria. And if you took extra BP in Houston, always at three or four in the afternoon, those service doors were wide-open, and the daylight from the outside would come spilling in, directly behind the center-field fence. It was like hitting into a setting sun. Brutal.

I take a second pull from the beer. The flight attendant brings another round.

This year is of immense importance to my status as a major league player. The past two seasons I had been Jekyll and Hyde. After tearing up the second half of '76, the '77 season had been a breakout year. I had finally gotten off to a much-needed good start (no hole to dig out from) and finished the year at .291, 15 home runs, and 91 RBI.

But not so fast, Mr. Hernandez. The next season, '78, I'd had a good first half but then fell apart in the second half, hitting a paltry .228 with only 21 RBI. The only good thing that had happened was winning my first Gold Glove Award for fielding excellence.

Big deal. Stargell hasn't won a Gold Glove and he's in his eighteenth season, a sure Hall of Famer. Pittsburgh's Herculean first baseman had mercifully sat out today's game, and there, spitting seeds on the Pirates' bench that afternoon, he had looked as relaxed and happy as a man at a country club. A year away from forty and he's hitting .333.

Yet I know that my glove is keeping me in the

---

* An 0-for-21 skid over 7 games in August cost me a .300 batting average and maybe a 100 RBI season.

lineup. Our manager, Kenny Boyer, had said as much to the press during the previous home series against the West-leading Astros. I'd gone 0 for 5 in the first game, while in the second game Roger Freed had come off the bench and launched a game-winning grand slam in the bottom of the eleventh. "Any chance you'll give Freed a couple of starts at first base?" some press members had asked.

Boyer had stuck by me, answering, "Freed realizes his role as a pinch hitter…Hernandez is so good defensively at first that I can't take him out, even when he's in a slump at bat."*

My dad had drummed into my head as a kid that if you excelled defensively, the manager would be less inclined to bench you when you were in a prolonged slump. Well, Boyer probably shudders at the thought of Roger Freed's glove "handling" our infielders, especially hard-throwing shortstop Garry Templeton. Last season, Tempy, who's a bit loose with his throws, made forty *errors at short, and my "golden" glove must have prevented twenty more.† So*

---

* *St. Louis Post-Dispatch,* May 2, 1979.

† Templeton threw from over the top, which made his ball rise and run either to the left or right. Plus, even when he was on top of me, coming in on a slow roller, Tempy still liked to

the Cardinals—and the St. Louis writers, who'd lobbied for that Gold Glove largely because of my adventures with Tempy's freewheeling style—were well aware of how important my skills were at first base.

Still, the day after Boyer's comments, I went 0 for 2, and the press descended on my locker. I survived the inquiry, mostly by agreeing with them. "First base has got to be a productive position," I said. "If you're not helping on offense, you're not doing your job. And batting no. 3—that guy's gotta hit."*

I tried to come across as confident, like I was weathering the storm, saying:

"The pitcher is out there doing the best job he can, and I'm sure not going to help him any if I'm upset about my hitting"

and

"It's a team effort and I have to contribute the same as always on the field"

and

"If I'm in a slump, I just wipe it out of my mind."

---

show off his incredibly strong arm, and I didn't have much time to react. As electrifying as he was to watch make plays, I still have nightmares about some of the throws.

* *St. Louis Post-Dispatch*, May 3, 1979.

What a load of crap! I can't just wipe it out of my mind, because I know that in the big leagues, shortstop and catcher are the only positions where managers can afford to keep a guy in the lineup just for his defense. First basemen are hitters, and sooner or later the team will reshuffle the deck.

The second beer is gone, replaced by a third.

And, yeah, sure, maybe my glove is keeping me in the lineup. But I don't want to be just another major league player. I want to be a Mickey Mantle. I want to be a star. My dreams, ever since I was a kid, were lofty. And I grew up a Cardinals fan. The uniform means a lot. I understood "Cardinals Pride" since day one, even before they drafted me and I thought, Holy cow, there's twenty-six teams and I get drafted by the Cardinals, the team I love!

So what? Lots of people have big dreams. When it comes down to it, maybe you're just a .250 hitter . . .

I close my eyes again—anything to slow down the train running at full steam inside my head. Keep this up and you'll never climb out of this. You're your own worst enemy . . .

When I open my eyes, I notice Ken Boyer strolling toward the rear of the plane. The same man who was my manager in Tulsa in '74 and

'75 when I was "wearing it out," and who took over the Cardinals last season. Now Boyer is making his way from first class, and he doesn't stop to chat with anyone until he's next to my seat.

He leans over to me and says, "Nice hitting today," referring to my 3-for-4 at the plate.

I say, "Thank you," and want to ask, Hey, Skip, any chance we can tell the pilot to go somewhere else—any place other than Houston and the lousy Astrodome? *Instead I take another long sip, and Boyer starts talking again.*

"I've seen you hit, Keith, and I know that you are something special. I knew that back in Tulsa. And I'm telling you right now that you are my first baseman. You'll be in the lineup every day, even if it costs me my job. So stop worrying. Go out there and have fun, and do the things on the field I know you're capable of doing." Finished, Boyer pats me on the arm, smiles, and moves on.

The next game, I'm in the Astrodome, facing Ken Forsch. I go 4 for 4, scoring a run in the 4–1 victory. My swing feels like a well-oiled machine. I'm no longer suffocating. I'm breathing.

I stand up from the table. It's been almost forty years since that plane flight, when Boyer came to my rescue. They were the most important words spoken to me over my career. Without them, I think maybe I wouldn't have made it in the big leagues. Who knows?

I glance at the digital clock above the stove (out of the game this long, but my eyes are still like a hawk's). Time to meet up with my friend Paton. But before going out, I walk into the guest bedroom and head to the closet. I turn on the light, and there, tucked in the corner, is the Silver Bat Award I got for winning the batting title that year, 1979. I should put it up on the wall with the artwork, but it's so damn heavy—it's pure silver.* Still, I need to get around to buying or constructing a wall mount.

I guess I've been saying that for a while now.

---

* I believe 1979 was the last year the bat contained a large amount of silver. After that, I heard, they were silver-plated only. I could be wrong, but my Silver Bat is darn heavy.

CHAPTER 33

MY SUCCESS IN 1979 was catalyzed by two events. One was the confidence booster from manager Kenny Boyer on the airplane—"You are my first baseman." *No matter what.* The second actually took place *a year earlier,* during a conversation with none other than the Reds' Pete Rose. Along with the Pirates' Willie Stargell, the Phillies' Dick Allen, and the Dodgers' Steve Garvey, Pete was often very encouraging to me during my early years when I struggled, despite being a rival player. He would land on first base and say things like "I like the way you swing the bat, Hernandez. You keep going the way you're going, and you'll be just fine." On this particular occasion in 1978, the Reds were in town, and I'd had a decent series so far. Pete was hanging around the batting cage, and he watched me take a couple of rounds of BP.

"Keith! You can hit!" he exclaimed as I exited the cage.

Wait, what? Pete Rose is saying that to me? Wow!

"Shoot, you're a .300 hitter, Keith!" he said. "And that's the goal, isn't it? To hit .300?"

"Sure," I said to Pete, who'd hit .300 or better in *thirteen* of the past fourteen seasons.

"Well, some guys make that tougher than it really is, Keith. You just gotta remember that baseball is every day over six months. That's a heck of a long time. You can't worry about your average on a day-to-day or even on a week-to-week basis. *It will drive you nuts.* Instead, think in terms of every 100 at-bats, which is about a month's worth of work."

I nodded. A full-time player got about 600 at-bats a year, depending on how often he walked and where he was in the lineup. So, yeah, 600 divided by a 6-month season was 100 at-bats a month.

Pete continued. "Now, 30 hits per 100 at-bats is a .300 average. So what's 30 multiplied by 6?"

I replied, "180."

"Right! So in 600 at-bats, 180 hits is .300 on the season. Now, what's 25 multiplied by 6?"

"150."

Pete nodded. "What's *that* batting average?"

".250, Pete."

"Precisely. The difference between a .250 hitter and a .300 hitter is 30 hits. Think about that: 30 hits spread out over the 600 ABs in a season is what separates the average from the great. That's less than one additional hit every five games! Now, think of all those at-bats you give away in the course of a season, like those last at-bats in a blowout game in the eighth or ninth. *Never* give those at-bats away! If you have 2 hits, you want 3; if you have 3, you want 4."

This all made perfect sense to me. *Don't let any at-bats go to waste—it might be that extra hit!*

Then Pete expounded, "If you hit .320 in the first 100 at-bats, you only have to get 28 in the next round to still be hitting .300. But *never* settle for that, Keith. Keep building your chips so after the fourth 100 you're playing with house money."

Pete Rose's words of wisdom—to break down the season per 100 at-bats—may sound obvious, but a simple outlook can be tough to practice if you're struggling like I was in 1978. I was just too anxious and uncertain to put Pete's words to good use. It wasn't until 1979—after Boyer's assuring me that I'd be in the lineup every day—that I settled down enough to digest the season per Pete's prescription.

In my first 100 at-bats of 1979, I got 22 hits—8 short of the goal of 30 (remember: 30 hits per

100 at-bats equals a .300 average). So, accordingly, my goal for the next 100 at-bats was the prescribed 30 hits plus 8 more to make up for those first 100 at-bats. That was a tall order, but I was just beginning that second set when Boyer had his chat with me on the airplane, and instead of 38 hits, I got 40, including one stretch where I was 20 for 43. That was more like it! Now, to maintain my .300, I only had to get 28 hits for my *third* set of 100 at-bats. But remember, Pete had said, "Be greedy." So once again I exceeded my quota, getting 34 hits and raising my season average to a fairly awesome .321.

Quite a turnaround.* What's more, I was killing both righties *and* lefties, and driving in runs at a monstrous clip: forty-one in fifty-five games. I couldn't wait to get to the ballpark every day.

Unfortunately, the team was headed in the opposite direction. Tied with the Expos for first place on June 11, 1979, we began the first trip of the season to California: Dodger town, San Francisco, and San Diego. We won the first game in L.A., but then proceeded to lose the next seven of eight. I stayed hot at the plate, going 17 for 38, and was now hitting .331 for the season. That was good enough for

---

* Since Boyer's talk, I'd batted .392 (47 for 120) with 5 HRs, 25 RBI, a .455 OBP, and an off-the-charts 1.064 OPS. Smokin'!

the sixth-best batting average in the NL, behind Pete Rose (.358), Dave Winfield (.354), Lee Mazzilli (.343), my teammate George Hendrick (.339), and George Foster (.332). But that early in the season, who cares? All I knew was that I was incredibly hot, in the top ten in batting average, and I wanted to help my team win more ball games.

After the West Coast disaster, we limped home in fourth place and then dropped 8 of 14 against the Mets, Expos, Phillies, and Pirates. We were a promising outfit—rebuilding since yet another disastrous season in '78, when we'd finished 74–88—but we just weren't ready for prime time against the more seasoned teams. By the All-Star break, we were taking our lumps (but were only six and a half games back, in fifth place).

But I was still going steady at .325, batting .356 (89 for 250) with 43 RBI, 27 extra-base hits, and a .961 OPS since May 1. In fact, the only hitters hotter from May through the break were the Padres' Dave Winfield and the Phillies' Mike Schmidt. Winfield, whose .331 average, 22 home runs, and 72 RBI made for one of the best first halves in baseball history, and Schmidt, who was on pace to hit 55 home runs that season,* were

---

* Thirty-one home runs at the break.

398

clear early favorites for National League MVP and two of the highest vote getters for the 1979 MLB All-Star Game.*

I, on the other hand, wasn't voted to the All-Star team. *How is that possible?* Three reasons: Steve Garvey, Pete Rose, and Willie Stargell. These first basemen were superstars, former MVPs with *twenty-six* National League All-Star selections between them. And though not as strong as mine, their first halves had all been solid: Garvey, "Mr. Clutch," had hit exactly .316 in each of the first three months of the season; Rose had cooled off a bit after a hot start but was still batting .304 at the break;† and Stargell, who didn't make the All-Star cut that year, was enjoying a .306, 18 home run, 41 RBI first half in just 51 starts. So imagine baseball fans sitting down in major league ballparks across the country, fill-

---

* The first "half" of the MLB season is actually longer than the second, as the All-Star break falls a few games or so *into* the last 81 games (there are 162 games in each season). In 1979, the break came after game 86, leaving 76 games left to play.

† Rose had batted .360 in his first 100 at bats, followed by .350 in his second 100 at bats, giving him plenty of breathing room for the following month-and-a-half-long slump when he hit just .234. In the game following the break, Pete would go 0 for 4, dropping his average to .301. But he would go no lower the rest of the season. Typical Pete, who was a pure force of will and determination.

ing out their All-Star ballots, and seeing those three guys as first base candidates along with their home team's first baseman. Then add my name to the mix. Outside of St. Louis, I'm sure the only consideration I got, if any, was *Who in the hell is Keith Hernandez?* Hence, I was left off the showcase's twenty-five-man roster,* and I resigned myself to spending the three off days at home. Was I disappointed? *Hell yes!* It wasn't going to be easy to break through that Garvey-Rose-Stargell ceiling.

Things changed, however, when I got an unexpected 10 a.m. phone call. We were back in Houston, playing the Astros for a final three-game series before the break. *Who's calling me at this hour?* I dragged the phone receiver across the hotel sheets to my ear and said a groggy hello.

It was John Claiborne, Bing Devine's replacement as the Cardinals' GM. "Congratulations, Keith!" he said. "You made the All-Star team."

Wow! Maybe Keith Hernandez was a household name! Not exactly—the manager of the National League's team, Tommy Lasorda, had cho-

---

* Set in 1939, the twenty-five-man roster increased to thirty in 1982, thirty-two in 2003, thirty-three in 2009, and its current number, thirty-four, in 2010.

400

sen me to replace an injured Dave Kingman on the roster.*

Later that afternoon, after Claiborne's phone call, Rick Hummel of the *St. Louis Post-Dispatch* asked if I planned to accept the invitation and head to Seattle for the game. "I'll go and I'll enjoy it," I told Rick, who wanted to know if I felt "slighted at all by being picked on the rebound." But I meant what I'd said, and bouncing back from that lousy April, I was thrilled that Lasorda, who had chosen me over Stargell, had recognized my effort.†

There was another reason I was happy to stay away from St. Louis for the break: I'd gotten

---

* Kingman was unavailable to play after being hit by a pitched ball on his left arm earlier that week in Atlanta. His comeuppance for bulldozing me in 1976! Speaking from experience, I'm sure the ball suffered more damage coming into contact with one of Kong's limbs than the other way around. Dave was out of action for ten days as a result of the hit-by-pitch but was back in action July 21, pinch-hitting for the Cubs in the ninth inning against the offending Braves to deliver the game-tying RBI and score the winning run. He would go on to be the NL home-run king that season, with forty-eight, beating out Mike Schmidt's forty-five.

† In today's game this could never happen, as managers no longer can name players to the roster, lest they be accused of "homerism" by selecting their own players and/or avoiding players from rival clubs. Sort of dumb, in my opinion.

married in the spring of 1978, and by 1979 the union was showing cracks in the foundation. Sue, the girl I'd spotted in the stands back in '76, and I just weren't well suited for a "baseball" marriage, in which I was more committed to my game than to her. We were able to avoid that obvious fact when I was playing ball every day. But the prospect of being stuck in the house for three days, going stir-crazy and waiting for the second half of the season to start, just wasn't my idea of a respite. (Sue did come to the All-Star Game, and we had a great time together.)

Crisis averted, for now . . .

When I flew into Seattle for the All-Star Game, the first day's routine was simple: head to the park, gather for a team meeting, take a few rounds of BP, and make yourself available to the media. But when you lace up your spikes in front of your locker, look up, and there's the likes of Johnny Bench, Joe Morgan, Dave Parker, Larry Bowa, Steve Garvey, Pete Rose, and Mike Schmidt, it's not just any "normal" day.

On All-Star weekend, even the guys who aren't too crazy about one another during the regular season genuinely enjoy one another's company. Take Expos All-Star catcher Gary Carter, for example. Gary had a knack for rubbing some players the wrong way during the regular season. I think it was the way he carried himself—always strutting, shoulders back, chest puffed out, and a smile you suspected was more adoration-loving than genuine. I didn't know him well, but we'd had our moments. Gary was very athletic behind the plate—he'd committed to going to UCLA out of high school as a quarterback on a full scholarship but decided on baseball instead—and I remember one game in Montreal when he ran me down, back toward third base, and tagged me out. But rather than just lay on the tag, he steamrolled me. It was completely unnecessary—like a boxer squeezing in an extra jab well after the bell. I never forgot that one. But now here was Gary, one of baseball's premier catchers, a few lockers down from me. I had tremendous respect for his game, and it was an honor to be around him and my other fellow All-Stars.

Behind the good-natured laughter and genuine camaraderie going on in the clubhouse was also a serious intent: *to win*. National League president Chub Feeney came into our clubhouse on the workout day and exhorted us to make good on his annual gentleman's bet with his American League counterpart, Lee MacPhail. He reminded us that the National

League had dominated the American League the previous seven meetings and had won fifteen of the last sixteen contests. It may have been called a "showcase," but the All-Star Game was no circus act. It was a real contest where a score was kept, and I sensed that every one of my teammates wanted to be on the winning side to prove ours was the better league.

The next day, after an All-Star luncheon, where each first-timer was presented with an oil-painted portrait of himself with his team cap on,* I went to perhaps the best cocktail party in history. The drinks were good, of course, but among the guests was a who's who of the morning-paper box scores when I was a kid—baseball's titans of yesteryear. I remember talking with the legendary Ernie Banks, "Mr. Cub," when Warren Spahn strode up. Cigarette in hand, the winningest left-hander in baseball history started bustin' Ernie's chops, saying, "I used to love to play you guys. I'd look ahead in the schedule for my next start, and if it was Chicago, I'd get all excited and send a limo for your lineup."

Well, I waited for Ernie to laugh first, which

---

* And first-timers with *new* teams, so I would receive another in 1984 with a Mets cap on.

he did with great joy, and I joined in.* *Somebody pinch me! I'm in absolute heaven!*

Spahn then turned to me and said, "Boy, Keith, I would've liked to have you at first base when I pitched."

"Warren," I said, "thank you very much, but you had Joe Adcock over there."

"Yeah, Joe could hit," replied Warren, "but I've never seen anyone with your glove. Plus, you can hit, too."

Holy shit! Here was Warren Spahn telling me — a twenty-five-year-old player who'd never hit .300 for a season—that I was his preferred first baseman! This is the same man I'd watched "toe the slab" and twirl a gem at Candlestick Park back in '63, when I was nine, my father remarking the whole game what a great pitcher he was.† Well, if that doesn't pump a player up, I don't know what will.

Bring on the American League!

I got my chance the next day, in the game's eighth inning, when Lasorda pinch-hit me with

---

* I looked it up, and sure enough, Mr. Spahn was 49–19 with 4 saves in his career against the Cubbies. He just may have sent that limo...

† Spahn would return to San Francisco that same season to throw another *complete* game, this time taking the loss after giving up the game's only run in the *sixteenth*!

two outs after Lee Mazzilli's home run to tie the game at 6–6. I stepped into the box to face Cleveland's stopper, Jim Kern. I'd battled Jim in AAA more than a few times in my Tulsa days, so I knew he had a blazing fastball but a slider he was uncomfortable throwing to lefties. I approached this virgin All-Star at-bat as if I had two strikes on me. I was ready to swing at the first pitch. It came, a fastball about nine to twelve inches outside at the knees.

"Strike one!" yelled home-plate umpire George Maloney.

I looked back at him. "That ball's a foot outside," I said.

"Swing the bat, sonny," Maloney retorted.

Swing the bat, sonny? I couldn't have hit that pitch with a ten-foot pole!

Of course, I didn't say anything. It was my first All-Star appearance, so it wasn't like I was going to argue with the umpire on the first pitch I saw. *I'm sure he'd be delighted to throw me out of the game if I beef.* But I was fuming—*Thanks, jackass, because now, instead of 1–0, a hitter's count, I'm down a strike*—and it got the best of me and my concentration. I went down swinging on three or four pitches.

Fortunately, we won the game (and Chub Feeney won his gentleman's bet) after Mazzilli drew a walk with the bases loaded off Ron Guidry in the ninth. But I never forgot that big, blind umpire, Maloney.* *Too bad the San Diego Chicken, the Padres' hilarious mascot, wasn't present in his white doctor's jacket with an eye chart.*

Oh well—on to the second half of the season.

---

* Actually, I did forget Maloney, because I thought for years the home-plate ump that night was Marty Springstead, and I told the story countless times as such. So, my apologies to Marty, who passed away in 2012. To George Maloney, who died in 2003, all is forgiven. *But, for crying out loud, how could you call that pitch a strike?*

CHAPTER 34

TWO WEEKS AFTER THE All-Star break, Winfield was leading the league in hitting at .345. But if I've said it once, I've said it a thousand times: *it's a long season,* and after a dismal August, when he batted just .175, Winfield was down to .312. I kept steadily climbing, hitting .333 in July and .384 in August—good enough for NL Player of the Month—and I sat atop the league at .345. It was while playing against Winfield and the Padres, in a series that stretched into September, that I began to really think about the batting title.

We'd arrived in San Diego on a roll, taking two of three in L.A., then two of three in San Francisco. No Cardinals team had done that—won both of those series on the same road trip—since 1969. *Could we finally exorcise the ghost of West Coast past?* First we had to deal with Winfield and the *three* southpaws the Padres were running out against us. In game one, Winfield reminded us that, despite the slump, he was still one of the most dangerous hitters in baseball, when he put the Padres on the board with a three-run shot in the bottom of the first. But fourteen innings later, I had the final say with a game-winning double—a bullet to left center—in the top of the *fifteenth* off lefty Bob Owchinko.

Now, that's a game-winning RBI!

I started game two with an RBI double off Randy Jones in the top of the first, and with the game tied 2–2 in the top of the seventh, I got Jones again, this time with a three-run bomb to put us ahead for good. Another game-winning RBI. I remember feeling positively on fire after that home run—like they couldn't get me out— and Mike Phillips, our backup shortstop from Texas, sat down next to me on the bench after that at-bat and asked, "Why do you take so many first pitches? You're starting off 0 and 1 most of the time. They're grooving you first-pitch fast-balls."

"Mike," I said, "I'm just too nervous! I go up there all wound up. I need a pitch to settle in."

It was true: I took the first pitch almost every at-bat that whole season. I was just too unsettled to go hacking away. Instead, I'd step in the box, take a deep breath, watch the pitch, take another deep breath, and get to hitting.

"Man," Mike said with that Texas drawl, "I wish I could do that."

But that's how well I was seeing the ball: I could be down 0–1 and still have the confidence to be patient, waiting for a pitch I could drive. And if the pitcher gave it to me, I drilled it; if, instead, he put it off the plate or in the dirt, I didn't chase. The knowledge of the strike zone that my father had drummed into me was paying off. I looked fastball on every pitch that year, even if I was facing a junk-baller. Again, I had the ability throughout my career to look fastball and adjust to any and all secondary pitches.

Part of the reason I was so hot at the plate was because our cleanup hitter, Ted Simmons, was back in the lineup. Ted had started off the first two months of the season on a tear, hitting .321 with 18 home runs (season pace of 48) and a whopping 52 RBI (season pace of 152), and his strong performance had helped open the door to my big rebound in May and June, because pitchers didn't want to come after Simmons, a proven veteran and .300 clutch hitter from both sides of the plate. Instead, the pitchers would come after me, a relatively unproven 3-hole hitter, hoping they could get the out and pitch around Simmons. In short, with Simmons striking fear into the opponents, I was seeing good pitches to hit.

But those rules of engagement went out the window when Ted went on the DL on June 25 for a month and George Hendrick bumped up to the cleanup spot. George was having a tremendous year, hitting .341 with 6 home runs and 31 RBI at the time. But it wasn't Ted Simmons–like power, and more important, George wasn't a switch-hitter.

So lefties still came after me, but righties were a bit more careful, and I was seeing fewer good pitches to hit. Proof of this was in those 26 games without Ted, when I hit only .299 but walked at a much higher rate. I was still contributing at a high level—with an on-base percentage of .417, and delivering in the clutch with 16 RBI—but Ted's absence was having an effect. Upon Ted's return on July 24, opposing pitchers resumed their caution, and that meant better pitches for me to hit the rest of the way.

Well, Simmons went deep in game three against the Padres, and we swept in San Diego. I remember feeling further energized when Ted did that, because he'd been in a slump since coming back to the lineup. *If he gets hot, the team could have a really good September.* The only problem was that the Pirates weren't losing. Even after we swept the Cubs, finishing our road trip at 9–2, we picked up only a half game on Pittsburgh, and we were seven games back with less than a month to play. That was a bit of a backbreaker for us. Anything was possible, but Willie Stargell's "We Are Family" campaign in Pittsburgh was turning into a movement, galvanizing the steel town and its baseball team, and they showed no signs of softening.

The Chicago series had been another boost for me. I went 4 for 7 in the 2 games with 2 walks and a double off Willie Hernandez, another lefty, and I finished the road trip 11 for 22 (.500!) with 3 doubles, 1 HR, and 6 RBI. I now sat "comfortably" atop the league at .348, with everyone else a good bit behind: my pitching teammates had checked Winfield, keeping him just 2 for 12 in our San Diego series, and his average dropped below .310;* the Braves' Bob Horner, the 1978 NL Rookie of the Year, who had put together a great month coming out of the All-Star break, batting .387 to raise his season average to .329, was now at .316; Lou Brock, who had been up to .327 on August 15, was at .314; and Garry Templeton, our Cardinals teammate, who'd batted .342 since the break, was still 22 points behind me at .326. So

---

* St. Louis pitching got the best of Winfield that season: 9 for 44 (.205 average).

despite my usual anxiety before every at-bat, I felt like the batting title was within reach.

Quite a turnaround from 1978's .255.

But just when I started to feel like *Oh my goodness, I can win this thing,* Pete Rose got hot. *Red-hot.* Never allowing himself to fall below .300 on the whole year, Pete hung around .310 for most of the second half. Then he batted a ridiculous .468 in 62 at-bats from September 1 through September 16, raising his average to .327, 18 points behind my .345, with two weeks left to go.

Could he get 18 points in fourteen days? Let's quantify that: Pete would have 59 more at-bats between September 17 and the end of the season on September 30. For him to jump the 18 points to .345, he'd need 30 hits in those 59 at-bats. That's a batting average of a whopping .509. But there was no guarantee that I was going to keep my stats up. What if I fell into a slump during those last fourteen days of the season? Let's say I got only 10 hits in my remaining 45 at-bats—a .222 average—then my season average would drop to .336, and I would meet Pete halfway. *Gulp.*

Well, who else would come to town for a three-game series to kick off those final two weeks but the Philadelphia Phillies and their tenacious and irrepressible first baseman, Pete Rose. *Folks, I* *can't make this stuff up.* Here we were, master versus apprentice, sharing the same field: me watching him, him watching me, and all the reporters and fans watching us both. Our respective teams may have been out of the divisional race and squabbling for third place, but we were just as much in the national spotlight as the Pirates and Expos, who were neck and neck atop the division. *Hey, Ma and Dad, look at me! I'm in every paper across the country!* Now I was becoming a household name *not* because I was winning the race, but because I was the man "Charlie Hustle" was chasing. And it didn't hurt that Pete himself was praising my accomplishments to the reporters huddled around his locker before and after every game. Even after Pete's 3 for 4 and my 0 for 2 in game one cut the lead to just 14 points, Pete had some pretty nice things to say to about me to the press: "If .335 is going to win the title, then I think I can do it. But Hernandez is a fine hitter. I think he should be the most valuable player. Me, I don't think I should get it. I've been having the same kind of year every year."*

Of course, and as the papers pointed out the next day, "beneath this facade [was] a hungry

---

* *St. Louis Post-Dispatch*, September 18, 1979.

man gunning for his fourth batting title."* In part, Pete's flattery was intended to get me to crumble a little—nothing burdens a man like strapping on medals before he's crossed the finish line. But by then, Pete wasn't the only one offering such praise. With the St. Louis press really getting behind me, and then the national attention of the batting race, I'd started to hear my name more and more frequently in the NL MVP conversation. As Kenny Boyer pointed out numerous times to the press during those final weeks, "How [else] do you rate a player who scores 100 runs, drives in 100 runs, hits the way he does and is the best fielding first baseman in the league?"† So my play—offensively and defensively—was making a pretty good argument for the league's highest individual accolade.

But none of that was in my control. The batting title, however, was mine to lose; and with the team's divisional chances gone,‡ it was the one thing I wanted. But first, I had to withstand Pete's relentless assault, and in that second game

---

* *St. Louis Post-Dispatch*, September 19, 1979.
† *St. Louis Post-Dispatch*, September 23, 1979.
‡ Ten games back on September 16, we were all but mathematically eliminated. That formality would come one week later, September 22, when we were twelve games back with eleven to play.

against the Phillies, Pete was 2 for 3 while I went 0 for 4, and the race was suddenly down to just 10 points. *10 points!* The Phillies then left town, and I broke out of my mini slump, going 2 for 5 in a doubleheader against the Cubs, but Pete kept the pressure on from afar, as reported by the *Post-Dispatch* the following day:

> The Phillies' Pete Rose continued his torrid hitting with three safeties in the two games [going 3 for 7]. He has 35 hits in his last 66 at-bats and has hit safely in his last 17 straight games. He's boosted his average from .306 to .333, nine points behind the Cardinals' Keith Hernandez in the fight for the NL batting title.*

Rose was like the mummy from those horror films that all kids growing up in the '50s loved but also dreaded. As a boy, I had this recurring nightmare in which I'd be running through the creek and into the woods near our house and the mummy would be chasing me—dragging one foot and limping, one arm outstretched to grab me—and no matter how fast I'd be running, I'd

---

* *St. Louis Post-Dispatch*, September 20, 1979.

turn around, and that son of a bitch would be gaining on me. Well, that was Pete, and in less than a week, my 18-point lead had been cut in half!

What was that "hypothetical" number I stated previously? Pete had to hit something ridiculous, like .509, to catch me? Well, he was bettering that by 21 points, hitting .530 over that week's span, and was now *30 for 50* since September 8. *That's batting .600 for over two weeks!** And what was that ridiculous *low* number to which I had to collapse in order to meet him halfway—.222? Well, I was worse than that, hitting just .214 over the previous two series.

Of course, I'm breaking this down six ways to Sunday and nearly forty years later, using newspaper articles, a calculator, and wonderful stat sites like Baseball-Reference.com. But I probably was doing some rough number crunching in my head at the time; regardless, the reporters were in my ear before *and* after every game with stat scenarios rounded off to the nearest millionth.

You have to remember what a batting title means to a player. Historically, there are *three* coveted batting stats: home runs, runs batted

---

* For his incredible September, Rose won his sixth, and final, Player of the Month.

in, and batting average. *The Triple Crown.* Of the three, batting average is the most prized (at least, it was before the earlier mentioned home-run craze), especially in a close race in which every at-bat counts. It gives September the air of a Kentucky Derby, and in 1979, base-ball's favorite horse, Pete Rose, was the one making the late charge, bringing the grandstand to its feet.

What was my MO now? Sure, I knew where I was: 78 at-bats into my sixth set, hitting .346 for the term. But so what? There were only ten games left in the season! There was no "next 100 at-bats" to make up lost ground. If I was going to beat Pete—who was 2 for 3 on September 20 and now just 8 points behind me—I had to get hits *now*! The only problem was we were heading up to New York to face the last-place Mets and their whole batch of September call-ups.

Advantage Hernandez? I think not!

Remember what Dick Selma told me back in 1974: to keep track of what pitchers threw me. "That way, the next time you face them, you've got an idea of what might be coming down the pike." Great advice, and it was certainly part of the reason I'd been able to do well in 1979. In the 698 plate appearances I had that season, 264, or

37.8 percent, were against pitchers I'd seen *ten* or more times; 534, or 76.5 percent, were against pitchers I'd seen five or more times. So I'd gotten a taste of pretty much everyone and had at least a little intelligence walking up to the plate. But in late September, against a team like the 1979 Mets, who had been mathematically eliminated from the divisional race for almost a month, such familiarity went out the window. Why? Because September call-ups—the young pups—take on the lion's share of the work, especially on the mound.

And the Mets, no longer with the services of Seaver and Koosman, Ltd., were tossing up new arms, right and left, hoping something would stick for the next season.* Names like Mike Scott, Jesse Orosco, Juan Berenguer, Jeff Reardon, Roy Lee Jackson, and John Pacella. *Wait…who?* Of course, a few of these guys would go on to have terrific careers, but at that point, they were all unknown. Their motions, deliveries, release points, pitch actions, strategies—

---

* Seaver was traded to Cincinnati midway through the 1977 season, and Koosman was now in Minnesota, earning his second 20-win season. Craig Swan remained with the team, managing 14 wins and a 3.21 ERA despite the lack of support.

it was all new information to be digested. And that lack of familiarity doesn't increase the odds for a good series at the plate.

So I would have to call on yet another piece of advice—this time from Dad and our BP rounds together since I was a kid: "Son, sometimes you're just gonna have to get up there, grit your teeth, and bear down." Well, that's exactly what I did. In game one of a doubleheader, I singled off the right-handed Pacella in the first; singled off Jackson, another right-hander, in the second; homered off Jackson in the fourth; singled off Dwight Bernard in the seventh; and hit the ball hard off Ed Glynn but right at the second baseman, Doug Flynn, for a groundout to lead off the ninth.* Boyer rested me the second game, and I was 0 for 3 in the finale, but I left New York (and their enigma pitching staff) 4 for 8, my average kicked up to .346, and we bussed down to Philly for one final series against Rose and his compadres, who'd just wrapped up three games against the Expos.

The next day, Pete was waiting for me by the batting cage. "How in the hell did you go into

---

* Neither Glynn nor Bernard was a September call-up, but I was 1 for 3 lifetime against the two of them *combined* prior to these at-bats. So, again, not a lot of familiarity.

New York and go 4 for 5 against all those September call-ups?" he asked. My performance that first game had put the pressure on him against Montreal, where a couple of 1 for 2s wouldn't do him much good; only more 3 for 4s and 4 for 5s could help him climb the ladder fast enough. He'd gotten a hit in each of those three games—extending a hitting streak to twenty-one games*—but concluded the series just 3 for 14, and we were back to double digits between us with a week to play.

Looking back, I relish the moment: here I was, standing with one of baseball's all-time greats, who later *that day* would collect his 200th hit of the season, setting a major league record for the most 200-hit seasons—ten—a record he had previously shared with Ty Cobb. And he was bustin' *my* chops, feigning incredulousness, about the batting title. I *should* have stopped right there, relaxed, smiled, and just taken it all in for what it was. But I couldn't. There would be no relaxing until I had nailed down the batting crown.

So while I remember being thrilled any time Rose or any of the big stars would come shoot the breeze around the batting cage or during a

---

* Pete's hitting streak lasted two more games.

game while standing on first base—and I could be a chatterbox—I didn't, in my core, feel like I was quite a peer yet. I guess I'd felt the same way during the All-Star Game—a bit of an outsider. *Why?* Who the hell knows, but not even with Pete basically conceding victory did I chill out. And looking back at the numbers now, with the pressure off, the race was essentially over. I'd clinched it in New York, and Pete, for all his competitive grit, knew it. With six games remaining in his season, there really wasn't enough time for him to catch me.

But each time Pete came up to the plate, I was intently hoping for an out. By the second game, my lead cut back down to 11 points, I felt like my head was going to explode: I hit a fly out to center, but Pete singled. *Oh shit.* He came up again and grounded out to the pitcher. *Phew.* I hit another fly out to center field. *Uh-oh* . . .

Round and round we went—him 1 for 3, me 0 for 3—until the top of the eighth, when I ripped a double to left-center field off reliever Tug McGraw. I ran by Pete, who was playing first base, going "Ooooooh!" all the way to second. Evidently I was still in battle mode, and Pete just looked at our first base coach and said, "What's wrong with him? Is he crazy? He still thinks I can catch him. I can't catch him."

So, yeah, Pete knew that I had it in the kipper, and a week later, after I went 7 for 15 at the plate over the remaining 5 games, it was apparent to all—even dumbass me. The season was over, and despite batting an incredible .421 for the month of September, Pete ended at .331, 13 points behind my .344.*

I'd won the National League batting title, becoming the first infielder to win a batting title and a Gold Glove in the same season.

---

* In Rose's 628 at-bats that season, 8 more hits would have given him .344. That's just 1 more hit every 78.5 of those at-bats. But with Pete, you know he never took any of those at-bats for granted. And my pitching teammates really picked me up, holding Pete to just 2 hits in 13 at-bats in that final series. In fact, had Pete hit St. Louis pitching that season (22 for 72) as well as he hit the Cubs (33 for 74), he would have had me.

KH BATTING PROGRESS (BY SEASON)

Year	Games (G)	At-Bats (AB)	Batting Average (BA)	On-Base Percentage (OBP)	Slugging Percentage (SLG)
1974	14	34	.294	.415	.441
1975	64	188	.250	.309	.362
1976	129	374	.289	.376	.428
1977	161	560	.291	.379	.459
1978	159	542	.255	.351	.389
1979	161	610	.344	.417	.513

CHAPTER 35

YOU KNOW THOSE SCENES in the movies where a character is stranded on an island, and to keep from going insane, he begins to tally on a big rock his total days marooned? Well, that was me in the weeks that followed the 1979 season. I was bored to tears, counting the hours until spring training, five *months* away. Again, domestic life just wasn't for me, especially on the heels of a batting race with Pete Rose and playing in front of 40,000 people on their feet every time I came up to the plate.

Why did I get married? I think when Sue and I started dating, she filled a void: she was a nice girl who kept me company during the long, cold winter months in St. Louis. And I'd spend weekends and Thanksgiving and part of the holidays with her big, loving family—she had great parents and younger siblings—and I took refuge in all of that during a time when I was lonely and

insecure. I also grew up with *Leave It to Beaver,*
The Donna Reed Show, I Love Lucy, My Three
Sons—all family-oriented television series that
probably influenced my expectations of what
adulthood should look like: wife, kids, dog, car,
mortgage, etc. I think this was typical of my generation, and perhaps it helped push many of us
into marriage before we really understood the
dedication and sacrifice it requires.

My father tried to warn me. Sue and I were
thinking of getting married after the '77 season,
but Dad asked me to wait another year. He was
leery of me taking on so much responsibility and
its effect on my burgeoning career. So we waited
the year, and then we got hitched. Had we waited
just one more year, the marriage never would've
happened.

Because I was taking off. And as my career,
along with my confidence, was being rocketed
into the stratosphere, I suddenly needed less
and less support to hold me up. One more push,
and I'd be weightless. As it turned out, that final
stage ignited with yet another morning phone
call:

Me: (groggily) Hello?
Caller: Keith, it's Jack Lang with the Baseball
    Writers' Association. You wouldn't mind shar-

ing the National League MVP with Willie
Stargell, would ya?
Me: No, sir, I would not!
Caller: Good. Congratulations.

For the first (and only) time in history, the vot-
ing for NL Most Valuable Player ended in a tie,
and Keith Hernandez—out of little Pacifica,
California—was one of the winners. I thanked
Mr. Lang, and called my parents and Gary. *If ever
there was a justified case of "black cord fever"!*

It was only after I'd hung up with my family that
I started to think about the strange way Mr. Lang,
the secretary-treasurer of the Baseball Writers'
Association of America, had dropped the news.
Actually, it was more of what he had *not* said that
I found odd. He didn't say:

*Keith, congratulations, this is Jack Lang from
the Baseball Writers' Association. I'm calling to
inform you that you have won the MVP along
with Willie Stargell. It's the first time there's
ever been a tie for MVP, but you and Willie
Stargell are the National League co-MVPs.
Congratulations.*

That would have been fine. But instead he had
asked *if I would mind* sharing it with Stargell.

Why was he asking *me*? I wasn't a writer—I had no say in who won the MVP. What if I had said, "Yes, sir, I do mind sharing the award"? Would that have yielded a different result? Because part of me felt that Willie Stargell, superstar that he was, didn't deserve the MVP that year. With 32 home runs and 82 runs batted in, he'd had a great season, but it wasn't a *full* season. In fact, with only 424 at-bats and 105 games started, it was two-thirds of a season. Yes, he was the glue that had kept that team together to win the World Series, whereas we had finished a distant third, but, again, he hadn't played close to every day.

I wasn't alone in this thinking: While the ever-popular Stargell led the way with ten first-place votes from the twenty-four writers who made the decision, *four* writers omitted him from their top ten, citing Stargell's frequent absence from the field. I, on the other hand, led in both second- and third-place votes and was the only candidate to make *every* writer's top ten—in fact, I cracked every writer's top five.*

---

* To be fair, I received only four first-place votes. But the reason the ballot is designed the way it is—with ten placed finishers—is to reduce the effect of any potential bias from hometown sports journalists and provide a more complete

Given Lang's choice of words—delivered in a seemingly sheepish, almost apologetic tone—I started to think that maybe I'd won the award outright and the powers that be were making it up to the twice-a-bridesmaid Stargell, who had placed second in '71 and gotten absolutely screwed in '73, when he'd led the league in home runs, runs batted in, doubles, slugging, and on-base plus slugging.* And maybe now they couldn't deny Willie a third time—not with all that "We Are Family" stuff. Whereas I was just the new kid on the block who'd never hit .300 in a season—a kid the Writers' Association thought would be content just to be included.

And if that was true—if the writers had produced such a convenient outcome—I couldn't help but wonder if my last name had made it easier for them. "Are you a wetback, Hernandez?" I never forgot what that heckling fan way back in AA ball had asked me, or that even some of my teammates failed to appreciate my European-

---

picture of the field. I should also note that while not one of the four journalists who omitted Stargell was from St. Louis, *two* were from Houston, which is head-scratching, given Stargell's success against the Astros that season (.302 in 43 ABs with 6 HRs and 13 RBI).

* The 1973 MVP results: Pete Rose (274 points); Stargell (250).

Spanish heritage: "C'mon, man, you're a Mexican." And though I'd never felt mistreated or racially targeted by the press, a teammate, a coach, or an organization, I'd heard comments from some of the Latino players suggesting Latinos were just as discriminated against as blacks, but without the national attention to combat it.* *Is that what this was with the MVP?* Would Lang have asked me if I'd "mind sharing" the award if my father, rather than my mother, had been Scots-Irish with the last name Jordan (my mother's maiden name)? *Did that name on the back of my jersey make a difference?*

Justified or not, all this entered my mind after that phone call.

Even so, my suspicions were minuscule compared to my delight that I'd won the award, and sharing it with Willie only further proved just how far I'd come after April's terrible start: here I was, sharing the spotlight with the great Willie Stargell, fellow Bay Area boy and the same cool and confident man spitting seeds on the bench

---

* I believe that in the '60s, '70s, and '80s, the Latin player was perhaps the most overshadowed, underappreciated player. Fortunately, with the great number of Latino players in today's game, times have changed.

that day in St. Louis while my average sat at .216, just hours before Boyer's fateful talk with me on the airplane. It never diminished the award, and I considered it an honor to share it with him.

I'd first met Stargell back in '74 at an awards dinner. It was a really big event, up in Napa somewhere, and Willie was there along with Pete Rose. Superstars. I was thrown in at the last moment simply because I was a Bay Area kid, and I remember the moderator, Lon Simmons, the broadcaster for the Giants and 49ers, saying, "I'm really sorry, Mr. Hernandez. Please forgive me. I don't have a lot of information on you." So I really had no business being there. (Willie, of course, was just a big ol' teddy bear who treated me like gold, as if I was a major leaguer.)

Six winters later, we were sharing the podium once again. Only this time it was in New York City, at the awards dinner hosted by the Baseball Writers' Association of America, *the biggest of all dinners*, where they handed out the Rookie of the Year Award, the Cy Young Award, and the MVP Award. DiMaggio came to these things, the commissioner and league presidents, too, and here I was, center stage with Willie, in front of the cameras and reporters in that huge ballroom with all those people.

Rubbing elbows with big shots.

Everywhere I turned, there was baseball royalty, past and current, and all of them were very conversational and wanted to talk baseball *with me*. Even Joltin' Joe, whose aloofness was well known, struck up a conversation. I was sitting next to him, and maybe it was an uncomfortable moment—I don't know—but he turned to me and asked what pitch gave me the most trouble. I was shocked that he'd asked me a question, so I just blurted out the first thing that came to mind: "The breaking ball." And he said, "No, no. I can't believe that. I loved the breaking ball." Then he said, "*I* didn't like the hard sinker, down and in from a right-hander." I said, "Well...I guess I don't like that pitch either."* So Joe was probably thinking, *Look at this stupid guy*, but that was fine: I was an MVP, the 136th ever selected in the history of Major League Baseball, talkin' shop with Joe DiMaggio.†

---

* Joe was a right-handed batter, so whereas he had problems with the right-handed pitcher's sinker, my fits came from the southpaws. Lefty versus lefty. Righty versus righty.

† Years later, around 1989, I would have a similar fumble with the actor Sean Connery. I was in London, at a dinner for, like, fifteen people, and Marty Bregman, the movie producer, was there, as was Connery and his wife, Micheline Roquebrune. And Connery, who was a super-gregarious guy, but intimidating—everything he is on the screen he is in person—suddenly looked at me from across the table and,

After New York, I spent much of the next month going around the country to different awards dinners. The various chapters of baseball writers from all over hold these things. It's like a circuit, and I loved every minute of it.

I'd go alone because Jessie was in school, and Sue, who was now pregnant, stayed at home. So while they were living in one reality, I was being swept up in another, where I was the center of attention on a grand scale. For a person with a history of poor self-esteem, the experience was intoxicating.

Here I was, coming off this amazing chase with Pete Rose and winning the batting title, only to have it all stop. Then they called me with the MVP thing and it kicked everything into high gear again. I was not playing ball, but it was fun to be on the road in the off-season. I did the dinners, and there were all these other players, the best of the best. And they were not only from baseball but from other sports as well. Like the Dapper

---

with a big smile and that confident Scottish cadence, asked, "Who are the toughest pitchers you faced and *why*?" Everyone turned to me, and I blanked and said, "I don't know." And he said, "I can't believe that you don't know." I continued to fumble for words, but nothing of substance came out—like Ralphie with Santa Claus in *A Christmas Story*, I was in such reverence of the big man that I sounded like an idiot.

Dan, the writers' event in Pittsburgh, included all the Steelers players: Terry Bradshaw, Joe Greene, Franco Harris. Then, a few days later, there was one up in Erie, Pennsylvania, and I got to talk with Joe Paterno, the legendary coach from Penn State. Even at the St. Louis dinner, I hung out with the best of all those sports teams—guys from the St. Louis Blues and the football Cardinals, like Jim Hart, Dan Dierdorf. All of the sudden, I wasn't just another baseball Cardinals player.

I also began to realize then that it wasn't that difficult to talk to girls I didn't know. They were there. Lots of beautiful women, and some of them had their eyes on me. And, yes, I cheated on Sue, who was home and pregnant. And I'm not proud of it, but it's true. It was like I'd suddenly broken out of a shell that had been containing me my whole life, and I wanted to exercise that new freedom and the elation that came from it. Well, I'm far from perfect, and it was hard not to want something I'd never had before—even if being married meant I was supposed to pass certain parts of that something up.

They always had huge cocktail parties, and reporters would come up to me, and then other athletes, and then the women. I'd shake hands and mingle and have a few drinks. I'd go from cocktails into dinner, and all the people who had been flown in were staying there at the hotel so the party kept going. There'd be drinks and girls.

Maybe even some cocaine. I say "maybe" only because I'm not positive that I did do it on any of those trips, but 1980 was the first time I tried the drug. (In the 1980s, coke was the drug of choice, so it was around.) Though I wasn't completely stupid. I knew it was a hard drug—much more serious than marijuana. But I remember that I felt on top of the world during that MVP cross-country circuit, and if someone offered me some coke, I probably said, "Sure." Because people were fawning over me, and I was riding the wave. I was now twenty-six years old, and for the first time in my life, I felt really good about myself.

Those were heady days for me: like that Frank Zappa and the Mothers of Invention album *Over-Nite Sensation,* I went from obscurity to stardom, and I just got swept up in it.

But it wasn't all peaches and cream. I do remember that when I went to the Dapper Dan, I got a frosty reception from the audience, which made sense because it was all Pirates country, and they didn't like Stargell sharing the MVP with a "singles hitter." I remember reading that in the Pittsburgh paper—this "slap guy" next to big powerful Willie. And when I went to Kansas City, I overheard Royals favorite George Brett make a snide remark. When I was being honored as the MVP, they played a highlight reel of my season. Brett was sitting behind me, about fifteen, twenty, feet away, and at one point the video showed me hit an up-and-in fastball that I had to inside-out, and I hit a freaking bullet down the left-field line. A great piece of two-strike hitting. Brett started giggling: "Inside-out Judy hitter." And that pissed me off. *I'd like to see you* pull *that ball, George.* But I didn't say anything to him. *What am I going to do, get in a fight with George Brett in Kansas City?*

I don't know why he felt compelled to do that. We were both the toast of Missouri: him in Kansas City, me in St. Louis. And I wasn't competing with George Brett. *He's in the other goddamn league!* I was just happy to meet him and talk baseball with a fellow hitter—not make some nasty remark about his game.

But I got the feeling from some of the big hitters in baseball that they didn't respect *my* game. Particularly those in the American League who just saw my stat lines, and because I hadn't hit a lot of home runs, they assumed I was just some inside-out hitter, when in fact I hit more line drives—gap to gap—than perhaps anyone else in the game. I just didn't try to lift the ball—I was trained to hit the top half of the ball, *not* the bottom half (and good thing, playing in Busch Stadium, the second-biggest park in the league). I'm not sure if my insecurity was reasonable or I was just being paranoid, but I sensed what I sensed.*

And I'd always think, *Well, all you guys are great players, but I'm pretty goddamn good, too.*

---

* Seventy of my 210 hits in 1979 were extra-base hits, exactly one-third, as reflected by my 105 RBI despite only hitting 11 home runs. That's not slap-hitting, folks, and that some people thought I was a Judy hitter still irritates me today. I most definitely was not.

CHAPTER 36

METS GAME THIS EVENING. I'll be in the booth.

But I'm already on my way into the city for a card show. That's where fans pay to have current and former ballplayers sign a bunch of their memorabilia, like baseball cards, bats, balls, and stuff. It'll be a few hours of autographs and taking pictures. Easy money.

The first time I heard about the memorabilia business, I thought it was a crock: *like someone's gonna stand in line and pay for that . . .* This was in the mid-1980s. I was playing for the Mets and hanging out with a buddy of mine, Brandon Steiner. I remember him telling me, over dinner, his idea to get a bunch of professional athletes under contract and start his own memorabilia company.

I told him, "You're crazy."

Well, Brandon, who was just out of college at the time, built Steiner Sports into a multimillion-dollar business, wound up selling it for, like, $80 million, and still runs the company today.

So what do I know?

I still do a few shows a year for Steiner. I may not have played ball in a while, but we old-timers can still pack 'em in. The events are very structured: there's someone to my left to put the fan's merchandise in front of me while I sign and pose for a quick photo with the fan; there's also someone to my right to move it all along when I'm finished. *Next!* It's not exactly intimate, but like kids waiting at the mall to see Santa, the fans don't seem to mind the assembly-line approach.

I wasn't such jolly company when I first started to make appearances. It was back in the '80s and I was still playing ball, and I was too on edge, as per usual. *I just played a doubleheader yesterday and now I gotta sign people's stuff for four hours?* Well, I guess my lack of enthusiasm showed because one of the assistants, a Brooklynite named Don Lipeles, got tired of my nonsense and let me have it: "You know, Keith, these people waited in line and paid a lot of money to get your autograph. And you're treating them like garbage. Quit being an asshole."

You have to love that New York honesty, and, moreover, Don was right—*It's not like anyone is forcing me to do this.* So I got my act together. Granted, there's always some Yankees fan who's a schmuck, and it's sometimes very stressful to move the line because there might be four hundred people in the queue. But it doesn't take much to say "Hello" and ask folks how they're doing. And people are lovely—they're excited to be face-to-face with ballplayers they've watched for a while, and I've enjoyed interacting with them over the years.

Those early days in the memorabilia business were like the Wild West: you were paid in cash, no oversight. I did a show in Brooklyn once where I signed for around four hours, and I left with a shopping bag full of dough. Maybe twenty-five grand—more money than I had made in either of my first two seasons in the bigs. (I negotiated my 1975 contract on my own with assistant GM Jim Toomey. It was the off-season, and I was on the kitchen phone in my parents' house. Dad said I should ask for $22K, which sounded reasonable to me, but Toomey started chuckling on the other end when I put the number to him, and without a leg to stand on, I wilted and signed a one-year deal for $18K. A year later, I again negotiated my contract, and I got $24K out of Toomey. *A 33 percent raise!* I hated doing those contracts, and later in 1976, I hired an agent.*)

---

* Late in the second half of the 1976 season, when I was wearing it out, I followed Lou Brock's advice and started using his agent, Jack Childers, out of Chicago. Phew!

Anyway, I probably could have made more than the twenty-five grand, but those fourteen letters that make up my name take a toll on the assembly-line production, plus I like to make sure that each fan gets a perfect signature. (The greatest name ever for autographs was Ed Ott—just five letters.)

Still, it was a lot of cash. I remember signing one day with Pete Rose, and Pete, who got paid a lot more per signature or inscription, went out the door with a briefcase full of bills. He and his buddies—*Pete always had a couple of buddies*—had a limo waiting to take them to Belmont:

Me: Pete, where you going?
Pete: The track.
Me: Okay.

But those trade shows were publicized events, and it didn't take long for the Feds and the IRS to get wind of them. Some guys, like Pete, went down because they failed to declare the income on their tax returns. (*Not even the standard 80 percent, fellas?*) So now it's all very much aboveboard: written contracts, W-2s and 1099s. And you're paid by check—no more shopping bags full of cash, which is probably a good thing because, sooner or later, someone was going to get robbed.*

Those early card shows were somewhat indicative of a star ballplayer's life from the late '70s to the early to mid-'80s: suddenly, there was a lot of money coming in, and nobody knew exactly what to do with it. Remember, guys like me who went pro in the early '70s did so when there was still a reserve clause. Even if we'd had success on the field, we didn't expect to make scads of dough. After retirement, we thought we'd have to do what all former ballplayers did: *go out and find a job.*

Baseball, for a *long* time, had a way of chewing up and spitting out everyone—even its stars—after their careers were over. For example, Whitey Ford, the future Hall of Famer for the Yankees and their winningest pitcher in franchise history, was given just two weeks' severance pay after he had to walk away from the game midseason in 1967 because of an elbow injury. He was thirty-eight years old, his one-in-a-million skill set suddenly expired, with no pension and little savings. He is still the winningest pitcher in that illustri-

---

* Because I was walking out with all that money, they had a limo waiting with two security guys in it—one of them packing a pistol—to take me home.

ous franchise's history. Makes you wonder what sort of treatment the non–Hall of Famers got . . .

But who needs to get a job when you're making $25K in one afternoon signing autographs?

What happened? How did we get here? The short answer is that beginning with free agency, organized labor—on the backs of the previous generations of ballplayers*—continued to win us a larger piece of the pie. And it was at a time

---

* Most notably, Curtis Flood, Dave McNally, and Andy Messersmith. After being traded to the Philadelphia Phillies in 1969, Flood filed a suit against MLB alleging that the reserve clause violated antitrust laws as well as the Thirteenth Amendment, which barred slavery and involuntary servitude. The case went to the Supreme Court in 1972. The Court ruled against Flood in a 5 to 3 decision, ultimately destroying the thirty-three-year-old's All-Star career. Three years later, another attempt was made to challenge the reserve clause when pitchers Dave McNally and Andy Messersmith refused to re-sign with their clubs and filed a grievance. The case went before an independent arbitrator, Peter Seitz, who decided in favor of the players on December 23, 1976. After a failed appeals process by MLB (owners), the reserve clause was finished. But so too was McNally, who retired at the end of 1975 after playing for the same salary he had earned the previous season. Messersmith, who also played on his previous year's contract terms, finished 19–14 with a 2.29 ERA in 40 starts and *321⅔ innings pitched.* So the Dodgers had pitched him to death, only to unceremoniously trade him to the very bad last-place Atlanta Braves after the season. A previous runner-up for the Cy Young, he was never quite the same after that abusive season.

when the pie itself was getting bigger, and bigger, and bigger. TV coverage, which had been growing steadily since the '60s, started to take off after the famous 1975 World Series, when Carlton Fisk hit his home run to cap Game Six, and by 1980, TV contracts with local and national broadcasts accounted for 30 percent of the game's $500 million in revenue.

That was a far cry from when I was a kid, when all you had was one Saturday *Game of the Week.*

Beyond the direct revenue from TV, the increased exposure had a trickle-down effect: more televised games meant more commercials and more player endorsement opportunities, resulting in even more exposure and, ultimately, additional revenue streams, like card and memorabilia shows with people lining up out the door to get autographs from baseball players—the famous men on TV.

So my generation of stars was fortunate in that we were just hitting our stride when all these things started happening. In 1976, the first year of free agency, the highest-paid player in the league was Hank Aaron, at $240K. The following year, that number more than doubled for baseball's new highest-paid player, Mike Schmidt, at $560K. Three years later, 1980, it was up above a million dollars—Nolan Ryan this time—with players like Dave Winfield reportedly asking for $2 million.*

For me, the timing was fortuitous: not only was 1979 the year I catapulted into the upper echelon of players, but it was also the final year of my contract, and in the 1980 off-season, I signed a $3.8 million contract for five years. Wow! My 1979 annual salary of $75K had just grown *ten times*.

The Cardinals didn't really have a choice—the market was what it was, as reported in the *St. Louis Post-Dispatch* by syndicated columnist Murray Chass of the *New York Times* just one month before my signing:

> The information, obtained from management officials and agents, shows that club owners, who often have lamented the spiraling salaries, committed themselves to spending nearly twice as much money on the first 22 players who signed in this market than on the first 22 who signed in last off-season's market.†

---

* Ryan signed a three-year deal for a guaranteed $3.5 million over the course. The next season, Winfield was signed for $1.4 million per year, almost six times what Aaron had made only six years previously.
† *St. Louis Post-Dispatch,* January 8, 1980.

Gussie Busch, who was as old-school as any owner out there, could bitch all he wanted about how players were making too much money, but the Cardinals' GM, John Claiborne, clearly understood the new cost of doing business: it was a seller's market, and you had to pay the players if you wanted to be competitive.

The only thing left to determine was my value, and after a batting title and an MVP at the tender age of twenty-five, with my prime years still in front of me, the Cardinals couldn't argue my elite status (especially when they were the ones who'd been saying that I was "the next Stan Musial"). Sure, they could have kicked the can down the road and negotiated a one-year deal, but that would have just raised the price: the benefit of a long-term deal is you secure a player for the future at today's rate, and by all indications, those rates are going to keep going up (the risk is that your "star" is just a flash in the pan and you wind up overpaying him in subsequent years).

Perhaps the biggest incentive for keeping me happy and playing ball in St. Louis for the next five years was that the Cardinals, who hadn't won the NL East since the two-divisional system was introduced in 1969, wanted to get back atop the league. And with Templeton, Hernandez, Simmons, and Hendrick in the top half of the lineup, they certainly had the pieces to build a successful franchise.*

So the timing was perfect: I suddenly had the security of a lucrative, long-term contract with guaranteed big money.

But, by the same token, it also raised the expectations of *Cardinals fans*. Every morning, those fans woke up and glanced at the paper, where they saw two trends: baseball players were getting richer by the day and the rest of the world was going in the toilet. Rising unemployment. Stagnant wages. Rising cost of living. Gas crisis. Hostages in Iran. Russians in Afghanistan. It was a pretty bleak time in the United States and the world beyond, and while we players felt justified in our pursuit of happiness—after all, a highly skilled and select labor force plying their trade in a meritocracy with an ever-growing demand is what capitalism is all about—it was impossible to ignore the hardships around us. Especially in a blue-collar town like St. Louis, where economic recessions always seem to strike the hardest. (The same week I signed my contract, General Motors announced it was shutting down a manufacturing

---

* Both Simmons and Hendrick were already tied to long-term deals. One month after the Cards made the investment in me, they signed Templeton to a long-term deal.

plant inside the city, resulting in the loss of thousands of jobs and $10 million in tax revenue for St. Louis.)*

So which Keith Hernandez was going to show up for the St. Louis fans: a premier player who "earned his bread" or an overpaid sub-.300-hitting "bum"? I wasn't sure—I might have just won an MVP and a batting title, and then gallivanted around the country thinking I was the cat's pajamas, but self-doubt about my abilities still lingered.

Again, what is greatness? To do something not only well but *consistently* well. Could I do that? Could I repeat my performance in the years following my MVP?

---

*   As reported by the *Post-Dispatch,* February 1, 1979. Other *P-D* headlines that month of my signing read: NEW ACTIVITY BY SOVIETS IN AFGHANISTAN; FORD SAYS IT LACKED PARTS TO FIX PINTO; NEIGHBOR CALLS GACY "NICE, GOOD MAN"; NO RELEASE BEFORE APRIL, KHOMEINI SAYS; CARTER CONSIDERS PLAN FOR 4-DAY WORKWEEK; MORTGAGE RATES HIGH, LIKELY TO REMAIN SO; WHO ARE THE REAL VILLAINS IN INFLATION?; STEEL INDUSTRY DOES NEED HELP; BUSCH COMPLETES ACQUISITION OF SCHLITZ BREWERY; FORGOTTEN VIETNAM VET?; US POWER LOSS AFFECTS ELECTION; CHILDREN CAN COUPON, TOO; CHRYSLER ASKS STATE WORKERS FOR A LOAN; BALLPARK FIGURES HARD TO CALCULATE; '79 COST IN BASICS CALLED LARGEST IN DECADE; FATHER OF 5 OFFERS TO SELL BODY PART.

CHAPTER 37

MY MEMORY STINKS. HERE'S the story I had planned to tell you:

I went into the 1980 season on pins and needles, wondering if 1979 was just a fluke, but I stepped into the batter's box on opening day against the Phillies' Dick Ruthven and ripped a one-out double down the line to short-hop the fence. My first at-bat of the season. And then and there—the ball careening off the wall—all the uneasiness that I'd had going into the season simply evaporated: With that one good swing, I knew not only that I belonged in the major leagues but that I was worthy to be considered among its elite players. The roller-coaster ride—one good year followed by one bad year—was over.

There's just one problem with this account: that at-bat against Ruthven didn't happen.

What?

At least not on opening day, 1980. Because I'm looking on Baseball-Reference.com, that all-knowing eye in the sky, and we didn't even match up against the Phillies on opening day. Rather, we opened up against Pittsburgh. So wrong team, *and,* to add insult to injury, I didn't even get a hit that first game: I went 0 for 3.

*Damn you, Baseball Reference! I've been telling folks that story for years!**

But my uneasiness going into the season was very real. It was all about April and getting off to a good start. Through 1975, 1976, 1977, 1978, 1979, and 1980, April was always front and center in my life, like a shadow hanging over me and the season ahead.

When I was very young, I sometimes had horrific nightmares. I'd wake up in the middle of the night, scared to death, determined to flee my bedroom. But I'd still be half asleep, dreaming, and if I moved too fast, my bedroom walls would suddenly grow in size and close in on me, or if I moved my hand or a foot too fast, it would appear

---

* I'm not sure what pisses me off more: the fact that I went hitless or that I'm getting too old to remember such things.

to suddenly start ballooning in size until it was smothering me. I was imagining it all, of course, but I was terrified, like I was living in my very own Wonderland.*

Well, that was April for me: a lurking nightmare. And the press during that 1980 spring training didn't help: *Sports Illustrated* put me on the cover of their Special Baseball Issue with the caption "Who's Keith Hernandez and What Is He Doing Hitting .344?" Rick Hummel put out a column in the *Post-Dispatch,* basically asking, "Will the real Keith Hernandez please stand up?"

But any doubts about my 1980 season at the plate were just like the phantoms of my childhood: unfounded. Because my approach at the plate was built on a solid foundation. There were simply no holes in my swing, and I could adjust to whatever pitchers had in store for me. So unless teams were going to walk me every time I

---

* The trick, I discovered, was that if I moved very slowly nothing would balloon and the walls would stay put. So I'd get out of bed—at a snail's pace—and cautiously make my way into the hall, calling out to my parents. Mom and Dad would come out of their bedroom, and I'd scream, "Slow down!" because if they moved too quickly, they, too, would grow in size. So Mom and Dad would inch their way over to me and sit me by the heater, then Mom would head into the kitchen, warm me up a glass of milk, and eventually I'd calm down and come back to my senses.

got up, I would get pitches to hit. It was now very rare that a pitcher could make me look bad. Like a master craftsman who puts ten thousand focused hours into his trade, I was an expert in my craft. And it wasn't just mechanics; I'd built an *approach*—between all those at-bats and advice sessions from veterans—and it had all come together. The year 1979 hadn't been a fluke. The year 1979 was proof that I'd arrived.

Sticking with Baseball Reference, I see that after the 0-for-3 opener, I went 2 for 4, including a triple off John Candelaria, for my first hit of the season. Really, when I look at my numbers, it just was a solid month for that entire April, hardened by my 5 for 5 on April 27 against the Phillies.* So it wasn't an opening day but an opening *month* success story—after a career in the majors, I should have recognized that 1 at-bat wouldn't make the difference. "Think in terms of every 100 at-bats..."

That 1980 April was when I first understood that I was a quality player. With my being the reigning MVP and a batting champ, pitchers were pitching me extra carefully. I still had Simmons

---

* The first two of those hits were off the right-handed starter Ruthven. But they were each singles—no doubles. I'll keep looking...

hitting right behind me, but opponents knew they had their hands full, and I was more than handling it. One month into the season—my *sixth* month in a row of hitting .300 or better—I was right where I had left off in 1979.*

And that's a legitimate confidence booster.

Especially when I think about the toll those opening weeks in previous seasons had taken on me. It was like I had to put my back up against the wall and feel that I was under attack in order to perform. I couldn't just relax—be a Lou Brock—and take it as it came. But after that April, I had my .300. *Okay, I'm on my way. I can hit, and this is where I belong.*

As for my peers, they seemed to agree. That first month of the 1980 season, Dave Parker, two-time NL batting champion for the Pirates and one of the most talented players I've ever seen, came strolling up to Ted Simmons and me after witnessing a round of BP in Pittsburgh, and exclaimed, "You two are the *hittingest* white boys I've ever seen!" Simmons laughed, and I loved it: *I'm Keith Hernandez, Hittingest White Boy.*

---

* I finished April at .329 in 73 at-bats. Nine days later, I completed my first set of 100 at-bats, and my average was up to .321 with 9 extra-base hits and *20* RBI. *Raking!*

*   *   *

I've talked a lot about Pete Rose because his example can't be overstated. Not only for me but for every other player of that era—from the majors down to Little League—because Charlie Hustle, like Derek Jeter in a later generation, *visibly* pushed himself on every play, in every game, in every season. "*Never* give those at-bats away!"

Simply put: Pete fought like hell.

This approach may seem standard for all major league players. It isn't. (Otherwise, Pete Rose wouldn't be Pete Rose, and Derek Jeter wouldn't be Derek Jeter.)

I remember José Cardenal, a veteran playing on the Phillies, landing on first base one game during the previous season, and asking me, "What are you doing hitting .330, Keith?"

I said, "What do you mean?"

"People will expect you to hit .330 every year. That's a lot of pressure. If you hit .305 next year, they'll say you had a bad year. Whereas you could hit .280 with one hand tied behind your back."

I chuckled, said something like "Yeah," and the game got back under way, but I was surprised that Cardenal had said this. In his prime, Cardenal had been solid for the Cubs, batting .296 over six seasons, and in 1979 he was a very good bench player on a talented, younger Phillies team. *The man could hit.* Yet here he was, suggesting I *not* give it my all. (José played the game free and easy, so maybe he thought I was just too high-strung for what was ahead.)

That year I was in the middle of the batting race, so it sorta went in one ear and out the other, but I remember thinking, *I can't do that. My father always taught me to be the best I can be. If I can hit .330, I'm gonna hit .330; if I can hit .350, I'm gonna hit .350.*

What Cardenal said may seem as unacceptable to you as it did to me, but when you think about it, it's also understandable. Like any other occupation in which you're expected to perform at a high level day in and day out, baseball gets to be a grind. And once you reach a place where you feel like *Okay, I've made it,* it's tempting to put the car into neutral and just coast down the hill. Especially when you're talking about *managing expectations*—the press, the fans, the organization, and, most important, yourself. I mean, here I was in 1980, having just won the MVP, and it seemed like the question on everyone's mind, including mine, was "Can Keith Hernandez repeat his MVP performance?" It's a completely legitimate question, but wearing nonetheless. And as a player, it soon gets interpreted as just another way of saying "Hey, Keith, what have you done for me lately?" Because the better you perform, the more will be expected of you.

From that perspective, José Cardenal's suggestion to temper those expectations by *not* grinding out every single at-bat begins to make a lot more sense. He wasn't advocating brilliance, certainly, but he also wasn't advocating mediocrity. Instead, he was advocating *sustainability* for the long road ahead.

What separated Rose from almost everyone else was his ability to say "Screw that" and approach every one of his 14,053 career at-bats like it was Game Seven of the World Series. But Pete was the exception, not the rule. *Could I even come close to that level of persistence and tenacity?* That was the challenge that lay ahead of me, not only in May, as I set off to make it my seventh month in a row of hitting .300, but for the rest of my career.

I still intended to be the best I could be.

Two weeks into that May, we were in San Francisco for a three-game series. It was the first time I'd been home since the MVP, and when I came into the house, Dad had the old film projector and screen set up in the living room. Just like when Gary and I were kids. He sat me down and said, "I want to show you something," then he turned off the lights and started the projector.

It was one of the old Little League films Mom used to shoot, and I saw myself up on the screen, eleven years old, at the plate. Dad said, "Look at this stance, look at this swing. That's when I knew you were special."

I was stunned. Seeing Dad behind the projector, so proud of what he was showing on the screen, I realized why he'd been so hard on me.

When I was thirteen, playing my first year in a Pony League, I hit a double and was rounding first when I felt something "pop" in my right quad muscle. After I scored that inning, Dad could see me limping and came out of the dugout, asking what was wrong. Later that night, when we got home and I was limping more and more because my leg had stiffened up, Dad just lit into me: "You shouldn't be pulling muscles! Those never go away, Keith! They come back and nag you!" He was just screaming at me, exclaiming, once again, that I must be lazy because "*active* thirteen-year-olds don't pull muscles." And I thought: *What are you talking about? I hit a double and I'm running to second base and I'm halfway there and something pulled. I don't know why! I'm playing ball. I'm playing sports. I'm riding around on my bike. I'm walking everywhere. I'm an active kid and I'm lazy?*

Thirteen years later, sitting in that living room with him, I finally understood: I might have won the batting title and MVP in 1979, but Dad had seen the potential years before. And anything that might derail my progress, like a lousy pulled muscle, had been a threat to his vision and had made him angry. I was his second chance to make the bigs...

The footage was his proof: "That's when I knew you were special."

EPILOGUE

I'M SITTING AT MY brother's kitchen table in San Francisco, drinking coffee to shake off the morning cobwebs. I arrived last night after broadcasting a three-game series in L.A., and we were up late reminiscing and looking over Dad's scrapbooks. There are four scrapbooks, covering his whole baseball career, starting with his time at Mission High School. Gary found them up in the rafters at my parents' house after Dad's death from cancer in 1992, eighteen months after I retired. Last night was the first time I'd seen them since before I left home for the minors in '72.

I sip my coffee and look at the collection still spread across the table. Dad probably put the clippings together himself, at least early on. Later, when he was playing in the minors and in Hawaii for the war, he probably sent the clippings home to his sister, Pep, who chronicled them.

I focus on a picture from 1945. A group of young

men in uniform—Stan Musial among them—squatting over a barbecue pit on Waikiki Beach. It is just after sunset; the men have dug a big pit in the sand, where the fire blazes as dinner roasts. The black-and-white photo was shot from the ocean, capturing Hawaii's most famous beach. The landscape in the background is so pristine—not one development or building, just palm trees.

The scrapbooks make it obvious how much Dad loved baseball. I remember sensing that even as a kid when Dad would go through the pages with us. Along with photos, there are some hand drawings. Sketches my dad did of his favorite players, most notably Charlie Gehringer, a Hall of Fame second baseman. The drawings are impeccable. Graceful yet direct strokes. He was a very talented man, my dad. If not for his love affair with baseball, I wonder what else he might have become.

But that seems impossible: *Dad without baseball.* I think about how these players, like Gehringer, must have lived inside my dad's head as a kid. When he was growing up in San Francisco in the '20s and '30s, there was no MLB team to follow locally. Just box scores and World Series radio broadcasts.* No TV.

---

* Regular season games for teams weren't nationally broadcast until 1950.

Perhaps we should be envious of a time when a kid was free to go about his day with mighty baseball heroes and their fantastic 3-for-4 adventures playing inside his head, unfettered by "the tube." I mean where would Greek mythology be if people way back when had had a TV camera and TV set to tell their stories instead of the oral tradition? *Would these stories have been as mystical and magical? As impressive?* Baseball is like that—there's something about the battle between hitter and pitcher that captivates a person's imagination. *Achilles vs. Hercules.*

It certainly was enough to stoke Dad, who, despite falling short of his dream to play in the major leagues, never lost his passion for the game.

And when baseball eventually went to the tube, Dad loved it. Every weekend when we were kids, we'd watch the Saturday *Game of the Week,* and Dad would always be commenting on the game, the swings, even though the coverage in the early days was terrible—they shot from above the press box behind home plate. I remember Dad always getting upset because we were looking down the back side of home plate, and it was impossible to tell where the pitch was. But when broadcasts later adopted the center-field camera, Dad was ecstatic, because we could now see the pitch and its location along with the action in the field: double plays, rundowns, outfielders making catches, hitting or missing cutoff men. It was all there in plain sight, and Dad would always comment on the mistakes or on the proper plays. It was like watching a game with a special instructor—unfettered color commentating at its best.

You couldn't get that from a box score.

I close the scrapbook with the drawings of Charlie Gehringer and move on. I come across a clipping from the Oklahoma City paper printed in 1947. The article explains that my father was given his outright release after a dustup with his minor league manager.

I remember the story well; my father narrated it for Gary and me on numerous occasions.

He had begun that season in the very tough Texas League (AA), playing for the Oklahoma City Indians, a Cleveland affiliate. On that team was future Hall of Famer Al Rosen. My father was the starting first baseman.

But Dad was in a slump and got benched by the manager. There were three managers for the Oak City squad that season. That particular manager was a big drinker, and his backup first baseman was a drinking buddy. Acting on his quick temper, his loathing of authority, and his aggressive nature when he felt wronged, my father stormed into the manager's office. I remember Dad saying he punched him out. Gary remembers it differently. He remembers Dad saying there was a heated exchange.

Either way, my father was released from the team, and the St. Louis Cardinals organization picked him up and sent him to their Houston AA club in the same Texas League. He had a terrific year, hitting over .300, with a team high of 18 homers, and led the team to the Texas League championship. He was named the club's MVP.

The irony isn't lost on me. In 1983, just seven months after we'd won the World Series, I was traded by the Cardinals to the New York Mets, while that same organization, thirty-six years earlier, gave my father a fresh start.

They picked him up. They let me go?

Being a Cardinal was everything I'd dreamed of as a kid. Everything I'd worked so hard for. (It wound up being for the best. I'm a New Yorker—not born and raised, but naturalized.)

And now, seeing my dad's scrapbooks and all the places he played and how so much of what's in these books represents his life, I wish that I had done a better job of holding on to things.

So now I've written a book. And I realize that, in a way, I've finally started to create a scrapbook of my own. Like my father before me, I've cut and pasted the memories together and tucked them into one place. I focused on the early years, and while those may not be the most celebrated, they were the "hard" ones. The most instructive.

When I first started this process, I thought, *There's so much there, and I'm not sure how to arrange it all.* But like a crossword puzzle, I just went one way, then another, and another, until it was put together. That's how I remember things. I always have. I can go up and down, left and right. It isn't a rigid progression. It's fluid.

Like a good baseball swing.

ACKNOWLEDGMENTS

Thank you, baseball. I've always said that when I leave the game I'll walk away for good, but this project has reminded me just how much baseball has shaped me. There's no leaving that.

The *St. Louis Post-Dispatch* and its writers, especially Rick Hummel, and Baseball-Reference .com. Thank you for providing such detailed windows into that baseball past.

Family, friends, former teammates, and colleagues. Thank you for indulging me with your stories and recollections these past two years. Especially my brother, Gary, who, as always, was willing to lend a hand, be it confirmation of a certain recollection or just chatting on the phone about this and that. Our stories are so intertwined that it is impossible not to benefit from even the most casual of our correspondence.

Kai Thompson Hernandez, for your remarkable literary eye, honesty, and intelligence. Thank you.

Ian Kleinert, for bringing this book to Little, Brown and steering it home. Philip Marino, John Parsley, and all those associated with the publisher over the course. Thank you for giving me the opportunity to share this story. Your patience has been remarkable.

Finally, to Mike Poncy, whose vision and dedication made this work possible. Mike promised me a year, and I took two. I'm extremely grateful to him and his family, and I look forward to our continued friendship. To Mike's support team and to the University of Virginia Library: public access to their periodical collection and digital archives, particularly from the *St. Louis Post-Dispatch*, ensured the team's investigative success.

ABOUT THE AUTHOR

Keith Hernandez is a former Major League Baseball first baseman who played the majority of his career with the St. Louis Cardinals and the New York Mets. A batting champion and five-time All-Star, Hernandez was corecipient of the 1979 NL MVP and won two World Series titles, one each with the Cardinals and Mets. He earned more Gold Glove Awards—eleven—than any first baseman in baseball history. Since 2000, Hernandez has served as an analyst on Mets telecasts for the SNY, WPIX, and MSG networks, and he is a member of the FOX Sports MLB postseason studio team. He divides his time between New York and Florida.

No. 3090
$25.95

THE LASER COOKBOOK

88 Practical Projects

Gordon McComb

TAB BOOKS Inc.
Blue Ridge Summit, PA

To my wife, Jennifer, who knows—and accepts—that
the books I write are only excuses to play with gadgets and toys.

FIRST EDITION
FIRST PRINTING

Copyright © 1988 by Gordon McComb
Printed in the United States of America

Library of Congress Cataloging in Publication Data

McComb, Gordon.
    The laser cookbook: 88 practical projects / by Gordon McComb.
        p. cm.
    Bibliography: p.
    Includes index.
    ISBN 0-8306-9090-5   ISBN 0-8306-9390-4 (pbk.)
    1. Lasers—Experiments. I. Title.
TA1675.M39 1988
621.36′6—dc19   88-25035
                                                 CIP

TAB BOOKS Inc. offers software for sale. For information and a
catalog, please contact TAB Software Department, Blue Ridge
Summit, PA 17294-0850.

Questions regarding the content of this book
should be addressed to:

    Reader Inquiry Branch
    TAB BOOKS Inc.
    Blue Ridge Summit, PA 17294-0214

Contents

Acknowledgments

Writing books (like this one) provides numerous rewards, including the chance to meet and exchange ideas with many interesting and helpful people. I am indebted to the help and consideration provided by the following people: Dennis Meredith of Meredith Instruments, Roger Sontag of General Science and Engineering, and Jeff Korman and Sam Frisher of Fobtron Components.

The ''behind the scenes'' people made a great impact in the preparation of this book and I gratefully acknowledge their assistance. Thanks go to Brint Rutherford and Roland Phelps at TAB BOOKS and to my agent Bill Gladstone. Finally, my brother and father, Lee McComb and Wally McComb, helped answer my endless questions about lasers, surveying, mathematics, and earthquakes.

Introduction

You've just bought a surplus helium-neon gas laser at a local swap meet. You get it home, plug it in, and marvel at the incredibly bright, red spot it projects on the wall. Your friends and family seem interested, but they keep asking you "What's it good for?" You mumble something about holography and gun sights, but your interest soon wanes.

You grow tired of playing "laser tag" with the cat or bouncing the beam off reflective objects in your living room. Your toy soon finds its place in the dusty confines of the closet. You've run out of things to do with the laser and you soon move on to other hobbies.

It's time to get that laser out of the closet! *The Laser Cookbook* shows you over 88 inexpensive laser-based projects from experimenting with laser optics to constructing a laser optical bench to using lasers to make stunning holograms. All the projects are geared towards garage/shop tinkering with a special emphasis on minimizing the budget. The book mixes the history of lasers, how lasers work, and practical applications in an easy-to-read and fun text that's suitable for experimenters of all ages.

Among the topics in this book, you'll learn how to use lasers for:

★ holography
★ optics and optical experiments
★ laser guns
★ laser light shows
★ laser beam intrusion and detection systems
★ aerodynamics and airflow study
★ coherent-light seismology

* laser beam communication
* laser and fiberoptics computer data link
* precision measurement

Though the laser is a relatively new invention, it has undergone many refinements and improvements since the first successful prototype was tested by Theodore Maiman in 1960. And its cost has been drastically reduced. Today, lasers are inexpensive, almost throw-away devices and are used in numerous consumer products and electronic systems. Lasers are everywhere—from the phone lines that connect home to office to the electronics that play back sound and pictures encoded on a videodisc to the bar-code scanning system used at the supermarket.

Lasers are available to even the most budget-conscious hobbyists, so if you don't already have one (whether in the closet or not), don't despair. Surplus laser kits can be purchased for less than $100, and the latest semiconductor lasers—the kind used in videodisc and audio compact disc players—cost under $15. The tools are here to bring laser technology to the common masses. All that's needed is a book to show how the pieces fit together. Such a book is *The Laser Cookbook*.

WHO THIS BOOK IS FOR

The Laser Cookbook is written for a wide variety of readers. If you're into electronics, you'll enjoy the many circuits you can build, including one that lets you carry your voice over a beam of light, or the project that can detect the presence of intruders around a campsite. A number of the projects are excellent springboards for science fairs. These include measuring—with astonishing accuracy—the speed of light, seismology, and hydrodynamics. Lastly, this book is a gold mine for the gadgeteer. Lasers represent the ultimate in space-age technology, but *The Laser Cookbook* presents numerous laser-based gadgets that you can readily build in your garage.

In all cases, the designs used in *The Laser Cookbook* have been thoroughly tested in prototype form. I encourage you to improve on the basic designs, but you can rest assured that the projects have actually been tried and field tested.

The projects in *The Laser Cookbook* include all the necessary information on how to construct the essential building blocks of high-tech laser projects. Suggested alternative approaches, parts lists, and sources of electronic and mechanical components are also provided, where appropriate.

HOW TO USE THIS BOOK

The Laser Cookbook is divided into 24 chapters. Most chapters present one or more actual hands-on projects that you can duplicate for your own laser creations. Whenever practical, I designed the components as discrete building blocks, so you can combine the blocks in just about any configuration you desire. That way, you are not tied down to one of my designs. You're free to experiment on your own!

If you have some experience in electronics, mechanics, or lasers in general, you can skip around and read only those chapters that provide the information you're looking for. Like the laser designs presented, the chapters are very much stand-alone modules. This allows you to pick and choose, using your time to its best advantage.

However, if you're new to lasers and the varied disciplines that go into them, you should take a more pedestrian approach and read as much of the book as possible. In this way, you'll get a thorough understanding of how lasers tick and the myriad ways you can use them.

CONVENTIONS USED IN THIS BOOK

You need little advance information before you can jump head-first into this book, but you should take note of a few conventions I've used in the description of electronic parts and in the schematic diagrams for the electronic circuits.

TTL integrated circuits are referenced by their standard 74XX number. The "LS" identifier is assumed. I built most of the circuits using LS TTL chips, but the projects should work with the other TTL-family chips—the standard (non-LS) chips, as well as those with the S, ALS, and C identifiers. If you use a type of TTL chip other than LS, you should consider current consumption, fan-out, and other design criteria, because these factors can affect the operation or performance of the circuit.

In some cases, however, a certain TTL-compatible IC is specified in a design. Unless the accompanying text recommends otherwise, you should use only the chip specified.

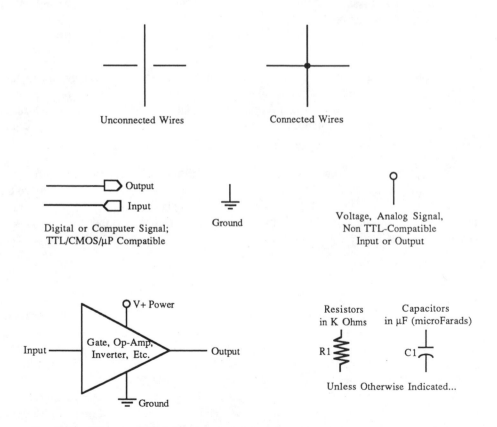

FIG. I-1. *Conventions used in the schematic diagrams in this book.*

Certain CMOS TTL-compatible chips offer the same functions as a sister IC, but the pinouts and operation might differ.

The chart in FIG. I-1 details the conventions used in the schematic diagrams. Note that unconnected wires are shown by a direct cross of lines, a broken line, or a "looped" line. Connected wires are only shown by a connecting dot.

Details on the specific parts used in the circuits are provided in the parts list tables that accompany each schematic. Refer to the parts list for information on resistor and capacitor type, tolerance, and wattage or voltage ratings.

In all schematics, the parts are referenced by component type and number.

- ★ IC# means an integrated circuit (IC).
- ★ R# means a resistor or potentiometer (variable resistor).
- ★ C# means a capacitor.
- ★ D# means a diode, a zener diode, and sometimes a light-sensitive photodiode.
- ★ Q# means a transistor and sometimes a light-sensitive phototransistor.
- ★ LED# means a light-emitting diode (most any visible LED will do unless the parts list specifically calls for an infrared LED).
- ★ XTAL# means a crystal or ceramic resonator.
- ★ S# means a switch, RL# means a relay, SPKR# means a speaker, and MIC# means a microphone.

SAFETY FIRST

It's hard to imagine that something as fun as lasers can be potentially dangerous. While the types of lasers commonly available to experimenters do not pose a great radiation emission hazard, they can do damage if mishandled. This point is reiterated in later chapters, but it's worth mentioning here: **NEVER LOOK DIRECTLY INTO THE LASER BEAM**. The intensity and needle-sharp focus of the beam can do your eyes harm.

Perhaps more importantly, gas lasers, such as the helium-neon type, require high-voltage power supplies. These power supplies generate from 1,000 to 10,000 volts. Though the current provided from these power supplies is low (generally under 7 milliamps), a 5,000- or 10,000-volt jolt is enough to at least knock you down. The power supply of a laser is not a toy and should be considered potentially lethal.

1

Introduction to Lasers

Think how boring science fiction movies would be if lasers did not exist. There would be no gallant laser sword fights between good guy and bad guy; no interstellar spaceships shooting darts of light at one another; no packets of photon energy hurled through the air like matterless handgrenades. Movies and television shows such as *Star Wars, Star Trek, War of the Worlds, Predator*, and *Day the Earth Stood Still*—along with countless others—owe a great deal of their spine-tingling suspense and fast-paced action sequences to the laser.

While lasers are most often regarded by the general public as exotic weaponry, this intriguing and fascinating scientific instrument enjoys a far greater involvement in peacetime applications. Lasers of one type or another are used in:

★ Supermarket scanning systems to instantly read the bar code label on packaged goods.

★ Audio compact disc players to play music with incredible fidelity.

★ Leveling instruments, used at construction sites to assure perfectly flat grading and absolutely straight pipe laying.

★ Light shows, where the beam of the laser dances to the beat of the music and makes beautiful sinuous shapes.

★ Holography, a special type of photography that captures a three-dimensional view of an object.

★ Communications systems, where voice, pictures, or computer data is transmitted through air or optical fibers on a beam of light.

Lasers are also used in gyroscopic inertial guidance systems on board commercial and military aircraft, in rifle and pistol range target practice, for rifle scopes, optical component testing, medicine (such as a high-tech substitute for the scalpel), optical radar, precision rangefinders, and many other diverse products and applications.

In this book, you'll learn how to design and build your own laser systems for holography, light-wave communications, target practice guns, light shows, and more. But first understand some basics. This chapter discusses the fundamentals of lasers: how they work, their history, forms of lasers, and the dynamics of laser light. So much has been written about laser physics that the fine details won't be covered here; only the basics of lasers are presented.

EINSTEIN AS THE SPARK

Albert Einstein was a theoretical physicist; he invented few actual things himself. As with many of the world's great thinkers, Einstein left the practical applications of his pioneering work in physics to other people. In addition to creating the theory of relativity—perhaps his best-known work—Einstein is responsible for first proposing the idea of the laser in about 1916.

Einstein knew that light was a series of particles, called *photons*, traveling in a continuous wave. These photons could be collected (using an apparatus not yet developed) and focused into a narrow beam. To be useful, all the photons would be emitted from the laser apparatus at specific intervals. As important, much of the light energy would be concentrated in a specific wavelength—or color—making the light even more intense and powerful.

Even in Einstein's day, photons could be created in a variety of means, including the ionization of gas within a sealed tube, the burning of some organic materials, or the heating of a filament in a light bulb. In all cases, the atoms that make up the light source change from their usual stable or *ground state* to a higher *excited state* by the introduction of some form of energy, typically heat or electricity. The atom can't stay at the excited state for long, and when it drops back to its comfortable ground state, it gives off a photon of light.

The release of photons by natural methods results in what is known as *spontaneous emission*. The photons leave the source in a random and unpredictable manner, and once a photon is emitted, it marks the end of the energy transfer cycle. The number of excited atoms is relatively low, so the great majority of photons leave the source without meeting another excited atom.

Einstein was most interested in what would happen if a photon hit an atom that happened to be at the excited, high-energy state. He reasoned that the atom would release a photon of light that would be an identical twin to the first. If enough atoms could be excited, the chance of photons hitting them would be increased. That would lead to a chain reaction where photons would hit atoms and make new photons, and the process would continue until the original energy source was terminated. Einstein had a name for this phenomenon, and called it *stimulated emission of radiation*.

RAISING ATOMS

Raising atoms to a high-energy state is often referred to as *pumping*. As already discussed, atoms can be pumped in a number of ways, including charging with electricity or heat. Another form of pumping is optical, with a bright source of light such as an arc lamp or xenon-filled flash tube.

In the common neon light, for example, the neon atoms are pumped to their high-energy state by means of a high-voltage charge applied to a pair of electrodes. The gas within the tube ionizes, emitting photons. If the electrical charge is high enough, a majority of the neon atoms will be pumped to the high-energy state. A so-called *population inversion* occurs when there are more high-energy atoms than low-energy ones. A laser cannot work unless this population inversion is present.

Photons scatter all over the place, and left on their own, they will simply escape the tube. But assume a pair of mirrors are mounted on either end of the tube, so some photons can bounce back and forth between the two mirrors.

At each bounce, the photons collide with more atoms. If many of these atoms are in their excited state, they too release photons. Remember: these new photons are twins of the original and share many of its characteristics, including wavelength, polarity, and phase. The process of photons bouncing from one mirror to the next and striking atoms in their path each time constitutes *light amplification*.

In theory, if both mirrors are completely reflective, the photons would bounce back and forth indefinitely. In reality, the tube would overheat and burn up because the light energy would not be able to escape. Rub a little of the reflective coating off one mirror, however, and it passes some light. Now a beam of photons can pass through the partially reflective mirror after the light has been sufficiently amplified. In addition, because the mirror is partially reflective, it holds back some of the light energy. This reserve continues the chain reaction inside the tube.

LET THERE BE LASER LIGHT

The combination of light amplification and stimulated emission of radiation makes the laser functional. As you probably already know, the word laser is an acronym for *light amplification of stimulated emission of radiation*.

We've used the neon tube to describe the activity of atoms and photons to make laser light, and while neon gas can be made to lase (emit laser light), it is not as efficient as some other materials.

Matter comes in three known states: solid, liquid, and gas. Lasers can be made from all three types of matter. While everyone assumed the first laser would be the gas variety, modeled after the neon sign, the solid laser was the first to be invented.

Theodore Maiman, a research physicist at Hughes Laboratories in Malibu, California, announced the first successful operation of the laser on July 7, 1960. Maiman's contraption was surprisingly simple and compact, consisting of a synthetic ruby rod with mirrored ends, a spiral-shaped photographic strobe lamp, and a high-voltage power supply (refer to FIG. 1-1). The laser head itself—ruby rod and flash lamp—measured only 1.5 inches long and could be held in one hand.

The operation of the ruby laser, still in use today, is straightforward. The power supply sends a short pulse of high-energy electricity to the flash lamp. The lamp flashes on quickly, bathing the rod in white light. Chromium atoms—which give the ruby its red color—absorb just the green and blue spectrum of the light. The absorption of this light raises the energy level of the chromium atoms. Shortly thereafter, the chromium atoms fall back to a transitory level called the *metastable state*.

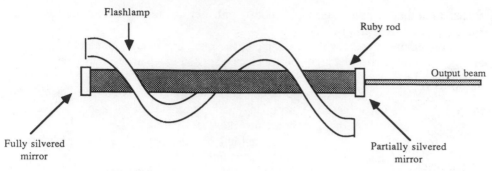

Flashlamp

Ruby rod

Output beam

Fully silvered
mirror

Partially silvered
mirror

FIG. 1-1. *The main optical components of the ruby laser: a flash tube and a specially-made synthetic ruby rod. The ends of the rods are reflectively coated to provide optical amplification.*

There they stay for a short period of time (a few milliseconds), and then they drop back to the unexcited ground state. In this final drop, as shown in FIG. 1-2, photons are emitted. Some of these photons bounce off of the mirrored ends of the rod. After being amplified by bouncing back and forth between the mirrors, a small stream of photons are emitted out one end. The entire process lasts less than a few hundredths of a second. Because of the way the ruby rod is energized, it is termed an *optically pumped laser.*

Development of Other Types of Lasers

Other forms of lasers were developed after Maiman completed his trials with his ruby device. A more thorough discussion of the history and development of lasers appears below, but it is worthwhile to note that lasers based on the other two forms of matter—gas and liquid—were invented just shortly after Maiman's historical announcement. For instance, the gas laser, using a form of modified neon tube, was tested in 1961. The first successful attempt at the semiconductor laser took place in 1962, using what was essentially a specially-made light emitting diode (LED) suspended in a cold liquid nitrogen bath.

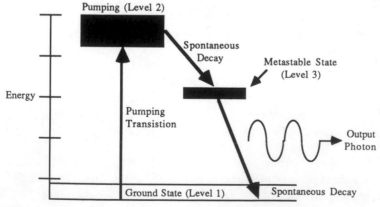

FIG. 1-2. *Energy levels of a ruby laser. After initial pumping by energizing the flash tube, the chromium atoms in the ruby rod spontaneously decay to a metastable state; it then decays once more and outputs a photon.*

4

Parts of a Laser

Lasers consist of the following components:

★ *Power supply*. All lasers use an electrical power supply delivering a potential of up to 10,000 volts and up to many hundreds of amps.

★ *Pumping device*. Electrical discharge lasers use the high-voltage power supply as the pumping device, but some lasers use a radio-frequency oscillator, high-output photoflash or lamp, or even another laser.

★ *Lasing medium*. The medium is the material that generates the laser light. The lasing medium can be a gas, solid, or liquid. There are thousands of lasing mediums, including specially-treated glass, argon, organic dyes, or even Jell-O.

★ *Optical resonant cavity*. The cavity encloses the lasing medium and consists of mirrors placed at each end. On most lasers, one mirror is completely reflective and the other mirror partially reflective.

TYPES OF LASERS

The three states of matter—gas, solid, or liquid—present a convenient way to generally classify lasers, but it offers no insight into the design and application of various laser mediums. While the list of possible lasing mediums is extensive, most commercial, scientific, and military lasers fall into one of these categories: crystal and glass, gas, excimer, chemical, semiconductor, and liquid. Let's take a closer look at each one.

Crystal and Glass Lasers

As you've already discovered, synthetic ruby makes the basis for a very good laser. *Synthetic ruby* is made with aluminum oxide doped with a small amount of chromium. Why synthetic ruby and not the real thing? Ruby made in the laboratory is far more pure than natural ruby. The purity is necessary or lasing action cannot occur.

Another common crystal laser is the *Nd:YAG* laser. Nd:YAG is composed primarily of the elements aluminum, yttrium, and oxygen, doped with a pinch of neodymium. The name YAG is an acronym for yttrium-aluminum garnet, a synthetic garnet sometimes used in jewelry. The Nd:YAG is similar to the synthetic ruby in that the crystal is the host for the neodymium atoms. These atoms are excited into high-energy states using optical pumping and emit light in the infrared region. Nd:YAG lasers can be operated continuously because the crystal is a good conductor of heat. Synthetic ruby is a poor conductor of heat and will explode if lased continuously.

The element neodymium can be mixed with glass to make a neodymium-glass, or *Nd:glass*, laser. The benefit of the Nd:glass laser is that the glass rod is less expensive than YAG. The largest drawback of this type of laser is that glass is a relatively poor conductor of heat. For this reason, Nd:glass lasers are used in pulsed mode only.

Gas Lasers

Gas lasers represent the largest group of lasers. Their popularity stems from their inexpensive components and ease of manufacture (in comparison to other types of lasers;

all lasers are relatively difficult to manufacture). A number of gases and gas compounds are used, including:

* Helium-neon.
* Helium-cadmium.
* Argon.
* Carbon dioxide.
* Krypton.
* CO_2.

Over 5,000 types of laser activity in gases are known, and several dozen have been made into working lasers. The *helium-neon* laser, as shown in FIG. 1-3, is the most common, finding wide use in general-purpose bar-code scanning systems in department stores and supermarkets, as well as in holography, surveying, and laboratory experiments. Most all helium-neon lasers emit a characteristic red beam. The power output of He-Ne lasers is limited, and all but unusual laboratory models are air-cooled by convection (some by forced air).

There is nothing exceptionally exotic about the average He-Ne laser, making it affordable and easy to use. Most of the projects in this book are centered around the common helium-neon tube, which you can purchase on the used or surplus market for $35 to $100.

CO$_2$ lasers are among the most powerful gas lasers. Whether operating in pulsed or continuous modes, a CO_2 laser can produce a beam that's intense enough to cut

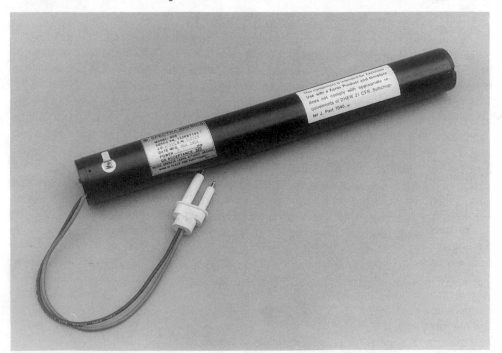

FIG. 1-3. *A commercially made helium-neon laser. The actual laser tube is encased in the aluminum tube; power leads extend from the rear of the laser.*

through almost any metal. CO_2 lasers actually contain a mixture of carbon dioxide, nitrogen, and helium that is continually pumped through the laser tube. To avoid overheating, CO_2 lasers are cooled by running water.

Argon and *krypton lasers* are used for their ability to produce two or more wavelengths of light, particularly in the short blue and green wavelengths. Though both types can produce a great deal of optical energy, depending on the model, they aren't used for cutting materials. They are mainly used for such applications as semiconductor manufacturing, medicine, color holography, and light shows. High-powered argon and krypton lasers are water-cooled; lower powered versions are forced-air cooled.

Excimer Lasers

Excimer lasers are gas lasers with a twist. A rare gas such as argon, krypton, or xenon electrically reacts with a halogen (chlorine, fluorine, iodine, or bromine) to form an excimer. Thinking back to high school chemistry, an excimer is a molecule that exists only in an electrically excited state. When the excimer molecule emits a photon, it doesn't go back to its ground state but breaks up into into constituent atoms. This provides the population inversion necessary for lasing action to occur.

The main benefit of excimer lasers is their ability to emit high-energy ultraviolet light, which is helpful in photochemistry and the manufacture of transistors and integrated circuits. By comparison, most all lasers emit their strongest radiation in the visible spectrum and infrared regions.

Chemical Lasers

Chemical lasers are high-powered beasts favored by the military as weapons against enemy aircraft or missiles. In the typical chemical laser, a flammable mixture of hydrogen and fluorine (or compounds thereof) acts as the lasing medium. The chemicals are pressurized and are sometimes ignited into a flame to initiate the lasing action. The typical chemical laser resembles a jet aircraft engine more than it does a James Bond-type laser. Obviously, chemical lasers are not for hobbyists.

Semiconductor Lasers

Semiconductor lasers are solid-state devices that—while almost as old as ruby and gas lasers—are just now catching on. You are probably aware of the semiconductor (or diode) laser used in compact audio and video discs, such as the one shown in FIG. 1-4. Semiconductor lasers are also used in fiberoptic telephone links, bar-code scanning devices, and military rangefinder equipment.

There are a number of different laser diode designs, with significant variations between each one. For our purposes, however, it is sufficient to say that the laser diode consists of a pn junction, as in a light-emitting diode (LED), but with specially cleaved and mirrored facets. In operation, current applied to the junction causes a glow of light. The mirrors comprise the optical cavity that amplifies the light generated within the diode junction. Laser diodes are made for either pulsed or continuous duty. Both types are widely available in the surplus electronics market.

FIG. 1-4. *A laser diode with heatsink attached. Although not apparent in the photograph, the laser and heatsink measure less than ¾ inch across.*

Liquid (Dye) Lasers

Liquid lasers use molecular organic dyes as the lasing material. The dye is directed through a cavity and pumped by an optical source, such as a CO_2 laser. The unique property of liquid dye lasers is that the output wavelength (see below) is tunable. By varying the mixture of the dyes, it's possible to change the color of the laser beam from a deep blue to a dark red.

LIGHT AND WAVELENGTHS

Light is part *particle* and part *wave*. The particles are called photons and the waves are a part of the *electromagnetic spectrum*. A graphic illustration of the electromagnetic spectrum appears in FIG. 1-5. Note that visible light comprises a relatively small portion of the entire spectrum.

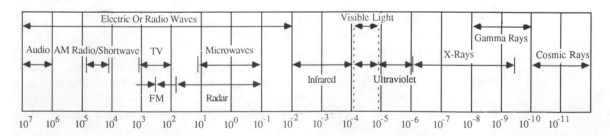

FIG. 1-5. *The electromagnetic spectrum, from long wavelength audio and AM radio signals to ultra-short gamma and cosmic rays. The visible light band is a relatively small section of the spectrum.*

You can best imagine the nature of light by thinking of the photons as bobbing up and down as they travel forward through space. Looking at the path of light sideways shows the photon drawing a sine wave, which is a wave that alternates up and down in a smooth, gradual motion, as shown in FIG. 1-6.

All sine waves—no matter how they are created and what they represent—share similar properties. They are composed of crests and troughs (or valleys). The distance between two consecutive crests determines the wavelength and thus the *frequency* of the wave. If the distance between two crests is small, the wavelength is small and the frequency is high. Increase the distance and the wavelength increases in proportion and the frequency drops. Frequency is most often expressed in *hertz*, or *cycles per second*. That is, frequency is the number of times the wave bobs up and down in one second.

Light travels at a velocity of 300,000 km per second (186,000 miles per hour). The different colors of visible light have different wavelengths and thus frequencies. The frequencies are in the terahertz range (thousand billions of cycles per seconds), as shown in FIG. 1-7. For convenience, light is usually expressed in wavelength, specifically *nanometers* (sometimes Angstroms). One nanometer is one billionth of a meter. TABLE 1-1 lists the different colors of the visible spectrum and their respective wavelengths. TABLE 1-2 compares the units of measurement common in the discussion of light and lasers.

Laser Wavelengths

One of the unique properties of lasers is their ability to emit light at a specific color, or wavelength. This is in contrast to the sun or an incandescent lamp, which both emit all the colors of the rainbow. The output wavelength is determined by the lasing medium. For example, the chromium atoms in synthetic ruby give off light at 694.3 nanometers (or nm), thereby making the wavelength of a ruby laser 694.3 nm.

The laser might emit light at just one specific wavelength or many distinct wavelengths. Light emission at any particular wavelength is called a *line*; if the laser emits light at many wavelengths, each individual wavelength is a *mainline*. The terms line and mainline are derived from the study of optical spectra, where white light passed through a prism is broken down into discrete lines or segments. TABLE 1-3 shows the chief wavelengths emitted by several common types of lasers.

Most helium-neon lasers emit light at one specific wavelength, namely 632.8 nm (632.8 billionths of a meter, equivalent to 6328 angstroms). Argon lasers generate two distinct mainlines, one at 488 nm and the other at 514 nm. Krypton lasers, popular in

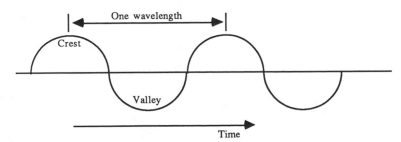

FIG. 1-6. *A sinusoidal wave, showing one wavelength from crest to crest.*

9

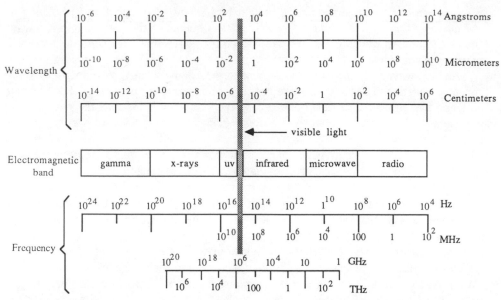

FIG. 1-7. *Comparing wavelength, frequency, and electromagnetic spectrum regions. Wavelengths are shown in three common units of measurement: angstroms, micrometers, and centimeters. A common unit of measurement for light wavelengths is the nanometer—to find the equivalent in nanometers, divide the number in angstroms by 10.*

professional light show systems, produce a mainline at 647 nm, but also produces weaker wavelengths all through the visible spectrum.

Note that mainlines are those wavelengths that greatly contribute to the intensity of the beam. Many lasers emit a whole slew of wavelengths but might be listed as having only one or two lines. These sub-lines are generally too weak to be useful, so they are usually ignored. In many laser systems, light at wavelengths other than at the desired lines are filtered out.

When using a multiple-line laser (such as argon or krypton), the individual colors can be separated by the use of prisms, filters, or diffraction gratings. These and other optical components are discussed in more detail in Chapter 3.

POWER OUTPUT

The intensity of the laser beam is measured in *joules* or *watts*. Both represent the amount of "work" that can be done during a particular period of time. In this case, the term *work* is used to denote the amount of energy or power released in some useful form, including heat. Electronic textbooks define one watt as the unit of electrical power equal to one volt multiplied by one ampere. The formula for computing watts is:

$$P = EI$$

where P equals power in watts, E equals EMF in volts, and I equals current in amps. One horsepower is also equal to 746 watts, an archaic but still-used measurement for determining the rate or amount of work performed by some device (usually a motor).

Table 1-1. Color Wavelengths

Color	Wavelength
Red	0.000066 cm; 660 nm
Orange	0.000061 cm; 610 nm
Yellow	0.000058 cm; 580 nm
Green	0.000054 cm; 540 nm
Blue	0.000046 cm; 460 nm
Violet	0.000042 cm; 420 nm

Infrared						Ultraviolet
Nanometers						
1200	700	600	550	500	400	200
Millimeters						
0.0012	0.00070	0.00060	0.00055	0.00050	0.00040	0.00020
Centimeters						
0.00012	0.00007	0.00006	0.000055	0.00005	0.00004	0.00002
	Red	Yellow	Green	Blue	Violet	

Watts, like horsepower, does not take time into consideration; joules does. One *joule* is equal to one ampere passed through a resistance of one ohm for one second (the joule is also a measurement of physical force). When wattage is measured against some factor of time, it is so indicated.

Rather than settle on one standard or another, laser manufacturers use a composite of watts and joules, although they mean different things. Generally, low-power, continuous-duty lasers are measured in watts; high-power, pulsed-duty lasers are measured in joules. And as a rule of thumb, radiant energy is expressed in joules and radiant power is expressed in watts.

Although laser light is most often defined as a pinpoint source, natural divergence and optics can cause the beam to spread. The area of the measured power output of a laser, in watts or joules, is often included in the specifications. A typical specification might be 5.0 joules cm^2. which means 5.0 joules in one square centimeter.

Most laser and helium-neon lasers are rated in milliwatts, or thousandths of a watt. The typical helium-neon laser has a power output of about two milliwatts, or two $\frac{1}{1000}$ of a watt. High-powered gas argon and krypton lasers generate several watts of optical power. Such *multiwatt* lasers are most often used in research, manufacturing, and light shows.

Table 1-2. Metric Prefixes

Prefix	Abbreviation	Power of Ten	Value
tera	T	10^{12}	thousand billion
giga	G	10^{9}	billion
mega	M	10^{6}	million
kilo	k	10^{3}	thousand
deci	d	10^{-1}	tenths
centi	c	10^{-2}	hundredths
milli	m	10^{-3}	thousanths
micro	μ	10^{-6}	millionths
nano	n	10^{-9}	billionths
pico	p	10^{-12}	thousand billionths

1 micrometer:

    1/1,000,000 meter; 10^{-6}m
    1000 nm
    10,000 A units

1 nanometer:

    1/1,000,000,000 meter; 10^{-9}m
    1/1000 μ
    10 A units

1 angstrom unit:

    1/10,000,000,000 meter; 10^{-10} m
    1/10,000 μ
    1/10 nm

The power output of a laser is dependent upon many factors, one of which is the efficiency of the conversion of optical or electrical power into photon power. Most lasers are extremely inefficient—about one or two percent of the incoming energy is converted to usable light energy. But even with poor efficiency, the beam from a laser is far more intense (per given area) than sunlight.

By comparison, a standard incandescent light bulb is roughly 2 to 3 percent efficient, yet its light intensity is only a fraction that of a low-power laser. Even a fluorescent lamp, with an efficiency of 10 to 15 percent, is not nearly as potent as a laser. CO_2 lasers are among the most efficient of the bunch, which is one reason why they emit such a powerful beam. Typical efficiency of a well-built CO_2 laser is about 30 to 35 percent.

COMPONENT PARTS OF THE LASER

A number of components go into making a laser. Because low-power gas and semiconductor lasers are the thrust of this book, we'll concentrate just on those. The

Table 1-3. Wavelengths of Popular Laser Types

Laser	Mainline	Comments
Argon	488.0 nm, 514.5 nm	Multiline: 351-528 nm
Carbon Dioxide	10,600 nm	
Dye laser	300-1,000 nm (typ.)	Tunable
Excimer	193-351 nm	
Helium-Cadmium	442 or 325 nm	
Helium-Neon	632.8 nm	Other lines at 543, 594, 652, 1,152, and 3391 nm
Nitrogen	337 nm	
Krypton	647 nm	Multiline: 350-800 nm
Nd:YAG	1,064 nm	
Ruby	694.3 nm	
Semiconductor	780, 840, 904 nm (typ.)	Range from 700-1,600 nm
(diode)		

typical helium-neon laser consists of a tube, high-voltage power supply, and power source, as shown in the block diagram in FIG. 1-8. Most He-Ne tubes are self-contained and include the facing mirrors, but some special tubes are available that use separate mirrors. The mirrors are mounted on a precision optical bench and adjusted so the laser beam properly exits the tube.

The high-voltage power supply converts the juice from the power source (usually either 12 volts dc or 117 volts ac) to between 1,200 and 3,000 volts. The high voltage

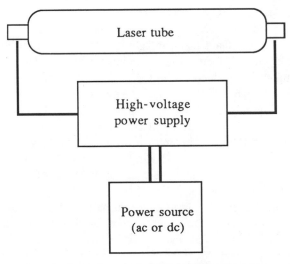

FIG. 1-8. *The major components of a gas laser, including tube, high-voltage power supply, and power source.*

is necessary to ionize the gas within the tube. The current output of the power supply is low—roughly 3 to 7 milliamps. You can calculate the approximate efficiency of the laser by multiplying the voltage (say 2,000 volts) by the current (such as five milliamps). The result is 10 watts of electrical power consumed by the tube. If the laser generates two milliwatts of light energy, the efficiency is only two percent (10 watts in times 0.002 watts out).

Semiconductor lasers consist of the laser chip or element, a power source, and possibly a drive circuit. Because the pn junction of the laser is so small, the chip is attached to a heatsink to dissipate unwanted heat. The chip and heat sink are encased in a metal canister and protected against dust and debris by a clear plastic or glass window. The power source is low-voltage dc. The exact voltage requirements depend on the type of diode used.

THE PROPERTIES OF LASER LIGHT

The light from a laser is special in many respects.

☆ *Laser light is monochromatic*. That is, the light coming from the output mirror consists of one wavelength, or in some instances, two or more specific wavelengths. The individual wavelengths can be separated using various optical components.

☆ *Laser light is spatially coherent*. The term *spatial coherence* means that all the waves coming from the laser are in tandem. That is, the crests and the troughs of the waves that make up the beam are in lock-step.

☆ *Laser light is temporally coherent*. *Temporal coherency* is when the waves from the laser (which can be considered as one large wave, thanks to spatial coherency) are emitted in even, accurately spaced intervals. Temporal coherence is similar to the precise clicks of a metronome that times out the beat of the music.

☆ *Laser light is collimated*. Because of monochromaticity and coherence, laser light does not spread (diverge) as much as ordinary light. The design of the laser itself, or simple optics, can collimate (make parallel) the laser light into a parallel beam.

The four main properties of laser light combine to produce a shaft of illumination that is many times more brilliant than the light of equal area from the sun. Because of their coherency, monochromaticity, and low beam divergence, lasers are ideally suited for a number of important applications. For example, the monochromatic and coherent light from a laser is necessary to form the intricate swirling patterns of a hologram. Without the laser, optical holograms would be much more difficult to produce.

Coherence plays a leading role in the minimum size of a focused spot. With the right optics, it's possible to focus a laser beam to an area equal to the wavelength of the light. With the typical infrared-emitting laser diode, for instance, the beam can be focused to a tiny spot measuring just 0.8 micrometers wide. Such intricate focusing is the backbone of compact audio discs and laser discs.

Minimum divergence (owing to the coherent nature of laser light) means that the beam can travel a longer distance before spreading out. The average helium-neon laser, without optics, can form a beam spot measuring only a few inches in diameter from a distance several hundred feet away. With additional optics, beam divergence can be reduced, making it possible to transmit sound, pictures, and computer code many miles on a shaft of light. A receiving station in the path intercepts the signal.

One experiment with the low divergence of laser light was performed during the historic Apollo 11 moon landings. A 1mm beam from a ruby laser was bounced to the moon and back, reflected by a matrix of highly polished mirrors. Although the moon is about 235,000 miles away, the laser beam spread to an area of only 1.5 miles when it reached the lunar surface.

THE BIRTH OF THE LASER

The concept of the laser is said to have occurred in 1951, brainstormed by Charles H. Townes, a physicist at Bell Labs (later a professor at Columbia University). Townes' first idea was to amplify stimulated emissions of microwave radiation. Using ammonia as the lasing medium, this device would emit radiation in the microwave region, below visible light and infrared. Three years later, along with graduate student James P. Gordon and Herbert Zeiger, Townes built and tested the first forerunner of the laser. They dubbed the device the *maser*, an acronym for *m*icrowave *a*mplification of *s*timulated *e*mission of *r*adiation.

In 1957, Townes sketched out an idea for the "optical maser," a device similar to his earlier invention but one that would emit radiation in the visible or at least near-infrared region of the electromagnetic spectrum. Townes joined forces with a researcher at AT&T, Arthur Schawlow, and began work on an optical maser using a large tube filled with gas (as an interesting aside, Schawlow is Townes' brother-in-law). By the time Townes and Schawlow were working on the optical maser in the late 1950s, researchers the world over were quickly drawing up plans of their own.

As mentioned previously, Hughes research scientist Theodore Maiman beat Schawlow and Townes to the punch with his crystalline ruby laser in 1960. The *gas discharge laser*, developed in 1961 by Ali Javan, William R. Bennett, and Dr. R. Herriott of Bell Labs, marked a major discovery, because unlike the ruby laser, it could be powered continuously instead of in short pulses.

The Bell Labs researchers used as the lasing mixture a combination of helium and neon gases. The gas was pumped into a long tube at relatively low pressure and mirrors were mounted on either end. When powered by a charge of high-frequency radio waves, the gas within the tube ionized, and photons began striking against the mirrors. Some photons escaped, and out one end of the tube came an invisible beam of infrared radiation. Later refinements to the helium-neon laser allowed it to emit visible light.

In 1962, a trio of groups including researchers at MIT, IBM, and GE developed the first semiconductor lasers. Shortly thereafter, groups at GT&E, Texas Instruments, and Bell Labs announced similar work. The small size and high energy output of the semiconductor laser required that it be cooled in liquid nitrogen—minus 196 degrees Celsius! Interesting things were done with the semiconductor laser, including transmitting a television picture along the beam of light and changing the characteristics of the diode so that the laser emitted a deep red glow instead of the characteristic invisible infrared radiation.

15

WILL THE REAL FATHER OF THE LASER PLEASE STAND UP?

Theodore Maiman, the scientists at Bell Labs, and others who built the first lasers are among those people credited with the introduction of the laser. But the actual inventor of the laser — the first person to have thought of it and worked out its principles—has been a debatable question since the late 1950's.

In the summer of 1958, Schawlow and Townes drew up a patent application for the optical maser (the term "laser" didn't come until later). Their patent was granted, and Townes, as well as two Russian scientists Nikolai G. Basov and Aleksander M. Prokhorov, received the Nobel Prize in 1964 for their work in developing the laser.

A graduate student at Townes' university by the name of Gordon Gould later claimed that he developed the basic principles of the laser earlier in November of 1957, more than half a year before the Townes/Schawlow patent application. Although Gould was not a graduate student of Townes, they knew each other and often spoke to one another.

Gould kept his ideas in a notebook which he later had notarized (the first page of this notebook is now at the Smithsonian Institution). Gould claimed he contemplated applying for a patent on his laser ideas, but an attorney gave him the mistaken impression that he needed a working model in order to be granted a patent. Apparently, before Gould could obtain more competent advice, Schawlow and Townes beat him to the punch and filed their application first.

Most textbooks on lasers, particularly those written before 1980, often credit Schawlow and Townes as the sole inventors of the laser. But today, it is Gordon Gould who owns the basic patents on the laser and enjoys a healthy sum from royalties paid by laser manufacturers.

This chapter has merely touched upon the fundamentals and history of lasers. A more thorough discussion of laser principles would have diluted the main purpose of this book—namely, to present a number of affordable and fun projects you can do with a gas or semiconductor laser. If you are serious about lasers and want to learn more, see Appendix B for a list of suggested further reading. A number of the books provide a technical, even scholarly, discourse on laser principles.

2

Working with Lasers

For the uninitiated, the thought of working with lasers means wearing dark tinted goggles and heavy lead-lined gloves while sitting in a concrete, air-conditioned bungalow. Behind a six-inch glass partition are several lab assistants, complete with white coats, clipboards, and solemn faces. Giant computers and monitoring equipment adorn the laser laboratory, soaking up enough electricity to light up Las Vegas. Is that a strain of Hollywood B-movie music in the background? Any moment now a mad scientist will come out and begin the final phase of his quest for world power.

The movies have done a considerable job selling a false and overly dramatic view of lasers (witness the James Bond classic ''Goldfinger''). On the contrary, the kinds of lasers available to the electronics hobbyist are so low in power that protective measures are unnecessary. The light radiation emitted by a helium-neon laser isn't even strong enough to be felt on skin.

Of course, precautions must still be taken, but for the most part, experimenting with lasers can be done in the comfort of the family living room, under normal temperatures, and with no more electrical power than the current from a set of flashlight batteries.

This doesn't mean hobby lasers are completely harmless. As with all electrical devices, some dangers exist, and it's vitally important that you understand these dangers and know how to avoid them. In this chapter, you'll learn about what you need to know to competently work with lasers, the basics of laser safety, and how to protect yourself and others from accidental injury.

BASIC SKILLS

What skills do you need as a laser experimenter? Certainly, if you are already well-versed in electronics and mechanical design, you are on your way to becoming a laser experimenter *extraordinaire*. But an intimate knowledge of neither electronics nor mechanical design is absolutely necessary.

All you really need to start yourself in the right direction as a laser experimenter is a basic familiarity with electronic theory and mechanics. The rest you can learn as you go. If you feel that you are lacking in either beginning electronics or mechanics, pick up a book or two on these subjects at the bookstore or library. See Appendix B for a selected list of suggested further reading.

Electronics Background

Study analog and digital electronic theory, and learn the function of resistors, capacitors, transistors, and other common electronic components. Your mastery of the subject does not need to be extensive but just enough so that you can build and troubleshoot electronic circuits for your laser systems. You'll start out with simple circuits and a minimum of parts and go from there. As your skills increase, you'll be able to design your own circuits from scratch, or at the very least, customize existing circuits to match your needs.

Schematic diagrams are a kind of recipe for electronic circuits. The designs in this book, as well as most any book that deals with electronics, are in schematic form. If you don't know already, you owe it to yourself to learn how to read a schematic diagram. There are really only a dozen or so common schematic symbols, and memorizing them takes just one evening of concentrated study. A number of books have been written on how to read schematic diagrams (see Appendix B).

Sophisticated laser systems use computers for process control. If you wish to experiment with these control circuits, you need to have at least some awareness of how computers operate. Although an in-depth knowledge of computers and program-ming is not required, you should have rudimentary knowledge of computers and the way computers manipulate data.

Mechanical Background

The majority of us are far more comfortable with the mechanical side of hobby laser building than the electronic side. It's far easier to see how a motor and lever work than to see how a laser tachometer operates. Whether or not you are comfortable with mechanical design, you do not need to possess a worldly knowledge of mechanical theory. Still, you should be comfortable with mechanical and electro-mechanical components such as motors and solenoids.

The Workshop Aptitude

To be a successful laser hobbyist, you must be comfortable with working with your hands and thinking problems through from start to finish. You should know how to use common shop tools and have some basic familiarity in working with wood, lightweight metals, and plastic.

LASER SAFETY

Lasers that are sold and used commercially are subject to compliance with a strict set of laws enforced by the Center for Devices and Radiological Health (CDRH, formerly the Bureau of Radiological Health, or BRH). The CDRH, a department of the Food and Drug Administration, serves a similar purpose as the Federal Communications Commission: to ensure that products comply with recognized standards and that the dangers of laser radiation are kept to a minimum.

For regulatory purposes, the CDRH has divided lasers into six groups, or classes. The classification of lasers depends on their power output (in joules or watts), their emission duration, and their wavelength. The classification is then affixed as a sticker to the laser, such as the one shown in FIG. 2-1.

✯ Class I applies to devices that have emissions in the ultraviolet, visible, and infrared regions of the electromagnetic spectrum, below which biological hazards have not been established (in other words, generally "harmless"). A helium-neon laser (at 632.8 nm), operating at less than a few microwatts, would be considered a Class I device.

FIG. 2-1. *This Class III helium-neon laser sticker is placed near the output of the laser and warns of possible danger to direct exposure to beam. The warning sticker is required of all commercially manufactured lasers, regardless of power output.*

★ Class IIa applies to products whose light output does not exceed Class I limits for emission duration of 1,000 seconds or less but are not intended for direct viewing. One example of a class IIa device is a hand-held bar-code scanner. Emission of Class IIa lasers is confined to wavelengths between 400 and 710 nm (visible spectrum).

★ Class II devices are identical to Class I lasers, except the permissible wavelengths are confined to visible light between 400 and 710 nm and the beam may not be on or motionless for a period greater than ¼ second. Power output can be as high as 1 milliwatt.

★ Class IIIa lasers comprise a large group of visible light devices (400 nm to 710 nm) with power outputs less than 5 milliwatts. Class IIIa lasers consist of most helium-neon lasers (the old BRH standards classified these He-Ne's as Class IIIb).

★ Class IIIb applies to devices that emit ultraviolet, visible, and infrared spectra. Class IIIb lasers can have power outputs ranging from 5 to 500 milliwatts in the visible spectrum; less if the beam is invisible. A low-output argon laser (100 mW for example) used in small light shows would be considered a Class IIIb product.

★ Class IV represents the "laser brutes." These devices exceed the limits of the other classes. The CDRH classifies a laser as a Class IV device if it produces light radiation (visible or invisible) that is dangerous to eyes and flesh whether or not the beam is direct, reflected, or diffused. CO_2, ruby, Nd:glass, and multi-watt gas lasers (such as 3- to 5-watt argons) fall into the Class IV umbrella.

Much of the laser components available on the surplus market do not comply with CDRH standards, although a few do. If they are in compliance, you will see a sticker, such as the one in the figure, affixed somewhere on the device. Note that individual components may not in themselves comply with the CDRH regulations, even though the device from which they were taken meets the standards.

Most of the CDRH regulations pertain to such simple functions as:

★ Placing the proper sticker(s) on the device.
★ Covering the power supply during operation.
★ Providing a power supply interlock that shuts the supply off if the case is opened.
★ Inserting a key switch in the power supply mains to prevent unauthorized use.
★ Adding a cover or slide to the output mirror to prevent accidental exposure to the beam when the laser is operating.
★ Providing adequate instructions for the user. In all cases, user information and basic service information are required.

Several of the projects in this book show you how to meet these compliance standards. As an experimenter working alone, however, the CDRH regulations do not strictly apply to you. As long as there is no danger of exposing others to harmful radiation or high voltages, you may do as you wish. It's up to you to decide if you want to add the safety features to your own, personal laser projects.

If you plan on developing laser systems for use by others or for use in public places (such as laser light shows), you need to be sure that you comply with all the pertinent regulations. Otherwise, you might be subject to fines. There is not enough room in this book to reprint the full text of regulations, but you can obtain a copy of the CDRH laser requirements (Part 1040 of Food and Drug Administration regulations) by writing to the bureau (there may be a publication or distribution charge—check first). Their address is provided in Appendix A. Be sure to state the section and topic of your inquiry. If you plan on producing a light show, you must file a variance and indicate the type of equipment and safeguards you plan on using.

LASER LIGHT RADIATION

Lasers emit electromagnetic radiation, usually either visible light or infrared. The level of "radiation" is generally quite small in hobby lasers and has about the same effect on external bodily tissues as sunning yourself with the living room lamp.

Skin is fairly resilient, even to exposure to several tens or hundreds of watts of laser energy. But the eye is much more susceptible to damage, and it is the effects of laser light on the retina that is the greatest concern. Even as little as 20 to 50 milliwatts of focused visible or infrared radiation can cause temporary and perhaps permanent blindness.

The longer the exposure to the radiation and the more focused the beam, the greater the chance that the laser will cause a lesion on the surface of the retina. Retinal lesions can heal, but many leave blind spots. In the worst case, with a laser that puts out a minimum of 100 to 200 milliwatts (such as an argon laser used in light shows), a constant exposure of a few seconds or more on the optic nerve of the retina can cause total blindness.

Retinal damage when using hobby lasers—those with outputs of less than 5 or 10 milliwatts—is rare. In fact, there have been only a handful of reported accidents involving lasers in the several decades since they became available, and many of these have involved electrocution by the high-voltage power supply, not exposure to the laser beam.

One reason laser radiation accidents are rare is the same reason that astronomers don't go blind looking through their telescopes. They know it's foolish to stare at the sun through even a low-power telescope, but if they did, the pain in their eyes would signal a potentially dangerous situation to the brain, and the eyelids would instinctively clamp shut.

Obviously, solar study through telescopes or staring down the shaft of a laser beam are not hobbies you would normally indulge in, but a potential danger still lies in accidental exposure. The effects of exposure of bright lights on the eyes are cumulative. Making a habit of carelessly shining a laser into your eyes only increases the chance of eye problems later on in life.

The Dangers of Focused Laser Light

Laser light is the most dangerous to the eyes when it is focused into a sharp point. The beam of the typical helium-neon laser, as it exits the tube, is about 0.8 millimeter in diameter. A simple lens system can focus the beam to a much smaller diameter of about 10 micrometers (10 millionths of a meter). This is equivalent to one hundredth of a millimeter, so the beam has been reduced by a factor of about 100. The output of the laser has not increased, but the energy is focused onto a much smaller area.

Laser Goggles

The welder uses tinted dark goggles to block the bright light emitted from the torch and melting metal. A pair of laser goggles can help prevent much of the light produced by a laser from reaching your eyes, even if the beam is inadvertently directed toward you.

Laser goggles, such as the ones in FIG. 2-2, are not an absolute necessity when experimenting with low power He-Ne and semiconductor lasers, though you will want a pair if your experiments often cause the beam to strike your eyes. Even with goggles, you should avoid direct exposure to the laser light. Some of the light can penetrate the goggles, and depending on the power output of the laser, can still be dangerous.

In all cases, you should use goggles when working with Class IV high-power lasers, such as ruby, Nd:glass and CO_2. Laser goggles are manufactured to restrict light at only a certain light wavelength, such as 332 nm (neon-nitrogen), 694.3 nm (ruby), and 840 nm (gallium arsenide). You must specify the wavelength or laser when ordering. Be aware that laser goggles are expensive; a new pair can cost over $100. A few laser goggles are designed to block a series of wavelengths and can be used effectively with many types of lasers.

The Invisible Ray

Infrared lasers pose a different threat, in that the light they produce cannot be readily seen. Don't be fooled by the false sense of security that just because you can't see the

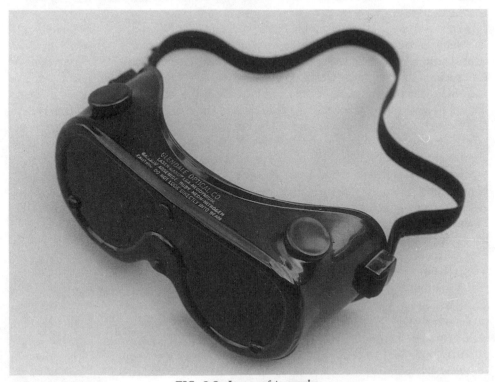

FIG. 2-2. *Laser safety goggles.*

beam that it isn't there—and won't harm your eyes. You might not know you are staring down a beam delivering 10 to 40 watts of pulsed infrared radiation until your vision becomes blurry and you see dark spots.

Most infrared lasers, particularly the semiconductor variety, emit *near-infrared* radiation. Most laser diodes emit light in the region between 780 and 904 nm. If you look directly at the laser you *might* see a faint red glow. Do not look at this light for an extended period, particularly if the beam has been collimated or focused. The visible glow might be dim, but the actual light output of the laser could be quite high.

A pulsed laser diode can easily deliver 5 to 10 watts of energy; many produce up to 50 watts of pulsed energy. Though the beam is pulsed, the repetition rate is very fast and appears as a steady stream. You can be assured that continual observation of a focused, 10-watt beam will cause at least some damage to the eye.

HIGH-VOLTAGE ELECTROCUTION

The latest semiconductor lasers operate from low-voltage dc power packs. A number of projects later in this book show how to construct semiconductor laser diode systems using flashlight batteries. These laser systems pose no threat of shock.

On the other hand, all gas lasers, including the popular helium-neon variety, require high-voltage power supplies. These power supplies boost the mains voltage from 12 volts dc or 117 volts ac to several thousand volts. The typical 12-volt-dc laser power supply produces up to 3,000 volts dc, an extraordinary amount when you consider that the electric chair puts out only 2,000 volts!

Some laser experimenters tend to disregard the high voltages. They assume that although the voltage is high, the current level is low. They rely on the old maxim "It's the volts that jolts but its the mills that kills." This is true but limited thinking. The current demand of the typical helium-neon laser is low, between 3 and 7 milliwatts. At normal dc levels (5 or 12 volts), this current is not enough to be felt. But at the 1.2 to 3 kV level of standard laser operating voltages, even a 7-milliwatt jolt can, depending on the circumstances, kill you.

Laser power supplies should be properly shielded and insulated. Avoid operating a power supply in the open, and always cover exposed high-voltage parts. Insulating material such as high-voltage putty (available at TV repair shops and electronic stores) restricts arcing and provides a relatively shock-proof layer. It's easy to forget that several thousand volts are coursing through a wire, and you might inadvertently touch it or brush across it. Even a direct contact is not necessary. A 3 kV arc can jump a quarter of an inch or more, and, like lightning, discharge on the nearest object. If that object happens to be your fingers or elbow, you will receive a painful shock.

Admittedly, most shocks from laser power supplies won't kill you, nor will they burn your skin. But don't underestimate the power of low-current high voltages. Your body's protective mechanism automatically reacts to the jolt. If you touch a live wire with your hand, your body quickly contracts to prevent further shock. If the jolt is large enough, you may be knocked backward onto the ground. Should you be holding the laser tube at the time, you might drop and shatter it, which adds the risk of cutting yourself on top of it all. Sound like the voice of experience? It is.

Phantom Current

Most laser power supplies use high-voltage capacitors at the output stage. Like all capacitors, these can retain current even after the power supply has been turned off. Though many laser supplies use bleeder resistors that drain the capacitors after power has been removed, not all do. Play it safe and assume that the output of any power supply—plugged-in or not—is potentially hot.

When working with the laser, make sure the power supply is off, then temporarily short the leads of the power supply together, or simply touch the positive terminal of the supply to ground (see FIG. 2-3). That will discharge any remaining current, making the power supply safe to work on. Likewise, the laser tube behaves like a Leyden jar, which is a type of capacitor. It, too, can retain a current after power has been removed. Drain the remaining charge by shorting the terminals or leads together.

High Voltage Precautions

Take these simple steps to avoid unnecessary shocks:

✶ Do not apply power to the laser until all the high-voltage wires and components are shielded or insulated.

✶ Do not work near a laser that has high-voltage components exposed.

✶ Provide an interlock switch to protect against accidental electrocution when servicing the laser.

✶ Discharge the tube and power supply to avoid shock after power has been removed.

✶ Affix a "Danger—High Voltage" sticker to the power supply and tube to warn others that high voltages are present.

✶ Install a power key switch to prevent unauthorized use.

✶ Never leave the laser or power supply unattended. A laser is not a toy, and children should not be allowed to use one without your supervision. For maximum security, lock the laser in a desk or filing cabinet to prevent unauthorized use.

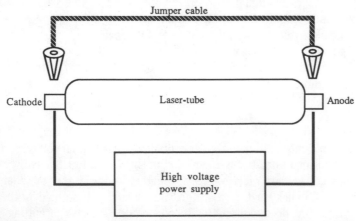

FIG. 2-3. *For safety's sake, always discharge the static remaining in a gas laser by shorting the terminals with a jumper cable (be sure power is removed first!). If you can't reach both terminals, short the anode to ground.*

Ac Electrocution

Some laser supplies and laser projects operate from the 117-volt ac house current. Observe the same precautions when working with ac circuits. A live ac wire can, and does, kill! Exercise caution whenever working with ac circuits and observe all safety precautions. If you are new to electronics and aren't sure what these precautions are, refer to Appendix B for a list of books that can help you broaden your knowledge.

You can greatly minimize the hazards of working with ac circuits by following these basic guidelines:

★ Always keep ac circuits covered.

★ Keep ac circuits physically separate from low-voltage dc circuits.

★ All ac power supplies should have fuse protection on the incoming hot line. The fuse should be adequately rated for the circuit but should allow a fail-safe margin in case of short circuit.

★ When troubleshooting ac circuitry, keep one hand in your pocket at all times. Use the other hand to manipulate the voltmeter or oscilloscope probe. Avoid the situation where one hand touches ground and the other a live circuit. The ac flows from one hand to the other, through your heart.

★ When possible, place ac circuits in an insulated Bakelite or plastic chassis. Avoid the use of metal chassis.

★ Double- and triple-check your work before applying power. If you can, have someone else inspect your handiwork before you switch the circuit on for the first time.

★ Periodically inspect ac circuits for worn, broken, or loose wires and components, and make any repairs necessary.

PROJECTS SAFETY

A number of the projects in this book require work with potentially hazardous materials, including glass, razor blades, and wood and metal tools. Glass and mirror-cutting should be done only with the proper tools and safety precautions. Wear eye protection whenever you are working with glass. If you can, wear gloves when handling cut glass and mirrors. Finish the edges with a burnisher, flame, or piece of masking tape.

Razor blades provide a well-defined and accurate edge and are helpful in a number of optical experiments. You need new, unused blades; nicks and blemishes on the blade surface can impair your results. Obviously, you must exercise extreme care when handling razor blades.

One good way to handle razor blades is to coat the edges of the blade with a soft wax or masking tape. When you are ready to position and use the blade, peel off the wax or tape. When cutting with razor blades, wear eye protection and gloves. For maximum safety, place the blade behind a large piece of clear plastic. If any pieces break off during cutting, the plastic will protect your body.

An optional experiment in Chapter 22 involves the use of liquid nitrogen, a cryogenic gas that has a temperature of minus 196 degrees Celsius. While liquid nitrogen is non-flammable and non-toxic, its extremely cold temperature can cause frost-bite burns. You should handle liquid nitrogen only in an approved container (a Thermos bottle with a hole drilled in the cap often works), waterproof gloves, and eye protection. Follow the recommendations and handling precautions given in Chapter 22 for more details. When treated properly, liquid nitrogen is safe and actually fun to use.

Construction plans require the use of wood- and metal-working tools. You can use hand or power tools; either way, carefully follow all operating procedures and use the tools with caution. Most power tools provide some type of safety mechanisms so don't defeat them! Thoroughly read the instruction manual that came with the tool. A number of good books have been written on wood and metal working and the tools involved. Check your library for available titles.

Common sense is the best shield against accidents, but common sense can't be taught or written about in a book. It's up to you to develop common sense and use it at all times. Never let down your guard. The laser projects in this book are provided for your education and enjoyment. Don't ruin the fun of a wonderful hobby or vocation because you neglected a few safety measures.

3

Introduction to Optics

Optics are an integral part of laser experiments. They allow you to manipulate the beam in ways similar to how electronic components control the flow of current through a circuit. In this chapter, you'll learn about optics and how they effect laser light. You'll also learn how to care for, clean, and store optics in order to preserve their light-manipulating characteristics. While the following text only scratches the surface of optics, it provides a clear understanding of the fundamentals and helps you start on your way to using optics in your own laser projects.

FUNDAMENTALS OF THE SIMPLE LENS

The speed of light in a vacuum is a constant, which is precisely 299,792.5 kilometers per second or 186,282 miles per second. By definition, a vacuum means the absence of matter; when matter is introduced, light slows down, because the beam of light actually bends. Imagine a ray of light as a line traversing from the sun to the Earth, as in FIG. 3-1. When the ray of light strikes the boundary between vacuum and matter (in this case air), the ray bends.

This is *refraction*, and it occurs whenever light passes through two mediums of different densities (a vacuum has no density; all matter has some density). The angle of the bend depends on three factors:

★ The density of the media.
★ The wavelength of the light.
★ The direction of light travel, whether it is passing from a less dense medium to a thicker one, or vice versa.

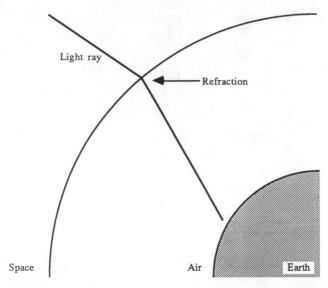

FIG. 3-1. *The effect of refraction on a ray of light entering the Earth's atmosphere.*

Refraction Based on Density

Light rays bend more in heavy density media. The amount of bending is called the *index of refraction*, which is calculated by dividing the density of the medium by that of a vacuum. A vacuum has a refractive index of 1; glass has a refractive index of about 1.6 (depending on the glass); and air has a refractive index of 1.0003. Note that the exact index of refraction for these and other media also depends on temperature, barometric pressure, and impurities, but not on thickness. Forgetting that the atmosphere gets thinner at higher altitudes, one foot of air has the same index of refraction as one mile of air. The slow-down of light rays through a refractive medium is not cumulative, where the light might eventually stop.

Refraction Based on Wavelength

Longer wavelengths of light bend less than shorter wavelengths. As you can see in the chart in FIG. 3-2, red light has a longer wavelength than violet light. If you were to direct a beam of red light through a refracting medium, such as water, its angle of bend would be less than that for a beam of violet light. Of course, this is how a prism, discussed more fully later in this chapter, breaks up white light into its component colors.

Refraction Based on Direction of Light Travel

Draw a line that bisects the border between two different media. Now draw a line at a right angle to the border, as shown in FIG. 3-3. This new line is called *line normal*, and is an important concept in optics. When a ray of light passes from a less dense medium to a more dense one, *the ray bends towards line normal*. The reverse is true when light passes from a dense medium to a less dense one: *The ray bends away from line normal*. So you can refer to this important concept more easily, let's summarize it. We'll use the terms ''rare'' and ''dense'' medium to denote less dense and more dense.

★ Rare-to-dense transition: light bends towards line normal.
★ Dense-to-rare transition: light bends away from line normal.

LENSES AS REFRACTIVE MEDIA

Lenses are refractive media constructed in a way so that light bends in a particular way. The refractive index of a lens is determined by its chemical makeup. Some lenses refract light more strongly than others. Two common lens glasses are *Schott* and *crown*. At the green light wavelengths of the middle (approximately 546 nm), Schott glass has a refractive index of 1.79 and crown glass has a refractive index of 1.52. Both crown and Schott glass lenses can be used separately or together.

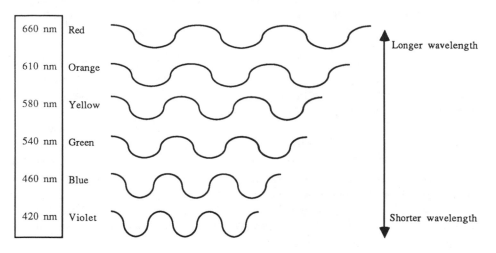

FIG. 3-2. *All colors have a specific wavelength; the wavelength increases as the colors approach the red end of the spectrum.*

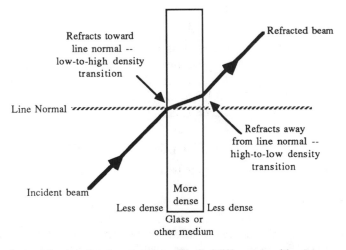

FIG. 3-3. *Light always refracts as it enters or exits mediums of different densities. Line normal shows the effect of refraction in relation to change in density.*

29

Unless you are a manufacturer of optics equipment like microscopes, telescopes, and binoculars, you won't know the exact makeup of the lenses you buy. Rather, you'll be concerned with three other lens specifications:

★ lens shape
★ lens focal length
★ lens diameter

Lens Shape

More than anything else, the *shape of the lens* determines how light is refracted through it. A flat piece of glass, although still a refractive medium, will bend all the light rays going through it equally. You won't see an apparent change when looking through the glass at some object on the other side (although you can experiment with the effects of refraction through a plane of glass with a laser, as described in Chapter 9).

But if you make the glass thicker in the middle than at the edges, light rays striking the glass are refracted at different angles. Why? Is it not the thickness of the glass that is causing the difference in the bending of light, but the difference in the direction of line normal throughout the radius of the glass.

Take a look at FIG. 3-4 for a better view. The lens curves at the edges, so line normal is bent away from the incoming light rays (assuming parallel light rays). The rays are traveling through a rare-to-dense transition, so the light is bent towards line normal. Because line normal is at a greater angle at the outer radius of the lens than it is at the middle, the rays at the edges are deflected more. Now, when you look through the glass—which in this form is more accurately called a lens—an object on the other side takes on a different appearance. Depending on how close you hold the lens to your eye, the object appears larger than it really is.

There are numerous shapes of lenses, and each shape manipulates light in a slightly different way. The next section discusses these shapes in more detail and how they are used.

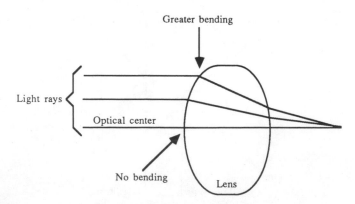

FIG. 3-4. *A lens is a piece of glass whose curvature bends light rays in a certain direction and amount. A common application for a lens is to focus parallel light rays to a point, as shown here.*

Lens Focal Length

The precise definition of *lens focal length* is rather involved and beyond the scope of this book but for our purposes, it is sufficient to say that the focal length of a lens is the distance from the lens where rays are brought to a common point. Rays entering one side of the lens are refracted so that they converge at a common point. Measuring the distance from the optical center of the lens to this point gives you the focal length. Later in this chapter, you'll learn that this definition applies to only certain kinds of lenses. Others behave in an almost opposite manner.

Focal length is an important consideration, because it tells you how much the lens is refracting light. A short focal length means that the light rays are brought to a point very quickly, so the rays must be heavily refracted in the lens. A long focal length means that the rays are gradually brought to a point and that the amount of refraction is mild. You choose a lens of particular focal length depending on the task you want to perform.

Lens Diameter

The *diameter of the lens* determines its light gathering capability. The larger the lens, the more light it collects. For example, you use the largest lens possible at the end of a telescope to bring distant planets and galaxies into view. In laser work, however, bigger isn't always better. The field of view of a laser beam is finite. That means you are interested in dealing with just the pencil-thin beam of the laser and nothing more.

Because the lenses can be small, it's easy to build compact laser optical systems. And perhaps more important to the hobbyist, smaller lenses are much cheaper than larger ones. Most of the lenses you purchase for your laser experiments should be surplus or seconds, but, the preference for small size pays off. Large, unblemished lenses are a rarity in the surplus lens market, and most of the big ones are usually practically useless for anything but paperweights anyway. In addition, most optics experimenters are mainly interested in large surplus lenses for components in telescopes, home-made projectors, and camera attachments. They tend to ignore the smaller ones, so you will probably have more to choose from.

LENS TYPES

There are six major types of lenses, as shown in FIG. 3-5. But before taking a look at each type of lens, let's define the meaning of plano, convex, concave, and meniscus.

- ★ *Plano* means flat.
- ★ *Convex* means curving outward (with respect to the other side of the lens).
- ★ *Concave* means curving inward (with respect to the other side of the lens).
- ★ *Meniscus* means curving in on one side and curving out on the other.

The combinations such as plano-convex and double-concave refer to each side of the lens. A plano-convex lens is flat on one side and curves outward on the other. A double-concave lens curves inward on both sides. Negative and positive refer to the focal point of the lens, as determined by its design. In actuality, all lenses are either positive or negative, but only meniscus lenses come in both flavors.

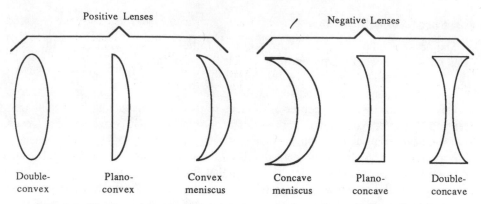

FIG. 3-5. *The six major types of lenses, broken into sub-groups of positive and negative.*

Lenses form two kinds of images: *real* and *virtual*. A real image is one that is focused to a point in front of the lens, such as the image of the sun focused to a small disc on a piece of paper. A virtual image is one that doesn't come to a discrete focus. You see a virtual image behind the lens, as when you are using a lens as a magnifying glass. Positive lenses, which magnify the size of an object, create both real and virtual images. Their focal length is stated as a positive number. Negative images, which reduce the size of an object, create only virtual images. Their focal length is stated as a negative number.

Lenses converge or diverge light. When light is *converged*, the rays are brought together at a common point. When light is *diverged*, it is spread out and the rays don't meet. The capacity to converge or diverge light also depends on the pattern of the light before it enters the lens.

In most cases when dealing with lasers, the light is *collimated*; that is, all of the light rays are traveling parallel (in actuality, the beam is spreading slowly, but the amount is small compared to the light from other sources). In some instances, however, the rays are diverging (spreading), and a given lens can serve to collimate the light (make it parallel).

All lenses have an *optical center*, that is typically in the middle of the lens. Refraction is absent or minimal at the optical center and increases with radius. In most lenses, refraction is the strongest at the outside edge of the lens.

Plano Convex

As noted above, a *plano convex* lens is flat on one side and curved outward on the other. Plano convex lenses have positive focal lengths; that is, they magnify an image when you look through them. Plano-convex lenses converge incident light to a common focal point and they form real or virtual images. They are most often used in telescopes, optical receivers and transmitters, and other applications where it is desirable to focus a beam of light to a common point.

Double-Convex

Double-convex lenses bulge out on both sides. The amount of curvature is typically the same for both sides, but not always. A double-convex lens that is the same on both sides is symmetrical. A lens that has different curvatures is asymmetrical.

Symmetrical lenses are often desired because they suffer from less distortion (covered later in this chapter). Like the plano-convex lens, double-convex lenses have positive focal lengths and converge light to a common point. They create both real and virtual images. Typically, a double-convex lens of a particular diameter has a shorter focal point (higher magnification) than a plano-convex lens of the same size.

Positive Meniscus

A meniscus lens has one surface concave (curved inward) and the other surface convex (curved outward). In a *positive meniscus* lens, the center of the lens is thicker than the edges (the reverse is true in a negative meniscus lens).

A meniscus lens is most often used with another lens to produce a device of a longer or shorter focal length than just the original lens used alone. For example, a positive meniscus lens can be used behind a plano-convex lens to shorten the effective focal length of the optical system. You can also use a positive meniscus lens as a magnifier; like the plano-convex and bi-convex lenses, they converge light rays to a common point, magnify images, and have a positive focal length.

Plano Concave

The *plano-concave* lens is flat on one side and curved inward on the other. Plano-concave lenses have negative focal lengths and diverge (spread) a beam of collimated light. They form virtual images only. Plano concave lenses are often used to expand a laser beam so that it covers a larger area, or they can be used to increase the focal length of optical equipment, such as telescopes.

Double-Concave

Double-concave lenses curve inward on both sides, and are similar in function and application as plano concave lenses. They have negative focal points so they create virtual images only; a double-concave lens can't be used to focus light at a common point.

Negative Meniscus

In a *negative meniscus* lens, the center of the lens is thinner than the edges. See the section above on positive meniscus lenses for a description of possible uses.

Lens Combinations

Lenses are often grouped together to manipulate the light in a way that can't be done by using just one lens alone. As discussed in the section on meniscus lenses, for instance, two or more lenses can be combined to shorten or lengthen the focal length of an optical device. Lenses can also be combined, usually by physical bonding with optically clear cement, to reduce or eliminate aberrations. These aberrations can distort the image or color rendition and are particularly annoying in systems that use large lenses (such as telescopes).

One lens used alone is a *singlet*. The majority of lenses are singlets, but they can be combined with others to create more complicated optical structures. Two lenses used together are called a *doublet* (or duplet); three lenses are called a *triplet*. Often, but not always, the individual lenses that make up a doublet or triplet are made of different substances, each with a different index of refraction.

Because of the monochromatic and pencil-thin nature of laser light, most lenses for laser projects needn't be anything more than singlets. Certain aberrations, particularly those that deal with the problems of faithful color reproduction, aren't of major concern to the laser enthusiast.

LENS COATINGS

The physics of optics says that even under the best circumstances, about 4 percent of incident light on a piece of glass (including a lens) will be reflected. The remaining 96 percent is passed through. This percentage varies depending on the angle of incidence. Reflectance is increased at the outer edges of a convex lens, for example, because the light strikes the lens surface at a greater angle.

The least expensive lenses are composed of bare glass with no special coating. An optical system that uses many uncoated lenses will suffer from an appreciable amount of light loss due to reflection. These reflections must go someplace, and they often strike the inner walls of the optical device or are bounced around in an unpredictable manner. Such reflections decrease contrast and cause flaring, ghosting, and other imperfections.

A thin coating of magnesium fluoride or some other material can decrease reflection to only 1.5 percent or so. That means 98.5 percent or more of the light passes through the lens. The coating applied to better quality lenses helps reduce unwanted reflection, and can also allow only one particular portion of the light spectrum to pass through.

Lens coatings take many forms, and the very expensive lenses have complex, multi-layer coatings applied in specific thicknesses (usually ¼ wavelength of visible light). Unless you order a coated lens directly from a lens manufacturer, you probably won't know the type of antireflection (AR) coating used. You can, however, tell if a lens is coated by tilting it at a 45-degree angle and looking at the reflected light. Coated optics designed to work with visible light have a blue or purplish hue to them. Often, but not always, lenses will be coated on both sides.

THE FUNCTION OF MIRRORS

Mirrors are used in laser experiments to re-direct a beam, to mix a beam with other light sources, and a number of other tasks. Mirrors differ in their reflective material, amount of reflection, flatness, and location of the reflective surface.

The Principles of Reflection

Recall the concept of line normal from the previous discussion of refraction. Line normal is also used in the analysis of reflection. The principle of reflection is simple: the angle of reflectance, in relation to line normal, is equal to the angle of incidence. That is, if you bounce a beam of light off a mirror at a 45-degree angle to line normal, the reflected ray will also be at a 45-degree angle. The reflected ray will be on the opposite side of line normal as the incident ray.

Front or Back Reflective Surface

Most household mirrors consist of a coat of silver applied to the rear side of a sheet of glass. To prevent tarnishing, a lacquer is applied over the silvering. Such a mirror is called *rear-surface* (also back or second surface), because the reflective material is applied to the rear of the glass.

If you look carefully at a back-surface mirror, you'll see two reflections: one from the silver and one from the front of the glass. The amount of reflection from the glass is small—about four to five percent—but it's enough to cause a ghost image when the mirror is used in fine optical equipment. Shining a laser on a mirror produces two beams: the main beam from the silver reflective surface and a ghost beam from the front of the glass.

Front-surface mirrors are coated with a reflective substance on the front of the glass. Looking closely at light reflected from a front-surface mirror, you see only one image — from just the reflective surface. There is no ghost because the glass substrate is behind the reflective layer.

Unless you're after an unusual effect or purposely trying to create image ghosts, you will always use front-surface mirrors in your laser projects. Front-surface mirrors are harder to find than ordinary back-surface mirrors, and they are more difficult to care for. Sources for front-surface mirrors, as well as all optical components discussed in this book, can be found in Appendix A. Look for local sources of front-surface mirrors; check the Yellow Pages under (guess what?!) "Mirrors." Call around until you find what you want. But before you do, be sure to read the section on buying optics below.

Reflective Coatings—Metal

Silver is seldom used as the reflective layer on front-surface mirrors because the exposed metal is liable to tarnish. However, some high-grade mirrors that require excellent reflection at all visible light wavelengths use silver front-surface mirrors that are protected with a thin, optically transparent overcoat.

The most common reflective material of front-surface mirrors is aluminum. Like silver mirrors, many front-surface aluminum mirrors are protected against scratches and marring by a clear overcoating. This overcoating must be optically pure and must be applied in precise layers, usually at a thickness equaling ¼ wavelength of green light (the middle of the spectrum).

Gold-coated mirrors provide the maximum amount of reflection at all visible wavelengths. The gold coating is soft and easily scratched, so a top coating is necessary. Again, the coating is applied in precise layers.

Reflective Coatings—Dielectric

Dielectric (non-electrically conducting) coatings are often used in mirrors designed for use in laser systems. A dielectric coating is extremely thin and semi-transparent and is applied to the glass substrate in a series of layers. The coating reflects light because its index of refraction is higher than that of the substrate (glass) underneath. The amount of reflection varies depending on the angle of incidence, coating type, and thickness of the coating.

Most dielectric coatings are sensitive to wavelength, making the mirrors suitable for different applications. Dielectrically coated mirrors designed for argon lasers have a different coating than those for helium-neon and diode lasers. If given a choice, you should pick the mirror coated for the type of laser you are using.

Note that the mirrors used in a helium-neon laser cavity are most often dielectrically coated. While light passing through these mirrors appears blue, light reflecting off the mirrors appears gold (or blue at some angles). The thickness of the dielectric coating, and hence the degree of reflectivity, is different for the two mirrors. One mirror is designed so that it reflects all or most of the light incident on it. The other mirror is designed so that only some of the light is reflected; the remaining portion passes through as the exiting laser beam.

Amount of Reflection

Even without a coating, glass will reflect about 4 percent of light when the rays are incident at an angle between about 0 and 30 degrees from the surface. Reflectance jumps considerably as the angle of incidence increases. At grazing incidence, reflection approaches 100 percent.

Although plate glass can be used as a kind of mirror, the exact amount of reflection is hard to control, especially without precision mounting equipment. Coatings are used to provide a known reflectance. The reflectance varies depending on the coating, coating thickness, and angle of incidence. Some mirrors are made to be 100 percent reflective at all angles. These generally use silver or aluminum reflective layers. Gold and dielectric coatings tend to be semi-transparent at angles of incidence other than 0 degrees.

OTHER OPTICAL COMPONENTS

There are numerous other optical components you can use in your laser-system building endeavors. Here is short rundown of the more popular ones.

Prisms

Most people learn about *prisms* in grade school as devices to break white light into its component colors. This breakup is more accurately called *dispersion,* as shown in FIG. 3-6, and is caused by refraction. As you learned earlier in this chapter, the longer the wavelength of light, the less it bends due to refraction.

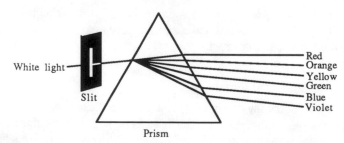

FIG. 3-6. *A prism refracts (or disperses) white light into its constituent colors. Dispersion allows you to use a prism with white light as a "rainbow maker."*

Prisms are used in laser systems for several important functions:

★ To disperse a multi-line laser beam into its component colors. You'd use a prism to separate the green and blue colors in an argon laser, for example.

★ To redirect a beam at some angle, as with a mirror.

★ To polarize a beam of laser light and direct it in one or more directions.

The most familiar type is the *equilateral prism* that is used mostly to disperse light but also to bend light at some angle. Viewed edge-on, an equilateral prism is an equilateral triangle with 60-degree angles between the equal faces.

Another common type is the *right angle prism* (one angle is 90 degrees; the others are typically 60 and 30 degrees). Right-angle prisms are designed primarily to direct light at a 90-degree angle; other angles are possible by varying the incident angle of the incoming light beam. A prism is often preferred over a mirror when vibration or stress are problems. The prism is a solid piece of glass and withstands mechanical stress better than a mirror. Right-angle prisms can use either an aluminized or coated hypotenuse or total internal reflection to bounce the light between the entrance and exit faces.

A *roof* or *amici roof prism* deflects light through a 90-degree angle. The roof prism is similar to a right-angle prism and almost always uses an uncoated hypotenuse. A *porro prism* (or retroflector) resembles a right-angle prism but is used to turn light around 180 degrees—it's sent back to where it came from. The light enters the hypotenuse of the prism, strikes one side, bounces off the opposite side, and is redirected out the hypotenuse.

Beam Splitters

A *beam splitter* does as its name implies: it takes one beam and divides it into two. Most beam splitters are also beam combiners—when positioned properly, the beam splitter can combine the light from two sources into one shaft of light.

Beam splitters come in two forms: cube and plate glass. Both are shown in FIG. 3-7. *Cube beam splitters* are made by cementing together two right-angle prisms so that their common hypotenuses touch. Usually, some form of reflective or polarizing layer is added at the joint. Anti-reflection coatings are typically applied to the entrance and exit faces to reduce light loss. The basic operation of the cube beam splitter is shown in FIG. 3-8A.

Note that the cube can be made to act as several beam splitters, depending on the coating at the hypotenuse. In many cube beam splitters, an entrance face can also act as an exit face. Most cube beam splitters divide the light equally between the two exit faces. These are called 50/50 beam splitters — 50 percent of the light goes out one face and 50 percent goes out the other (in actuality, less than 50 percent exits the cube at each face due to inherent reflection and transmission losses).

Plate beam splitters use a flat piece of glass to reflect and pass light. Although you can use an uncoated piece of glass, the best plate beam splitters are those designed for the job. An anti-reflection coating is applied to the glass to control the amount of reflection. Plate beam splitters can be made to transmit and reflect light equally (50/50) or unequally. Common ratios are 10/90 (10 percent reflection, 90 percent transmission) and 25/75 (25 percent reflection, 75 percent transmission).

Plate beam splitters often suffer from satellite images—you get two reflected beams instead of one. The first spot of light, as shown in FIG. 3-8B, is the primary beam (the one you want). It is produced when light bounces off the reflective or first surface of the glass. The second spot is the satellite, caused by internal reflection. You can

FIG. 3-7. *Two types of beam splitters: plate and cube (the cube beam splitter is shown attached to a metal mounting bracket).*

sometimes eliminate or reduce the intensity of the satellite by reversing the plate. The reason: some beam splitters are coated on one side only. Turning them over directs the coating toward the laser. You can also eliminate the satellite by carefully placing black tape on the beam splitter. Direct the laser beam so that only one spot is reflected.

Filters

Filters accept light at certain wavelengths and block all others. The color of the filter typically determines the wavelength of light that it accepts, thus rejecting all others. For example, a red filter passes red light and blocks other colors. Depending on the design of the filter, the amount of light blockage can be small or large.

Many filters for laser experiments are designed to pass infrared radiation and block visible light. Such filters are commonly used in front of photo sensors to block out unwanted ambient light. Only infrared light—from a laser diode, for instance—is allowed to pass through and strike the sensor.

Filters for light experiments come in three general forms: colored gel, interference, and dichroic. *Colored gel filters* are made by mixing dyes into a Mylar or plastic base.

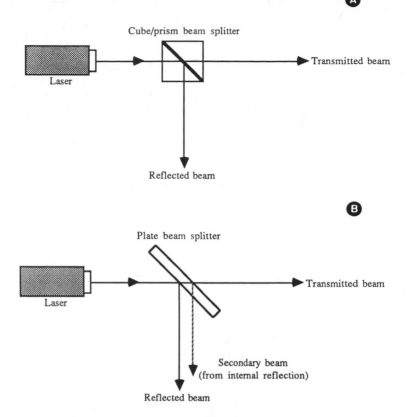

FIG. 3-8. *How cube and plate beam splitters work. The cube beam splitter (A) is composed of two right-angle prisms cemented together. The plate beam splitter (B) is a piece of flat glass that may or may not be coated with a reflective layer.*

Good gel filters use dyes that are precisely controlled during manufacture to make filters that pass only certain colors. Depending on the dye used, the filter is capable of passing only a certain band of wavelengths. A good gel filter might have a bandpass region (the spectrum of light passed) of only 40 to 60 nanometers.

Interference filters consist of several dielectric and sometimes metallic layers that each block a certain range of wavelengths. One layer might block light under 500 nm and another layer might block light above 550 nm. The band between 500 and 550 nm is passed by the filter (see FIG. 3-9). Interference filters are sometimes referred to as bandpass filters, because they are made to pass a certain band of light wavelengths. Interference filters can be made either narrowband, accepting only a very small portion of wavelengths, or broadband, accepting a relatively large chunk of the spectrum.

Dichroic filters use organic dyes or chemicals to absorb light at certain wavelengths. Some filters are made from crystals, such as cordierite, that exhibit two or more different colors when viewed at different axes. Color control is maintained by cutting the crystal at a specific axis. Dichroism is also used to create polarizing materials (colored and uncolored), as discussed more fully in Chapter 8.

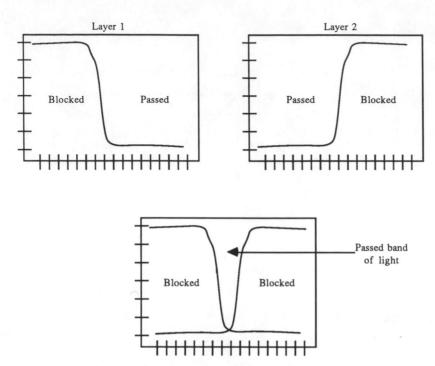

FIG. 3-9. *Interference filters are composed of two (or more) layers that selectively block light beyond a certain wavelength. By sandwiching two complementary layers together, it's possible to pass only light in a very restricted band.*

Both interference and dichroic filters exhibit a rainbow of colors as you tilt them against a white light source. Their coloration gives you no clue to the wavelengths they are designed to pass. Peering through the filter, you might see a bluish or greenish tinge, but tilting the filter or reflecting light off one surface can reveal other striking colors such as gold, purple, or yellow.

Pinholes

A *pinhole* is a small hole drilled or punched into an opaque sheet. The hole can be as small as 1 or 2 micrometers to as large as a millimeter. Pinholes are used to make spatial filters (see below) or to diffract light.

Spatial Filter

Imagine looking at a laser beam head on (don't actually do it— just imagine it!). The spot has a bright central portion and an almost fuzzy outer sheath. Some advanced laser experiments require a near-perfect beam (one that lacks the fuzz). *Spatial filters* are used to "clean up" the beam spot by taking just the center portion and excluding the perimeter noise.

A spatial filter is a pinhole coupled with a microscope objective. As depicted in FIG. 3-10, the lenses in the microscope objective focus the beam of light to a tiny spot, often not more than 25 to 50 micrometers in diameter. That spot is squeezed through a pinhole

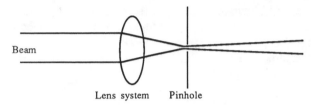

Beam

Lens system   Pinhole

FIG. 3-10. *The basic operation of the spatial filter. A lens system (typically a microscope objective) squeezes the light into a fine point. The light is then passed through a pinhole. The size of the pinhole must complement the magnification power of the lens system.*

of similar diameter. Spatial filters require precision optics and focusing, and though you can make your own, it's often better to buy one (surplus if possible).

The spatial filter won't work without the objective, because the pinhole alone causes the beam to diffract (see Chapter 8 for some experiments with diffraction). Instead of cleaning up the beam, you smear it even more. And without the pinhole, the beam expands too much as it comes out of the objective, producing a large, fuzzy dot.

Slits

A *slit* is a pinhole that has been enlarged to make a long, narrow rectangle. It is designed to produce diffraction in a laser beam. The *width* of the slit is the important consideration, not the length. Slits can be made by precision tooling, with photographic film, and with sharp, unused razor blades (again, see Chapter 8, for ideas on making slits). Slits can either be single or double, depending on the application.

Diffraction Gratings

Diffraction in a spatial filter is an undesirable side-effect, but diffraction in general is a highly useful optical phenomenon. Diffraction is what makes laser holograms work and gives the colorful rainbow to compact discs and some metallic "mood" jewelry.

A *diffraction grating* diffracts light in a controlled manner. The amount of diffraction and the size of the interference fringes that the diffraction produces is determined by the number of lines or scribes made in a transparent or reflective material. Many diffraction gratings are made with up to 15,000 parallel lines scribed into the material.

A diffraction grating can be either transmissive or reflective. *Transmissive gratings* are made by etching a piece of clear film with a precision tool (a diamond or laser). You see the diffraction effects by looking through the material. *Reflective gratings* are made with an opaque metallic sheet. You view the diffraction effects by reflecting light off of it.

Diffraction gratings can be used to split a laser beam into many smaller beams or to experiment with diffraction, light wavelength, metrology (the science of measurement), and much more.

Ronchi Rulings

A *Ronchi ruling* is a coarse diffraction grating but is made with more precision. Instead of 15,000 lines per inch, a Ronchi ruling has from 50 to 400 lines per inch. The lines are etched or scribed in glass and are held to a much tighter tolerance than the lines in a diffraction grating.

You can use a Ronchi ruling for many of the same tasks as a diffraction grating, although the principle use of a Ronchi is to test the flatness of optical components. Holding a Ronchi ruling up to a laser beam causes diffraction, and because the lines in the ruling are precise, you can use the diffraction pattern as an aid in measuring distances, light wavelengths, and more.

Miscellaneous Optics

There are more optical components than the few mentioned above, such as polarizers, quarter-wave plates, and cylindrical lenses. These and others of interest to the laser experimenter are introduced throughout the rest of this book. If you would like to learn more about optics and how to use them, consult Appendix B for a list of books on optical components. Also check your local library for additional titles on the subject.

BUYING OPTICS

Most of the lenses and mirrors you are likely to buy will be surplus, either from equipment taken out of service or no longer in manufacture, or from components that are defective in one way or another. Serious laser endeavors need the best quality optics you can afford, but routine experiments can effectively use second-and third-grade lenses and mirrors. You'll especially want to confine yourself to low-grade optics when just starting out. There's nothing worse than spending $20 on a high-quality lens only to have it ruined because you didn't know how to care for it.

Never-before-used prime surplus optics are the best choice. Why? They are the highest quality, yet they cost less because they are no longer needed by the original manufacturer or purchaser. But such surplus is hard to find, and depending on the source, is not much cheaper than buying components brand new, straight from the factory. Contact a number of optics manufacturers (see Appendix A) and ask for their latest catalog and price list. Use the price list as a "blue book" to know when you are getting a good deal.

Lenses

Optics that are damaged in some way are often referred to as "seconds." The amount of damage can be slight or severe, but in any case, the fault was major enough that the manufacturer or user rejected the component. Lenses suffer from three major faults:

★ *Scratches*. Most scratches are hairline marks that you can't ordinarily see without using a microscope or magnifying glass. The scratch is deep enough that it can't be rubbed out, so it's a permanent scar. If the scratch is large (over about 50 micrometers, visible with a good magnifier), and extends through the optical center, the lens can't be used for laser experiments. Toss the lens or use it for some other less demanding application.

★ *Digs*. Digs are gouges in the lens surfaces. These are usually large enough to see with the unaided eye. Obviously, a dig in the usable portion of the lens makes it worthless. Some digs are small, however, and might not be easily seen. Their presence might only be revealed when shining a laser beam through the lens.

★ *Edge chips*. Most lenses are designed to use the inner 60 to 80 percent of the surface, leaving the outside edge for mounting with retainer rings. Chips at the edges generally don't pose problems. But a large chip can extend into the usable area of the lens and adversely affect the light. Look carefully for edge chips, and reject those lenses where the chip extends beyond 10 percent of the radius.

If you are buying lenses from a surplus dealer, make it a habit to test for the presence of anti-reflection (AR) coating. Although you can use uncoated optics, the coated variety is always better. To test for the coating, hold the lens so that white light glances off the surface. A lens with an AR coating will be tinted.

Mirrors

A scratch on a mirror can smear a laser beam and distort it beyond recognition. Closely inspect the reflective side of the mirror and look for scratches, digs, and chips. Small imperfections around the periphery of the mirror can be tolerated, as long as the center of the mirror is free of blemishes.

Even though an aluminum-or silver-coated mirror might seem 100 percent reflective to you, the metallic coating could be uneven and spotty. Being careful to grasp it by the edges only, hold the mirror up to a light and peer through it. Can you see any small pinholes or other imperfections in the coating? If so, pick another mirror. Even 100 percent reflective mirrors might have a thin enough coating that you can see through it. This is fine as long as the coating appears even.

CARE, CLEANING, AND STORAGE OF OPTICS

The bane of laser optics is dust, dirt, and grime, a trio that can quickly ruin even the best engineered project. Lenses, mirrors, beam splitters, filters, and other optical components must be absolutely free of dust, or the laser beam could be undesirably diffused and diffracted. Obviously, it's impossible to prevent all contamination without a sophisticated "clean-room," but every step you take to control dust goes a long way to assure success in your experiments.

Keep your optics wrapped in lint-free tissue (not facial tissue) until you use them. The tissue paper for wrapping gifts inside boxes is a good choice. Cut the tissue into small, manageable pieces and carefully wrap each lens, mirror, or other component. Use cellophane tape to keep the tissue closed. Don't write directly on the tissue or tape; you'll damage the optics. If you must mark the component, write the description on white paper tape and affix the tape to the outside of the tissue.

Store like items in closeable plastic sandwich bags. Mark the contents on the bag with a label. The seal on the bag prevents contamination from moisture. Leave a little bit of air in the bag as you seal it to provide a soft protective cushion.

Avoid touching optical components unless you have to, and then handle the components by the edges only. Oil from your skin acts as an acid that etches away glass and anti-reflection coatings. Use optics-quality cleaning tissue (or a cotton swab) to remove oil and grime from lenses and mirrors. Never use the tissue dry, as the slightly abrasive surface of the tissue can cause micro-scratches on the surface of the components.

Use an approved lens-cleaning fluid or pure alcohol, but not eyeglass cleaner containing silicone. Apply the cleaner to the tissue, not directly to the optical component. Use only enough cleaner fluid to lightly wet the tissue. Let the component dry on its own; avoid wiping a lens or mirror dry or you might scratch it. Clean plastic lenses with distilled water.

Clean optics with a tissue and cleaning fluid or water sparingly. Use a bulb brush (available at photographic stores) to remove dust from optics each time you use them. A can of compressed air can also be used to blow away light dust particles. Be sure to hold the can upright so that the propellant is not expelled. If the valve has a pressure control, dial it to the lowest setting.

If the optical component is fragile and easily marred, clean it by dipping it in alcohol or optics grade cleaner. If this isn't practical, you may also use an eye-dropper to splash cleaner on the component. Allow to dry or blow away the excess moisture with a can of compressed air.

The best way to prevent dust contamination is to use the optics in the cleanest environment possible. Dusty garages are not the place for laser optics experiments. Choose a place inside that is thoroughly dusted and vacuumed. If possible, aim a small fan *into* the area to create a high-pressure region. Be sure that you don't stir up dust with the fan. Place an air filter in front of the fan to block dust from entering the room.

Laser projects you construct using an optical bench or prototyping board can be protected overnight by taping a large sheet of tissue over the optics. Avoid the use of towels or blankets, as they leave lint on lenses and mirrors. Apply the bulb brush to the optics before continuing the project the next day.

Some laser projects, like the Michelson interferometer described in Chapter 9, are designed to be built with optics left intact. But the optics are delicate and can be ruined if exposed. Find a cardboard box large enough for the project and spray the inside of the box with a clear lacquer. This mats the inside of the box and helps prevent cardboard dust from contaminating the optics. Next, add fiber fill or other bonded interfacing or padding on the bottom and sides of the box and carefully place the project inside. Tape up the top and mark ''Fragile'' on it along with the contents so you know what's inside. Store the box so that nothing heavy will be placed on top of it.

4

Experimenting with Light and Optics

Laser radiation is light, and with few exceptions, all light behaves the same way. One of the best ways to learn about lasers and optics—without having to bother with the cost of laser equipment nor all the sundry safety precautions—is to construct a high-intensity simulated laser. The simulated laser described in this chapter emits a powerful beam of visible light that can be focused, directed, and controlled in much the same way as real laser light.

The parts for the simulated laser, or "simu-laser," are affordable and easy to find, and because you are not dealing with real laser light, there is no worry of accidentally exposing your eyes to potentially harmful radiation. The light from the simu-laser is bright, but it is no more damaging to your eyes than a momentary glint of sunlight from a car mirror.

HIGH-OUTPUT LEDS

The simu-laser is designed around a high-intensity visible light-emitting diode. These exceptionally bright LEDs are enormously efficient, emitting several hundred—and sometimes several thousand—times the light of ordinary LEDs. Visible LEDs are rated by their millicandela output. One millicandela is equal to one thousandth of a standard candle, a common measurement of light intensity. Typical undiffused red LEDs produce from 5 to 20 millicandelas (mcd); diffused LEDs emit even less, often under 2 mcd.

High-output LEDs, usually referred to as "Super Brights" or "Kilo Brights," put out 300 mcd or more. Such LEDs are routinely available at Radio Shack and other hobbyist electronics outlets. You can use a 300 mcd LED for the simulated laser, but you can achieve better results with a component rated at a higher value. A number of companies, including Stanley and Texas Instruments, offer LEDs with light outputs of 1,000, 2,000, even 3,000 mcd. Higher outputs can be obtained—up to 5,000 or 6,000 mcd—when driving the LED with more current.

The simulated laser project detailed in this chapter uses the Stanley Electric Co. H2, which is a 2,000 mcd LED imported by A.C. Interface. This LED, or one like it, is available from a number of industrial electronics outlets. Look in the Yellow Pages under Electronics and call around. Some outlets don't sell on a retail level, but you might have luck striking a deal if you are a part of a group or school.

A number of mail order outfits, such as Allied Electronics and General Science and Engineering, also carry high-output LEDs and are accustomed to dealing with individuals. See Appendix A for a list of mail order companies that offer service to electronics hobbyists. The remaining parts used in the project are commonly available from new and surplus dealers.

The output of LEDs increase linearly as you increase current. The H2 is rated at 2,000 mcd when powered with a current of 20 mA. The output is roughly doubled—4,000 mcd—when the LED is biased with a current of 40 mA.

Although some high-output LEDs can function with currents as high as 50 mA, I found that this much juice heated up and burned out several of the sample H2 LEDs I had. To be on the safe side, don't operate any high-output LED above 45 mA unless the manufacturer's literature says otherwise. As you may expect, high-output LEDs are more expensive than their standard cousins. Typical prices are $2 to $4 for a 2,000 mcd LED. At these prices, you don't want to carelessly burn too many out.

Measurement of light output of LEDs, including the high-output variety, is often made with an *integrating sphere*, a device that measures the total radiant power of the component. The sphere collects light emitted in all directions, including the off-axis radiation that spills out the sides. The simulated laser project detailed here focuses only the light that comes out the top of the LED; no reflector is used to collect the off-axis light. You can increase the brightness of the device by adding a penlight flashlight reflector behind the LED.

BUILDING THE SIMULATED LASER

Follow the schematic in FIG. 4-1 for wiring the high-output LED. The parts list appears in TABLE 4-1. The circuit is simple and runs off a single 9-volt transistor battery. The switch is a miniature single-pole, single-throw (SPST) type. The lens I used for

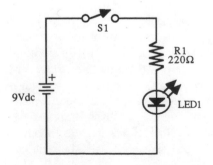

FIG. 4-1. *The basic schematic for the simu-laser. With the supply voltage and resistor shown, forward current through the LED is approximately 34 mA. You can safely increase the forward current to about 45 mA by reducing R1 to 165 ohms (150-ohm and 15-ohm resistors in series).*

Table 4-1. Simu-laser Parts List

R1	220 ohm resistor
LED1	High-output light-emitting diode
S1	SPST miniature switch
1 each	9-volt battery, battery clip, project box (3¼ by 2⅛ by 1 ⅛ inches), 16 mm diameter, 34 mm focal length, positive double-convex lens.

All resistors are 5 to 10 percent tolerance, ¼ watt

the prototype was double-convex, 16 mm in diameter by 34 mm in focal length. You can use a lens with different specifications, but you should avoid a lens with a focal length greater than about 35 mm. A longer focal length means that you must provide more space between the lens and the LED. The project box specified in the parts list is just long enough to accommodate the focal distance between LED and lens.

Mount the components as shown in a small project box. Everything fits in a compact box measuring 3¼ by 2⅛ by 1⅛ inches (Radio Shack catalog number 270-230). Drill a ½-inch hole in one end of the box, and countersink it lightly to conform to the rounded shape of the lens. Use a general-purpose glue (such as Duco cement) to carefully tack the edges of the lens to the outside wall of the box. Use a toothpick to apply small drops of glue to the edge of the lens.

Mount the LED and current-limiting resistor on a small piece of perf board and attach a metal or plastic angle bracket to the back of the board. Suitable brackets are available at hobby stores that specialize in radio-control model airplanes. Cost is under $1 for a set of four or five brackets. You can also salvage the bracket from an Erector Set toy kit.

Measure the diameter of the switch shaft and drill a hole accordingly in the top of the box. Wire the snap-on battery cap, switch, and circuit board and turn the switch on. The LED should glow a bright red (some high-output LEDs emit red-orange light). If all checks out, point the box toward a light-colored wall (no more than a couple feet away), and place the circuit board inside. Aim the LED at the lens and adjust its position and distance until the spot on the wall is bright and well defined. Mark the location on the side of the box with a pencil, then check for proper focal length by measuring the LED-to-lens distance. It should be very close to the rated focal length of the lens.

With the proper mounting position marked off, use a #19 bit to drill a hole in the side of the box and mount the circuit board using ⅜₂-by-¼-inch hardware (available from a hardware store or Erector Set). The simu-laser, mounted in its box with all components, is shown in FIG. 4-2.

Place the cover on the box and flick on the power switch. Point the simu-laser at a wall and watch for a bright red spot. Note that the beam spreads out considerably when the wall is more than 4 or 5 feet away. This is due to the wide divergence of the beam, even when optics are used. Later in this chapter you'll see how to add more lenses to control the size of the beam, or even focus it to a bright, pin-point spot.

BEAM COLLIMATION

Depending on the exact distance between the lens and wall, the spot from the simu-laser beam should have a bright center, with concentric light/dark rings around it. This

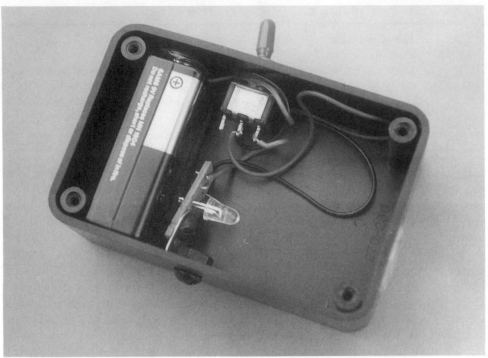

FIG. 4-2. *The simu-laser, with cover removed to show the arrangement of the components.*

"ring" effect is caused by the internal construction of the LED. Place the simu-laser a few inches from the wall and you can see the chip inside the LED, along with a dark spot and line that denotes the contact wire stretching from anode to cathode. You will also see shadows from the glue placed at the edge of the lens.

In a dark room, place the simu-laser on a table and aim the beam at a solar cell. Make sure that all of the spot falls on the surface of the cell. Connect a meter to the cell as shown in FIG. 4-3 and measure the output. Now change the distance between the simu-laser and the cell.

Note that as you increase the distance by a factor of two, the reading on the meter falls off roughly by 50 percent. This is due to the inverse-square law, familiar to photographers. The inverse-square law states that for every doubling in the distance between a light source and subject, the intensity of the light falling on the subject decreases by 50 percent.

What causes this phenomenon? At first glance, it might appear that the light loses its energy the farther it travels. But this can't be the answer, because energy can never be lost, just transformed into something else. The reason behind the apparent weakening in the light intensity is due to the spread—or divergence—of light. Physical law dictates that as light propagates through a vacuum or any medium, the light waves must spread transversely, making it impossible to have a perfectly collimated (parallel) beam.

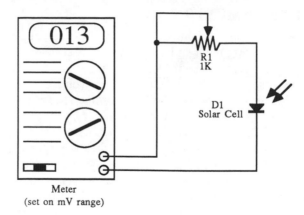

Meter
(set on mV range)

FIG. 4-3. *How to detect and measure light level using a silicon solar cell. Potentiometer R1 allows you to adjust the sensitivity of the cell.*

Light from the simu-laser, though focused by a lens, spreads out as it travels through air or space. The amount of spreading is measured using the metric radians or milliradians (thousandths of a radian). One milliradian is equal to:

★ 0.057296 degrees
★ 3.438 minutes
★ 206.265 seconds of arc

The simu-laser uses a simple lens to focus the light from the LED, so the divergence is wide, on the order of 500 to 750 milliradians. A more elaborate lens system with two or more lenses can decrease the divergence so the light is held in a tighter beam of perhaps 250 milliradians. However, no matter what kind of optics are used, the light beam eventually suffuses to a point where its individual photons are miles apart. Note that the divergence of a real laser is extremely small, on the order of 1 to 5 milliradians, even without optics. This is just one of the properties of lasers that make them so special.

In later experiments in this book, you will find that the inverse-square law does not apply to most lasers when used at close distances. The light beam from a helium-neon gas laser, for example, has so little divergence that its diameter increases an imperceptible amount at close ranges. Only after traversing several hundred meters does the diameter of the beam enlarge to appreciable amounts.

Table 4-2. Parts List for Light Intensity Measurements	R1 1K potentiometer D1 Silicon solar cell Volt ohm meter

OPTICAL EXPERIMENTS

The double-convex lens mounted on the case of the simu-laser does not do an adequate job of collimating the light in a fine beam. A second lens, positioned in front of the simu-laser, can act to make the light rays more parallel. The exact distance between the two lenses is a function of the type of lens you are using and the focal lengths of both lenses. But you can experiment with the proper spacing by adjusting the distance while looking at the spot projected on a nearby wall.

The spot should be well-defined, focused, and smaller than the spot made by just the simu-laser lens. There should be little or no light spilling past the sides of the second lens (light spill is normal in an optical device and is usually countered by the use of apertures or stops). If you can't focus the beam on the wall without a lot of light spilling past it, choose a larger diameter lens. The second lens used in the prototype was a 16 mm diameter, 124 mm focal length positive meniscus placed 5⅜ inches (about 137 mm) in front of the simu-laser. It reduced the beam divergence by about a factor of two.

You can temporarily fix the simu-laser and lens in position with modeller's clay. Use a small piece of wood or plastic (about 12 by 4 inches) and build up the clay to the proper height. Now repeat the test with the solar cell. Note that the simu-laser can be moved farther away without a drastic loss in power. Take another reading without the second lens and compare it to the measurements you just made.

Focusing Light to a Point

Light from the simu-laser can be focused to a sharp point by using two additional supplementary lenses. Remove the meniscus lens used for the previous experiment and mount a 17 mm diameter, 70 mm focal length, double-concave lens approximately two inches from the front of the simu-laser. Use clay to keep it in place. Position a 30 mm diameter, 55 mm focal length, plano-convex lens 6½ inches from the double-concave lens. Adjust the position of the lenses so that their optical centers are aligned and that the lens faces are parallel to one another.

Place a sheet of white paper approximately 2¾ inches in front of the plano-convex lens. What happens? The light is focused to a point a little less than ⅛-inch diameter. Move the paper closer to or farther away from the lens and note that the spot gets larger. A side view of the focused beam is shown in FIG. 4-4. The beam is at its smallest when the paper is located at the focal point.

Table 4-3. Parts List for Simu-laser Optics Experiments

1	Simu-laser
1	16 mm diameter, 124 mm focal length, positive meniscus lens
1	17 mm diameter, 70 mm focal length double-concave lens
1	30 mm diameter, 55 mm focal length plano-convex lens
1	2-by-2-inch front-surface mirror
1	Plate glass beam splitter (approx. 1-by-1 inch); ⅟₁₆- to ¼-inch thick
1	Polarizing film
1	Right-angle prism

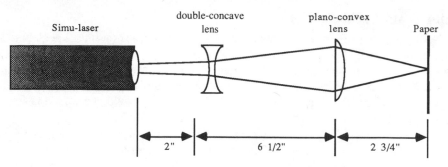

FIG. 4-4. *Arrangement of simu-laser and optics for demonstrating the focusing of light into a point. Experiment with the distances between components if your lenses are different from those specified in the text.*

The double-concave lens acts to diverge the light to approximately the diameter of the plano-convex lens. This beam spreading allows most or all of the surface of the plano-convex lens to be used (and hence the beam is more subject to certain aberrations, as detailed in Chapter 3, "Introduction to Optics"). You can test the effectiveness of the double-concave lens by removing it from the light path. The beam, still focused in front of the plano-convex lens, is enlarged to about ¼ inch. Experiment with the effects of different lenses placed at various spots along the length of the test board.

Using Mirrors

Mirrors allow you to direct the beam from the simu-laser in any direction you desire. Note that a flat mirror doesn't alter divergence or convergence of a beam. A converging beam of light still converges after bouncing off a mirror. Concave or convex mirrors, however, act as reflective lenses and spread or focus the light. Concave mirrors are often used in holography to provide a heavily diverged beam in order to cover a large area. The mirror is a more effective diverger than a lens.

Place a 2-by-2-inch, front-surface, aluminized mirror in the path of the light beam, and position it at a 45-degree angle. The light should now bounce off the mirror and be perpendicular to the beam of the simu-laser. Move the mirror closer to the focusing lens and position the paper to catch the light reflected off the mirror, as shown in FIG. 4-5. Note that the focal length between the focusing lens and paper is the same whether or not the mirror is in place. If the focal length is approximately 2¾ inches, the same distance will be covered between lens, mirror, and paper.

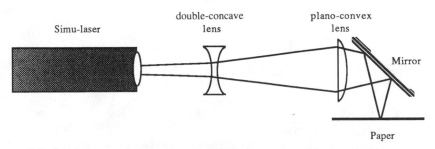

FIG. 4-5. *A flat mirror does not alter the convergence or divergence of light rays.*

Using Beam Splitters

Now exchange the mirror with a small piece of plate glass (any thickness between ¹⁄₁₆- and ¼-inch will do). When positioned at a 45-degree angle to the simu-laser, the glass acts as a beam splitter. With uncoated glass, approximately 10 to 15 percent of the light is reflected off the first surface and the rest is transmitted through the glass (there is some light loss due to internal reflections). You should see a spot in front of the simu-laser and another, less strong one to the right or left.

Rotate the glass. The transmitted beam remains but the reflected beam will spin in an arc around the beam splitter. Use the solar cell to measure the amount of light reflected from the glass. The amount of reflection should change as the glass is turned. The amount of reflectance is minimal when the glass is positioned between 0 and 30 degrees to the simu-laser, but it begins to increase dramatically at angles greater than 40 degrees. At 90 degrees (glancing angle), reflection is almost 100 percent. Be sure to take your readings in a darkened room.

Light reflecting off a glass medium is partially polarized, and if the angle is just right, one plane of polarization will be almost extinguished. Try this experiment. Place a piece of polarizing film in front of the simu-laser. Position the glass plate at about 55 degrees to the lens of the simu-laser. Locate the solar cell so that it collects the reflected light. Now slowly rotate the polarizing film. See any change? You should. If you don't, change the angle of the glass a small amount and try again. The light should be strongest with the polarizer in one position and weakest when it is rotated 90 degrees.

Future chapters deal with the nature of polarized light in more detail, but it's worth describing here how this phenomenon works. Polarized light has two components, typically identified as p and s. These two components are *orthogonal* to one another, or at 90-degree angles.

When a piece of glass is positioned at a special angle called *Brewster's angle*, the p component vanishes, and only the s component remains. Brewster's angle for most glass is 56 degrees 39 minutes, or roughly 1 radian. By placing a polarizer in the light path, you can control polarization of the light. Rotate it so that the s component passes and you see light reflected off the glass (the p component is "absorbed" by the glass, so only the s component remains). When you rotate the polarizer so that the s component is blocked, the light dims. With both the s and p components reduced or eliminated, the light level drops.

You can visually see the dimming effect as you rotate the polarizer. To assure yourself that you are not just seeing things, use the solar cell to make a graph of the light output. A plastic protractor can be used to help you rotate the polarizer in even 5- or 10-degree intervals.

Using Prisms

Most people think of prisms as rainbow makers—glass objects that break up sunlight into its component colors. While prisms are indeed often used in this role of light dispersion, they also find great application as re-directors of light. Prisms have an advantage over mirrors, in that because they are made of thick glass, they are less susceptible to the effects of stress and vibration. The reflective surface of a prism is typically inside the glass, making it far less susceptible to scratches and blemishes. Prisms can also be designed with unique shapes so that the light passing through it is reflected without flipping it upside down or sideways, as in a regular mirror.

A right-angle prism is used to deflect light at a 90-degree angle. The corner opposite the hypotenuse forms a right angle. Usually, but not always, the sides opposite the hypotenuse are the same length. That leaves a 30- and 60-degree angle for the other two corners. Shine a light into the prism through one face, and it is internally reflected at the hypotenuse and then exits the second face.

You can readily experiment with a right-angle prism by placing it in front of the simulaser. You'll need a prism that is at least 25 mm wide with faces 25 mm to 30 mm long. Glass and plastic prisms of this size (and larger) are available on the new and surplus markets for under $10. Optical quality for these less expensive prisms might not be high, but prime optics are not required for these experiments.

Position the prism so that the light enters one face and is bounced off the hypotenuse at a 90-degree angle. If the room lights are low, you might be able see the beam in the prism reflecting off of the hypotenuse and exiting the glass.

5

All About
Helium-Neon Lasers

The helium-neon tube is the staple of the laser experimenter. He-Ne tubes are in plentiful supply, including in the surplus market. They emit a bright, deep red glow that can be seen for miles around. Although the power output of He-Ne tubes is relatively small compared to other laser systems—such as CO_2, argon, and ruby—the helium-neon laser is perfectly suited for most any laser experiment. Its moderate power supply requirements coupled with its slim, coherent beam lend the He-Ne laser to inexpensive projects in holography, interferometry, surveying, lightwave communications, and much more.

In this chapter you'll learn all about helium-neon lasers: what they are, how they work, and what you need to put a complete system together. In Chapter 6 you'll learn how to place a bare He-Ne laser tube in an enclosure to make it easier to use, along with plans on building a He-Ne laser experimenter's system. With the experimenter's system, you'll be able to perform numerous optical experiments with your helium-neon laser.

ANATOMY OF A HE-NE LASER TUBE

The helium-neon laser is a glass vessel filled with 10 parts helium with 1 part neon and is pressurized to about 1 mm/Hg (exact gas pressure and ratios vary from one laser manufacturer to another). Electrodes placed at the ends of the tube provide a means to electrify (ionize) the gas, thereby exciting the helium and neon atoms. Mirrors mounted at either end form an *optical resonator*. In most He-Ne tubes, one mirror is totally reflective and the other is partially reflective. The partially reflective mirror is the output of the tube.

The first helium-neon tubes were large and ungainly and required external cooling by water or forced air. The modern He-Ne tubes, such as the one in FIG. 5-1, are about the size of a cucumber and are cooled by the surrounding air. The length and diameter of He-Ne tubes varies with their power output, as detailed later in this chapter.

Most helium-neon laser tubes are composed of few parts, all fused together during manufacture. Only the very old He-Ne tubes, or those used for special laboratory experiments, use external mirrors. The all-in-one design of the typical He-Ne tube means they cost less to manufacture and the mirrors are not as prone to misalignment.

Helium-neon lasers are actually composed of two tubes: an outer *vacuum* (or plasma) tube that contains the gas, and a shorter and smaller inner *bore* or capillary, where the lasing action takes place. The bore is attached to only one end of the tube. The loose end is the output and faces the partially reflective mirror. The bore is held concentric by a metal element called the *spider*. The inner diameter of the bore largely determines the diameter width of the beam, which is usually 0.6 mm to 1 mm.

The ends, where the mirrors are mounted, typically serve as the *anode (positive)* and *cathode (negative)* terminals. On other lasers, the terminals are mounted on the same end of the tube. A strip of metal or wire extends the cathode (sometimes the anode) to the other end.

Metal rings with hex screws are often placed on the mirror mounts as a means to tweak the alignment of the mirrors. Unless you suspect the mirrors are out of alignment, you should *not* attempt to adjust the rings. They have been adjusted at the factory for maximum beam output, and tweaking them unnecessarily can seriously degrade the performance of the laser.

The partially silvered mirror, where the laser beam comes out, can be on either the anode or cathode end. I found that on the many tubes I've tested, the beam extends out the cathode end. Many manufacturers prefer this arrangement, claiming it is safer and provides more flexibility. You can usually tell the output mirror by holding it against a light. You should see the blue tint of the anti-reflective coating. The totally reflective

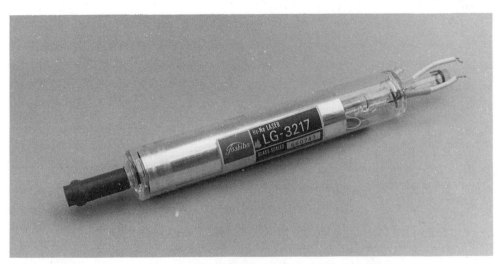

FIG. 5-1. *A bare helium-neon laser tube. This one measures about 1¼ inches in diameter by 12 inches in length.*

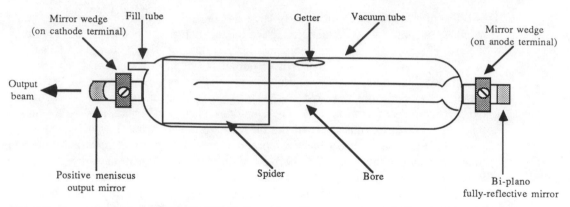

FIG. 5-2. *A cross-sectional view of a typical He-Ne laser tube, with component parts indicated. The arrangement and style of your laser tube might be slightly different.*

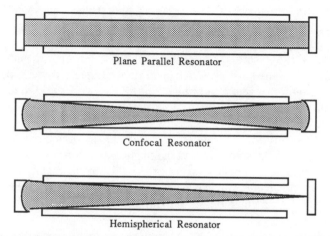

FIG. 5-3. *Three ways to implement the optical cavity in a laser—plane parallel, confocal, and hemispherical. Most laser tubes use the latter method or a derivative of it.*

mirror generally is not treated with an AR coating. A cutaway view of a laser tube with all the various components is shown in FIG. 5-2.

The facing mirrors of the He-Ne tube comprise what is commonly referred to as a *Fabry-Perot interferometer* or *resonator*. With the mirrors aligned *plane parallel* to one another, as shown in FIG. 5-3, the light bounces back and forth until the beam achieves sufficient power to pass through the partially reflected output mirror. In practice, the plane parallel resonator is seldom if ever used, because it is unstable and suffers from large losses due to diffraction.

A *confocal resonator* uses two concave spherical mirrors of equal radius, each placed at the center of curvature of the other. The cavity uses a large portion of the gas volume and produces high power, but mirror adjustment is relatively critical. Yet another approach is the *hemispherical resonator*, which is primarily a plane mirror coupled with a spherical mirror. This type of resonator is very stable and easy to align, but its design wastes plasma volume, so power output of the laser is reduced.

56

The exact configuration of the resonator mirrors in a laser is not a major consideration to the hobbyist experimenter. You'll have little choice of the engineering of the tube when buying parts through surplus outlets. However, you might have a choice if you buy your tubes new or if you purchase a particular type of tube for a special application.

LASER VARIETIES

He-Ne lasers are available in three forms: bare, cylindrical head, or self-contained. *Bare tubes* are just that—the plasma tube is not shielded by any type of housing and should be placed inside a tube or box for protection. *Cylindrical head* lasers (or just ''laser heads'') are housed inside an aluminum tube. Leads for power come out one end of the laser. The opposite end might have a hole for the exiting beam or be equipped with a safety shutter. The shutter prevents accidental exposure to the beam. Both the bare tube and cylindrical head laser require an external high-voltage power supply (discussed below).

Lastly, *self-contained* (or lab) lasers contain both a laser tube and a high-voltage power supply. To use the laser, you simply plug it into a wall socket and turn on the switch.

Each form of laser has its own advantages and disadvantages:

★ Bare tubes are ideal for making your own self-contained laser projects, such as laser pistols and rifle scopes, and fit in confined spaces. But because the tube and high-voltage terminals are exposed, they are more dangerous to work with. You must exercise considerable caution when working with bare tubes to avoid electrocution and injury from broken glass.

★ Cylindrical head lasers are easy to use because the tube is protected and the high-voltage terminals are not exposed (but care must still be exercised to avoid shock from power applied to the leads). Laser heads are ideal for optical benches and holography (with the right type of mount). On the down side, the tubes tend to be large and are not easily mounted for use in hand-held devices.

★ Self-contained lasers are designed to provide protection against tube breakage and high-voltage electrocution. They are often used in schools and labs where they can be easily set up for optical experiments. The built-in power supply operates from a wall socket, however, so the laser cannot be used where 117 volt ac current is not available. Also, the bulk of the self-contained laser prohibits it from being used in hand-held devices.

THE POWER SUPPLY

Owning a plasma tube doesn't mean you have a laser. The tube is only half the story; just as important is the power supply. You also need electricity for the power supply, either directly from a 117-volt ac wall socket or a 12-volt dc battery. Power supplies for lasers generate a great deal of volts but relatively few milliamps. The typical power supply generates from 1,200 to 3,000 volts at 3.5 to 7 mA. Generally, the larger the tube (and the higher the power output), the more juice it requires.

You have a number of choices for the power supply:

★ *Commercially-made* laser supply, either ac or dc operated. These are the easiest to use and often come completely sealed as a precautionary measure. A common type

FIG. 5-4. *The latest commercially made He-Ne power supplies are available in convenient, sealed packages, such as the one shown in the photograph. The power supply is about the size of a sandwich.*

of ac-operated commercially made He-Ne power supply is shown in FIG. 5-4. Cost on the retail market is about $225; surplus is between $50 and $100. A high-voltage Alden connector (see end of chapter) is common on cylindrical head lasers. The female connector on the power supply matches with the male connector on the laser.

★ *Home-built* power supply kit. Low-current power supplies can be built in your shop but require some specialized, hard-to-find parts. Building your own supply saves money and helps teach you about laser power requirements. Cost: $10 to $25 for parts; pre-packaged kits of parts and circuit board (available from some sources listed in Appendix A) cost $30 to $150.

★ *Salvaged high-voltage TV flyback transformer or module* power supply. Many compact TVs use a self-contained flyback transformer that operates from 12 to 24 Vdc. The transformer, intended as the high-voltage source for the picture tube, generates up to 15 kV at a few milliamps. The modules are cheap ($10 to $20 on the surplus market) but their low current output makes them suitable only for small tubes.

If you are just starting out with lasers, your first power supply should be a commercially made and tested unit, preferably new and not a take-out from existing equipment. Armed with a tube and ready-to-go supply, you'll be able to start experimenting with the laser the moment you get it home. Then as you gain experience, you might want to build one or two supplies as extras or to power the various tubes you are bound to acquire. Chapter 12 presents several power supply circuits you can use to power tubes with outputs from 1 to about 5 mW.

Inside a Power Supply

Although the exact design of He-Ne power supplies varies, the principle is generally the same. He-Ne power supplies are familiar to anyone who has dabbled in high-voltage circuits, such as those required for amateur radio.

Here's how a typical power supply works. An input voltage, say 12 Vdc, is applied to an oscillator circuit, such as a simple transistor, resistor, and capacitor. The values of the resistor and capacitor determine the time constant of the oscillator circuit. The oscillating input is fed to the windings of a step-up transformer. The voltage is stepped up to somewhere between 300 to 1,000 volts by the transformer and then passed through a series of high-voltage diodes and capacitors. These components act to rectify and multiply the voltage presented by the transformer. Depending on the number of capacitors and diodes used, the voltage multiplier doubles, triples, or quadruples the potential.

Power supplies that operate from 117 Vac usually don't need the front-end oscillator circuit since the juice is already in the alternating current format required by the transformer (most transformers can't pass dc current). The transformer steps up the voltage to anywhere between 300 and about 2,000 volts. If the output voltage is high enough, voltage multiplication by means of diodes and capacitors is not required, but the ac component is removed by one or more diodes.

Some of the more advanced power supply circuits use a separate 6 to 10 kV *trigger transformer* to initially start or "ignite" the laser. The trigger transformer, similar to the kind used in photoflash equipment, fires only when the tube first turns on (but might continue firing if the tube doesn't ignite). A circuit in the power supply senses when the laser starts to draw current (indicating that it has started), and shuts the trigger transformer off. A silicon-controlled rectifier (SCR) serves as the switch to turn the trigger transformer on and off.

High-voltage triggering is not required for all tubes, especially those under 2 to 3 mW, but it is usually needed with higher output types. If your tube is hard to start—either refusing to ignite at all or just flickering—you may need to use a supply that has a high voltage trigger or at least one that supplies extra current. Most all commercially-made supplies have a built-in trigger transformer (or something equivalent) but home-brew supply circuits generally do not.

Using a high-powered laser with a power supply that can't deliver the required current may actually damage the supply. TABLE 5-1 lists the average voltage and current requirements for a variety of tubes. The tubes are rated by their output only so the chart should be used only for estimating power requirements. Many other factors, such as polarization of the beam and operating mode, can affect the power output and change the voltage and current requirements. Obtain descriptive literature from the seller of the laser tube if you need more precise information.

Note that most He-Ne tubes can be safely operated over a range of currents. Manufacturer's specifications usually list the recommended operating current for optimum performance. You can often safely increase or decrease the current slightly, for example,

Table 5-1. Voltage/Current Levels for Typical He-Ne Tubes

Power Output	Dimensions	Voltage w/Ballast	Tube Voltage	Typical Current
0.5 mW	5.00/1.00	1250	900	3.5 mA
0.5 mW	6.00/1.12	1390	1050	4.5 mA
1.0 mW	8.90/1.12	1890	1400	5.0 mA
2.0 mW	8.90/1.45	1890	1400	5.6 mA
2.0 mW	10.60/1.45	1990	1500	6.5 mA
5.0 mW	13.80/1.45	2390	1900	6.5 mA
7.0 mW	16.15/1.45	2930	2400	7.0 mA

Notes:
* Dimensions are in inches, length by diameter.
* Tube voltage is without ballast resistor.
* Current rating is recommended maximum; many tubes will fire and lase at currents 20 to 30 percent less.
* Note higher current and voltage requirements for larger tubes in same power output class.

to produce a more powerful beam or to conserve battery power. Unless the specifications state otherwise, you should not exceed 7-8 mA operating current.

A Warning About High Voltage Power Supplies

You've undoubtedly read this before in this book, but the warning can't be stressed enough: *beware of high voltage power supplies*. Never touch the output terminals of the supply when it is on or you may receive a bad shock. Turn the supply off and unplug it before working with the laser.

The capacitors in the voltage multiplier section of the supply can retain current even when the system is turned off. Before touching the tube or power supply, *short the anode and cathode terminals together*. If you can't easily bring them together, keep a heavy-duty alligator-clip test cable handy. String it across the anode and cathode and short the leads.

The laser tube itself can also retain current after power has been removed. *Always short out the anode and cathode terminals of the laser before handling the tube*. Cylindrical head lasers with a male Alden connector can be discharged by touching the prongs of the connector against the metal body of the laser.

POWER OUTPUT

The greatest difference among helium-neon laser tubes is power output. There are some He-Ne tubes designed to put out as little as 0.5 mW of power, while others generate

10 mW or more of light energy. The difference in power output is not always visible to your eye because the spot made by a laser beam is brighter than your eye can register.

By far, the majority of helium-neon tubes are rated at 1-2 mW. This is adequate for most laser experiments and you rarely need more. In fact, lower power lasers are often easier to work with because the power supply requirements are not as stringent. You can get by with a smaller, lighter-weight power supply with a 1-2 mW tube. The higher power comes in handy, however, if you are engaged in holography (the more power the faster the exposure), outdoor surveying, and other applications where a bright beam is necessary.

Cylindrical head lasers, generally designed for use in telecopiers, laser facsimile machines, and supermarket bar code scanners, are generally engineered for high output. Most tubes in this class are rated at 5-8 mW, though a few—such as those made for laser facsimile devices—generate in excess of 10 mW. If you need lots of power check these out. Just be sure that the power supply delivers sufficient current and voltage to the tube.

Bear in mind that power output varies with tube age. A tube that originally produces two milliwatts when new may only generate 1.5 mW after several thousand hours of use. Careless handling also reduces the power output. Every shock or jolt may tweak the mirrors out of alignment, which reduces the power output. If the laser is abused, as it often is in industrial or commercial applications, the mirrors may become so out of whack that the tube no longer generates a beam.

The loss of output power is important to remember when buying used or surplus tubes. Even though the tube may have been rated at 2 mW, there is no guarantee that it's still providing that much power. You can readily measure the power output of a laser if you use a calibrated power meter, such as the Metrologic 45-450.

PHYSICAL SIZE

Helium-neon laser tubes come in a variety of sizes, depending on power output. Most are about 1 to 1¼ inches in diameter by 5-10 inches long. Some very small tubes are designed for use in hand-held bar code readers and generate less than 0.5 mW. Such ''pee-wee'' tubes are available from a few surplus sources and are fun to play with, but they are extremely fragile. They can be permanently damaged by even a moderate jolt.

Few He-Ne lasers put out more than 10 to 15 milliwatts. These tend to be the largest are usually enclosed in a cylindrical head. The tube may measure about 1.5 inches in diameter and 13 inches long; the entire enclosure is 1.75 inches in diameter by 15 inches in length. A typical aluminum-housed laser head is shown in FIG. 5-5.

Self-contained lab lasers can be most any size depending on the power output. Average size is approximately 24 by 4 by 3 inches (LWH).

BEAM CHARACTERISTICS

The beam emitted from most helium-neon tubes doesn't vary much between laser to laser. Except in special cases, the light has a wavelength of 632.8 nm, and can measure between 0.5 to 2 mm in diameter. The diameter (or *waist*) of the laser beam is measured in a variety of ways and under different operating modes of the laser; hence the wide

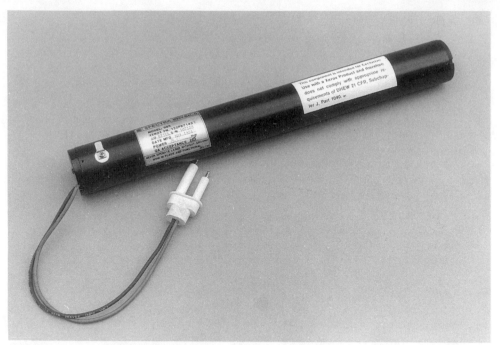

FIG. 5-5. *A typical cylindrical laser head, removed from a Xerox laser printer. Laser heads such as these are common finds in the surplus market.*

disparity in sizes. The diameter is less than the actual side-to-side measurement of the laser beam. Most manufacturers eliminate the outer 13.5 percent of the beam diameter, leaving the bright inside core.

As background, *single-mode* operation (sometimes called TEM_{00}-mode) of the laser produces a solid beam from side to side (looking from head-on). *Multi-mode* operation, which provides higher output power, causes the beam to separate into bands, as shown in FIG. 5-6. Note that most He-Ne tubes work in TEM_{00} mode only and the tube must be specially built to operate in multi-mode.

In TEM_{00} mode, the round beam of a laser has a plane wavefront and a Gaussian transverse irradiance profile. This mode experiences the minimum possible diffraction loss, has minimum divergence, and can be focused to the smallest possible spot.

The plane wavefront, as illustrated in FIG. 5-7, is a natural by-product of spatial coherence. All the waves in the beam are in lock-step, as if it were one big wave. The locking is constant across the diameter of the beam. This is in contrast to a circular wavefront, also shown in the figure, where the waves toward the outside radius of the beam are slightly behind the center waves. Note that you can easily convert the plane wavefront of laser light to circular wavefront simply by placing a lens in the path of the beam.

The Gaussian irradiance profile of a laser operating in TEM_{00} mode is shown in FIG. 5-8. The center 86 percent of the beam is the brightest; the irradiance of the beam falls off as you approach the edges of the beam. You can visually see this effect when the beam is spread using a bi-concave lens. Shine the light at a green or black card and note how the intensity of the beam is greatest at the center and less at the edges. If the

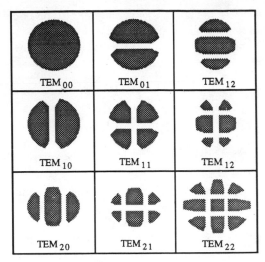

FIG. 5-6. *Only the single mode TEM$_{00}$ provides a solid beam throughout its diameter. Multi-mode operation increases the overall power output of the laser but splits the beam into many segments. The blank areas in the beam are nulls.*

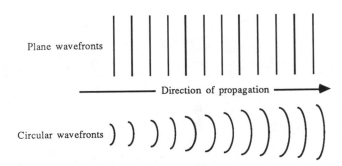

FIG. 5-7. *A comparison of plane and circular wavefronts. The plane wavefront geometry of the typical laser decreases divergence and provides coherency across the entire diameter of the beam.*

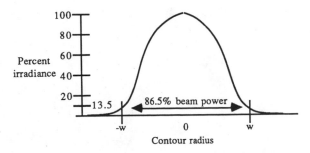

FIG. 5-8. *The Gaussian irradiance profile of an He-Ne laser (in TEM$_{00}$ mode). The peak of the irradiance profile is the center of the beam.*

beam is so bright that it causes a halo even on a green or black card, wear dark green glasses or pass the beam through a deep green filter.

Even without external optics, the divergence (spreading) of the laser beam is typically not over 1.2 milliradians (mrads). That means that at 100 meters, the beam will spread 120 millimeters, or about 4.7 inches. Computing beam divergence is more thoroughly covered in Chapter 14.

He-Ne lasers exhibit *random plane polarization*. That is, the beam is plane polarized (as discussed in Chapter 8) in either one direction or 90 degrees in the other. The polarization randomly toggles back and forth, but the switch-over is extremely fast and generally not detectable. In this regard, all laser tubes are polarized, but there is no control over the plane of polarization.

Some helium-neon tubes are designed with internal polarizing optics that block one of the planes. These are called *linearly polarized* tubes. Polarization of the beam is accomplished not with filters but with a clear window placed at *Brewster's angle* at the rear of the tube. The window is visible at the rear of the tube, as shown in FIG. 5-9, and is a clear indicator that the tube is linearly polarized. In some lasers, the rear of the tube is terminated with the Brewster window but lacks a totally reflective mirror. You must then add an external mirror to operate the laser.

Linearly polarized tubes are more expensive than randomly polarized ones and are generally low in power—typically less than 2 mW (higher power polarized tubes do exist,

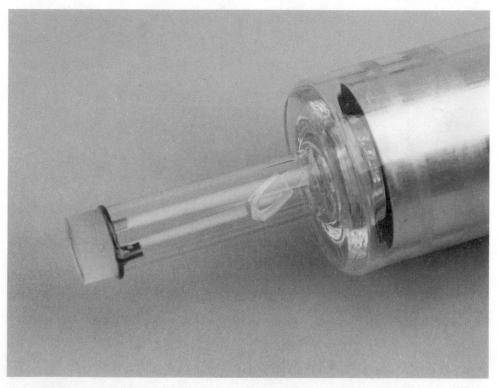

FIG. 5-9. *The tiny piece of glass positioned near the plane parallel mirror in this tube causes polarized beam output.*

but at a cost). However, polarized tubes are particularly handy in advanced holography, interferometry, high-speed modulation, and other applications where you need a stable output and a linearly polarized beam.

Of course, you can always polarize a laser by placing a polarizing filter in the path of the beam, but this significantly reduces the intensity of the beam. In most applications you need as much beam intensity as possible.

Most linearly polarized tubes are rated by their polarization purity. The purity is expressed as a ratio, such as 300:1 or 500:1. That is, under normal operating conditions, the tube is 300 or 500 times per likely to emit one plane of polarization over the other. Few applications, even precisely controlled laboratory experiments, require polarization purity greater than 500:1.

A laser beam might appear grainy or spotty when reflected off a white or lightly colored wall. This effect is called *speckle* and is caused by local interference. Even a smooth, painted surface has many hills and valleys in comparison to the wavelength size of the laser beam. These small imperfections in the surface bounce light in many directions. The uneven reflection causes constructive and destructive interference, where the light waves from the beam either reinforce or cancel one another.

Speckle is also produced in your eye as the beam strikes the surface of the retina. If you move your head, the speckle appears to move, too. Interestingly, beam speckle can be used to detect near- or short-sightedness. The speckle moves in the same direction as the head when viewed by a person with normal vision. But the speckle will appear to move in the opposite direction as the head when viewed by persons suffering from near- or far-sightedness. If you and any of your friends wear glasses, you can try this experiment for yourselves.

HE-NE COLORS

A He-Ne tube generates many different colors. You can see these colors by looking at a bare tube with a diffraction grating (an example is shown on the cover of the book, taken with a criss-cross diffraction grating). The diffraction grating disperses the orange glow of the plasma tube into its component colors. Note that just about every primary and secondary color is present, with dark lines between each one. The dark areas represent in-between colors that are not generated within the tube.

Most all colors (plus infrared wavelengths you can't see) are transmitted out of the tube before they can be amplified. That prevents them from turning into laser light. Here's how it's done: The cavity mirrors of the laser are coated with a highly reflective material that reflects the wavelength of interest (such as 632.8 nm) but transmits the others. As the beam inside the laser grows in strength, it overcomes the reflectance of the output mirror and exits the tube. You can verify the purity of the output beam by examining the red spot of the beam with the diffraction grating. You will see only one, well-defined color.

He-Ne's emit a deep red beam at 632.8 nm because it is the strongest line. The other colors are weak or may not be sufficiently coherent or monochromatic. Yet there are some special helium-neon lasers that are made to operate at different wavelengths, namely 1.523 micrometers (infrared) and 543.5 nm (green). Green and infrared He-Ne lasers are exceptionally expensive (rare in the surplus market) and are designed for special applications.

You can see the 543.5 nm green line by examining a regular red He-Ne tube with a diffraction grating. You will also notice a second, darker red line at 652 nanometers. These and other spectra are created as the helium and neon atoms drop from their raised, excited state to various transition levels. FIGURE 5-10 shows a diagram of the energy levels within a typical He-Ne tube. As an aside, the invisible 1.523 micrometer line is the wavelength of the first helium-neon tubes that were developed by Javan, Bennett, and Herriott at Bell Telephone Labs.

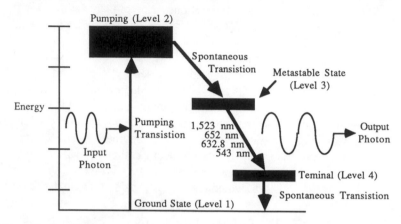

FIG. 5-10. *This simplified view of the energy levels of the He-Ne laser shows how photons are created as the atoms decay from their level 3 metastable state to an intermediate level 4 terminal state. Many wavelengths of light are created in the helium-neon gas mixture, but selective filtering provides a beam with a nearly pure wavelength of 632.8 nm (some He-Ne tubes operate at 1523 nm and 543 nm).*

THE ROLE OF THE BALLAST RESISTOR

Laser tubes operate at voltages between 1.2 and 3.0 kV (though some are higher or lower), but their current requirements are much more stringent. Most tubes in the 1- to 5-mW power output range are designed to consume between 3.5 and 5 milliamps of current. If consumption is any less, the tube won't fire anymore and could be damaged.

A helium-neon laser tube uses a ballast resistor to limit its current and to provide stable electrical discharge. The value of the ballast resistor varies depending on the tube and power output, but it's generally between 47kΩ and 230kΩ. The ballast resistor is usually placed close to the anode of the tube to minimize anode capacitance and to provide more stable operation.

You can safely operate most lasers between the 3.5- to 7-mA band gap recommended for He-Ne tubes, but the lower the current, the better. The tube will last longer and the power supply will operate more efficiently. If you have a choice of ballast resistor values, choose the highest one you can that fires the tube and keeps it running. If the tube sputters or blinks on and off, it might be a sign that it's not receiving enough current. Lower the value of ballast resistor and try again.

Commercially made power supplies designed for use with cylindrical head lasers are typically engineered *without* a ballast resistor. Rather, the resistor is housed in the end cap of the aluminum laser head—never forget this. If you use the power supply with a bare tube that lacks a ballast resistor, you can permanently ruin the laser. If in doubt, add the ballast resistor; you can always take it out later.

BUYING AND TESTING HE-NE TUBES

Not all helium-neon laser tubes are created equally. Apart from size and output power, tubes vary by their construction, reliability, and beam quality. After buying an He-Ne tube, you should always test it; return the tube if it doesn't work or if its quality is inferior.

Should you need a laser for a specific application that requires precision or a great deal of reliability, you might be better off buying a new, certified tube. The tube will come with a warranty and certification of power output. Because you're the only one handling the laser, you won't be bothered with such headaches as misaligned or chipped mirrors—unless you misalign or chip the mirrors yourself!

The documentation—a sort of pedigree that comes with the best tubes—will specify actual output, often within a tenth of a mW. For example, the tube may be rated by the manufacturer at 1 mW. That's the nominal output figure, but the documentation for the particular tube you receive might state the output was tested at exactly 1.3 mW. If you purchase many new tubes, you'll quickly discover that no two lasers are the same. Even though manufacturing tolerances are extremely tight, slight variations still exist. Much of this variation is due to mirror alignment.

Visual Inspection

The first step in establishing the quality of the tube is to inspect it visually. If the tube is used, be on the lookout for scratched, broken, or marred mirrors. Check both mirrors and use lens tissue and pure alcohol to clean them. Gently shake the tube and listen for loose components. Most tubes have a metal spider that holds the bore in place, and though it may rattle a bit, the spider should not be excessively loose. If the tube is an old one, it might have externally mounted mirrors (with most He-Ne tubes, the mirrors are mounted within the glass envelope). Carefully check the mirrors and mounts for loose components and scratches.

Inspect the tube carefully under a bright light and look for hairline cracks. If the tube is encased in a housing that contains a shutter, be sure the shutter opens when the laser is turned on (open the shutter manually if it is not electrically controlled).

Checking Laser Operation

After inspection, connect the tube to a suitable power supply. Be sure to read the section below if you are unsure how to connect the tube to the supply. Place the tube behind a clear plastic shield or temporarily cover it with a piece of cardboard. Flick the power supply on and watch for the beam. Listen for a sputtering or cracking sound; immediately turn off the power supply if you hear any anomalies. Point the laser toward a wall. If the laser is working properly, the beam comes out one end only and the beam spot is solid and well-defined.

Although one of the mirrors in an He-Ne tube should be completely reflective, they aren't always so. Occasionally, the totally reflective mirror allows a small amount of light to pass through and you see a weak beam coming out the back end (this is especially true if the mirror is not precisely aligned). Usually, this poses no serious problem unless the coating on the mirror is excessively weak or damaged or if the mirrors are seriously out of alignment.

All lasers exhibit satellite beams—small, low-powered spots that appear off to the side of the main spot. In most cases, the main beam and satellites are centered within one another, so you see just one spot. But slight variations and adjustment of the mirrors can cause the satellites to wander off axis. This can be unsightly, so if it matters enough to you, you might want to choose a tube that has one solid beam.

The satellites are caused by internal reflection from the output (partially reflective) mirror. The main and satellite beams are out of phase to one another because their path lengths are different. Some applications, such as advanced holography or interferometry, require you to separate the satellite beams from the main beam. You can do so with a spatial filter or metal flap.

When projected against a white or lightly colored wall, the beam from the laser might "bloom" with a visible, lightly colored ghost or halo. The ghost, which generally has a blue cast to it, sometimes makes it difficult to see the shape of the beam itself. Wearing a pair of green safety goggles helps to reduce the ghost, allowing you to see just the beam spot. You can also tack a piece of flat black or dark green paper on the wall and project the beam at it to reduce the effects of the ghost.

With just the beam itself cast on the wall or paper, inspect it for any irregularities. It should be perfectly round. If there are smears, try cleaning the output mirror and try again. Note that the beam will show nulls (dark spots) if the tube is not operating in TEM_{00} mode, as described above. These cannot be eliminated by cleaning.

Should the tube start but no beam comes out, check to be sure that nothing is blocking the exit mirror (or, is the laser an infrared type?). Clean it and try again. If the beam still isn't visible, the mirrors might be out of alignment. You cannot re-align mirrors that are fused to the glass tube unless the tube has alignment rings or wedges—and then the process depends largely on trial and error (and usually results in error).

Each ring is equipped with three or four hex screws. You readjust the mirrors by tightening and loosening one or all of the screws. Use a hex wrench that is *completely insulated* with high-voltage tape and take care not to touch any exposed metal parts. With the laser on, watch the output mirror and try loosening one of the screws. Does a beam appear? Keep trying, noting how you adjust each screw.

You might be able to make the beam appear by pressing down slightly on the wrench. That stresses the ends of the tube and can bring the mirrors into partial alignment. The idea is to work slowly and note the positions of the mirrors at each adjustment interval. Alignment becomes very difficult if both mirrors are out of whack.

If the tube doesn't ignite at all, check the power supply and connections. Try a known good tube if you have one. The tube still doesn't light? The problem could be caused by:

★ *Bad tube.* The tube is "gassed out," has a hairline crack, or is just plain broken.

★ *Power supply too weak.* The tube may require more current or voltage than the levels provided by the power supply.

★ *Insulating coating or broken connection on terminal.* New and stored tubes may have an insulating coating on the terminals. Be sure to clean the terminals thoroughly. A broken lead can be mended by soldering on a new wire.

Sputtering Tubes and Other Problems

Some ''problems'' with laser tubes are really caused by the power supply. In fact, if your laser doesn't work, suspect the power supply first. Even commercially made power supplies can burn out, especially if they are used with a tube they aren't designed for.

One common problem is when the tube sputters when you turn it on. This fault is most often caused by a tube that isn't receiving enough current. Inspect the connections from the power supply to the tube—make sure that there is no arcing. An arcing connection can cause the tube to blink.

If the tube is not designed for the power supply you are using, the supply (or tube) might have a ballast resistor that excessively restricts current. Locate the ballast resistor—it's usually on the power supply or mounted directly on the anode terminal of the tube. Try a slightly lower value, but be sure the resistor is rated for at least 3 watts (5 watts is even better).

Note that the tube may be unstable if the ballast resistor is too high or too low. The trick is to find the value that works with the tube. Specifications that accompany new tubes may indicate the recommended ballast resistor value; in most cases, you must experiment until you find the one that yields the best results.

The ballast resistor is often located in the end cap of laser tubes that are encased in an aluminum housing. Remove the end cap, if possible, by twisting it off. You might need to loosen one or more set screws. The ballast resistor is typically sealed inside the end cap with silicone rubber. Peel the rubber away and exchange the resistor with a lower value. If the new resistor works, repot it in the end cap with fresh silicone rubber sealant.

Long lead lengths can also cause sputtering. The longer the lead, the greater the loss of current. Most laser power supplies cannot power a laser with leads longer than about 12 to 18 inches. Small ''pee-wee'' power supplies, particularly those that run on 12 volts dc, should have no longer than 2- to 4-inch leads. Bear in mind that the length of the anode lead is of most importance; the cathode lead can be any reasonable length.

Some laser power supplies have a current adjust pot; turn it to see if it makes a difference. Exercise caution, however, and avoid yanking the current so high that you cause damage to the tube. You can test the current consumption of any tube by inserting a meter between the laser and power supply. Chapter 6, ''Build a He-Ne Laser Experimenter's System,'' provides the details. Few helium-neon lasers can be safely operated above 7 mA of current.

Hard-to-start tubes flick on but quickly go out. If the power supply incorporates a trigger transformer, the tube might ''click'' on and off once every 2 to 3 seconds (correlating to the time delay between each high-voltage trigger pulse). Tubes that haven't been used in a while can be hard to start, so once you get it going, keep it on for a day or two. In most cases, the tube will start normally.

Hard starting can also be caused by age and de-gassing, two factors you can't fix. A tube that simply won't start might suffer from inadequate current, regardless of ballast resistor, power lead length, and other variables. Be sure to use a power supply that delivers sufficient current. You will have better luck starting the tube if the power supply incorporates a high-voltage trigger transformer.

POWERING THE TUBE

Most surplus He-Ne tubes are sold without instructions of any type. It's up to you to know how to use it. For the uninitiated, this can seem frightening, but the detective work is actually simple. Follow these steps and you can get just about any tube working in a manner of minutes.

All He-Ne tubes have an anode (positive terminal) and cathode (negative terminal). In some cases, the terminals are marked with an "A" and "C" (sometimes "K") or simply "+" and "-." A few others have a red dot that indicates the anode. Following the polarity specified, connect the power supply so that the positive lead connects to the anode and the negative (or ground) lead connects to the cathode.

By far, most He-Ne tubes have no markings at all, and you are left wondering which one is which. Connecting the tube backwards to the power supply can damage the supply, the tube, or both. Also note that some power supplies must have a load on the output terminals or damage to the high-voltage components could result.

You can readily identify the cathode of most tubes by looking for the ring-shaped "getter" that rests near the inside wall of the tube. The getter is usually made of a zirconium-aluminum alloy and serves to remove trace gas residues after the tube is sealed during manufacture. In most all cases, the getter is connected to the cathode or at least to the spider, which is connected to the cathode. The area around the getter might have a silver discoloration, but this is not an indication that the tube is bad nor that it has been used excessively.

Another tip-off is the filling line originally used to pump the gasses into the tube. The filling line usually (*but not always*) denotes the cathode end. In fact, the line often doubles as the cathode connection.

Lasers enclosed in aluminum housings typically have leads coming out of an end cap. These leads terminate in a male high-voltage Alden connector, designed for use with a corresponding female connector attached to commercial laser power supplies. The thin prong of the connector denotes the anode.

If there is no connector, or another connector type is used, you can often identify the polarity of the leads by their color. As usual, red denotes positive (anode) and black (or sometimes white) denotes negative (cathode). Lasers that use a shielded coaxial cable use the inside conductor for the anode and the outside shield for the cathode.

USING THE TUBE

If you have not used your He-Ne laser yet, test it by connecting the power supply and applying juice. If the supply is one that's commercially made, there might be a 1- to 3-second delay before the laser turns on. This time delay allows the capacitors to charge and is also a CDRH requirement. If nothing happens after about 5 seconds, disconnect the power and check all the connections.

Once you get the laser running, keep it on for an hour or so. The tube will become warm, but if the supply is properly adjusted (that is, it's not delivering too much current), the laser will not be damaged. The "burn in" period provides a safety net; if the tube and supply are going to fail, it will likely be within the first hour or so of use. This allows you plenty of time to return the tube and/or power supply and obtain a replacement.

6

Build a He-Ne Laser
Experimenter's System

Bare laser tubes have a "shocking" personality—you'll want to enclose yours in a protective housing to make using it easier. You can place just the tube in the enclosure or make an all-in-one lab laser that incorporates both laser and high voltage power supply in one compact package. You might also want to house a cylindrical laser head in a box to keep it from rolling around the table.

This chapter provides plans on how to bundle a bare or cylindrical laser head in an easy-to-manage plastic enclosure. Several versions of laser housings are provided, including hand-held cylindrical pointers, box-type lab lasers, and mini optical breadboards.

BUILD AN ALL-IN-ONE LAB LASER

Small, 1- to 2-mW bare He-Ne's—along with their high-voltage power supplies—can be neatly packaged within a small plastic enclosure. Depending on the size of the enclosure, you should be able to use any commercially made power supply, as well as the home-brew power supply presented in Chapter 11.

Although plastic is a poor conductor of heat, neither power supply nor tube generate enough heat to do damage. However, you should avoid placing the tube or power supply components directly against the plastic of the enclosure. Allow some breathing room and provide ventilation slots or holes.

Basic Assembly

An assembly diagram for the all-in-one lab laser, using a 1.12-by-.9-inch, 1 milliwatt He-Ne tube and compact, commercially made 12-volt dc power supply, is shown in FIG.

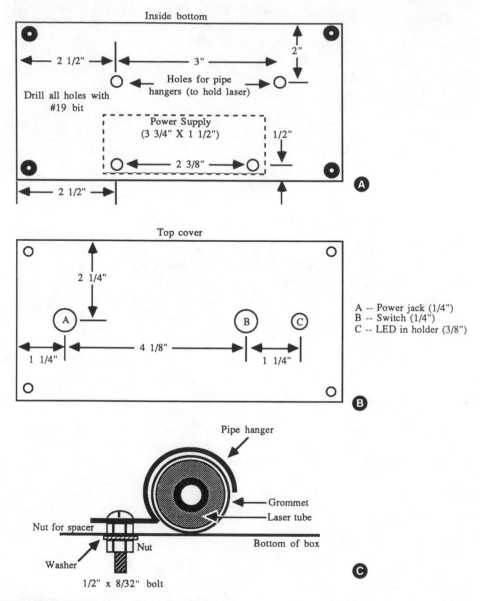

FIG. 6-1. *Drilling guide for the lab laser enclosure, using the components detailed in the text. (A) Drilling guide for the inside bottom of the enclosure; (B) Drilling guide for the top cover; (C) Mounting detail for the laser tube, pipe hanger, and grommet.*

6-1 (the power supply is available new and surplus). A parts list is provided in TABLE 6-1. The dimensions provided in the plans are for the power supply and He-Ne tube specified and fit well in a 7¾- by-4⅜- by-2⅜-inch plastic project box (available at Radio Shack).

Note that the actual size of your enclosure depends on the dimensions of your components. Measure the power supply and tube and buy parts to fit. Don't be afraid

Table 6-1. Lab Laser Parts List

R1	470 ohm resistor
R2	80 kilohm ballast resistor, 3 to 5 watts
LED1	Light-emitting diode
S1	SPST switch
J1	¼-inch phone jack
1	He-Ne laser tube (as specified in text)
1	12 Vdc modular power supply (as specified in text)
1	Plastic project box (7¾ by 4⅜ by 2⅜ inches)
2	¾- or 1-inch pipe hangers
2	⁸⁄₃₂ by ½-inch bolts
4	⁸⁄₃₂ inch nuts
2	#8 locking washers
Misc.	Rubber grommets or weather stripping, fuse clips or springs.

All resistors are 5-10 percent tolerance, ¼-watt, unless otherwise indicated.

of making the enclosure on the large side. Unless you are specifically after miniaturization, the larger the enclosure, the better the cooling of the components within.

Place stand-offs under the power supply and large grommets to support the tube. The grommets provide ventilation space between the laser and enclosure as well as shock absorption for the tube. You can use rubber weather stripping, O-rings, or high-voltage dielectric tape for the grommets.

Electrical Connection

You must connect the high voltage anode and cathode leads to the terminals on the tube. With most tubes, the terminals are the metal mirror mounts on each end of the laser. It's decidedly a bad idea to solder the leads directly to the terminals, yet the electrical connection must be solid and stable.

One method for attaching the high-voltage leads to the tube is to use a ⅝-inch compression spring (such as Century Spring S-676), as illustrated in FIG. 6-2A. These are readily available at most hardware stores. If the spring is too long, cut it with a pair of heavy clippers. Use a file to remove the outer coating of the spring (many are plastic coated), and then solder the power lead to the spring. Slip the spring over the terminal and inch it into place. If the spring won't fit over the terminals on your laser, use a larger or smaller type. Don't use a spring that's too heavy. A lightweight compression spring maintains electrical contact without stressing the mirror mount.

Another method is to use ¼-inch fuse clips (see FIG. 6-2B). You can buy these at most any electronics store, including Radio Shack. The clip is just about the right size for most laser tube terminals and can be easily soldered to the high- voltage leads. If the clip has small indentations for holding the fuses, bend these out with a pair of needle-nose pliers. You might need to tweak the clip a bit to get it to fit around the ends of the mirror mounts.

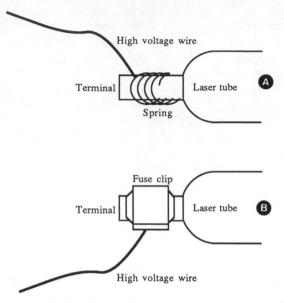

FIG. 6-2. *Two ways to attach the high-voltage leads to the laser tube terminals: by compression spring, and fuse clip. Be sure to file away any coating that might be on the spring, or electrical contact will be impaired.*

Final Assembly

Before permanently mounting the laser and power supply, note the position of the output mirror and drill a hole for the beam to escape. A ⁵⁄₁₆-inch hole provides plenty of room for mounting error and is about the size of the output mirror. You can drill a smaller hole, but you must be sure to precisely align the tube in the enclosure.

Next, drill holes in the top cover for the 12 Vdc power socket, on off switch, and LED indicator. Use a ¼- or ⁹⁄₃₂-inch bit for the ¼-inch phone jack; measure the diameter of the switch and LED and use the proper size drill bits for each. When drilling plastic, start with a small pilot hole, then enlarge it with bigger drill bits until the hole is the proper size. Place a block of wood behind the plastic to prevent chipping.

You can use a metal enclosure only if the power supply is completely sealed and all interconnections are insulated (this includes the leads that connect to the terminals on the tube). Use heat-shrinkable tubing rated for at least 20 kV, high-voltage heat-shrinkable dielectric tape, or high-voltage putty. You might also want to coat the inside of the enclosure with a non-conductive paint. I've had great success using brush-on plastic coating, the stuff designed as a covering for tool handles. Many plastics outlets sell this coating, which is available in brush- and dip-on forms.

Solder the connections between all components, as shown in the schematic in FIG. 6-3, and mount them in the enclosure. Avoid long wire lengths; keep all lead lengths as short as possible. Place the ballast resistor close to the anode terminal of the tube. Be sure that no leads interfere with the output beam of the laser. You might want to tie down the leads to keep them from wandering about in the enclosure. Use plastic tie wraps and secure the leads to the inside of the enclosure with a small piece of double-sided foam tape. Keep low-voltage and high-voltage leads separate. Finish the lab laser

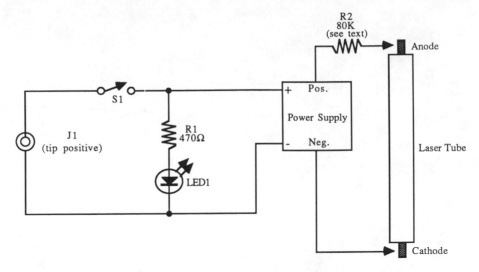

FIG. 6-3. *Wiring diagram for the lab laser. Be careful of the very high voltages present at the terminals of the laser and the output of the power supply.*

by adding rubber feet to the bottom of the enclosure. The finished laser is shown in FIG. 6-4A and B.

Power Supply

Power for the lab laser comes from a 12 Vdc battery pack or a 12 Vac adapter/battery eliminator. The battery or ac adapter must provide at least 350 mA current, or more, depending on the tube and high-voltage power supply used. Construction details for a battery pack and charger/adapter, suitable for use with the all-in-one lab laser, appear in Chapter 21.

BUILD AN ENCLOSED LASER HEAD

The all-in-one lab laser doesn't lend itself to hand-held portability. A bare laser tube can be easily shielded in a pipe that is suitable for hand-held use, or you can even mount one on an optical bench. You can use metal or plastic for the laser enclosure. Metal conducts heat more readily and is recommended if you plan on keeping the laser turned on for long periods of time. However, a plastic enclosure provides insulation against the high-voltage potentials present at the terminals of the laser.

The laser head used in this project is designed around a 2- mW Melles Griot plasma tube. The tube measures 1.45 inches in diameter by 10.6 inches in length. A piece of 1½-inch PVC pipe, cut to a length of 12 inches, serves as the enclosure. The pipe is capped off on both ends and a removable plug is attached to the enclosure to provide a shutter—a guard against accidental exposure to the beam.

The power supply pack, a separate component to the laser head, is designed to run off 117 Vac and includes a fuse, key switch, and pilot lamp. The design of this laser incorporates many of the safeguards required by the CDRH for a commercially sold Class II or Class IIIa device.

FIG. 6-4. *The completed lab laser: (A) With the cover removed, showing the mounting of the components, and (B) with cover in place.*

Table 6-2. Cylindrical Laser Head Parts List

R1   80 kilohm ballast resistor (3 to 5 watts)
1   He-Ne laser tube (as specified in text)
1   12-inches of 1½-inch, schedule 40 PVC
2   1½-inch plastic test plugs
1   1½-inch PVC end cap
Misc.   O-rings or grommets, fuse clips or springs, silicone sealant, 24-inch length
        of miniature plastic or metal chain, two eyelets for chain, two ¼-inch
        grommets.

Building the Laser Head

Refer to TABLE 6-2 for a parts list. FIGURE 6-5 shows the construction details of the laser head. Cut a piece of 1½-inch schedule 40 PVC to 12 inches. Make sure the cuts on both ends are square. Remove the rough edges with a file or fine-grit sand paper (300-grit wet/dry paper, used dry, is a good choice). Drill a hole, using a number 48 bit, a distance of ⅝-inch from the back end of the tube. This hole is for attaching the eyelet used to secure the protective cap chain (see below).

Solder the high-voltage leads to pair of springs or fuse clips, as detailed above. Insert a ballast resistor (80 kΩ, or more) between the anode terminal and anode lead, as shown in FIG. 6-6, and wrap the connections in heat-shrinkable tubing. Waft a lighter or match under the tubing or use a heat gun to shrink it around the resistor and other connections.

Thread the wires through a grommet and poke the grommet inside a ¼-inch hole drilled in the center of a 1½-inch test plug. Secure the grommet and resistor by applying a layer of silicone rubber over the inside surface of the test plug and let dry.

Once the sealant has set, attach the springs or fuse clips to the terminals on the laser tube. Wrap O-rings, electrical tape, or rubber bands around the tube, as shown in FIG. 6-7, and insert the tube in the PVC pipe. The output mirror should be

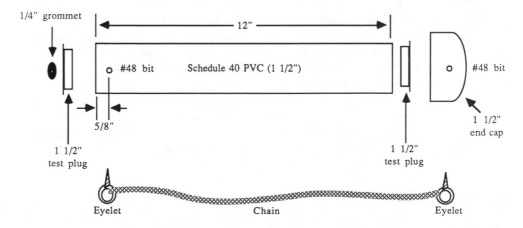

FIG. 6-5. *Construction details for the cylindrical laser head. Adjust pipe diameter and length to accommodate the exact dimensions of the tube you are using.*

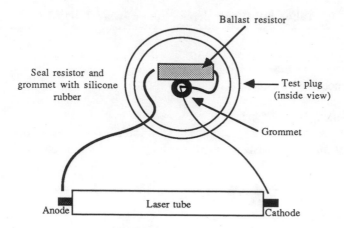

FIG. 6-6. *After soldering the leads to the ballast resistor, secure the resistor to the test plug with silicone rubber sealant. For a professional look, feed the high-voltage leads through a grommet mounted in the center of the plug. Be sure to use high-voltage dielectric wire (rated 3 kV or more) or you can receive a bad shock.*

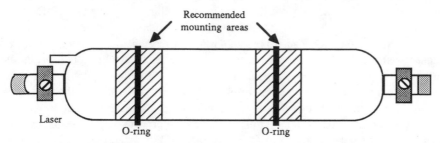

FIG. 6-7. *Recommended mounting areas on a bare glass He-Ne tube. You can use large O-rings or grommets as shock absorbers (shock absorption reduces "microphonic noise" that can impair the coherent operation of the laser).*

approximately ½-inch from the end of the tube. Secure the test plug to the other end of the tube with a dab of all-purpose adhesive.

Next, drill a ¼-inch hole in the center of another test plug and mount it on the output end of the tube. Secure the plug with glue (not PVC solvent cement).

Construct the protective plug using a 1½-inch PVC end cap. Secure it to the tube using a miniature eyelet and 24-inch length of lightweight metal or plastic chain. Insert another eyelet in the small hole previously drilled in the PVC pipe. Secure the other end of the chain to the eyelet. Be sure that the eyelet doesn't interfere with the tube, ballast resistor, or high-voltage leads. If the threads of the eyelet contact internal parts, cut the shaft of the eyelet so that it doesn't protrude inside the pipe. Apply glue to hold the eyelet in place.

Building the Power Pack

Refer to TABLE 6-3 for the parts list for the power pack. The power pack uses a commercially available 117 Vac high-voltage laser power supply. You can use a dc power supply if you need a completely portable and self-contained laser. Many new and surplus

Table 6-3. Laser Head Power Supply Parts List

S1	Key switch
L1	Neon lamp (with dropping resistor)
1	Plastic project box (6½ by 3¾ by 2 inches)
Misc.	Fuse holder, ac plug and cord, two ¼-inch grommets

ac power supplies are modular, sealed in a box measuring 1⅜-by-4¼-by-3⁵⁄₁₆-inches. The power supply may be equipped with an Alden high-voltage connector or flying leads (tinned pigtail leads, with no connector). If the supply has an Alden connector, cut it off and save it for future use—female Alden connectors are hard to find. Use the two or three holes in the module to mount the supply in a 6½-by-3¾-by-2-inch plastic experimenter's box (you can use any plastic box that is large enough for the power supply, switch, and other components). *Do not* drill holes in the module—you'll undoubtedly drill through the components sealed inside.

Follow the drilling guide shown in FIG. 6-8, and drill holes in the enclosure for the power cord (allowing extra for the grommet), indicator lamp, and key switch. Use a rotary

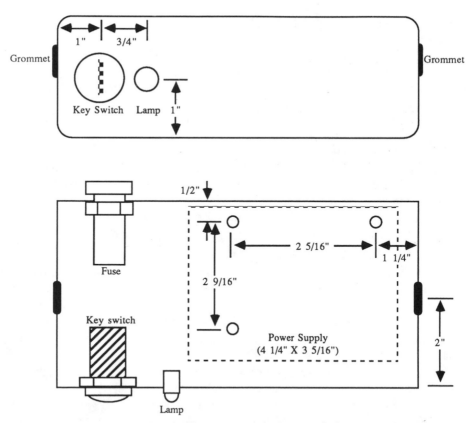

FIG. 6-8. *Layout and drilling guide for the laser head power supply. Drill holes large enough to accommodate the fuse holder, key switch, and neon lamp that you are using. The drilling guide assumes you are using a commercially made modular power supply (dimensions indicated in the figure).*

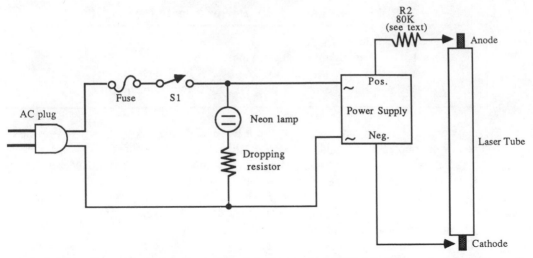

FIG. 6-9. *Wiring diagram for the laser head power supply. Beware of potentially lethal voltages throughout this circuit.*

rasp or countersink bit for the larger holes. Drill small pilot holes first to avoid chipping or cracking the plastic with large bits.

Use 16-gauge wire and solder the components as shown in FIG. 6-9. Keep wire lengths as short as possible. After soldering is complete, mount the components in the enclosure and route the grommet and power cord in the appropriate hole. Wrap all high-voltage leads in 20 kV heat-shrinkable tubing or tape and apply high-voltage putty to eliminate arcing. You may also insulate the wiring using clear aquarium tubing. Double check your work (use a meter as a safety measure) and insert a 2-amp fast-acting fuse in the fuse holder.

Test the laser by plugging in the power supply and turning the key switch to the ON position. The indicator light should turn on, and within 3 to 5 seconds, the laser should fire. If the indicator lamp and laser do not turn on, it could indicate a wiring problem or blown fuse. Recheck your work to make sure the wiring is correct.

BUILD A COMPACT LASER BREADBOARD

A breadboard allows you to experiment with lasers and other optical components without elaborate mounting and construction. The laser breadboard presented here is a semi-permanent mount for a commercial- or home-made cylindrical laser head and serves as a "head-end" for the optical breadboards detailed in the next chapter. The laser and optical breadboards are constructed with the same inexpensive materials, allowing you to mix and match as you desire.

Follow the construction details shown in FIG. 6-10 (parts list in TABLE 6-4). Cut a piece of ¼-inch pegboard to 6- by 18-inches. Sand the front, back, and edges and spray on a coat or two of clear lacquer (this seals the wood). Cut lengths of 2-by-2-inch lumber and use nails or screws to attach the wood to the pegboard. You may wish to substitute 4¹/₆₄-by-½-by-¹/₁₆-inch aluminum channel for the 2-by-2 lumber. Refer to the next chapter on how to use aluminum channel stock.

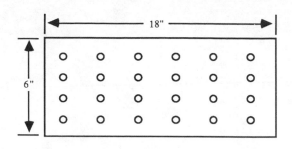

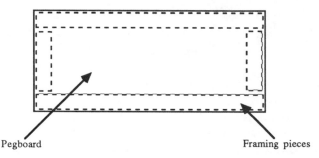

Pegboard   Framing pieces

FIG. 6-10. *A simple optical breadboard can be constructed using an 18- by 6-inch piece of ¼-inch Masonite pegboard and lengths of 2-by-2 framing lumber. Cut the lumber as indicated in the parts list in* TABLE 6-4.

Cylindrical laser heads mount easily in a clamp made with PVC pipe. Cut a length of 2-inch PVC to 3 inches. Next, carefully split the pipe in half down the middle using a hacksaw or table saw. Finish all edges with a file. Use the holes already in the pegboard as a template, and drill two holes in each PVC half. Next, mount the pipe halves in the breadboard. Use $^8/_{32}$-by-¾-inch bolts, $^8/_{32}$ nuts, and washers. Before tightening the hardware, slip the loose end of a 3-inch adjustable hose clamp under each piece of pipe. Tighten the hardware and close the clamp. Mount small rubber feet on top of the four bolt heads, then slide the laser head into the mount, as shown in FIG. 6-11. Tighten the clamps.

Table 6-4. Parts List for Mini Optical Breadboard

1	18- by 6-inch sheet of ¼-inch pegboard
2	18-inch length of 2-by-2-inch framing lumber
2	3-inch length of 2-by-2-inch framing lumber
2	3-inch lengths of 2-inch schedule 40 PVC (cut lengthwise)
4	$^8/_{32}$ by ¾-inch bolts, nuts, and washers
2	3-inch (approx.) adjustable hose clamps
Misc.	Nails or screws for securing pegboard to framing lumber, rubber feet or rubber weather stripping

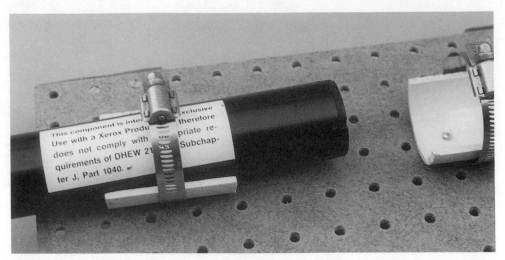

FIG. 6-11. *Secure the laser on the breadboard using lengths of 2-inch PVC cut lengthwise and fastened to the pegboard with ¹⁰⁄₂₄ hardware. The laser can be lashed in place with an adjustable car radiator hose clamp.*

You can mount the power supply in a number of locations, depending on its size and design. Sealed, modular power supplies can be mounted on top of the breadboard next to the laser. If it's small enough, you can tuck the power supply underneath the breadboard. Unsealed supplies should be placed in a protective housing and can be mounted on the breadboard or simply placed along side of it.

7

Constructing an
Optical Bench

An optical bench is a device that allows you to experiment with lasers and optics by mounting them securely on a rigid base. Components can be easily added or deleted, using any of a number of fastening systems, including nuts and bolts, magnets, sand, styrofoam, or even clay. The optical bench is the equivalent of the solderless breadboard used in electronics. Once you are satisfied that your project works, you can disassemble it and start on another project or re-assemble the components in a permanent housing.

There are a number of useful design approaches to optical benches in this chapter. You can make an optical bench of just about any size, up to a practical limit of 4 by 8 feet. Projects that follow show how to build a 2-by-4 foot bench as well as a 4-by-4 foot model. Construction materials are cheap and easy to get, and you're free to use more exotic materials if you desire.

You'll also learn how to construct components for an optical breadboard system. Small, Lego-like blocks can combine to facilitate just about any design. The mounting of lenses, mirrors, and other optical parts is tricky business; this chapter includes several affordable approaches that make the job easier.

BASIC 2-BY-4-FOOT OPTICAL BENCH

The basic 2-by-4-foot optical bench is made completely of wood. Using the parts indicated in TABLE 7-1, start with a 2-by-4-foot chunk of ¼-inch pegboard.

After sizing the pegboard, sand the edges as well as the front and back (the back will have a coarse finish and the front will be smooth). Seal the wood by spraying or brushing on one or more coats of clear lacquer or enamel. Let dry completely, then proceed to the next step.

Table 7-1. 2-by-4-Foot Optical Bench Parts List

1	2-by-4-foot, ¼-inch pegboard
2	48-inch lengths of 2-by-2-inch framing lumber
2	18-inch lengths of 2-by-2-inch framing lumber
Misc.	Nails or screws to secure pegboard to lumber, weather stripping

Now for the frame of the bench. Cut two 4-foot lengths of 2-by-2 lumber. Use nails or screws and attach the lumber pieces to the long sides of the pegboard. Next, cut two 18-inch lengths of 2-by-2 lumber and secure them to the ends. Center the 18-inch lengths so that there is an even gap on either side. You can use just about any size lumber for the frame, but you should be consistent in case you build more optical benches. By using the same framing lumber, you maintain a constant height for each bench. Several benches can be used together on a large table.

While you can use the bench as is, it's a good idea to paint it with flat black paint. The black paint helps cut down light scatter and also imparts a more professional look. Rubber feet (for electronics projects) or rubber or foam weather stripping make for good cushions and shock absorbers, and they prevent marring desks and tabletops. Apply the rubber to the underside of the frame.

ENHANCED 4-BY-4-FOOT OPTICAL BENCH

The enhanced 4-by-4-foot optical bench is also made with ¼-inch pegboard, but the frame is of all-metal construction. You may use aluminum or steel shelving standards or ⁴¹⁄₆₄-by-½-by-¹⁄₁₆-inch extruded aluminum channel for the frame.

The parts list for the 4-by-4-foot bench is included in TABLE 7-2. Use a hacksaw (with a fine-tooth blade) to cut the metal to size as shown in FIG. 7-1. Be sure to cut each piece with the proper 45-degree miter. Use a miter box and C-clamps for best results. After cutting, remove the flash and rough edges from the ends of the metal with a file. Secure the framing pieces to the underside of the pegboard using ⁸⁄₃₂-by-½-inch hardware. A diagram of the completed bench is shown in FIG. 7-2.

Because of the size of the pegboard sheet, it might buckle in the middle under the weight of a heavy object. If this is a problem, add one or more reinforcing struts to the underside of the bench. An extra piece of shelving (standard or aluminum channel) can be mounted down the center of the bench. Secure the extra piece to the frame using ½-inch angle-iron brackets (available at the hardware store).

Table 7-2. 4-by-4-Foot Optical Bench Parts List

1	4-by-4-foot, ¼-inch pegboard
4	48-inch lengths of ⁴¹⁄₆₄- by ½- by ¹⁄₁₆-inch aluminum channel stock
4	1½- by ⅜-inch flat corner irons
8	⁸⁄₃₂ by ½-inch bolts, nut, lock washers
Misc.	Weather stripping or rubber feet for bottom of channel stock

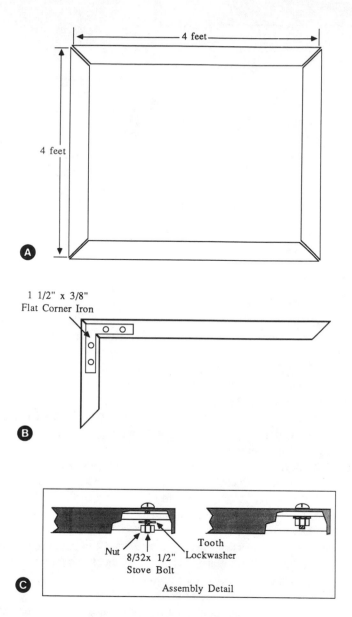

FIG. 7-1. *(A) Cutting guide for the aluminum channel used as a frame for the 4-by-4-foot optical bench. Be sure to miter the ends as shown. (B) Use 1½-by-⅜-inch flat corner irons to secure the ends. (C) Assembly detail for the framing pieces and corner irons showing ⁵⁄₃₂ hardware.*

Note: when drilling through metal, use only a new or sharpened bit. The drill motor should turn slowly—less than 1,000 rpm. Exert only enough pressure to bite into the metal, not enough to bend the metal or bit while drilling. Remove the flash around the drilled hole with a file.

As with the smaller version of the optical bench, paint this one a flat black to reduce light reflections. Also be sure to paint over the shiny heads of the machine screws.

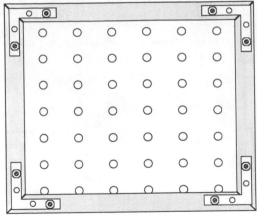

FIG. 7-2. *The underside of the optical bench, showing aluminum channel framing pieces, corner irons, and mounting hardware.*

Bottom View

Adding a Sheet-Metal Top

The pegboard optical bench is suitable for most hobbyist applications. The wood is sturdy, absorbs many vibrations, and is easy to drill. However, experiments that require greater precision need an all-metal optical bench. One can be constructed using medium-to thin-gauge aluminum, steel, or regular sheet metal. Large sheets or plates of metal are not routinely available at a hardware store, so look in the Yellow Pages under headings such as aluminum, metal specialties, sheet metal work, and steel.

Many sheet-metal shops work with thin-gauge metal—20- to 24-gauge or thinner. This is too thin to be used alone, but you can laminate it over the pegboard. The thickness of plate aluminum and steel is most commonly listed in inches, not gauge. A ⅛- or ³⁄₁₆-inch thick piece of aluminum or steel does nicely as the top of the optical bench. Steel is cheaper, but aluminum is easier to work with. The average price for a 2-by-4-foot piece of ³⁄₁₆-inch hot roll steel is about $25 to $30. The same size plate in un-anodized aluminum is approximately three times as much.

You might be lucky and find an outlet that sells pre-drilled stock. More than likely, however, you have to do the work yourself if you want the convenience of pre-drilled holes in your optical bench. Use a large carpenter's square to lay out a matrix of lines spaced either ½- or 1-inch apart (I prefer holes at ½-inch centers, but obviously this requires you to drill four times as many holes).

You might find it easier to place masking tape on the metal and mark the lines with a pencil. Use a carbide-tipped bit (#19 bit for ⁸⁄₃₂ hardware) and heavy-duty drill motor. A drilling alignment tool, available as an option for many brands of drill motors, helps to make perpendicular holes.

Using Plastic Instead of Metal

Another approach to the benchtop is acrylic plastic (Plexiglas, Lexan, and so forth). The advantages of plastic are that it is extremely strong for its weight and is easier to work with than metal. A steel top adds considerable weight to the bench (which in some cases is desirable), while a plastic top adds little weight.

A 2-by-4-foot piece of ³⁄₁₆- or ¼-inch acrylic plastic costs $6 to $8; you can buy sheets of plastic at most plastic fabricator outlets. Have them cut the plastic to size and finish the edges. You can drill through the plastic for the mounting holes using a regular bit, but better results are obtained when using a special plastic/glass drill bit.

USING OPTICAL BENCHES

Because pegboard stock already has holes, you probably won't need to drill new ones to mount the laser and other optical components. The holes are pre-drilled with better-than-average accuracy so you can use them for alignment. You can place a series of mirrors and lenses along one row of holes, for example, and they will all line up to one another.

There might be occasion, however, to drill new holes in the pegboard. Extra holes (⁵⁄₃₂-inch or #19 bit for ⁸⁄₃₂ hardware) should be ¼ inch or more away from existing holes, or the bit might slip while you are drilling. Schemes for mounting the laser and optical components appear later in this chapter.

As you complete a project or make changes to an existing experiment, keep notes and record the placement of all components. You might want to mark the rows and columns of holes as a reference for indicating the location of components. For example, you can mark all the rows with a letter and all columns with a number. A mirror placed at the intersection of C6 could be marked on a piece of graph paper. You can develop your own shorthand for identifying various optical components, but here are some suggestions:

- ✸ S-FSM—small front-surface mirror
- ✸ L-FSM—large front-surface mirror
- ✸ P-BS—plate beam splitter
- ✸ C-BS—Cube beam splitter
- ✸ RAP—right-angle prism
- ✸ EQP—equilateral prism
- ✸ SPP—special prism
- ✸ POL—polarizer
- ✸ EXP—beam expander
- ✸ SPA—spatial filter
- ✸ L(XXX)—Lens (with type, size, and focal length)

You might also want to provide shorthand notation for any special components you use, such as single and double slits, diffraction gratings, optical fibers and fiber couplers, diode lasers, LEDs, sensors, and more.

OPTICAL BREADBOARD COMPONENTS

Small versions of the optical benches described above make perfect optical breadboards. Each breadboard, measuring perhaps 8- by 12-inches, can contain a complete optical sub-assembly, such as a laser and power supply (as described in the previous chapter), beam expander, beam director or splitter, sensing element, or lens array. You can construct a breadboard for each sub-assembly you commonly use. For example, if you often experiment with lasers and fiberoptics, one breadboard would consist of a laser/power supply and the other a fiberoptic coupling, cable, and sensor.

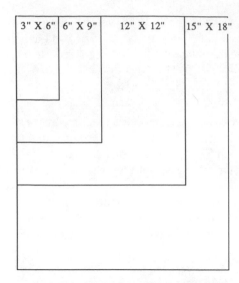

3" X 6"	6" X 9"	12" X 12"	15" X 18"

FIG. 7-3. *Suggestions for possible sizes for optical breadboards, but you can make your breadboards any size you wish.*

Construct the small breadboards in the same fashion as the larger optical benches detailed earlier in this chapter. Use the same materials for each breadboard to maintain consistency. Several sizes of breadboards are shown in FIG. 7-3. Use the scrap from the construction of the optical bench for the short lengths of framing pieces.

To use the breadboard pieces, lay them out like building blocks on a large, flat surface. The dining room table is a good choice, but be sure to place a drop cloth or large piece of paper on the table surface to prevent marring and scratching. You can also add rubber feet, rubber weather stripping, or foam weather stripping to the bottom of the breadboard pieces.

Lay out the pieces in the orientation you require for the project. If you've used paper as a drop cloth, you can draw on it to mark the edges of the breadboards. This is helpful in case you want to repeat an experiment and need to replace the breadboard pieces in the same spot.

LASER AND OPTICS MOUNTS

The optical bench or breadboard serves as a universal surface for mounting lasers and various optical components. The type of mounting you use for your laser and optics depends on their individual design, and most parts can be successfully secured to a bench or breadboard using one or more of the following techniques. Keep in mind that you might need to adjust the dimensions and design for each mounting configuration to conform to your particular components.

Laser Mounts

One of the most versatile yet easiest to construct laser mounts uses a piece of 2-inch (inside diameter) PVC cut in half lengthwise. Building plans are provided in Chapter 6. The mount is designed for use with cylindrical laser heads, either commercially-made versions or ones you build yourself using bare laser tubes.

Another approach to laser mounting is shown in FIG. 7-4. A pipe hanger, designed for electrical and plumbing pipe, secures a bare laser tube to the optical bench. This

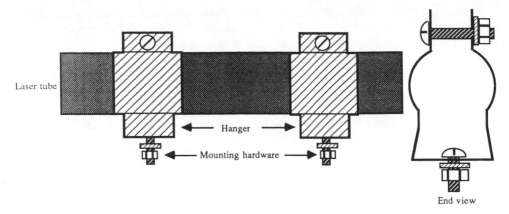

FIG. 7-4. *Cylindrical laser heads can be secured to optical benches and breadboards using pipe hangers. Choose a hanger large enough to accommodate the diameter of the laser, and avoid overtightening.*

approach is not recommended unless you shield the tube with an insulating box or cover the anode and cathode terminals on the laser with high-voltage putty or high-voltage heat-shrinkable tubing.

Pipe hangers come in various sizes to accommodate pipe from ½-inch to 2½-inches (outside dimension is approximately ¾ inch to 3 inches). Get a size large enough to easily fit the tube. Add a few layers of plastic tape around the tube where the hanger touches. *Do not* overtighten the hanger, or you run the risk of cracking or breaking the tube! You may use bigger hangers to mount cylindrical laser heads. Most commercially manufactured cylindrical heads measure 1.74 inches in diameter and can be successfully mounted using a 1½- or 2-inch hanger. All-in-one lab lasers (commercial or home-built) don't usually need mounting, because their housing lets you place them just about anywhere, yet some projects require you to secure the laser to the optical bench so that it doesn't move. Use straps or wood blocks to hold the laser in place, or drill mounting holes in the housing and attach the laser to the bench using nuts and bolts. The latter technique is not recommended if you are using a commercially made lab laser, because any modification voids its CDRH certification. Your own home-built lab laser (as detailed in Chapter 6, can be modified by locating a spot inside where the hardware will not interfere with the tube or power supply.

Lens Mounts

Lenses present a problem to the laser experimenter because they come in all sizes and shapes. Unless you are very careful about which lenses you buy (and purchase them new from prime sources), you will have little choice over the exact diameter of lenses

Table 7-3. Tube Hanger Laser Mount System Parts List

2	Plumbing pipe hanger (see text for diameters)
2	$^{10}/_{24}$ by ¾- or 1-inch carriage bolts, nuts, lock washers
2	$^{8}/_{32}$ by ½-inch bolts, nuts, and lock washers

you use. That makes it hard to build lens mounts using tubing and retaining rings, which come in only a few standard sizes. Another problem is that many lenses suitable for laser experiments are small, which makes them difficult to handle.

With a bit of ingenuity, however, you can make simple lens holders for most any size lens you encounter. The basic ingredient is patience and a clean working environment. As much as possible, handle lenses by the edges only and work in a well-lit, clean area— free from dust, cigarette smoke, and other contaminates.

A basic lens mount is shown in FIG. 7-5, and is useful for lenses as small as 4 mm to as large as 30 mm. Start by cutting a ledge in one end of a piece of ¾-inch PVC pipe coupling. Use a fine-toothed hacksaw to make two right-angle cuts. Smooth the rough edges with a file or wet/dry sandpaper (used dry). Next, use a caliper or accurate steel rule to measure the diameter of the lens. Choose a drill bit just slightly smaller than the diameter of the lens, and drill a hole in the remaining stub on the pipe coupler. Remember: you can always enlarge a hole to accommodate the lens, but you can't make it smaller.

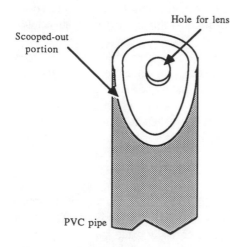

Hole for lens

Scooped-out portion

PVC pipe

FIG. 7-5. *One of the best (and easiest) ways to mount a lens is inside one wall of a piece of PVC pipe or coupler. You can make the hole the same size as the lens (for a friction fit) or slightly smaller (glue the lens on the outside wall of the pipe using all-purpose adhesive).*

Press the lens into the hole. Don't exert excessive pressure or you may crack the lens. If the hole is too small, use a larger bit or enlarge the hole with a fine rat-tail file (the kind designed for model building works nicely). After careful drilling and filing, you should be able to pop the lens into the hole but still have enough friction-fit to keep it in place. The lens is not mounted permanently, so it can be removed if you have another use for it. Clean the lens using an approved lens cleaner. Refer to Chapter 3 for details on lens care and cleaning.

The PVC coupling holder can be mounted on the optical bench in a number of ways. Several methods are shown in FIG. 7-6. The hole for the thumbscrew does not require tapping but tapping makes the job easier. Use a ⁴⁄40 or ⁶⁄32 thumbscrew or regular pan-head machine bolt as the set screw. The hardware used for mounting the holder on the bench is a ¹⁰⁄24- or ¼-inch 20 carriage bolt, secured in place with a threaded rod coupler (cut the coupler if it is too long for the PVC holder). You can adjust the height and angle of the lens by loosening the thumbscrew and adjusting the holder.

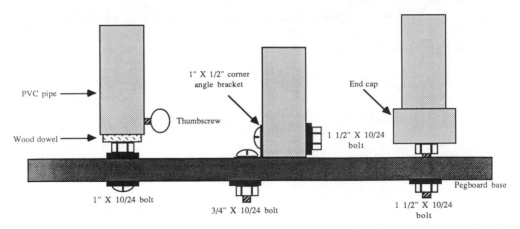

FIG. 7-6. *Various ways to attach PVC pipe to a pegboard optical bench. If the bench is ferrous metal (steel, not aluminum), you can build a magnetic base by gluing a magnet to the bottom of the pipe.*

White PVC plastic can cause light to scatter, so you might want to coat the lens holders with flat black paint. The small spray paints sold by Testor (and available wherever model supplies are sold) adhere well to PVC.

The PVC pipe can be used simply as a holder for mirrors, beam splitters, and other components. A length of 1- or 1¼-inch PVC, pressed in a vise, can be used to hold thin Masonite board or acrylic plastic. You can mount mirrors, lenses, plate beam splitters, and other components on the Masonite. Cut the Masonite to a width just slightly larger than the inside diameter of the PVC (1¼-inches for schedule 40 1¼-inch PVC). Clamp the pipe in a vise until it deforms into an ellipse. Stick the Masonite board in the pipe and slowly release the vise. The pipe will spring back into shape, holding the Masonite. You can also directly mount thick plate beam splitters and mirrors into the PVC. Don't try it with thin optics, or they could shatter as the PVC springs back into shape.

A way to mount lenses of almost any size is to tack them on a piece of ⅛-inch acrylic plastic. The acrylic pieces needn't be much larger than the lens itself, but you should allow room for mounting hardware. Black plastic with a matte finish is the all-around best choice, although you can always coat the plastic with black matte paint.

Drill a hole in the plastic just smaller than the lens, leaving enough room for the edges of the lens to make contact with the plastic. After drilling, place the lens directly over the hole. Apply two or three small dabs of all-purpose adhesive (such as Duco cement) to the outside edges of the lens. Use a syringe applicator or toothpick to dab on the adhesive.

Be sure that no ''strings'' of the cement cover or come in contact with the usable area of the lens. If you make a mistake, immediately remove the lens, wash it in water, and clean the lens with approved cleaner. Although you can remove undried cement with chemicals such as acetone and lacquer thinner, these compounds could have an adverse effect on lens coatings.

Some lenses are square as opposed to round and can be mounted on the top of a short length of PVC pipe or small piece of ⅛-inch acrylic plastic. Be sure to mount the lens perpendicular to the plastic, or the laser beam might not follow the path you want.

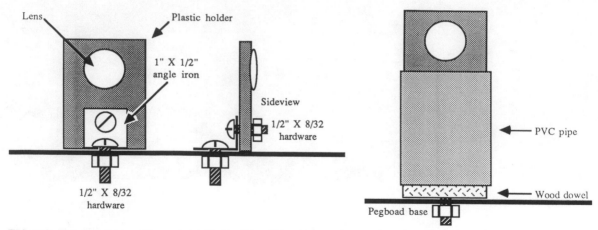

FIG. 7-7. *Two ways to mount lenses to acrylic plastic and how to secure the plastic to the optical bench. You can use angle irons (available at the hardware store) or insert the plastic into a short length of PVC pipe.*

Let the adhesive dry completely, then mount the lens and holder as shown in FIG. 7-7. The illustration provides a number of mounting techniques. In one, the holder is mounted to a pipe, which is attached to the shaft of a bolt. The length of the bolt depends on the size of the holder and lens but is generally between 1 and 3 inches long. You can alter the height of the bolt by adjusting the mounting nuts, as illustrated in FIG. 7-8. Parts lists for the lens-mounting systems are included in TABLE 7-4.

Round lenses measuring between 21 and 26 mm in diameter can be inserted inside ¾-inch PVC coupling. The lenses are held in place with thin pieces of ¾-inch pipe. Follow the instructions shown in FIG. 7-9. Cut a ¾-inch slip coupling in half, discarding the

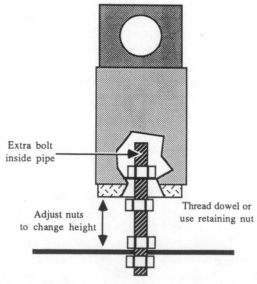

FIG. 7-8. *A set of nuts and a long bolt allow you to adjust the height of the PVC pipe in relation to the surface of the optical bench.*

Table 7-4. Lens Holders and Mounts Parts List

For PVC Lens Mount/Thumbscrew Adjustable Height (Fig. 7-6)
1   ¾- or 1-inch schedule 40 PVC pipe, length 2 to 5 inches
1   2- to 4-inch length of ¾- or 1-inch wood dowel (trim to fit in pipe)
1   ⁸⁄₃₂ machine thumbscrew
1   ¹⁰⁄₂₄ by 1-inch bolt, nut
2   # 10 flat washers

For PVC Lens Mount/Angle Bracket Bench Mount (Fig. 7-6)
1   ¾- or 1-inch schedule 40 PVC pipe, length 2 to 5 inches
1   ¹⁰⁄₂₄ by 1½-inch bolt, nut, washer
1   ¹⁰⁄₂₄ by ¾-inch bolt, nut, washer
1   1- by-½-inch corner angle bracket

For PVC Lens Mount/Bolt Adjustable Height (Fig. 7-6)
1   ¾- or 1-inch schedule 40 PVC pipe, length 2 to 5 inches
1   ¾- or 1-inch PVC end cap
1   ¹⁰⁄₂₄ by 1½-inch bolt
4   ¹⁰⁄₂₄ nuts, flat washers

For Simple Lens Holder Only (Fig. 7-7)
1   ½- by ¾-inch, ⅛-inch-thick acrylic plastic (adjust size to accommodate lens)

For Simple Lens Holder and Bench Mount (Fig. 7-7)
1   ½- by ¾-inch, ⅛-inch-thick acrylic plastic (adjust size to accommodate lens)
1   1-by-½-inch corner angle bracket
2   ⁸⁄₃₂ by ½-inch bolts, nuts, split lock washers

For PVC Lens Holder and Mount/Adjustable Height (Fig. 7-8)
1   ½- by ¾-inch, ⅛-inch-thick acrylic plastic (adjust size to accommodate lens)
1   ¾- or 1-inch schedule 40 PVC pipe, length 2 to 5 inches
1   2- to 4-inch length of ¾- or 1-inch wood dowel (trim to fit in pipe)
1   2- to 4-inch length ⁸⁄₃₂ threaded rod
4   ⁸⁄₃₂ nuts, flat washers

innermost portion to avoid the raised pipe-end stops. Thoroughly smooth the ends with a file, fine-grit sandpaper, or grinding wheel. Next, cut two ⅛- to ³⁄₁₆-inch pieces of ¾-inch PVC pipe, sand the edges, and insert one into the coupling (the inside diameter of the coupling is tapered, so the pipe will only fit one way). Drop in the lens, center it, and press in the other small piece of pipe.

You can use the mounted lens in a number of ways, including cementing it to a PVC holder (using PVC solvent cement) or using it in the optical rail system described later

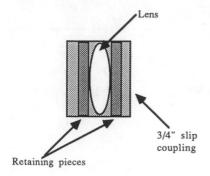

Lens

Retaining pieces

3/4" slip coupling

FIG. 7-9. *Lenses can be mounted inside a ¾-inch PVC clip coupling using the scheme shown in this diagram. The retaining pieces are small slivers of ¾-inch PVC. Paint all parts flat black to prevent light scatter.*

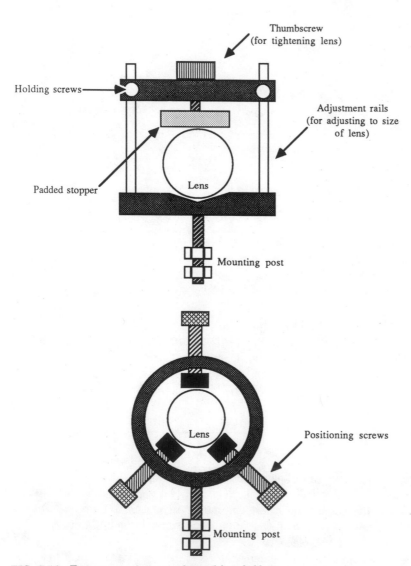

Thumbscrew (for tightening lens)

Holding screws

Adjustment rails (for adjusting to size of lens)

Padded stopper

Lens

Mounting post

Positioning screws

Lens

Mounting post

FIG. 7-10. *Two ways to construct advanced lens holders.*

94

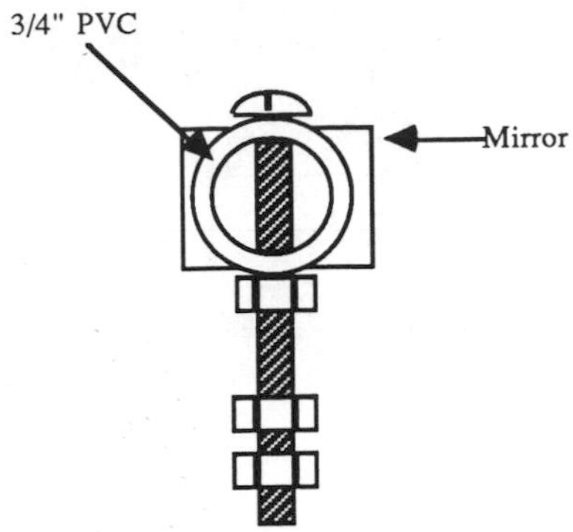

3/4" PVC

Mirror

FIG. 7-11. *Build a simple mirror mount by gluing it to a short length of ¾-inch PVC. Mount the PVC to the optical bench with a nut and bolts, and adjust the height and angle of the mirror by turning the bolts.*

in this chapter. As mentioned before, the white PVC pipe can cause light scattering. Reduce the scatter by painting the coupling and pipe pieces flat black. If you must use smaller lenses, ½-inch PVC pipe couplers accommodate optics between 16 and 21 mm in diameter.

Advanced, adjustable lens holders are shown in FIG. 7-10. These can be made using metal or acrylic plastic and require some precision work on your part. The holders are adjustable and can be used with most any size of circular lenses. On one, change the size by loosening the holding screws and sliding the top along the rails. Clamp the lens in place by turning the top screw. Delete the rounding on the bottom when using cylindrical or square lenses.

Mirror Mounts

Front-surface mirrors are often used to redirect the beam or to increase or decrease its height in relation to the surface of the bench. A simple mirror mount, using just about any thickness and size of mirror, is shown in FIG. 7-11. Here, ¾-inch PVC pipe is cut into short ½-inch sections with a mirror glued onto one end and a hole drilled through the top and bottom. Mounting hardware, such as ¹⁰⁄₂₄- or ¼-inch 20 (detailed in TABLE 7-5), is used to secure the pipe to the optical bench. You can swivel the mirror right and left by loosening the retaining nut. By attaching the mirror/pipe to an angle-iron

Table 7-5. Mirror Mounts Parts List

For Stem PVC Pipe Mount (Fig. 7-11)	
1	1- to 4-inch length of ¹⁰⁄₂₄ machine bolt
1	½-inch length of ¾-inch schedule 40 PVC pipe
3	¹⁰⁄₂₄ nuts, flat washers
For Swivel PVC Pipe Mount (Fig. 7-12)	
1	¹⁰⁄₂₄ by 1½-inch bolt, washer, nut
1	½-inch length of ¾-inch schedule 40 PVC pipe
1	⁸⁄₃₂ by ½-inch bolt, washer nut

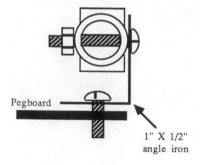

Pegboard

1" X 1/2"
angle iron

FIG. 7-12. *A swivel mirror mount (allowing 2 degrees of freedom) can be built using PVC pipe and an angle iron. Choose the right size of angle iron to fit the application.*

bracket, as illustrated in FIG. 7-12, you can provide two axes of freedom—right and left, and up and down.

Because you might never know what you'll need to complete an optical experiment, build several mounted mirrors in the following configurations (note that "small" means approximately ½-inch square and "large" means 1-inch square).

* Small mirror mounted to ^{10}/$_{24}$-by-1-inch bolt (bench hugger)
* Small mirror mounted to ^{10}/$_{24}$-by-2½-inch bolt
* Large mirror mounted to ¼-inch 20 by 3-inch bolt
* Small mirror mounted to ½-inch angle-iron bracket and ^{10}/$_{24}$-by-1-inch bolt
* Small mirror mounted to ½-inch angle-iron bracket and ^{10}/$_{24}$-by 2-inch bolt
* Large mirror mounted to 1½-inch angle-iron bracket and ½-inch 20 by 3-inch bolt

You can make other mounts by using different mirrors, bolt lengths, and angle-iron sizes, as needed. Be sure that the mirror is small enough to clear any hardware. For instance, an overly large mirror might interfere with the angle bracket.

Commercially made mirror mounts are occasionally available from surplus sources. The components are optically flat, dielectric mirrors designed (in this case) for use with helium-neon lasers. The mounts can be secured to the bench in a variety of ways including angle irons, hold-down brackets, and clamps. Many of the mounts come with holes pre-drilled and pre-tapped at ½- or 1-inch centers. The holes can be used to facilitate quick and easy mounting to the bench.

The major benefit of commercially made mirror mounts is their precision. Many have fine-threaded screws for adjusting the inclination or angle of the mirror. If you're handy with tools, you can fashion your own precision mirror mounts from aluminum or plastic. Best results are obtained when you use a precision metal-working lathe or mill.

Another method of mounting mirrors, popular among holographers, is depicted in FIG. 7-13. Here a mirror is cemented inside a nook sawed into a piece of 1¼-inch PVC pipe. The pipe can be mounted on a stem, placed in sand (see below and in Chapters 17 and 18), or simply balanced on the bench. You can mount extra large mirrors on the pipe (use bigger pipe) and the pipe pieces can be any length to suit your requirements.

One method of securing the pipe is to use a dowel and short piece of PVC. Secure the dowel inside a short pipe end (¾- to 1-inch long). This pipe holds the mirror. A thumbscrew set in another length of pipe (1 to 4 inches) lets you adjust the height of the mirror. The bottom pipe piece can be secured to the bench using hardware or a

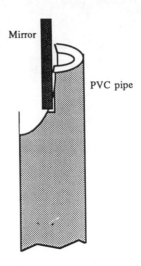

Mirror

PVC pipe

FIG. 7-13. *A mounting method popular with holographers is to glue the mirror onto a piece of scooped-out PVC pipe.*

magnet. The magnet obviously requires a metal benchtop. You can add metal to a wood benchtop with pieces of galvanized sheet metal. Small squares (up to about 6 by 12 inches) are available at many better hardware stores. The sheet metal comes with holes pre-drilled and can be cut to size with a hacksaw.

Cement the mirror in the pipe using gap-filling glue (Duco works well, and the mirror can be removed later if necessary). On occasion, you may want to make the mirror mount temporary, for example, if you have one extra-nice mirror and don't want to commit it to any one type of mount. You can temporarily secure the mirror to the pipe using florist or modeling clay. Build up a bead of clay around the pipe and press the mirror into place. You can vary the angle of the mirror by adding extra clay to one edge.

Mounting Prisms, Beam Splitters, and Other Optics

Prisms and beam splitters require unusual mounting techniques. A porro prism, often found in binoculars and a common find on the surplus market, can be used as laser retroreflectors (or corner cubes). The prisms act as mirrors where the axis of the outgoing beam is offset, yet parallel, from the incoming beam. You'll find plenty of uses for porro prisms, including using them to change the height of the beam over the bench.

The porro prism is easy to mount on a small piece of ⅛-inch acrylic plastic. Cut the plastic to accommodate the size of prism you have. Secure the plastic holder on a sliding post mount (as described above for mirror mounting) and you have control over the height and angle of the prism.

A prism table is a device that acts as a vise to clamp the component in place. The table can be used with most any type or shape of prism. A basic design is shown in FIG. 7-14; the parts list is provided in TABLE 7-6. Construct the table using small aluminum, brass, or plastic pieces. The thumbscrew is a 8/32-by 1-inch bolt; the top of the table is threaded to accommodate the bolt.

Beam splitters require an open area for both reflected and refracted beams. Cube beam splitters can often be used in prism tables. Alternatively, you can build a number of different mounts suitable for both cube and plate beam splitters, as shown in FIG. 7-15. The idea is to not block the back or exit surface(s) of the component.

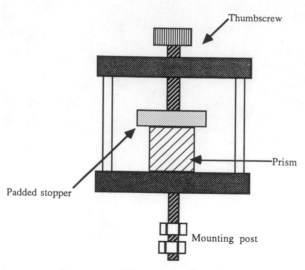

FIG. 7-14. *A prism or cube beam splitter table can be constructed using ordinary hardware and acrylic plastic. Secure the component by tightening the thumbscrew.*

Filters can be secured using adjustable lens mounts, as shown above. Commercially available filter holders designed for photographic applications (camera and darkroom) can also be used. Filters can be mounted on plastic or, if small enough, held in place inside a PVC pipe.

ADVANCED OPTICAL SYSTEM DESIGN

The projects in this section deal with advanced optical system design. Included are plans on building an optical rack for testing lenses and their effect on the laser beam, as well as motorizing mirrors, beam splitters, and other components for remote control or computerized applications. You can adopt these plans for any number of different optical system requirements such as laser light shows, laboratory experiments, laser rangefinders, and more.

Building an Optical Rack

An optical rack provides a simple means of experimenting with optical components such as lenses and filters. A common optical rack used by hobbyists is the meter or

Table 7-6. Prism Table Parts List

2	3-inch lengths of ¼-by-¼-inch acrylic plastic square extruded rods
2	3-inch lengths of 3⁄16-inch-diameter acrylic plastic round extruded rods
1	10⁄24 by 2-inch thumbscrew with knurled knob
1	10⁄24 by 1½-inch flat heat machine bolt (for mounting post)
2	10⁄24 nuts, washers
1	½-by-½-inch padded rubber

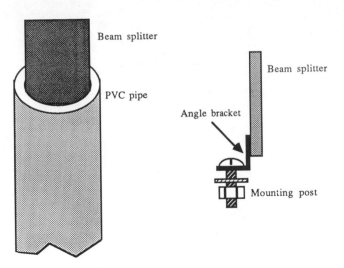

FIG. 7-15. *Plate beam splitters can be attached to an optical bench by inserting them into a length of PVC or by gluing them onto a small angle bracket. Be sure you can adjust the angle of the beam splitter and the transmitted and reflected beams are not obscured.*

yardstick. You place various clamps along the length of the stick to mount optical components. Meter sticks and their clamps, such as the set shown in FIG. 7-16, are available from a number of sources, including Edmund Scientific. The clamps hold only lenses of certain sizes (usually 1 inch or 25 mm), so be sure you get lenses to match.

Another approach to the optical rack is shown in FIG. 7-17. Here, aluminum channel is used as a "trough" for the optical components. The lenses are mounted in tubes such

FIG. 7-16. *A yardstick with inexpensive optical components attached. The stick provides an easy way to align optics and measure their distances.*

99

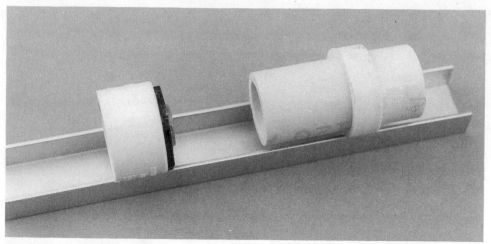

FIG. 7-17. *A homemade optical rail can be constructed using an aluminum channel and lenses mounted inside PVC pipe.*

as PVC or brass pipe. Each lens is centered in the tube and the outside dimension of the pipe is the same for all components. That means the light will pass through the optical center of each lens. You may use smaller or larger tubes for some components, but you must adjust the optical axis with shims or blocks.

Cut a piece of $^{57}/_{64}$-by-$^{9}/_{16}$-by-$^{1}/_{16}$-inch aluminum channel stock to whatever length you need for the rack. A 1-to-3-foot length should be sufficient. Mount the lenses (and/or filters) in PVC pipe, as explained in the lens-mounting section previously in this chapter. With ¾-inch PVC, you are limited to using lenses that measure between 21 mm and 26 mm in diameter. That comprises a large and popular (not to mention inexpensive) group of lenses, so you should have no trouble designing most any optical system of your choice. When using ½-inch PVC, you can use lenses with diameters between 16 mm and 21 mm.

A sample lens layout using the optical rack is shown in FIG. 7-18. A parts list is provided in TABLE 7-7. The two lenses together comprise a beam expander, which is a common optical system in laser experiments. The laser beam is first diverged using a plano-concave or double-concave lens and is then collimated using a plano-convex or double-convex lens. The focal length of the plano-convex (or double-convex) lens deter-

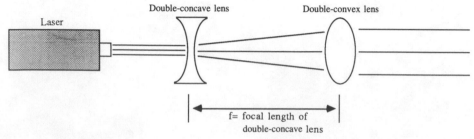

FIG. 7-18. *A double-concave lens and a double-convex lens make a laser beam expander. Adjust the distance between lenses to match the focal length of the double-convex lens.*

Table 7-7. Optical Rack Beam Collimator Parts List

1	1-3 foot length of $^{57}/_{64}$- by $^{9}/_{16}$- by $^{1}/_{16}$-inch extruded aluminum channel stock
1	Double-convex lens, in ¾-inch PVC holder
1	Double-concave lens, in ¾-inch PVC holder

mines whether the beam will be collimated for focusing to a point. You can experiment with different lenses and distances until you get the results you want.

A good way to use the rack is to calculate on paper the effects of the lenses in the system. Then see if your figures hold true. Armed with some basic optical math (see Appendix B for a list of books that provide formulas), you should be able to compute the result of just about any two- or three-lens combination.

R/C TRANSMITTER/RECEIVER

Servo motors designed for use in model airplanes and cars can be used as remote-control beam-steering units. Perhaps the easiest way to use the motors is with their intended receiver and transmitter. Unless you need to control many mirrors or other optical components, a two- or three-channel transmitter should do the job adequately. That allows you direct control over two or three servo motors. More sophisticated radio control (R/C) transmitters exist, of course, but they can be expensive. Fortunately, several Korean companies have recently joined the R/C market and offer low-cost

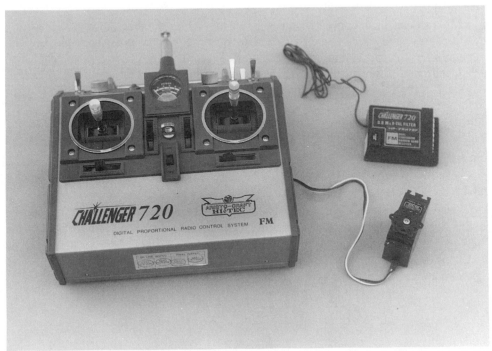

FIG. 7-19. *A complete R/C transmitter/receiver/servo setup. This transmitter provides complete digital proportional control of four independent servos (additional channels provide "on/off" functions only).*

101

Table 7-8. Beam Steering Servo Parts List

1	Four-channel (or more) R/C transmitter, with batteries
1	R/C receiver, with batteries
4	R/C servos
4	Plastic bell cranks and angle brackets (for mounting mirrors to servos)
4	First-surface mirrors (approx. ½-inch square, or size as needed)

alternatives to the more expensive brands. While these might not be as well made as the name brands, they provide similar functionality.

FIGURE 7-19 shows a six-channel R/C transmitter and companion receiver. The servo motors, which contain a small dc motor, feedback potentiometer, and circuit, connect to the receiver. This transmitter is designed for model aircraft use, so some of its channels are dedicated to special purposes, such as raising and lowering the landing gear. These channels are effectively on or off, without intermediate steps, as are the aileron and rudder controls. Even with the extra channels, only three or four can be adequately used for optical bench beam-steering.

The transmitter and receiver operate on battery power. The servos are designed for use in many types of airplane fuselages, so a variety of mounting hardware is included. If you don't find what you need in the parts included with the R/C transmitter and receiver, you can always take a trip to the hobby store and get more. A well-equipped hobby store, particularly those that specialize in R/C components, will stock everything you need.

Mirrors can be mounted to the servo motors in a number of ways. Gap-filling cyanoacrylate glue can be used to secure the mirror to the various plastic pieces. The hubs on servo motors are interchangeable by removing the set screw. If you can't find a hub that works for you, you can fashion your own using metal or plastic.

Control the motors by turning on the transmitter and receiver. Rotate the control sticks as necessary to move the motors. If the transmitter is set up correctly, the servo motors should return to their midway position when the control sticks are centered. If this is not the case, adjust the trimmer pots located on the transmitter. A parts list for a typical servo-controlled system is included in TABLE 7-8.

ELECTRONIC SERVO CONTROL

You can also control the servos using the circuit and computer program that appears in Chapter 20, "Advanced Light Shows." The circuit is designed for interfacing with the Commodore 64 and allows you to control two servo motors. Additional projects in that chapter and in Chapter 19 show how to adapt the servos for electronic control using a potentiometer. These approaches can be easily adapted for optical bench beam-steering.

8

Laser Optics Experiments

You can use lasers for almost any experiments customarily associated with a non-coherent or white light source. For example, laser light refracts and reflects the same as ordinary light, allowing you to use a laser for experimenting with or testing the effects of refraction and reflection.

Moreover, laser light provides some distinct advantages over ordinary white light sources. The light from a laser—such as a helium-neon tube—is highly collimated. The pencil-thin beam is easily controllable without the use of supplementary lenses. That makes routine optics experiments much easier to perform.

Because laser light is comprised of so much intense, compact illumination, you can readily use it to demonstrate or teach the effects of diffraction, total internal reflection, and interference. When using ordinary light sources, these topics remain abstract and hard to comprehend because they are difficult to show. But with laser light, the effects are clearly visible. You can readily see the effects of diffraction and other optical phenomena using simple components and setups.

This chapter shows how to conduct many fascinating experiments using visible laser light. While you don't need to complete each experiment, you should try a handful and perhaps expand on one or more for a more in-depth study. For example, the effects of polarization by reflection is a fascinating topic that you can easily develop into a science fair project.

EXPERIMENTING WITH REFRACTION

Recall that refraction is the bending of light as it passes from one density to another. Light bends away from line normal at a dense-to-rare transition; light bends toward line

Table 8-1. Parts List for Refraction Experiments

1	Laser
1	Plate glass (approx. 2 inches square)
1	Plastic sheet or block
1	Clear glass or plastic container to hold water, mineral oil, isopropyl alcohol, glycerin, etc.
1	Plastic protractor
1	Equilateral prism

normal at a rare-to-dense transition. TABLE 8-1 lists the materials you'll need to carry out the experiments in this section.

Refraction Through Glass Plate

You can most readily see the effects of refraction by placing a piece of clear plate glass in front of the laser. The beam will be displaced some noticeable distance. Try this experiment: place a laser at one end of the room so that the beam strikes a back wall or screen. Tape a piece of paper to the wall and lightly mark the location of the beam with a pencil.

Next, have someone place a small piece of regular window glass in front of the laser. Position the glass so that it is canted at an angle to the beam. The spot on the paper should shift. Mark the new location.

If you know the distance between the glass and wall as well as the distance between the two spots, you can calculate the angle of deflection (see FIG. 8-1). (With that angle, you can then compute the refractive index of the glass; consult any book on basic

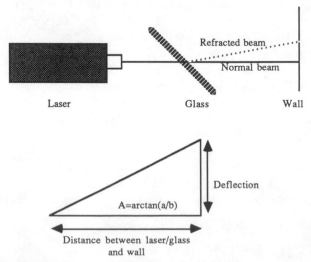

FIG. 8-1. *Measuring the deflection of the beam enables you to calculate the refractive index of glass, lenses, and other optical components.*

trigonometry for the formula.) The figure shows how the distance between (A)—glass to wall—and (B)—spot to spot, or deflection—are the equivalent of the adjacent and opposite sides of a right triangle. The illustration shows the particular formula to use to find the angle of deflection: $A = \arctan(a/b)$. Use trig tables or a scientific calculator to solve for it.

Try the experiment with different types of glass, plastic, and other transparent materials. Move the paper each time you try a new material. Note that not all glass is made of the same substances, and refractive indexes can vary. For example, one piece of glass may have a refractive index of 1.55 and another may have a refractive index of 1.72. The two may look identical on the outside but refract light differently. The higher the index of refraction, the greater the distance between the two beams.

Refraction Through Water

Bears, eagles, and others of the animal kingdom know a lot about refraction; how else could they catch fish out of lakes and streams with such precision! Because water is more dense than air, it has a higher index of refraction. Images in water not only look closer, but they appear at a different place than they really are. If you don't take refraction into account, you'll come up with nothing after throwing your spear into the water.

One easy way to demonstrate refraction in water is to place a narrow stick, like a dowel, in a jar. Fill the jar with water and the stick seems to bend. If the water is a little cloudy (as it often is after coming out of the tap), you can demonstrate the actual refraction of light with a laser. Fill the jar with water. Position the laser above the jar but at a 10 to 15 degree angle to the water line. Turn off the room lights so that the beam can be more readily seen in mid-air (chalk dust or smoke helps bring it out). You'll see the shaft of light from the laser ''magically'' bend when it strikes the water.

By dipping a protractor in the water, you can visually measure the angles and compute the index of refraction using the classic formula $n = \sin i/\sin r$. That is, the index of refraction is equal to the sin of the angle of incidence over the sin of the angle of refraction (this is often referred to as Snell's Law). Repeat the experiment with other liquids, including glycerin, alcohol, and mineral oil. Correlate the refractive indexes of these fluids with the glass and plastic from above (you can use Snell's Law for these materials, too).

Equilateral prisms are most often used to disperse white light (break up the light into its individual component colors). The light from a helium-neon laser is already at a specific wavelength, so it cannot be further dispersed. However, prisms can be used to show the effects of refraction and how the light can be diverted from its original path.

To demonstrate refraction in a prism, place the prism at the edge of a table. Aim the laser up toward the prism at a 45 degree angle. The beam should strike one side and then refract so that the light exits almost parallel to the surface of the table. For best results, you'll need to clamp the laser in place so that the beam doesn't wander around.

EXPERIMENTING WITH REFLECTION

The law of reflection is simple and straight-forward: the angle of reflectance, in relation to line normal, is equal but opposite to the angle of incidence. As an example, light incident on a mirror at a 45-degree angle, as shown in FIG. 8-2, will also bounce off the mirror

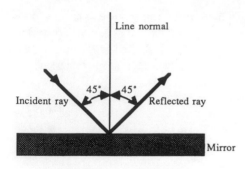

FIG. 8-2. *The law of reflection.*

at a 45-degree angle. The total amount of deflection between incident and reflected light will be 90 degrees. Materials needed for conducting the experiments in this section are found in TABLE 8-2.

Front-Surface Versus Rear-Surface Mirrors

Light is reflected off almost any surface, including plain glass. An ordinary mirror consists of a piece of glass backed with silver or aluminum. Light is reflected not only off the shiny silver backing but the glass itself. You can readily see this effect by shining a laser at an ordinary rear-surface mirror. With a relatively large distance between mirror and wall, you will note two distinct spots. The bright spot is the laser beam reflected off the silver backing; the dim spot is the beam reflected off the glass itself.

Now repeat the experiment with a front-surface mirror. Because the highly reflective material is applied to the front of the glass, the light is reflected just once. Only a single spot appears on the wall (see FIG. 8-4)

Total Internal Reflection

When light passes through a dense medium toward a less dense medium, it is refracted into the second medium if the angle of incidence is not too great. If the angle of incidence is increased to what is called the *critical angle of incidence*, the light no longer exits the first medium but is totally reflected back into it. This phenomenon, called *total internal reflection*, is what makes certain kinds of prisms and optical fibers work.

Consider the right-angle prism shown in FIG. 8-4. Light entering one face is totally reflected at the glass-air boundary at the hypotenuse. The reflected light emerges out of the adjacent face of the prism. Depending on how you tilt the prism with respect to the light source, you can get it to reflect internally in other ways.

Table 8-2. Parts List for Reflection Experiments

1	Laser
1	Rear-surface mirror (approx. 1 inch square)
1	Front-surface mirror (approx. 1 inch square)
1	Right-angle prism
1	Large paper sheet (such as 11 by 17 inches) to make cylinder
1	Long lens (for laser scanning)

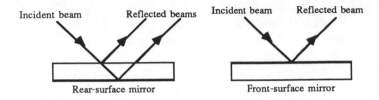

FIG. 8-3. *A rear-surface mirror creates a ghost beam along with the main beam; a front-surface mirror reflects just one beam.*

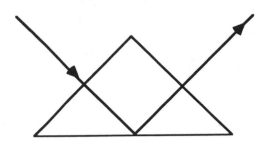

FIG. 8-4. *A right-angle prism allows you to deflect and direct light in a number of interesting ways.*

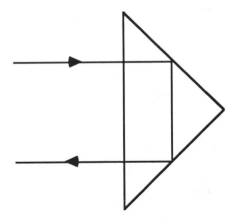

The main advantage of total internal reflection is that it is more efficient than even the most highly reflective substances. Reflection is almost 100 percent, even in optics of marginal quality. Another advantage is that the reflective portion of the prism is internal, not external. That lessens the chance of damage caused by dust and other contaminants.

You can readily experiment with total internal reflection (TIR) using just about any prism. A right-angle or equilateral prism works best. Shine the beam of a laser in one side of the prism. Now rotate the prism and note that at some angles, the beam is refracted out of the glass without bouncing around inside. At other angles, the light is reflected once and maybe even twice before exiting again.

If the prism is poorly made—the glass has many impurities, for example—you can even see the laser beam coursing around inside the prism. This effect is best seen when the room lights are turned low or off. To see the effect of total internal reflection and refraction in a prism, make a tube by wrapping a large piece of white construction paper or lightweight cardboard around the prism. Poke a hole for the light beam to go through and turn on the laser. If the paper is thin enough, you can see the laser beam striking it (looking from the outside). If the paper is thick, you'll have to look down the tube to see the beam on the inside walls.

Rotate the prism (or the laser and tube) and note how the beam is either refracted or internally reflected. Keep a notebook handy and jot down the effects as the prism is rotated. Use a protractor if you want to record the exact angles of incidence.

Another experiment in total internal reflection uses a lens. A long, single-axis lens (the kind shown in FIG. 8-5 like those used for laser scanning) works the best. Shine the light through the lens in the normal manner. Depending on the type of lens used, the beam will refract into an oval or slit. Now cant the lens at an oblique angle to the laser beam, as shown in the figure. If you hold the lens just right, you should see the laser beam internally reflected several times before exiting the other end. You can see the internal reflections much more clearly if the room lights are off.

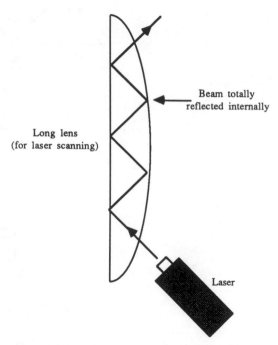

FIG. 8-5. *A long beam-spreading lens (or something similar) can be used to readily demonstrate total internal reflection. A solid glass rod can also be used.*

EXPERIMENTING WITH DIFFRACTION

TABLE 8-3 provides a parts list for the diffraction experiments that follow. Diffraction is a rather complex subject, thoroughly investigated by Thomas Young in 1801. Young's aim was to prove (or disprove) that light traveled in waves, and were carried along as particles in some invisible matter (the early physicists called this invisible matter the *ether*). If light was really made of waves, those waves would break up into smaller waves (or secondary wavelets) when passed through a very small opening (according to Huygens'

Table 8-3. Parts List for Diffraction Experiments

For Single Slit

2 Utility knife razor blades
1 2-by-3-inch acrylic plastic (⅛-inch thick)
2 ⁶/₃₂ by ½-inch bolts, nuts, washers

For Double Slit

2 Utility knife razor blades
1 2-by-3-inch acrylic plastic (⅛-inch thick)
1 Tungsten, wire, or other thin filament
4 ⁶/₃₂ by ½-inch bolts, nuts, washers

For Spectroscope

1 1-inch-diameter, 6-inch-long cardboard tube
1 Single slit (in cardboard or razor blade, as above)
1 Diffraction grating

General Experiments

1 Laser
1 Single slit
1 Double slit
1 Screen
1 Transmission diffraction grating (1-inch square or larger)

principle). The same effect occurs when water passes through a small opening. One wave striking the opening turns into many, smaller waves on the other side.

Young used a small pinhole to test his lightwave theory technique. Light exiting the pinhole would be *diffracted* into many small wavelets. Those wavelets would act to constructively or destructively interfere with one another when they met at a lightly colored screen. *Constructive interference* is when the phase of the waves are closely matched—the peaks and valleys coincide. The two waves combine with one another and their light intensities are added together. *Destructive interference* is when the phase of the waves are not in tandem. A peak may coincide with a valley, and the two waves act to cancel each other out.

What Young saw convinced him (and many others) that light was really made up of waves. Young saw a pattern of bright and dark bands on the viewing screen. The brightest and biggest band was in the middle, flanked by alternating light and dark bands. Bright bands meant that the waves met there on the screen constructively. Dark bands denoted destructive interference.

Making Your Own Diffraction Apparatus

Young's original experiments have been repeated in many school and industrial laboratories. Monochromatic light sources are the best choice when experimenting with diffraction. A laser is the perfect tool not only because its light is highly monochromatic but that its beam is directional and well-defined.

Use a slit instead of using a pinhole for your diffraction experiments. You can make a high-precision slit using two new razor blades, as shown in FIG. 8-6. You can use almost any type of blade, but be sure that they are new and the cutting surfaces aren't nicked. Mount the razor blades on a small piece of plastic by drilling a hole in the metal (if there isn't already one) and securing it to the plastic with 6/32 or smaller hardware. Adjust the space between the blades using an automotive spark gap gauge. A gap of less than 0.040 inches is sufficient.

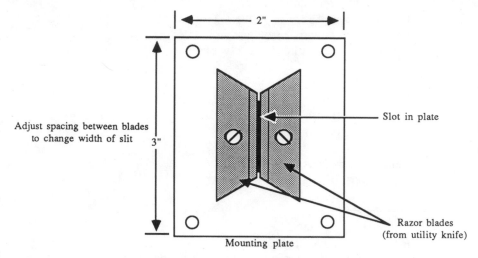

FIG. 8-6. *A single slit made by two razor blades butted close together. Mount the blades on a piece of ⅛-inch arylic plastic. Drill or cut a large slot in the center of the plastic for the beam to pass through.*

Shine the laser beam through the gap and onto a nearby wall or screen (distance between blades and wall: 2 to 3 feet). You should see a pattern of bright and dark bands. If nothing appears, check the gap and be sure that the laser beam is properly directed between the two blades. If the beam is too narrow, expand it a little with a lens. Note that the center of the diffraction pattern is the brightest. This is the *zero order fringe*.

If the fringe pattern is difficult to see, increase the distance between the blades and the screen. As the distance is increased, the pattern gets bigger. If the screen is 10 feet or more away (depending on the gap between the razor blades), the light-to-dark transitions of the fringes can be manually counted. Experiment with the gap between the razor blades. Note that, contrary to what you might think, the fringes become closer together with wider gaps. You achieve the largest spacing between fringes with the smallest possible gap.

Experiments with Double Slits

You can perform many useful metrological (measurement) experiments using a double slit. Follow the arrangement shown in FIG. 8-7. Place a single slit in front of a laser so that it is diffracted into secondary wavelets. Then place a double slit in the light path. The fringes that appear on the screen will be an interference/diffraction pattern similar to the fringes seen in the single-slit experiment above. With the double slit, however,

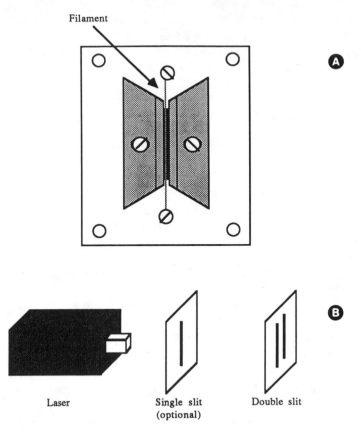

Filament

A

B

Laser   Single slit   Double slit
(optional)

FIG. 8-7. *A double slit using a small filament (I used 30-gauge wire-wrap wire. Stretch the filament be-tween the blades; adjust the gap between the blades so that it is even on both sides of the filament. (A) Details of the double slit. (B) arrangement of laser, single slit, and double slit for experiments to follow.*

it's possible to perform such things as measuring the wavelength of light, measuring the speed of light, or measuring the distance between the double slit and the screen.

Make a double slit by opening the gap between two razor blades and inserting a thin strip of tungsten filament. Secure the filament using miniature watch or camera screws. You can also use small gauge wire (30 gauge or higher) or a strand of hair (human hair measures about 100 micrometers across). Measure the filament or wire with a micrometer. Next, adjust the spacing between the razor blades so the gap is less than a millimeter or so across. The filament should be positioned in the middle of the gap.

Another more accurate method is to use a *Ronchi ruling*, which is a precision-made optical component intended for testing the flatness (or equal curvature) of lenses, mirrors, and glass. The ruling is made by scribing lines in a piece of glass. The spacing between the lines is carefully controlled. Typical Ronchi rulings come with 50, 100, and 200 lines per inch. At 50 lines per inch, the distance between gaps is 0.02 inch, or 0.508mm.

With the distance between gaps known, you can now perform some experiments. Set up the double slit precisely 1 meter (1,000 mm) from a white or frosted glass screen. Turn on the laser, and as accurately as possible, measure the distance between fringes. With a red helium-neon laser, the distance should be approximately 1.25 mm between fringes. If this proves too difficult to measure, increase the distance to 5 meters (5,000 mm). Now you are ready to perform some calculations.

Here is the formula for computing light wavelength.

$$w = \frac{f \times b}{d}$$

where w is the wavelength of the light, f is the distance between two bright fringes, b is the distance between the slits, and d is the distance between the slits and the viewing screen.

Measuring the fringes indicates they are 1.25 mm apart using a 50-line-per-inch Ronchi ruling. And you know that the distance between the slits is 0.508 mm. Multiply 1.25 times 0.508 and you get 0.635. Now divide the result by 1,000 (for the distance between slits and screen) and you get 0.000635. That is very close to the wavelength, in millimeters, of red He-Ne light.

You can interpolate the formula (using standard algebra) to find the distance between the slits and screen. The formula becomes:

$$d = \frac{f \times b}{w}$$

As an example, if the fringes measure 6.25 mm apart with a slit distance of .508 mm and the wavelength of the laser light is 0.000632 mm, the distance is 5,017 mm, or a little over 5 meters.

If you aren't sure of the spacing between slits, you can use the formula:

$$b = \frac{w \times d}{f}$$

The result is the spacing, in millimeters. Calculating the space between slits is handy if you use the tungsten-and-razor-blade method. Two other (less accurate) methods of making double slits include:

★ Photograph two white lines with color slide film and use the film as an aperture.
★ Scribe two lines in film, electrical tape, or aluminum foil.

You might also use this technique to measure small parts like machine pins, needles, and wire. The spacing of the fringes reveals the diameter or width of the part. Keep in mind that the best diffraction effects are obtained when the slits (and center object) have the thinnest edges possible. The fringes disappear with thicker edges.

Calculating Frequency, Wavelength, and Velocity

Knowing the wavelength of the light used in the diffraction experiments can be used to calculate the frequency of the light as well as its velocity. Use the following formulas for calculating frequency, wavelength, and velocity of light:

$$\text{velocity} = \text{frequency} \times \text{wavelength}$$

$$\text{frequency} = \frac{\text{velocity}}{\text{wavelength}}$$

$$\text{wavelength} = \frac{\text{velocity}}{\text{frequency}}$$

These figures will help you in your calculations:

* ✯ Speed of light in a vacuum: 299,792.5 km/sec
* ✯ Approximate speed of light in air: 299,705.6 km/sec (sea level, 30°C)
* ✯ He-Ne laser light: 632.8 nm
* ✯ Green line of argon laser: 514.5 nm
* ✯ Blue line of argon laser: 488.0 nm

As an example, to calculate the frequency of red He-Ne laser light, take velocity (299,792.5) divided by wavelength (632.8). The result is 473.7555 terahertz.

Using Diffraction Gratings

A *diffraction grating* is a piece of metal or film that has hundreds or thousands of tiny lines scribed in its surface. The grating can be either transmissive (you can see through it) or reflective (you see light bounce off of it). Although the reflective type makes interesting-looking jewelry, it has limited use in laser experiments. A small piece (1-inch square) of transmissive diffraction grating can be used for numerous experiments. The exact number of scribes is not important for general tinkering, but one with 10,000 to 15,000 lines per inch should do nicely. Edmund Scientific and American Optical Center (see Appendix A) sell diffraction gratings and kits at reasonable cost.

The diffraction grating acts as an almost unlimited number of slits and disperses white light into its component colors. When used with laser light, a diffraction grating splits the beam and makes many sub-beams. These additional beams are the secondary wavelets that you created when experimenting with the diffraction slits detailed above. The beams are spaced far apart because the scribes in the diffraction grating are so close together.

The pattern and spacing of the beams depends on the grating. A criss-cross pattern shows a grating that has been scribed both horizontally and vertically. You can obtain the criss-cross material from special effects "rainbow" sunglasses sold by Edmund. Most gratings, particularly those used in compact disc players and scientific instruments, are scribed in one direction only. In that case, you see a single row of dots.

Besides breaking up the beam into many sub-beams, one interesting experiment is what might be called "diffraction topology." The criss-cross rainbow glasses material shows the effect most readily. Put on the glasses and point the laser beam at a point in front of you. Tilt the glasses on your head and note that the sub-beams appear almost 3-D, as if you could reach out and grab them. Of course, they aren't there but the illusion seems real.

Now move the beam so that it strikes objects further away and closer to you. Not only does the apparent perspective of the sub-beams change, but so does the distance between the spots. The closer the object, the greater the perspective and the closer the spots are spaced to one another. Scan the laser back and forth and the perspective and distance of spots changes in such a way that you can visually see the topology of the ground and objects in front of you.

One practical application of this effect is to focus the diffracted light from the film onto a solid-state imager or video camera, then route the signal to a computer. A program running on the computer analyzes the instantaneous arrangement of the dots and correlates it to distance. If the laser beam is scanned up and down and right and left like the electron beam in a television set, the topology of an object can be plotted. The easy part is setting up the laser, diffraction grating, and video system; the hard part is writing the computer software! Anybody want to give it a try?

While you've got your hands on a diffraction grating, look at the orange gas discharge coming from around the tube. You'll be startled at all the bright, well-defined colors. Each band of light represents a wavelength created in the helium-neon mixture. The dark portions between each color represents wavelengths not produced by the gases.

If you can't readily see the lines with the diffraction grating you're using, you might have better luck with a home-built pocket spectroscope. Place a plastic or cardboard cap on the end of a 1-inch diameter tube. Saw or drill a slit in the cap, or make a gap using a pair of razor blades, as detailed earlier in this chapter. On the other end of the tube, glue on a piece of transmissive diffraction grating. Aim the slit-end of the spectroscope at the light source and view the spectra by looking at the inside of the tube, as shown in FIG. 8-8. Don't look directly at the slit.

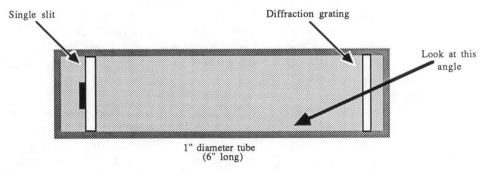

FIG. 8-8. *You can construct your own pocket spectroscope with a a short 6-inch long cardboard tube, slit (cutout or razor blade), and diffraction grating. View the diffracted light by looking at the inside wall of the tube. Rotate the tube (and grating) to increase or decrease the width of the spectra lines.*

POLARIZED LIGHT AND POLARIZING MATERIALS

When I was a kid, I learned about polarized light the same way that most other people did at the time—in ads for sunglasses. Specially made sunglasses somehow blocked glare by the magic of polarization. Not until I began experimenting with lasers did I learn the true nature of polarized light and how the sunglasses perform their tricks. Be aware that the subject of polarized light is extensive and at times complicated. The following is just a brief overview to help you understand how the experiments in this section work.

Table 8-4. Parts List for Polarization Experiments

1	Laser
2	Polarizing sheets (1-inch in diameter or larger)
1	Plate glass (approx. 1 inch square)
1	Block of calcite (as clear as possible)
1	Quarter wave (retardation) plate

Consult a book on optics for more details. TABLE 8-4 indicates the materials necessary to performs the experiments in this section.

What Is Polarized Light

Light is composed of two components: a magnetic field component and an electrical field component (thus the term *electromagnetic*). These components, or vectors, are both waves that travel together, but at 90-degree angles. That is, if one vector travels up and down, the other travels right and left. FIGURE 8-9 shows a diagram of the magnetic and electric field vectors traveling as waves through space.

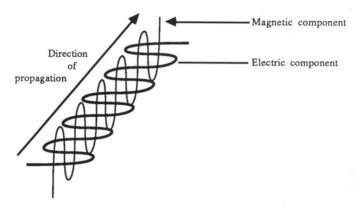

FIG. 8-9. *A pictorial representation of the electric and magnetic components of light waves.*

In sunlight, the phase of the electrical and magnetic vectors are constantly changing (but the two are 90 degrees out of phase to one another). At one moment, the phase of, say, the electric field vector might be 0 degrees; at another time it might be 38 degrees. An instant later it might be at 187 degrees. Such light is said to be *unpolarized*. This is the nature of light from the sun, desk lamp, flashlight, and most any other illumination source.

By locking the phase of the fields vectors or by filtering out those phases that don't match up to the ones desired, it's possible to *polarize* light. There are three general types of polarized light:

★ *Plane (or linearly) polarized*, where the electric and magnetic vectors do not change phase.

✱ *Circularly polarized*, where the phase of the electric field vector rotates from 0 to 360 degrees in even and well-defined steps.

✱ *Elliptically polarized*, same as above but the instantaneous amplitude of the electric field vector constantly changes or is not the same amplitude as the magnetic field vector.

The terms *plane, circular,* and *elliptical* refer to the imaginary pattern the light would make on a viewing screen. Looking at a beam of plane-polarized light head-on, it would appear as in FIG. 8-10A, with the electric field vector occupying a horizontal or vertical plane. Circularly and elliptically polarized light take on a more two-dimensional figure—either a circle or ellipse. The symmetry of the ellipse depends entirely on the instantaneous amplitude of the electric field vector. Their head-on patterns are shown in FIG. 8-10B and 8-10C.

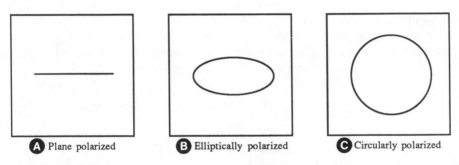

Ⓐ Plane polarized   Ⓑ Elliptically polarized   Ⓒ Circularly polarized

FIG. 8-10. *The "end-view" of three types of polarized light: plane, elliptical, and circular.*

Polarized light is most commonly created from unpolarized light by the use of a filter. A polarizing filter, typically made from organic or chemical dyes, blocks out those phases that don't lie along a specific axis. As you might guess, this means that a good portion of the light won't get through; but in practice, no polarizing filter is 100 percent efficient at absorbing off-axis phases. That means that only about 35 to 50 percent of the light is eventually blocked.

You can most easily experiment with polarized light using two polarizing filters (one is the *polarizer*, the other the *analyzer*, as shown in FIG. 8-11). Sandwich the filters together and rotate one of them as you view a light source. The intensity of the light will increase and decrease every 90 degrees of rotation.

All lasers emit polarized light, with either of two orthogonal planes of polarization. But the exact phase of the polarization varies over time as does the relative amplitude of the polarization components. You can repeat the experiments with the two polarizing filters with your He-Ne laser. As you rotate one of the filters, the intensity of the beam increases or decreases.

Lasers can be linearly polarized in one plane with the use of *Brewster's window* placed in front of the fully reflective mirror. This window is a piece of clear glass titled at an angle (precisely 56 degrees, 39 minutes) that "absorbs" one of the planes of polarization. As a result, the output beam is plane-polarized with a purity exceeding 300:1.

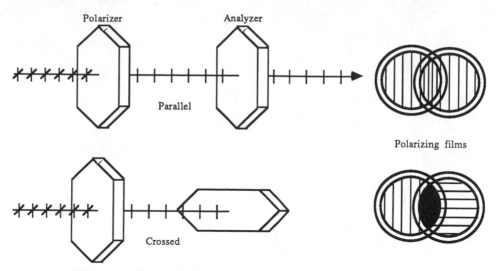

FIG. 8-11. *How to align two polarizers to alternately pass or block light.*

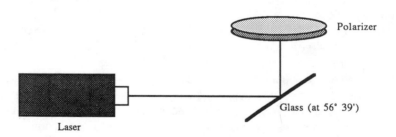

FIG. 8-12. *A laser, piece of glass, and polarizer are the components you need to experiment with polarization by reflection. Watch the intensity of the beam change as you rotate the polarizer.*

The Brewster's Angle window works by *polarization by reflection*. You can experiment with this technique using a coated or uncoated piece of plate glass (1-inch square should do it). Position the laser, glass, and polarizing filter as shown in FIG. 8-12. With the glass tilted at an angle of approximately 57 degrees, rotate the polarizing filter while watching the *reflected* (not transmitted) beam. The intensity of the beam should increase and decrease. If you don't witness a discernible effect, alter the angle of the glass a bit and try again. A precision metal protractor can help you position the glass at the required Brewster's Angle. FIGURE 8-13 shows what happens to the polarization components as they reflect on contact with the glass.

Experimenting With Calcite

There are a number of polarizing materials designed for use with optics and lasers, including birefringent polarizers, Wallaston prisms, dichroic sheet polarizers, and Glan-Taylor polarizers. Polarization through *birefringence* is an interesting effect that you can

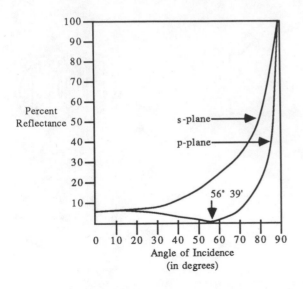

FIG. 8-13. *A graphic illustration of the amount of reflectivity of the p and s planes at different angles of incidence.*

readily investigate with a dollar chunk of *calcite* and a polarizing filter. Calcite is a commonly occurring mineral that takes on many forms, including limestone and marble. In one form it is an optically clear rhombohedral crystal.

Although some optics-grade calcite polarizing prisms are priced in excess of $500, you can make your own (for experimental purposes) for about a dollar. Many rock stores and natural history museum gift stores sell chunks of calcite at reasonable cost. This calcite is far from optically pure, but it's good enough for routine experiments. You can always tell a calcite crystal by looking at its shape and what it does to printed material when you place it on a page from a book. As shown in FIG. 8-14, a calcite crystal creates two images through a process called *birefringence*, or double refraction.

Look for a piece that's relatively clear and large enough so that you can work with it. A few inclusions here and there won't hurt. If the crystal has rough edges or is broken into an unusable shape, you can repair it by cleaving new sides. A calcite crystal will retain its rhomboid shape even if recleaved. You can best cleave the crystal by using a small- bladed flat screwdriver or chisel and hammer. Use the screwdriver to chip away a small layer of the crystal to expose a new face.

You may, if you wish, finish the sides using very fine-grit (300 or higher) wet/dry sandpaper, used wet. The faces of the crystal will turn a milky white, but they can be repolished using jeweler's rouge and a buffing wheel. Rouge is available at many hardware and glass or plastics shops; you can outfit your drill motor with a suitable buffing wheel.

Point the laser into the crystal and look at the opposite side. You'll see two beams instead of one, as indicated in FIG. 8-15. One ray is called the *ordinary ray* and the other is the *extraordinary ray*. Depending on the optical quality of the crystal and how well you have polished its sides, the beams should project on a wall or screen located a few inches away. The interesting thing about these two beams is that they are orthogonally polarized. That is, beam A is polarized in one direction and beam B is polarized at a 90-degree angle. You can test this by rotating the polarizing filter in front of the two beams (look at the projected beams, not the spots on the filter). As you rotate the filter, one beam will become bright as the other dims. Keep rotating and they change states.

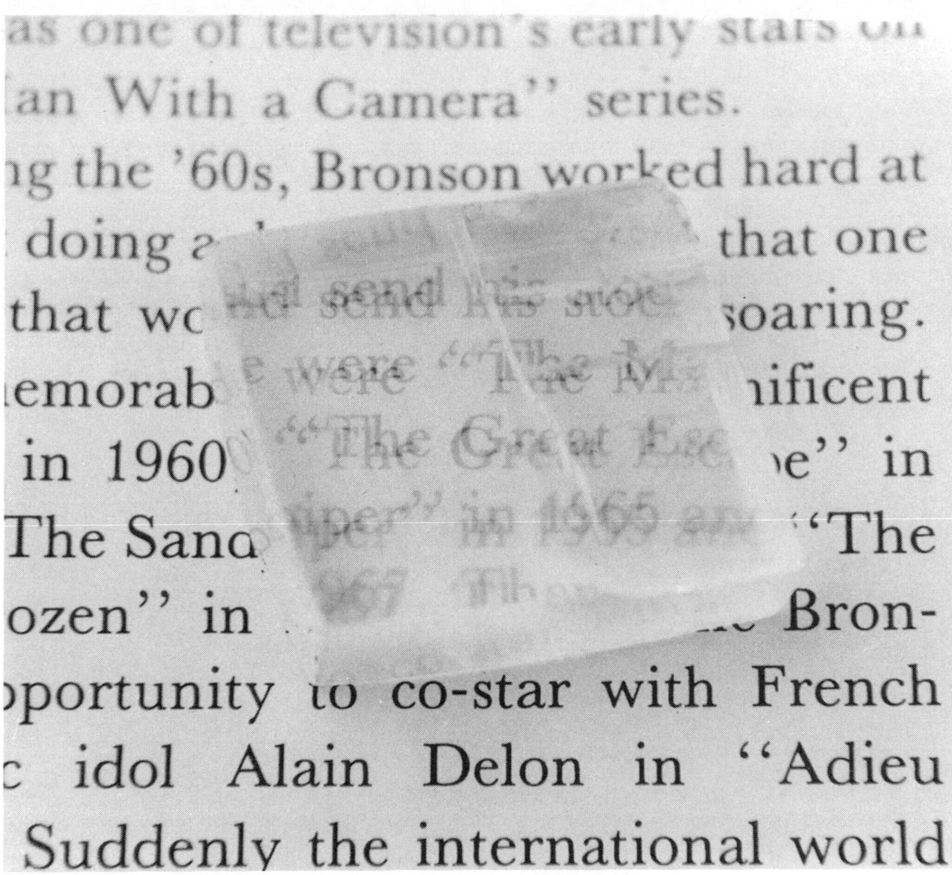

as one of television's early stars on
an With a Camera'' series.

1g the '60s, Bronson worked hard at
doing a [ ] that one
that wc [ ] soaring.
emorab [ ] ificent
in 1960 [ ]e'' in
The Sanc [ ] ''The
ozen'' in [ ] Bron-
pportunity to co-star with French
c idol Alain Delon in ''Adieu
Suddenly the international world

FIG. 8-14. *Calcite exhibits birefringence, causing double images.*

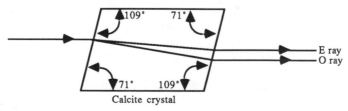

FIG. 8-15. *A single beam entering a calcite crystal is refracted into two beams—E and O rays. The refracted beams are orthogonally polarized.*

Retardation Plates

Retardation plates, typically made of very thin sheets of mica or quartz, are elements primarily used in the synthesis and analysis of light in different states of polarization. There are several types of retardation plates (also called *phase shifters*):

★ A *quarter-wave retardation plate* converts linearly polarized light into circularly polarized light, and vice versa.

119

★ A *half-wave retardation plate* changes the polarization plane of linearly polarized light. The angle of the plane depends on the rotation of the plate.

Both quarter- and half-wave plates find use in some types of holography, interferometry, and electro-optic modulation. They are also used in most types of audio compact disc players as one of the optical components. When coupled with a polarizing beam splitter, the quarter-wave plate prevents the returning beam, (after being reflected off the surface of the disc) from re-entering the laser diode. If this were to happen, the output of the laser would no longer be coherent. A quarter-wave plate can be similarly placed in front of a polarizing filter and laser (see FIG. 8-16) for use in the Michelson interferometer project detailed in Chapter 9. The retardation plate prevents light from reflecting back into the laser and ruining the accurate measurements possible with the interferometer.

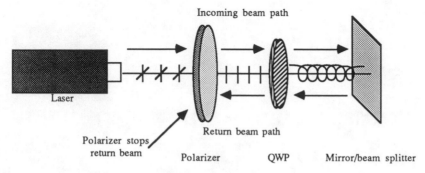

FIG. 8-16. *A quarter-wave plate, in conjunction with a polarizer, can be used to prevent a reflected beam from re-entering the laser.*

MANIPULATING THE LASER BEAM

Simple and inexpensive optics are all that's required to manipulate the diameter of the beam. You can readily focus, expand, and collimate a laser beam using just one, two, or three lenses. Here are the details. Refer to TABLE 8-5 for a parts list.

Focusing

Any positive lens (plano-convex, double-convex, positive meniscus) can be used to focus the beam of a laser to a small point. For best results, the lens should be no more than about 50 to 100 percent larger than the diameter of the beam, or the light won't be focused into the smallest possible dot. To use a particular lens to focus the light from

Table 8-5. Parts List for Beam Manipulation Experiments

1	Double-convex lens (in PVC or similar holder)
1	Double-concave lens (in PVC or similar holder)
1	Ruler (for measuring focal length)
1	Focusing screen

120

your laser, it might be necessary to first expand the beam to cover more area of the lens. Refrain from expanding the beam so that it fills the entire diameter of the lens.

Note that the beam is focused at the focal point of the lens, as illustrated in FIG. 8-17. The size of the spot is the smallest when the viewing screen (or other media such as the surface of a compact disc) is placed at the focal length of the lens. The spot appears out of focus at any other distance.

If you don't know the focal distance of a particular lens, you can calculate it by holding it up to a strong point source (laser, sun, etc.) and varying the distance between lens and focal plane. Measure the distance, as shown in FIG. 8-18, when the spot is the smallest.

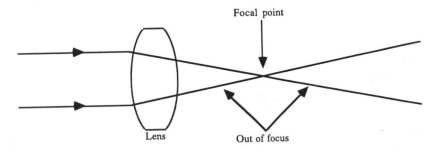

FIG. 8-17. *Positive lenses focus light to a point. The size of the beam increases at distances ahead or beyond this focal point.*

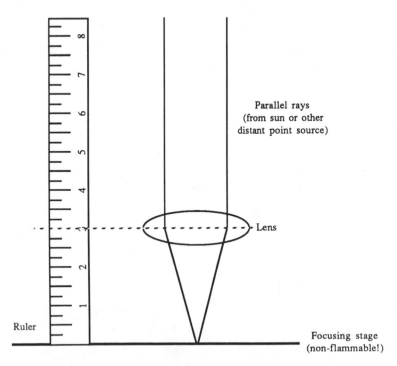

FIG. 8-18. *Measure the focal length using the setup shown here. The ruler can be marked off in inches or centimeters, as you prefer.*

Expanding

Any negative lens (plano-concave, double-concave, negative meniscus) can be used to expand the beam. An expanded beam is useful in holography, interferometry, and other applications where it is necessary to spread the thin beam of the laser into a wider area. You might also want to expand the beam to a certain diameter before focusing it with a positive lens.

The degree of beam spread depends on the focal length of the lens (remember that negative lenses have negative focal points because their focal point appears behind the lens instead of in front of it). The shorter the focal length, the greater the beam spread. If you need to cover a very wide area with the beam, you may combine two or more negative lenses. The beam is expanded each time it passes through a lens. Remember to use successively larger lenses as the beam is expanded.

Collimating

By carefully positioning the distance between the negative and positive lens, it's possible to enlarge the beam and make its light rays parallel again. A double-concave

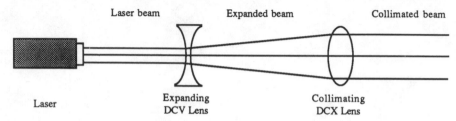

FIG. 8-19. *A common optical arrangement for lasers is the beam expander/collimator, created by coupling a negative and positive lens. Note that this arrangement is modeled after the design of a simple Galilean telescope, used in reverse.*

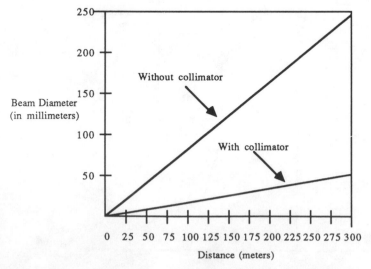

FIG. 8-20. *Beam divergence is greatly reduced over long distances by the use of an expander/collimator. This graph shows the approximate beam spread of an He-Ne laser with and without collimating optics.*

and double-convex lens positioned as shown in FIG. 8-19 make it a collimator, a useful device that can be used to enlarge the beam yet still maintain collimation and to reduce divergence over long distances. FIGURE 8-20 shows a graph that compares the divergence of the beam from a He-Ne laser with and without collimating optics. Although the collimator initially makes the beam wider, it greatly decreases divergence over long distances.

In order for the beam to be collimated, the distance between lenses A and B must be equal to the focal length of the double-convex lens B. Again, if you don't already know the focal length of this lens, determine it using a point light source and ruler. Collimation allows for the sharpest focus of the beam. Rather than simply expand the laser beam to fill the focusing lens, first expand and collimate it.

A small telescope (such as a spotting scope or rifle scope) makes a good laser beam collimator. Just reverse the scope so that the beam enters the objective and exits the eyepiece. An inexpensive ($10) sports scope can be used as an excellent collimating telescope. Mount the scope in front of the laser using clamps or brackets. Adjust for the smallest divergence by focusing the scope.

9

Build a Michelson Interferometer

Albert A. Michelson was the first U.S. citizen to win the Nobel prize for science. The 1907 award was given to him for his "precision optical instruments and the spectroscope and metrological investigations conducted herewith." Michelson was the inventor of a unique *interferometer* that opened up new vistas in the science of light and optics. With the interferometer, Michelson was able to determine—with unprecedented accuracy— the speed of light, the wavelength and frequency of light emitted by different sources, and the constancy of the speed of light through any given medium, among other feats.

Michelson's apparatus (actually a modified version of it) can be reasonably duplicated in the home shop or garage using a minimum of optical components. When finished, you'll be able to use your interferometer for many of the same experiments conducted by Michelson and others. You will learn first-hand about lightwave interference and discover some interesting and useful properties of laser light. The interferometer project presented provides an excellent springboard for a science fair project.

A SHORT HISTORY

Before launching into the construction plans for the interferometer, let's take a moment to review Michelson and his exotic contraption.

Albert A. Michelson was born in Prussia in 1872. As with many Europeans at the time, Michelson moved at the age of two with his parents to the United States. They settled in the wide expanse of Virginia City, Nevada, which was then experiencing a mining boom. Michelson's father was not a miner but a shopkeeper. He serviced the miners and local community with his dry goods store.

Even at an early age, Michelson showed great interest and adeptness in mathematics. His parents could not afford a private college but Michelson did manage to be accepted by the U.S. Naval Academy. After graduation and a short stint at sea, he accepted a job as instructor at the academy.

Michelson's foray into light and light physics came after one of his instructors asked him to prepare a demonstration of the Foucault method of measuring the speed of light. After studying the Foucault device, Michelson saw several ways that it could be made more accurate, and set about building an improved homemade version himself. In 1878 he repeated Foucault's earlier speed of light measurements and achieved results that were the most accurate to date.

A few years later, Michelson began designs on another apparatus that he believed could measure the speed of light with unmatched accuracy. Michelson also wanted to learn more about what scientists of his time called *ether*, an invisible and undetectable material that surrounded all matter, including space, planets, and stars. Though physical evidence of the ether had never been found, physicists knew it had to exist.

In the 1860s, James Clerk Maxwell had determined, on a theoretical level, that light consists of electromagnetic waves. Others postulated that if light really consists of waves, like water or sound waves, it must travel in some medium. That medium, though invisible, must be in every nook and cranny in the universe.

With a grant of about $500 from the Volta fund, Michelson began work on his first interferometer. The brass device, shown in the sketch in FIG. 9-1, consisted of two optical bench arms, each about three feet long. The arms were positioned in an asymmetrical cross, and in the apex of the cross, a beam splitter was placed. At the four ends of the arms he positioned a light source, two mirrors, and a viewing eyepiece.

In operation, a beam of light from an Argand lamp (popular in vehicles and drinking pubs as well as in the laboratory) was passed through a slit and lens, then separated by the beam splitter. The two beams were directed to a pair of fully silvered mirrors and re-directed back through the beam splitter, arriving superimposed over one another at the eyepiece.

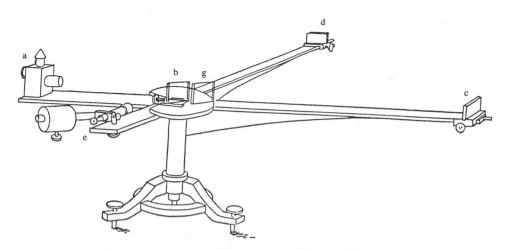

FIG. 9-1. *A preliminary sketch of the original Michelson interferometer.*

The function of Michelson's interferometer was to split the nearly monochromatic light from the lamp two ways. The two beams then traveled at right angles to one another, proceeding the same distance, and then recombined at some common converging point. As with all waves, *fringes* appeared as the two light beams recombined.

The fringing is the result of alternating reinforcement and canceling of the waves. Where the crests of two waves meet, the light is reinforced and Michelson saw a bright glow. Where the crest and valley of two waves meet, the light is canceled, causing a dark spot.

Though Michelson's device worked, it was extremely sensitive to vibration. Minute disturbances such as the changing of air temperature, the tap of a dog's tail on the floor 20 feet away, even human breathing causes the fringes to disappear. Serious experiments with the interferometer were not generally conducted until Michelson took the device to the Potsdam Astrophysical Observatory in Berlin and mounted it on the stable foundation designed for an equatorial telescope.

To test for the presence, direction, and speed of the ether, Michelson rotated the interferometer and looked for minute changes in the speed of light. If the ether existed, Michelson and others postulated, it would take longer for light waves to travel "upstream" through the medium than down or across it. By rotating the device at 90-degree intervals, Michelson hoped to find a direction where a shift in the fringes would show that the light was indeed taking longer to travel one path over the other.

Alas, Michelson could detect no differences or changes in the speed of light. Though the interferometer worked and promised many breakthroughs, he was disappointed and vowed to try again with a larger and more complex version.

It wasn't until 1905 that Albert Einstein declared that the ether did not exist and announced that light travels at the same speed in all directions. That explained why Michelson's interferometer detected no change. In the meantime, Michelson had devised several versions of his unpatented interferometer, including the interferential comparator for the standardization of the meter, a mechanical harmonic analyzer for testing the harmonic motions of interference fringes, and a stellar interferometer for measuring the size of stars. By the turn of the 20th Century, a number of firms regularly manufactured bench models of the interferometer, and it became common in laboratories around the world.

Even up to his death in 1931, Michelson kept busy trying to improve on his basic ideas. His last project was to measure, with greater accuracy then ever before, the speed of light through a mile-long vacuum tube. It's a pity that Michelson was not born later, or at least that the laser was not invented earlier. Had Michelson used a laser in his interferometer experiments, he would have realized an even finer measure of accuracy. With the benefit of hindsight, it's easy to see that modern physics owes a lot to Michelson's pioneering work. Devices and processes such as holography and the laser gyroscope are a direct outgrowth of the interferometer.

BUILDING YOUR OWN INTERFEROMETER

Michelson was plagued by the problems of weak fringes in his early interferometers because the light source he used was not entirely monochromatic, and it was certainly not coherent. With the aid of a helium-neon laser, you can construct a complete and working interferometer that displays vivid, easy-to-see fringes. The interferometer plans provided below are a modification of the Michelson apparatus. The design presented is generally referred to as the Twyman-Green interferometer, after its creators.

As with most optics experiments, a certain level of precision is required for the interferometer to work satisfactorily. However, careful construction and attention to detail should assure you of a properly working model. The design outlined below uses commonly available components and yields a device that is moderately accurate in determining the speed of light, light frequency, rate of rotation, and other observations. You might want to improve upon the basic design by adding components that provide a greater level of precision.

Component Overview

A parts lists is included in TABLE 9-1. The interferometer consists of an acrylic plastic base. Four bolts allow you to make fine adjustments in the level and position of the base. A single plano-concave or double-concave lens spreads the pencil beam of the laser to a larger spot. This allows you to see the fringes. In the center of the base is a glass plate beam splitter, positioned at a 45-degree angle to the lens. The beam splitter breaks the light into two components, directing it to two fully silvered mirrors.

One mirror is mounted on a sled that can be moved back and forth by means of a micrometer. The second mirror, placed at right angles to the first mirror, is stationary. The final component is a ground-glass viewing screen. After reflecting off the mirrors, the two beams are re-directed by the beam splitter and are projected onto the rear of the screen. When adjusted properly, the two beams exactly coincide and fringes appear. You can conveniently view the fringes on the front side of the screen.

Constructing the Base

Cut a piece of ⅜-inch acrylic plastic (Plexiglas) to 9½ by 7 inches. Keep the protective paper on the plastic until you are through with cutting and drilling to prevent chipping.

Be sure the plastic is square. Finish the edges by sanding or burnishing. Drill a series of mounting holes using the drilling guide shown in FIG. 9-2. Although there is room for some error, you should be as accurate as possible. Measure twice and use a drill press to ensure that the holes are perpendicular. Remove the protective paper from the plastic and set the base aside.

Constructing the Micrometer Sled

The micrometer sled is perhaps the most complicated component of the interferometer and will take you the longest to make. Note that the sled is optional; you don't need it if all you want to do is observe laser light fringes. The sled is required only if you wish to perform some of the more advanced experiments outlined in this chapter.

The sled consists of two 2½-inch lengths of $^{41}/_{64}$-by-½-by-$^{1}/_{16}$-inch extruded aluminum channel stock. The channel stock serves as a guide rail for the sled and is available at most hardware and building supply stores. Cut the stock with a hacksaw and miter box (to assure a perfect right-angle cut), then finish the edges with a file.

To avoid a mismatch, use the holes you drilled in the base as a template for marking the mounting holes for the channel stock. Place the stock on the base and mark the holes

Table 9-1. Michelson Interferometer Parts List

Base and Legs
1   9½-by-7-inch, ⅜-inch-thick acrylic plastic
4   ¼-inch 20 by 2-inch hex-head machine bolt
4   ¼-inch 20 nut
4   Plastic discs (for feet)

Micrometer Sled (One-Axis Translation Table)
2   2½-inch lengths of ⁴¹⁄₆₄ by ½-by-¹⁄₁₆-inch aluminum channel stock
2   1½-by-2¾-inch, ⅛-inch-thick acrylic plastic
2   ⁸⁄₃₂ by ½-inch bolts, nuts
4   #8 flat washers
2   #8 or #10 fender washers
4   ⁶⁄₃₂ by ½-inch bolt, nuts
12 #6 flat washers
2   ¼-by-¾-inch metal mending plate (one flat, one bent to make an angle bracket)
1   4-inch length ²⁄₅₆ threaded rod
2   ²⁄₅₆ locking nuts
3   ²⁄₅₆ brass nut (one for soldering to straight metal mending plate)
1   ²⁄₅₆ self-tapping wood screw
1   Plastic wheel (from R/C servo; for turning rod)

Sled Mirror
1   1¼-by-1½-inch front-surface mirror
1   Small metal bracket (Erector Set)

Side Mirror
1   1¼-by-2½-inch front-surface mirror
1   Small metal bracket (from Erector Set)
1   ⁸⁄₃₂ by ½-inch bolt, nut, flat washer

Beam Splitter
1   1-by-3-inch plate (coated) beam splitter
1   1½-inch, L-shaped metal girder (from Erector Set)
1   ⁸⁄₃₂ by ½-inch bolt, nut, flat washer

Lens
1   8 to 10 mm diameter double-concave lens, in plastic or metal holder (measuring 1-inch square)
2   2-inch flat metal strip (sheet metal, brass, or similar, from Erector Set)
1   1⅜-by-¾-inch, ⅛-inch-thick acrylic plastic
1   ⁸⁄₃₂ by ½-inch bolt, nut, flat washer

Screen
1   2½-by-3½-inch ground glass
1   1½-inch, L-shaped metal girder (Erector Set)
1   ⁸⁄₃₂ by ½-inch bolt, nut, flat washer

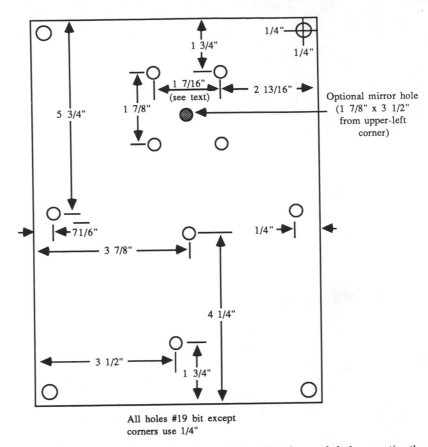

All holes #19 bit except
corners use 1/4"

FIG. 9-2. *Drilling guide for the Michelson interferometer base. Note the gray hole for mounting the second mirror directly to the base.*

with a pencil. Drill the holes with a 5/32-inch bit. Remove the flash from the aluminum with a file.

During extrusion, the aluminum channel might develop slight ridges and imperfections along the surfaces and edges. Remove these blemishes by rubbing the top (undrilled side) and edge with a piece of 300-grit wet/dry sandpaper, used wet. The object is to make the surface as smooth as possible. Don't use a file, grinding stone, or other coarse tool, as these introduce heavy and difficult-to-remove ridges.

Set the aluminum pieces aside and construct the sled from two ⅛-inch-thick acrylic plastic pieces cut to 1½ inches by 2¾ inches. Sand and burnish the edges of the plastic to make them smooth (the exact dimensions of the plastic is not important, so you may safely remove some of it when finishing the edges). Clamp the two pieces together and drill two holes are shown in FIG. 9-3.

Finish the sled by attaching the hardware shown in FIG. 9-4. The angle bracket is a flat mending plate (¼-by-¾-inch, available at most hobby stores), bent 90 degrees at the middle. Before inserting the fender washers, select two, butt them together, and check for size. The two washers should be exactly the same size and should not have

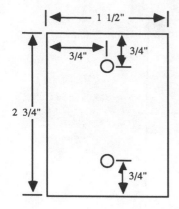

FIG. 9-3. *Cutting and drilling guide for the sled pieces (top and bottom).*

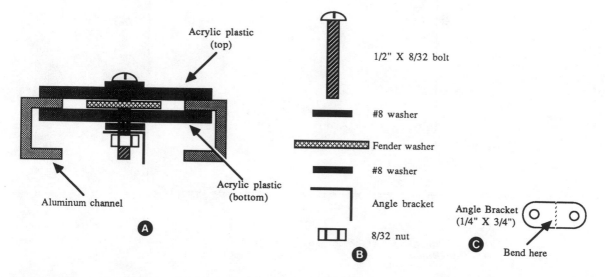

FIG. 9-4. *Use the hardware shown to assemble the sled. (A) Assembled sled (end view); (B) exploded view showing the hardware to use; (C) Bend a small, flat metal plate (available at hobby stores) to make the angle bracket.*

any ridges. Continue the selection process until you find two washers that are exactly the same size.

The mirror mount in the prototype was salvaged from an Erector Set. You can use a similar mounting bracket as long as it is sturdy yet can be bent slightly. Metal is the best choice because it prevents excessive vibration, yet heavy angle irons can't be easily bent. If you can't scrounge up a bracket from an Erector Set, check around a hobby shop for ideas. You are bound to find something.

Assemble the pieces of the sled using the ½-by-⁸⁄₃₂-inch hardware as shown, but don't tighten the bolts just yet. Mount the two aluminum rails using ⁶⁄₃₂-by-½-inch bolts. Use two #6 washers stacked on top of one another as spacers. Attach nuts to each bolt but don't tighten them. A mounting assembly detail is shown in FIG. 9-5.

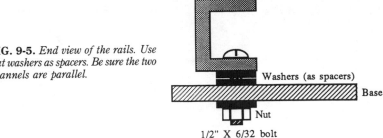

FIG. 9-5. *End view of the rails. Use flat washers as spacers. Be sure the two channels are parallel.*

Carefully insert the sled between the rails and jiggle things around until everything fits. Center the sled between the two rails and tighten the rails. Be absolutely sure that the rails are parallel or the sled won't travel properly. Once the rails are tightened in place, slip the sled back and forth until it rides evenly on both rails. Slowly tighten the nuts sandwiching the top and bottom sled pieces together.

If everything fits properly, the sled should mount on the rails with little or no side-to-side motion. If there is excessive play, loosen the nuts holding the rails and push the rails closer together, remembering to keep them parallel. After careful adjustment, you should be able to get the rails close enough together so that the sled still has freedom to move back and forth, but with no side-to-side play.

If the sled doesn't move even when the rails are pushed apart, the washers might be too thin, causing the top and bottom plastic pieces to clamp against the rails. Try slightly thicker washers. A micrometer comes in handy at this point to accurately measure the thickness of the washers. The aluminum rail should be $\frac{1}{16}$-inch thick, or very close to it. The washers should be just slightly thicker.

Should you find that the sled binds at one end or another, the rails are not parallel. Loosen and readjust them as necessary. If both ends of the sled are not centered between in the rails, it might move at an angle and cause considerable problems when you attempt to use the interferometer. Assuming that the plastic pieces of the sled are square, there should be equal distance between the edges of the sled and the rails. If not, loosen the two nuts holding the sled together and readjust as necessary.

The sled is now almost complete. Pull the sled out of the rails. Attach two $\frac{2}{56}$ locking nuts and a 4-inch length of $\frac{2}{56}$ threaded rod to the angle bracket on the underside of the sled, as shown in FIG. 9-6. Solder a $\frac{2}{56}$ brass nut to a $\frac{1}{4}$-by-$\frac{3}{4}$-inch flat mending iron (the same kind used to make the angle bracket above), being careful not to spill molten solder inside the threads. One or two small spots of solder tacked to the outside of the nut should be sufficient (it took me three tries to get it right, so don't despair if your first attempt doesn't work out).

With a small bit, drill a hole 3½ inches from either side of the base (see FIG. 9-7). Thread the free end of the rod through the nut/mending iron, insert the sled between the rails, then secure the mending iron using a $\frac{2}{56}$ self-tapping screw. Finish the sled by mounting a small pulley or plastic wheel to the end of the rod. I used a 1³⁄₁₆-inch diameter plastic hub designed for model airplane servos. The finished sled, mounted on the base and with mirror attached (plans below), is shown in FIG. 9-8.

131

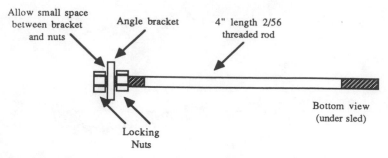

Allow small space
between bracket
and nuts

Angle bracket

4" length 2/56
threaded rod

Bottom view
(under sled)

Locking
Nuts

FIG. 9-6. *The micrometer screw is a 4-inch length of ⅔₆ threaded rod. Secure it to the angle bracket (from FIG. 9-4) with two ⅔₆ locking nuts.*

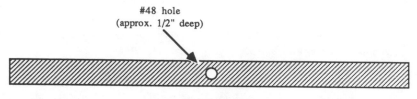

#48 hole
(approx. 1/2" deep)

End view of base

FIG. 9-7. *Drilling guide for the micrometer screw.*

FIG. 9-8. *The finished sled (shown with mirror attached).*

Note that although the micrometer sled is fairly accurate and has a usable resolution of a fraction of a millimeter, it is not precise enough for some light measurement applications. Methods of improving accuracy are provided later in this chapter.

Mounting the Mirrors

One of the fully silvered mirrors attaches to the bracket on top of the sled. Use epoxy or a general-purpose adhesive to stick the mirror against the bracket. The prototype used Duco cement, which dries fairly quickly, cures overnight, and does not discolor or fog the mirrors. The mirror attached to the sled should measure approximately 1¼ wide by 1½ inches tall.

If you don't use the adjustable sled, you can mount the mirror and bracket directly to the base. The drilling template for the base shows the location for the rear mirror when no sled is used.

The second fully silvered mirror is mounted along the right edge of the base, using the same kind of bracket as the one attached to the sled. The second mirror should measure approximately 1¼ by 2½ inches. Secure the bracket for the second mirror using a 8/32-by-½-inch bolt and matching hardware. Do not overtighten.

Mounting the Beam Splitter, Lens, and Viewing Screen

The beam splitter can be ordinary plate glass, but its thickness should not exceed 3/32-inch. Internal reflections in thicker glass can cause a separate satellite beam (that beam can be removed using electrical tape, as shown in Chapter 3, but the close distances between optics make this a difficult task). The prototype used a coated, flat, glass plate measuring 1 by 3 inches. You can get by with a piece that's shorter, but stay away from beam splitters that are less than one inch wide.

A right-angle girder piece stolen from an Erector Set serves as an excellent mount for the beam splitter. Cut a piece of girder to a length of three holes wide, as shown in FIG. 9-9, and glue the beam splitter to the outside edge. When the cement is dry, attach the beam splitter and bracket to the center hole of the base using an 8/32-by-½-inch bolt and hardware. Before tightening, position the beam splitter so that it is at a 45-degree angle to the sides of the base. Don't overtighten.

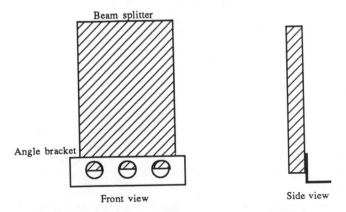

FIG. 9-9. *Mount the beam splitter on an Erector Set (or equivalent) metal angle bracket.*

The small beam from the laser must be expanded before passing through the beam splitter. A suitable choice is a plano-concave or bi-concave lens approximately 8 to 10 mm in diameter. Focal length isn't a major consideration, but you might need to choose another lens if the spot on the screen is excessively small or large.

Mount the lens using one of the techniques outlined in Chapter 7, "Constructing an Optical Bench." A metal or plastic frame is a good choice. Use flat girders from an Erector Set or similar toy, bent at right angles at the bottom. Cement the bottom of the bracket to a piece of 1⅜-by-¾-by-⅛-inch acrylic plastic. Drill a hole with a #19 bit in the center of the plastic and attach it to the base using 8/32-by-½-inch bolt and hardware.

The screen is made from a 2½-by-3½-inch piece of ground glass (plastic can also be used). Mount the glass on the same type of girder used for the beam splitter. Once the cement is dry, attach the glass to the base using an 8/32-by-½-inch bolt and matching hardware. Position the screen so that it is parallel to the front edge of the base. Once more, don't overtighten the hardware.

Attaching the Legs

Finish the interferometer by attaching the legs to the four corners. Tap the four corner holes with a ¼-inch 20 tap. Thread ¼-inch 20 with 2-inch machine bolts (threaded all the way) into the holes, and secure them into position with a ¼-inch 20 nut. You can adjust the overall height of the interferometer by loosening the nut and turning the bolt. Retighten the nut when the base is at the proper height.

Leveling discs or "feet" can be added to the tips of the bolts, as shown in FIG. 9-10. The discs used in the prototype were ¾-inch-diameter by ¼-inch-deep plastic chassis spacers. You can use just about anything for the feet in your interferometer, including plastic or metal stand-offs, acrylic discs drilled and tapped for ¼-inch 20 hardware, or plastic torriod coil cores. A visit to any well-stocked industrial surplus or supply outlet should yield several good alternatives. You can compensate for slight differences in height by turning the discs one way or the other. The finished interferometer, with sled and feet, is shown in FIG. 9-11.

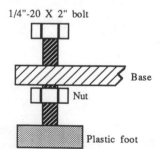

1/4"-20 X 2" bolt

Base

Nut

Plastic foot

FIG. 9-10. *Hardware detail for the leveling feet.*

Adjustment and Checkout

Now comes the fun part. Set the interferometer on a hard surface, preferably on a concrete floor or sturdy table covered with carpet or foam. Even minute vibrations will upset the fringes, so it is important that the interferometer be placed on a stable platform. Thoroughly clean all of the optics, including the lens. Smudges, dirt, and

134

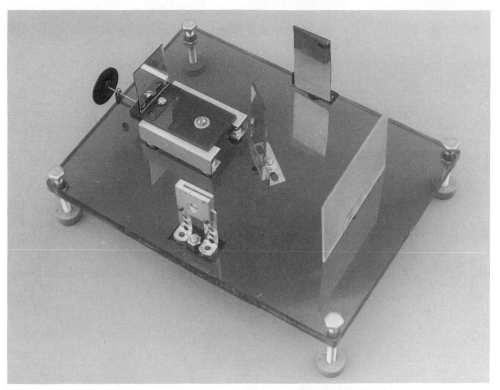

FIG. 9-11. *The finished interferometer, with all components attached and aligned.*

fingerprints may prevent the appearance of the fringes or make them extremely difficult to see.

Turn the wheel on the sled so that the distance between the mirrors and beam splitter is approximately the same (about 3 inches). Exact positioning of the sled is not important. (Obviously, if you didn't construct the sled, you can ignore this step.)

Position a laser in front of the lens and direct the beam through its center. Shim the front or back of the laser so that the beam is parallel to the base. Start out with the lens perpendicular to the left edge of the base. If the expanded beam doesn't strike the center of the beam splitter, move the laser to the right or left as needed.

As depicted in FIG. 9-12, one half of the beam should pass through the beam splitter and strike the side (say the #1) mirror. The other half of the beam should reflect off the beam splitter and strike the rear (#2) mirror. If the beam doesn't hit the #2 mirror, adjust the angle of the beam splitter as needed.

The reflected beam from the #2 mirror should pass directly through the beam splitter and hit the rear of the screen. It should appear as a round, fuzzy, red dot. The reflected beam from mirror #1 should strike against the beam splitter and also project onto the rear of the screen. Most likely, this beam will not match up with the first one. Adjust differences in horizontal spacing by rotating the #1 mirror on its mount. You can compensate for differences in vertical alignment by *carefully* bending the #1 and/or #2 mirrors up or down. Bend the brackets to stress the metal only, not the mirror, or you might break the glass.

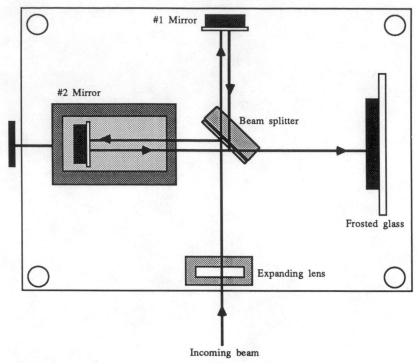

FIG. 9-12. *The beam from the laser should follow the path shown here. Be sure both reflected beams from the mirrors align perfectly at the frosted glass.*

Continue adjusting the mirrors, lens, and beam splitter until the beams coincide on the screen. It's vitally important that the two beams be as parallel as possible. Any slight incline, either horizontally or vertically, of one beam to the other will prevent the fringes from appearing.

After each adjustment, especially after bending the mirror mounts, wait 15 to 30 seconds for the vibrations in the interferometer to settle. Once you are satisfied that the beams are as parallel to one another as possible, wait a few minutes and see if the fringes appear. Although the fringes should have a concentric bullseye or ring appearance, the pattern you see may begin at the outside edges of the patch. You can center the beam with the rings simply by moving the laser. You will note that moving the laser doesn't disturb the rings nor their position on the screen. Moving the laser too much will cause the fringes to disappear.

Once the fringes show up on the screen, you can lightly tighten the optical components to the base. After tightening a nut and bolt, inspect the beam to make sure that the fringes are still visible. You'll note that even a small thump on the base of the interferometer causes the fringes to disappear. Depending on where you placed the interferometer, vibrations through the ground or table can also cause the fringes to go away. Once the vibrations settle, the fringes should reappear.

The loss of distinct fringes is a nuisance in many laser projects such as interferometry and holography, but it is handy in other applications. For example, you can detect even faint motion around a given perimeter by placing a phototransistor in front of the ground glass screen. Changes in the fringes appear as voltage or current fluctuations in the transistor, and an alarm circuit can announce a possible breach of security. You can even hear the disturbance by connecting an audio amplifier to the phototransistor.

If you built the sled, you can experiment with the effects of changing the distance of the two light paths. Slowly turn the sled wheel and watch the fringes. Even a slight movement of the wheel should cause the fringe rings to move in and out. Turning the wheel one way causes the rings to grow from the inside. Turning the wheel the other way causes the rings to shrink towards the center.

By looking at the center spot of the rings, you can move the sled in precise increments. Each change from light to dark denotes a movement of one-half of one wavelength. When using a helium-neon laser, one half a wavelength is 316.4 nanometers (632.8 nm ÷ 2), or 316.4 billionths of a meter! As you might guess, it's hard to turn the wheel so that you see only one complete light-to-dark or dark-to-light transition. The section below shows how to increase the precision of the sled so that you can use it for accurate laboratory experiments.

If the Fringes Don't Appear

In some instances, no amount of tweaking and adjustment can coax the fringes to appear. What now? If you have constructed the interferometer as described in the text and both beams of light are transversing the paths as indicated in FIG. 9-12, above, then the fringes are bound to show up sooner or later. Continue experimenting with the position of the optics until they appear.

Misalignment isn't the only cause of absent fringes. Excessive vibrations, even ones that you and your dog can't feel, can mask the fringes. Be sure that the interferometer is on a solid base. I first tried the prototype on a carpeted floor and obtained adequate but frustrating results. Things got better when I took the contraption outside and placed it on the concrete in the garage.

If you suspect excessive vibration and just can't seem to find a vibration-free spot, try planting the interferometer in a sand box. A similar type of sandbox is used for homebrew holography and is used for the same reason: to eliminate vibrations that cause the fringes to shift.

Loosely mounted optics can amplify even minute vibrations. Be sure the mirrors are securely cemented to their mounts and that the brackets are fairly tight on the base.

As you learned in Chapter 3, "Introduction to Optics," air is a refracting medium. Like a lens, air causes light to bend and change speeds. If the air is moving around the interferometer, the density and therefore the index of refraction is constantly changing. Understandably, this has a dramatic impact on the appearance of fringes. Avoid placing the interferometer in a drafty place or where there may be a sudden change in temperature.

If you've just taken the interferometer from a cool to a warm atmosphere, the optics will slowly warm up and expand. This expansion, invisible to the eye, can also inhibit the appearance of the rings. Wait at least 15 to 30 minutes to acclimate the interferometer to a change in environment.

MODIFYING THE INTERFEROMETER

There are a number of ways to improve on the basic interferometer. By using a rod that has more threads per inch, you achieve greater accuracy over linear position. A quick bit of math, however, reveals that no single rod can be machined accurately enough to give a resolution good enough to turn the wheel precisely at ½-wavelength intervals.

For example, with the 2/56 threaded rod used, there are 56 threads per inch. Each revolution, then, is 1/56 of an inch, or about 0.45 mm. With practice, you can move the wheel in 1-degree increments, or 0.00125 mm at a time. Smaller hardware exists with up to 160 threads per inch, equal to about 0.159 mm per revolution, or 0.00044 mm per degree of rotation. Hardware this fine is hard to get and is fragile. In order for you to "dial" in a half wavelength of time, the sled needs to have a positional accuracy of greater than 0.0003164 mm! (316.4 nm); that's even less than you can hope for using the extremely small rods with 160 threads per inch.

An easier way to approach this accuracy is by using a gearing mechanism that reduces your movements to a snail's pace. A suitable gearbox can be obtained by salvaging the gearing mechanism of a small stepper or dc motor. Attach the control wheel to the input of the gear box; attach the output of the gearbox to the interferometer sled using a rubber band or rubber belt. The belt helps isolate the interferometer from vibration.

Using the more commonly available 2/56 threaded rod, you can achieve a positioning accuracy of about 0.00014 mm (140 nm) using the 16:1 gear box supplied with a typical surplus dc stepper motor (the gear ratio may differ depending on the exact model).

Even with an improved gearing system, however, the sled may still not offer sufficient provision for some applications. There is a limit to what garage shop tinkering can do. A machinist can rebuild the sled using aluminum stock and a manual or numerically controlled mill. In addition, a number of ready-made products that do the same thing are available. Industrial manufacturers sell optical bases (called *translation stages*) that have extremely fine precision. Similar (but generally less expensive) models with micrometer adjustment bases are available at most any machinist supply outlet.

One other method is to use the works of a student's micrometer. These are available for $20 or less at many hardware stores and have a measurement accuracy of 0.001 of an inch (0.0254 mm), but you can dial in smaller amounts. With proper gearing and careful control of the knob, you can obtain far greater resolution. A 16:1 gear ratio—which you can make yourself using small plastic or brass gears pulled from a small dc motor—should provide enough accuracy to move the mirror at half-wavelength steps.

Another modification of the interferometer is removing the viewing screen. By removing the screen, you can project the fringe pattern on a wall or other surface. The larger bullseye makes viewing and counting the fringes easier. Calibrate and graduate the screen for easier measurements.

Try bouncing the fringe pattern onto a separate, larger, rear-projection (frosted glass or plastic) screen. A graduated and calibrated magnifier (such as those used in the optics and publishing trades), can then be placed directly against the screen without worry of upsetting the interferometer.

The Michelson interferometer can be used with a number of light sources. If you have other lasers that operate at different wavelengths such as argon or krypton, you can compare fringe patterns and calculate the differences in wavelengths. Both argon and krypton lasers emit several strong lines of visible light; you can separate these with a prism or dichroic filter. After separation, the beam can be sent through the lens of the device.

INTERFEROMETRIC EXPERIMENTS

While the Michelson interferometer provides a wealth of hands-on experience in optics, interference, and lasers, it's nice to be able to actually do something with the contraption. Here are some ideas.

Structural Stress

Remove mirror #2 from the slide and mount it on a wall. Position the interferometer base close to the wall but make sure the device doesn't touch the wall. Apply pressure on the wall (anywhere) and you should see a shift in the fringes. Even a brick wall under light pressure by a child's hand will show some movement.

If the stress on the wall is not too great, project the fringe pattern on a larger surface. This enables you to more accurately measure the distance of travel. Each light-to-dark or dark-to-light transition of the center bullseye in the pattern denotes a change of 316.4 nanometers. You'll find that a wood or plaster wall can bow so much that you'll spend the greater part of the evening counting fringes!

Linear Measurement

By attaching a small pointer to the sled, you can measure the size of objects with amazing accuracy. Again, each transition of the bullseye patterns marks a change of 316.4 billionths of a meter. With an extra bit of work, it's possible to locate the stage of a microscope on the base of the interferometer and sled. With the microscope, the pointer (such as a tungsten filament or even a strand of human hair) can be more easily seen than with the unaided eye.

Study Effects of Refraction

Placing any object in front of either mirror #1 or #2 causes a shift in the time it takes for light to traverse the two paths. You can study the effects of refraction in air by blowing gently through a tube. Place the end of the tube in either optical path and watch the fringes move. Try other objects like lenses, smoke, and water.

Similarly, you can explain the shimmer of a desert mirage by heating up the air around the interferometer and watching the fringes appear and disappear. Although a mirage doesn't involve lasers, you can easily see how a rise in temperature causes a change in the refractive index of air. A "real" mirage looks like a shimmering oasis that awaits a weary traveler, but in reality, it is air set in motion by the heat. The different densities of the air cause unusual refraction effects.

Fringe Counter

Some experiments move the fringes too quickly and all you see is a blur. A counter circuit can be used to count the number of light-to-dark or dark-to-light transitions of the shifting fringe pattern, even if the fringes move several thousand times per second. See FIG. 9-13 and parts list in TABLE 9-2.

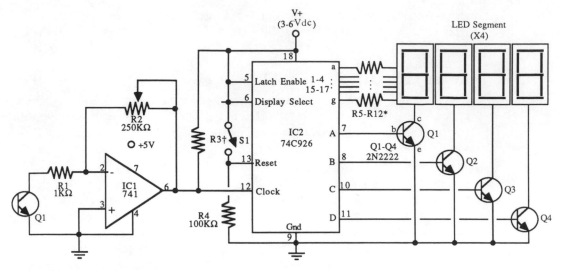

* Not required if +V is 4V or less
† Optional, 10KΩ to 10MΩ, for sensitivity

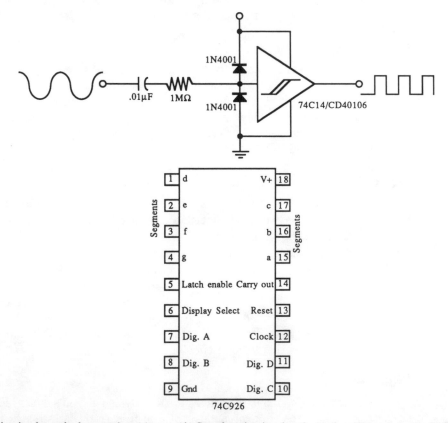

FIG. 9-13. *Circuit schematic for counting fringes. (A) Complete circuit using the National Semiconductor 74C926 all-in-one counter chip; (B) Adding a Schmitt trigger to provide a clean square wave input for the counter chip (insert it between pin 6 of IC1 and pin 12 of IC2; (C) Pinout diagram for the 74C926.*

Table 9-2. Fringe Counter Circuit Parts List

Full Counter

IC1	741 op amp
IC2	National Semiconductor 74C926 integrated four-digit counter IC
R1	1 kilohm resistor
R2	250 Kilohm potentiometer
R3	10 kilohm to 10 megohm resistor
R4	100 kilohm resistor
R5-R12	330 ohm resistor (not required if supply voltage is under 5 Vdc)
Q1-Q4	2N2222 transistor
Q5	Infrared phototransistor
LED1-4	Common-cathode seven-segment LED display
S1	SPST switch

Optional Wave-Shaping Electronics

1	0.01 μF disc capacitor
1	1 megohm resistor
2	1N4001 diode
1	74C14 or 40106 Schmitt trigger IC

All resistors are 5 to 10 percent tolerance, ¼ watt. All capacitors are 10 to 20 percent tolerance, rated 35 volts or more.

Remove the ground-glass viewing screen on the interferometer. Place the phototransistor behind a simple focusing lens (such as a 20 to 40 mm focal length bi-convex lens), at least two or three feet from the interferometer. At this distance, the fringe pattern should be fairly large and the lens and transistor should be able to discriminate separate circular fringes.

Connect the counter to the output of the amplifier and reset it to 0000. Move the sled and watch the counter. It should read some number. Note that the accuracy won't be 100 percent, but the counter should be able to read at least 90 to 95 fringe changes out of 100 (accuracy drops dramatically if the interferometer is exposed to vibrations). You can improve the count accuracy by turning out all room lights.

OTHER TYPES OF INTERFEROMETERS

The Michelson/Twyman-Green apparatus is only one of many types of interferometers developed over the last 75 years or so. A variety of interferometer types are shown in FIG. 9-14. These interferometer designs using corner cubes do not reflect the the beam back into the laser cavity. This back-to-the-source reflection can perturb the laser wavelength, making fringe counts meaningless. Note that more accurate fringe counts can also be obtained using thick plate beam splitters or cube beam splitters, where unwanted reflections and satellite beams are either non-existent or can be masked off

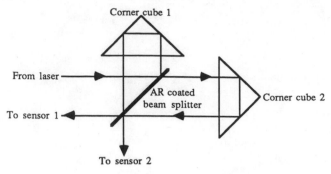

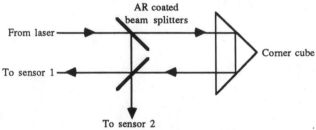

FIG. 9-14. *Corner cubes can be used to make interferometers that don't cause reflected light to re-enter the laser. Three different approaches are shown here.*

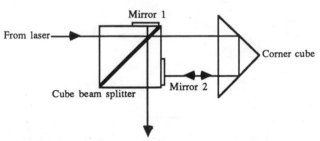

using black tape. (Full details on both plate and cube beam splitters, as well as corner-cube (porro) prisms, are in Chapter 3, "Introduction to Optics.")

the laser wavelength, making fringe counts meaningless. Note that more accurate fringe counts can also be obtained using thick plate beam splitters or cube beam splitters, where unwanted reflections and satellite beams are either non-existent or can be masked off using black tape. (Full details on both plate and cube beam splitters, as well as corner-cube (porro) prisms, are in Chapter 3, "Introduction to Optics.")

Another type of interferometer is shown in FIG. 9-15 (a parts list for this and the remaining experiments in this chapter is in TABLE 9-3). This is called a Lloyd's Mirror interferometer and consists of a double-concave lens, a double-convex lens, and a

Table 9-3. Lloyd's Mirror Interferometer Parts List

1	Laser
1	Double-concave lens (10 to 20 mm in diameter)
1	Double-convex lens (20 to 30 mm in diameter)
1	Microscope slide
1	Viewing screen

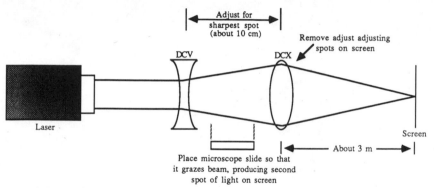

Adjust for
sharpest spot
(about 10 cm)

Remove adjust adjusting
spots on screen

DCV

DCX

Laser

Screen

About 3 m

Place microscope slide so that
it grazes beam, producing second
spot of light on screen

FIG. 9-15. *A Lloyd's Mirror interferometer consists of a laser, two lenses, and microscope slide (or other piece of flat glass). Arrange the components as shown and watch the interference fringes appear at the screen.*

microscope slide. By placing the components as shown in the figure, it's possible to calculate the wavelength of the light using the formula for double-slit diffraction (see the previous chapter for more details). Note that the double-convex converging lens is removed from the light path in order to see the fringes on the viewing screen.

One interesting interference effect can be used to dazzle an audience during a light show. Simply shine a laser beam onto a front-surface mirror and position the mirror so that the beam strikes a wall or ceiling. Dip a cotton swab in rubbing alcohol and spread the alcohol over the mirror. As the alcohol dries, you see constantly moving lightforms swirling on the wall or ceiling. Tilt the mirror at an angle and some of the alcohol will run down the mirror producing more effects.

Other effects of interference can be demonstrated using a microscope slide. Hold the slide up to a slightly expanded laser beam, as shown in FIG. 9-16. Some of the light is internally reflected inside the slide until it finally exits and strikes the screen. Interference fringes appear on the screen because of the many reflections of light inside the glass.

Another experiment shows the effects of interference caused by heat expansion. Spread the beam slightly with a double-concave lens and shine it through a microscope slide. Touch a hot soldering iron to the glass and watch the the fringes appear around the point of contact with the iron.

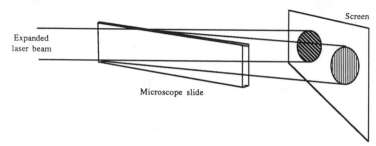

Screen

Expanded
laser beam

Microscope slide

FIG. 9-16. *An expanded beam passed through a microscope slide shows interference fringes when the beam spots are projected on a screen.*

143

10

Introduction to Semiconductor Lasers

The typical 5 mW helium-neon gas laser measures almost two inches in diameter by 10 to 15 inches in length. Imagine stuffing it all into a size no larger than the dot in the letter *i*! Such is the semiconductor laser. A close relative to the ordinary light-emitting diode, the semiconductor laser is made in mass quantities from wafers of gallium arsenide or similar crystals.

In quantity, low- to medium-power semiconductor lasers cost from $5 to $35. Such lasers are used in consumer products such as compact audio disc players and laser disc players, as well as bar-code readers and fiberoptics data links. With the proliferation of these and other devices, the cost of laser semiconductors (or laser diodes) is expected to drop even more.

This chapter presents an overview of the diode laser: how it's made, the various types that are available, and how to use them in your experiments. The low cost of semiconductor lasers— typically $10 on the surplus market—make them ideal for school or hobbyist projects where a tight budget doesn't allow for more expensive gas lasers.

THE INSIDES OF A SEMICONDUCTOR LASER

The basic configuration of the diode laser (sometimes called an *injection laser*) is shown in FIG. 10-1. The laser is composed of a pn junction, similar to that found in transistors and LEDs. A chunk of this material is cut from a larger silicon wafer, and the ends are cleaved precisely to make the diode chip. Wires are bonded to the top and bottom. When current is applied, light is produced inside the junction. As it stands, the device is an LED—the light is not coherent.

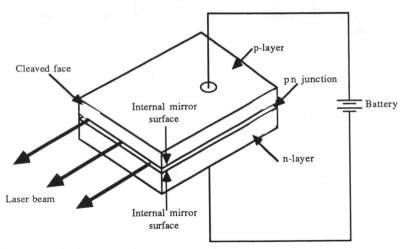

FIG. 10-1. *Design of a semiconductor laser chip showing cleaved face and pn junction.*

An increase in current causes an increase in light output. The cleaved faces act as partially reflective mirrors that bounce the emitted light back and forth within the junction. Once amplified, the light exits the chip. This light is temporally and spatially coherent, but because of the design of the diode chip, is not very directional. The beam of most laser diodes is elliptical, with a spread of about 10 to 35 degrees.

The first laser diodes, created in 1962 shortly after the introduction of the ruby and helium-neon lasers, were composed of a single material forming one junction—a *homojunction*. These could be powered only in short pulses because the heat produced within the junction would literally cause the diode to explode. Continuous output could only be achieved by dipping the diode in a cryogenic fluid such as liquid nitrogen (with a temperature of −196 degrees C, or −320 degrees F).

As manufacturing techniques improved, additional layers were added in varying thicknesses to produce a *heterojunction diode*. The simplest heterojunction semiconductor lasers have a gallium arsenide (GaAs) junction topped off by layers of aluminum gallium arsenide (AlGaAs). These can produce from 3 to 10 watts of optical output when driven by a current of approximately 10 amps. At such high outputs, the diode must be operated in pulsed mode.

Typical specifications for *single heterostructure* (sh) lasers call for a pulse duration of less than 200 nanoseconds. Most drive circuits operate the diode laser conservatively with pulse durations under 75 or 100 nanoseconds. Output wavelength is generally between 780 nm and 904 nm.

A *double heterostructure* (dh) laser diode is usually made by sandwiching a GaAs junction between two AlGaAs layers. This helps confine the light generated within the chip and allows the diode to operate continuously (called *continuous wave*, or *cw*) at room temperature. The wavelength can be altered by varying the amount of aluminum in the AlGaAs material. The output wavelength can be between 680 nm and 900 nm, with 780 nm being most common.

Power output of a double heterostructure laser is considerably less than with a single heterostructure diode. Most dh lasers produce 3 to 5 mW of light, although some high-output varieties can generate up to 500 mW yet can still be operated at room temperature (indeed, some high-cost cw lasers can produce up to 2.6 watts of optical power, but these are rare and very expensive). High-output laser diodes come in T0-3 transistor-type cases and are mounted on suitable heat sinks. A typical application for high-output lasers is long-haul (long distance) fiberoptic data links.

POWERING A DIODE LASER

Drive circuits for both sh and dh lasers are presented in Chapter 11, ''Laser Power Supplies.'' But it's worthwhile here to discuss the drive requirements necessary for operating diode lasers.

Single heterostructure lasers are typically driven by applying a high-voltage, short-duration pulse. The duration of the pulse is controlled by an RC network, as shown in the basic schematic in FIG. 10-2, and the pulse is delivered by a power transistor. Care must be exercised to ensure that the pulse duration does not exceed the maximum specified by the manufacturer. Longer pulses cause the laser to overheat, annihilating itself in a violent puff of smoke.

Double heterostructure semiconductor lasers can be operated either in pulsed or cw mode. In pulsed mode, the diode is driven by short, high-energy spikes, as with an sh laser. Power output may be on the order of several watts, but because the pulses are short in duration, the average power is considerably less. In cw mode, a low-voltage constant current is applied to the laser outputs in a steady stream of light. Cw lasers and drive circuits are used in compact disc players where the light emitted by the laser is even more coherent than the beam from the revered He-Ne tube.

Forward-drive current for most cw lasers is in the neighborhood of 60 to 80 mA. That's 50 to 200 percent higher than the forward current used to power light-emitting diodes. If a cw laser is provided less current, it can still emit light, but it won't be laser light. The device lases only when the threshold current is exceeded—typically a minimum of 50 to 60 mA. Conversely, if the laser is provided too much current, it generates excessive heat and is soon destroyed.

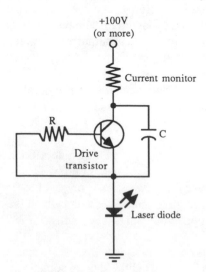

FIG. 10-2. *One way to drive a single heterostructure laser diode. The transistor is driven in avalanche mode, producing short-duration pulses of current.*

Monitoring Power Output

All laser diodes are susceptible to changes in temperature. As the temperature of a semiconductor laser increases, the device becomes less efficient and its light output falls. If the temperature decreases, the laser becomes far more efficient. With the increase in output power, there is a risk of damaging the laser, so most cw drive circuits incorporate a feedback loop to monitor the temperature or output power of the device and adjust its operating current accordingly.

Sensing temperature change requires an elaborate thermal sensing device and complicated constant-current reference source. An easier approach is to monitor the light output of the laser. When the output increases, current is decreased. Conversely, when the output decreases, current is increased.

To facilitate the feedback system, the majority of cw laser diodes now incorporate a built-in photodiode monitor. This photodiode is positioned at the opposite end of the diode chip, as shown in FIG. 10-3, and samples a small portion of the output power. The photodiode is connected to a relatively simple comparator or op amp circuit. As the power output of the laser varies, the current (and voltage) of the photodiode monitor changes. The feedback circuit tracks these changes and adjusts the voltage (or current) supplied to the laser. The feedback circuit can be designed around discrete parts or a custom-made IC. Actual driving circuits using both designs are presented in the following chapter. There is also a schematic for driving a cw laser in pulsed mode.

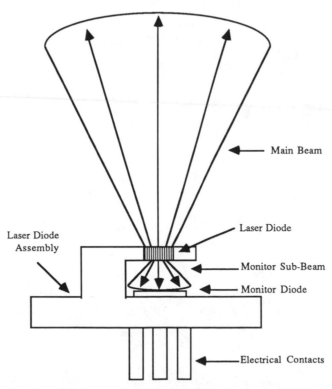

FIG. 10-3. *The orientation of the laser and monitor photodiode chips in a typical double-heterostructure semiconductor laser.*

Connecting the Laser to the Drive Circuit

The laser and photodiode are almost always ganged together, using one of two approaches. Either the anode of the laser is connected to the cathode of the photodiode, or the cathodes are grouped together. That leaves three terminals for connecting the diode to the control circuits. Schematic diagrams for the two approaches are illustrated in FIG. 10-4. A sample terminal layout for the popular Sharp laser diodes (as used in bar code readers and compact disc players) is shown in FIG. 10-5.

There is a danger of damaging a laser diode by improperly connecting it to the drive circuit. Connecting a 60 to 80 mA current source to the photodiode will probably burn it out and can destroy the entire laser. Moral: follow the hook-up diagram carefully. If no diagram came with the laser diode you received, write to the seller or manufacturer and ask for a copy of the specifications sheet or application note.

HANDLING AND SAFETY PRECAUTIONS

While the latest semiconductor lasers are hearty, well-made beasts, they do require certain handling precautions. And, even though they are small, they still emit laser light that can be potentially dangerous to your eyes. Keep these points in mind:

★ Always make sure the terminals of a laser diode are connected properly to the drive circuit (I've covered this already but it's most crucial).

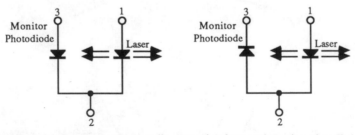

FIG. 10-4. *Two ways of internally connecting laser and monitor photodiode.*

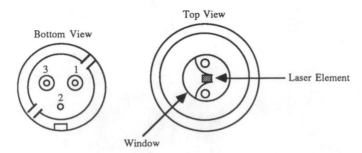

FIG. 10-5. *Package outline and terminal configuration for the Sharp LT020 laser diode.*

★ Never apply more than the maximum forward current (as specified by the manufacturer), or the laser will burn up. Use the pulser drive (see Chapter 11) if you are not using the laser with a monitor photodiode feedback circuit.

★ Handle laser diodes with the same care you extend to CMOS devices. Wear an anti-static wrist strap while handling the laser, and keep the device in a protective, anti-static bag until ready for use.

★ Never connect the probes of a volt-ohmmeter across the terminals of a laser diode (the current from the internal battery of the meter can damage the laser).

★ Use only batteries or *well-filtered* ac power supplies. Laser diodes are susceptible to voltage transients and can be ruined when powered by poorly filtered line-operated supplies.

★ Take care not to short the terminals of the laser during operation.

★ Avoid looking into the window of the laser while it is operating, even if you can't see any light coming out. This is especially important if you have added focusing or collimating optics.

★ Mount the laser diode on a suitable heatsink, preferably larger than 1 inch square. Use silicone heat transfer paste to assure a good thermal contact between the laser and the heatsink. You can buy heatsinks ready made or construct your own. Some ideas for heatsinks appear in the next section.

★ Insulate the connections between the laser diode and the drive to minimize the chance of short circuits. Use shielded three-conductor wire to reduce induction from nearby high-frequency sources.

★ Laser diodes are subject to the same CDRH regulations as any other laser in its power class. Apply the proper warning stickers and advise others not to stare directly into the laser when it is on.

★ Use only a grounded soldering pencil when attaching wires to the laser diode terminals. Limit soldering duration to less than 5 seconds per terminal.

★ Unless otherwise specified by the manufacturer, clean the output window of the laser diode with a cotton swab dipped in ethanol. Alternatively, you can use optics-grade lens cleaning fluid.

MOUNTING AND HEATSINKS

Most laser diodes lack any means by which to mount them in a suitable enclosure. Their compact size does not allow for mounting holes. However, with a bit of ingenuity, you can construct mounts that secure the laser in place as well as provide the recommended heatsinking. One approach is to clip the laser in place using a fuse holder, as shown in FIG. 10-6. You might have to bend the holder out a bit to accommodate the laser. Mount the clip on a small piece of aluminum or a TO-220 heatsink. Use silicone paste at the junction of all-metal pieces; this assists in proper heat transfer.

Another method, detailed in FIG. 10-7, is to drill a hole the same diameter as the laser in an aluminum heatsink. Use copper retaining clips (available at the hobby store) to secure the laser in place. Once again, apply silicone paste to aid in heat transfer.

Some lasers are available on the surplus market, like that shown in FIG. 10-8, and are already attached to a heatsink and mount. The mount doubles as a rail for collimating and beam-shaping optics. You can use the laser with or without these optics, of course, or substitute with your own.

FIG. 10-6. *A fuse clip can be used as a simple heatsink for a semiconductor laser.*

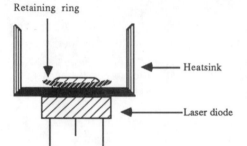

Retaining ring

Heatsink

Laser diode

FIG. 10-7. *Use a flexible copper retaining ring to hold a diode to the heatsink. Use silicone heatsink paste to aid in proper heat transfer.*

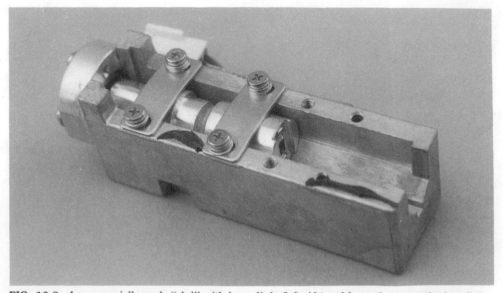

FIG. 10-8. *A commercially made "sled" with laser diode (left side) and beam-shaping optics installed.*

SOURCES FOR LASER DIODES

Laser diodes are seldom sold at the neighborhood electronics store, and as of this writing, Radio Shack does not carry the device as a replacement or experimenter's item. That leaves buying your laser diodes directly from the manufacturer, through an authorized manufacturer's representative, or through surplus. Buying direct from the manufacturer or rep assures you of receiving prime, new goods, but the cost can be high. Average cost for a new 3 to 5 mW laser cw diode is about $30. Names and addresses of manufacturers are in Appendix A. You can locate local representatives by writing to the manufacturer, or look in the Yellow Pages under "Electronics—Wholesale and Retail."

The same or similar device on the surplus market is about $10 to $15, depending on the power output. Several of the surplus mail-order dealers listed in Appendix A offer sh and dh laser diodes; write them for a current catalog. Many also provide kits and ready-made drive/power supply circuits. Be aware that, at this time, most surplus laser diodes are take-outs, meaning that they were used in some product that was later retired and scrapped. While buying used He-Ne tubes can be a chancy affair, the risk of buying pre-owned laser diodes is minimal. Like all solid-state electronics, the life span of a laser diode is extremely long—in excess of 5,000 to 10,000 hours of continuous use.

BUILD A POCKET LASER DIODE

You can build a complete laser in a box about the size of a pack of cigarettes. FIGURE 10-9 shows the basic layout; TABLE 10-1 provides the parts list. You can use just about any of the drive circuits presented in Chapter 11 to power the laser. In all cases, you can mount the components on a universal solder PCB and fit the whole thing in a 3¼-by-2⅛-by-1⅛-inch plastic experimenter's box. Drill holes for the switch, power jack, and lens tube. The lens hole should be ¾-inch in diameter.

Saw off a solderless RG59U coaxial connector and mount the laser inside (check the connector style first to be sure the diode fits snugly). Use all-purpose adhesive to secure a 10-mm double-concave lens (with a focal length of about 15 mm) inside one end of a 1-inch length of a ⁷⁄₁₆-inch (I.D.) brass tube. The tube is available at most hobby stores. Fit the laser diode in the lens tube and mount the tube in the enclosure. Use all-purpose adhesive to keep it in place. You can adjust the spacing between the laser and lens later.

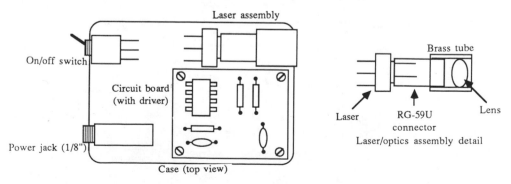

FIG. 10-9. *Basic layout for the pocket laser showing ON/OFF switch, power jack, laser assembly, and driver board.*

Table 10-1. Pocket Laser Parts List

1	Laser diode; Sharp LT020, LT022, or equivalent
1	RG59U solderless video connector
1	1-inch length 7/16-inch (I.D.) brass tube
1	10 mm diameter, 15 mm focal length double-convex lens
1	SPST switch (DPDT switch for dual-ended supply)
1	1/8-inch jack (2- or 3-conductor, depending on supply)
1	Driver board (see Chapter 12)
1	3 1/4-by-2 1/8-by-1 1/8-inch plastic project box

Wire the components as shown in FIG. 10-10. Install the switch, power jack, and drive board in the box. Temporarily apply power to the circuit board and dim the lights. Point the lens toward a lightly colored wall at a distance of no more than a few inches. Adjust the distance between laser and lens by sliding the RG59U connector in or out of the brass tube until the spot on the wall is bright and well-defined. You will see rings in the beam; this is normal. A grainy speckle in the spot means that the diode is emitting laser light. If you don't see the speckle, the laser might not be driven with enough current.

When everything looks ok, dab a small drop of all-purpose adhesive on the RG59U connector and brass tube to keep the laser from coming loose. Don't apply too much glue, because you might need to readjust the laser later on. Close up the box and fit a set of four "AA" batteries in a battery holder. Place the battery holder in a box measuring at least 2 1/2 by 2 1/2 by 1 inch (see FIG. 10-11). Use three-conductor shielded microphone cable as the power cord, as shown, and solder a 1/8-inch stereo plug on the end. To use the battery pack, simply plug it into the power jack on the laser box.

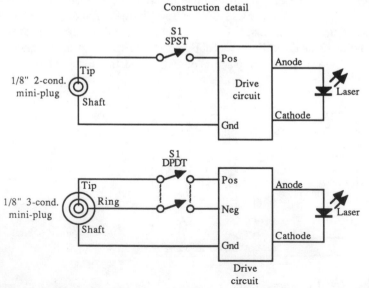

FIG. 10-10. *Two ways to wire the pocket laser. Use the dual-ended power supply if the driver board requires it.*

Table 10-2. Pocket Laser Power Pack Parts List

1	4-cell "AA" battery holder
1	⅛-inch plug (2- or 3-conductor, depending on supply)
1	2½-by-2½-by-1-inch (minimum) project box Batteries

Note that the 6-volt battery pack is meant for use with the pulsed drive circuit described in Chapter 12. Other drive schemes call for a 12-volt supply or for a split ±5-volt supply. Use the appropriate type of batteries, connected in parallel and/or in series, to provide the required voltage level. You might need to add voltage regulators (small TO-92 case) or zener diodes to maintain or regulate the supply voltages.

You might want to combine the laser/drive components in the same box as the batteries. You can fit everything in a project box measuring 6¼ by 3¾ by 2 inches, or even less if you are careful how you mount the components. Make sure that the batteries are placed in a convenient location so that they can be easily changed when they wear out.

USING THE POCKET LASER

The light from the pocket laser is largely invisible unless you happen to own see-in-the-dark infrared glasses or an IR viewing card (a card coated with a chemical that reacts to infrared radiation). The faint red glow of the laser is discernible only in darkness and when the lens is focused on a nearby wall. That makes applications such as laser pointers out of the question. But the pocket laser is far from useless. As you'll learn in future chapters, you can use this basic configuration to create a collimated free-air laser light communicator.

You can also use the pocket laser as the head-end for a fiberoptic data link or as a means to experiment with interferometry. Although the beam is difficult (if not impossible) to see without some sort of IR viewing device or infrared viewing card, you

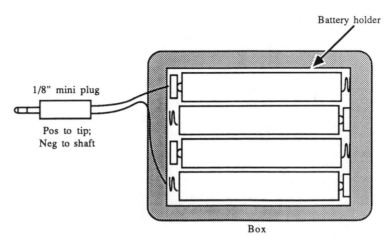

FIG. 10-11. *Install the batteries in a project box and terminate the battery holder leads with a ⅛-inch mini plug (two- or three-conductor as needed).*

can detect the interferometric fringes with an ordinary photodetector. Connect the photodetector to an audio amplifier, as shown in Chapter 9, and you can *hear* the fringes move. Connected to a counter, you can even count the number of fringes that go by.

An advanced project might be to use the laser to make near-infrared holograms. Although most films are already sensitive to near-infrared radiation, you can obtain better results if you use an emulsion specifically formulated for the 780 to 880 nm range of most laser diodes. Be sure that the film has very high resolution, or the hologram won't turn out.

11

Laser Power Supplies

Imagine a world without electricity. Without the motive force of electricity and more importantly a way to harness it, we would be without 90 percent of our creature comforts. Everything from the family car to the kitchen food processor operates on electrical power, and without juice, these things would come to a grinding halt.

The same is true of lasers and their support systems. Without power, your laser is useless and no more worthwhile than a rock paperweight. In this chapter, you'll learn how to construct universal power supplies, including:

★ High-voltage power supplies for operating a helium-neon laser; both 117 volt ac and 12 volt dc versions.

★ Regulated power supplies for diode lasers.

Low-voltage power supplies for operating electronic equipment are in the next chapter. There you'll find designs for single- and dual-voltage regulated supplies, including an all-purpose adjustable version and battery pack regulators.

ABOUT HELIUM-NEON POWER SUPPLIES

A helium-neon laser tube must be connected to a high-voltage power supply or it won't work. You have two options to provide the required juice: buy a ready-made laser power supply or build your own. Commercially made power supplies for helium-neon lasers are available from a variety of sources, and if you are just starting out, this is the best route to go. As detailed in Chapter 5, you need to be sure that the supply is rated for the tube you are using. Some tubes require more operating current than others and might not work properly with a power supply that can't deliver the milliamps.

He-Ne laser power supplies you build yourself are not overly complicated and they don't need lots of parts. But the parts they do require can be hard to find. Specifically, the laser power supply must use high-voltage diodes and capacitors—the higher the rating, the better. The 1N4007 diode is rated at 1 kV, the minimum you can use. Such diodes are bound to burn out when running a laser that consumes more than 5 milliamps, so 3- to 10-kV diodes are preferred. High-voltage capacitors of the typical values used in laser power supplies—.1 to 0.001 μF, are even harder to find. Most high-voltage capacitors have very low values, usually in the tens of picofarads.

Perhaps the most troublesome component is the transformer. The *ideal* laser power supply transformer is specially made to conform to the specifications required by the job, but a number of ready-made step-up switching type transformers can effectively be used. The hard part is finding them. The typical transformer for use in a dc-operated helium-neon laser steps up 12 volts to between 300 and 1,000 volts. High-voltage transformers designed for use with photocopiers can also be used. These transform 117 Vac to 1,000 to 4,000 Vac. Most laser tubes require between 1,200 and 3,000 volts.

A local surplus or electronics outlet can carry suitable high-voltage diodes, capacitors, and transformers, but you might have better luck trying surplus mail-order outlets. See Appendix A for a list of mail-order surplus dealers. Ask for their latest catalog, and if you don't see the items you want, write or call. Some outlets carry stock that is not included in the general distribution catalog.

Appendix A also lists several sources for laser components. These include Meredith Instruments, MJ Neal Co. Information Unlimited, and General Science & Engineering. These mail-order companies are prime sources of laser power supply components, and you should obtain their catalogs before beginning any serious laser project.

Many also offer power supply kits, with all the parts conveniently pre-packaged for you. In fact, one of the dc power supplies discussed below is available (at the time of this writing) in kit form from General Science & Engineering. In the event that the kit is no longer available, you can still construct the power supply using the schematic and parts list, provided in this chapter.

Before building any of the laser power supplies described in this chapter, read the following very carefully:

☆ Any laser power supply delivers high voltages that, under certain circumstances, can injure or kill you. Use extreme caution when building, testing, and using these power supplies.

☆ Do not attempt to build your own power supply unless you have at least some knowledge of electronics and electronic construction.

☆ Although the power supply projects are not difficult to construct, they should be considered suitable only for intermediate to advanced hobbyists.

☆ Power supplies and laser tubes retain current even after electricity has been removed. Be sure to short out the output of the power supply before touching the laser or high-voltage leads.

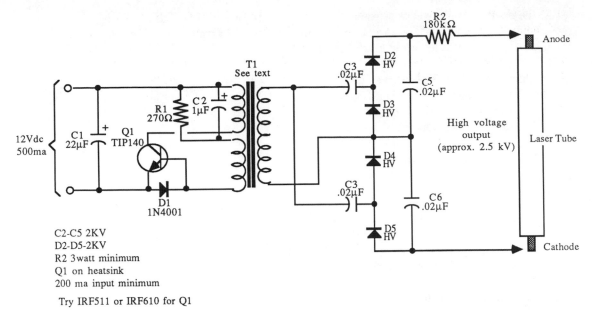

FIG. 11-1. *An easy approach to building a high-voltage He-Ne power supply. Be wary of the high voltages present at the secondary of T1.*

BASIC HE-NE 12-VOLT POWER SUPPLY

The schematic in FIG. 11-1 shows a basic, no-frills power supply suitable for use with helium-neon tubes rated at 0.5 to 1 milliwatt. TABLE 11-1 contains the parts list. The circuit is shown more as a lesson in high-voltage power supply design than a full-fledged project. You will probably want to supplement the supply with additional features, such as a 10-kV trigger transformer or current feedback circuit. A number of books provide details on advanced high-voltage power supplies; see Appendix B for a selected list.

Table 11-1. Basic Dc He-Ne Power Supply Parts List

R1	270 ohm resistor
R2	180 kilohm resistor, 3 to 5 watt
C1	22 μF electrolytic capacitor
C2	1 μF electrolytic capacitor
C3-C6	0.02 μF capacitor, 1 kV or more
D1	1N4001 diode
D2-D5	High-voltage diode (3 kV or more)
Q1	TIP 140 power transistor
T1	High-voltage dc-to-dc converter transformer; see text for specifications.

All resistors are 5 to 10 percent tolerance, ¼ watt, unless otherwise indicated. All capacitors are 10 to 20 percent tolerance, rated 35 volts or more, unless otherwise indicated.

At the heart of the power supply is a dc switching transformer, T1. This oscillation transformer is designed for use as a dc-to-dc converter and is available from Meredith Instruments. It has the following characteristics:

* ✶ Input voltage (primary): 6 volts
* ✶ Output voltage (secondary): 330 volts
* ✶ Ferrite core size: EE19
* ✶ Maximum power output: 7 watts
* ✶ Oscillation frequency: 15 kHz
* ✶ Winding ratio (Ns/Np): 57.4

Operation of the Power Supply

Here's how the power supply works: Q1, R1, and C1 form a Hartley-type astable multivibrator (a free-running oscillator) that switches the incoming 12 volts dc between the two secondary windings of the transformer. T1 is a high-turns-ratio transformer that steps up the incoming voltage to about 660 volts. Capacitors C2 through C5 as well as diodes D2 through D5 form a voltage multiplier that increases the voltage to about 2,500 volts at approximately 3 to 4 mA.

Resistor R2 is an important component. All laser tubes are current-sensitive and try to consume as much current as the power supply will deliver. The resistor limits the current to a safe level; without it, the tube might burn out. Resistor R2 is chosen for a typical 1 mW laser tube. If your laser sputters or doesn't fire, the resist or value might be too high or too low, causing the tube to be unstable. Later you will see how to test the power supply to discover how much current the tube is drawing and to adjust R2 to deliver just the minimum to keep the tube lasing.

Note that the battery power requirement is rather steep. The power supply consumes about 350 mA of current, so you should use only heavy-duty batteries. Although the supply will work on "C" alkaline cells, you'll have better luck with "D" cells. The best results are obtained when using high-output lead-acid or gelled electrolyte batteries. A pair of 6-volt, 4 AH batteries will power the laser for several hours before needing a recharge.

The power supply works best when the input voltage is as close to 12 volts as possible. Because most batteries deliver a range of voltages during their discharge period, you might want to add the regulator circuit provided in FIG. 11-2 (parts list in TABLE 11-2). The schematic uses a positive 12-volt regulator that requires about 1 volt as "overhead."

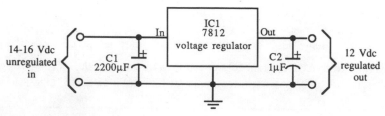

FIG. 11-2. *Use a 7812 voltage regulator with a 14- to 16-volt supply to regulate the voltage to the high-voltage power supply presented in FIG. 11-1.*

Table 11-2. 12 Vdc Battery Regulator Parts List

IC1	7812 +12 Vdc voltage regulator
C1	2200 μF electrolytic capacitor
C2	1 μF electrolytic capacitor

All capacitors are 10 to 20 percent tolerance, rated 35 volts or more.

When fed by the typical lead-acid or gelled electrolyte battery—which have an average output of about 13.8 volts—approximately 12 volts reaches the power supply.

Components R1 and C1 determine the frequency rate of the circuit. By adjusting R1, you change the frequency and therefore the output voltage of T1. If your supply is having trouble igniting and running your laser tube, try a slightly higher or lower value for R1.

Building the Circuit

The basic power supply should be constructed on a printed circuit board. Component placement is not crucial, but you should allow as much room as possible for the high-voltage components. Keep the anode lead as short as possible (2 to 4 inches) and place the ballast resistor close to the anode terminal on the laser tube.

Testing the Current Output

Resistor R2, the ballast resistor, determines the amount of current delivered to the tube. Although you can calculate the exact value of the resistor using design formulas, you need to know the parameters of the particular tube you are using. Dial the meter to read dc milliamps. Turn on the power supply and watch the meter. The current should not exceed 6 or 7 mA (it probably won't with the basic power supply described earlier, anyway). If the current is too high, you should immediately remove the power. Short the leads of the power supply to remove any remaining current, and replace R2 with

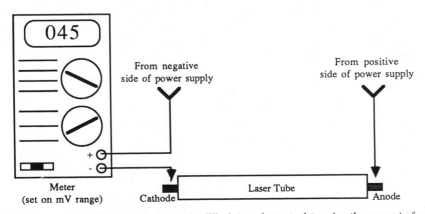

FIG. 11-3. *Connect a volt-ohmmeter (set to read millivolts) as shown to determine the amount of current consumed by the laser tube.*

a higher value resistor. Be sure to use a resistor rated to at least 3 to 5 watts. Re-apply power and take a new reading.

Most likely, the laser will sputter or not turn on at all. The usual cause is a ballast resistor that is either too high or too low; either way, the sputtering is caused by unstable operation and can usually be corrected by selecting another ballast resistor. The tube will not ignite or lase if the current is less than about 3.5 mA. If the tube stays on without sputtering and the current output is between about 3.5 and 6 mA, you have selected the proper ballast resistor.

If the ballast resistor is too low, excessive current will flow through the tube, damaging it or at the least severely shortening its life. Besides doing harm to the tube, the power supply consumes excessive current, prematurely draining battery power. You will realize the longest battery life by careful selection of the ballast resistor.

Note that some sputtering is caused by arcing of the anode and cathode leads. Be sure the leads are securely attached to the power supply and the laser. You can often see the result of arcing by turning off the lights and looking carefully for a tell-tale blue glow around the anode and cathode terminals. The glow is a corona caused by the ionization of air by high-voltage discharge.

PULSE-MODULATED DC-OPERATED HE-NE SUPPLY

The basic helium-neon laser power supply is good for low-output tubes, but it doesn't deliver sufficient current for higher power and hard-to-start tubes. The advanced power supply shown in FIG. 11-4 can be used with 1- to 5-mW tubes, depending on the transformer you use. The parts list for this supply is included in TABLE 11-3.

About the Circuit

The advanced laser power supply uses an LM555 timer IC as a pulse width modulator (PWM). Two potentiometers, R12 and R13, adjust the width of the output pulses from the 555, and therefore change the currents used to trigger and operate the tube.

Capacitor C5 and resistors R8, R9, R12, and R13 determine the pulse width of the 555. Initially, the R12 and R13 are dialed to their center positions and relay R1 is de-energized, effectively removing R8 and R13 from the circuit. When 12 volts is applied to the circuit, the 555 pulses and triggers Q1, C1, and R2. This in turn drives transformer T1. This transformer steps up the 12 volts to approximately 1,000 volts. Capacitors C7 through C10 and diodes D4 through D19 form a four-stage cascaded voltage multiplier that increases the output to about 3,500 volts.

If the tube doesn't fire, R12 adjust to increase the duty cycle of the 555 pulses. When the tube ignites, sensing resistors R3 through R6 trigger Q2, which closes relay R1. That brings R8 and R13 into the circuit. Adjusting R13 controls the duty cycle of the 555 while the tube is operating. Shortening the duty cycle of the pulses decreases the current delivered to the tube; lengthening the duty cycle increases the current.

Building the Circuit

The PWM power supply can be built on a perforated board or printed circuit board. When using a perforated board, be sure that lead lengths are kept to a minimum and

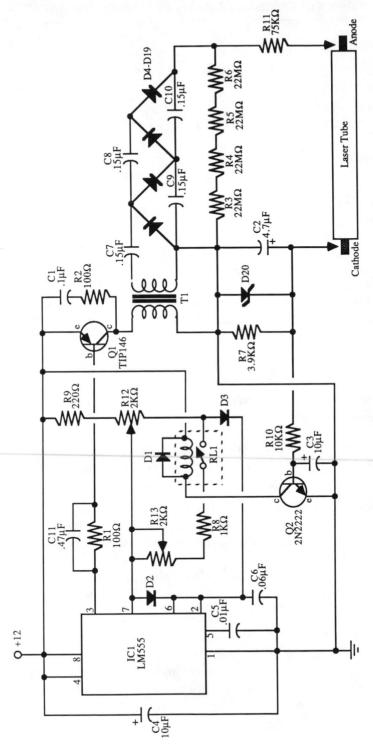

FIG. 11-4. *The circuit schematic for the pulse-width-modulated power supply.*

Table 11-3. Pulse Width Modulated Power Supply

IC1	555 timer IC
R1-R2	100 ohm resistor
R3-R6	22 megohm resistor
R7	3.9 kilohm resistor
R8	1 kilohm resistor
R9	220 ohm resistor
R10	10 kilohm resistor
R11	75 kilohm resistor, 3-5 watt
R12,R13	2 kilohm potentiometer
C1	0.1 μF
C2	4.7 μF electrolytic capacitor
C3,C4	10 μF electrolytic capacitor
C5	0.01 μF disc capacitor
C6	0.06 μF disc capacitor
C7-C10	0.15 μF capacitor, 3 kV or more
C11	0.47 μF capacitor
D1-D3	1N914 diode
D4-D19	High-voltage diodes (3 kV or more; four diodes in series for each diode symbol in schematic)
Q1	TIP146 (on heatsink)
Q2	2N2222
RL1	12-volt SPST relay
T1	High-voltage step-up transformer; 9-volt primary, 375-volt secondary
Misc.	Heatsink for Q1, high-dielectric wire for connecting tube to supply

All resistors are 5 to 10 percent tolerance, ¼ watt, unless otherwise indicated. All capacitors are 10 to 20 percent tolerance, rated 35 volts or more, unless otherwise indicated.

that the high-voltage capacitors and diodes are not placed too close together. To prevent arcing, place the diodes at 45-degree angles.

The leads for the anode and cathode should be 6 inches or shorter. Reduce the chance of arcing by wrapping high-voltage dielectric tape around the leads. Or, slip a length of neoprene aquarium tubing over the wires.

Construct clips for the laser terminals as detailed in Chapter 6, "Build a He-Ne Laser Experimenter's System." You can also form heavy-duty steel or copper wire and bend it in a clip shape. Make the clip slightly smaller than the diameter of the laser tube terminals. When made properly, the wire should clip securely around the tube. Wrap a length of high-voltage dielectric tape around the clip and terminal to hold them in place. Be sure that you don't cover the mirrors on either end of the laser.

Using the Power Supply

Operating the power supply is straightforward. Once the tube is secured, rotate potentiometers R12 and R13 to their center positions. Apply power and watch the tube. Slowly rotate R12 until the tube triggers. You will hear the relay click in. If it chatters and the tube sputters, keep turning R12. If the tube still won't ignite, rotate R13 slightly.

Once the tube lights and stays on, rotate R13 so that the tube begins to sputter and the relay clatters. This marks the threshold of the tube. Advance R13 just a little until the tube turns back on and remains steady. Every tube, even those of the same size and with the same output, have slightly different current requirements, so you will need to readjust R12 and R13 for every tube you own.

Resistor R11 is the ballast, limiting current to the tube. The schematic shows a 80-kilohm resistor, but you can experiment with other values to find one that works best with your tube. If the laser doesn't trigger or run after adjusting R12 and R13, try reducing the value of the ballast resistor. Use a voltmeter, as explained in the previous section, to monitor the output current to ensure against passing excessive current through the tube.

AC-OPERATED HE-NE POWER SUPPLY

The schematic in FIG. 11-5 shows a basic ac-operated helium-neon power supply (parts list in TABLE 11-4). A high-voltage transformer converts the 117 Vac line current to 1,000 volts or more. The voltage multiplier increases the working voltage while rectifying the ac. The circuit shows a transformer with a 1,000 volt secondary and the voltage multiplier section used in the basic dc-operated power supply presented earlier in this chapter. The output voltage is about 4 to 5 kV (rectified and unloaded). Some tubes require extra

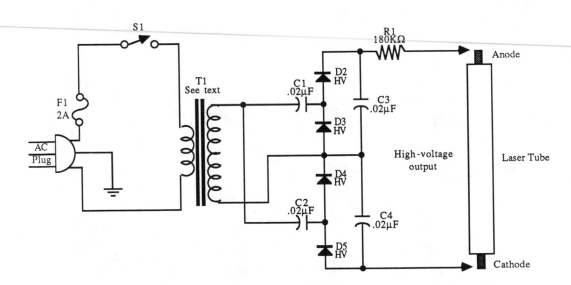

FIG. 11-5. *Minimum configuration for an ac-operated high-voltage He-Ne power supply.*

Table 11-4. Basic Ac He-Ne Power Supply Parts List

R1	180 kilohm resistor, 3 to 5 watt
C1-C4	0.02 μF capacitor, 1 kV or more
D1-D4	High-voltage diode (3 kV or more)
T1	High-voltage step-up transformer; see text for specifications.
S1	SPST switch
F1	Fuse (2 amp) and holder ac plug

voltage to start and might need a transformer with 2,000- to 2,500-volt secondary. Note that the circuit is basic and lacks current sensing or high-voltage start capabilities.

ENCLOSING THE HE-NE POWER SUPPLIES

Laser power supplies should never be used without placing them in protective, insulating enclosures. After you have built and tested your power supply, tuck it safely in a plastic enclosure. If you plan on using the supply to power a variety of tubes, mount heavy-duty (25-amp) banana jacks to provide easy access to the anode and cathode leads. Keep the jacks separated by *at least* 1 inch and apply high-voltage putty around all terminals to prevent arcing.

A functional schematic for a completely self-contained, rechargeable battery pack/power supply is shown in FIG. 11-6. The parts list for the battery pack/power supply is provided in TABLE 11-5. Note the addition of the key switch, power-on indicator, and battery-charging terminal. The key switch prevents unauthorized used of the power supply and acts as the main ON/OFF switch. For maximum security, you should get the

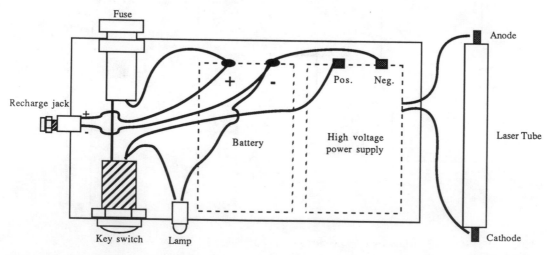

FIG. 11-6. *Hookup diagram for building an all-in-one battery-operated helium-neon laser power supply. The battery can be recharged in the enclosure without removing it.*

164

Table 11-5. Battery Pack/He-Ne Supply Parts List

B1	12 Vdc battery
PS1	Modular 12 Vdc He-Ne high-voltage power supply
F1	Fuse holder (fuse: 2 amps)
S1	SPST key switch
LA1	LED indicator (with built-in dropping resistor)
J1	¼-inch, 2-conductor phone jack
Misc.	Project box, grommet (for output leads), high-dielectric wires for connection to laser

kind of switch where the key can be removed only when it is in the OFF position (CDRH requirements call for a key that cannot be removed in the ON position).

The power-on indicator is simply an LED with a current-dropping resistor. The battery-charging terminal provides a means to recharge the batteries without removing them from the enclosure. Note that you can operate the laser while the battery recharger is connected, but in most cases, the power supply will consume too much current and the batteries will not be recharged.

A fuse is added to provide protection against an accidental short circuit in the battery compartment. Lead-acid and gelled electrolyte batteries can easily burn plastic and even metal when their terminals are shorted. The fuse helps prevent accidental damage and fire.

ABOUT LASER DIODE POWER SUPPLIES

As discussed in Chapter 10, laser diodes come in two basic forms: single- and double-heterostructure. The single-heterostructure (or sh) diodes are regarded as the "older" variety and can only be operated in pulsed mode (unless you cool them with a cryogenic fluid, such as liquid nitrogen). Sh laser diodes are capable of multi-watt operation, but only when the pulses are 200 nanoseconds or shorter. Therefore, sh diode supplies may be built around some type of astable multivibrator.

Double-heterostructure (dh) laser diodes can be operated in pulsed or CW modes. Like any diode, excessive currents can destroy the laser, so you must take precautions to operate the unit within its design parameters. Dh lasers are capable of multi-watt operation when used in pulsed mode, but most are designed for CW operation and emit 1 to 10 mW of light energy. Remember that although you can often see a red glow from a diode laser, this light represents only a fraction of the total radiation from the diode. The bulk of the radiation is in the near-infrared spectrum and is largely invisible to your eyes.

PULSED SINGLE-HETEROSTRUCTURE INJECTION DIODE SUPPLY

A common method for powering an sh injection diode is shown in FIG. 11-7 (see the parts list in TABLE 11-6). The power supply provides pulses of about 10 to 20 amps at a short duration of around 50 ns. The supply provides sufficient drive current to exceed the threshold of the laser (typically about 7 or 8 amps), with some room to spare. The

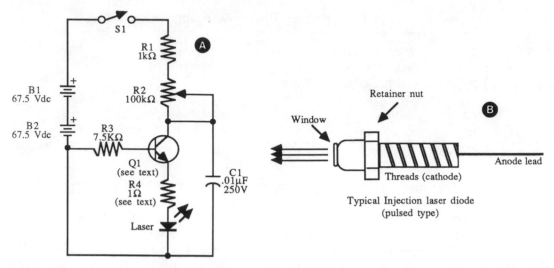

FIG. 11-7. *(A) High-current drive circuit for a single heterostructure laser diode. (B) Power leads for the typical sh laser diode, showing single lead for the anode.*

Table 11-6. Single Heterostructure Laser Pulsed Driver Parts List

R1	1 kilohm resistor
R2	100 kilohm potentiometer
R3	7.5 kilohm resistor
R4	1 ohm resistor, carbon composition
C1	0.01 μF capacitor, 250 V or higher
Q1	2N2222 or equivalent; see text
B1,B2	67.5 Vdc batteries
Misc.	Single heterostructure laser diode, heatsink

All resistors are 5 to 10 percent tolerance, ¼ watt, unless otherwise indicated.

laser might still glow at currents less than threshold, but the light won't be stimulated emission. In other words, the device will not emit laser light but behave like an expensive LED.

The sh laser diode circuit uses a common npn transistor operated in avalanche mode. The batteries are 67.5-volt type (NEDA 217, Eveready number 416) used in older tube-type equipment. You'll have better luck finding the required batteries at an electronic store specializing in communications or ham gear. The price can be steep—up to $10 each depending on the source—so make sure they are fresh before you sign the check.

Quality control in low-cost plastic npn transistors is not great, so not all transistors will work in the circuit. The schematic calls for a 2N2222, but you might need to experiment with several until you find one that oscillates in the circuit. Construct the circuit using component leads that are as short as possible and test the transistor by substituting the laser with a short piece of copper wire (magnet wire works well). Use an oscilloscope across current-monitor resistor R4 (1 ohm, carbon composition) and watch for the pulses from the transistor. Avoid the use of a logic probe, as most are not designed for circuits exceeding 18 volts.

After you have determined that the transistor is oscillating (adjust R2 as needed), substitute the laser, being careful to observe polarity. Most sh lasers use the case as the cathode and the single lead as the anode. Yours *might be different*, so be sure to check the specifications or information sheet that came with the unit. The diode operates at a wavelength of about 904 nm, which is beyond that of normal human vision, so don't expect the same bright red beam that's emitted by a helium-neon laser. You can test the operation of the laser by using one of the infrared sensors described in the previous chapters.

PULSED DOUBLE-HETEROSTRUCTURE INJECTION DIODE SUPPLY

The popularity of compact audio discs, as well as many forms of laser bar-code scanning, have made double-heterostructure laser diodes plentiful in the surplus market. A number of sources (many of which are listed in Appendix A) offer dh laser diodes for prices ranging from $5 to $15. Depending on the power output of the laser, new units are even affordable. A typical 5 mW laser diode lists for about $25 to $30 in low quantities. Sharp is a major manufacturer of dh laser diodes; write them for literature and a price list.

As discussed in the previous chapter, one of the most attractive features of dh laser diodes is that they work with low voltage power supplies. A dh laser can easily be run off a single 9-volt transistor battery. However, dh laser diodes are sensitive to temperature. They become more efficient at lower temperatures, and their power output increases. Unless the temperature is very low (such as when the diode is immersed in liquid nitrogen, as described in Chapter 22), the increase in power output can damage the laser. That's why most dh lasers are equipped with a monitor photodiode. The current output of the monitor photodiode is used in a closed-loop feedback circuit to keep the power output of the laser constant.

Although dh lasers are designed for CW operation, they can also be used in pulse mode. An astable multivibrator, such as a 555 timer, can be used to pulse the laser. A circuit is shown in FIG. 11-8, with a parts list in TABLE 11-7. Because the laser is pulsed, the forward current can exceed the maximum allowed for CW operation (generally 60 to 80 mA). However, care must be taken to keep the pulses short. Pulses longer than about a 50 percent duty cycle (half on, half off) can cause damage to the laser. Duty cycle is not a critical consideration when the current is maintained under 80 mA. The circuit shown in the figure lets you alter the frequency of the astable multivibrator (and therefore the duty cycle).

A closed-loop feedback system constantly watches over the output of the monitor photodiode and maintains the proper current to the laser diode. One such circuit is shown in FIG. 11-9. This circuit is designed around the IR3C02 chip, which is a special-purpose IC manufactured by Sharp. See TABLE 11-8 for a list of required parts. This IC is made for use with their extensive line of dh lasers, and while hard to find, it is relatively inexpensive (obtain the chip through Sharp's parts service or from a distributor dealing with Sharp components).

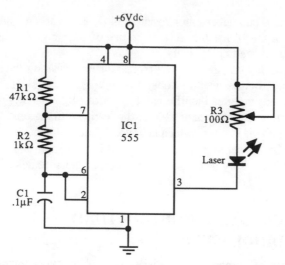

FIG. 11-8. *A double heterostructure laser can be connected to a 555 timer IC for pulse operation. With the components shown, pulse rate is about 300 Hz; pulse repetition is about 3 milliseconds.*

Table 11-7. Pulsed Double Heterostructure Laser Power Drive Parts List

IC1	555 timer IC
R1	47 kilohm resistor
R2	1 kilohm resistor
R3	100 kilohm potentiometer
C1	0.1 µF disc capacitor
Misc.	Double heterostructure laser diode, heatsink

All resistors are 5 to 10 percent tolerance, ¼ watt. All capacitors are 10 to 20 percent tolerance, rated 35 volts or more.

Another method using discrete components is shown in FIG. 11-1 (parts list in TABLE 11-10). Here, an op amp, acting as high-gain comparator, checks the current from the monitor photodiode. As the current increases, the output of the op amp decreases, and output of the laser drops. The gain of the circuit—the ratio between the incoming and outgoing current—is determined by the settings of R1, R4, and R5.

The circuit in the schematic was adapted from an application note for a General Electric C86002E laser diode and uses a CA3130 CMOS op amp. You can readily modify the circuit if you use another op amp or laser diode. Both output transistors are available through most larger electronics outlets, but if you have trouble locating them, you might have luck substituting them with a single TIP120 Darlington power transistor.

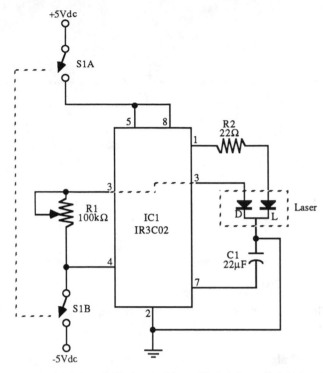

FIG. 11-9. *Basic schematic for the Sharp IR3C02 laser diode driver IC.*

Table 11-8. Sharp IC Laser Drive Parts List

IC1	Sharp IR3C02 laser diode drive IC
R1	100 kilohm resistor
R2	22 ohm resistor
C1	22 μF electrolytic capacitor
S1	DPDT switch
Misc.	Double heterostructure laser diode (such as Sharp LT020), heatsink

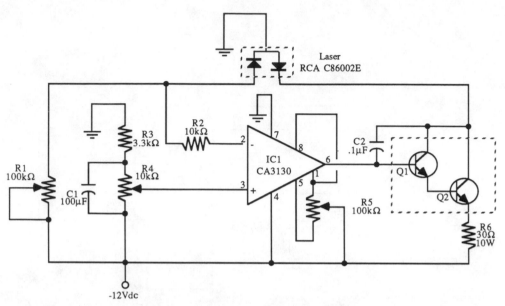

FIG. 11-10. *One way to automatically adjust drive current using a discrete op amp. Use the transistors specified or replace with a suitable Darlington power transistor (such as TIP 120).*

Table 11-9. Op Amp Laser Drive Parts List

IC1	RCA CA 3130 operational amplifier
R1,R5	100 kilohm potentiometer
R2	10 kilohm resistor
R3	3.3 kilohm resistor
R4	10 kilohm potentiometer
R6	30 ohm, 10 watt resistor
C1	100 μF electrolytic capacitor
C2	0.1 μF disc capacitor
Q1	2N2101 transistor
Q2	2N3585 transistor
Laser	RCA C86002 (or equivalent laser diode)

All resistors are 5 to 10 percent tolerance, ¼ watt, unless otherwise indicated. All capacitors are 10 to 20 percent tolerance, rated 35 volts or more.

12

Build an Experimenter's Power Supply

Many laser projects require a steady supply of low-voltage dc, typically between 5 and 12 volts. You may use one or more batteries to supply the juice, but if you plan on doing lots of laser experiments, you'll find that batteries are both inconvenient and anti-productive. Just when you get a circuit perfected, the battery goes dead and must be recharged.

A stand-alone power supply that operates on your 117 Vac house current can supply your laser system designs with regulated dc power without the need to install, replace, or recharge batteries. You can buy a ready-made power supply (they are common in the surplus market) or make your own.

Several power supply designs follow that you can use to provide operating juice to your laser circuits. The designs show you how to construct a:

- ★ 5-volt dc regulated power supply
- ★ 12-volt dc regulated power supply
- ★ Quad ±5- and ±12-volt regulated power supply
- ★ Adjustable (3 to 20 volts dc) regulated power supply.

Note that the power supplies presented within this chapter are similar with the exception of different values for capacitors, diode bridges, and other components. You may use the schematics to create power supplies of different voltage levels. The multi-voltage supply is designed to provide the four voltages common in laser support systems: +5 volts, +12 volts, −5 volts, and −12 volts. These voltages are used by motors, solenoids, and ICs.

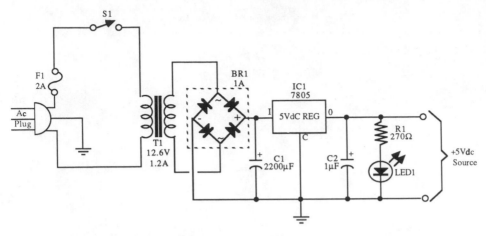

FIG. 12-1. *Schematic diagram for the 5 Vdc regulated power supply.*

SINGLE-VOLTAGE POWER SUPPLY

Refer to FIGS. 12-1 and 12-2 for schematics of the single-voltage power supplies. FIG-URE 12-1 shows the circuit for a +5-volt supply; FIG. 12-2 shows the circuit for a +12-volt supply. There are few differences between them, so the following discussion applies to both. For the sake of simplicity, we'll refer just to the +5-volt circuit. Parts lists for the two supplies are provided in TABLES 12-1 and 12-2.

For safety, the power supply must be enclosed in a plastic or metal chassis (plastic is better as there is less chance of a short circuit). Use a perforated board to secure the components and solder them together using 18- or 16-gauge insulated wire. Do not use point-to-point wiring where the components are not secured to a board.

Alternatively, you can make your own circuit board using an etching kit. Before constructing the board, collect all the parts and design the board to fit the specific parts you have. There is little size standardization when it comes to power supply components and large value electrolytic capacitors, so pre-sizing is a must.

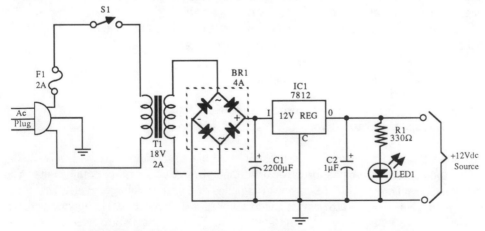

FIG. 12-2. *Schematic diagram for the 12 Vdc regulated power supply.*

Table 12-1. 5 Vdc Power Supply Parts List

IC1	7805 +5 Vdc voltage regulator
R1	270 ohm resistor
C1	2200 μF electrolytic capacitor
C2	1 μF electrolytic capacitor
BR1	Bridge rectifier, 1 amp
LED1	Light-emitting diode
T1	12.6-volt, 1.2-amp transformer
S1	SPST switch
F1	Fuse (2-amp)
Misc.	Ac plug, cord, fuse holder, cabinet

All resistors are 5 to 10 percent tolerance, ¼ watt. All capacitors are 10 to 20 percent tolerance, rated 35 volts or more.

To explain the circuit in FIG.12-1, note the incoming ac routed to the primary terminals on a 12.6-volt transformer. The "hot" side of the ac is connected through a fuse and a single-pole single-throw (SPST) toggle switch. With the switch in the OFF (open) position, the transformer receives no power so the supply is off.

The 117 Vac is stepped down to about 12.6 volts. The transformer specified here is rated at 2 amps, sufficient for the task at hand. Remember that the power supply is limited to delivering the capacity of the transformer (and later, the voltage regulator). A bridge rectifier, BR1, converts the ac to dc (shown schematically in the dotted box). You can also construct the rectifier using discrete diodes (connect them as shown within the box).

When using the bridge rectifier, be sure to connect the leads to the proper terminals. The two terminals marked with a "~" connect to the transformer. The "+" and "–"

Table 12-2. 12 Vdc Power Supply Parts List

IC1	7812 +12 Vdc voltage regulator
R1	330 ohm resistor
C1	2200 μF electrolytic capacitor
C2	1 μF electrolytic capacitor
BR1	Bridge rectifier, 4-amp
LED1	Light-emitting diode
T1	18-volt, 2-amp transformer
S1	SPST switch
F1	Fuse (2-amp)
Misc.	Ac plug, cord, fuse holder, cabinet

All resistors are 5 to 10 percent tolerance, ¼ watt. All capacitors are 10 to 20 percent tolerance, rated 35 volts or more.

terminals are the output and must connect as shown in the schematic. A 5-volt, 1-amp regulator, a 7805, is used to maintain the voltage output at a steady 5 volts.

Note that the transformer supplies a great deal more voltage than is necessary. This is for two reasons. First, lower-voltage 6.3- or 9-volt transformers are available, but most do not deliver more than 0.5 amp. It is far easier to find 12- or 15-volt transformers that deliver sufficient power. Second, the regulator requires a few extra volts as "overhead" to operate properly. The 12.6-volt transformer specified here delivers the minimum voltage requirement, and then some.

Capacitors C1 and C2 filter the ripple inherent in the rectified dc at the outputs of the bridge rectifier. With the capacitors installed as shown (note the polarity), the ripple at the output of the power supply is negligible. LED1 and R1 form a simple indicator. The LED glows when the power supply is on. Remember the 270-ohm resistor; the LED will burn up without it.

The output terminals are insulated binding posts. Don't leave the output wires bare, or they could accidentally touch one another and short the supply. Solder the output wires to the lug on the binding posts, and attach the posts to the front of the power supply chassis. The posts accept bare wires, alligator clips, or even banana plugs.

Differences in the 12-Volt Version

The 5- and 12-volt versions of the power supply are basically the same, but with a few important changes. Refer again to FIG. 12-2. First, the transformer is rated for 18 volts at 2 amps. The 18-volt output is more than enough for the overhead required by the 12-volt regulator and is commonly available. You may use a transformer rated at between 15 and 25 volts.

The regulator, a 7812, is the same as the 7805 except that it puts out a regulated +12 volts instead of +5 volts. Use the T series regulator (TO-220 case) for low-current applications and the K series (TO-3) for higher capacity applications. Lastly, R1 is increased to 330 ohms.

MULTIPLE-VOLTAGE POWER SUPPLY

The multi-voltage power supply is like four power supplies in one. Rather than using four bulky transformers, however, this circuit uses just one, tapping the voltage at the proper locations to operate the +5, +12, -5, and -12 regulators.

The circuit, as shown in FIG. 12-3, is composed of two halves. One half of the supply provides +12 and -12 volts; the other half provides +5 and -5 volts. Each side is connected to a common transformer, fuse, switch, and wall plug. See TABLE 12-3 for a parts list.

The basic difference between the multi-voltage supply and the single-voltage supplies described earlier in this chapter is the addition of negative power regulators. Circuit ground is the center tap of the transformer. Make two boards, one for each section. That is, one board will be the ±5-volt regulators and the other board will contain the ±12-volt regulators. The supply provides approximately 1 amp for each of the outputs.

Use nylon binding posts for the five outputs (ground, +5, +12, -5, -12). Clearly label each post so you don't mix them up when using the supply. Check for proper operation with your volt-ohmmeter.

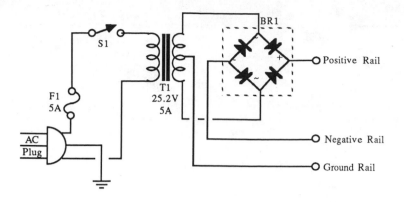

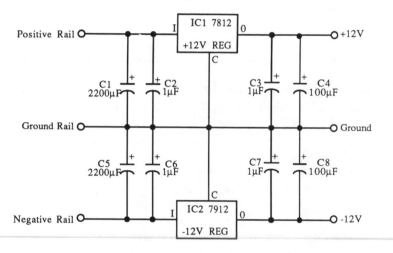

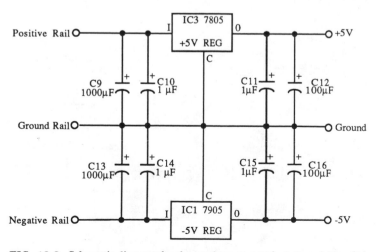

FIG. 12-3. *Schematic diagram for the quad power supply (±5 and 12 volts).*

Table 12-3. Quad Power Supply Parts List

IC1	7812 +12 Vdc voltage regulator
IC2	7912 −12 Vdc voltage regulator
IC3	7805 +5 Vdc voltage regulator
IC4	7905 −5 Vdc voltage regulator
C1,C5	2200 μF electrolytic capacitor
C2,C3,	1 μF electrolyic capacitor
C6,C7,C10,C11,C14,C15	
C4,C8,	100 μF electrolytic capacitor
C12,C16	
C9,C13	1000 μF electrolytic capacitor
C1,C5	2200 μF electrolytic capacitor

All capacitors are 10 to 20 percent tolerance, rated 35 volts or more.

ADJUSTABLE-VOLTAGE POWER SUPPLY

The adjustable power supply uses an LM317 adjustable voltage regulator. With the addition of a few components, you can select any voltage between 1.5 to 37 volts. By using a potentiometer, you can select the voltage you want by turning a knob.

The circuit shown in FIG. 12-4 is a no-frills application of the LM317, but it has everything you need to build a well-regulated, continuously adjustable, positive-voltage power supply. See TABLE 12-4 for the parts list. The regulator is rated at over 3 amps so you must mount it on a heavy-duty heatsink. Although you don't need to forcibly cool the regulator and heatsink, it's a good idea to mount them on the outside of the power supply cabinet, for example on the top or back.

Remember that the case of the regulator is the output, so be sure to provide electrical insulation from the heatsink, or a short circuit could result. Use a TO-3 transistor mounting

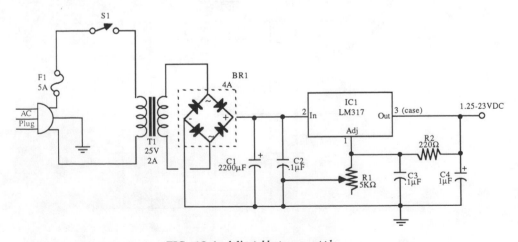

FIG. 12-4. *Adjustable power supply.*

176

Table 12-4. Adjustable Power Supply Parts List

IC1	LM317 adjustable positive voltage regulator
R1	5 kilohm potentiometer
R2	220 ohm resistor
C1	2200 μF electrolytic capacitor
C2,C3	0.1 μF disc capacitor
C4	1 μF electrolytic capacitor
BR1	Bridge rectifier, 4-amp
T1	25-volt, 2-amp (or more) transformer
S1	SPST switch
F1	5-amp fuse
Misc.	Ac plug, cord, fuse holder, cabinet

All resistors are 5 to 10 percent tolerance, ¼ watt. All capacitors are 10 to 20 percent tolerance, rated 35 volts or more.

and insulator kit. It has all the hardware and insulating washers you need. Apply silicone grease to the bottom of the regulator to aid in heat transfer.

INSPECTION AND TESTING

All of the dc power supplies should be inspected and tested before use. Be particularly wary of wires or components that could short out. Visually check your wiring and check for problems with a volt meter. When all looks satisfactory, apply power and watch for signs of problems. If any arcing or burning occurs, immediately unplug the supply and check everything again. When all appears to be operating smoothly, check the output of the power supply to ensure that it is providing the proper voltage.

BATTERY PACK REGULATORS

Voltage regulators can also be used with battery packs for portable equipment. A 5-volt regulator can be used with a single 6-volt battery to provide a steady supply of 5 volts. The schematic in FIG. 12-5 shows how to connect the parts. Refer to TABLE 12-5 for a parts list. Alternatively, use a 12-volt regulator. The battery should put out a nominal 13 volts to accommodate for the 1- to 1.2-volt drop across the regulator. Most lead-acid and gelled electrolyte batteries put out 13.8 volts when fully charged. See TABLE 12-6 for a chart of voltage values for various types of batteries.

BATTERY RECHARGERS

With a rechargeable battery, you can use it once, zap new life into it, use it again, and repeat the process several hundred—even thousands—of times before wearing it out. The higher initial cost of rechargeable batteries more than pays for itself after the third or fourth recharging.

Rechargeable batteries can't be revived simply by connecting them to a dc power supply. The dc supply delivers too much current and tries to charge the battery too

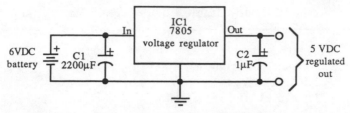

FIG. 12-5. *Battery pack regulator.*

quickly. If you are recharging gelled electrolyte or lead-acid batteries, you might be able to get away with using an ac power adapter, the kind designed for video games, portable tape recorders, and other battery-operated equipment (the output *must* be dc). By design, these adapters limit their maximum current to between 250 to 600 mA. A 300 mA recharger can be effectively used on batteries with capacities of 2.5 AH to 5 AH. A 400 mA or 500 mA ac adapter can be used on batteries with capacities of 3.5 AH to 6.5 AH.

However, one problem is that you must be careful the battery doesn't stay on charge much longer than 12 to 16 hours. Leaving it on for a day or two can ruin the battery. This is especially true of lead-acid batteries. The circuit shown in FIG. 12-6 minimizes the danger of overcharging.

Table 12-5. 5 Vdc Battery Voltage Regulator

IC1	7805 +5 Vdc voltage regulator
C1	2200 μF electrolytic capacitor
C2	1 μF electrolytic capacitor

All capacitors are 10 to 20 percent tolerance, rated 35 volts or more.

Table 12-6. Battery Voltage Levels

Battery	Newly Charged	Nominal	Discharged
Alkaline Ni-cad	1.4 volts	1.2 volts	1.1 volts
Power/1 cell*	2.3 volts	2.0 volts	1.6 volts
Power/multi	6.5 volts	6.0 volts	4.8 volts
Power/multi	13.8 volts	12.0 volts	9.6 volts

*Gelled electrolyte and lead-acid battery; single cell, 6 volt (three cells in series), 12-volts (six cells in series).

178

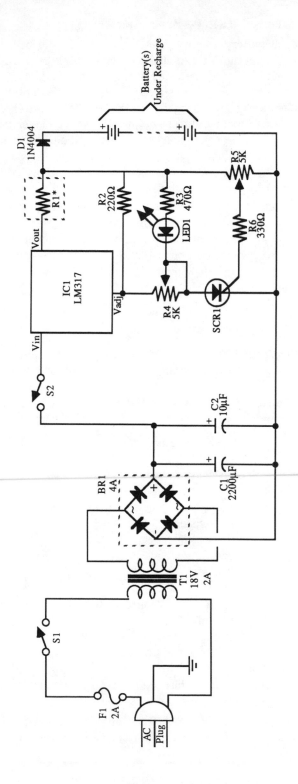

FIG. 12-6. *Circuit diagram for the battery charger. See page 180 for values of R1 and pg 182 for settings for R4 and R5.*

Build the Universal Battery Recharger

The universal battery recharger shown in FIG. 12-6 is built around the LM317 adjustable voltage regulator IC. As indicated in TABLE 12-7, this IC comes in a TO-3 transistor case and should be used with a heatsink to provide for cool operation. The heatsink is absolutely necessary when recharging batteries at 500 mA or higher.

The circuit works by monitoring the voltage level at the battery. During recharging, the circuit supplies a constant-current output; the voltage level gradually rises as the battery charges. When the battery nears full charge, the circuit removes the constant-current source and maintains a regulated voltage to complete or maintain charging. By switching to constant-voltage output, the battery can be left on charge for periods longer than recommended by the manufacturer.

Before you build the circuit, you should consider the kind of batteries you want recharged. You'll have to consider whether you will be recharging 6-volt or 12-volt batteries (or both) and the maximum current output that can be safely delivered to the battery (use the 10 percent rule or follow the manufacturer's recommendations).

Resistor R1 determines the current flow to the battery. Its value can be found by using this formula:

$$R1 = 1.25/Icc$$

where Icc is the desired charging current in mA. For example, to recharge a battery at 500 mA (0.5 amp), the calculation for R1 is 1.25/0.5 or 2.5 ohms. TABLE 12-8 lists

Table 12-7. Universal Battery Charger Parts List

IC1	LM317 adjustable positive voltage regulator
R1	See text; Table 12-8
R2	220 ohm resistor
R3	470 ohm resistor
R4,R5	5 kilohm, 10-turn precision potentiometers
R6	330 ohm resistor
C1	2200 μF electrolytic capacitor
C2	10 μF electrolytic capacitor
D1	1N4004 diode
BR1	Bridge rectifier, 4-amp
SCR1	200-volt silicon controlled rectifier (1 amp or more)
LED1	Light-emitting diode
S1,S2	SPST switch
T1	18-volt, 2-amp transformer
F1	2-amp fuse
Misc.	Ac plug, cord, fuse holder, cabinet, heatsink for LM317, binding posts for battery under charge

All resistors are 5 to 10 percent tolerance, ¼ watt, unless otherwise indicated. All capacitors are 10 to 20 percent tolerance, rated 35 volts or more.

Milliamperes	Ohms
50	25.00
100	12.50
200	6.25
400	3.13
500	2.50

**Table 12-8. Common
Currents and Resistor Values**

common currents for recharging and the calculated values of R1. For currents under 400 mA, you can use a 1-watt resistor. With currents between 400 mA and 1 amp, use a 2-watt resistor.

If the resistor you need isn't a standard value, choose the closest one to it as long as the value is within 10 percent. If not, use two standard-value resistors, in parallel or in series, to equal R1. If you'd like to make the charger selectable, wire a handful of resistors to a one-pole multi-position rotary switch, as shown in FIG. 12-7. Dial in the current setting you want.

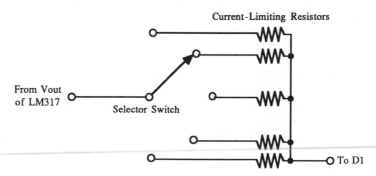

FIG. 12-7. *Rotary switch for selectable change currents.*

The output terminals can be banana jacks, alligator clips, or any other hardware you desire. You might want to use banana jacks and construct cables that can stretch between the jacks and the batteries or systems you want to recharge. For example, you can connect the charger to a 12-volt He-Ne laser battery pack. The pack is outfitted with a common ¼-inch phone plug for easy connection to the laser. To recharge the battery, you simply remove the cable attaching it to the laser and replace it with the one from the recharger.

Building The Circuit. For best results, build the circuit on a printed circuit board. Alternatively, you can wire the circuit on perforated board. Wiring is not critical, but you should exercise the usual care, especially in the incoming ac section. Be sure that you provide a fuse for your recharger.

Calibrating The Circuit. After the circuit is built, it must be calibrated before use. First set R4, the voltage adjust. This potentiometer sets the end-of-charge voltage. Then set the trip point, which is adjusted by R5. Follow these steps.

1. Before attaching a battery to the terminals and turning the circuit on, set variable resistors R4 and R5 to their mid ranges. With the recharger off, use a volt-ohmmeter to calibrate R4, referring to TABLE 12-9. Adjust R4 until the ohmmeter displays the proper resistance for the current setting you've chosen for the charger.
2. Connect a 4.7k, 5-watt resistor across the output terminals of the charger (this approximates a battery load). Apply power to the circuit. Measure the output across the resistor. For 12-volt operation with gelled electrolyte cells and lead-acid batteries, the output should be approximately 13.8 volts; for 6-volt operation, the output should be approximately 6.9 volts. If you don't get a reading or if it is low, adjust R5. If you still don't get a reading or if it is considerably off the described mark, turn R4 a couple of times in either direction.
3. Connect the volt-ohmmeter between ground and the wiper of R5, the trip-point potentiometer. Turn R5 until the meter reads zero. Turn the charger off.
4. Remove the 4.7k resistor, and in its place connect a partially discharged battery to the output terminals (be sure to use a *dis*charged battery), observing the correct polarity. Turn the charger on and watch the LED. It should not light.
5. Connect the volt-ohmmeter across the battery terminals and measure the output voltage. Monitor the voltage until the desired output is reached (see step 2, above).
6. When you reach the desired output, adjust R5 so that the LED glows. At this point, the constant-current source is removed from the output, and the battery float charges at the set voltage.

Application Notes. If you have both 6- and 12-volt batteries to charge, you might find yourself readjusting the potentiometers each time. A better way is to construct two battery rechargers (the components are inexpensive) and use one at 6 volts and the other at 12 volts.Alternatively, you can wire up a selector switch that chooses between two sets of voltage adjustment and trip-point pots.

At least one manufacturer of the LM317, National Semiconductor, provides extensive application notes on this and other voltage regulators. Refer to the *National Linear Databook Volume 1 (1987)* if you need to recharge batteries with unusual supply voltages and currents.

Table 12-9. Values for R4

$R1^5$	6-volt (in ohms)	12-volt (in ohms)
25.00	1578	2950
12.50	1497	2799
6.25	1457	2724
3.13	1437	2686
2.50	1433	2679

Depending on your battery and the tolerances of the components you use, you might need to experiment with the values of two other resistors. If the output voltage cannot be adjusted to the point you want (either high or low), increase or decrease the value of R2. If the LED never glows, or glows constantly, adjust the value of R6. Be careful not to go under about 200 ohms for R6, or the SCR could be damaged.

When recharging a battery, you know it has reached full charge when the LED goes on. To be on the safe side, turn the charger off and wait five to 10 seconds for the SCR to unlatch. Reapply power. If the LED remains lit, the battery is charged. If the LED goes out again, keep the battery on charge a little longer.

BATTERY MONITORS

A battery monitor simply provides an aural or visual indicator that a battery is either delivering too much or too little voltage. FIGURE 12-8 shows a schematic for a simple "window comparator" battery monitor (see TABLE 12-10 for a parts list). It is designed to be used with 12-volt batteries, but you can substitute one or more of the zener diodes for use with other voltages.

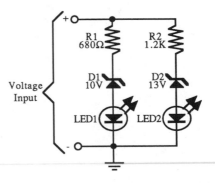

FIG. 12-8. *A simple battery condition indicator. Choose the zener diodes to provide a "window" for over/under voltage indication.*

Table 12-10. Battery Monitor Dual LED Parts List

R1	680 kilohm resistor
R2	1.2 kilohm resistor
D1	10 volt zener
D2	13 volt zener
LED1,2	Light emitting diodes

All resistors are 5-10 percent tolerance, ¼-watt.

In normal operation, LED1 glows when the voltage from the battery is at least 10 volts. It is also desirable to know if the battery is delivering too much voltage, so a second zener diode is used. If LED2 is on, the circuit is receiving too much power, and it could be damaged. More likely, however, the battery level will drop, and LED1 will grow dim or flicker off completely. If LED1 is not lit or is dim, the battery needs to be recharged.

13

Free-Air Laser Light Communications

Because light is at such a high frequency in the electromagnetic spectrum, it is an even better medium for communications than radio waves. Lasers are perfect instruments for communications links because they emit a powerful, slender beam that is least affected by interference and is nearly impossible to intercept.

This chapter explains the basics of laser light communications using both helium-neon and semiconductor lasers. You'll discover the different ways light can be modulated and cajoled into carrying an analog signal from a microphone or FM radio. The following chapter details advanced projects in laser light communications.

LIGHT AS A MODULATION MEDIUM

Higher frequencies in the radio spectrum provide greater bandwidth. The bandwidth is the space between the upper and lower frequencies that define an information channel. Bandwidth is small for low-frequency applications such as AM radio broadcasts, which span a range 540 kHz to 1600 kHz. That's little more than 1 MHz of bandwidth, so if there are 20 stations on the dial, that's only 50 kHz per deejay.

Television broadcasts, including both VHF and UHF channels, span a range from 54 MHz to 890 MHz, with each channel taking up 6 MHz. Note that the 6 MHz bandwidth of the TV channel provides more than 100 times more room for information than the AM radio band. That way, television can pack more data into the transmission.

Microwave links, which operate in the gigahertz (billions of cycles per second) region, are used by communications and telephone companies to beam thousands of phone calls in one transmission. Many calls are compacted into the single microwave channel because the bandwidth required for one phone conversation is small compared to the overall bandwidth provided by the microwave link.

Visible light and near-infrared radiation has a frequency of between about 430 to 750 terahertz (THz)—or 430 to 750 trillion cycles per second. Thanks to the immense bandwidth of the spectrum at these high frequencies, one light beam can simultaneously carry all the phone calls made in the United States, or almost 100 million TV channels. Of course, what to put on those channels is another thing!

Alas, all of this is theoretical. Transmitters and receivers don't yet exist that can pack data into the entire light spectrum; the current state of the art cannot place intelligent information at frequencies higher than about 25 or 35 gigahertz (billion cycles per second). It might take a while for technology to advance to a point where the full potential of light beam communications can be realized.

Even with these limitations, light transmission offers additional advantages over conventional techniques. Light is not as susceptible to interference from other transmissions, and when squeezed into the arrow-thin beam of a laser, is highly directional. It is difficult to intercept a light beam transmission without the intended receiver knowing about it. And, unlike radio gear, experimenting with even high-power light links does not require approval from the Federal Communications Commission. Businesses, universities, and individuals can test lightwave communications systems without the worry of upsetting every television set, radio, and CB in the neighborhood (however, CDRH regulations must be followed).

On the down side, light is greatly affected by weather conditions, and unlike low frequencies such as AM radio, it does not readily bounce off objects. Radar (low-band microwave) pierces through most any weather and bounces off just about everything.

EXPERIMENTING WITH A VISIBLE LED TRANSMITTER

It's easy to see how laser lightwave communication links work by first experimenting with a system designed around the common and affordable visible light-emitting diode. The LED provides a visual indication that the system is working and allows you to see the effects of collimating and focusing optics.

The LED communications link, like any other, consists of a transmitter and receiver. An LED is used as the transmitting component and a phototransistor is used as the receiving component. To facilitate testing, a radio or cassette player is used as the transmission source. You listen to the reception at the receiver using headphones. In Chapter 14, "Advanced Projects in Laser Communication," you'll learn how to transmit computer and remote-control data through the air via a laser beam.

Just about any LED will work in the circuit shown in FIG. 13-1, but if you want to operate the link over long distances (more than 5 or 10 feet), you should use a high-output LED, such as the kind described in Chapter 4, "Experimenting with Light and Optics." After you test the visible LED, you can exchange it with one or more high-output infrared LEDs to extend the working distance. However, you enjoy the greatest range using an infrared or visible laser (we'll get to that shortly).

Building the Transmitter

The transmitter, with parts indicated in TABLE 13-1, is designed around a 555 timer IC. The 555 generates a modulation frequency upon which the information you want

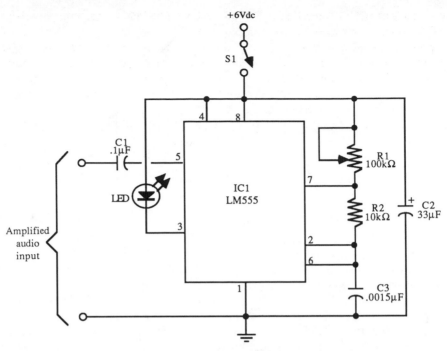

FIG. 13-1. *Schematic diagram for the pulse frequency modulated LED transmitter. Adjust frequency by rotating R1. With components shown, frequency range is between 8 and 48 kHz.*

to send is placed. The output frequency of the 555 changes as the audio signal presented to the input changes. This modulation technique is commonly referred to as pulse frequency modulation, or PFM, and is shown diagrammatically in FIG. 13-2. The signal can be received using a simple amplifier, as shown later in this section, but for best response, a receiver designed to "tune in" to the PFM signal is desired. Advanced receivers are discussed later.

IC1	LM555 timer IC
R1	100 kilohm potentiometer
R2	10 kilohm resistor
C1	0.1 µF disc capacitor
C2	33 µF electrolytic capacitor
C3	0.0015 µF mica or Hi-Q disc capacitor
LED1	Light-emitting diode (see text)
S1	SPST switch

All resistors are 5 to 10 percent tolerance, ¼ watt. All capacitors are 10 to 20 percent tolerance, rated 35 volts or more, unless otherwise indicated.

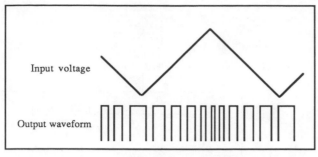

FIG. 13-2. *Comparison of input voltage and width of the output waveform.*

Construct the transmitter in a small project box. Power comes from a single 9-volt transistor battery. The switch lets you turn the circuit on and off and the potentiometer allows you to vary the relative power delivered to the LED. In actuality, adjusting the pot changes the modulation frequency, which in turn changes the pulse width, which in turn changes the current delivered to the LED. Got that?!

In any case, the entire range is beyond human hearing and above the audio signals in frequency that you will be transmitting. You can readily increase the modulation frequency to the upper limit of the components used in the transmitter and receiver, but lowering them into the 20-to 20,000-Hz region of the audio spectrum causes an annoying buzz. Any sourcebook on using the LM555 timer IC will show you how to calculate output frequency for astable operation.

Mounting details are provided in FIGS. 13-3 and 13-4; parts are shown in TABLE 13-2. Solder an LED to the terminals of a ⅛-inch phone plug jack, and mount the jack in the base of a ¾-inch PVC end plug, as shown in FIG. 13-3. If the plug is rounded on the end, file it flat with a grinder or file. Lightly countersink the hole so that the shaft of the phone jack is flush to the outside of the plug. Countersinking also helps the shaft of the jack to poke all the way through the thick-walled PVC fitting.

The transmitter and LED connect via an ⅛-inch plug that is mounted so that it extrudes through the project box, as detailed in FIG. 13-4. Use a ⁵⁄₁₆-inch 18 nut to hold the plug in place. The ⅛-inch mini plug used in the prototype is threaded for ⁵⁄₁₆-inch 18 threads, but not all plugs are the same. Check yours first.

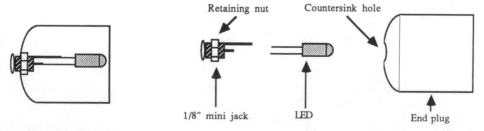

FIG. 13-3. *How to mount the LED in a PVC end plug. The same approach is used for the receiver phototransistor.*

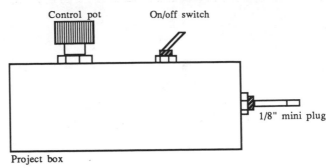

FIG. 13-4. *The project box, shown with ⅛-inch mini plug for connecting to the LED.*

Table 13-2. Plug and Box Transmitter Parts List

1	¾-inch schedule 40 PVC end plug
1	⅛-inch miniature phone jack
1	⅛-inch miniature phone plug
1ea.	Project box, knob for potentiometer, 6 Vdc battery holder (4 "AA").

Attach the transmitter into the LED by plugging it in. Install a 9-volt battery and turn the transmitter on. The LED should glow. You won't be able to test the transmitter circuit until you build the receiver.

Building the Receiver

The receiver, shown in FIG. 13-5, is designed around the common LM741 op amp and an LM386 audio amplifier. See TABLE 13-3 for a parts list. Power is supplied via two 9-volt batteries (to provide the 741 with a dual-ended supply). A switch turns the circuit on and off (interrupting both positive and negative battery connections) and a potentiometer acts like a volume/gain control.

You can listen to the amplified sounds through headphones or a speaker, or you can connect the output of the receiver to a larger amplifier. A good, handy outboard amplifier to use is the pocket amp available at Radio Shack. The pocket amp accepts an external input and has its own built-in speaker.

Construct the receiver in a plastic project box. The one used for the prototype measured 2¾ by 4⅛ by 1⁹⁄₁₆ inches and was more than large enough to accommodate the circuit, batteries, switch, potentiometer, and output jack.

The receiving phototransistor is built into a PVC end plug in the same manner as the transmitter LED, described above. Mount the phototransistor as shown in FIG. 13-3, being sure to note the orientation of the transistor leads and jack terminals. Although the circuit will work if you connect the phototransistor backwards, sensitivity will be greatly reduced.

Connect the receiver to the phototransistor, install two batteries, plug in a set of headphones, and turn the power switch on (but don't put the headphones on just yet). Adjust the potentiometer midway through its travel and point the phototransistor at an

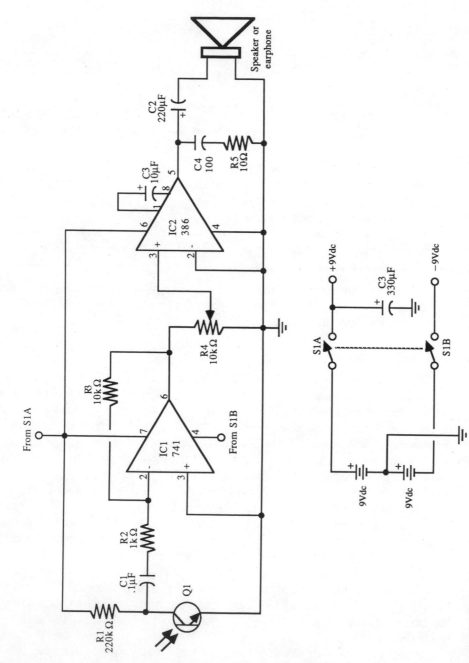

FIG. 13-5. *The universal laser light detector. The output of the LM386 audio amplifier can be connected to a small 8-ohm speaker or earphone. Two 9-volt batteries provide power. Decrease R1 to lower sensitivity; increase R3 to increase gain of the op amp (avoid very high gain or the op amp might oscillate).*

Table 13-3. Universal Receiver Parts List

IC1	LM741 operational amplifier IC
IC2	LM386 audio amplifier IC
R1	220 kilohm resistor
R2	1 kilohm resistor
R3	10 kilohm resistor
R4	10 kilohm potentiometer
R5	10 ohm resistor
C1	0.1 μF disc capacitor
C2	220 μF electrolytic capacitor
C3	10 μF electrolytic capacitor
C4	100 μF electrolytic capacitor
Q1	Infrared phototransistor
S1	DPDT switch

All resistors are 5 to 10 percent tolerance, ¼ watt. All capacitors are 10 to 20 percent tolerance, rated 35 volts or more.

incandescent lamp. You should hear a buzzing sound through the headphones (the buzzing is the lamp fluctuating under the 60-cycle current).

If you don't hear the buzz, adjust the volume control until the sound comes in. Should you still not hear any sound, double check your wiring and the batteries. Even with the phototransistor not plugged in you should hear background hiss. No hiss might mean that the circuit is not getting power or the headphone jack is not properly wired.

The receiver can be used with the LED lightwave link as well as all the other communications projects in this chapter (as well as most of those in the remainder of this book). Its wide application makes it an ideal all-purpose universal laser beam receiver. When I refer to the "universal receiver," this is the one I'm talking about.

Using the Lightwave Link

Once the receiver checks out, you can test the transmitter. Switch off the lights or move to a darkened part of the room. Turn on the transmitter source (radio, tape player) and aim the transmitter LED at the receiver phototransistor. Adjust the controls on the receiver and transmitter until you hear sound. You might hear considerable background hiss and noise, caused by other nearby light sources. If you use the communications link outdoors in sunlight, the infrared radiation from the sun might swamp (overload) the phototransistor, and the sound could be drastically reduced or cut off completely. The transmitter and receiver works best in subdued light.

Test the sensitivity and range of the communications link by moving the receiver away from the transmitter. Depending on the output of the LED, the range will be limited to about 5 feet before reception drops out.

Extending the Range of the Link

Most all phototransistors are most sensitive to infrared light. The peak spectral sensitivity depends on the makeup of the transistor, but it is generally between about 780 and 950 nm in the near-infrared portion of the spectrum. A red LED has a peak spectral output of about 650 nm, considerably under the sensitivity of the phototransistor. A solar cell offers a wider spectral response and can provide greater range. The best type of solar cell to use is the kind encased in plastic like the phototransistor (many have a built-in lens). Connect the cell in the circuit as shown in FIG. 13-6.

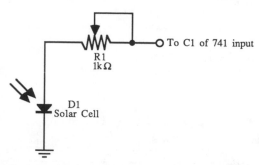

FIG. 13-6. *How to connect a solar cell to the input of the universal laser light detector. The cell provides better sensitivity in the visible light range than an infrared phototransistor.*

The solar cell is sensitive to a wide range of colors. The light spectrum above or below the red radiation from the LED isn't needed for reception, so block it with a red filter. Test the effectiveness of the filter by temporarily taping it to the front of the solar cell.

You can also use the filter with the phototransistor to help limit the incoming radiation to the red wavelengths. Even though the phototransistor is designed to be most sensitive to near-infrared radiation, it can still detect light at other wavelengths, especially red. One or two layers of red acetate placed over the phototransistor can increase the range in moderate light conditions by several feet.

The best way to increase the working distance of the communications link is to add lenses to the LED and/or the phototransistor. The PVC end plug makes it fairly easy to add lenses to both transmitter and receiver components. Mount a simple double-convex or plano-convex lens in the end plug. The PVC rings hold the lens in place and let you easily adjust the distance between the lens and phototransistor. If the lens has a focal length of more than 10 to 15 mm, attach a coupling to the end plug and stuff the lens in the coupling. Again, use PVC rings to hold the lens in place.

Be sure that you position the lens at the proper focal point with respect to the *junction* of the LED or phototransistor. If you don't know the focal length of the lens you are using, test it following the instructions provided earlier in this book.

You can see the effect of the lens on the transmitted light by pointing the LED against a lightly colored wall. At close range and with the lens properly adjusted, you should actually see the junction of the LED projected on the wall (assuming you are not using an LED with a diffused case). You might also see a faint halo around the junction; this is normal and is caused by light emitted from the sides of the LED.

With the lens(es) attached, try the lightwave link again and test its effective range. With extended range comes increased directionality, so you must carefully aim the transmitter element at the receiver. A simple focusing lens on both receiver and transmitter should extend the working distance to a hundred feet or more. Test the real effectiveness of the system at night outside. The darkness will also help you better aim the transmitter. At 100 feet, the light from the LED will be dim, but you should be able to spot it if you know where to look for it.

Note that the plastic case of the LED and phototransistor acts as a kind of lens, and that can alter the effective focal length of the system. Experiment with the position of the lens until the system is working at peak performance.

ACOUSTIC MODULATION

In 1880, Alexander Graham Bell, with his assistant Sumner Tainter, demonstrated the first *photophone,* a mechanical contraption using sunlight or collimated artificial light to transmit and receive voice signals over long distances. Its operation was simple. The system used a lightweight membrane similar to reflective Mylar as a voice diaphragm. A bright beam of light, typically from the sun, was pointed at the diaphragm, which vibrated when a person talked into it. The vibration then caused the light to fluctuate in syncopation with the sound. A receiver, located some distance away, demodulated the fluctuating light levels and turned the beam back into the talker's voice.

Bell had great hopes for the photophone, and in fact had predicted that it would be a bigger hit than the telephone. But the problems of poor range in inclement weather doomed the photophone as just another scientific curiosity. Had Bell used a laser with his photophone, he would have been able to greatly increase the range of the device. Of course, clouds, fog, and heavy rain would have still reduced the working distance of the laser photophone, limiting it to a clear-weather communications device.

You can easily duplicate Bell's photophone, adding the laser as a high-tech improvement. The process of transmitting low-frequency audio signals via a photophone-like device is more accurately termed *acousto-modulation*. You can use a stretched membrane as the acoustic vibrating element or adapt a surplus speaker as a "light switch."

Stretched Membrane Modulator

Thin reflective Mylar is a fairly common find among the mail order surplus outfits, as well as local army/navy surplus shops. Reflective Mylar, or a reasonable facsimile made with generic acetate, is used to produce parachutes for radiosonde equipment, the thermal layer on camping blankets, high-tech jewelry, radar jammer streamers, and lots more. Price is reasonable. A small 2-by-2-foot square sheet of reflective (or "aluminized") acetate costs about a dollar on the surplus market and a little more when you buy it from a commercial dealer. One small square is all you need.

Refer to TABLE 13-4 for a parts list for the stretched membrane modulator. Secure the Mylar sheet inside a 4- to 6-inch diameter embroidery hoop as shown in FIG. 13-7. The hoop allows you to open the two halves, insert the material, and pull it tight as the two halves are tightened together. The idea is to pull the Mylar as taut as possible.

Mount the hoop on a wooden or plastic base. Set up a speaker behind the hoop and direct a laser beam at the Mylar. Activate the speaker using a radio, tape player, or

Table 13-4. Mylar Hoop Modulator Parts List

1	4- to 6-inch diameter circular wood or plastic embroidery hoop
1	4- to 6-inch diameter full-range speaker
2	3-by-3-inch wood block (for base and speaker mount); ½-inch plywood or pine
2	1-by-½-inch corner angle bracket
4	⁸⁄₃₂ by 1½-inch bolts, nuts, flash washers
1	¼-inch 20 nut and washer (for tripod)
1	Portable camera tripod

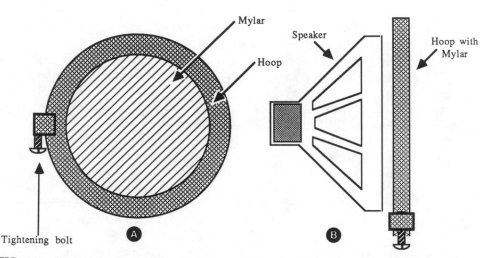

FIG. 13-7. *Basic arrangement for the Mylar speaker modulator. (A) Front view with Mylar stretched in embroidery hoop; (B) Side view with speaker behind the hoop.*

amplified microphone. As the speaker vibrates, it oscillates the Mylar and thus modulates the laser beam.

The modulation is not electronic or electromechanical, but *positional* or *geometrical*. You can see the effect of the modulation by positioning the laser so the beam strikes a distant target. When the Mylar vibrates, the beam is displaced at the target, making squiggles and odd shapes. Position a receiving element such as a solar cell at the target and you can register the movement by sensing the varying intensity of the beam (actually, the intensity falls off as the beam moves off-axis to the center of the cell).

The universal laser receiver, described earlier in this chapter, can be readily used to capture and demodulate the signal transmitted over the beam. The solar cell is connected to the receiver as shown in FIG. 13-6.

The ideal size for the solar cell depends on the divergence of the beam and the distance between the laser and receiver. Beam divergence with most helium-neon lasers is only about one milliradian (less on high quality tubes). Placing the target 50 meters away produces a spot of about 50 mm across (about 2 inches). That means you can use a silicon solar cell that's 2 inches in diameter and capture all or most of the beam. Modulation that causes the beam to wander off-axis to the cell generates a change of voltage.

You can readily calculate the approximate beam spread at any distance by multiplying the divergence in radians by the distance in meters. For example:

$$\text{Divergence (radians)} = 0.001$$
$$\text{Distance} = 200$$

0.001 times 200 equals 0.2, or 200 millimeters.

Another example: What is the spread at 1 km using a laser with a divergence of 1.2 mrad? Answer: 1.2 meters. That's a small amount considering that the beam travels over half a mile. You can reduce beam divergence by adding collimating optics to the output of the laser. Chapter 8 provides details on building laser collimating optics.

Speaker Cone Modulator

An interesting effect used in many light shows is created by mounting a mirror in front of a speaker (the mirror can also be mounted directly on the speaker). A laser beam, reflected off the mirror, bounces around on the wall or screen in time to the music (various mirror/speaker mounting techniques are discussed more fully in Chapter 19).

You can use the same technique to transmit audio information over the air. Simply place a receiving element at the spot where the beam lands. For best results, keep the amplitude of the speaker at a low level so the beam doesn't deflect more than a few degrees. Use a 2- or 3-inch diameter silicon solar cell as the receiver element. You can use the speaker to transmit music from a radio or tape player, or rig up the speaker to an amplifier and microphone and broadcast your own voice.

Even with the speaker turned down low, wide deflection of the beam becomes a problem when transmitting over long distances. The beam covers a larger area at the target as the distance between the receiver and transmitter is increased. It is generally impractical to enlarge the sensing area by more than 4 or 5 inches in diameter, so another approach is recommended. This idea comes from Roger Sontag at General Science and Engineering. Instead of bouncing the light off of a mirror, cut an edge off the cone of a speaker and use it as a "shutter". As the speaker cone vibrates, it alternately passes and cuts off the laser beam. The system requires careful alignment, but the deflection of the beam at the receiver is minimal.

The best speakers to use are those that measure 4 to 6 inches in diameter and have a deep taper. Avoid using a speaker where the cone lies flat in the frame.

Mount the speaker in a swivel mount so that you can adjust its height and angle. Place a helium-neon or cw diode laser to one side of the speaker so that the beam skims across the top of the cut portion of the cone. Energize the speaker with a fairly powerful amplifier (but don't exceed the wattage rating of the speaker), and watch for the cone to move in and out in response to the sound. Now look at the target and watch it flicker as the speaker moves. If the cone doesn't block the beam, or blocks the beam entirely, readjust the position of the speaker as needed.

You can use the universal laser beam receiver described earlier in this chapter to capture the signal on the modulated beam. The intensity of the beam could swamp the phototransistor, so place a set of polarizers in front and vary their rotation to reduce the beam intensity to a usable level.

ELECTRONIC MODULATION OF HELIUM-NEON LASERS

Agreeably, using a sheet of plastic or a dissected speaker does not represent a high-tech approach to laser modulation. Although it might appear otherwise, it's fairly easy to modulate the beam of a helium-neon laser, and using only a handful of parts at that. Two approaches are provided here: both have an effective bandwidth of around 0 Hz to 3 kHz, making them suitable for most voice and some music transmission schemes.

Transformer

A transformer placed in line with the high-voltage power supply and cathode of the tube can be used to vary the current supplied to the tube. This causes the intensity of the beam to vary. This is amplitude modulation, the same technique used in AM radio broadcasts.

Although you can use a number of transformers as the modulating element, Dennis Meredith of Meredith Instruments suggests you use a public address power output transformer. It's ideal for the job because of its high turns ratio—the ratio of wire loops in the primary and secondary. You wire the transformer in reverse to the typical application: the speaker terminals from a hi-fi or amplifier connect to the ''output'' of the transformer and the laser connects to the ''input.''

PA transformers are available from almost any electronics parts store, including Radio Shack, who offers a good one for under $5. PA transformers are rated by their voltage, usually either 35 or 70 volts. Get the higher voltage rating. There are several terminals on the transformer. Connect the speaker terminals to the common and 8-ohm terminals; connect the laser cathode, as shown in FIG. 13-8, to the common and one of the wattage terminals (parts list in TABLE 13-5). Experiment with the wattage terminal that yields the most modulation. The prototype seemed to work best using the 5-watt terminal.

The cathode passes some current, so touching its leads can cause a shock. Isolate the transformer and wires in a small project box, like the one shown in FIG. 13-9. Five-way binding posts (fancy banana jacks) are used for the cathode connections; the audio input is an ⅛-inch miniature phone jack.

Transistor

Who wants to lug around a bulky and heavy transformer when you can provide modulation to the He-Ne tube using a simple silicon transistor? This next mini-project provides a seed that you can use to design and build an all-electronic analog or digital

1	70-volt PA transformer
1	⅛-inch miniature jack
2	5-way binding posts (25-amp)
1	Project box

Table 13-5.
Transformer Modulator Parts List

196

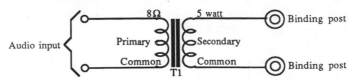

FIG. 13-8. *Wiring diagram for the He-Ne laser transformer modulator.*

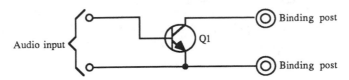

FIG. 13-9. *Wiring diagram for the He-Ne laser transistor transformer. Experiment with different transistors and test the results. Both the transistor and transformer modulation schemes require a well-amplified audio signal.*

laser communications link. I have not fully tested the upward frequency limits of the transistor modulator, but I successfully passed a 4 kHz tone through the prototype circuit using a 2 mW He-Ne tube.

You can employ just about any transistor, but I found the common 2N2222 signal transistor to be adequate. Connect the transistor between the high-voltage power supply and cathode of the laser tube, as shown in FIG. 13-10. Heatsinking is not required

FIG. 13-10. *The finished transformer modulator, enclosed in a project box with insulated binding posts added.*

in most applications; after an hour of testing the transistor, it remained cool. The transistor is all you need for the basic setup, but you might want to add a 390-ohm resistor to the base of the transistor. To make the "circuit" more permanent, mount it on a small piece of perf board or wire it into one of your He-Ne laser enclosures.

Apply a well-amplified signal to the base of the transistor and aim the laser at the universal laser light receiver. You should hear sound. If the sound is weak, double-check your wiring and try turning up the volume. You might need one or two watts of power to produce a measurable amount of modulation.

You can build a completely portable He-Ne laser modulation system using a Walkman cassette player, IC amplifier, helium-neon tube, and 12-volt power supply. Suitable amplifier circuits appear later in this chapter.

ELECTRONIC MODULATION OF CW DIODE LASER

A cw diode laser can be modulated using the circuit provided earlier in this chapter for the LED transmitter. Although it's always better to limit current to the laser using feedback from the monitor photodiode, this system provides a safety net because the laser is driven with pulses at the modulation frequency of about 40 kHz.

Laser diodes exhibit a great deal of divergence, so collimating optics are necessary if you want to use one in a lightwave communications project. Many surplus cw diode lasers come with collimating optics or have suitable optics available for them (most are pulled from existing equipment, such as compact disc players or bar-code scanners). Alternatively, you can build your own collimator using a simple bi-convex lens, as described in Chapter 8, "Laser Optics Experiments."

Mount the battery pack, modulating circuit, and laser in a project box. The box used in the prototype measured 6¼ by 3¾ by 2 inches. Construction details for the project are shown in FIG. 13-11; the parts list is included in TABLE 13-6.

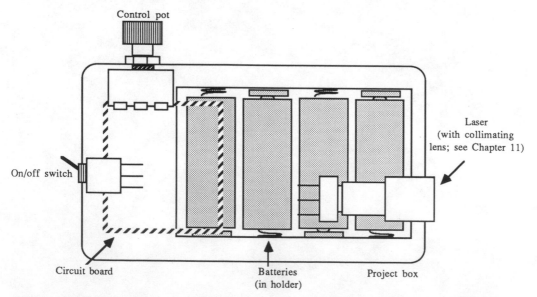

FIG. 13-11. *Layout diagram for the laser diode transmitter. Use "C" or "D" size batteries for long-life performance.*

198

Table 13-6. Cw Modulated Laser Diode Transmitter Parts List

1	Laser diode with collimating optics (see Chapter 10)
1	Driver board
1	Control potentiometer and knob
1	SPST switch
1	Battery holder—"C" size
1	Project box (approximately 3¾ by 6¼ by 2 inches)

Be aware that aiming a laser diode is tough at best. Although the laser emits a deep red glow, the visible illumination is not enough to see in anything but absolute darkness. Looking directly into the laser for any length of time is decidedly a bad idea: the collimating lens acts to focus the light in a narrow beam. Don't let the red glow of the laser fool you. Your eye loses its sensitivity as it approaches the near-infrared band, but its susceptibility to damage from radiation is not lessened.

You can try aiming the laser using trial and error but the results might be frustrating. Another approach is to use an infrared imaging card, such as that sold by Kodak. The card is coated with a substance that's sensitive to infrared light. Directing an infrared source at the card causes it to glow. Before you use the card, you must first "charge" it under the white light of the sun or a desk lamp.

Still another approach is to use an infrared inverter tube. These are expensive "see-in-the-dark" devices used by police, soldiers, and voyeurs. The tube—usually mounted in a pair of binoculars, goggles, or glasses—blocks most visible light and amplifies infrared light. They are normally used with a separate infrared light source, but in this instance, the diode laser provides the needed IR radiation.

The phototransistor used with the receiver could be swamped by the power emitted by the diode laser. Use a pair of polarizers, as shown in FIG. 13-12, to control the amount of infrared radiation that reaches the phototransistor. A filter placed in front of the

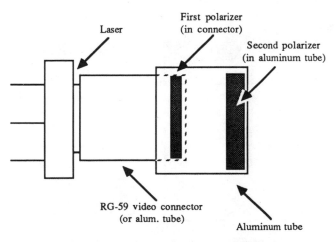

FIG. 13-12. *The output beam of the laser can be controlled by adding polarizing films to a connector and tube, as shown. The same method can be used on the receiver phototransistor.*

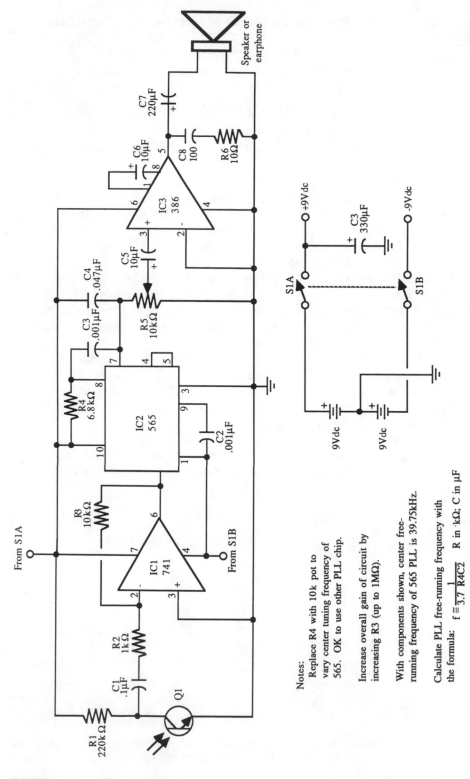

FIG. 13-13. *Circuit schematic for the 555-based PLL laser light PFM receiver. Although R4 is shown as a resistor, you might want to substitute it with a 10k precision potentiometer so that you can "dial in" the center frequency of the transmitter. Experiment with the value of C1 for best high-frequency response. Note that circuit is functionally identical to the laser light detector/receiver shown in FIG. 13-5 but with the addition of the 565.*

Notes:

Replace R4 with 10k pot to vary center tuning frequency of 565. OK to use other PLL chip.

Increase overall gain of circuit by increasing R3 (up to 1MΩ).

With components shown, center free-running frequency of 565 PLL is 39.75kHz.

Calculate PLL free-running frequency with the formula: $f \cong \dfrac{1}{3.7\ R4C2}$ R in 'kΩ; C in μF phototransistor can also increase sensitivity and reduce background noise. Infrared filters are available at most photographic stores; surplus is another good source. Many IR filters may appear dark red or purple or even completely black. You might not be able to see through the filter, but it is practically transparent to near-infrared radiation.

OTHER MODULATION AND DEMODULATION TECHNIQUES

Amplitude modulation is susceptible to interference from changing light levels. This can lead to noise and poor system response. The pulse frequency modulation technique used with the visible LED and diode laser system rejects noise and is not as sensitive to changes in the intensity of the source beam.

The universal laser light receiver can be used to capture the signal transmitted over an AM or PFM modulated beam. A better approach is the circuit shown in FIG. 13-13. It uses a LM565 phase-locked loop (PLL) adjusted so that its center frequency matches the center frequency of the transmitter—about 40 kHz.

An audio signal impressed upon the 555 in the transmitter changes the center frequency. This change is detected by the PLL as an error signal. The amount of error

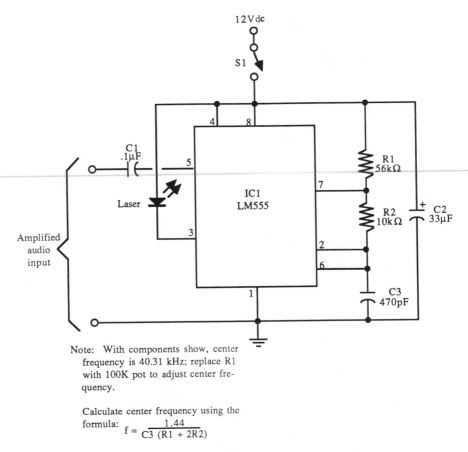

Note: With components show, center frequency is 40.31 kHz; replace R1 with 100K pot to adjust center frequency.

Calculate center frequency using the formula:
$$f = \frac{1.44}{C3\ (R1 + 2R2)}$$

FIG. 13-14. *Circuit diagram for the laser diode transmitter.*

signal is proportional to the frequency of the original audio signal. Therefore, tapping the error signal pin on the PLL chip and then amplifying it retrieves the audio that was transmitted over the beam.

The circuits for the transmitter and receiver appear in FIGS. 13-13 and 13-14 (see TABLES 13-7 and 13-8 for a list of required parts). The transmitter is virtually the same as the one presented earlier in the chapter but with no provision for adjusting the center frequency. The receiver uses the 565 PLL (other PLLs can be used) and a trim pot to adjust the circuit for the exact center frequency of the transmitter. You can connect the transmitter as discussed above, or amplify it and apply the signal to the laser diode.

With the circuits complete and set up, aim the laser at the phototransistor and provide an audio signal for transmission. Adjust the trim pot on the receiver until you hear the audio carried over the light beam. The components used in both receiver and transmitter can drift, so you might need to touch up the trim pot control to re-align the center frequency.

IC1	LM741 op amp IC
IC2	LM565 PLL IC
IC3	LM386 audio amplifier IC
R1	220 kilohm resistor
R2	1 kilohm resistor
R3	10 kilohm resistor
R4	6.8 kilohm resistor
R5	10 kilohm potentiometer
R6	10 ohm resistor
C1	0.1 μF disc capacitor
C2	0.001 μF silvered mica capacitor
C3	0.001 μF disc capacitor
C4	0.047 μFdisc capacitor
C5,C6	10 μF electrolytic capacitor
C7	220 μF electrolytic capacitor
C8	100 μF electrolytic capacitor
Q1	Infrared phototransistor
S1	DPDT switch

Table 13-7. Pulse Frequency Modulator Receiver Parts List

IC1	LM555 timer IC
R1	56 kilohm resistor
R2	10 kilohm resistor
C1	0.1 μF disc capacitor
C2	33 μF electrolytic capacitor
C3	470 pF silvered mica capacitor
S1	SPST switch
	Laser

Table 13-8. Pulse Frequency Modulator Transmitter Parts List

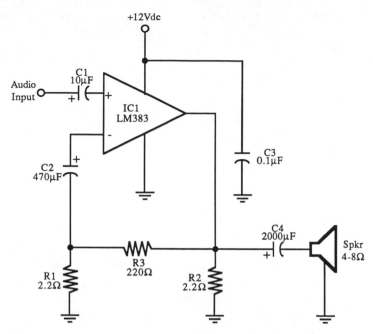

FIG. 13-15. *An 8-watt audio amplifier, designed around the LM383 integrated amp. The IC must be installed on a suitable heatsink.*

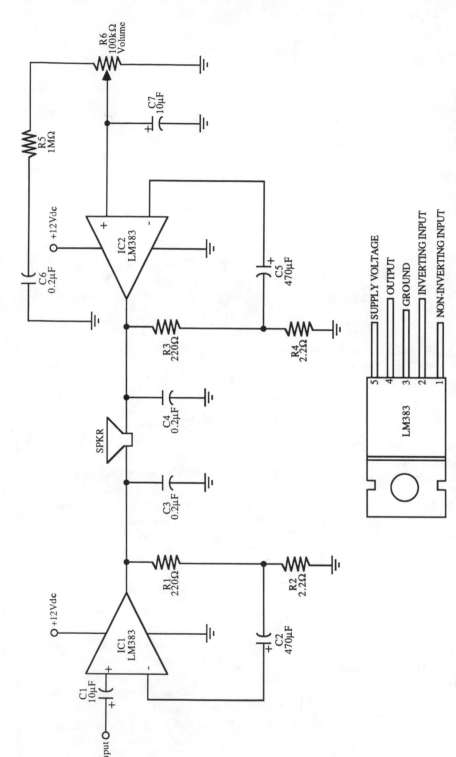

FIG. 13-16. *A 16-watt audio amplifier, designed around two LM383 integrated amps. The ICs must be installed on a suitable heatsink.*

AUDIO AMPLIFIER CIRCUITS

The universal receiver has a built-in LM386 integrated amp. The sound output is minimal, but the chip is easy to get, it's cheap, and it can be wired up quickly. It's perfect for experimenting with sound projects.

If you need more sound output or must amplify the audio input for the transformer or transistor modulator, try the circuit in FIG. 13-15 (parts list in TABLE 13-9). You can use it instead of the LM386 in the receiver or in addition to it. The circuit is designed around an LM383 8-watt amplifier IC. The IC comes mounted in a TO-220-style transistor package, and you should use it with a suitable heatsink. FIGURE 13-16 shows a higher output 16-watt version using two LM383's (parts list in TABLE 13-10). Note that the LM383 IC is functionally identical to the TDA2002 power audio amplifier.

14

Advanced Projects in Laser Communication

The last chapter presented a number of basic free-air laser light communications projects. You learned how to modulate a He-Ne laser beam using a transformer, transistor, and even a piece of Mylar foil stretched in a needlepoint hoop. You also learned various ways to electronically modulate laser diodes and recover the transmitted audio signal. This chapter presents advanced projects in free-air laser-beam communication. Covered are methods of remotely controlling devices and equipment via light and how to link two computers by a laser beam.

TONE CONTROL

Everyone is familiar with Touch-Tone dialing: pick up the phone and push the buttons. You hear a series of almost meaningless tones, but to the equipment in the telephone central office, those tones are decoded and used to dial the exact phone you want out of the millions in the world. You can use the same technique as a remote control for actuating any of a number of devices, such as motors, alarms, lights, doors, you name it. The tone signals are sent from transmitter to receiver via a laser light beam. With the right setup, you can remotely control devices up to several miles away, and without worry of interference or FCC regulations.

The Touch-Tone (or more simply "tone control") system supports up to 16 channels. Each channel is actuated by a pair of tones. Tone selection depends on the buttons pressed on the keypad. Dividing a common 16-key keypad into a matrix of 4 by 4, as illustrated in FIG. 14-1, shows how the tones are distributed. For example, pressing the number 5 key actuates the 770 Hz and 1336 Hz tones. Pressing the number 9 key actuates both the 852 Hz and 1477 Hz tones.

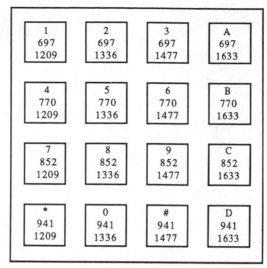

FIG. 14-1. *Keypad tones for tone dialing matrix.*

The dual tones help prevent accidental triggering, but they also present a somewhat difficult decoding dilemma. The first tone dialing circuits used tuned components that were expensive and difficult to maintain. As tone dialing caught on, custom-made ICs were developed that dispensed with the tuned circuits. Until recently, these ICs have been rather costly and required some sophisticated interface electronics. Now, Touch-Tone decoding ICs cost under $15 and operate with only two or three common components.

Most telephones use a matrix of 12 keys, not 16, so the last column of buttons isn't used. The circuits in the phone may or may not be able to reproduce the tones for the last column, but most off-the-shelf Touch-Tone dialing ICs are capable of the full 16-channel operation.

Making Your Own Controller

Dialing other phones is not the goal of this project, but using a phone dialer as a remote controller is. You have several alternatives for making the controller.

★ Salvage the innards of a discarded phone (must have tone dialing).
★ Use a portable, hand-held tone dialing adapter.
★ Build the controller from scratch using a keypad and dialing chip.

The last approach allows you full access to all 16 combinations of tones. The other two approaches limit you to the 12 keys on a standard telephone—digits 0 through 9 as well as the # and * symbols.

Salvaging the keypad and circuits from a phone requires some detective work on your part, unless you happen to receive a schematic (not likely), but the advantage is you get the entire controller as one module. The biggest disadvantage is that the dialing circuits may require odd operating voltages.

FIG. 14-2. *A battery-operated portable pocket tone dialer (shown with hookup leads attached).*

The portable tone-dialing adapter, such as the one in FIG. 14-2, is an easier approach, with the added benefit of an easy-to-carry (fits in your pocket) module that runs on battery power. The adapter is meant for use with rotary or pulse dial phones when you need to access services that respond to Touch Tones (long-distance services, computer ordering, etc.). You place the adapter against the mouthpiece of the phone and press the buttons.

FIGURE 14-3 shows how easy it is to modify the dialer for use as a tone source for the PFM laser diode modulator. Alternatively, you can connect the output of the dialer to an audio amp and process it through the transformer or transistor He-Ne laser modulator described in the previous chapter. The connections to the dialer's speaker can remain in place, thereby providing you with audible feedback that the controller is working and sending out tones.

1	Pocket Touch-Tone dialer	
1	⅛-inch miniature plug	
Misc.	Wire	

Table 14-1. Pocket Dialer Parts List

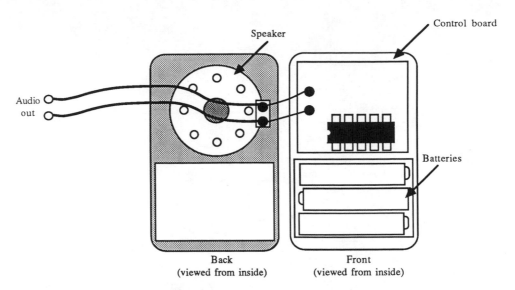

FIG. 14-3. *Wiring diagram for adding external hookup leads to the pocket dialer.*

The Tone Receiver

A number of electronics outlets, such as Radio Shack, sell an all-in-one tone receiver chip. This chip deciphers the dual tones and provides a binary weighted decoded output (8, 4, 2, 1). Add to the basic circuit a 4-of-16 demultiplexer, as shown in FIG. 14-4, and you can control up to 16 different devices. When used with a telephone keypad or dialing adapter, you can decode the first 12 digits. Use the universal laser light detector (presented in the last chapter) to capture the beam and amplify it for the receiver. See the parts list for the tone receiver in TABLE 14-2.

INFRARED PUSH BUTTON REMOTE CONTROL

The Motorola MC14457 and MC14458 chips form the heart of a useful remote control receiver-transmitter pair. The chips are available through Motorola distributors as well as several mail-order outlets and retail stores (including, at the time of this writing, Digikey and Circuit Specialists; see Appendix A for addresses). Price is under $15 for the pair.

Table 14-2. Tone Dialer Receiver Parts List

IC1	SSI202 tone decoder IC
IC2	74154 IC
RI	10 megohm resistor
R2-R5	1 kilohm resistor
LED1-4	Light-emitting diode
XTAL1	3.57 MHz (colorburst) crystal

All resistors are 5 to 10 percent tolerance, ¼ watt. All capacitors are 10 to 20 tolerance.

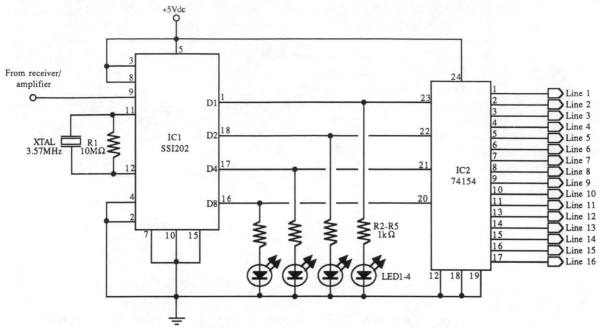

FIG. 14-4. *A schematic diagram for the SSI202 tone-decoding chip and how to decode the outputs with 74154 IC. The LEDs provide a visual indication of the binary output of the tone-decoding chip.*

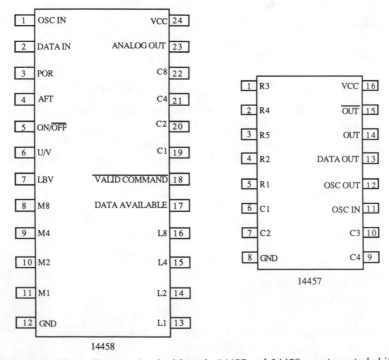

FIG. 14-5. *Pinout diagrams for the Motorola 14457 and 14458 remote control chips.*

The 14457 is the transmitter and can be used with up to 32 push-button switches (we'll be using 12). Pushing a switch commands the chip to send a binary serial code through the laser (preferably a diode laser). The 14458 chip receives the signal. Decoded output pins on the 14458 receiver chip can be connected directly to a controlled device, such as a relay or LED, a counter, or a computer port.

FIGURE 14-5 shows the pinout diagrams for the two chips. The 14457 comes in a small, 16-pin DIP package, and with all the other components added in, takes up a space of less than 2 inches square. The chip uses CMOS technology to conserve battery power, and when no key is pressed, the entire thing shuts down. Battery power is used only when a key is depressed.

Building the Transmitter

The basic hookup diagram for the 14457 transmitter circuit is shown in FIG. 14-6; the parts list is provided in TABLE 14-3. Note the oscillator and tank circuit connected to pins 11 and 12. The oscillator required by the 14457 (and a matching one for the 14458 receiver) is a hard-to-find ceramic resonator, not a standard crystal.

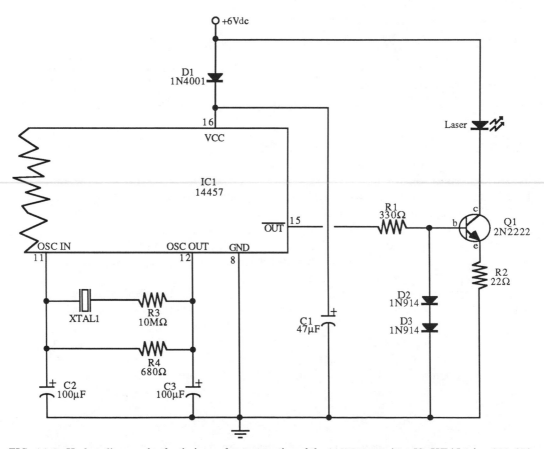

FIG. 14-6. *Hookup diagram for the timing and output portion of the 14457 transmitter IC. XTAL1 is a 300-650 kHz ceramic resonator, as discussed in the text.*

211

Table 14-3. Remote Control Transmitter Parts List

Transmitter

IC1	Motorola MC14457 remote control transmitter IC
R1	330 ohm resistor
R2	22 ohm resistor
R3	10 megohm resistor
R4	680 ohm resistor
C1	47 μF electrolytic capacitor
C2,C3	0.001 μF disc capacitor
Q1	2N2222 transistor
D1	IN4001 diode
D2,D3	IN914 diode
XTAL1	300 to 600 kHZ ceramic resonator
Misc.	Laser diode

Keypad

Q1-Q4	2N2222 transistor
Misc.	Matrix keypad or switches

All resistors are 5 to 10 percent tolerance, ¼ watt. All capacitors are 10 to 20 percent tolerance, rated 35 volts or more.

The ceramic resonator works just like a crystal but comes in frequencies under 1 Mhz. The exact value of the resonator isn't critical, I found, as long as it is within a range of about 300 to 650 kHz and the resonators for both chips are identical. I successfully used a 525 kHz resonator in the prototype circuit. A common ceramic resonator is 455 kHz, used as an intermediate frequency in many receivers. The inverted output of the 14457 ($\overline{\text{OUT}}$') is applied to the modulating input of the laser (see the previous chapter).

So much for the output stage of the transmitter; what about the input stage? FIGURE 14-7 shows how to connect a series of 12 push-button switches to the column and row inputs of the 14457. You can use separate switches, but a cheaper way is with a surplus telephone keypad.

Just about any wiring technique can be used to construct the 14457 transmitter, but because you'll probably want to make the unit handheld, stay away from wire-wrapping. The stems of wire-wrapping posts and sockets are too long and will fatten the controller considerably. Use a set of four "AA" batteries or a 9-volt transistor battery to power the transmitter. You might need additional batteries for the amplifier and modulator, depending on the type used. And, you must also provide power to the laser itself.

Building the Receiver

Short-haul communications links do not require amplification on the input stage of the receiver. But if you plan on using the receiver some distance from the transmitter

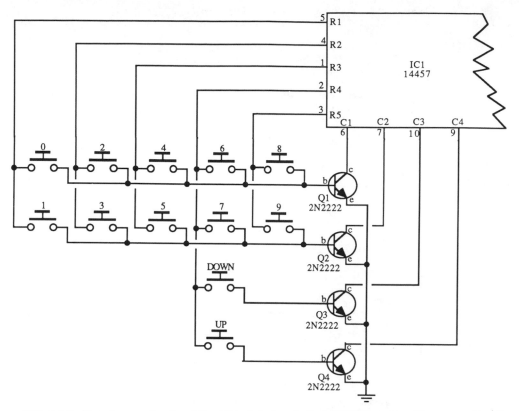

FIG. 14-7. *Keypad connection for adding 12 push buttons to the 14457 transmitter. You may easily add additional rows of buttons by connecting them to Q3 and Q4 in the manner shown for Q1 and Q2.*

(500 meters or more), an extra amplification stage is recommended. You may use the universal amplifier found in Chapter 13.

The basic wiring diagram for the 14458 receiver chip is shown in FIG. 14-8 (parts list in TABLE 14-4). Once again, the ceramic resonator is used as a timing reference for the IC. One inverter from a 4069 is used to provide an active element and driver for the oscillator circuit.

All that's required now is to connect the devices to be controlled to the output lines, shown in FIG. 14-9. Note the various sets of outputs and the $\overline{VC}$' function pin. The $\overline{VC}$' line goes HIGH when all but the number keys are pressed. The pin is used in some advanced decoding schemes as a function bit. The chart in TABLE 14-5 shows what happens when the 12 keys are pressed (the chip can accommodate another 20 push buttons; see the manufacturers data sheet for more information).

For most routine applications, you need only to connect the controlled device to pins 19 through 22 (labeled C1, C2, C4, and C8). These are binary weighted, and by connecting a 4028 one-of-ten decoder IC to the receiver, you can individually control up to 10 control devices or functions.

The receiver is wired to accept a single keypress on the transmitter as a complete command. The receiver can also be made to wait until *two* keys are pressed (this is used because in television and VCR applications, you are able to dial in multi-digit

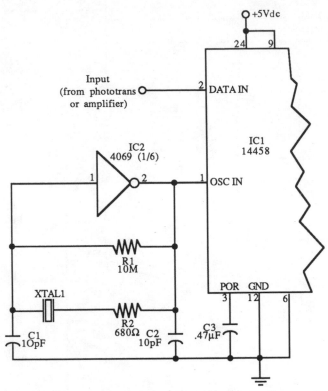

FIG. 14-8. *The timing portion of the 14458 receiver IC. XTAL must be the same value as the resonator used with the 14457 transmitter. Connect a phototransistor or amplifier to pin 2 of the chip (see Chapter 13 for details).*

Table 14-4. Remote Control Receiver Parts List

Receiver

IC1	Motorola MC14458 remote-control receiver IC
IC2	4069 CMOS hex inverter gate
R1	10 megohm resistor
C1,C2	10 pF disc capacitor
C3	0.47 µF disc capacitor
XTAL	300 to 600 kHz ceramic resonator

All resistors are 5 to 10 percent tolerance, ¼ watt. All capacitors are 10 to 20 percent tolerance, rated 35 volts or more.

Output Enhancements

IC2	4028 CMOS decoder IC
or	
IC2	4001 NOR gate IC
IC3	4029 CMOS counter IC

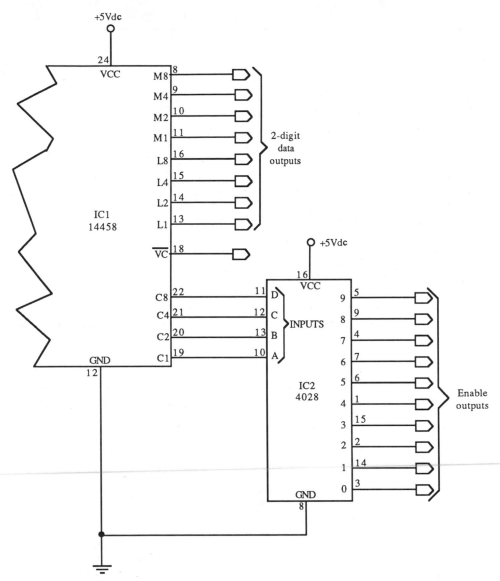

FIG. 14-9. *A 4028 CMOS IC can be used to decode the binary output of the 14458 transmitter chip.*

channels). The two-digit data outputs are used when the chip is this two-digit mode. To change from one- to two-digit mode, disconnect the power leads to pins 9 and 6.

FIGURE 14-10 shows how you can use the UP and DOWN functions with a counter to provide variable step control. Note the DOWN ENABLE and UP ENABLE lines. When pressing the UP or DOWN buttons on the transmitter, the UP and DOWN codes are sent continually rather than just one per push, as with the other buttons.

The enable outputs from the 4028 can only handle 10 functions, so the UP and DOWN functions are integrated with the number functions. That is, when the DOWN button is pressed, the output at the 4028 chip is the same as if you pressed the number 6 button

Table 14-5. Key Decoding

Key	Row	Column	FB	C8	C4	C2	C1	$\overline{VC}$ Pulse
0	1	1	0	0	0	0	0	
1	1	2	0	0	0	0	1	
2	2	1	0	0	0	1	0	
3	2	2	0	0	0	1	1	
4	3	1	0	0	1	0	0	
5	3	2	0	0	1	0	1	
6	4	1	0	0	1	1	0	
7	4	2	0	0	1	1	1	
8	5	1	0	1	0	0	0	
9	5	2	0	1	0	0	1	
Toggle1	1	3	1	0	0	0	0	X
Toggle2	1	4	1	0	0	0	1	X
CONT1	2	3	1	0	0	1	0	X
CONT2	2	4	1	0	0	1	1	X
CONT3	3	3	1	0	1	0	0	X
CONT4	3	4	1	0	1	0	1	X
DOWN	4	3	1	0	1	1	0	X
UP	4	4	1	0	1	1	1	X
MUTE	5	3	1	1	0	0	0	X
OFF	5	4	1	1	0	0	1	X

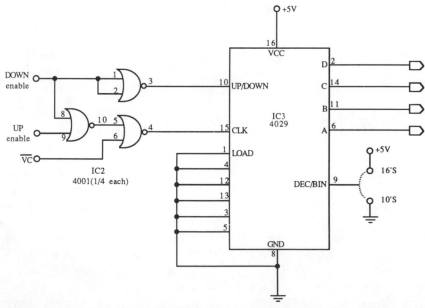

FIG. 14-10. *Decoding for the UP and DOWN functions. The BCD output of the 4029 can be interfaced to a display or computer. The 4029 chip can be made to count by 16s or 10s by connecting pin 9 to ground or V+ as shown.*

(binary code 0110). However, the $\overline{VC}$ pin is toggled HIGH, which can be used in further decoding. Similarly, when the UP button is pressed, the output of the 4028 chip is the same as if you pressed the number 7 button (binary code 0111).

To enable you to count the number of UP and DOWN pulses, connect the UP ENABLE input of the circuit shown in the figure to the number 7 output of the 4028 and the DOWN ENABLE input to the number 6 output. The $\overline{VC}$ pin acts to gate the circuit so that the counter doesn't count when numbers 7 and 6 are pressed.

DATA TRANSMISSION

The UART (Universal Asynchronous Receive/Transmit) chip converts parallel to serial and serial to parallel. It's much more involved than a shift register that simply converts parallel data to pure serial form, or vice versa.

The UART allows you to send data to devices like printers, plotters, and modems and yet be assured that all the information you are sending is getting there intact. Built into the chip are provisions for sending and receiving at the same time, for adding parity

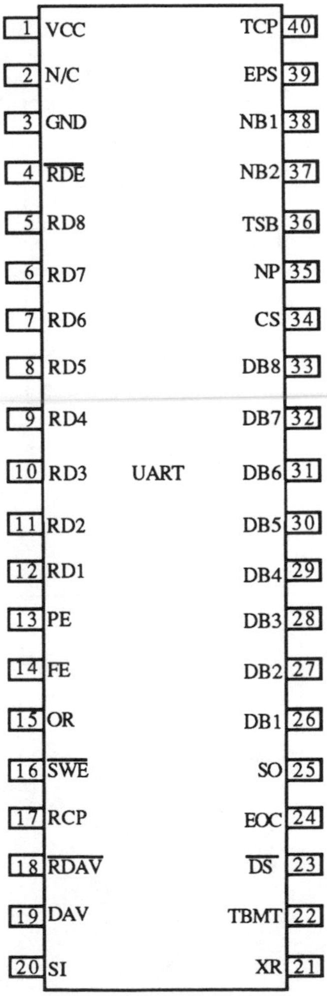

FIG. 14-11. *Pinout diagram for the AY3-1015 (or equivalent) UART chip.*

	UART	
1 VCC		TCP 40
2 N/C		EPS 39
3 GND		NB1 38
4 RDE		NB2 37
5 RD8		TSB 36
6 RD7		NP 35
7 RD6		CS 34
8 RD5		DB8 33
9 RD4		DB7 32
10 RD3		DB6 31
11 RD2		DB5 30
12 RD1		DB4 29
13 PE		DB3 28
14 FE		DB2 27
15 OR		DB1 26
16 SWE		SO 25
17 RCP		EOC 24
18 RDAV		$\overline{DS}$ 23
19 DAV		TBMT 22
20 SI		XR 21

217

bits and stop bits to the serial data train, and more. A pinout diagram for the IC is shown in FIG. 14-11. Note that a number of other UARTs will work as well and that these chips might even have the same pinouts. The functions of the pins are listed in any UART spec sheet.

For all their sophistication, however, UART chips are surprisingly inexpensive—under $5 or $6. They require accurate timing, however, which means the addition of a crystal and a baud-rate generator (the generator can be replaced by other circuits, but in the long run, the generator is a better choice). With all the components added, a UART system costs about $15.

You can arrange the UARTs in a number of ways. For example, a computer such as the IBM PC has its own UART built into it. You can connect it to a laser modulator and send serial data through the light beam. You can either receive the data and process it through the serial port on the remote computer, or convert it to parallel form with a receiver UART.

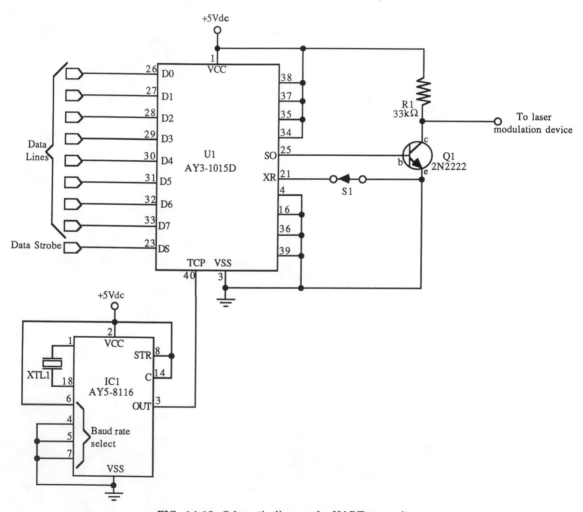

FIG. 14-12. *Schematic diagram for UART transmitter.*

Table 14-6. Transmitter UART Parts List

IC1	AY3-1015D UART IC
IC2	AY5-8116 baud-rate generator
R1	33 kilohm resistor
Q1	2N2222 transistor
S1	SPST switch (momentary, normally closed)
XTL1	3.57 MHz (colorburst) crystal

All resistors are 5 to 10 percent tolerance, ¼ watt.

The Commodore 64 computer lacks a UART device and is ideal for the UART link used in this project. The link connects to the Commodore by way of the computer's User Port. The User Port is a bidirectional parallel port, though this project uses it as an output device only—the UART connected to the Commodore 64 is a transmit-only device. You can convert to transceiver operation by rewiring it.

The circuit in FIG. 14-12 shows how to connect the transmitter UART to the User Port of the "host" Commodore 64. The circuit, with a parts list provided in TABLE 14-6, is shown connected to the laser diode PFM modulator (introduced in the last chapter). Alternatively, you can connect the transmitter UART to an audio amplifier and transformer or transistor modulator to operate a helium-neon laser tube. The receiver UART (with amplifier), shown in FIG. 14-13, can be used as a stand-alone remote-control device. Or, it can be connected to another computer, such as a Commodore 64, for the purpose of receiving signals from the host machine. See TABLE 14-7 for a list of parts for the receiver UART.

The output of the receiver UART is an 8-bit binary code. This code can be used to remotely control up to 256 functions. One way to operate up to 16 devices, such as solenoids, alarms, or motors, is shown in FIG. 14-14. The UART is connected to a 4028 1-of-10 decoder. The first 10 digits (00000000 through 00001010) are decoded and applied to relays or opto-isolators where they can be used to drive any of a number of output devices.

How The UART Works

In the schematic in FIG. 14-12, 8-bit parallel data from the Commodore 64 (or other computer) is routed to the data lines on the UART. When the computer is ready to send the byte, it pulses the STROBE line high (the line might be called DATA READY or something similar). The UART converts the data to serial format and sends it through the serial output (SO) pin. The speed of the data leaving the output is determined by the baud-rate generator. The COM8116 dual baud-rate generator sets the speed of the transmission and reception, and it is hooked up here to be rather slow—about 300 baud. This means that the UART sends serial data at the rate of roughly 300 bits per second (equivalent to 30 bytes per second).

The receiving UART is connected almost in reverse to the transmitting UART. The receiver uses a baud-rate generator that is operating at the same frequency as the

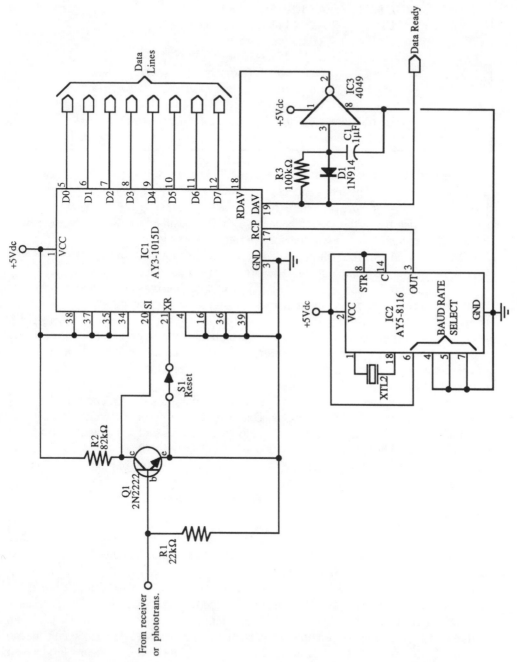

FIG. 14-13. Schematic diagram for UART receiver.

Table 14-7. Receiver UART Parts List

IC1	AY3-1015D UART IC
IC2	AY5-8116 baud-rate generator
IC3	4049 CMOS hex inverter IC
R1	22 kilohm resistor
R2	82 kilohm resistor
R3	100 kilohm resistor
C1	1 μF tantalum capacitor
Q1	2N2222 transistor
D1	1N914 diode
S1	SPST switch (momentary, normally closed)
XTL1	3.57 MHz (colorburst) crystal

All resistors are 5 to 10 percent tolerance, ¼ watt. All capacitors are 10 to 20 percent tolerance, rated 35 volts or more.

transmitter. The receiver is equipped with an IR photodetector. If you could see infrared light, you'd see the LED flash on and off very rapidly as the data passed. The ON and OFF periods are equal to 0's and 1's, or "spaces" and "marks" as they are called in serial communications.

The amplified output is applied to the serial data pin on the UART. When an entire word is received, the UART places it on the parallel data output pins and pulses the

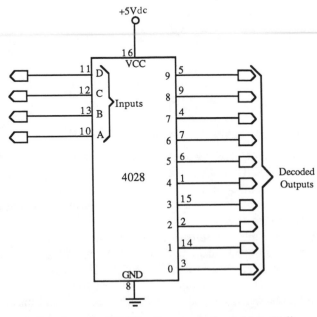

FIG. 14-14. *Four lines from the UART receiver can be decoded into 10 lines using a 4028 IC.*

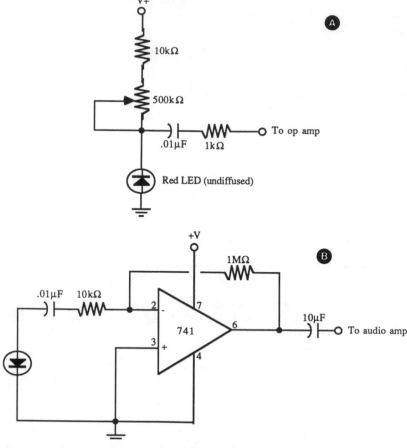

FIG. 14-15. *Ways to connect an undiffused red LED to an op amp. (A) Adjustable sensitivity; (B) Preset sensitivity.*

DATA AVAILABLE pin. In this circuit, a short time delay is used to automatically reset the UART so it processes the next word.

ALTERNATE HE-NE LASER PHOTOSENSOR

Conventional photodiodes are engineered to be most sensitive to light wavelengths in the near-infrared region. That automatically reduces their effectiveness in receiving a modulated signal over the red beam of a helium-neon laser. This loss in sensitivity is not a major concern in most laser communications links, but it can present problems if the laser-to-receiver distance is very long.

More importantly, an infrared-sensitive phototransistor or photodiode is suscepti-ble to swamping by the infrared radiation of the sun. Even with red filters, it's difficult to "tune out" the sun while receiving the modulated signal over the laser beam. A better approach is to use a red light-emitting diode. Though not specifically designed to detect light, an LED can be easily adapted for the purpose. Inventor and magazine columnist

222

Forrest Mims III has written extensively on this topic; check out back issues of *Popular Electronics* and *Modern Electronics* for details.

Sensitivity in the red region of the visible spectrum is accentuated, because the LED is designed to emit red light. You obtain best results when using clear, non-diffused red LEDs. Sample hookup diagrams appear in FIG. 14-15. In my tests, the white light and infrared content of a nearby desk lamp changed the output of the circuit by a few tenths of a volt. But shining a red He-Ne laser at the LED caused the output to swing to about a volt or two of the supply voltage.

15

Lasers and Fiberoptics

Most everyone has encountered fiberoptics at one time or another. Many telephone calls—both local and long distance— are now carried at least partway by light shuttling through a strand of plastic or glass. Fiberoptics are now used on some of the higher end audio systems as a means to prevent digital signals from interfering with analog signals. And fiberoptic sculptures, in vogue in the late 1960s but coming back in style today, look like high-tech flowers that seem to burst out in brightly colored lights.

An optical fiber is to light what PVC pipe is to water. Though the fiber is a solid, it channels light from one end to the other. Even if the fiber is bent, the light will follow the path in whatever course it takes. Because light acts as the information carrier, a strand of optical fiber no bigger than a human hair can carry the same information as about 900 copper wires. This is one reason why fiberoptics is used increasingly in telephone communications.

Laser light exhibits unique behavior when transmitted through optical fiber. This chapter discusses how to work with optical fibers, ways to interface fibers to a laser, and many interesting applications of laser/fiberoptic links.

HOW FIBEROPTICS WORK

The idea of optical fibers is over 100 years old. British physicist John Tyndall once demonstrated how a bright beam of light was internally reflected through a stream of water flowing out of a tank. Serious research into light transmission through solid material started in 1934 when Bell Labs was issued a patent for the *light pipe*.

224

In the 1950's, the American Optical Corporation developed glass fibers that transmitted light over short distances (a few yards). The technology of fiberoptics really took off in about 1970 when scientists at Corning Class Works developed long-distance optical fibers.

All optical fibers are composed of two basic materials, as illustrated in FIG. 15-1: the core and the cladding. The *core* is a dense glass or plastic material where the light actually passes through as it travels the length of the fiber. The *cladding* is a less dense sheath, also of plastic or glass, that serves as a refracting medium. An optical fiber may or may not have an outer *jacket*, a plastic or rubber insulation for protection.

Optical fibers transmit light by *total internal reflection (TIR)*. Imagine a ray of light entering the end of an optical fiber strand. If the fiber is perfectly straight, the light will pass through the medium just as it passes through a plate of glass. But if the fiber is bent slightly, the light will eventually strike the outside edge of the fiber.

If the angle of incidence is great (greater than the critical angle), the light will be reflected internally and will continue its path through the fiber. But if the bend is large and the angle of incidence is small (less than the critical angle), the light will pass through the fiber and be lost. The basic operation of fiberoptics is shown in FIG. 15-2.

Note the *cone of acceptance*; the cone represents the degree to which the incoming light can be off-axis and still make it through the fiber. The angle of acceptance (usually 30 degrees) of an optical fiber determines how far the light source can be from the optical axis and still manage to make it into the fiber. Though the angle of acceptance might seem generous, fiberoptics perform best when the light source (and detector) are aligned to the optical axis.

Optical fibers are made by pulling a strand of glass or plastic through a small orifice. The process is repeated until the strand is just a few hundred (or less) micrometers in diameter. Although single strands are sometimes used in special applications, most optical fibers consist of many strands bundled and fused together. There might be hundreds or even thousands of strands in one fused optical fiber bundle. Separate fused bundles can also be clustered to produce fibers that measure ¹⁄₁₆ of an inch or more in diameter.

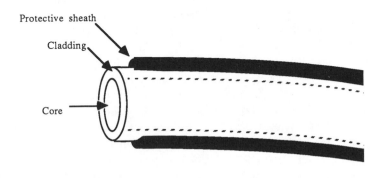

FIG. 15-1. *Design of the typical optical fiber.*

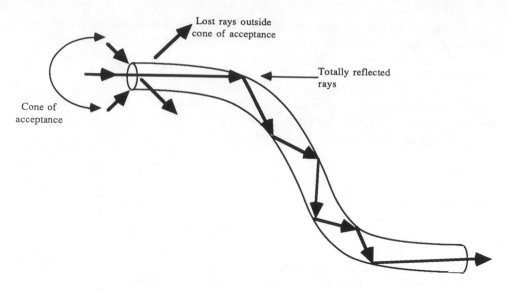

FIG. 15-2. *Operation of an optical fiber, with cone of acceptance.*

TYPES OF OPTICAL FIBERS

The classic optical fiber is made of *glass*, also called *silica*. Glass fibers tend to be expensive and are more brittle than stranded copper wire. But they are excellent conductors of light, especially light in the infrared region between 850 and 1300 nm. Less expensive optical fibers are made of *plastic*. Though light loss through plastic fibers is greater than with glass fibers, they are more durable. Plastic fibers are best used in communications experiments with near-infrared light sources—in the 780 to 950 nm range. This nicely corresponds to the output wavelength and sensitivity of commonplace infrared emitters and detectors.

Optical fiber bundles can be coherent or incoherent. The terms don't directly relate to laser light or its properties but to the arrangement of the individual strands in the bundle. If the strands are arranged so that the fibers can transmit a pictorial image from one end to the other, it is said to be coherent. The vast majority of optical fibers are incoherent, where an image or special pattern of light is lost when it reaches the other end of the fiber.

The cladding used in optical fibers can be one of two types—step-index and graded-index. *Step-index* fibers provide a discrete boundary between more dense and less dense regions between core and cladding. They are the easiest to manufacture, but their design causes a loss of coherency when laser light passes through the fiber. That means coherent light in, largely incoherent light out. The loss of coherency, which is due to light rays traveling on slightly different paths through the fiber, reduces the efficiency of the laser beam. Still, it offers some practical benefits, as you'll see later in this chapter.

There is no discrete refractive boundary in *graded-index* fibers. The core and cladding media slowly blend, like an exotic tropical drink. The grading acts to refract light evenly, at any angle of incidence. This preserves coherency and improves the efficiency of the fiber. As you might have guessed, graded-index optical fibers are the most expensive of the bunch. Unless you have a specific project in mind (like a 10-mile fiber link), graded-index fibers are not needed, even when experimenting with lasers.

WORKING WITH FIBEROPTICS

Where do you buy optical fibers? While you could go directly to the source, such as Dow Corning, American Optical, or Dolan-Jenner, a cheaper and easier way is through electronic and surplus mail order. Radio Shack sells a 5-meter length of jacketed plastic fiber; Edmund Scientific offers a number of different types and diameters of optical fibers. You can buy most any length you need, from a sampler containing a few feet of several types to a spool containing thousands of feet of one continuous fiber.

A number of surplus outfits, such as Jerryco and C&H Sales, offer optical fibers from time to time (stocks change, so write for the latest catalog before ordering). You might not have much choice over the type of fiber you buy, but the cost will be more than reasonable.

Although it's possible to use an optical fiber by itself, serious experimentation requires the use of fiber couplings and connectors. These are mechanical splices used to connect two fibers together or to link a fiber to a light emitter or detector. Be aware that good fiberoptic connectors are expensive. Look for the inexpensive plastic types meant for non-military applications. You can also make your own home-built couplings. Details follow later in this chapter.

Optical fibers can be cut with wire cutters, nippers, or even a knife. But care must be exercised to avoid injury from shards of glass that can fly out when the fiber is cut (plastic fibers don't shatter when cut). Wear heavy cotton gloves and eye protection when working with optical fibers. Avoid working with fibers around any kind of food serving or preparation areas, because tiny bits of glass can inadvertently and invisibly settle on food, plates, etc.

One good way to cut glass fiber is to gently nick it with a sharp knife or razor, then snap it in two. Position your thumb and index finger of both hands as close to the nick as possible, then break the fiber with a swift downward motion (snapping upwards increases the chance of glass shards flying off toward you).

Whether snapped apart or cut, the end of the fiber should be prepared before splicing it to another fiber or connecting it to a light emitter or detector. The ends of the cut fiber can be polished using extra fine grit aluminum oxide wet/dry sandpaper (330 grit or higher). Wet the sandpaper and gently grind the end of the fiber on it. You can obtain good results by laying the sandpaper flat on a table and holding the fiber in your hands. Rub in a circular motion and take care to keep the fiber perpendicular to the surface of the sandpaper. If the fiber is small, mount it in a pin vise.

Inspect the end of the fiber with a high-powered magnifying glass (a record player stylus magnifier works well). Shine a light through the opposite end of the fiber. The magnified end of the fiber should be bright and round. Recut the fiber if the ends look crescent shaped or have nicks in them.

FIBEROPTIC CONNECTORS

Commercially made fiberoptic connectors are pricy, even the plastic AMP Optimate Dry Non-Polish (DNP) variety. A number of mail-order firms such as Digi-Key and Jameco

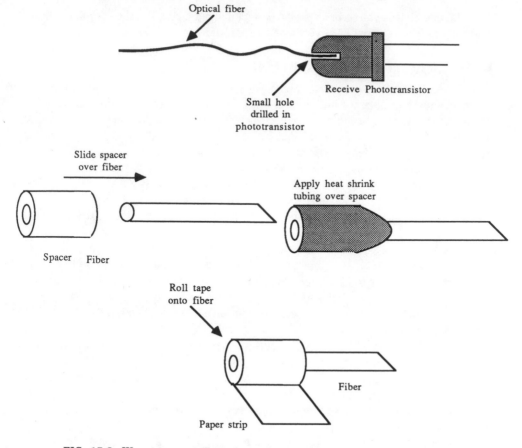

Optical fiber

Receive Phototransistor

Small hole
drilled in
phototransistor

Slide spacer
over fiber

Apply heat shrink
tubing over spacer

Spacer   Fiber

Roll tape
onto fiber

Fiber

Paper strip

FIG. 15-3. *Ways to connect fiberoptics to phototransistors, LEDs, and laser diodes.*

offer splices, for joining two fibers, and connectors, for attaching the fiber to emitters and detectors. Depending on the manufacturer and model, the connectors are made to work with either the round- or flat-style phototransistors and emitters.

You can make your own connectors and splices for home-brew laser experiments. FIGURE 15-3 shows several approaches. An easy way to splice fibers is to use small heat-shrink tubing. Cut a piece of the tubing to about ½ inch. After properly cutting (and polishing) the ends of the fiber, insert them into the tubing and heat lightly to shrink. Best results are obtained when the tubing is thick-walled.

Optical fibers can be directly connected to photodiodes by drilling a hole in the casing, inserting the fiber, and bonding the assembly with epoxy. Be sure that you don't drill into the semiconductor chip itself. Keep the drill motor at a fairly slow speed to avoid melting the plastic casing. Work slowly.

A strand of optical fiber can be held in place using a pin vise (remove the outer jacket, if any, and tighten the chuck around the fiber) or by using solderless insulated spade tongues. These tongues are designed for terminating copper wire but can be successfully used to anchor almost any size of optical fiber to a bulkhead. The laser, be it He-Ne or semiconductor, can then be aimed directly into the cone of acceptance of the fiber.

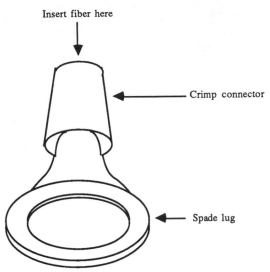

Insert fiber here

Crimp connector

Spade lug

FIG. 15-4. *A solderless crimp lug can be used to secure the end of an optical fiber to a circuit board or bulkhead.*

Spade tongues, as shown in FIG. 15-4, are available in a variety of sizes to accommodate different wire gauges. Use #6 (22 to 18 gauge) for small optical fibers and #8 (16 to 14 gauge) for larger fibers. Secure the fiber in the spade tongue by crimping with a crimp tool. Do not exert too much pressure or you will deform the fiber. If the fiber is loose after crimping, dab on a little epoxy to keep everything in place.

The "FLCS" package, shown in FIG. 15-5, is a low-cost fiberoptic connector available from a variety of sources including Radio Shack, Circuit Specialists, and many Motorola

FIG. 15-5. *The popular plastic "FLCS" optical fiber connector.*

semiconductor representatives. It can be easily adapted for use with laser diodes by cutting off the back portion. This exposes the optical fiber.

After removing the emitter diode, file or grind off the back end of the connector, as shown in FIG. 15-6. You can also drill out the back of the connector with a ⁵⁄₃₂-inch bit. Mount the connector and laser on a circuit board or perf board, and be careful to align the laser so that its beam directly enters the end of the fiber.

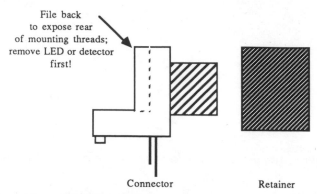

FIG. 15-6. *How to modify an "FLCS" connector to open the back portion. With the back open, you can shine a laser beam inside the connector and into the optical fiber.*

BUILD A LASER DATA LINK

A number of educational fiberoptic kits are available (see Appendix A for sources) and at reasonable cost. For example, the Edu-Link (available through Advanced Fiberoptics Corp., Circuit Specialists, Edmund, and others) contains pre-etched and drilled PCBs for a small transmitter and receiver along with a short length of jacketed plastic or glass fiber. The emitter LED and photodetector are housed in plastic connectors, and the circuits provide input and output pins for sending and receiving digital data.

You can use the Edu-Link or the circuits shown in FIGS. 15-7 and 15-8 to build your own fiberoptic transmitter and receiver. Parts lists for the two circuits are provided in TABLES 15-1 and 15-2. Note that the Edu-Link, as well as other fiberoptic data communications kits, use a resistor to limit current to the emitter LED. The value of the resistor is typically 100 to 220 ohms. At 100 ohms and a 5 Vdc supply, current to the emitter LED is 35 milliamps (assuming a 1.5-volt drop through the LED). That isn't enough to operate a dual-heterostructure laser diode, so the resistor must be exchanged for a lower value. A 56 ohm resistor will provide about 62 mA current to the laser diode; a 47-ohm resistor will deliver about 74 mA current. A feedback mechanism for controlling the output of the laser diode is not strictly required because the device is used in pulsed mode.

If you are using the Edu-Link system and have not yet assembled the boards, construct the transmitter and receiver circuits, but don't mount the emitter LED. Connect a Sharp LT020, LT022, or equivalent low-power dh laser diode to the transmitter circuit. Dismantle the emitter and modify the connector for use with the laser diode as detailed in the previous section.

230

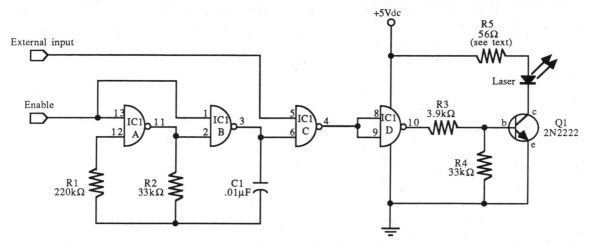

FIG. 15-7. *Schematic for experimenter's data transmitter using optical fibers and a laser diode. Transmission frequency of the free-running oscillator is approximately 3 kHz.*

The transmitter circuit of FIG. 15-7 includes a built-in oscillator. Trigger it by placing the ENABLE and DATA IN lines HIGH. Next, connect a logic probe to the DATA OUT pin of the receiver. Apply power to the two circuits and watch for the pulses at the DATA OUT pin. If pulses are not present, double-check your work and make sure that the fiberoptic connection between the transmitter and receiver is aligned and secure and that the output laser diode is properly aligned to the fiber. Remove power and disconnect the logic probe.

In normal operation, place the ENABLE pin LOW and connect any serial data to the DATA IN pin. Be sure the incoming signal is TTL compatible or does not exceed the supply voltage of the transmitter. You can use the circuit to transmit and receive ASCII computer

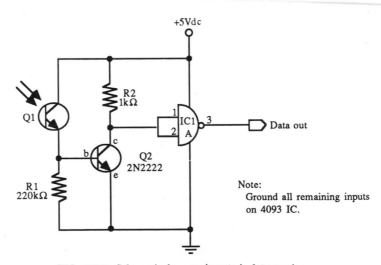

FIG. 15-8. *Schematic for experimenter's data receiver.*

Table 15-1. Optical Fiber Transmitter Parts List

IC1	4093 CMOS NAND gate IC
R1	220 kilohm resistor
R2	33 kilohm resistor
R3	3.9 kilohm resistor
R4	33 kilohm resistor
R5	56 ohm (nominal) resistor
C1	0.01 μF disc capacitor
	Laser diode
Q1	2N2222 transistor

All resistors are 5 to 10 percent tolerance, ¼ watt. All capacitors are 10 to 20 percent tolerance, rated 35 volts or more.

data, remote-control codes, or other binary information. A number of circuits in Chapter 14, "Advanced Projects in Laser Communication," show how to transmit computer data by laser over the air.

A number of these projects can easily be adapted for use with the fiberoptic transmitter and receiver. For example, you can connect the output pin of the Motorola 14557 remote control transmitter chip to the DATA IN pin of the Edu-kit transmitter circuit. The matching Motorola 14558 receiver chip connects to the DATA OUT terminal on the Edu-kit receiver circuit.

The CMOS chips in the transmitter and receiver can be operated with supplies up to 18 volts, but care must be taken to adjust the value of R5, the resistor that limits current to the laser diode. An increase in supply current must be matched with an increase in resistance or the laser diode could be damaged.

Use Ohm's law to compute the required value ($R = E/I$). Assume a 1.2- to 1.5-volt drop through the diode.

Example:
Supply voltage—12 volts.
Voltage drop through laser diode—1.5 volts.
Working voltage—10.5 volts (12 – 1.5).
Desired current (60 to 80 mA)—70 mA nominal..
Resistor to use—150 ohms (10.5 / 0.070 = 150).

Table 15-2. Optical Fiber Receiver Parts List

IC1	4093 CMOS NAND gate IC
R1	220 kilohm resistor
R2	1 kilohm resistor
Q1	Infrared phototransistor
Q2	2N2222 transistor

All resistors are 5 to 10 percent tolerance, ¼ watt.

MORE EXPERIMENTS WITH LASERS AND FIBEROPTICS

Besides data transmission, fiberoptics can be used to:

★ Transmit analog data (modulate a diode or He-Ne laser and pass it through the fiber).

★ Detect vibration and motion.

★ Route laser light to remote locations.

★ Separate a laser beam into several shafts of light.

This is only a partial listing; there are literally dozens of useful and practical applications for lasers and fiberoptics. Some hands-on projects follow.

Vibration and Movement Detection

A fiberoptic strand doesn't make the best medium for transmitting laser-light analog data. Why? The fiber itself can contribute to noise. As mentioned earlier, when a beam of coherent laser light is passed through a conventional step-index optical fiber, the rays travel different paths, and the light that exits is largely incoherent. You can see the effects of this interference by shining a helium-neon laser through an optical fiber. Point the exit beam at a white piece of paper and you'll see a great deal of speckle. The speckle is the constructive and destructive interference, created inside the fiber, as the laser light rays travel from one end to the other.

This interference—which is most prominent in low-cost plastic optical fibers—is normally an undesirable side effect. However, it can be put to good use as a vibration and motion detection system. Connecting a phototransistor to the exit-end of the fiber lets you monitor the light output. Movement of the fiber causes a change in the way the light is reflected inside, and this changes the coherency (or incoherency, depending on how you look at it) of the beam. A simple audio amplifier connected to the phototransistor allows you to hear the movement.

FIGURE 15-9 shows a setup you can use to test the effects of fiberoptic vibration and motion. A parts list for the system is provided in TABLE 15-3. More advanced projects using this technique are in Chapter 16, "Experiments in Laser Seismology." The noise is sometimes a hiss and sometimes a "thrum." Depending on the length of the fiber and type of motion, you might also hear low- or high-pitched squeals. These squeals can change pitch as the fiber or phototransistor is slowly moved.

The squeals are caused by the Doppler effect of *optical heterodyning*, a process whereby two rays of light at slightly different frequencies meet. The two basic (or fundamental) frequencies mix together, creating two additional frequencies. One is the sum of the two fundamental frequencies and the other is the difference.

How are the different frequencies of light created in the first place? Remember that the speed of light slows down as it passes through a refractive medium. There is a strict relationship between the wavelength, speed, and frequency of light. Because the wavelength of light can't be altered (at least by ordinary refraction), that means the frequency must be shifted in direct proportion to the change in the speed of light.

The change in frequency caused by refraction is rather small (on the order of a few hundred hertz) and is dependent on the original light frequency and the refractive index

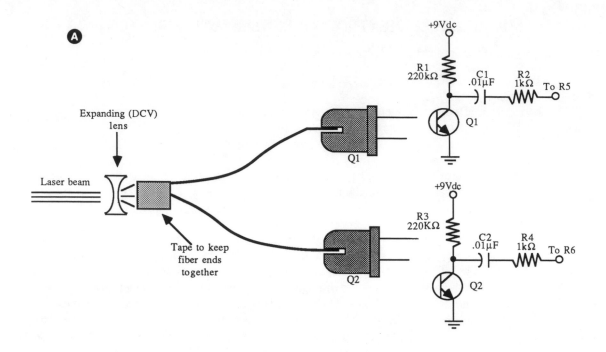

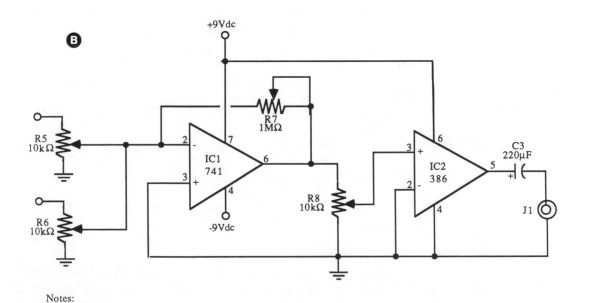

Notes:
Vary R5 and R6 to adjust
sound levels from Q1 and
Q2.

FIG. 15-9. *Hookup diagram for connecting a pair of phototransistors to op amp and audio amplifier. (A) Physical connection (showing beam expansion into both fibers) and phototransistor hookup; (B) Op amp and audio amplifier.*

Table 15-3. Vibration Detection System Parts List

IC1	LM741 operationsl amplifier IC
IC2	LM386 audio amplifier IC
R1,R3	220 kilohm resistor
R2,R4	1 kilohm resistor
R5,R6,R8	10 kilohm potentiometer
R7	1 megohm potentiometer
C1,C2	0.01 μF disc capacitor
C3	220 μF electrolytic capacitor
Q1,Q2	Infrared phototransistors
J1	Audio output jack (¼- or ⅛-inch)
Misc.	DCV expansion lens (approx. 6 to 10 mm diameter)

All resistors are 5 to 10 percent tolerance, ¼ watt. All capacitors are 10 to 20 percent tolerance, rated 35 volts or more.

of the medium. The sum frequency is extremely high and can't be heard, but the difference frequency might only be 200 to 500 Hz and can be readily detected with an ordinary phototransistor and audio amplifier.

Optical heterodyning is most conspicuous when only two coherent rays of light meet. In an optical fiber, dozens and even hundreds of rays of internally reflected laser light might meet at the phototransistor, and the result can sound more like cacophonous noise than a distinct tone. A Michelson interferometer (see Chapter 9) reveals optical heterodyning much more readily.

You might also notice a varying tone when sampling the beam directly from the laser. Even though lasers are highly monochromatic, they can still emit several frequencies of light, with each frequency spaced only fractions of a nanometer apart. As these frequencies meet on the surface of the photodetector, they cause heterodyning or beat frequencies. When the difference frequency is 20 kHz or less, you can hear them. You can precisely measure the difference frequencies using an oscilloscope. The tones heard when sampling the beam directly from a laser are most prominent with short tubes and when they are first turned on.

Separating Beam With Optical Bundles

By grouping together one end of two or more fused bundles, you can separate the beam of a laser into many individual sub-beams. The laser light enters the common end (where all the bundles are tied together), and exits the opposite end of each individual fiber. Some optical fibers come pre-made with four or more grouped strands (used most often in automotive dashboard application) or you can make your own.

The pencil-thin beam of the typical He-Ne laser is too narrow to enter all the fibers at once, so the beam must be expanded. Place a bi-concave or plano-concave lens in front of the entrance to the bundles. Adjust the distance between the lens to the bundle until the beam is spread enough to enter all the fibers.

Split bundles can be used to experiment with optical heterodyning as well as to split the beam of one laser into several components. Each beam can be used in a separate optical fiber system. For example, you must use a four-fiber split bundle to provide illumination for four-fiberoptic intrusion detection systems. Each sub-system is placed in a quadrant around the protected area and has its own phototransistor, making it easier to locate the area of disturbance.

Interfacing Fiberoptics to a Computer

Many of the advanced applications of lasers and fiberoptics require interface to a computer. In Chapter 16, "Experiments in Laser Seismology," you'll learn how to connect a phototransistor to a computer via an analog-to-digital converter.

16

Experiments in Laser Seismology

At first you hear it. It sounds like the low rumbling of a woofer speaker, yet the sounds are coming from nowhere and everywhere. Then the windows join the strange session of music-making and begin to rattle, followed by the eerie creaks of the wooden beams in the house.

Then you feel it, a swaying and pumping motion like a carnival ride gone haywire. Within a few seconds, you realize it's not a large truck passing outside or the heavy thump of a jet breaking the sound barrier, but an earthquake.

Earthquakes are among the most frightening natural phenomenon, feared most because of their stealthy suddenness. Even though geologists and seismologists have been measuring earthquakes for decades with sophisticated instruments on land, in the air, and even in space, predicting tremors is an inexact science. The best seismologists can do is warn that a "big earthquake is due soon"—expect it anytime between now and the next century.

Fortunately, massive earthquakes on land are rare. Many of the largest earthquakes occur out at sea, and while they can cause enormous tidal waves (such as the Japanese tsunami), earthquakes at sea seldom topple buildings or swallow up people. Earthquakes on the West Coast in Southern California are almost a dime a dozen, and most of them so faint that they cannot be felt.

Earthquakes can happen anywhere, and even tremors that occur hundreds of miles away can be detected with the proper instruments. Most seismographs use complex and massive electromagnetic sensors to detect earthquakes, both near and far, but you can readily build your own compact seismograph using a laser and a coil of fiberoptics.

When constructed properly, a laser/fiberoptic seismograph can be just as sensitive as an electromagnetic seismograph costing several thousand dollars.

This chapter covers construction details of a laser/fiberoptic seismograph as well as useful information on how to attach the seismograph to a personal computer.

THE RICHTER SCALE

A number of scales are used to quantify the magnitude of earthquakes. The best known and most used is the Richter scale, named after Charles F. Richter, a pioneer in seismology research. The Richter scale is a logarithmic measuring system ranging from 1 to 10 (and theoretically from 10 to 100), where each increase of 1 represents a ten-fold increase in earthquake magnitude. However, the actual energy released by the earth during the quake can be anywhere between 30 and 60 times for each increase of one digit. Each numeral is further broken down into units of 10, so earthquakes are often cited as 4.2 or 5.6 on the Richter scale.

To give you an idea of how the Richter scale works (and why it can cause confusion), consider the difference between a 3.0 and 4.0 earthquake. Both are difficult to detect without instruments (although some people say they can feel the swaying motion of a 4.0 earthquake). But because the magnitude is increased logarithmically by a factor of 10 per numeral and the actual energy released could be 60 times as great, the difference between a 3.0 and 5.0 earthquake is quite large. That is, the 5.0 earthquake is 10 X 10 (or 100) times more powerful than the 3.0 earthquake.

Similarly, a 6.0 earthquake can cause extensive structural damage and close down buildings for repair; and an earthquake measuring 7.0, if it continues for any length of time, can result in massive destruction of buildings, bridges, and roads. An earthquake measuring 9.0 or 10.0 would level any town.

Most earthquakes occur at a *fault*, which is a crack or fissure in the earth's crust. The majority of earthquakes occur at the boundaries of crustal plates. These plates slip and slide over the earth's inner surface. Sudden motion in these plates is released as an earthquake. Major faults, such as the San Andreas in California, create many thousand "mini-faults" or fractures that spread out like cracks in dried mud. These fractures are also responsible for earthquakes. In fact, two recent large earthquakes in southern California, occurring in 1971 and 1987, were caused by relatively small faults lying outside the San Andreas line.

Though faults are long—some measure thousands of miles—the earthquake occurs at a specific location along it. This location is the *epicenter*. The magnitude of earthquakes is measured at the epicenter (or more accurately, at a standard seismographic station distance of 100 km or 62 miles) where the amount of released energy is the greatest. The shock waves from the earthquake fan out and lose their energy the further they go. Obviously, there can't be a seismograph every 50 or even 100 miles along a fault to measure the exact amplitude of an earthquake. When the epicenter is some distance from a seismograph, its magnitude is inferred, based on its strength at several nearby seismograph stations, past earthquake readings, and the geological makeup of the land in-between.

This accounts for the uncertainty of the exact magnitude of an earthquake immediately after it has occurred and why different seismologists can arrive at different readings. It takes some careful calculations to determine an accurate Richter scale reading for an

238

earthquake, and the precise measurement is sometimes debated for months or even years after the tremor.

HOW ELECTROMAGNETIC SEISMOGRAPHS WORK

The most common seismograph in use today is the electromagnetic variety that uses a sensing element not unlike a dynamic microphone. Basically, the case of the seismograph is a large and heavy magnet. Inside the case is a core, consisting of a spool of fine wire. During an earthquake, the spool bobs up and down, inducing an electromagnetic signal through the wires. A similar effect occurs in a dynamic microphone. Sound vibrates a membrane, which causes a small voice coil (spool of wire) to vibrate. The voice coil is surrounded by a magnet, so the vibrational motion induces a constantly changing alternating current in the wire. As the sound varies, so does the polarity and strength of the alternating current.

To prevent accidental readings of surface vibration, the seismograph is buried several feet into the ground and is sometimes attached to the bedrock. In other cases, it is encased in concrete or secured to a cement piling sunk deep into the ground. Wires lead from the seismograph to a reading station, that might be directly above or several miles away. Telephone lines, radio links, or some other means connect the distant seismographs to a central office location.

The signal from the seismograph is amplified and applied to a galvanometer on a chart recorder (the galvanometer is similar to the movement on a volt-ohmmeter). The galvanometer responds to electrical changes induced by the moving core of the seismograph. The bigger the movement, the larger the response. Attached to the galvanometer is a long needle that applies ink to a piece of paper wound around a slowly rotating drum.

An advance over the chart recorder is the computer interface. The pulses from the seismograph are sent to an analog-to-digital converter (ADC), which connects directly to a computer. The ADC transforms the analog signals generated by the seismograph into digital data for use by the computer. Software running on the computer records each tremor and can perform mathematical analysis.

Laser/Fiberoptic Seismograph Basics

The laser/fiberoptic seismograph (hereinafter referred to as the laser/optic seismograph) doesn't use the electromagnetic principle to detect movement in the earth. Though there are several ways you can implement a laser/optic seismograph, we'll concentrate on just one that offers a great deal of flexibility and sensitivity. The system detects the change in coherency through a length of fiberoptics.

As discussed in Chapter 15, ''Lasers and Fiberoptics,'' when a laser beam is transmitted through a stepped-index optical fiber, some of the waves arrive at the other end before others. This reduces the coherency of the beam in proportion to the design of the fiber, its length, and the amount of curvature or bending of the fiber. Given enough of the right optical fiber, a laser beam could emerge at the opposite end that is totally incoherent.

It is not our intent to completely remove the coherency of a laser beam, but just to alter it slightly through a length of 10 or 20 feet of fiber. Movement or vibration of the fiber causes a displacement of the coherency, and that displacement can be detected with a phototransistor. You can even hear this change in coherency by connecting the phototransistor to an audio amplifier. The "hiss" of the light coming through the fiber changes pitch and makes odd thuds, pings, and thrums as the fiber vibrates. The sound settles as the fiber stops moving or vibrating. In a way, the optical fiber makes a unique form of interferometer that settles quickly after the external vibrations have been removed.

Reducing Local Vibrations

The laser/optic seismograph is susceptible to the effects of local vibrations, movement caused by people walking or playing nearby, passing cars, trucks, and trains, even the vibration triggered by the sound of a jet passing overhead.

To be most effective, the seismograph should be placed in an area where it won't be affected by local vibrations. Those living on a ranch or the outskirts of town will have better luck at finding such a location than city dwellers or those conducting earthquake experiments in a school or other populated area.

Even if you can't move away from people and things that cause vibration, you can reduce its effects by firmly planting the seismograph in solid ground. Avoid placing it indoors, especially on a wooden floor. Most buildings are flexible, and not only do they readily transmit vibrations from one location to the next, they act as a spring and/or cushion to the movement of an earthquake, improperly influencing the readings.

The cement flooring or foundation of the building is only marginally better. Small vibrations easily travel through cement, so if you attach your seismograph to the floor in your room, you are likely to pick up the movement of people walking around in the living room and kitchen.

The best spot for a seismograph is attached to a big rock out in the back yard, away from the house. Lacking a rock, you can fasten the seismograph to a cement piling, and then bury some or all of the piling into the ground. You can also spread out four to eight cement blocks (about 75 cents each at a builder's supply store), and partially bury them in the ground. Fill the center of the blocks with sand and mount the seismograph on top. Other possible spots include (test first):

- ★ The base of a telephone pole.
- ★ A heavy fence post.
- ★ A brick retaining wall or fence.
- ★ The cement slab of a separate garage, work shop, or tool shed.

CONSTRUCTING THE SEISMOGRAPH

Cut a piece of optical fiber (jacketed or unjacketed) to 15 feet. Polish the ends as described in the last chapter. Using a small bit (to match the diameter of the fiber), drill a hole in the top of a phototransistor. Be sure to drill directly over the chip inside the detector, but do not pierce through to the chip. Epoxy the fiber in place. Alternatively, you can terminate the output end of the fiber using a low-cost FLCS-type connector. You can also use a modified FLSC connector for the emitter end of the fiber (as detailed in Chapter 15) or one of the other mounting techniques described.

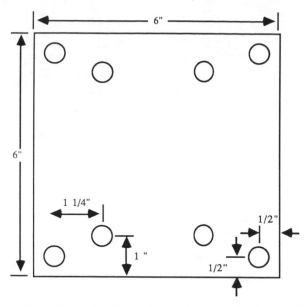

FIG. 16-1. *Drilling and cutting guide for the laser/optic seismograph base.*

Put the fiber aside and construct the base following the diagram in FIG. 16-1. A parts list is included in TABLE 16-1. You can use metal, plastic, or wood for the base, but it should be as dimensionally sturdy as possible. The prototype used ³⁄₁₆-inch-thick acrylic plastic. Cut the base to size and drill the post and mounting holes as shown. Insert four ¼-inch-20-by-3-inch bolts in the inside four holes. Starting at one post, thread the fiber around the bolts in a counterclockwise direction (see FIG. 16-2). Leave 1 to 2 feet on either end to secure the laser and photodiode. If the fiber slips off the bolts, you can secure it using dabs of epoxy.

Mount the photodetector and laser diode (on a heatsink, as shown in FIG. 16-3), in the center of the platform. Alternatively, you can use a He-Ne laser as the coherent light source. Mount the laser tube securely on a separate platform and position the end of the optical fiber so that it catches the beam.

You can use the universal laser light detector presented in Chapter 13 to receive and amplify the laser light intercepted by the phototransistor. You can use either a pulsed or cw drive power supply for the laser diode. Schematics for these drives appear in

Table 16-1. Fiberoptic Seismograph Parts List

1	6-inch-square acrylic plastic base (³⁄₁₆-inch thick)
4	3-inch by ¼-inch 20 carriage bolt, nuts, washers
1	Laser diode on heatsink
1	Sensor board (see Fig. 16-4)
Misc.	15 feet (approx.) jacketed or unjacketed fiberoptics, connector for receiver photodiode, connector or attachmnent for laser to fiber

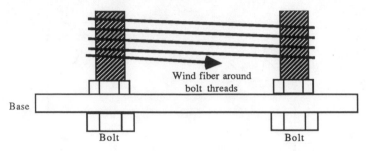

FIG. 16-2. *How to wind the optical fiber around the bolts.*

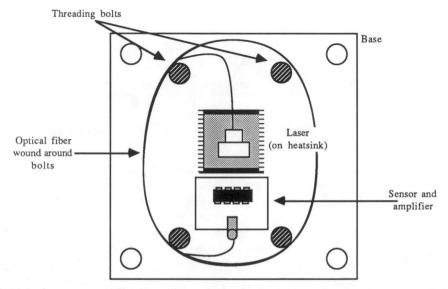

FIG. 16-3. *Arrangement of fiber, laser (on heatsink) and sensor/amplifier board on the seismograph base.*

Chapter 11, ''Laser Power Supplies.'' In either case, be sure that the laser diode does not receive too much current. In pulsed mode, the laser doesn't operate at peak efficiency, but it is not required in this application.

Note that when using a He-Ne tube, you don't need excessive power—a 0.5 or 1 mW He-Ne is more than enough. This simplifies the power supply requirements and allows you to operate the seismograph for a day or two on each charge on a pair of lead-acid or gelled electrolyte batteries.

Test the seismograph by turning on the laser and connecting the output of the amplifier to a speaker or pair of headphones. A small vibration of the base will cause a noticeable thrum or hiss in the audio output. You might need to adjust the control knob on the amplifier to turn the sound up or down.

The mounting holes allow you to attach the seismograph to almost any stable base. Whatever base you use, it should be directly connected to the earth. Use cement or masonry screws to attach the seismograph to concrete or a concrete pylon. When you get tired of listening to earthquake vibrations, connect the output of the amplifier to a volt-ohmmeter. Remove the ac coupling capacitor on the output of the amplifier.

Table 16-2. Commodore 64 Seispograph ADC Parts List

Basic Setup
IC1   TLC548 serial ADC
R1   10 kilohm potentiometer

Light-Dependent Resistor Setup
IC1   TLC548 serial ADC
R1,R2   1 kilohm resistor
R3   22 kilohm resistor

Phototransistor Setup
IC1   TLC548 serial ADC
R1,R2   1 kilohm resistor
R3   100 kilohm potentiometer
Q1   Infrared phototransistor
Misc. $^{12}/_{24}$ pin connector for attaching to Commodore 64 User Port

Computer Interface of Seismograph Sensor

A small handful of readily available electronic parts are all that is necessary to convert the voltage developed by the solar cell or phototransistor into a form usable by a computer. The circuit shown in FIG. 16-4 uses the TLC548 serial ADC, connected to a Commodore 64. The Commodore 64 provides the timing pulses, so only a minimum number of parts are required. See TABLE 16-2 for a parts list for the circuit. Construct the TLC548 circuit on a perforated board using soldering or wire-wrapping techniques.

Software

The software is relatively simple. You might want to collect a number of samples and either print them out for future reference or graph them in a chart. Such programs are beyond the scope of this book, but if you are interested in pursuing the subject, you can find suitable charting programs using the Commodore 64 in *Practical Interfacing Projects with the Commodore Computers* (Robert Luetzow, TAB BOOKS, catalog #1983), as well as a number of other publications. Check back issues of magazines that cater to owners of the Commodore 64.

LISTING 16-1

```
10   POKE 56579, 255
20   POKE 56577, 0
30   POKE 56589, 127
40   FOR N = 0 TO 7
50   POKE 56577, 0
60   POKE 56577, 1
```

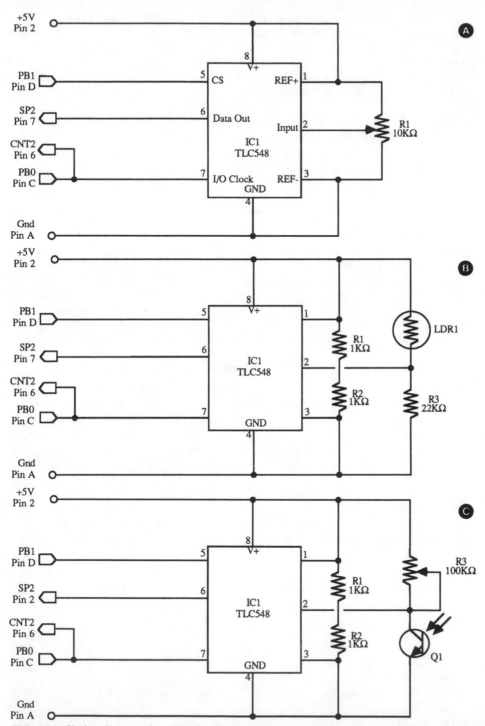

FIG. 16-4. *Hookup diagrams for connecting the TLC548 serial analog-to-digital converter to a Commodore 64 computer. (A) Test circuit (vary R1 and watch change in values); (B) Interfacing the circuit with a photoresistor; (C) Interfacing the circuit with a phototransistor. Adjust R3 to vary the sensitivity.*

```
 70   NEXT N
 80   IF (PEEK (56589) AND 8) = 0 THEN 80
 90   N = PEEK (56588)
100   PRINT N;
110   POKE 65677, 2
120   GOTO 40
```

CORRELATING YOUR RESULTS

I had just put the finishing touches on the coherency change seismograph prototype using a Commodore 64, when Los Angeles, my home town, was racked by a 6.1 Richter-scale earthquake (October 1, 1987). Although the epicenter of the earthquake was more than 50 miles distant with the Hollywood mountains in between, the entire area still shook violently. The earthquake could be felt for about 45 seconds but the remains of the tremor continued for several minutes (with lots of aftershocks).

I immediately checked the computer and found that it had recorded the full duration of the quake. I jotted down the results (I had not yet implemented a recording feature to save the data on disk or tape), and then waited until the seismologists in southern California could settle on an accurate magnitude for the tremor. At the epicenter, the earthquake measured 6.1 on the Richter scale. In my area, however, it was calculated that the earthquake measured only about 5.6 on the Richter scale. I used that information to "calibrate" the results from the computer. That way, with the digital data I recorded more accurately compared to a known value, I could better estimate the magnitude of future quakes.

17

Beginning Holography

Remember the first time you saw a real hologram? The image seemed to float in space, as if a piece of invisible film hung in mid-air in front of you. Moving your head back and forth verified the image was more than two-dimensional. You could actually see around the object to examine its top, bottom, and sides.

If experimenting with fiberoptics, modulators, and power supplies is the technical side of lasers, then holography is the artistic side. Armed with a helium-neon laser, some assorted optics, and a pack of film, you can create your own holograms. Your subjects can be anything that is small enough to illuminate with the laser beam and patient enough to sit still for the exposure.

After development of the film, you can display your holograms for others to see and appreciate. As you gain experience, you can tackle more complex forms of the laser holographic art—rainbow holograms, holographic interferometry, and even motion picture holograms.

This chapter introduces you to the art and science of making holograms, including how holograms work and what you need to set up shop. You'll learn how to build a holographic table and create, and later view, a transmission hologram. The next chapter continues with plans and procedures for a more advanced holographic table as well as how to create elaborate two- and three-beam reflection holograms.

A SHORT HISTORY OF HOLOGRAPHY

The idea of holography is older than the laser. Dr. Dennis Gabor, a researcher at the Imperial College in London, conceived and produced the first hologram in 1948.

Because Gabor was of a scientific bent, he published his ideas in a paper titled "Image Formation by Reconstructed Wavefronts," a phrase that aptly describes the technology behind holography. Gabor was later awarded the Nobel prize for Physics in 1971 for his pioneering work in holography.

Dr. Gabor's first holograms were crude and difficult to decipher. Compared to regular photography, the first Gabor holograms were scratchy throwbacks to pre-Civil War Daguerreotypes. Part of the problem was the lack of a sufficiently coherent source of light. No matter how complex the setup, the images remained fuzzy and indistinct. The introduction of visible-light lasers in the early sixties provided the final ingredient required to make sharp and clear holograms.

Gabor left much of the exploration of holography to other pioneers such as Lloyd Cross, T.H. Jeong, Emmett Lieth, Pam Brazier, Juris Upatnieks, Fred Unterseher, and Robert Schinella. Much of the original developments of laser holography—first developed by Leith at the University of Michigan—had scientific and even military applications. Today, holography is used in medicine, fluid aerodynamics, stress testing, forensics, and even art.

In the 1960s and most of the 1970s, the equipment required to make professional-looking holograms was beyond the reach of most amateur experimenters. Now, however, with the wide proliferation of visible-light helium-neon lasers and the availability of surplus optical components, it's possible to build a workable holography setup for less than a few hundred dollars. And, that includes the materials required to construct a vibration-free isolation table.

If you're apprehensive of holography because you are afraid you won't understand how it works, consider that you don't need to know how the silver halide crystals in photographic emulsion react to light to take a snapshot of your family. You just pick up the camera, set some dials, focus, and press the shutter release.

Although you are encouraged to understand how coherent laser light is used to create, and later reconstruct, a multi-dimensional image, you needn't have a college degree in physics to make a hologram. Photographic experience is also not required, though it comes in handy. You will find the process of developing holographic films similar to processing ordinary black-and-white films and papers. If you've never been in a dark-room before, you might want to pick up a basic book on the subject and read up on the various processes and procedures involved. Obviously, you can't learn everything you need to know about holography in the two chapters in this book, and you are urged to expand your knowledge by further reading. A partial list of titles on holography is in Appendix B.

WHAT A HOLOGRAM IS—AND ISN'T

Many people hold misconceptions about the nature of holograms. A hologram is a photographic plate that contains interference patterns that represent the light waves from a reference source as well as from the photographed object itself. The patterns, like those in FIG. 17-1, contain information about the intensity of the light (just as in regular photography), as well as its instantaneous phase and direction. These elements together make possible the three-dimensional reproduction of the hologram.

The interference patterns constitute a series of diffraction gratings, and form what is, in effect, an extremely sophisticated lens. The orientation of the gratings, along with

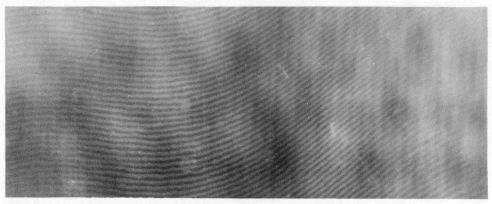

FIG. 17-1. *A thumbprint? No, it's a close-up of the interference fringes of a hologram, captured on high-resolution film.*

their width and size, determine how the image is reconstructed when viewed in light. In most types of holograms, the image becomes clear only when viewed with the same wavelength of coherent light used to expose the film.

Not all holograms are the same. As you'll see later in this chapter and in the next chapter, there are two general forms of holograms: transmission and reflection. The terminology refers to how the hologram is viewed, not exposed. The typical transmission hologram needs a laser for image reconstruction. The reflection hologram, while made with a laser, can be viewed under ordinary light.

The hologram stores an almost unlimited number of views of a three-dimensional object. Put another way, specific areas on the surface of the film contain different three-dimensional views of the object. You see these views by moving your head up and down or right and left. This effect is most readily demonstrated by cutting a hologram into small pieces (or simply covering portions of it with a piece of cardboard). Each piece contains the entire image of the photographed object but at a slightly different angle. As you make your own holograms, you get a clearer view of how the image actually occupies a three-dimensional space.

Some other types of images impart a sense of multi-dimensional imagery, but they are not true holograms. The coin-in-the-bowl scientific novelty, popular in mail-order catalogs, uses concave lenses to project an image of a coin into your eyes. The image appears closer than it is and when you reach out for it, it's not there. Another example: The famous shots of Princess Leia projecting out of the R2-D2 robot in the movie *Star Wars* was created with the aid of photographic trickery.

WHAT YOU NEED

You need relatively few materials to make a hologram:

★ Stable isolation table (often nothing more than a sandbox on cement pillars)

★ Laser—a 1 mW, 632.8 nm helium-neon is perfectly suited for holography, though other visible-light lasers will do as well; it must operate in TEM_{00} mode.

★ Beam expander lens

★ Film holder

★ Film and darkroom chemicals
★ Object to holograph

Other materials are needed for more advanced holographic setups, but this is the basic equipment list. These and other materials are detailed throughout this chapter.

THE ISOLATION TABLE

If you built the Michelson interferometer described in Chapter 9, you know how sensitive it is to vibration. The circular fringes that appear on the frosted glass shake and can even disappear if the interferometer is bumped or nudged. Depending on the table or workbench you use, vibrations from people walking nearby or even passing cars and trucks can cause the fringes to bob.

Because the interference fringes create the holographic image in the first place, you can understand why the table you use to snap the picture must be carefully isolated from external vibrations. If the laser setup moves at all during the exposure—even a few millionths of an inch—the hologram is ruined. Optical tables for scientific research cost in excess of $15,000 and weigh more than your car. But they do a good job at damping vibrations in the lab and preventing them from reaching the laser and optical components.

Obviously, a professional-grade optical table is out of the question, but you can build your own with common yard materials. Your own isolation table uses sand as the heavy damping material. The sand is dumped in a box that is perched on cement blocks. The homemade sandbox table is not as efficient as a commercially made isolation table, but it comes close. Add to your sand table a reasonably vibration-free area (California during an earthquake is out!) and you are on your way to making clear holograms.

Selecting the Right Size

The size of the table dictates the type of setups you can design as well as the maximum dimensions of the holographed object. The ideal isolation table measures 4-by-8 feet or larger, but a more compact 2-by-2-foot version can suffice for beginners. You will be limited to fairly simple optical arrangements and shooting objects smaller than a few inches square, but the table will be reasonably portable and won't take up half your garage.

The design for the sand table is shown in FIG. 17-2. The table consists of four concrete blocks (the kind used for outside retaining walls), a 2-by-2-foot sheet of ¾-inch plywood, some carpeting, four small pneumatic inner tubes, and an 8-inch-deep box filled with sand. You can build this table using larger dimensions (such as 4-by-4 or 4-by-8 feet), but it requires considerably more sand. You can figure about one 75- or 100-pound bag of fine sand for each square foot of table area.

Building the Table

First, build the box using the materials indicated in TABLE 17-1. Use heavy-duty construction—heavy screws, wood glue, and battens. Make the box as sturdy as possible—strong enough for an adult to sit or stand on. Next, lay out the blocks in a 2-foot-square area, inside the house or shop. You'll need a fairly light-tight room to work in, so a garage with all the cracks, and vents, and windows covered up is a good area. In addition, be sure that the room is not drafty. Air movement is enough to upset the fringes. You need a solid, level floor, or the sand table might rock back and forth.

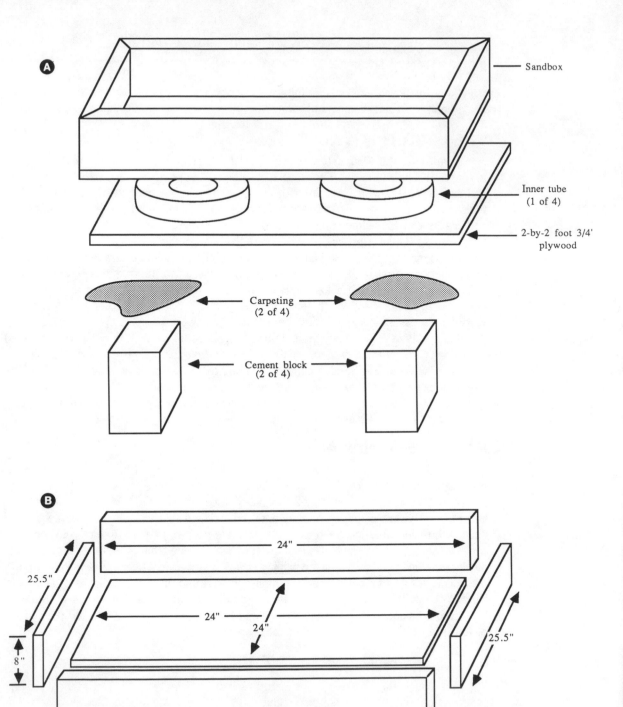

FIG. 17-2. *Design of the 2-by-2-foot sand table. (A) Blocks, carpet, plywood base, inner tubes, and sandbox and how they go together. (B) Construction details of the sandbox. Use ¾-inch plywood for the sandbox.*

Table 17-1. Small Sand Table Parts Lists

Base and Pedestal

4	Cement building blocks
4	8-inch-square pieces of carpet
1	2-foot-square piece of carpeting
4	10- to 14-inch inner tubes
1	2-by-2-foot sheet of ¾ inch thick plywood

Sand Box

1	2-by-2-foot sheet of ¾-inch thick plywood
2	8- by 25.5-inch, ¾-inch thick plywood
2	8- by 24-inch, ¾-inch thick plywood
4	75- or 100-pound bags of washed, sterilized, and filtered sand

Place the 2-by-2-foot sheet of plywood over the blocks, then cover the plywood with one or two layers of soft carpeting (plush or shag works well). Partially inflate the four inner tubes (to about 50 to 60 percent) and place them on the carpet. Don't over-inflate the tubes or fill them with liquid. If possible, position the valves so that you can reach them easily to refill the inner tubes. You may need to jack up the sand box to access the valves, but if the tubes are good to begin with, you won't need to perform this duty often.

Carefully position the box over the inner tube. Don't worry about stability at this point: the table will settle down when you add the sand. Be sure to evenly distribute the sand inside the box as you pour out the contents of each bag. There should be little dust if you use high-quality, pre-washed and sterilized play sand. Fill the box with as much sand as you can, but avoid overfilling where the sand spills over the edges.

Testing the Table

You can test the effectiveness of the sand table by building a makeshift Michelson interferometer, as shown in FIG. 17-3. The optical components are mounted on PVC pipe, as described more fully in Chapter 7, "Constructing an Optical Bench." You can place the laser inside the box, on the top of the sand, or locate it off the table. As long as the beam remains fairly steady, any slight vibration of the laser will not affect the formation of the interference fringes necessary for successful holography.

Once you have the optics aligned and the laser on, wait for the table to settle (5 to 15 minutes), then look at the frosted glass. You should see a series of circular fringes. If the fringes don't appear, wait a little longer for the table to settle some more. Should the fringes still not materialize, double-check the arrangement of the laser and optics. The paths of the two beams must meet exactly at the frosted glass, and their propagation must be parallel—vertically as well as horizontally.

Determining Settling Times

Test the isolation capabilities of the table by moving around the room and watching the fringes (you might need someone to stand by the glass and closely watch the fringes).

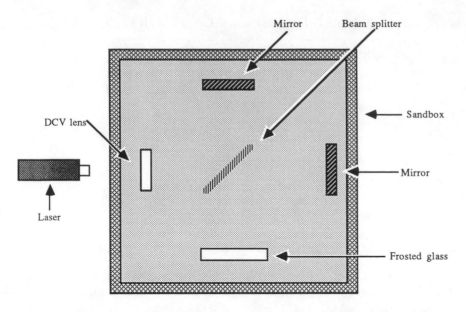

FIG. 17-3. *Optics arranged as a Michelson interferometer for testing the stability of the table.*

The fringes shouldn't move at all, but if they do, it should be slight. More energetic movement, such as bouncing up and down or shaking the walls, will greatly affect the formation of the fringes.

Watch particularly for the effects of vibrations that you can't control, such as other people walking around or cars passing by. Adequate isolation might require a more advanced table (such as the one detailed in the next chapter), more sand, or a change in location. You might also want to wait until after hours, where activity of both people and automobiles is reduced. Keep in mind that you will have better luck when the sand table is located on a ground floor and on heavy wood or cement.

Note the time it takes for the table to settle each time you change the optics or disturb the sand. You will need to wait for at least this amount of time before you can make a holographic exposure. Also note how long it takes for the table to recover from small shocks and disturbances; recovery time for most tables should be a matter of seconds.

THE DARKROOM

Part of holography takes place in the darkroom, where the film is processed after exposure. Although it's most convenient to place the isolation table and processing materials in the same room, they can be separate. As with the isolation table, the darkroom must be reasonably light-tight. It should have a source of running water to rinse processed film and a drain to wash away unwanted chemicals. A bathroom is ideal, as long as you have room to move and can work uninterrupted for periods up to 15 to 20 minutes.

If the bathroom has windows, cover them with opaque black fabric or painted cardboard. If you plan on making many holograms, arrange some sort of easily installed curtain system. Drape some material over the mirror and other shiny objects, like metal towel racks and fixtures. You'll need access to the sink and faucet, so leave these clear.

Only two chemicals are needed for basic holography (advanced holographers use many more chemicals, as detailed in the next chapter). You need to set out two shallow plastic bowls or trays large enough to accommodate the film. If space is a premium inside your bathroom, place a wooden rack over the tub and set the trays on it. The bathtub makes a good location for the trays, because the processing chemicals might stain clothing, walls, floors, and other porous materials. If any drips into the tub, you can promptly wash it away.

OPTICS, FILM, FILM HOLDERS, AND CHEMICALS

Here's a run-down of the basic materials you need to complete your holographic setup.

Optics

Basic holography requires the use of a plano-concave or double-concave lens and one or more front-surface mirrors. The lens can be small—on the order of 4 to 10 mm in diameter. Focal length is not a major consideration but should be fairly short. Mount the lens in 1- or 1¼-inch PVC pipe, painted black, as detailed in Chapter 7.

The purpose of the lens is to expand the pencil-thin beam of the laser into an area large enough to completely illuminate the object being photographed. The area of the beam is expanded proportionately to the distance between the lens and object, and the basic 2-by-2-foot table doesn't allow much room for extreme beam expansion. If the beam is not adequately expanded, use a lens with a shorter focal length, or position two negative lenses together as shown in FIG. 17-4.

The direct one-beam transmission hologram setup described below does not require the use of mirrors or beam splitters, but multiple-beam arrangements do. The size of the mirror depends on the amount of beam spread and the size of the object, but in general, you need one or more mirrors measuring 2-by-3 inches or larger. Some setups also require beam steering or transfer mirrors. These are used before the beam has been expanded, so they can be small. See Chapter 7 for ideas on how to mount mirrors and other optics.

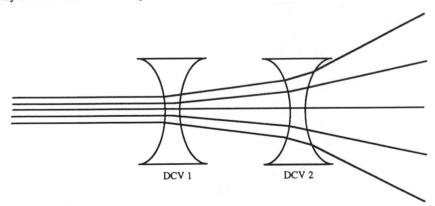

DCV 1   DCV 2

FIG. 17-4. *How to obtain maximum beam spread by using two double-concave lenses.*

Holographic Film

Holography requires a special ultra-high resolution film emulsion that is most sensitive to the wavelength of the laser you are using. Kodak Type 120 and S0-173 or Agfa-Gevaert Holotest 8E75 and 10E75, for example, are made for 632.8 nm helium-neon lasers and are most sensitive to red light (a relatively insensitive wavelength for orthochromatic film). You can handle and develop this film using a dim (7-watt or less) green safelight—a small green bug light works well as long as it is placed 5 feet or more from the sand table and film handling areas. Holographic film comes in various sizes and base thicknesses. Film measuring 2¼ inches square to 4-by-5 inches is ideal for holography.

Holographic films are available with and without antihalation backing. This backing material, which comes off during processing, prevents halos during exposure. The backing is semi-opaque, which prevents light from passing through it. Transmission holograms are made with the laser light striking the emulsion surface, so you can use a film with antihalation backing. Reflective holograms are made with light passing *through* the film and striking the emulsion on the other side. Unless you are eager to make exposures lasting several minutes or more, you'll want a film without the antihalation backing when experimenting with reflection holography.

When buying or ordering film, be sure to note whether the stuff you want comes with antihalation backing. If you want to try both basic forms of holography (transmission and reflection) but don't want to spend the money for both kinds of films, use stock without the backing. Note that this film does not make the best transmission holograms, but the results are more than adequate. Be sure to place a black matte card (available at art supply stores) in back of the film when making the exposure. This prevents light from entering the film through the back and fogging the emulsion.

Another alternative is to use glass plates for your first holograms. These consist of a photographic emulsion sprayed onto a piece of optically clear glass. The benefit of the glass is that it is easier to handle for beginners and is not as susceptible to buckling and movement during the exposure.

Where do you get holographic film? Good question. Start by opening the Yellow Pages and looking under the Photographic heading. Call the various camera stores and ask if they carry it or can special-order it for you. But in the interest of saving you the disappointment, be aware that the personnel at most camera stores are not even aware of such a thing as holographic film. You will probably have better luck calling those outlets that specialize in professional photography or darkroom supplies.

You might also happen to live in an area close to a Kodak or Agfa-Gevaert field office. Call and ask for help. A few companies, such as Metrologic, offer film suitable for holography; check Appendix A for the address. Lastly, write directly to the film manufacturers and ask for a list of local dealers that handle the materials you need. You might even be able to order holographic film through the mail.

Film Holder

You will need some means to hold the film in place during the exposure. One method is to sandwich the film between two pieces of glass held together by two heavy spring clips, as shown in the photograph in FIG. 17-5. The glass must be spotlessly clean. The disadvantage of this method is that the contact of the glass and film can create what's known as Newton's Rings, a form of interference patterns.

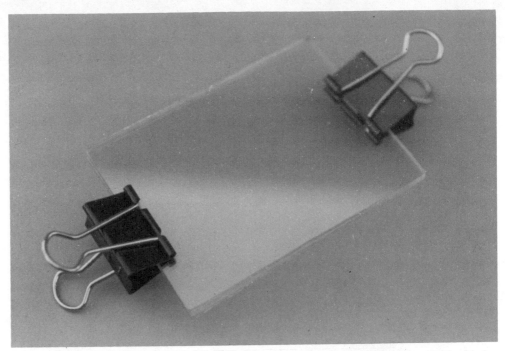

FIG. 17-5. *A homemade film pressure plate consisting of two pieces of optically clear glass and two binder clips. The film is inserted between the glass and pressed tightly together to eliminate air bubbles.*

If you plan on using a glass-plate film holder, remember to press the plates together firmly and keep constant pressure for 10 to 20 seconds (use wooden blocks for even pressure). This removes all air bubbles trapped between the glass and film. Snap the binder clips around the glass and position the holder in front of the object. The handles of the clips can be secured to the table by butting them against two pieces of PVC pipe. Depending on the arrangement of the optics, you might be able to locate the film holder between the PVC pipes that contain the expansion lenses.

Yet another approach is to use a commercially-made film holder, the kind designed for processing plate film. The holders come in a variety of sizes and use novel approaches to loading and holding the film. Most any camera store that carries professional dark-room supplies has a variety of film holders to choose from. You can also make your own following the diagram in FIG. 17-6. Construct the holder to accommodate the size of film you are using. You might need to make several holders if you use different sizes of film.

To use any of the holders, load the film (in complete darkness or under the dim illumination of a small green safelight) into the holder, and stick the holder in the proper location in the sand. If the holder does not allow easy mounting in the sand, attach it to small wood or plastic pieces, as illustrated in FIG. 17-7.

Processing Chemicals

You can use ordinary film developer to process most holographic film emulsions. A good choice is Kodak D-19, available in powder form at some photographic shops. If D-19 is not available, you may use most any other high-resolution film developer. Agfa,

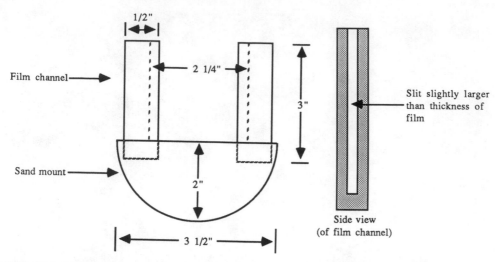

FIG. 17-6. *Construction details for a homemade wooden film holder. The holder shown is made for 2¼-by-2¼ film.*

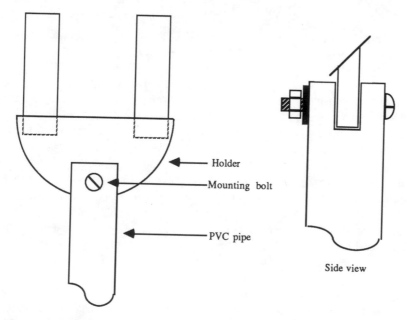

FIG. 17-7. *You can raise the distance between film and sand by mounting the holder on a piece of PVC pipe.*

Nacco, and Kodak make a variety of high-quality powder and liquid developers that you can use.

Both transmission and reflection holograms require bleaching as one of the processing steps. If you can't buy pre-made bleach specifically designed for holography, you can mix your own following the directions that appear below. Note that transmission and reflection holograms need different bleach formulas. Chemicals for making the bleach

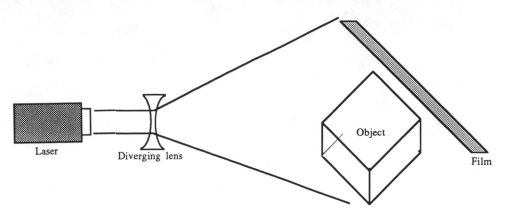

FIG. 17-8. *The basic arrangement for making a single-beam transmission hologram.*

are available at many of the larger industry photographic outlets. If you can't find what you want, dial up a chemical supply house and see if you can buy what you need in small quantities.

The remaining, optional chemicals are available at most camera stores. These include acetic acid stop bath, fixer (with or without hardener), photoflo, and hypo clear.

SINGLE-BEAM TRANSMISSION SETUP

The layout in FIG. 17-8 shows how to arrange the laser, lens, photographic object, and film plate for a direct, one-beam transmission hologram. A parts list is provided in TABLE 17-2. Note that the term "transmission" has nothing to do with the arrangement of the film, optics, or object for making the hologram but rather the method of viewing the image after it is processed. You look through transmission holograms to see an image; you shine light off the emulsion side of a reflection hologram to see the picture.

You can use almost anything as the object, but for your first attempt, choose something small (about the size of a pack of cigarettes or less), with a smooth but not highly reflective surface. A pair of dice, a coffee mug, a chess piece, a small electronic circuit board, or an electronic component make good subjects. Things to avoid include silverware, highly reflective jewelry, the family TV set, and your cat. These and other reflective, large, and/or animate objects can be subjects for holograms, but only after you gain experience.

Making the Exposure

After you arrange the laser and optics as shown above, turn the laser on. The distance between the lens and object/film should be 1.5 to 2 feet. Be sure the beam covers the

Table 17-2. Single-Beam Transmission Hologram Setup Parts List	
1	He-Ne laser
1	8 to 10 mm bi-concave lens
1	Holographic film in film holder
1	Object

object and the film, as shown in the figure. Now block the beam with a black "shutter" card.

Turn off all the lights and switch on the safelight. The safelight should emit only a tinge of illumination, hardly enough for you to see your hand out in front of you. The idea is to help you see your way in the dark, not provide daylight illumination. You can test for excessive safelight illumination by placing a piece of film on the sand table for 5 minutes with half of it covered with a piece of black cardboard. Process the film and look for a darkening on the uncovered side. A dark portion means that the film was fogged by the safelight.

Load the film into the holder, emulsion side towards the laser, and place the holder at a 45-degree angle to the laser beam (you can tell the emulsion side by wetting a corner of the film; the emulsion side becomes sticky). The film should be close to the object but not touching it. Wait 10 minutes or so for the table to settle, then quickly but carefully remove the card covering the laser. After the exposure is complete, replace the card. *Do not* control the exposure by turning the laser on and off. The coherency of lasers improves after they have warmed up. For best results, allow the laser to warm up for 20 to 30 minutes before making any holographic exposure.

Exposure times depend on the power output of the laser. As a rule of thumb, allow 3 to 4 seconds for a 1 mW laser and 1 to 2 seconds for a 3 mW laser. You might want to make a test exposure using the technique shown in FIG. 17-9. Place a card in front of the film and make a 1 second exposure. Move the card so that it exposes a little more of the film and make another 1-second exposure. Repeat the process four to six times until you have a series of strips on the film. Each strip along the length of the film denotes an increase in exposure of 1 second.

Develop the test strip film following the steps below, then choose the exposure used for the best-looking strip. In the average transmission hologram, the film should be dark gray with distinct fringe patterning. When viewed with laser light, underexposure causes

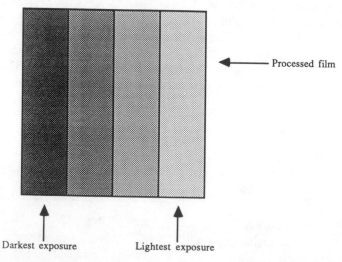

Darkest exposure   Lightest exposure

FIG. 17-9. *The results of a sample test strip with increasingly dark stripes of gray across the film. Choose the exposure (and development time) that yields the proper density, as noted in the text.*

258

the film to be excessively light and lack contrast. Overexposure makes the image hard—if not impossible—to see.

Processing Steps

Once the hologram is exposed, place it in a light-tight container or box. Mix the processing chemicals (if you haven't already) as follows:

★ D-19 developer—Full strength as detailed in the instructions printed on the package (when using another developer, mix according to instructions to obtain the highest resolution).

★ Bleach—One tablespoon of potassium ferrocyanide mixed with one tablespoon of potassium bromide in 16 ounces of water. Alternatively, you may dissolve 5 grams of potassium dichromate in 1 liter of water. Add 20 ml of diluted sulfuric acid.

Use water at room temperature (68 to 76 degrees F), and be sure the temperature is roughly the same between each chemical bath. High temperatures or wide variations in temperature can soften the film and introduce reticulation—two side effects you want to avoid. Place the developer and bleach in large plastic bowls or processing trays (available at photo stores). The chemicals have a finite shelf life of a few months when stored in stoppered plastic bottles. Use small or collapsible bottles to minimize the air content, and store the bottles in a cool place away from sunlight.

In the dark or with a green safelight, remove the film from the light-tight box and place it in the developer. Use plastic tongs to handle the film (avoid using metallic implements and your fingers). Swish the film in the developer and knock the tongs against the side of the tray or bowl to dislodge any air bubbles under or on the film. Maintain a slow and even agitation of the film. After about 2 to 5 minutes, the image on the film will appear and development is complete.

If you have a safelight, you can see the image appear and can better judge when the development is complete. As a rule of thumb, when held up to a safelight, a properly exposed and developed transmission hologram allows about 70 to 80 percent of the light to pass through it (reflective holograms pass about 20 to 30 percent of the light).

After development, rinse the film in running water or a tray filled with clean water. You can also use an acetic stop bath, mixed according to directions. The stop bath more completely removes traces of developer and helps prolong the life of the bleach used in the next step.

After 15 seconds or so of rinsing, place the film in the bleach. Keep it there for 2 to 3 minutes. After a minute or two of bleaching, you can turn on the lights. Follow bleaching with another rinse. Use lots of water and keep the film in the wash for 5 to 10 minutes. A cyclonic rinser, used in many professional darkrooms, does a good job of removing all the processing chemicals.

The hologram is almost ready for viewing. Before drying it, dip the film in Kodak Photoflo solution—a capful in a pint of water is sufficient. The Photoflo reduces the surface tension of the water and helps promote even drying without spotting. It also removes minerals left from the water bath. You may also use a squeegee to remove excess liquid. Darkroom squeegees cost $5 to $10 and are good for the purpose, or a new car windshield wiper blade costs $2 and is just as good.

Use clothespins or real honest-to-goodness film clips to hang up the film to dry. Place the film in a dust-free area. A specially made drying cabinet is the best place, but the shower or bathtub is another good choice.

Wait until the film has completely dried before trying to view it (the fringes might not be clear until drying is complete). Depending on the temperature, humidity, and other conditions, it takes 30 to 120 minutes for the film to dry completely. Glass plate film dries more quickly. Note that when wet, photographic emulsion becomes soft and scratches easily. Be sure to handle the film with care and avoid touching it (with hands or tongs) except by the edges.

Let's recap the processing steps:

* Develop for 2 to 5 minutes.
* Rinse for 15 seconds (water or stop bath).
* Bleach for 2 to 3 minutes.
* Rinse for 5 to 10 minutes in constantly running water.
* Dip in Photoflo for 15 seconds (optional step).
* Squeegee to remove excess liquid (don't scratch the emulsion!).
* Let dry at least 30 minutes.

Viewing the Hologram

Part of the fun of holography is making the picture; the rest is seeing the result with your own eyes. If you haven't disturbed the setup used to take the picture, simply replace the film in the film holder. The emulsion should face the laser. View the image by looking through the film. The image might not be noticeable unless you move your head from side to side or up and down.

Note that if you have dismantled the sand box setup, you must replace the laser, optics, and film holder in the same arrangement to reconstitute the image. The simple layout used in the single-beam direct transmission exposure makes it relatively easy to reconstitute the image.

Problems

Having problems? The image in the hologram isn't clear or the exposure just isn't right? Most difficulties in image quality are caused by motion. The fringes must remain absolutely still during the exposure or the hologram could be ruined. Consider that a more powerful laser decreases the exposure time, reducing the problems of vibration. For example, a 5 to 8 mW laser might require an exposure of only 0.5 to 1 second. If at all possible, use the most powerful laser you can get your hands on, but don't give up on holography if all you own is a tiny 0.5 mW tube.

Like regular photography, it takes time, patience, and practice to make really good holograms. Don't expect to make a perfect exposure the first time around. Odds are the exposure will be too short and the development too long, or vice versa. If your first attempt doesn't come out the way you want it (or doesn't come out at all!), analyze what went wrong and try again.

Check the layout and be sure that the film is inserted in the holder with the emulsion side out (that is, towards the laser). If you use a film with an AH backing (recommended for transmission holograms), the light won't pass through to the emulsion if the film is inserted backward in the holder. Be sure that the chemicals are mixed right and that you are following the proper procedure.

INTERMEDIATE HOLOGRAPHY

You can learn more about holography by actually making a hologram than reading an entire book on the subject (however, that *is* recommended, see Appendix B for a list of books on holography). Below are some observations that will help you better grasp the technology and artistry of holograms.

Field of Vision

Here's an important point to keep in mind as you experiment further. You might have realized that the film holder represents the frame of a window onto which you can view the subject. Place your head against the film holder, close one eye, and look at the object from up close. Without actually moving your eye, scan your head vertically and horizontally and note the different views you can see of the subject. They are the same views you see in a hologram. Use this technique to view the perspective and field of vision for your holograms. You can then adjust the position of the object, film, or even the optics to obtain the views you want.

Varying Exposure

Unless you have a calibrated power meter and lots of experience, expect mistakes in estimating exposure times when experimenting with different types of holographic setups. The direct, one-beam setup detailed previously conserves laser light energy, thus reducing exposure time. Some multi-beam setups (see below and in the next chapter) require exposure times of 15 to 25 seconds, assuming a 3 to 5 mW laser.

Light Ratios

All holograms are made by directing a reference beam and an object beam onto a film plate. The reference beam comes directly from the laser, perhaps after bouncing off a beam splitter and a mirror or two. The object beam is reflected off the object being photographed. The ratio between the reference and object beams is a major consideration. If the ratio isn't right, the hologram becomes "noisy" and difficult to see. The reflectivity of the object largely determines the ratio, but with most commonly holographed subjects, the reference-to-object light ratio for a transmission hologram is about 4:1 (four parts reference to one part object).

Intermediate and advanced holography requires careful control over light ratios, which means you must take readings using a calibrated power meter (available through Metrologic) or a light meter.

You may adjust the light ratios by repositioning the optics or by using a variable-density beam splitter. A variable-density beam splitter is a wheel (or sometimes a rectangular piece of glass) with an anti-reflective coating, applied in varying density, on one side. An area with little or no anti-reflection coating reflects little light and passes much. The opposite is true at an area with a high amount of AR coating. You can "dial" in the ratio of transmitted versus reflected light by turning the wheel. Note that basic holography doesn't require a variable-density beam splitter, which is good because they're expensive.

Reverse Viewing

If you flip the hologram over top to bottom, you'll see the image appear in front of the film, looming toward you. You see the image inside-out as you view it from the back side. This effect is created by light focusing in the space in front of the hologram. Although the entire image can't be focused onto a plane, you can see the formation of three-dimensions by placing a piece of frosted glass at the apparent spot where the hologram appears. As you move the plate in and out, different portions of the picture will come in and out of focus.

Projected Viewing

The image in a hologram can be projected in a variety of ways. Try this method. Replace the hologram so that its emulsion faces the laser. Remove the beam-expanding lens so that just the pencil-thin beam of the laser strikes the center of the hologram film. Place a white card or screen behind the film to catch the light going through the hologram. The screen or card should be located where your eyes would be if you were viewing the hologram. Watch the image that appears. You'll see the complete object, but the image will be two-dimensional.

Now move the film up and down and right and left. Notice how the picture of the object remains complete but the perspective changes. This is the same effect you get if you cut a hologram into many pieces. Each piece contains a full picture of the subject but at slightly different views.

Transfer Mirrors

Some holographers prefer to place the laser in the sand table. This is perfectly acceptable, as long as you mount the laser on a wood or plastic board. Position it along one side of the table and direct the beam diagonally across the table with a transfer mirror. Aiming the beam diagonally across the surface of the sand table gives you more room and allows you to create more elaborate setups. The general idea is shown in FIG. 17-10.

Alternate Single-Beam Transmission Setups

FIGURE 17-11 shows the setup for an alternate single-beam transmission hologram. This arrangement requires a white card measuring about 4-by-4 inches and a 5- or 6-inch square mirror. Position the film holder as shown and locate the mirror at about an 80-degree angle to the film. Place the card so that no direct light from the laser strikes the film. All of the light used for exposing the film should be reflected off the mirror.

Yet another single-beam transmission hologram can be created by using the simple setup shown in FIG. 17-12. It is similar to the first arrangement, but the film is positioned at almost a 90- degree angle to the path of the laser light. Here, no white card or mirror is used. TABLES 17-3 and 17-4 provide the parts lists for these two setups.

The film can actually be beside, under, or over the object. Place the film angled downward on a hill of sand. Underneath, place a piece of painted airport runway from

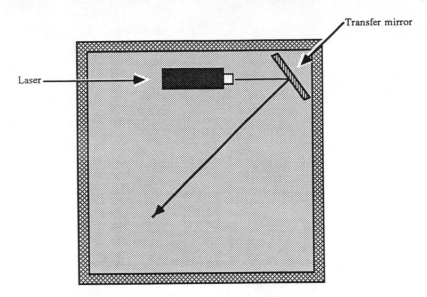

FIG. 17-10. *The idea of transfer mirrors.*

Table 17-3. Alternate #1 Single-Beam Transmission Hologram Parts List

1	He-Ne laser
1	8 to 10 mm bi-concave lens
1	Holographic film in film holder
1	5- or 6-inch-square front-surface mirror
1	Black blocking card
1	Object

Table 17-4. Alternate #2 Single-Beam Transmission Hologram Parts List

1	He-Ne laser
1	8 to 10 mm bi-concave lens
1	Holographic film in film holder
1	Object

a model airplane kit. The finished hologram will have a startling 3-D image of the runway that will appear as if you are actually landing an airplane. Try this technique the next time you exhibit your best model airplane. You're sure to win first place!

SPLIT-BEAM TRANSMISSION HOLOGRAM

The visual effect of a single-beam hologram is limited due to the single source of light. Objects photographed in this manner can look dark or lack detail in shadowed areas. Only one side of the hologram might be illuminated, and as you move your head to see

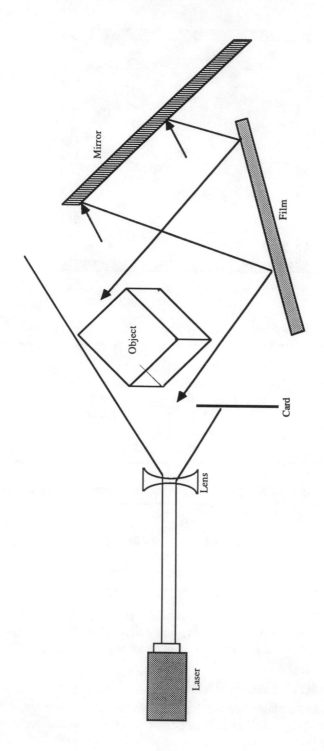

FIG. 17-11. A single-beam transmission hologram using a large mirror. The mirror provides the reference beam as well as a large portion of light for the illumination of the object.

264

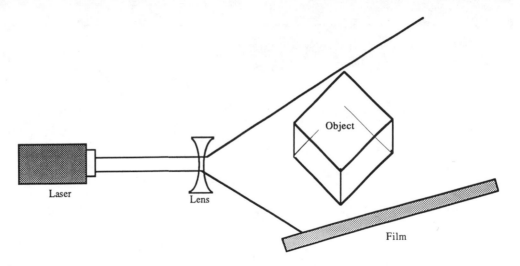

FIG. 17-12. *A simple single-beam transmission hologram arrangement, shown with film set at a 75 to 80 degree angle to the beam path.*

different views, the image grows dim. In portraiture photography, two, three, and sometimes four different light sources are used to illuminate different parts of the head or body. The amount of illumination from each light is carefully controlled to make the picture as pleasing as possible.

A similar approach can be used in holography by splitting the laser beam and providing two or more sources of light to illuminate the object (there is still only one reference beam). The setup in FIG. 17-13 shows how to illuminate an object by splitting the laser light and directing two expanded beams to either side of the object. See TABLE 17-5 for a list of required materials.

The main consideration when splitting the light is that the reference and object beams should travel approximately the same distance from the laser. That is, the reference beam should not travel 2.5 feet and the object beam(s) only 1.2 feet. Use a fabric tape to measure distances. Accuracy within one or two inches will assure you of good results. Longer distances might exceed the coherency length of the laser, and your holograms might not come out right. Note that high-power lasers generally have longer coherency lengths than low-power ones.

The arrangement requires three diverging lenses, three mirrors, and two beam splitters. A slightly different variation, using fewer components, is presented in the holography gallery found in the next chapter. The first beam splitter reflects the light to a reference mirror. This light is then expanded by a bi-concave lens and directed at the film. The transmitted light through the first beam splitter is divided again by a second beam splitter. These two beams are bounced off positioning mirrors, expanded by lenses, and pointed at the object.

It's very important that no light from the two object mirrors strikes the film. It is a good idea to baffle the light by placing black cards on either side of the film holder, as illustrated in the figure.

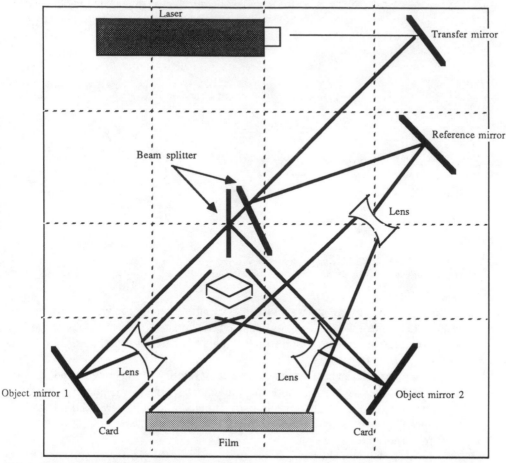

FIG. 17-13. *Optical arrangement (shown in the sandbox) for a multiple-beam transmission hologram. The object is illuminated on two sides, providing even lighting and better contrast.*

Exposure time should be similar to the one-beam method described earlier in this chapter, but you should probably make another test strip to make sure. Although roughly the same total amount of light is striking the film in both single- and multiple-beam setups, there is inherent light loss through the beam splitters as well as additional light scattering through the three lenses.

Table 17-5. Split-Beam Transmission Hologram Parts List

1	He-Ne laser
3	8 to 10 mm bi-concave lens
1	Holographic film in film holder
4	1- to 2-inch-square front-surface mirror
2	Plate beam splitter (50:50)
2	Black blocking card
1	Object

Process the film in the usual manner, and when dried, place it back in the film holder, emulsion side facing the reference beam. Remove the object you photographed as well as the object mirrors and second beam splitter because you need only the reference beam to reconstitute the image. An image should now appear.

You can visually see how the processed hologram must be placed in the exact same position relative to the reference beam, or the image won't appear. Try turning the film in the holder. Notice that the image disappears if you rotate the film more than a few degrees in either direction.

18

Advanced Holography

Most people have enjoyed looking at a hologram, but few people have made one. But if just looking at a hologram is such fun, imagine what its like to make your own. The last chapter introduced the basics of holography and showed you how to make your own transmission-type holograms. This chapter takes you several steps further, revealing how to make colorful reflection holograms, circular holograms, or even holographic movies. There are also several alternative setups for both transmission and reflection holograms you might like to try.

ADVANCED SANDBOX

The 2-by-2-foot sandbox described in the last chapter is fine for tinkering around, but serious holography requires a bigger work area. FIGURE 18-1 shows a design for a 4-by-4-foot sandbox using plywood, concrete blocks, poured concrete, and automobile inner tubes. A parts list is provided in TABLE 18-1. The table uses basic masonry and concrete-pouring techniques, so if you aren't familiar with these, pick up any good book on the subject at the library. Although the procedure of pouring and leveling concrete might seem too involved, it's actually a simple process that takes just one or two hours.

Start the table by laying a 4-by-4-foot carpet on the floor. Place five concrete blocks, each measuring 8 by 8 by 16 inches, over the carpet, as shown in FIG. 18-2. Add small pieces of carpet on top of the blocks, then set a ¾-inch piece of 4-by-4-foot plywood squarely over the blocks. Add yet another piece of carpet over the plywood.

Inflate four small automobile or motorcycle inner tubes to 50 to 60 percent full. Don't overfill—just inflate enough so that the inner tube starts to expand and that a heavy weight

268

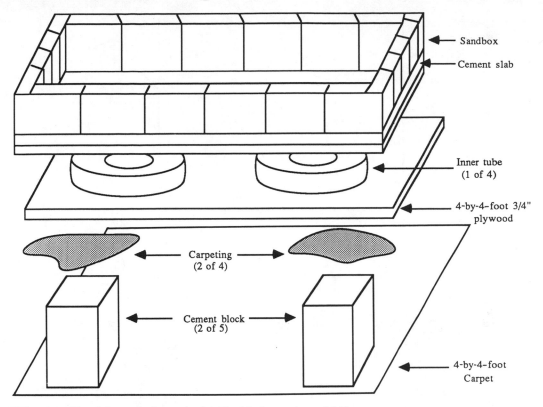

FIG. 18-1. *Materials required to make the 4-by-4-foot concrete sand table.*

Table 18-1. Large Sand Table Parts Lists

Base and Pedestal

5	Cement building blocks (8 by 8 by 16 inches)
5	8-inch-square pieces of carpet
1	4-foot-square piece of carpeting
4	10- to 14-inch inner tubes
1	4-by-4-foot sheet of ¾-inch-thick plywood

Sand Box

1	4-by-4-foot sheet of ¾-inch-thick plywood
16	12-by-12-inch-square stepping stones (or equivalent)
4	48-inch lengths of 2-by-4 framing lumber (for cement slab)
2	Bags Redi-Mix (or similar) cement
1	Bag mortar mix
1	4-by-4-foot piece of chicken wire
4	75- or 100-pound bags of washed, sterilized, and filtered sand

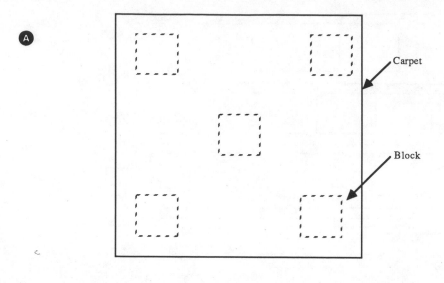

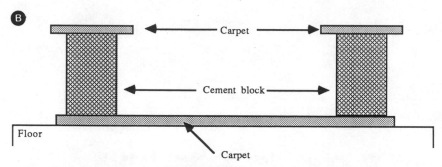

FIG. 18-2. *Placement of the carpet and blocks. (A) Top view; (B) Side view.*

placed on top will not squeeze the rubber together. Inner tubes for small 12- or 13-inch car wheels work well. Alternatively, you can use wide motorcycle-tire inner tubes. Use a fifth tube in the middle of the table if the tubes are very small.

Cut a piece of plywood to 4 by 4 feet. Nail 2-by-4 framing to the outside edge of the plywood. Use only a few nails for each side; the framing is temporary. Mix two bags of Redi-Mix (or similar) cement according to instructions. In most cases, all you add is water. An old washbucket makes a good mixing bin. Lay a piece of plastic tarpaulin in the box to prevent cement from oozing out the sides. Fill the box about ⅓-full with cement, then place a piece of 4-by-4-foot chicken wire (trim the chicken wire so that it fits) on top of the cement. Pour the remaining concrete over the chicken wire.

The concrete should reach the top of the box. If it doesn't, mix a little more, but you don't need to use a whole bag. Use a piece of scrap 2-by-4 as a leveling board to smooth out the concrete. Once the cement is leveled, leave it alone overnight. Read the instructions that came with the cement to see if you should water the slab as it dries to prevent cracking. If watering is recommended, sprinkle a small amount of water on the slab every few hours. Should the slab be cracked after drying, fill it using concrete filling cement, available at most building supply stores. After the slab has dried (the cement is now concrete), remove the 2-by-4 frame pieces and trim away the tarpaulin.

Now arrange a series of stepping stones around the perimeter of the slab as shown in FIG. 18-3. The size of the stepping stones doesn't matter as long as they are about 1 inch thick. A common stepping stone size is 12 by 12 inches; you don't need anything fancy (don't buy colored or fluted stones).

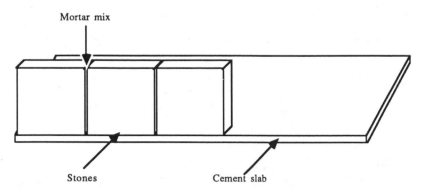

FIG. 18-3. *Adding square stepping stones to the perimeter of the concrete slab. Use mortar to set the stones.*

Prepare a bucket of mortar mix according to instructions. With a trowel, glop the mortar onto the bottom and sides of the stones and apply them to the perimeter of the slab (you might need to wet the slab and stones first with clean water). Work slowly and try to use just the right amount of mortar, but you can scrape off mortar that oozes between the stones with the trowel.

If the stones you use won't fit evenly around the perimeter of the slab—the corners don't meet, for example—you can cut them into smaller pieces by first making a scoring line. Score the stone with a hacksaw at the place where you want to make the cut. After the score is ⅛- to ¼-inch deep, place the stone at a curb or other ledge. Press down with both hands to break the stone at the score. Your first attempt might not work, but with practice, you'll get the hang of it. You can also use smaller stepping stones or even red brick to fill in corners that don't meet.

The mortar takes about a day to dry and might also require a sprinkle now and then with water to prevent cracking. After the mortar has set, add 16 to 18 100-pound bags of sand. Fill to about 2 inches from the top of the table. At this point, you may want to remember that the table will weigh about a ton when filled with sand, so if you put the table on a rickety floor, you'll soon regret it.

The sand table is now complete. Some holographers like to paint the concrete flat black to reduce light scatter and to improve the looks. Painting is not necessary, but do as you please.

MAKING A REFLECTION HOLOGRAM

Transmission holograms require you to shine the expanded beam of a laser through them in order to see an image. Another type of hologram that doesn't require a laser for viewing is the reflection hologram. These work by shining light (white or colored)

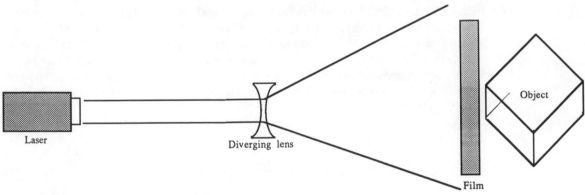

FIG. 18-4. *Basic single-beam reflection hologram arrangement.*

off the diffraction grating surface of the hologram. If viewed under white light, the hologram gives off a rainbow of dazzling colors.

Mixing the Chemicals

Reflection holograms are no more difficult to make than transmission holograms, although the processing chemistry is a bit different. White-light reflection holograms can use Kodak D-19 developer but should be bleached using one of the following formulas:

★ Carefully mix 20 grams (or about one tablespoon) of potassium bromide and 20 grams mercuric chloride *(fatal if swallowed)* in one liter of water. This stuff is dangerous and highly caustic, so never touch it with bare fingers or allow it to splash on skin, clothes, or eyes.

Or,

★ Dissolve two grams of potassium dichromate with 30 grams of potassium bromide in one liter of water. After these have thoroughly mixed, carefully add two cm^3 of concentrated sulfuric acid (always add acid to water, not the other way around). This is also nasty stuff and will burn skin if you touch it. Wear gloves and safety goggles when mixing, and use gloves or tongs when processing the film.

The best reflection holograms need a fixing step, just like regular photographic film and paper. Fixer comes pre-made (in powder or liquid), making it easy to use. Kodak Rapid Fixer with hardener is a good choice. Mix according to instructions.

Setting Up

FIGURE 18-4 shows the most rudimentary arrangement for making a reflection hologram. See TABLE 18-2 for a parts list. Position the laser, lens, film, and object in a direct line. For best results, the object used in reflection-type holography should be relatively small in comparison to the film and should be placed within a few inches of the film. Larger images or those placed far away tend to be dark and fuzzy.

As you read in the last chapter, reflection holograms require a film without the antihalation backing; be sure to use this type. When you are ready to make the exposure, turn out the lights, remove the film, and place the film in the holder.

If you are using a glass-plate film holder, remember to press the plates together firmly and keep constant pressure for 10 to 20 seconds to remove air bubbles trapped between the glass and film. Use wood blocks to apply even pressure. Snap the binder clips around the glass and position the holder in front of the object. If necessary, mount the film holder between two PVC or dowel pillars.

As with the transmission hologram, the beam should be expanded so that the outer ⅓ of the diameter falls off the edge of the film. You want the inner ⅔ of the beam, which is the brightest portion. Unlike transmission holograms, reflection holograms call for a ratio between reference and object at a more even 1:1 or 2:1. Use a photographic light meter or power meter to determine proper beam ratios.

Exposure time depends on the power output of the laser as well as the size of the film (or more precisely, the amount of beam spreading), but you might have luck using trial exposures of 3 to 5 seconds with a 1 mW laser and a 1 to 2 seconds for a 3 mW laser.

Processing the Film

In dim or green-filtered light, dip the film in the developer tray and process for 2 to 5 minutes. As a general rule of thumb, a reflection hologram should pass about 20 to 30 percent of the light when held up to a green safelight. After developing, rinse in water or stop bath for 15 seconds.

Dip the film in the first fixer bath for 2 to 3 minutes. After fixing is complete, the room lights can be turned on (fixer renders the film insensitive to further exposure to light). Wash again in water for 15 seconds.

Place the film in the bleach mixture for 1 to 2 minutes or until the film clears. Rinse once more in water for 15 seconds. Finally, place the film in a second fixer bath for 3-5 minutes or until the hologram turns a brown color.

Wash all the chemicals away by rinsing the film under running water for at least five minutes. Then, dip the hologram in Photoflo, squeegee it, and hang it up to dry (details on these last steps are in the previous chapter). Be aware that you can't see a holographic image until the film is completely dried, so don't judge your success (or failure) at this point.

If you are impatient and can't wait for the film to dry on its own, you can hurry up the process by blow-drying the film with a hair dryer. Set the dryer on no heat (air only) and gently waft it 6 to 8 inches in front of the film. The backing will dry quickly but the emulsion takes 5-10 minutes. Always remember to dry film in a dust-free place. Amateur photographers like to use the tub or shower in the bathroom, a place where airborne dust usually doesn't stay for long.

To sum up:

✶ Develop in D-19 (or similar) developer for 2 to 5 minutes.

Table 18-2. Single Beam Reflection Hologram Setup Parts List		
	1	He-Ne laser
	1	8 to 10 mm bi-concave lens
	1	Holographic film in film holder
	1	Object

★ Rinse in water or stop bath for 15 seconds.
★ Fix in first fixer for 2 to 3 minutes (light on after fixing).
★ Rinse in water for 15 seconds.
★ Bleach for 1 to 2 minutes (or until the film clears).
★ Rinse in water for 15 seconds.
★ Fix in second fixer for 3 to 5 minutes.
★ Wash thoroughly under running water for 5+ minutes.
★ Dip in Photoflo for 15 seconds; squeegee.
★ Dry for at least 30 minutes.

Alternate Method

A slightly less complex processing method can be used to make reflection holograms. Develop the film in D-19 for 2 to 5 minutes, then wash in running water for 5 minutes. Bleach the film using the sulfuric acid bleach described above for 2 minutes or until the film clears (becomes transparent). Wash another 5 to 10 minutes and dry it.

VIEWING REFLECTION HOLOGRAMS

Reflection holograms don't require a laser for image reconstruction. Just about any source of light will work, including sunlight or the light from an incandescent light. Avoid greatly diffused light such as that from a fluorescent lamp, or the hologram will look fuzzy. The ideal light source is a point-source, such as an unfrosted filament bulb. You will see the image as you tilt the hologram at angles to the light.

Note the many colors in the picture, particularly green. Although made with a red helium-neon light, the film shrinks after processing, so it tends to reflect shorter wavelength light. The amount of shrinkage varies depending on the film, but it often correlates to 50 to 100 nanometers, reducing the red 632.8 nm wavelength of the a helium-neon laser to about 500 to 550 nm.

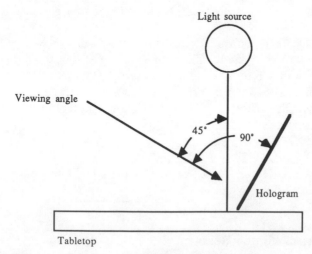

FIG. 18-5. *How to view the processed (and dried) reflection hologram in white light.*

274

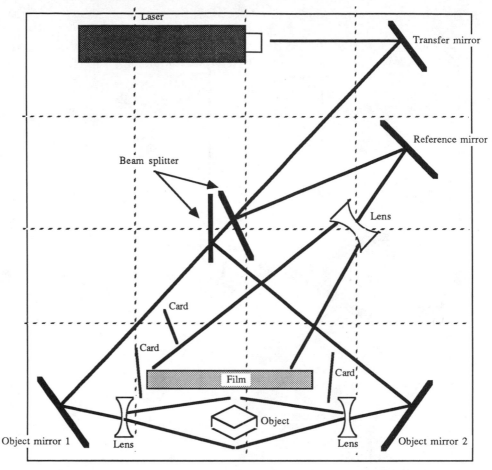

FIG. 18-6. *Optical arrangement (shown in the sandbox) for a multiple-beam reflection hologram. The object is illuminated on two sides, providing even lighting and better contrast.*

The best viewing setup for a reflection hologram is shown in FIG. 18-5. Place the light from a desk lamp straight down at the table. Tilt the hologram toward you until the image becomes clear (about 45 to 50 degrees).

IMPROVED REFLECTION HOLOGRAMS

There are a number of methods to make better and more interesting reflection holograms. One is to use a casting or mold for an object and place the mold directly behind the film. The hologram that results has an eerie 3-D quality to it where you can't tell if the object is concave or convex. Try it.

A split-beam reflection hologram provides more even lighting and helps improve the three-dimensional quality. FIGURE 18-6 shows one arrangement you can use. Except for the angle of some of the objects, it is nearly identical to the split-beam transmission hologram setup described in the last chapter.

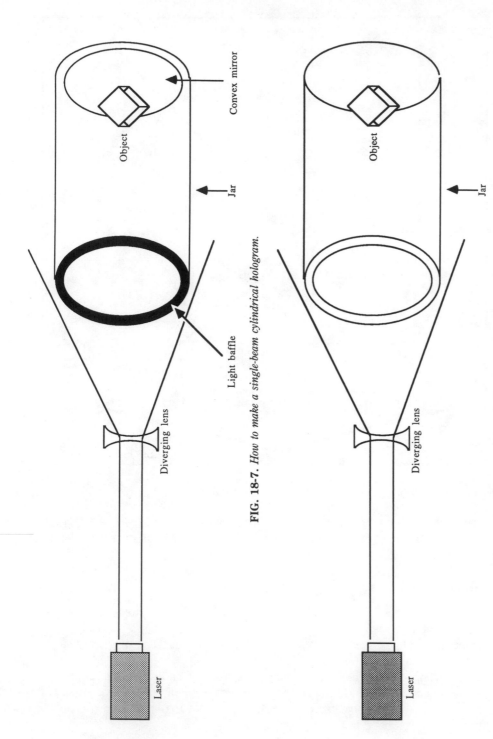

FIG. 18-7. *How to make a single-beam cylindrical hologram.*

Convex mirror

Object

Jar

Light baffle

Diverging lens

Laser

FIG. 18-8. *Another approach to the cylindrical hologram, without the mirror and light baffle.*

Object

Jar

Diverging lens

Laser

Table 18-3. Split-Beam Transmission Hologram Parts List

1	He-Ne laser
3	8 to 10 mm bi-concave lens
1	Holographic film in film holder
4	1- to 2-inch-square front-surface mirror
2	Plate beam splitter (50:50)
3	Black blocking card
1	Object

Table 18-4. Cylindrical Hologram Setup Parts List

1	Laser
1	8 to 10 mm bi-concave lens
1	3-inch diameter (approximately) clear glass or plastic jar (length 2 to 4 inches)
1	3-inch diameter (approximately) convex mirror
1	Object on pedestal
1	Film Strip
1	Light baffle

ADVANCED HOLOGRAPHIC SETUPS

A one-mirror cylindrical transmission hologram can be made using the basic arrangement depicted in FIG. 18-7 (refer to TABLE 18-4 for a parts list). You need wide film for this project; you can either buy it in 70-by-250-mm strips, or cut even larger film to size. The setup is relatively simple. A glass or plastic jar (approximately 3 inches in diameter) holds a convex mirror and the object. Inside the jar, wrap a strip of film so that the emulsion is facing inward. A light baffle made of black artboard, placed at the neck of the jar, prevents laser light from spilling directly onto the film.

In operation, the laser light directly illuminates the object as well as the mirror. The light from the mirror acts as the reference beam. The light from both object and mirror meets at all areas around the circumference of the jar, exposing the entire piece of film. The object shows up better if it is mounted on a pedestal. A small piece of wood painted flat black works well as a pedestal.

Process the film as usual, but be sure the trays are large enough to accommodate the film. To view the hologram, wrap it in a circle and shine an expanded laser beam through the top and against one inside wall. View the film by rotating it. You can support the film by placing it back inside the jar you used for making the hologram.

A reflection hologram is made by changing the convex mirror for a concave one (many such mirrors are coated on both sides so that they are concave/convex). To view the hologram, shine a point source of white light through the top and against one inside wall.

Any object that you can fit in the jar and place on the pedestal can be used for a cylindrical hologram. Good choices for first attempts include chess pieces, old coins (held upright on one edge), and playing dice. If the object doesn't sit the way you want on the pedestal, secure it in place using black modeling clay (not the best method) or Super Glue. Most objects will snap off even with Super Glue, particularly if you apply just a dab on top of the pedestal.

The biggest problem with this method is movement of the film during exposure. Wait at least 5 minutes after loading the film to expose it to allow time for the film to shift and settle. You might want to tap the jar once or twice after placing the film to help set it in position. Leave it alone while you take a coffee break (or better yet, take in a half-hour sitcom).

Direct Beam Cylindrical

Another type of cylindrical hologram doesn't use a mirror. The direct beam cylindrical arrangement shown in FIG. 18-8 makes transmission-type holograms of objects you've mounted on a black pedestal. See TABLE 18-5 for a parts list. The setup requires a well-expanded beam of laser light, so you might need to use two bi-concave lenses, positioned one after the other, to achieve the desired effect.

If you use non-AH film (film without an antihalation backing), you might want to cover the outside of jar with black construction paper to prevent the film from being fogged by stray light that strikes the outside of the jar. Once again, be sure to place the film securely in the jar. Place tape on the top portion of the film to keep it from moving; wait at least 10 to 15 minutes for the film to settle.

Directing the Beam

It is easiest to expose objects by placing the jar sideways on the sand table. That requires you to mount the pedestal and object to the mirror and secure the mirror to the base of the jar. When this isn't practical or desirable, you may place the jar upright and direct the beam into the jar with a large front-surface mirror.

While this approach works, it's not highly recommended, because dust, fingerprints, and other contamination on the mirror can upset the exposure. Reflected laser light is never as pure when it is expanded to cover a wide area. Whenever possible, laser light should should be unexpanded when bounced off mirrors.

Multiple-Channel Holograms

A transmission hologram must always be positioned so that the illumination from the laser is at the same angle as the reference beam when the picture was first taken.

Table 18-5. Cylindrical Hologram Setup Parts List

1	Laser
1	8 to 10 mm bi-concave lens
1	3-inch diameter (approximately) clear glass or plastic jar (length 2 to 4 inches)
1	Object on pedestal
1	Film strip

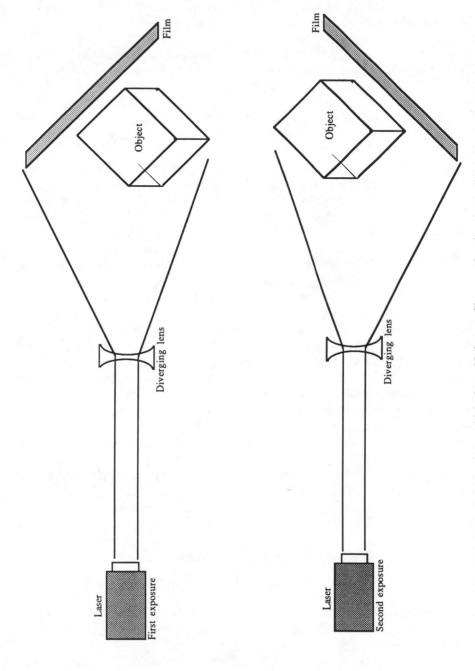

FIG. 18-9. *How to make a multiple-channel hologram. Shown are locations for the film holder for the first and second exposures of the same object.*

279

Canting the film at an angle makes the image disappear. While this is often considered a nuisance by beginning holographers, it's actually a considerable benefit because it means you can expose the same piece of film with an almost unlimited number of scenes! You see each scene by rotating the film or by shifting its angle relative to the illumination beam. This process is most often called multiple-channel holography, and it takes many forms.

In practice, you want to limit the number of exposures to two or four. The more scenes recorded on the film, the more chance they will interfere with one another. The objects for multiple-channel holography should be relatively small in comparison to the size of film you are using. A good rule of thumb for a two-channel hologram (one that has two separate images on it) is that the subjects should be about half the size of the film. In a four-channel hologram, the subjects should be approximately one-quarter the size of the film.

Other forms of multiple channel holograms, including multiplex still-film holography, can accommodate hundreds and even thousands of separate images when the area of exposure is controlled. *Multiplex still-film holography* (or *holographic stereograms*) use frames of movie film recorded as slits on the hologram. After processing, the film is wrapped in a circle and you see each "frame" as the slits roll by.

A famous example is this "Kiss," created by Lloyd Cross and Pam Brazier, where a woman blows a kiss, then winks. The technique is fascinating but beyond the scope of this book. For more information on this holographic technique (as well as numerous others), consult *Holography Handbook*, by Fred Unterseher, et al (Ross Books, 1982; see Appendix B for other titles).

To make a simple multiple-channel hologram, arrange the laser and optics as shown in FIG. 18-9. Position the film to produce a standard direct-beam transmission hologram. Make the first exposure but at about half the normal time. Shift the position of the film and change subjects (you can also use the same subject, if desired). Make the second exposure, again at about half the normal time. Be sure that the emulsion faces the object and reference beam for both exposures. For best results, the angle of the film should change by 60 to 90 degrees.

After processing, illuminate the hologram in the usual manner. Note how you see object A when the film is tilted one way, then object B when the film is tilted the other way. If you used the same object for both exposures and the angle of the film was roughly 90 degrees, rotating the film will reveal almost 180 degrees of the object.

Instead of physically moving the film, you can rotate it in its holder. For example, you can make a four-channel hologram by rotating the film 90 degrees for each new exposure (exposure time about one-fourth of normal). When viewing the hologram, you see the different views of different objects by spinning the film.

HOLOGRAM GALLERY

Below are several setups you might want to use to create a wide variety of holograms. Included are both transmission and reflection types, using single and multiple beams. In all cases, remember to follow standard holographic practices:

★ Allow time for the table and film to stabilize before taking the exposure.

★ When using glass-plate film holders, be sure the glass is perfectly clean. Press both pieces firmly together for about 30 seconds. Use blocks of wood to exert even

280

pressure. Remove all the trapped air, or the film might move during the exposure.

★ Be sure to place the film so that the emulsion faces the subject and/or reference beam. This isn't always necessary for reflection-type holograms, but it is a good habit.

★ Observe proper lighting ratios between reference and object beams. Generally, transmission holograms have a 3:1 or 4:1 ratio between reference and object beams (but up to 10:1 is sometimes required to eliminate noise); reflection holograms have a 1:1 or 2:1 ratio.

★ Measure distances for reference and object beams to ensure they are approximately equal. Use a cloth or flexible tape.

★ Use the proper chemicals mixed fresh (or stored properly), as per directions. Throw out exhausted chemicals—flush them down the sink and run plenty of water to wash away the chemical residue.

Holographic Interferometry

FIGURE 18-10 shows the basic setup for experimenting with holographic interferometry, a type of metrologic study where you can visually see how an object moves under stress. An interferometric hologram is made with two exposures: one where the object under test is "at rest," and other when it is "under stress." Slight differences in shape and structure can occur between the two states, causing movement that shows up in the two exposures. The amount and type of movement is clearly visible in the form of interference lines.

To make an interferometric hologram, take one exposure of the object (a ruler in the example) at about half-normal time—that is, if the usual exposure is 3 seconds reduce it to 1.5 seconds. Then, without disturbing anything, apply stress (the weight) to the object and after allowing time for settling, take another exposure. It is important that you do not disturb anything in the setup other than to carefully apply the weight.

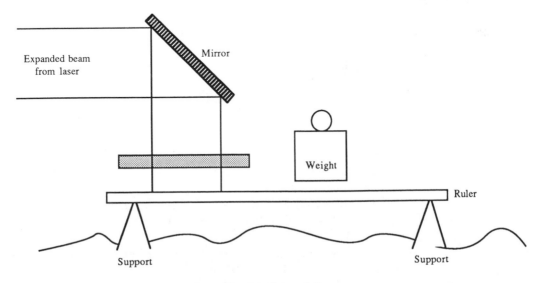

FIG. 18-10. *The basic arrangement for making interference holograms.*

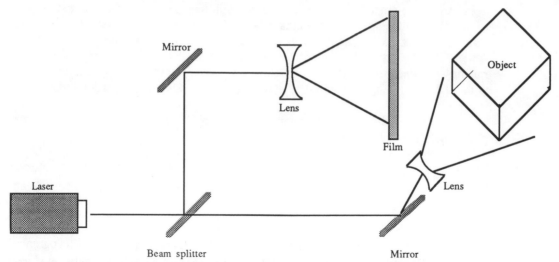

FIG. 18-11. *An alternative scheme for producing a multiple-beam reflection hologram.*

If the ruler, film, or other components shift even a few millionths of an inch, the hologram will be ruined. Don't expect to get this one right the first time. It requires a great deal of patience and careful arrangement.

If the ruler doesn't prove a cooperative subject, try another. One good choice is a small C-clamp pressed tightly around a steel plastic block. Take one picture with the clamp tightened, but not overly so, on the block. Cinch down on the clamp and take another exposure. You will see stress marks around the C-shaped mouth of the clamp as well as at the point of contact on the block. Other possible subjects include a light bulb in both cold and hot states (turn the bulb on for a few minutes between exposures, but be sure to block the film from exposure), and the strain on a piece of metal from an increased electromagnetic current.

Multiple-Beam Reflection Hologram

The setup in FIG. 18-11 shows another arrangement you can use to make a multiple-beam reflection hologram. It is a more simple approach to the multiple beam plan described earlier in this chapter and doesn't provide the same even lighting of the object, but it's easy to arrange for classroom study.

Soft Lighting Technique

Transmission holograms often suffer from high-contrast lighting where the shadows have little detail. While this can enhance the three-dimensional quality of the image, the lighting effect is unnatural. FIGURE 18-12 shows how you can soften the lighting to achieve a less dramatic appearance. The reference beam is directed towards the film as usual, but the object beam is diffused using opal or frosted glass.

Note that the glass acts as a mirror on the back side so you should add black cards as necessary to avoid light spills. Expand the beam slightly before striking the back of the glass to avoid a hot spot in the center. Try exposure times slightly longer than normal.

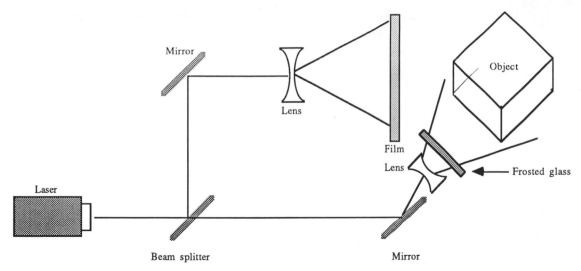

FIG. 18-12. *One way to provide soft lighting for the object is to place a piece of frosted glass in the path of the expanded object beam.*

Downward Facing Hologram

A simple form of single-beam transmission holography entails pointing the film toward the sand. The object must be relatively small and should be lightly colored, because shadows will be heavy (the object is back-lit only).

MISCELLANEOUS IDEAS AND TIPS

Here are a collection of ideas and tips you might find useful.

Holography Groups

Holographers are generally a friendly group and like to share ideas and techniques. If you don't know other holographers in your area, ask at your local camera store or college (the photography, chemistry, or physics departments are good choices). One of the best ways to learn about holography is to watch someone else do it. Offer to help out on the next shoot. You'll gain useful practical knowledge that could otherwise take you years to uncover by yourself.

You will also find it less expensive if you join a holography group. If the group is well organized, it might have community-property equipment such as spatial filters, collimating mirrors, or even argon and krypton lasers. Or, look for someone who is willing to loan you the equipment you need for your next holographic masterpiece. Rental should either be free or modest, but in any case it will be considerably less than if you rented the items from a commercial outfit. You might even have gear that's worth sharing as a way of returning the favor.

Holography groups often put on their own public shows where others can come to wonder in astonishment "How do they do it?" With experience comes more professional results, and you might find yourself submitting your holograms for judging at regional shows and fairs (photo contents often have a special holography category). If prize money is involved, you can use it to help pay for your holographic habit.

Making Money With Holography

Besides contests (which are rare and usually don't provide much money), you might be able to turn your holographic expertise into cash. Consider making holograms of jewelry, gemstones, and other artifacts and selling them at swap meets or flea markets. You don't need to tend the booth yourself; be a distributor and sell them to other retailers. Of course, you can offer your wares to gift and card shops, but you are competing against national companies that specialize in low-cost, ''general-purpose'' holograms.

Holograms as Gifts

Though it doesn't offer monetary pay, you can make holograms for everyone for Christmas or other gift-giving seasons. Because you pick the subject, you can personalize the holograms for each recipient. Unless your friends and family own their own laser, however, you'll want to make reflection-type holograms so that they can be viewed under white or filtered light. You can complete your holographic offerings by placing them in frames or even housings that include a point light source (an unfrosted 15-watt night-light works well).

Adding an Aperture Card

Most low-cost helium-neon lasers emit a faint glow around the periphery of the beam. Because this glow is low power, it doesn't often interfere with your holograms. But to ensure that the glow doesn't wreck a hologram that you've spent hours preparing, place a card with a hole in it in front of the laser. Make the hole large enough for the entire beam to pass through (about 1mm in diameter), but nothing else. Avoid making the hole too small or the beam will diffract as it passes through. A better approach to cleaning up the laser beam is to use a spatial filter. See Chapter 3 for details on what a spatial filter is and how it works.

Using View-Camera Film Backs

A view camera is a little more than a lens attached to a bellows. At the focal point of the lens is a removable ground glass. The photographer frames and focuses the subject on the ground glass and then takes it out and replaces it with a film back. A black slide inserted in the film back prevents the film from being fogged in daylight. The slide is removed, the exposure taken, and the slide is returned.

Film backs for view cameras come in various sizes and styles, and many can be adopted for use for transmission holograms. The backs are unique in that they use a pressure plate to hold the film steady. This is a real boon to the holographer who is constantly struggling to keep the film from moving during an exposure. Because of the pressure plate, however, film backs can't be used for reflective holography were the expanded laser beam must pass through the film. You can find film backs in larger photographic stores that cater to professionals. A used film back is just as good as a new one, so don't be shy about saving a few dollars.

Chemical Alternatives

Some holographers like to dilute the D-19 developer 4:1 (four parts water, one part developer) in order to improve the resolution of the film. Because the chemical is diluted, development takes about four times longer. Dilute the developer only as you need it.

If potassium ferrocyanide is not available for making bleach for transmission holograms, you may substitute cupric bromide. An alternative bleach for reflection holograms consists of 30 grams potassium bromide, 15 grams of borax, two grams of potassium dichromate, and two grams of p-benzoquinone (check photo or industrial chemical houses for the last ingredient). The mixture, although still poisonous, is safer than the mercuric chloride bleach mixture described earlier in this chapter.

Displaying Your Holograms

You don't need the sand table to view your finished holograms, so if you want to show your work to others, there is no need to lug around 2,000 pounds of luggage with you. Presentations and shows with transmission holograms can be simplified by building a portable laser hologram table. This table, which can be set up in 10 minutes or less, houses the laser, beam expanding optics, and hologram.

The table can simply be an optical breadboard (see Chapter 7) engineered for permanent use to display holograms. One way of arranging the laser and optics is shown in FIG. 18-13. A parts list for the table appears in TABLE 18-6. The beam-steering mirrors are used to "fold" the light path, enabling you to use a smaller table. The laser is placed on one side and the beam diverted to the middle rear of the table. One or two bi-concave lenses are used to expand the beam, which is directed toward the hologram. The amount of expansion depends on the size of the finished holograms. If your holograms are different

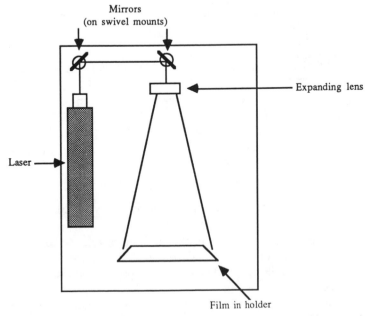

FIG. 18-13. *Top view of the laser, mirrors, lens, and film holder for a portable transmission hologram viewing table.*

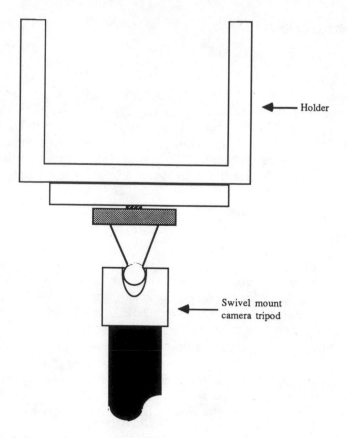

Holder

Swivel mount
camera tripod

FIG. 18-14. *A swivel mount from a portable camera tripod can be used to position the film holder at angle to a laser or white light source.*

Table 18-6. Portable Hologram Viewing Table Parts List

1	18-by-24-inch piece of ¼-inch Masonite or ⅜-inch plywood
1	Laser
2	Mirrors on swivel mounts (see Chapter 7)
1-2	8 to 10 mm diameter bi-concave lenses, in mounts (see Chapter 7)
1	Film holder, with swivel mount

sizes, you can control the beam spreading by making the second lens removable and adjustable.

The film holder is designed so that it can be tilted in relation to the laser beam. A ball-and-socket joint from a low-cost portable tripod can be used to adjust the angle. Simply loosen the knob and tilt the film holder into the position you want. Lock the knob and the holder stays in place.

Although some people might want to see the inner workings of your holographic setup, you'll probably want to enclose it to block stray light. A frame made of plastic or metal can be constructed and placed over the table. Alternatively, you can position the table behind a partition and expose just the holographic film for viewing. Use pieces of black velvet or other material as drapes. This technique can be used when your holograms are on display at the fair, photo show, or museum.

An even simpler arrangement can be built for reflection holograms. The laser is not necessary, nor are the beam-expanding optics. You need a fairly bright point source of light, positioned above the hologram. The hologram should be mounted in a tiltable holder, as illustrated in FIG. 18-14, to allow you to set the proper angle of view. You can also motorize the holder so that the angle of the hologram shifts slowly, revealing its 3-D nature. An animation motor (designed for point-of-sale promotional signs), hooked up to a cam for the forward and backward motion, should do nicely.

Manual and Automatic Beam Shutter

Using a card as a shutter has its disadvantages: it's clumsy to use and you could actually disturb the table as you lift it out of the sand. Just being close to the sand table during the exposure can cause unwanted air movements that can upset the optics, beam, and film. And if you use a high-powered 8 to 10 mW He-Ne for your holograms, the light might be so strong that you only need exposure times of less than 1 second. With short exposure times come inaccuracy: it is hard to manually control the shutter card with accuracy of better than ½ second.

One way of providing more accurate shutter control is to use the shutter mechanism on a discarded camera. Use an old camera with a leaf-type shutter—the kind resembling an iris. Don't use a focal plane shutter such as those used in most 35 mm SLRs. You can find old cameras at flea marts and garage sales.

Inspect the camera to make sure that the shutter is still working, then take the camera home and dismantle it. Remove the shutter and mount it on a stand where you can easily reach the shutter speed control, release, and cocking mechanism (some shutters are self-cocking).

With the shutter, you can set the desired short-exposure time by dialing it in on the speed control knob, cocking the shutter, and pushing the shutter release. Most of the old shutters open and close with an unmistakable clang that can vibrate through the table and disturb the optics and film. Therefore, for best results, locate the laser and shutter off the table. As long as the laser is on a fairly sturdy mount, any slight movement will not affect the hologram (assuming the laser is well made and doesn't loose coherency when vibrated; a check with the Michelson interferometer can visually show you how well the laser maintains coherency).

Old camera shutters usually don't have settings longer than one second. For time exposures, you place the speed control ring in ''bulb'' position and manually control the duration that the shutter is open. Use a cable release and a darkroom timer to manually control the shutter.

A fully electronic shutter system is shown in FIG. 18-15. Here, a 12-volt solenoid is mounted on a piece of ⅛-inch thick acrylic plastic. The plunger of the solenoid connects to the shutter plate as well as a spring. When the solenoid is not energized, the shutter is at rest and blocks the beam. Energize the solenoid and the shutter moves, unblocking the beam. The finished solenoid shutter is shown in the photo in FIG. 18-16. A parts list for the solenoid shutter is provided in TABLE 18-7.

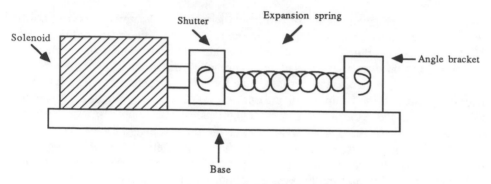

Solenoid   Shutter   Expansion spring   Angle bracket   Base

FIG. 18-15. *Layout for the solenoid shutter.*

FIG. 18-16. *The completed solenoid shutter.*

POWER/LIGHT METER

A photographic light meter can be used to test the output of a laser or to make sure that the beam ratios are correct for a given holographic setup. Best results are obtained using a well-made meter with a white diffusing filter placed over the sensing element. The filter prevents the laser light from forcing the sensor into non-linear operation. The filter isn't strictly needed when measuring expanded laser light.

You can make your own power/light meter using an ordinary solar cell and a volt-ohmmeter (VOM). Connect the solar cell to the voltmeter as shown in Chapter 4. Place a small piece of white diffusion over the cell. To use the meter, dial the VOM to the mV range, and position the cell in the path of the beam.

Table 18-7. Solenoid Shutter Parts List

1	12 Vdc solenoid, with mounting bolts or screws
1	½-inch-long expanded spring (length when relaxed)
2	1-by-½-inch corner angle irons
1	½-by-¾-inch plastic (for shutter)
1	6/32-by-½-inch bolt, nut, washer

These past two chapters have only lightly covered the art and science of holography, leaving many topics untouched. If you would like to learn more about holography, refer to Appendix B for a list of selected books on the subject. One in particular, *Holography Handbook* (Unterseher, Hansen, and Schlesinger) offers an excellent tutorial in making many types of basic and advanced holograms.

19

Basic Laser Light Shows

Over 16 million people have seen the Laserium light show, and just about every one of those 16 million have gone home afterward wishing they could create the same kind of mind-boggling special effects. If you have a laser, you are already on the road to producing your own laser light shows. A small assortment of basic accessories is all you need to make dancing, oscillating shape on the ceiling, wall, or screen.

This chapter details some basic approaches to affordable laser light shows. You'll learn how to produce light shows using dc motors and mirrors that make interesting and controllable "Spirograph" shapes, how to make a laser beam dance to the beat of music, and how to make "sheet" and "cone" effects using mirrors and lenses.

The Laserium "laserists" use advanced components and lasers costing many tens of thousands of dollars. A few of these more sophisticated components are detailed in the next chapter (there, you'll discover the use of servos and galvanometers to control the laser beam, how to make exciting smoke effects, and ways to use argon, krypton, and other laser types to add more colors to the show).

THE "SPIROGRAPH" EFFECT

Imagine your laser drawing unique, "atom-shaped," repeating spiral light forms, with you adjusting their size and shape by turning a couple of knobs. The "Spirograph" light show device (named after the popular Spirograph drawing toy made by Kenner) uses three small dc motors and an easy-to-build motor speed and direction control circuit.

Depending on how you adjust the speed and direction of the motors, you alter the shape and size of the spiral light forms. And because the motors used are not constant

Table 19-1. "Spirograph" Light Show Device Parts List

3	Small 1.5 to 6 Vdc hobby motor
3	Lincoln penny
3	1-inch diameter or square, thin, front-surface mirror
3	¾-inch electrical conduit pipe hanger
3	^{10}⁄₂₄-by-¾-inch bolt, flat washer, tooth lock washer
6	^{10}⁄₂₄ nut
1	8-by-24-inch pegboard (¼-inch thick)
2	24-inch lengths of 2-by-2-inch framing lumber
2	4-inch lengths of 2-by-2-inch framing lumber

speed, slight variations in rotation rate cause the light forms to pulse and change all on their own. A complete parts list for the "Spirograph" light show device is in TABLE 19-1.

Mirror Mounting

Got a penny? That and a little bit of glue is all you need to mount each mirror to a motor. The best motors to use are the 1.5- to 6-volt dc hobby motors that are made by Mabuchi, Johnson, numerous other companies and are sold by Radio Shack and most every other electronics outlet in the country. Measure the diameter of the shaft; it can vary depending on the manufacturer and original application for the motor. Then drill a hole in the exact center of a penny using a bit just slightly smaller than the motor shaft.

Use a drill press to hold the penny in place and to prevent the bit from skipping. You'll find drilling easier if you turn the coin over and position the bit in the middle column of the Lincoln Memorial (for a penny less than about 25 years old). Note that the newest pennies are easiest to drill. Don't worry; the hole can be off a few fractions of an inch, but it should not be larger than the motor shaft. If anything, strive for a press fit. File away the flash left by the bit so the surface of the penny is smooth.

Next, apply a drop of cyanoacrylate adhesive (Super Glue) to a 1-inch-square or diameter mirror to the center of the penny. Best results are obtained when using a fairly thin mirror and gap-filling glue. The Hot Stuff Super "T" glue made by HST-2 (available at hobby stores) is a good choice. Wait an hour for the adhesive to dry and set. Repeat the procedure for the other three mirrors.

Avoid gaps between the mirrors and pennies. Although a small amount of misalignment is desirable, a large gap will cause excessive beam displacement when the motor turns. You'll see exactly why this is important once you build the Spirograph light show device.

Finally, mount the penny and mirror on the end of the motor shaft, as depicted in FIG. 19-1. Apply several drops of adhesive to the shaft and let it seep into the hole in the penny. Wait several hours for the adhesive to set completely before continuing. Alternatively, you can solder the penny to the shaft. This requires a heavy-duty soldering iron or small, controllable torch. Mount the penny on the motor shaft first, then tack on the mirror.

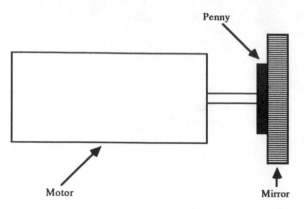

FIG. 19-1. *Mirror and penny mounting detail for the dc motors used in the "Spirograph" light show device.*

Mounting the Motors

Ideal motor mounts can be made with 1-inch plumbing pipe hangers, sold at a plumbing supply outlet or hardware store. The hanger is made of formed, u-shaped metal with a mounting hole on one end and an adjustable open end at the other (many other styles can also be used). Secure the motor in the hanger by loosening the bolt on the end, slipping the motor in, and then finger-tightening the bolt.

Secure the hanger on an 8-by-24-inch piece of ¼-inch hardwood pegboard, as shown in FIG. 19-2. Add wood blocks to the underside of the pegboard to make an optical breadboard, as explained in Chapter 7, "Constructing an Optical Bench." Arrange the hangers as shown in FIG. 19-3, and lightly secure the hangers to the pegboard using ¹⁰⁄₂₄-by-½-inch bolts and matching hardware. Use flat and split washers as indicated in FIG. 19-2 to prevent movement when the motors are turning (and vibrating).

Building the Motor Control Circuit

The motor control circuit allows you to individually control each motor. You have full command over the speed and direction of each motor by flicking a switch and turning a dial.

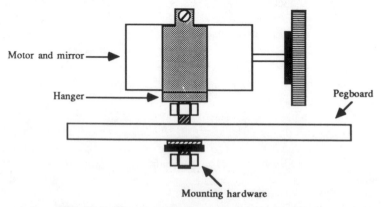

FIG. 19-2. *How to mount the motors to a pegboard base.*

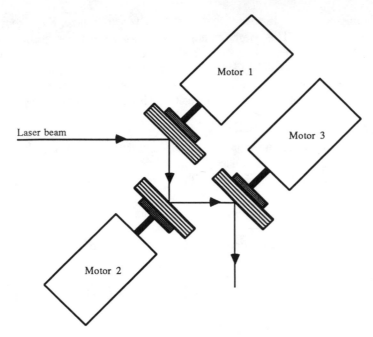

FIG. 19-3. *Arrangement of the motors on the pegboard base.*

The schematic for the motor control circuit is shown in FIG. 19-4. The illustration shows the circuit for only one motor; duplicate it for the remaining two motors. The prototype used a 3½-by-4-inch perforated board and wire-wrapping techniques. Your layout should provide room for the electronics, switches, potentiometers, and transistors on heatsinks (the latter are very important). Lay out the parts before cutting the board to size. Power is provided by a 6 Vdc battery pack consisting of four alkaline "D" cells.

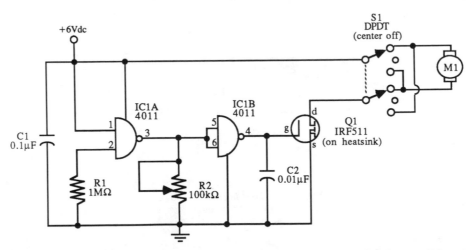

FIG. 19-4. *An easy-to-build pulse width modulation speed control and direction switch for a small dc motor. Q1 must be mounted on a heatsink.*

The double-pole, double-throw switches allow you to control the direction of the motors or turn them off. The potentiometers let you vary the speed of the motors from full to about ½ to ⅔ normal. Different speeds are obtained by varying the "on" time, or duty cycle, of the motors. The more the duty cycle approaches 100 percent, the faster the motor turns. The design of this circuit does not allow the motors to turn at drastically reduced speeds which, in any case, is not really desirable to achieve the spiral light-form effects.

Alternative speed control circuits are shown in FIGS.19-5 through 19-7. FIGURE 19-5 details a similar control circuit using 2N3055 heavy-duty transistors. This circuit also works on the duty-cycle principle (more accurately referred to as pulse width modulation). These transistors should be placed in a suitable aluminum heatsink with proper case-to-heatsink electrical insulation. The 2N3055s and heatsinks require more space than the IRF511 power MOSFET transistors used in the schematic outlined earlier, so make the board larger.

FIGURE 19-7 shows a basic approach using 2- to 5-watt power potentiometers. Be sure to use pots rated for at least 2 watts, or you run the risk of burning them out. Bear in mind that the potentiometer approach consumes more power than the pulse width modulated systems. No matter how fast the motors are turning, a constant amount of

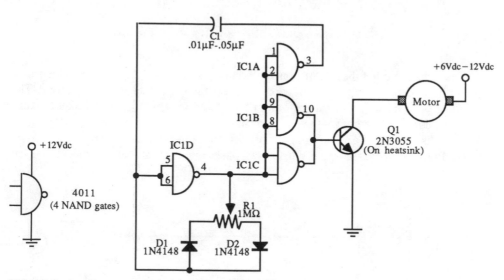

FIG. 19-5. *An alternate method of providing pulse width modulation using a 2N2055 power transistor.*

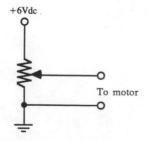

FIG. 19-6. *How to connect a high-wattage rheostat or potentiometer to control the speed of a dc motor.*

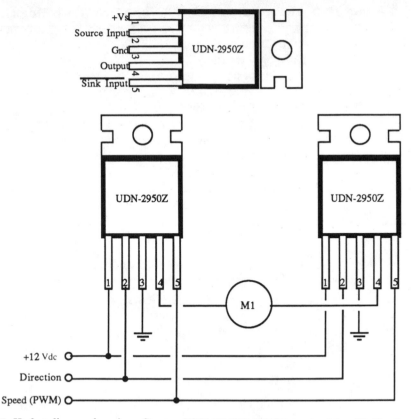

FIG. 19-7. *Hookup diagram for using a Sprague UDN-2950Z half-bridge motor driver IC. Use the output of the circuits in* FIG. *19-4 or 19-5 to supply the Speed (PWM) signal.*

current is always drawn from the batteries. Current not used by the motors is dissipated by the potentiometer as heat.

FIGURE 19-7 shows speed and direction control using a Sprague motor control IC (others are available). You can obtain the IC through most Sprague reps as well as from Circuit Specialists (see Appendix A for sources). Use the pulse width modulation circuit shown in FIG. 19-4 or 19-5 and apply to the speed pin (pin 5) of the UDN-2950Z IC. Parts lists for the three alternative speed control circuits are provided in TABLES 19-2 through 19-4.

Mount the circuit board on one end of the optical breadboard using $^{10}/_{24}$ by $^{1}/_{2}$ bolts and $^{10}/_{24}$ nuts. Make sure there is sufficient space between the bottom of the board and the wire-wrap posts and top of the optical breadboard.

Mounting the Laser

Cut a 3-inch length of 2-inch plastic PVC pipe lengthwise in half. Using $^{10}/_{24}$-by-$^{1}/_{2}$-inch bolts and hardware, mount the two halves on the optical breadboard. Insert a 2½-to 3-inch diameter worm-gear pipe clamp under the PVC half before tightening the nuts and bolts. Use silicone adhesive to attach rubber feet above the four bolt heads. The

Table 19-2. Motor Control Circuit Parts List (Each Motor)

IC1	4011 CMOS NAND gate IC
R1	1 megohm resistor
R2	100 kilohm potentiometer
C1	0.1 μF disc capacitor
C2	0.01 μF disc capacitor
Q1	IRF511 MOSFET power transistor (or equivalent)
S1	DPDT switch, center off
Misc.	Heatsink for Q1

All resistors are 5 to 10 percent tolerance, ¼ watt. All capacitors are 10 to 20 percent tolerance, rated 35 volts or more.

Table 19-3. Alternate #1 Motor Control Circuit Parts List (Each Motor)

IC1	4011 CMOS NAND gate IC
R1	1 megohm potentiometer
C1	0.01 or 0.05 μF capacitor
D1,D2	1N4148 diode
Q1	2N3055 power transistor
Misc.	Heatsink for Q1

All resistors are 5 to 10 percent tolerance, ¼ watt. All capacitors are 10 to 20 percent tolerance, rated 35 volts or more.

Table 19-4. Alternate #2 Motor Control Circuit Parts List (Each Motor)

IC1,2	Sprague UDN-2950Z half-bridge motor driver
1	Speed control circuit (minus drive transistor) from Fig. 19-4 or 19-5

rubber feet serve as a cushion between the laser tube and bolts, as well as to increase the height of the beam over the optical bench. More details on this and other laser-mounting methods can be found in Chapter 7.

The PVC pipe laser holder is designed for a cylindrical laser head. If you are using a bare laser tube, install it in a suitable enclosure as detailed in Chapter 6, ''Build a He-Ne Laser Experimenter's System.''

Aligning the System

Slip the laser into the holder and tighten the two clamps. The distance between the front of the laser and the motors is not critical, but be sure that there is no chance that the mirror on the first motor will touch the end of the laser. Turn the laser on but do not apply power to the motor control circuit. Rotate the hangers on each motor so that the beam is deflected from mirror 1 to 2 to 3.

Fine-tune the alignment by rotating each motor 90 degrees. The misalignment inherent in the mirror mounting should displace the beam on the mirrors. Avoid fall-off where the beam skips off the mirror. Beam fall-off causes a void in the spiral when the motors turn.

If you cannot align the motors so that the beam never falls off the mirrors, check the gap between the mirrors and pennies. Place the motor with the largest gap at the end of the chain as motor number 3. If beam fall-off is still a problem, try mounting a mirror and penny on a new motor.

Place all three switches to their center position and apply power to the motor control circuit. Flick switch #1 up or down and rotate the potentiometer. The motor should turn. If the motor whines but refuses to turn, flick the switch off, turn the pot all the way on, and reapply power. The motor should turn.

Test the speed control circuit by turning the pot. The motor should slow down by an appreciable amount (you'll be able to hear the decrease in speed). If nothing happens, double-check your work. A motor that won't change speed could be caused by improper wiring or a bad transistor. A blown transistor could cause the motor to spin at about a constant 80 percent of full speed. Next reverse the motor by moving the switch to the opposite position. The motor should momentarily come to a halt, turn in its tracks, and go the other way.

Turn the first motor off and repeat the testing procedure for the other two. After all motors check out, turn them back on and point the #3 mirror so that the beam falls on a wall or screen. Watch the spiral light form as all three motors turn. Do you notice any beam fall-off—if so, *stop all the motors* and readjust them. Note that the motors vibrate a great deal at full speed, and that can cause them to go out of alignment. When you get the motors aligned just right, tighten the hangers to prevent them from coming loose.

Test the different types of light forms you can create by turning off the #1 motor and using just #2 and #3. Depending on how the direction is set on the motors, you should see an "orbiting atom" shape on the screen, as depicted in FIG. 19-8. If the form looks more like constantly changing ellipses, reverse the direction of one of the motors. Adjust the speed control on both motors and watch the different effects you can achieve. Now try the same thing with motor #1 and #3 on. Try all the combinations and note the results.

What happens if the light form doesn't show up or appears very small, even when the screen is some distance from the light show device? This can occur if the mirror is precisely aligned with the rotation of the motor. Although this is rare using the construction technique outlined above, it can happen. You can see how much each motor contributes to the creation of the light form by turning on each one in turn. You should see a fairly well-formed circle on the screen. The mirror is too precisely aligned if a dot appears instead of the circle. Replace the mirror and motor with another one and try again.

Note that the size of the circle does not depend on where the beam strikes the mirror. The circle is the same size whether the beam hits the exact center of the mirror or its edge.

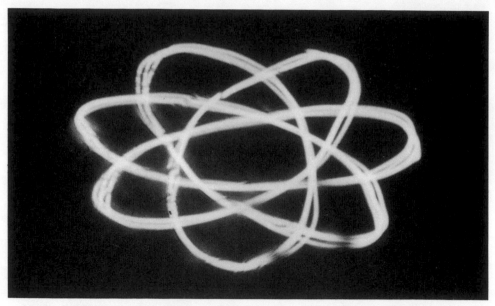

FIG. 19-8. *The "atom" laser lightform made with the "Spirograph" device.*

Notes On Using and Improving the "Spirograph" Device

Here are some notes on how to get the most from the spiral light-form device:

★ Keep the mirrors clean and free of dust or the light forms will appear streaked and blurred.

★ *Never* adjust the position of the motors when they are turning. The mirrors are positioned close together, and moving the motors could cause the glass to touch. The mirrors will then shatter and fragments of glass will fly in all directions. It is a good idea to use protective goggles when adjusting and using the spiral light show device.

★ Cheap dc motors like those used in this project make a lot of noise. You might want to use higher quality motors if you plan on using the "Spirograph" maker in a light show. Get ones with bearings on the shaft. You can also place the device in a soundproof box. Provide a clear window for the beam to come out.

★ The "Spirograph" device is designed for manual control. With the right interface circuit, you can easily connect it to a computer for automated operation. The motor direction and speed control circuit used in this project is similar to the robotic control schemes outlined in my book *Robot Builder's Bonanza* (TAB BOOKS, catalog number 2800). Refer to it for ideas on how to control motors via computer.

★ You can obtain even more light forms by adding a fourth motor. Try it and see what happens.

★ Don't be shy about turning some of the motors off. Some of the most interesting effects are achieved with just two motors.

SOUND-MODULATED MIRRORS

In the early seventies, during the psychedelic light show craze, Edmund Scientific Company offered an unusual device that transformed music into a dancing beam of light.

298

The system, called MusicVision, was simple: Thin front-surface mirrors were attached to a sheet of surgical rubber. The rubber sheet was then pulled taut across the front of an 8- or 10-inch woofer. A projector was positioned off to one side so that it cast one or more beams on the mirrors mounted on the rubber.

When the hi-fi was turned on, the speaker would move, vibrating the rubber sheet and causing the mirrors to bob up and down. The beam of light from the projector would follow the mirror, projecting an undulating and constantly changing pattern on a wall or the back side of a rear-projection screen. A filter wheel added color to the light shapes, which then colorfully bounced and jumped in time to the music.

Imagine what would happen if you replaced the projector and color wheel with a laser. Point the thin beam of a laser at the mirror and you would get a projected image of it on the wall doing a dance. There are numerous ways to build sound-modulated mirror systems. Below are just a few of them; you are free to experiment and come up with some of your own.

The Old Rubber Sheet Over the Speaker Trick

A simple yet effective light show instrument can be made using a small mirror, a sheet of rubber, and a discarded peanut can. This design, with parts indicated in TABLE 19-5, comes from laser light show designer and consultant Jeff Korman, who calls it ''PeanutVision.'' Using an all-purpose adhesive, mount a thin front-surface mirror—measuring approximately ½ inch in diameter—onto a 6-inch square sheet of surgical rubber.

Surgeon's gloves (available at many surplus stores) are a good source of surgical rubber, but a better choice is to use flat squares of the stuff. Check an industrial supply outlet and don't be afraid to improvise. If the rubber dates some time back, however, check to be sure it's still in its protective wrapper. The rubber dries out in time when exposed to air. In a pinch, you can get by using the rubber from balloons, but if possible, use thin-walled balloons.

While waiting for the adhesive to dry, drill 5 to 10 small holes in the metal end of a Planter's Peanuts can. Mount a 3-inch round speaker over the holes. Use small hardware, epoxy, or glue to hold the speaker in place.

Stretch the rubber over the open end of the can. Pull the rubber tight while making sure that the mirror is placed in the approximate center of the opening. Wrap one or more rubber bands around the sheet to secure it, as indicated in FIG. 19-9. Solder a pair of wires to the speaker terminals and connect the leads to a low-wattage stereo or hi-fi. Unless you use a high-capacity rated speaker, don't connect it to a stereo system that delivers more than a few watts—otherwise you'll burn out the voice coil in the speaker.

Table 19-5. PeanutVision Parts List

1	Peanut can measuring approx. 4 inches in diameter by 3¾ inches tall
1	2- to 3-inch diameter speaker
1	Latex rubber; approximately 6 inches square
1	Thin, ½-inch diameter, front-surface mirror
1	Rubber band

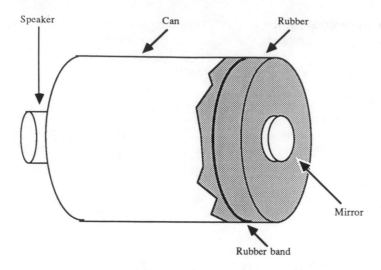

Speaker   Can   Rubber

Mirror

Rubber band

FIG. 19-9. *How to build the PeanutVision, using a peanut can, rubber sheet, mirror, and speaker.*

Connecting the light show speaker in parallel with the main speakers of the hi-fi reduces the chance of burnout, but it also changes the output impedance and might affect the sound. Instead of the usual 8 ohms of impedance of regular hi-fi speakers, adding the light show instrument in parallel reduces the output impedance to 4 ohms (assuming you use an 8-ohm speaker in the light show instrument). This generally causes no damage, but the sound quality of the stereo could be affected.

Use the sound-modulated mirror system by attaching it to a swivel mount and frame. Place the frame in front of the laser and adjust the swivel until the beam strikes the mirror and is reflected to a back wall or screen. The further the wall is from the instrument, the larger the beam pattern will be. You can also control pattern size by adjusting the volume. Again, be careful you don't turn up the volume too much, or the speaker could be ruined.

Enhancing the Light Show

Your light shows look even better if you are the proud owner of an argon, krypton, green He-Ne, helium-cadmium, or other non-red, visible-light gas plasma laser tube. The argon and krypton lasers produce light with many distinct wavelengths. These are mainlines and can be separated by using an equilateral prism or dichroic filters. Send each beam to a different PeanutVision system. An argon laser with its 488.0 and 514.5 mainline beams separated can be used with two sound-modulated mirrors. Alter the appearance of the light forms by feeding the right channel to one mirror and the left channel to the other.

Alternatively, you can add a filter to the sound output of your hi-fi and separate the highs from the lows. Route the high-frequency sounds to one mirror and the lows to the second mirror. Position the mirrors so that the beams converge on the screen. The colors will appear as if they are dancing with one another. Each has its own dance steps, but both are moving together to the beat of the music.

Direct Mirror Mounting

Instead of mounting the mirror on a sheet of surgical rubber, mount it directly onto the speaker cone. The best mounting location is in the center, above the voice coil. If the mirror is thin enough (0.04 inch or so), its mass won't overload the speaker and it should vibrate in unison with the sound.

Frequency response using this mounting technique is excellent—almost the frequency response of the speaker itself. Note that higher frequency sounds don't move the speaker cone and mirror as much as low-frequency sounds so the visual beam pattern effect is more marked at low frequencies.

If you want the visuals only and don't want the speaker to emit sound, you can reduce its audio output by carefully cutting away the cone material. Use a razor blade to cut the cone at the outer edges. Next, cut out the inside where the cone attaches to the voice coil, but keep the *spider*—the portion attaching the voice coil to the frame of the speaker—intact. The electrical connection for the voice coil might be physically attached to the outside of the cone, so be sure to leave this part attached.

The speaker will still produce sound, even with all or most of the cone removed. However, the sound level will be low and not generally audible when the room is filled with music from the main sound system. If sound from the speaker is a problem, mount it in a small wooden box. Fill the box with fiberglass padding (the kind made for speaker stuffing), and provide a clear window for the laser beam. Or, you can make the speaker and laser self-contained by making the box large enough for the tube. Keep the fiberglass away from the tube and add one or two small holes for ventilation.

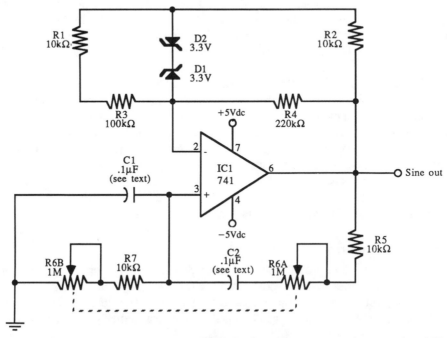

FIG. 19-10. *Adjustable-frequency sine-wave oscillator. For lower frequency tones, increase value of C1 and C2 (make them the same). R6 is a dual-ganged 1-megohm precision potentiometer.*

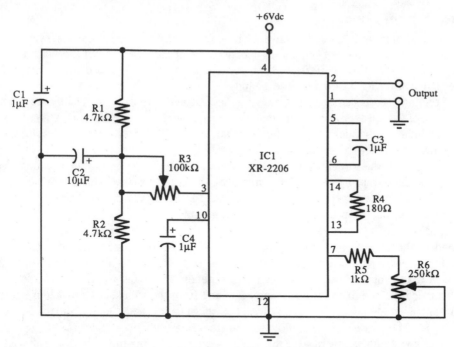

FIG. 19-11. *How to build a sine-wave generator using an XR-2206 function generator IC.*

The soundproof box comes in handy if you are controlling the beam with an audio oscillator. The oscillator, operating under your control, produces a buzzing or whining noise that is distracting when accompanied with a music soundtrack. With the speaker systems stuffed in the box, the oscillator noise will be largely inaudible (unless you are standing right next to the box).

Schematics for useful audio oscillators appear in FIGS. 19-10 and 19-11. Both oscillators produce sinusoidal ac signals that cause the speaker cone to move both in and out from its normal centered position (a waveform that is positive only moves the cone all the way out but not in). The op-amp circuit shown in FIG. 19-10 is the cheapest to build but requires a healthy assortment of parts. The circuit in FIG. 19-11 is based around the versatile Exar XR-2206 monolithic function generator. Many mail-order electronics firms, such as Circuit Specialists, offer this chip. Its higher cost (about $4 to $5) is offset by the minimum number of external components required to make the circuit function. TABLES 19-6 and 19-7 include parts lists for the generators.

Bell-Crank Mounting

Both speaker systems outlined above cause the mirror to bob up and down, thereby moving the beam across a wall or screen. Moving the apex of the mirror back and forth—in an arc motion—produces better pattern effects. You can build a sound-modulated mirror system using a speaker, mirror, and a model airplane plastic bell-crank. The bell-crank and other mounting hardware are available at hobby shops that carry radio control (R/C) model parts.

You can use the speaker as-is or remove the cone, as described above. Devise the crank and mount as shown in FIG. 19-12. Use a gap-filling cyanoacrylate glue to bond the parts to the metal speaker frame. Note: be sure the bell crank and other model parts are not made of nylon; these don't adhere well to any glue.

After the glue used to attach the mirror and mount has set (allow at least 30 minutes), secure the frame of the speaker to a tiltable stand. Position the speaker so that the laser beam glances off the mirror at a 45-degree angle. The mirror should rock the beam right and left (or up and down, depending on how the laser and speaker are arranged). Some "sloppiness" is inherent in this and other sound-modulated mirror systems. The beam will not trace a perfect line as it moves back and forth.

The beam pattern using just one mirror is more-or-less one-dimensional. You can create two-dimensional patterns using two mirror/speaker systems. Position the two speakers at 90 degrees off-axis to one another, and aim the laser so that the beam strikes one mirror and then the next.

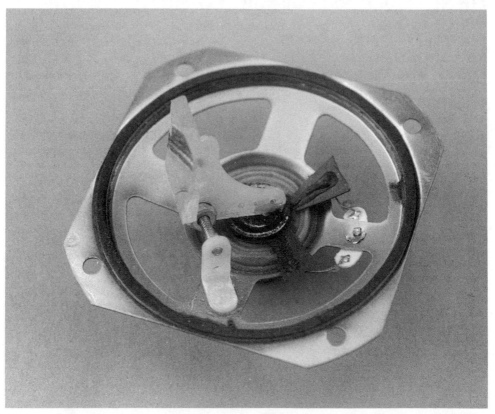

FIG. 19-12. *One way to attach a mirror to a speaker. The bell-crank arrangement, when used with the proper lever/fulcrum geometry, can greatly increase the deflection of the mirror.*

Table 19-6. Op-Amp Sine Wave Generator Parts List

IC1	LM741 op-amp IC
R1,R2 R5,R7	10 kilohm resistor
R3	100 kilohm resistor
R4	220 kilohm resistor
R6	1 megohm dual precision potentiometer
C1,C2	0.1 μF silvered mica capacitor (capacitors must be closely matched for best operation)
D1,D2	3.3-volt zener diode

All resistors are 5 to 10 percent tolerance, ¼ watt. All capacitors are 10 to 20 percent tolerance, rated 35 volts or more, unless otherwise indicated.

SOUND MODULATION OF AIRPLANE SERVOS

Radio-controlled (R/C) model airplanes use motorized servo mechanisms for controlling such things as the rudder, ailerons, and landing gear. The servos, which connect to a central receiver on board the craft, consist of a miniature dc motor, a control board, a potentiometer, and a gear reduction system. All work together to provide closed-loop feedback, a system where the position of the servo arm is known and maintained at all times.

How Servos Work

The servo operates from a 4.5 to 8 volts dc source. That provides power to the motor and circuitry. To actuate the servo, the receiver (acting under command from the radio control transmitter), sends a series of pulses. The width of the pulses varies from 1.0 to 2.0 milliseconds and determines the direction and distance of travel.

Table 19-7. Function Sine Wave Generator Parts List

IC1	Exar XR-2206 function generator IC
R1,R2	4.7 kilohm resistor
R3	100 kilohm potentiometer
R4	180 kilohm resistor
R5	1 kilohm resistor
R6	250 kilohm potentiometer
C1,C2,C4	1 μF electrolytic capacitor
C2	10 μF electrolytic capacitor

All resistors are 5 to 10 percent tolerance, ¼ watt. All capacitors are 10 to 20 percent tolerance, rated 35 volts or more.

When a pulse is received, the servo circuit actuates the motor, which turns the gearing system as well as an output potentiometer. The position of the potentiometer wiper indicates the position of the servo arm (connected to some linkage on the aircraft). The servo circuit monitors the position of the potentiometer and turns off the motor when the pot reaches a given point. Very fine movement—much less than 1 degree of revolution—is possible with most servo systems.

Although R/C servos are meant to be used with the proper type of receiver, you can rig up your own actuating circuit using only a handful of components. By applying an audio input to the circuit, you can make the servos dance back and forth to the music. Laser light is deflected by a mirror mounted on the end of the servo arm. Note that servos are not as nimble as other light-show devices (such as the galvanometer described in the next chapter), but they can be used to create interesting "sweeping scan" effects. Using two motors placed at right angles to one another lets you create two-dimensional light forms.

Building the Sound Servo Systems

FIGURE 19-13 shows the circuit for the sound-modulated servo (parts list in TABLE 19-8). The project is is designed around the 556 IC, a dual version of the venerable 555 timer chip (two timers in one integrated circuit). One half of the 556 provides a series of pulses, and the other half varies the width of the pulses based on the voltage presented at the modulation input. Potentiometer R2 provides a threshold adjustment that lets you find a suitable "mid-point" where the servo arm swings both clockwise and counterclockwise when music is applied to pin 3, the modulation input.

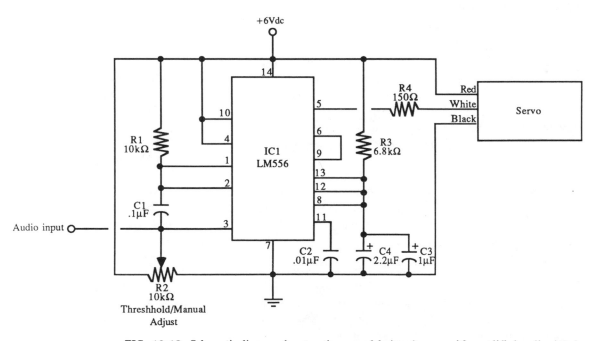

FIG. 19-13. *Schematic diagram for operating a model aircraft servo with amplified audio signals.*

305

Table 19-8. Sound Modulated Servo Parts List

IC1	LM556 dual timer IC
R1	10 kilohm resistor
R2	10 kilohm potentiometer
R3	6.8 kilohm resistor
R4	150 ohm resistor
C1	0.1 μF disc capacitor
C2	0.01 μF disc capacitor
C3	2.2 μF electrolytic capacitor
C4	1 μF electrolytic capacitor
M1	Servo motor

All resistors are 5 to 10 percent tolerance, ¼ watt. All capacitors are 10 to 20 percent tolerance, rated 35 volts or more.

Most R/C servos work the same, but a few odd-balls can present problems. The prototype circuit used Aristo-Craft Hi-Tek HS-402X servos, which are low-cost Korean copies of the popular Futaba servo motor. Capacitors C4 and C3, with resistor R3, determine the pulse width. If you don't get the results you want with the servo you use, try varying the values of these components.

The servo has three color-coded wires: red, white, and black. The red and black wires are the positive and ground leads, respectively. The white wire is the pulse lead, and connects to the output of the circuit. Build two identical circuits if you are controlling a pair of servo motors.

Using the Sound Servo System

Connect the output of an amplified music source to pin 3, the input of the circuit (a 500 mW to 1 watt amplifier provides more than enough power). Connect the circuit to the servo motor as indicated in the schematic. Turn up the volume on the amplifier and watch for a racking motion of the servo. If nothing happens or the servo immediately travels to the far end of its rotation and stays there, adjust R2 to modify the input voltage. If the servo moves to one extreme and makes a chattering noise, disconnect the power immediately. The chattering is caused by the gears in the gear train skipping. If allowed to continue, the gears will strip and the servo will be useless.

When adjusted properly, the servo should move back and forth in syncopation with the music. The amount of movement depends on the relative sound level of the music. The servo tends to react more to low-frequency sounds, which generally have a higher power content than higher frequency ones. The higher the volume, the more the servo will wiggle back and forth.

Note that the frequency response of the servo depends on the amplitude of rotation. The more the servo rotates, the lower the frequency response. If the servo is allowed to swing too far in both directions, the motor won't respond to changes in the music of more than 8 to 10 Hz. When the motor is set so that it slightly vibrates, frequency response is increased to a more respectable 30 to 50 Hz.

Mirror Mounting

Your local hobby store should stock a variety of plastic and hardware items that can be used to mount a suitable mirror on the servo. The output shaft of the servo is designed to accommodate a number of different plastic wheels, armatures, and brackets. You can glue the pieces together or use miniature 4/40 or 3/56 hardware (or whatever happens to be handy). Attach the mirror to the bracket using epoxy.

Positioning the Servos

Mount the servos on an optical breadboard (as discussed in Chapter 7) using the hardware provided with the servo or purchased separately. By mounting two servos at a 90-degree angle (one vertical and one horizontal) and positioning the mirrors so that the beam is deflected off one mirror and then the other, you gain complete control of the X and Y coordinates of the laser beam. If you provide each servo with a slightly different signal (left and right stereo channels, for example), you can create unusual lithesome patterns. Using active or passive filtration you can divert high-frequency sounds to one servo and low-frequency sounds to the other.

Remember that the servo is not really sensitive to frequencies, just the relative amplitude of the music generated by these frequencies. The servos respond best to such sounds as drums and bass and other low-frequency, short-duration instruments. Filter these out with a circuit that rolls off at about 300 to 500 Hz, and the servo will no longer respond to them but act on the amplitude of the remaining frequencies.

One of the best advantages of the sound-modulated servo system is it doesn't reproduce the music—unlike the speaker/mirror light-show instrument detailed earlier. This is especially important if you're putting on a light show. It can be disconcerting to an audience to hear the squeaky, raspy sounds of the speaker/mirror system along with the high fidelity of the auditorium audio system.

SIMPLE SCANNING SYSTEMS

Not all light-show effects are designed to bob with the music. Some effects are made by scanning the beam using prisms, mirrors, mirror balls, and other rotating reflecting optics. Depending on how you arrange the optical components and laser, you can create unique "sheet" and "cone" effects.

A sheet is a one-dimensional scan where the pinpoint laser beam is spread out in a wide arc. When projected on a screen, the beam draws out a long, streaking line. A cone is a three-dimensional scan where the beam is moved both up and down as well as right and left. When projected on a screen, the beam draws a circle or oval.

You need an extremely powerful laser (100 mW or more) to see the scanning effect in mid air, and then the beam is most visible when it shoots towards you, rather than away from you. As an example, light-show experts rig up mirrors of fiberoptics so the rays of laser light are directed toward the audience. Of course, the beams are aimed so that they don't actually strike anybody but are deflected to "beam stops"—flat-black fabric or metal baffles that prevent the beam from bouncing around the room.

Unless you fill the room with smoke or fake fog, the scanned beam from a 10 mW He-Ne is invisible, and even with the smoke it is extremely weak. Details on adding smoke can be found in Chapter 20, "Advanced Laser Light Shows."

Sheet Effects

There are three basic ways to create sheet-effect scanned images (more sophisticated approaches are shown in the next chapter).

★ Reflect the beam off a mirror attached to the shaft of a motor, as shown in FIG. 19-14. The arc of the scan is approximately 170 degrees with a one-sided mirror (silvered on one side only).

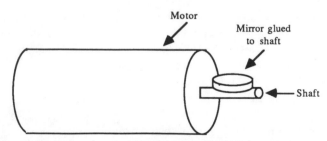

Motor

Mirror glued to shaft

Shaft

FIG. 19-14. *Mount a mirror on the shaft of a small dc motor as shown to produce a sweeping scan effect.*

★ Bounce the beam off a holographic scanner, which is a specialized mirrored wheel used in laser-based supermarket checkout systems. The scanner is a wheel with mirrored or flat, polished edges. The number of facets on the outside of the wheel determine the arc of the scan.

★ Pass the beam through a cylindrical lens. The lens expands the beam in one direction only. The angle of the arc is determined by the focal length of the lens. Most cylindrical lenses expand the beam to cover a 90- to 120-degree arc.

In all approaches, the intensity of the beam is reduced by a factor determined by the arc of the scan as well as any time the beam is stopped or blocked. Beam intensity is reduced the most with the one-sided mirror techniques. If you were to slow down the motor spinning the one-sided mirror, you'd see that the beam is not reflected for half the period of rotation (that is, when the beam strikes the back of the mirror). When the reflective side of the mirror faces the laser, the beam is directed outward in an arc. The beam intensity along the arc is only a fraction of what it is when the beam is stationary.

Holographic scanners must be precisely mounted on the motor shaft. Wobble of the scanning wheel causes multiple scan lines when the beam is projected. The multiple lines might be desirable when using certain smoke effects because the width (not arc) of the scan is increased. The scan width increases from the diameter of the actual beam to the distance between the far right and left lines.

The cylindrical lens does not suffer from excessive reduction in beam intensity or multiple scan lines. The beam is refractively widened into an arc so that no motors or mirrors need be used to provide the scanning action. The only requirement of the cylindrical lens is that its focal length must be carefully chosen if you desire a specific scanning arc.

Cone Effects

A cone effect is made by mounting a mirror off-axis on the shaft of a motor. A similar mounting technique was described for the "Spirograph" laser light show device, detailed at the beginning of this chapter. These mirrors are mounted slightly off-axis to produce a small circle shape on a screen. In the cone-scanning system, the mirror is mounted at a greater off-axis angle to produce a larger circle.

Altering the Speed of the Scan

With the exception of the cylindrical lens system, the scanning systems described here use motors that can be accelerated or decelerated as desired for a particular effect. Beyond a certain speed, the scanning rate is not detectable to the human eye and further speed increase is not necessary. This can help prolong the life of your motors as well as make the light show system quieter.

Both the one-sided mirror and cone systems use optical components that could present an uneven load on the motor shaft. That can lead to excessive noise and wear on motors that are not equipped with shaft bearings. You can reduce wear and noise by decreasing the speed of the motor without adversely affecting the visual effects of the scan. Use the motor speed circuits provided earlier in this chapter.

Slow "sweeping" effects can be achieved by reducing the motor speed to a crawl. Most speed control circuits cannot slow down a motor beyond a certain point without stalling the motor or causing the shaft to jerk instead of turn smoothly. If you can't get the motor to turn slowly enough, consider adding a gear reduction system to decrease the rotation of the mirror.

Sweeping scans can also be created using R/C servos. Even at top speed, the scan of one servo is slow enough to see, so the beam appears as a comet with a streaking tail. For a repetitive sweep, the servo circuit described earlier requires a low-frequency sinusoidal waveform. The oscillators depicted back in FIGS. 19-10 and 19-11 serve as excellent tone sources for the servos.

20

Advanced Laser
Light Shows

Want to put on a neighborhood light show that will dazzle your friends and family? Considering going into the professional laser light show business? Or just interested in experimenting with new art forms? The projects described in this chapter can turn you into a light show wizard. You'll learn how to make complex geometric patterns using devices known as galvanometers. You'll also find details on making your own galvanometers and the basics of how to effectively use argon and krypton lasers in light shows. Finally, this chapter provides important information on restrictions and rules governing public light show performances.

WHERE TO HAVE A LIGHT SHOW

Before discussing the hows of advanced light shows, let's take a moment to examine where to have them. Your choice of location goes a long way toward the overall enjoyment of the show and the ease with which you can produce it. You must consider the size of the room or auditorium, the location of screens or backdrops, the degree of light-proofing for doors and windows, and several other factors.

Even high-powered lasers look dim when they are used to create flashing beams and undulating light forms on the screen. A truly professional light show uses high-powered 2- to 5-watt argon and krypton lasers that cost $15,000 to $35,000. Unless you find one of these that has fallen off some truck (in which case you probably don't want it), you'll be using a trusty red helium-neon laser for your light shows. The higher the output of the laser, the brighter the beam. However, note that a 10 mW laser might not necessarily appear twice as bright as a 5 mW laser. Beyond a certain level the eye can no longer

310

discern brightness. But the higher output tube will deliver more light as the beam is swept across the screen.

Speaking of screens, you must provide some type of light colored background or the laser beam may not be clear or easy to see. A beaded glass screen designed for movie projection is not a good idea because the little beads of glass act as prisms and mirrors. Not only will the beam be reflected back into the audience, it will appear fuzzy due to dispersion inside the glass.

Any light-colored wall, preferably one painted with flat white paint, will do. If such a wall is not handy, bring one in the form of a well-pressed sheet, a piece of photographic background paper (this stuff comes in convenient rolls), or a scenery flat. A flat, used in live theater, is a piece of painted muslin stretched taut in a wood frame. The flat is lightweight, but its size makes it hard to transport.

Obviously, the room or auditorium must be large enough to accommodate the number of people attending the show, but it must also be spacious enough to allow the light show pattern to spread to a respectable size. The distance between the laser and the projection surface is called the *throw*. The longer the throw, the larger the light show image. An image that is 1 foot high at a distance of 6 feet will measure 2 feet high at a throw distance of 12 feet. An easy rule of thumb is that every time you double the throw, the image size increases by 100 percent.

Because the laser beam is so compact, the effects of the inverse square law are minimized (recall from Chapter 3 that the inverse square law requires the intensity of light to fall off 50 percent for every doubling of light-to-subject distance). It doesn't really matter if the laser is 10 feet from the wall or 20 feet, but remember the effects of a long throw. Too much distance can cause the light show patterns to fan out excessively. Beam divergence also becomes a problem at long distances. A laser beam with a divergence of two milliradians will diverge to a spot approximately two inches in diameter at 80 feet.

How will you seat the audience? The conventional chairs- facing-the-screen seating arrangement is only marginally useful in laser light shows. Projecting the laser beam like a movie image requires that the laser projector be placed high above the audience, and your room might not easily allow for this.

EXPERIMENTING WITH GALVANOMETERS

Professional light shows don't use R/C servos or stepper motors as laser beam scanners. Rather, they use a unique electromechanical device called the *galvanometer*. A galvanometer—or galvo for short—provides fast and controllable back-and-forth oscillation. Mount a mirror on the side of the shaft and the reflected light forms a streak on the wall. Position two galvanometers at a 90-degree angle, apply the right kind of signal, and you can project circles, ovals, spirals, stars, and other multi-dimensional geometric shapes.

What Is a Galvanometer?

Most electronics buffs are familiar with the basic galvanometer movement of an analog meter. The design of the movement is shown in FIG. 20-1. A coil of wire is placed in the circular gap of a magnet. Applying current to the coil causes it to turn within the

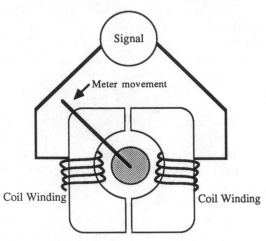

FIG. 20-1. *The basic operation of the galvanometer.*

electromagnetic field of the magnet. The amount of turning is directly proportional to the amount of current that is applied. The needle of the meter is attached to the coil of wire.

Some meter movements are designed so that the needle rests in the center of the scale. Applying a positive or negative voltage swings the needle one direction or the other. Say that at full deflection the meter reads + and – 5 volts. When charged with + 5 volts, the needle swings all the way to the right. When charged with – 5 volts, the needle sways all the way to the left. Current under 5 volts (positive or negative) causes the needle to travel only part way right or left.

Meter movements are designed for precision and are not capable of moving much mass. But by using a stronger magnet and a larger coil or wire, a galvanometer can be made to motivate a larger mass. Heavy-duty scanning galvanometers are often made to actuate the needles in chart recorders and they have more than enough "oomph" to rack a small first-surface mirror back and forth. Some galvo manufacturers, most notably General Scanning, make units specifically designed for high-speed laser light deflection. These are best suited to laser light show applications but their cost is enormous. Surplus galvanometers, available from several sources including Meredith Instruments, Fobtron Components, and General Science & Engineering, cost from $30 to $60 apiece; new high-speed models cost upwards of $350.

You may use either commercially made galvanometers for the projects that follow or make your own using small hobby dc motors. Be aware that commercially-made galvos work much better than homemade types, but if you are on a budget and simply want to experiment with making interesting light show effects, the dc motor version will prove more than adequate.

Using Commercially-Made Galvos

FIGURE 20-2 shows a typical commercially made galvanometer. The General Scanning model GVM-735 galvanometers illustrated in the picture are actually Cadillacs among

FIG. 20-2. *A commercially made precision galvanometer.*

scanners, so the units are not representative of typical quality. There are other makers of fine galvanometers, including C.E.C., Minneapolis-Honeywell, and Midwestern.

Galvanometers carry a number of specifications you can use to judge quality, versatility, and practicality. Among the most useful specifications are:

☆ **Rotation**. The amount of deflection of the shaft, in degrees. Usually stated in both + and − about a center point. A deflection of 10 to 20 degrees is fine for light show applications.

☆ **Natural frequency**. Often stated as the resonance frequency, in hertz, and provides an indication of top speed. Most galvo applications call for a top frequency of 80 percent of the resonance frequency. For example, with a resonance frequency of 225 hertz, top operating frequency is about 180 Hz.

☆ **Rotor inertia**. The measurement of the ability to move mass. A higher inertia means the galvanometer can move a greater amount of mass. The rotor inertia is relatively small—1 to 2 g/cm², but it's sufficient to move a small, mounted mirror.

☆ **Coil resistance**. The resistance, in ohms, of the drive coil. Helpful in designing and applying drive circuits.

☆ **Operating voltage**. Nominal and/or maximum operating voltage, typically 12 volts. Also useful in designing and using drive circuits.

★ **Power consumption**. The power consumption, in milliamps or amps, of the galvanometer, typically under worst-case conditions (full rotor deflection, full voltage, etc.). The drive circuit you use must be able to deliver the required current.

Driving Galvanometers

Galvanometers can be driven in a variety of ways, including power op amps, audio amplifiers, and transistors. A basic, no-frills drive circuit appears in FIG. 20-3 (refer to TABLE 20-1 for a parts list). The input can be an audio signal from the LINE OUT jack of a hi-fi or an unamplified input from a frequency generator (more on these later). You *can* apply an amplified signal to the input of the drive circuit, but the op amp will clip the output if the input is excessively high.

The two drive transistors, a complementary pair consisting of TIP31 and TIP32 power types mounted on heatsinks, interface the output of the op amp to the coil of the galvanometer. The circuit works with a variety of voltages from ±5 volts to ±18 volts. Most scanners operate well with supply voltages of between ±5 and ±12 volts. Check the specifications of your galvanometers and make sure you don't exceed the rated voltage.

If anything, operate the galvos at a reduced voltage. They will still operate satisfactorily but the rotor might not deflect the full amount. This is not a problem for most applications, including laser light shows, where full deflection is not always desired.

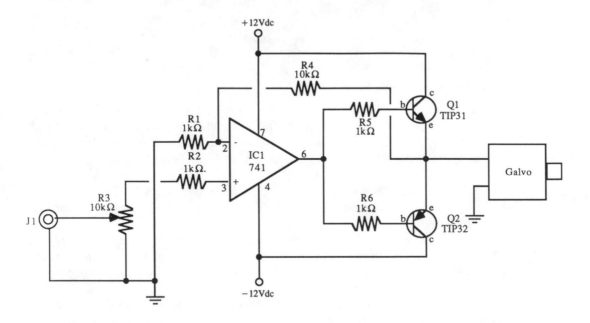

Notes:
Q1 and Q2 must be on heasinks!

Use supply voltage to complement galvanometer; up to ± 18 VDC.

FIG. 20-3. *Driver circuit for operating a galvanometer from line-level audio source. Build two circuits for controlling two galvanometers.*

314

Table 20-1. Galvanometer Drive Parts List

IC1	LM741 op amp IC
R1,R2 R5,R6	1 kilohm resistor
R3	10 kilohm potentiometer
R4	10 kilohm resistor
Q1	TIP 31 npn transistor
Q2	TIP 32 pnp transistor
J1	⅛-inch jack
G1	Galvanometer
Misc.	Heatsinks for Q1 and Q2.

All resistors are 5 to 10 percent tolerance, ¼ watt.

One by-product of full deflection is a "ringing" that occurs when the rotor hits the stop at the ends of both directions of travel. The ringing appears in the laser light form as glitches or double-streaks.

To make two-dimensional shapes, you need two galvanometers positioned 90 degrees apart, as illustrated in FIG. 20-4. Mount mirrors on the shafts using aluminum or brass tubing. Add a set screw (see FIG. 20-5) so that you can tighten the mirror mounts on the rotor shaft of the galvanometer.

You can use any number of mounting techniques to secure the galvos to an optical breadboard or table, but the mounts you use must be sturdy and stable. Vibrations from the galvos can be transferred to the mounts, which can shake and disturb the light forms.

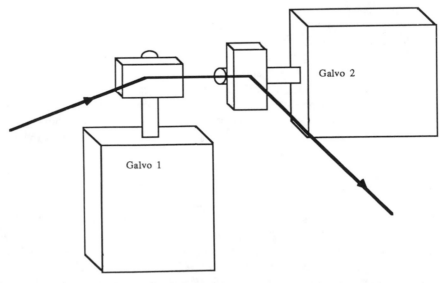

FIG. 20-4. *How to arrange two galvanometers to achieve full X and Y axis deflection. Place the mirrors of the galvanometers close together to counter the effects of beam deflection.*

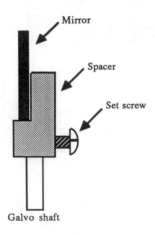

Mirror

Spacer

Set screw

Galvo shaft

FIG. 20-5. *You can mount a thin, front-surface mirror to the galvanometer shaft using an aluminum spacer that has been filed down.*

Build a separate drive circuit for both galvanometers and enclose it in a project box (or you can include the driver circuit in a larger do-everything light-show console). I built the prototype drive circuit on a universal breadboard PCB and had plenty of room to spare. The enclosure measured 4⅜ by 7¾ by 2⅜ inches. Subminiature ⅛-inch phone jacks were provided for the audio inputs and scanner outputs and potentiometers were mounted for easy control of the input level.

To test the operation of the galvanometers and drive circuits, plug in the right and left channels of the hi-fi and turn the gain controls (R1 for both drives) all the way up. The galvos should shake back and forth in response to the music. Shine a laser beam at the mirrors so the light bounces off one, is deflected by the other, and projects on the wall. The light forms you see should undulate in time to the music.

Providing An Audio Source

The test performed above only lets you test the operation of your galvanometer setup. With the arrangement detailed above, the light form will always be squeezed into a fairly tight line that crawls up and down the wall at a 45-degree angle. Full flexibility of a pair of galvanometers, physically set apart 90 degrees, requires an audio source that has two components — both of which are set 90 degrees apart in phase.

Audio signals are sine waves, and sine waves are measured not only by frequency and amplitude but by phase. The phase is measured in degrees and spans from 0 to 360 degrees. FIGURE 20-6 shows two sine waves set apart 90 degrees. Notice that the second wave is a quarter step (90 degrees) behind the first one.

If you could somehow delay the sound coming from one channel of your stereo, you can broaden the 45-degree line into a full two-dimensional shape. The closer the delay is to 90 degrees out of phase, the more symmetrical the light form will be. Imagine a pure source of sine waves—a sine wave oscillator. The oscillator is sending out waves at a frequency of 100 Hz. It has two output channels called sine and cosine. Both channels are linked so they run at precisely the same frequency, but the cosine channel is delayed 90 degrees. The lightform projected on the screen is now a perfect circle.

The circuit in FIG. 20-7 provides such a two-channel oscillator. Two controls allow you to change the frequency and ''symmetry'' of the sine waves. The symmetry (or

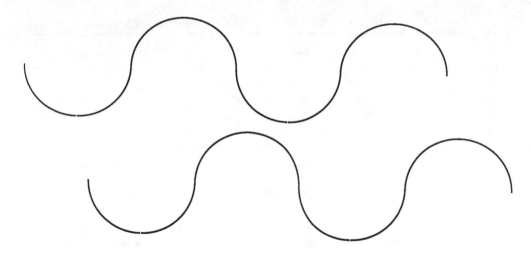

FIG. 20-6. *Two sine waves; the bottom wave is delayed 90 degrees from the top wave.*

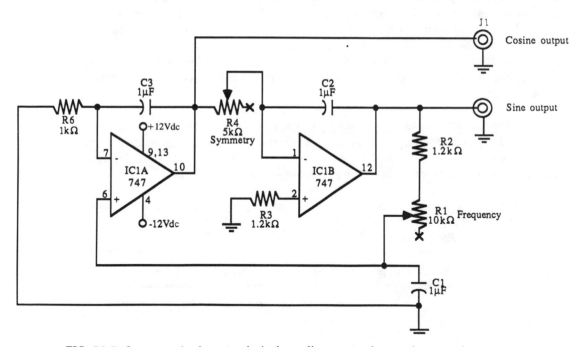

FIG. 20-7. *One way to implement a sine/cosine audio generator for operating two galvanometers.*

phase) control counters the destabilizing effects caused by rotating the frequency knob. This circuit, with parts list provided in TABLE 20-2, is designed so that the resistors and capacitors are the same value. Changing the value of one resistor throws off the balance of the circuit, and the symmetry control helps rebalance it. Note that the frequency and symmetry controls provide a great deal of flexibility in the shape of the projected beam. Fiddling with these two potentiometers allows you to create all sorts of different and unusual light forms.

317

Table 20-2. Sine/Cosine Generator Parts List

IC1	LM747 dual op amp IC
R1	10 kilohm potentiometer
R2,R3	1.2 kilohm resistor
R4	5 kilohm potentiometer
R5	1 kilohm resistor
C1-C3	1 μF electrolytic capacitor
J1,J2	⅛-inch miniature phone jack

The circuit is designed around the commonly available 747 dual op amp (two LM741 op amps in one package). You can use almost any other dual op amp, such as the LM1458 or LF353, but test the circuit first on a breadboard. For best results, use a dual op amp.

You can obtain even more outlandish light forms when combining the sine and cosine signals from two separate oscillator circuits. On a perf board, combine two oscillators using two LM741 op amps. An overall circuit design is shown in FIG. 20-8. One set of switches allows you to turn either oscillator on and off and the input controls let you individually control the amplitude from each sine/cosine channel (for a total of four inputs). A parts list for the general circuit is in TABLE 20-3.

The switch lets you flip between mixing the sine inputs together or criss-crossing them so that the sine channel of one oscillator is mixed with the cosine of the other oscillator, and vice versa.

★ When the switch is in the "pure" position(A)—sine with sine and cosine with cosine—you obtain rounded-shape designs, such as spirals, circles, and concentric circles.

★ When the switch is in the "cross-cross" position (B)—sine with cosine for both channels—you obtain pointed shapes, like diagonals, stars, and squares.

Like the drive circuit, you should place the oscillator, with all its various potentiometers, in a project box or tuck it inside a console. Provide two ⅛-inch jacks for the outputs for the two galvos.

Table 20-3. Complete Light Show Circuit Parts List

2	Sine/Cosine generators (see Fig. 20-7)
IC1,IC2	LM741 op amp IC
R1,R2	10 kilohm potentiometer
R6,R7	
R3,R4	1 kilohm resistor
R8,R9	
R5,R10	10 kilohm resistor
J1,J2	⅛-inch miniature phone jack
S1-S3	DPDT switch

All resistors are 5 to 10 percent tolerance, ¼ watt.

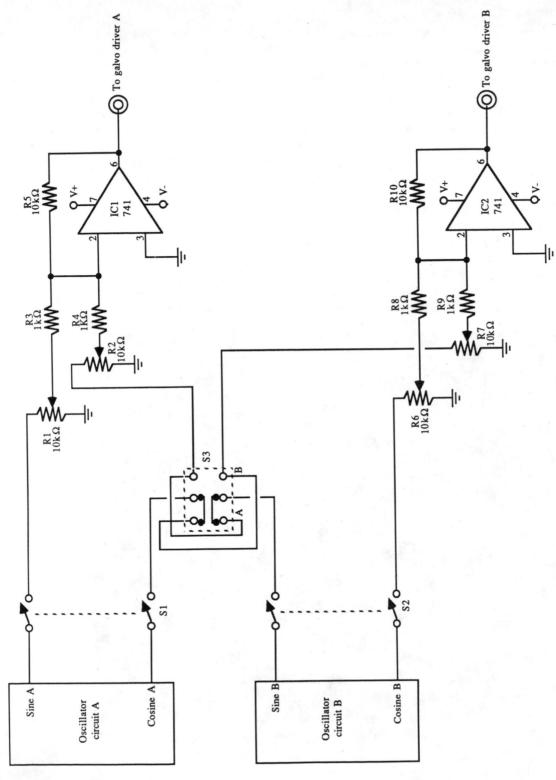

FIG. 20-8. *A schematic for designing a two-channel sine/cosine audio generator, with dual op amp mixers (note: use separate op amps for the mixers).*

319

Using the Oscillator

Connect the outputs of the oscillator to the inputs of the drive circuit. Apply power to both circuits and rotate the mixer input controls (R1, R2, R6, and R7) to their fully on positions. Flick on switch #1 so that only the signals from one oscillator are routed to the mixer amps and turn switch #3 to "A" position. Slowly turn the control knobs until the galvanometers respond.

If the galvanometers don't seem to respond, temporarily disconnect the jumpers leading between the oscillator and drive circuits and plug an amplifier into one of the oscillator output channels. You should hear a buzzing or whining noise as you rotate the frequency and symmetry controls. If you don't hear a noise, double-check your wiring and be sure the mixer controls are turned up. When turned down, no signals can pass through the mixing amps.

Aim a laser at the mirrors and watch the shapes on a nearby wall or screen. Get the feeling of the controls by turning each one and noting the results. With the symmetry control turned down and the frequency control almost all the way down, you should see a fairly round circle on the screen. If the circle looks like an egg, adjust the mixer controls to decrease the X or Y dimension, as shown in FIG. 20-9.

If the egg is canted on a diagonal, the phase of the cosine channel is not precisely 90 degrees. Try adjusting the symmetry control and fine tuning it with the frequency

FIG. 20-9. *The basic circle produced by turning on one sine/cosine generator and adjusting the frequency and symmetry controls to produce a pure sine wave.*

FIG. 20-10. *One of many spiral light forms created by turning on both sine/cosine generators.*

control. There should be one or more points where you achieve proper phase between the sine and cosine channels.

Now turn off the first oscillator and repeat the testing procedures for the second oscillator. It might behave slightly different than the first due to the tolerance of the components. If you need more precise control over the two oscillators, use 1-percent tolerance resistors and High-Q capacitors.

For really interesting light forms, turn on both oscillators and adjust the controls to produce various symmetrical and asymmetrical shapes. At many settings, the light forms undulate and constantly change. At other settings, the shape remains stationary and can appear almost three-dimensional. FIGURES 20-10 and 20-11 show sample lightforms created with the circuit and galvanometers described above.

Alternate between "A" "B" settings by flicking switch #3. Note the different effects you create when the switch is in either position.

Powering the Oscillator and Drive Circuits

So far we've discussed using galvo oscillator and drive circuits but have paid no attention to the power supply requirements. Although you can build your own dual-polarity power supply to run the galvo system, I strongly recommend that you use a well-made commercial supply, one that has very good filtering. *Sixty cycle hum*, caused by insufficient filtering and poor regulation, can creep into the op amps and make the galvos shudder continuously.

Output voltage and current depend on the galvanometers you use. I successfully used two General Scanning GVM 734 galvos with a power supply that delivered ±5

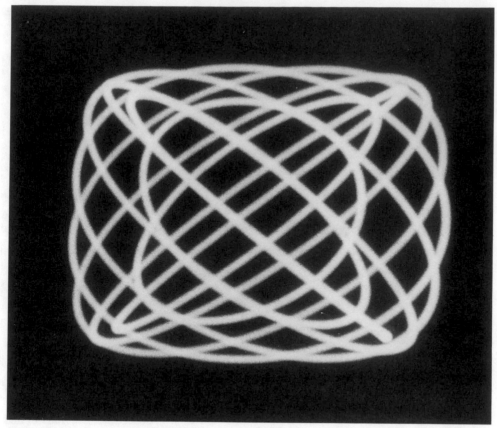

FIG. 20-11. *A clearly definable "Lissajous" figure, made with the galvanometer light show device.*

volts at about 250 mA for each polarity. You might need a more powerful power supply if you use different galvanometers (some require ±12 at 1 amp or more). The power supply I used for the prototype system was surplus from a Coleco computer system that cost $12.95. Look around and you can find an equally good deal.

Useful Modifications and Suggestions

Not shown in the driver circuit above is an additional switch that allows you to change the polarity to one of the galvanometers. This provides added flexibility over the shape of the light forms. Wire the switch as shown in FIG. 20-12.

The drive circuit detailed above might not provide adequate power for all galvanometers. If the galvos you use just don't seem to be operating up to par, use the drive circuit shown in FIG.20-13, developed by light show producer Jeff Korman (see parts list in TABLE 20-4). This new driver is similar to the old one but provides better performance at low frequencies. Korman also uses a special-purpose sine/cosine oscillator chip made by Burr-Brown. The chip, called the 4423, is available directly from Burr-Brown or from Fobtron Components (see Appendix A).

322

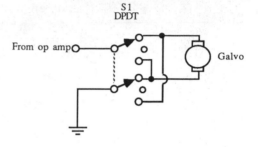

FIG. 20-12. *Wire a DPDT switch to one of the galvanometers to reverse its direction in relation to the other galvanometer.*

Cost is high ($25 to $35) but it provides extremely precise control over frequency without the worry of knocking the signals out of 90-degree phase.

Other useful tips:

★ Whenever possible, try to reduce the size of the light forms; it makes them appear brighter.

★ Connect an audio signal into one channel of the drive circuit and connect the sine/cosine oscillator into the other channel. The light form will be modulated in 2-D to the beat of the music.

★ You can record a galvanometer light show performance by piping the output of the oscillators into two tracks of a four- track tape deck. Use the remaining two tracks to record the music. When played back, the galvanometers will exactly repeat your original recording session. This is how most professional light show producers do it.

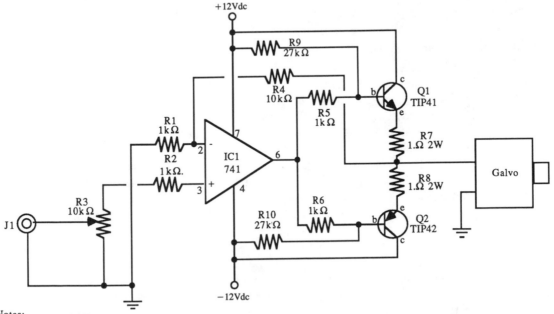

Notes:
Q1 and Q2 must be on heatsinks!

Use supply voltage to complement galvanometer; up to ± 18 Vdc.

FIG. 20-13. *An enhanced high current galvanometer circuit designed by light show consultant Jeff Korman.*

323

Table 20-4. Enhanced Galvanometer Driver Parts List

IC1	LM741 op amp IC
R1,R2, R5,R6	1 kilohm resistor
R3	10 kilohm potentiometer
R4	10 kilohm resistor
R3	10 kilohm potentiometer
R7,R8	0.1 ohm, 2-watt resistor
R9,R10	27 kilohm resistor
Q1	TIP 41 npn transistor
Q2	TIP 42 pnp transistor
J1	⅛-inch jack
G1	Galvanometer
Misc.	Heatsinks for Q1 and Q2.

All resistors are 5 to 10 percent tolerance, ¼ watt, unless otherwise indicated.

★ Try adding one or two additional oscillators. Combine them into the mixing network by adding a 10k pot (for volume control) and a 10k input resistor. Wire in parallel as shown in the FIG. 20-8 schematic, above.

★ Triangle or sawtooth (ramp) waves create unusual pointed-star shapes, boxes, and spirals. You can build triangle and sawtooth generators using op amps, but an easy approach is to use the Intersil 8038 or Exar XR-2206 function generator ICs.

Making Your Own Galvos

A set of commercially-made galvanometers can set you back $100 to $200, even when they are purchased on the surplus market. If you are interested in experimenting with laser graphics and geometric designs but are not interested in spending a lot of money, you can make your own using small dc motors.

Follow the diagram shown in FIG. 20-14 to make your own galvanometers. You can use most any 1.5- to 6-volt dc motor, but it should be fairly good quality. Test the motor by turning the shaft with your fingers. The rotation should be smooth, not jumpy. Measure the diameter of the outside casing. It should be about 1 inch. Refer to TABLE 20-5 for a list of required parts.

Use a high-wattage soldering iron or small brazing torch to solder a penny onto the side of the motor shaft. For best results, clean the penny and coat it and the motor shaft with solder flux. Make sure the penny is thoroughly heated before applying solder or the solder may not stick. You'll need to devise some sort of clamp to hold the penny and motor while soldering—you need both hands free to hold the solder and gun.

Let the work cool completely, then mount a small ½-by-¾-inch front-surface mirror to the front of the penny. You can use most any glue: Duco adhesive or gap-filling cyanoacrylate glue are good choices. Note that the mirror should not be exceptionally thick. You get the best results when the mirror is thin—the motor has less mass to move, so it can vibrate faster.

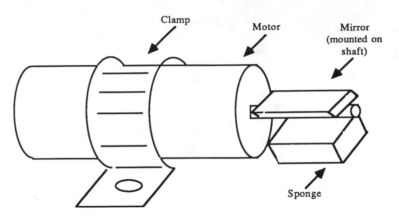

FIG. 20-14. *Basic arrangement for making galvanometers using small dc motors. The sponge prevents the mirror and shaft from turning more than 20-25 degrees in either direction and helps dampen the vibrations.*

Table 20-5. Dc Motor Galvanometer Parts List

1	Small 1.5- to 6-Vdc hobby motor
1	¾- to 1-inch pipe clamp
1	2-by-3-inch, ⅛-inch-thick acrylic plastic
1	⁸⁄₃₂-by-½-inch bolt, nut, washer
1	½-by-¾-inch thin, front-surface mirror
1	Lincoln penny
1 ea.	Small piece of sponge, anti-static foam

Snap the motor into a ¾-inch electrical conduit clamp and fit it into position (the clamp will have a 1-inch opening and will hold most small hobby motors). If the clamp is too small, widen the opening by gently prying it apart with a pair of pliers. Mount the motor and clamp to a 2-by-3-inch acrylic plastic base (⅛-inch thickness is fine). Drill holes as shown in FIG. 20-15. Use a ⁶⁄₃₂ by ½-inch bolt and a ⁶⁄₃₂ nut to secure the pipe clamp to the base.

Use a treated, synthetic sponge and cut into two 1-by-½-inch pieces. The sponge should be soft but will dry out when left overnight. After the sponge has dried out, compress it and secure it under the penny using all-purpose adhesive. Now slide a 1-by-½-inch piece of anti-static foam into the gap between the sponge and penny. The fit should be close but not overly tight. If you need more clearance, compress the sponge by squeezing it some more. The finished dc motor galvanometer is shown in FIG. 20-16.

As an alternative, cut a piece of ½-inch foam and stick it under the penny. Try different foams to test their "suppleness." The foam should be soft enough to let the penny and mirror vibrate but not so soft that it acts as a tight spring and bounces the penny back after only a small movement.

Using the Motor/Galvanometers

Attach leads to the motor terminals and connect the homemade galvanometers to the drive circuit and oscillator detailed earlier in this chapter. Repeat the testing

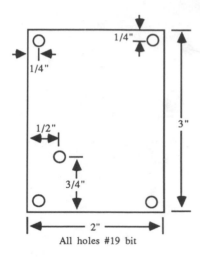

1/4"

1/4"

1/2"

3/4"

3"

2"

All holes #19 bit

FIG. 20-15. *Cutting and drilling template for the base for the homemade motor galvanometers.*

FIG. 20-16. *A completed motor galvanometer, secured to the base with a ¼-inch electrical conduit clamp.*

326

procedures outlined for commercially made galvos. Position the motors so that they are 90 degrees off-axis and shine a laser onto both mirrors. You should see shapes and patterns as you adjust the controls on the oscillator.

The motor/galvanometers can be mounted in a variety of ways. One approach is to use metal strips bent 90 degrees at the bottom. Drill matching holes in the strip and attach the base of the motor/galvos to the strips using 6/32 hardware. You can also secure the base of each motor/galvanometer using ½-inch galvanized hardware brackets (available at the hardware store).

The light forms might not be perfectly symmetrical. Depending on the motors you used and the type and thickness of foam backing you installed, one motor might vibrate at a wider arc than the other. Try adjusting the foam and sponge on both motors to make them vibrate the same amount.

SMOKE EFFECTS

Smoke effects are obtained by spreading the laser beam into an arc (the light is projected as a straight line) and filling the room with smoke or vapor. Because you see only a thin slice of the smoke through the arc of laser light, you can clearly view the air currents as they swirl and shift.

Smoke effects in professional light shows require multi-watt lasers—a 2- to 5-watt argon laser makes wonderful smoke effects. The "smoke" is often vapor left by heating dry ice. Dry ice vapor is heavier than air so it must be blown through the stream of laser light. Small blowers keep the air circulating.

You can experiment with laser smoke effects by using a helium-neon laser (1 mW or more). Although the smoke is not visible at any distance, it can be used for small, amateur light shows. You can also use laser smoke effects to view fluid aerodynamics (see Chapter 22) or just to see what happens to smoke particles in a ventilated room. You can use dry ice vapor (buy the dry ice from a local ice-packing company), smoke from a cigarette, incense stick, or match.

In all cases, exercise reasonable care. Dry ice can cause frostbite, so handle it only with gloves and place it in Pyrex or metal containers (plastic and regular glass could shatter). Cigarettes, incense, and matches present a fire hazard. Get help if you are not sure of what you are doing.

Note that smoke—and all particles in the air—are seen when laser light shines through them. You see them best when you are on one side of the smoke particles and the laser is on the other. You see the outline of the smoke particles as they swirl around.

Casting the Arc

Spread the laser beam into an arc using the sheet effects described in the last chapter. As a recap, you can spread light out in an arc by:

* Spinning a mirror on the side of a motor shaft.
* Rotating an off-axis mirror mounted on the end of a motor shaft.
* Spinning a holograph scanner mirror wheel.
* Spreading the light with a cylindrical lens.

These approaches do not allow you to change the spread of the arc. You can obtain more control over the angle—make it narrow or wide—by using a single galvanometer (commercially made or homemade) and by adjusting the amplitude of the drive signal. You can use the oscillator and driver circuits detailed previously in this chapter.

Making the Smoke Effect

Turn off all the lights except for a dim pilot light that you can extinguish remotely. Light the cigarette, incense, or match, and waft the smoke under the laser light arc. Alternatively, dunk the dry ice in a pail of tepid water. Move to a position that allows you to clearly see the smoke and turn off the pilot light. Depending on the spread of the arc, the power of the laser, and the amount of smoke or vapor, you should clearly see particles swirling in the air.

Watch the effect as you add more smoke or vapor or make the spread of the arc smaller. If the air is moving too fast, the smoke/vapor might disperse too quickly. Turn off blowers, air conditioners, and other appliances that may be agitating the air. On the other hand, if the room gets too filled with smoke, you'll see a general haze in the light and the swirling won't be as easy to see. Clear the room by airing it out. Use blowers or fans to speed up the process.

USING ARGON AND KRYPTON LASERS

Most professional laser light shows use argon or krypton lasers. Both of these are manufactured in high-output versions and provide two or more colors. As you learned in earlier chapters, argon lasers emit light at two principle wavelengths or mainlines—488.0 nm and 514.5 nm. Krypton lasers have the unique ability to produce light at just about any wavelength, providing a spectrum of colors. Because they can produce all three primary colors—red, green, and blue—krypton lasers are often used in color holography. The three primary colors can also be created by using an argon and helium-neon laser.

Using a prism or set of dichroic filters allows you to separate the mainlines. The prism disperses the light into its component colors so that each color can be individually manipulated. Dichroic filters let you block all but the color you want. For example, a "red" filter placed in front of an argon laser will block the green 514.5 nm mainline.

Serious light-show applications require a laser with a minimum power output of 100 mW. Better, more dramatic results are obtained with even higher wattages; it's not uncommon to see 3- to 5-watt argon lasers used in professional light shows. These Class IV devices are downright dangerous unless you know precisely what you are doing. They also require water cooling and extensive plumbing, making them a hassle to use.

High-output krypton and argon lasers are unreasonably expensive but if you are serious about laser light shows, you might locate a used specimen at an affordable price ($3,500 or so). If you keep an eye out and make plenty of contacts, you might luck onto a high-output industrial-grade argon laser—used for such applications as medicine, optical disc manufacturing, and forensics—that is no longer functioning but is repairable. Perhaps the tube is gassed out or maybe the power supply is fried, but the cost of fixing the laser will be less than buying a new one. Before you sign the check, make sure you know what the problem is and that you are confident the laser can be fixed.

High-output lasers can't be plugged into the ac socket and aimed at the wall. Most require 220-volt, three-phase ac (wall outlets provide 110-volt single-phase ac). The laser generates too much heat for air cooling and must be shrouded by water to keep it cool. The water supply must be continually circulating from the faucet to a drain. Adequate filtration and pressure regulation is needed to prevent deposits in the cooling jacket or rupturing the tube.

Finally, but most importantly, the power supplies used to operate high-output lasers produce high current at high voltage. Touching a high-voltage component or wire on the power supply or tube will kill you—*no exceptions*. Thoroughly familiarize yourself with the safe operation of the laser before using it.

YOU AND UNCLE SAM

They say the government has its fingers in everything, and lasers are no exception. Uncle Sam's interest in lasers is purely one of safety—the federal government wants you to comply with minimum safety requirements before you put on a light show. As you learned in Chapter 2, "Working With Lasers," the branch of the government that regulates the laser industry is the Center for Radiological Health, or CDRH (formerly BRH, or Bureau of Radiological Health). The CDRH monitors the manufacture and use of lasers so that harmful laser radiation does not befall unsuspecting people.

Most of the CDRH regulations concern the manufacture of lasers, but some sections deal with the use of lasers in public arenas, including light shows. Briefly stated, anyone wishing to conduct a laser light show for public viewing or otherwise demonstrate the operation of lasers to the public, must fill out forms and submit them to the CDRH. These forms provide necessary information on the type and class of laser and how you intend to use it.

You must also provide details, as precisely as possible, of how the light show equipment will be arranged, where beam stops will be placed, and the number and type of fail-safe mechanisms used. You must also demonstrate an understanding of the regulations and that you intend to comply with them. In the case of a traveling light show, you must indicate how your laser system can adapt to different rooms and auditoriums.

The complete CDRH requirements for laser light shows is too involved to repeat here. You can obtain compliance regulations and application forms directly from the CDRH; their address is given in Appendix A.

GOING PROFESSIONAL

Laser light shows can be both fun and rewarding, both on a personal and financial level. Although permanent laser shows, most notably Laserium, are the most visible, they represent only a small number of light shows conducted in the U.S. Many rock bands like to play to the accompaniment of a light show, especially one that includes lasers. Contact local bands and clubs and ask if they would add a laser show to their gig.

A local non-laser light show producer who has not had the time, inclination, or background to include lasers in his repertoire, might be delighted to have you as a consultant. If you can't find music groups or nearby light show producers, ask at the radio stations in town (call or drop by). You will probably need to start small and work your way to the big time, all the while adding to your laser system.

On a smaller scale are light shows for schools and organizations. What boys' or girls' club wouldn't like to be treated to a light show? These gigs are mostly non-paying, but they are an excellent way to hone your light show talents.

Even if you don't take your light show on the road and perform before a live audience, you can doodle with the artforms created by the assortment of mirrors, motors, servos, galvanometers, and other sundry equipment on film or videotape. A telecine adapter, used primarily for converting Super-8 movies and 35 mm transparencies to videotape, can be used to capture the light-show images on film. Simply replace the film projector with the laser projector. You can use a video camera or still camera to capture the images on the rear-projection plate.

Another alternative is to aim the laser at the wall or screen and photograph or videotape the images directly. This method doesn't yield the best results, because you pick up the pattern on the wall or screen and the images aren't generally as brilliant.

To photograph the light show artforms, place the camera (video or film) on a tripod and focus the lens on the front of the screen. You might need to use the zoom or macro feature of the lens, or else attach supplementary positive diopter lenses in front of the camera in order to take sharp pictures.

Persistence of vision is the capacity of the eye to blend a series of still pictures into smooth motion. A movie is made up of thousands of individual still pictures. These pictures are flashed on the screen faster than our eyes can detect, so the image appears to be in motion. The same technique is used in laser light shows. The scanning of motors, R/C servos, or galvanometers produces a two-dimensional shape on the screen. What appears as a spiral or circle is actually one beam of light, moving so fast that our eyes (and brain) synthesize it into a complete, moving picture.

While your eye smooths the scanning of the laser beam to create the illusion of motion, the eye of the camera may be faster, so the results you see on film might not match those you see in person. When taking still pictures of a laser image, choose a shutter speed $\frac{1}{15}$th of a second or longer. Shorter (higher in number) shutter speeds might result in only partial images.

Television pictures are also created by flashing a series of still pictures on the screen. The video frame rate for a complete picture is $\frac{1}{30}$ of a second. That's faster than your eye can detect, so you don't witness any flicker. Videotaping a laser light show image could result in objectionable flicker. You can see the flicker on your TV set while recording. However, you can often minimize the flicker by adjusting the speed or frequency knob on the light-show motor/galvanometer controller.

21

Experimenting with Laser Weapons Systems

Even before the laser was invented, science fiction writers told of incredible weapons and machines that emitted a bright saber of light, a death ray that disintegrated everything in its path. In the 1951 classic *The Day the Earth Stood Still*, a 7-foot tall "police robot" was equipped with a powerful disinto-ray gun. The gun was mounted behind a visor in the robot's helmet and shot its high-intensity, pencil-thin flame with great precision.

Even today, science fiction movies and books place high emphasis on weapons that use light instead of bullets. But real science hasn't kept up with science fiction; most lasers do little or no harm to human flesh, and many can't cut through a piece of paper, let alone tanks, automobiles, and spaceships.

As unlikely as practical laser-based weapons seem given the current limitations of the state-of-the-art, it's possible that weapons using an intense form of light could someday be developed. In 1983, President Ronald Reagan outlined a plan for outfitting land- and space-born satellites with laser weapons as a defensive measure against ballistic missiles. What are the possibilities of developing powerful laser weapons that thwart nuclear destruction? Can weapons be placed on the ground, installed in tanks or towed on trailers? And what about non-war use of laser guns: could they be used—as they are in the "Star Trek" TV show and movies—to either kill or stun an opponent?

Let's take a brief look at laser weapons and the technology that's currently available. Then read the plans for constructing a useful but relatively harmless laser "gun" using a helium-neon tube. The emphasis of the laser gun is to show you what goes into hand-held lightwave weapons, not to make an effective munition. On a more practical standpoint, laser pistols and rifles provide a means for target practice without wasting bullets, pellets, or B-B's and with much less risk of bodily injury.

AN OVERVIEW OF LAND/SPACE LASER WEAPONS

Lasers are already used in the battlefield, but not as offensive weapons. The U.S. Army and North Atlantic Treaty Organization (NATO) use laser rangefinders for determining the distance between the firing line and the target. The laser system can be mounted on a rifle stock and carried by one person. A number of high-caliber cannon, tanks, and helicopters use their own laser rangefinders, controlled by an on-board firing computer.

Laser rangefinders operate in a variety of ways, but many work by means of transmitting short modulated pulses, then waiting for an echo. The timing of the return signal indicates distance. Accuracy is within 10 to 20 feet for most systems and range is up to 7 miles.

Reagan's Strategic Defense Initiative (SDI), which he announced in a widely publicized speech on March 23, 1983, calls for the deployment of land- and space-based weapons using one or all of three possible technologies:

★ Particle beam weapons, shooting atoms of neutral or charged particles from ground- or space-based platforms.

★ Kinetic energy weapons, from ground-based cannon, that fling high-speed projectiles at the target.

★ Laser weapons, which use short-wavelength electromagnetic energy to heat up the target, damaging its electronics or flight control mechanism.

Of the three types, kinetic energy weapons (KEW) have received the greatest attention. Battlefield KEWs are believed to be technologically possible, and may provide the greatest amount of firepower. The most common variety of KEW is the electromagnetic rail-gun, which shoots specially designed heavy metal "bullets" at about six miles per second (the bullet from an M-16 rifle travels at about ⅔ of a mile per second). Rail-guns require a great deal of energy and many designs are one-shot affairs: the gun is severely damaged after just one firing.

To be effective, the wavelength of a laser weapon must be short, at least in the visible band but preferably in the ultraviolet or x-ray band. The greatest difficulty in designing short-wavelength lasers is power—the shorter the wavelength, the more energy that is required. Optical (visible or ultraviolet) lasers work by heating the skin of the target. The beam must remain at the same spot for several seconds until the skin is hot enough to do internal damage to the target. This is tough because the typical ballistic missile travels in excess of 6 miles per second. Imagine focusing on the same 2- or 3-foot spot over a distance of 50,000 feet and you have an idea how accurate such a laser weapon must be.

In addition to the problems of accuracy, laser weapons of any power tend to be monstrous. That limits them to ground-based ray guns, using mirrors to direct the beam to the target. High-powered lasers using turbine-powered chemical jets have been developed and even placed aboard aircraft, but the wavelength of the light is long—6 to 10 micrometers—far in the infrared region. This makes the laser relatively inefficient at destroying their targets.

X-ray lasers, still in the "so secret they don't exist" category, emit an extremely high powered beam that can literally destroy a missile in mid-flight. X-rays can't be deflected by mirrors, however, which means that the weapon must be easily aimed and in a direct line of sight to the target. Fortunately, x-ray lasers can be built small, experts say, making them suitable for space-based operation. The biggest disadvantage to x-ray lasers is that they use an internal atomic explosion to work, so they are essentially one-shot devices.

A relative newcomer to the SDI (or "Star Wars") scene is the free-electron laser, which is being developed at several national laboratories and universities. The free-electron laser uses a stream of electrons that is made to emit photons of light after being oscillated by giant electromagnets. Free-electron lasers (FELs) have been built and they do work. But if put into production, an actual anti-ballistic missile FEL would take up a football field or more. Obviously, such a device would be useful only as a stationary ground-based weapon. It's possible, though unlikely, that it would be built over a span of several years on a low-orbiting space platform.

SMALL-SCALE WEAPONS USING LAB-TYPE LASERS

So far, we've discussed high-power laser weapons designed to counter a nuclear attack. Laser guns in the movies are often hand-held devices, or at most, small enough to prop on a vehicle. Lasers powerful enough to inflict damage but small enough to be carried have been developed, but they are not used in any current military application. It's relatively easy, for example, to build a hand-held ruby laser that puts out bursts of large amounts of light energy. When focused to a point, the light from a ruby laser can cut through paper, cloth, skin, or even thin metal.

Ruby crystals are poor conductors of heat, so ruby lasers emit only short pulses of light to allow the crystal to cool between firings. Nd:YAG lasers operate in a similar fashion as ruby lasers but can produce a continuous beam. Making a hand-held Nd:YAG laser is no easy feat, however. The Nd:YAG crystal must be optically pumped by another high-powered laser or by an extremely bright flash lamp or light source. Though the power output of an Nd:YAG laser is extremely high, considering the current state-of-the-art, a hand-held model is impractical. However, such a weapon could be built as a "laser cannon," transported on an armored vehicle or on a towed trailer.

CO_2 lasers are often used in industry as cutting tools. This type of laser is known for its efficiency—30 percent or more compared to the 1 to 2 percent of most gas and crystal lasers. A pistol-sized CO_2 laser would probably be difficult to design and manufacture because the CO_2 gas mixture (which includes helium and nitrogen) must be constantly circulated through the tube. What's more, the laser requires a hefty electrical power supply. Still, such a weapon could be built in an enclosure about the same size as a personal rocket launcher. These are designed to be slung over a shoulder and fired when standing in an upright position.

BUILD YOUR OWN HELIUM-NEON LASER PISTOL

The small lab-type laser weapons described above would cost several thousand dollars to build and require expert machining and tooling. You can readily build your own low-power, hand-held laser using a commonly available and affordable helium-neon tube and 12-volt dc power supply. The pistol is made from 2- and 1¼-inch schedule PVC plumbing pipe that you can cut with an ordinary hack saw.

Defining Barrel Length

The exact length of the pistol barrel depends on the laser tube and power supply you use. The laser used in the prototype pistol is a common variety 2 mW tube measuring 1½ inches in diameter by 7½ inches. You can obtain even smaller tubes through some laser dealers and make your pistol more compact.

The power supply is one of the smallest commercially made, measuring a scant ⅞-inch in diameter by slightly under 4 inches in length. This particular power supply was purchased through Meredith Instruments (see address in Appendix A) but is also available from Melles Griot and several laser manufacturers.

Cutting the Barrel and Grip

TABLE 21-1 provides a parts list for the laser pistol. Assuming you use the same or similar tube and power supply, cut a piece of 2-inch schedule 40 PVC to 12½ inches. Sand or file the cut ends to make them smooth. Drill a ⅜-inch diameter hole four inches from one end of the tube, as shown in FIG. 21-1. This hole serves as the leadway for the power wires.

Next, cut a length of 1¼-inch schedule 40 PVC to 6¼ inches. Using a wide, round file, shape one end of this piece so that its contour matches the 2-inch PVC. The angle of the smaller length of pipe, which serves as the grip, should be approximately 10 to 15 degrees. The match between the barrel and grip does not need to be exact, but avoid big gaps. Cut the grip a little long so to allow yourself extra room for shaping the contour. The grip is about the right length if it measures 6 inches top to bottom.

Cut a ¼-inch hole 1¼ inches from the bottom of the grip and another ¼-inch hole 90 degrees to the right but at a distance of 4¾ inches from the bottom (see FIG. 21-2). The lower hole is for the ¼-inch phone jack for the power, and the upper hole is for the push button switch. Note that the size of the upper hole depends on the particular switch you use. The switch detailed in the parts list is commonly available at Radio Shack and other electronics outlets. If you use another switch, you should measure the diameter of the shaft and drill a hole accordingly.

Cut two ⅙-inch-wide slits approximately ½ inch from the top of the grip. The slits should be opposite one another and at right angles to the top hole (used for the switch). Unthread the loose end of a 12-inch-long (3½-inch diameter) hose clamp through the slits. Tighten the clamp one or two turns, but not so much that you can't insert the barrel into it. The pistol so far should look like FIG. 21-3.

Table 21-1. Laser Pistol Parts List

1	12½-inch length, 2-inch schedule 40 PVC pipe
1	6¼-inch length, 1¼-inch schedule 40 PVC pipe
1	3-inch adjustable hose clamp
2	2-inch test plugs
1	1¼-inch PVC end cap
J1	¼-inch phone jack
S1	SPST momentary switch (normally open)
Misc.	Miniature 12 Vdc He-Ne power supply (see text), laser tube (see text)

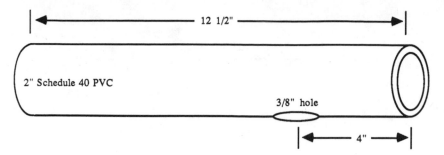

FIG. 21-1. *Cutting and drilling guide for the He-Ne laser pistol barrel.*

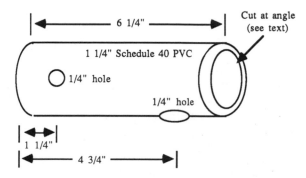

FIG. 21-2. *Cutting and drilling guide for the He-Ne laser pistol grip.*

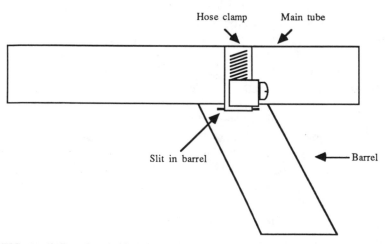

FIG. 21-3. *Barrel and grip held in place with an adjustable car radiator hose clamp.*

Wiring the Jack and Switch

Use 20- or 22-gauge stranded wire to connect the components as shown in FIG. 21-4. The wire lengths are approximate and provide some room for easily fitting the jack, switch, power supply, and tube into the PVC enclosure. After you have soldered the jack and

335

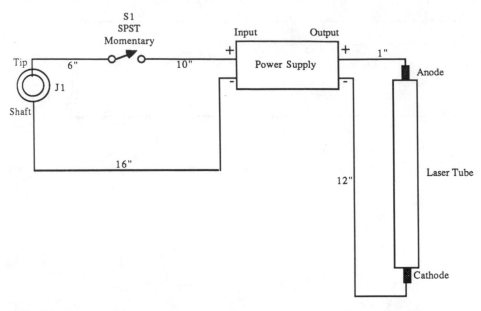

FIG. 21-4. *Wire the He-Ne laser pistol as shown in this diagram. Be aware of the high voltages present at the output of the power supply.*

switch, mount them in the grip, feed the wires through the hole in the barrel, and mount the grip to the barrel. Center the hole in the grip and tighten the clamp.

Mounting the Laser Tube and Power Supply

Attach the power supply leads to the tube. With the power supply and tube used, the anode lead from the supply connects directly to the anode terminal of the tube. This wire must be kept short to minimize current loss and high-voltage arcing. The cathode lead stretches from the supply to the opposite end of the tube. This design works well because the tube emits light from the cathode side, opposite the power supply. Because not all He-Ne lasers operate this way, you'll want to choose the tube carefully. The tube must emit its light from the cathode side or the power supply will get in the way. Loosely attach the power supply to the tube by wrapping them together with electrical tape.

The tube should be protected against shock by wrapping it in a thin styrofoam sheet, the kind used for shipping fragile objects. One or two wraps should be sufficient. Close up the sheet with electrical tape.

Final Electrical Connection and Assembly

Solder the wires from the jack and switch to the power supply. Be sure to observe proper polarity. Slide the tube and power supply into the barrel so that the output end of the laser faces forward. Drill a ⅜-inch hole in the approximate center of a 2-inch knockout "test" plug (available in the ABS plumbing pipe department of most hardware stores). Because the tube might not rest in the exact center of the barrel, determine the proper spot for drilling by first inserting the plug and observing the location of the output mirror. Mark the spot with a pencil, remove the plug, and drill out the hole.

After drilling, replace the plug and push the tube into the barrel so that the output window is just flush with the inside of the plug. Don't allow the window to protrude outside the plug, or you run a greater risk of chipping or breaking the output mirror. Insert another 2-inch plug in the rear of the barrel.

Test plugs are not routinely available for 1¼-inch pipe, so you must use an ordinary end cap for the bottom of the grip. Slip the end cap over the pipe; the fit should be tight. If not, try another end cap.

Building the Battery Pack

The battery pack for the laser is separate, not only because it allows you to build a smaller gun but allows you to power the device from a variety of sources.

The main battery pack consists of two 6-volt 8 AH lead-acid batteries contained in a 4⅜-by-7¾-by-2⅜-inch phenolic or plastic experimenter's box (available at Radio Shack). The batteries are held in place inside the box with heavy double-sided foam tape. The battery pack contains a fuse and power jack, mounted as shown in FIG. 21-5. A parts list for the pack is provided in TABLE 21-2.

The fuse is absolutely necessary in case of a direct short. Lead-acid batteries of this capacity produce heavy amounts of current that can easily burn through wires and cause a fire. A 5-amp fast-acting bus fuse provides adequate short-circuit protection without burning out during the short-term shorts that can occur when plugging in the battery pack cable.

Wire the battery pack as indicated in FIG. 21-6. When wired in series, the two 6-volt batteries produce 12 volts. The high capacity of the batteries means you can operate

FIG. 21-5. *The internal arrangement of the twin six volt batteries, fuse, and power jack for the battery pack.*

Table 21-2. Battery Pack Parts List

B1,B2	6 Vdc high-output (4 AH or more) gelled electrolyte or lead-acid rechargeable battery
F1	5-amp fuse
J1	¼-inch phone jack
1	Project box, measuring 4⅜ by 7¾ by 2⅜-inches
2	⅝-inch eyelets
1	Camera or guitar strap

the laser for at least an hour before needing a recharge. I have operated the prototype pistol for up to 6 hours before needing a recharge.

To make the battery pack conveniently portable, insert two ⅝-inch eyelet screws near the top of the box. Snap on a wide camera strap and adjust the strap for your shoulder. You can sling the battery pack over your shoulder while holding the pistol in your hands.

Current is delivered from the battery pack to the pistol by means of a 6- to 12-foot coiled guitar extension cord. These are available at Radio Shack and most music stores. Buy the two-wire mono variety; you don't need the three-wire stereo type. Remember to double-check the hookup of the power jacks in the battery pack and pistol. Make sure that the positive terminal connects to the tip of the jack.

Battery Recharger

The battery recharger is a surplus battery eliminator/charger pack designed for 12-volt systems. The pack outputs 13 to 18 volts at about 350 mA. The batteries can be recharged in the box by unplugging the power cord that stretches between the pack and pistol and plugging in the recharger. At 350 mA, recharging takes from 10 to 14 hours. Because the battery eliminator/recharger is not "intelligent," be sure to remove it after the recharge period. Otherwise the batteries could be damaged by overcharging.

ADDING ON TO THE LASER PISTOL

There are several modifications you can make to the laser pistol to increase its functionality and versatility. These include a power indicator, modulation bypass jack, and single-shot circuit.

Power Light Add-on

A power light provides a visual indication that the laser gun is on. The light is especially helpful if you are using the pistol in daylight when the beam is hard to see and you want to be sure that the gun is working.

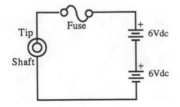

FIG. 21-6. *The wiring diagram for the battery pack. Do not omit the fuse.*

The power light consists of a light-emitting diode and current-limiting resistor. Drill a hole for the LED in the rear test plug and mount it using all-purpose glue. The LED is connected in parallel with the laser power supply: when you pull the switch, current is delivered to the power supply and LED.

Modulation Bypass Add-on

The modulation bypass permits you to easily modulate the beam with an analog or digital signal. The bypass consists of a ⅛-inch miniature earphone jack connected between the cathode lead of the power supply and the cathode terminal of the tube. Both LED and modulation bypass add-ons are shown in FIG. 21-7.

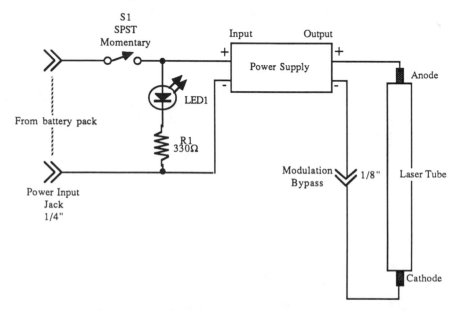

FIG. 21-7. *Schematic diagram for adding the modulation bypass and LED indicator enhancements to the He-Ne laser pistol.*

To add the bypass to the pistol, drill a hole for the jack in the rear test plug. Apply high-voltage putty around the terminals to the jack; be sure that none of the putty interferes with the contacts of the jack. The putty helps prevent arcing due to high voltages. When not using the bypass jack, insert a shorting plug into the jack (the shorting plug has its internal contacts shorted together).

To use the modulation bypass, remove the shorting plug and insert the leads from a modulation transformer, as detailed in Chapter 13, ''Free-Air Laser Light Communications.'' The transformer can be driven by an audio amplifier so signals can be transmitted via the laser beam. Depending on what you connect to the modulation transformer, you can transmit audio signals or digital data over distances exceeding 1 mile.

Aiming Sights or Scope

If you plan on using the pistol for target practice, you'll want to add front and rear sights along the top of the barrel. Because the beam comes out of the barrel almost

1¼ inches from the top, you are bound to experience parallax problems with any type of sight system you use. For best results, mount the sights as close the barrel as possible—the further away they are from the barrel, the more pronounced are the effects of parallax error.

Effective homemade sights can be made inserting two small, flat or pan-head machine screws into the top of the barrel (use flat-blade screws, not hex or Philips). The screws should be short and should not overly extend inside the barrel. If they do, the tips of the screws could interfere with the laser and power supply.

Adjust the leveling of the sights by turning the screws clockwise or counter-clockwise. Position the "slits" of the tops of the screws to that they are parallel to the length of the barrel. By adjusting the height of the screws you compensate for the differences in parallel between the sight and the laser tube. Note that there is no need to adjust for windage because the light is not affected by the wind, nor do you need to compensate for bullet trajectory, because the light beam will continue in a straight path.

Painting

Although painting the laser pistol won't make it work better, it certainly improves its look. Prior to painting, you should remove the end caps, tube, switch, and jack, or else use masking tape to prevent paint from spraying on them. Be particularly wary of paint coming into contact with the output mirror of the tube and the internal contacts of the power plug.

Black ABS plastic pipe does not need to be painted, saving you from this extra step. However, straight pieces of 1¼- and 2-inch black ABS plastic is hard to find. Most plumb-

FIG. 21-8. *The completed He-Ne laser pistol, with modulation bypass shorting plug installed.*

ing and hardware stores carry only pre-formed fittings for drains and other waste-water systems.

Spray on a light coast of flat black paint; Testor's hobby paints are a good choice, and when used properly, won't sag during drying. The paint dries to a touch in 10 to 15 minutes, but it isn't cured until overnight. You can, of course, paint the pistol any color. A complete, painted pistol is shown in FIG. 21-8.

APPLICATIONS FOR THE LASER PISTOL

Let's face it, the He-Ne laser pistol isn't going to make you Luke Skywalker, so there is little chance you'll be going around the galaxy disintegrating bad guys. The output of the tube used in the pistol (like all other helium-neon lasers) isn't enough to be felt on skin, it won't burn holes in anything nor is it capable of any kind of destruction. That leaves rather peaceful applications of the pistol.

Before detailing some of the fun you can have with the laser pistol, I need to stress the safety requirements once more. The hand-held nature and design of the pistol might prompt you to use it in a Laser Tag-like game. Don't. The eyes of you and your opponent (man or beast) could be exposed to the laser beam—a definite health hazard. Point the pistol only at inanimate "blind" objects.

Hand-Held Pointer

Although the He-Ne pistol is rather large for the task, it can be effectively used as a hand-held pointer. Even in a large auditorium with a brightly lit movie, the laser pointer can be easily seen on the screen.

If you don't care for the pinpoint of light, try shaping the beam with optics and a shape mask. Use a double-concave lens to expand the beam from its nominal 0.75 mm to about 10 millimeters. A bi-convex lens collimates the beam—makes the rays parallel again. In front of the collimating lens you place a mask of an arrow, cut from a piece of thick black plastic, aluminum foil or photographic film (your local offset printer can provide a high-contrast mask of any artwork). When using aluminum foil, paint both front and back sides to cut down light reflections.

Because the positioning of the optical components depends on the focal lengths of the lenses, you should experiment with some lenses and try out the system before building it onto the pistol. When you have determined the proper placement of the lens and mask, mount them in PVC pipe or paper tube and attach the pipe to the end of the pistol. A 2-inch coupler can be used to easily attach extensions to the front of the laser.

The Ultimate Cat Toy

Believe it or not, many owners of helium-neon lasers spend countless hours using the bright red beam as a high-tech cat toy. If you have a cat and it's fairly playful, try this experiment: When the animal is least expecting it, shine the beam on the floor (not into its eyes). Most cats will react to the beam by pouncing on it. Of course, they can never get it because it's simply a spot of light on the carpet. Scan the beam at a fairly slow rate and have the cat chase after it.

Dogs don't seem to be much interested in laser beam spots. Mine just licks the end of the laser and wags his tail.

22

Laser Projects Potpourri

In the past several hundred pages, you've discovered numerous applications for your helium-neon and diode laser. Yet there are many, many more, enough to fill several volumes twice the size of this book. This chapter briefly reviews additional applications for lasers and details the components and procedures involved. Feel free to expand upon the ideas presented in the pages that follow; consider the projects as springboards for your own advanced experiments.

OPTICAL SWITCH USING LCD PANEL

An ordinary liquid crystal display (LCD) can be used as a type of laser shutter. Instead of using the display to indicate letters or numbers, you shine a laser through it. When voltage is applied to the terminals of the display, the crystals alternately rotate between their aligned and non-aligned states, breaking and passing the beam.

The basic construction of an LCD is shown in FIG. 22-1. To use the panel as a laser beam switch, remove the back reflective paper. If you accidentally remove the polarizing sheet, replace it with another. Be sure the replacement sheet is oriented in the proper direction.

Connect a 5-volt battery source to the terminals on the display. One or more segments should blink on. You can use any of the segments as long as it is wide enough to block the entire beam. If the segments dim out after you apply current, drive the display with 5- to 10-Hz pulses provided by a 555 timer IC (any book on the 555 can provide details on how to wire it as a pulse generator). You can also drive the panel with an audio source such as a tape recorder, radio, or amplified microphone.

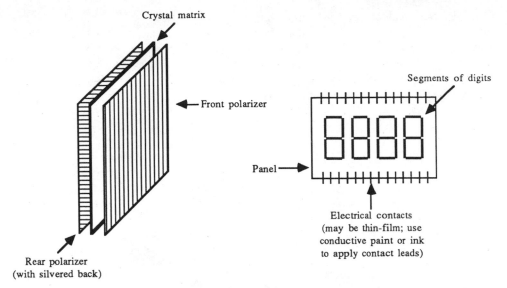

FIG. 22-1. *Construction of a reflective liquid crystal display (LED) panel. To use the panel as a shutter, remove the silver backing on the reverse side of the rear polarizer. Activate the panel by applying low-voltage dc to the electrical contacts. Shine the laser through one or more segments.*

To use the panel, position it in front of the laser and turn the segment on and off. Note that even when the segment is on, some of the laser beam will pass through, so the LCD panel can't be used as an absolute shutter. If you are using the panel as a modulation system, place a phototransistor in the path of the light and amplify the signal using the universal laser light receiver detailed in Chapter 13.

LASER SURVEILLANCE

Not long ago, Radio-Electronics magazine ran a cover story on using a helium-neon laser as a way to intercept the private conversations of others. The article provided step-by-step instructions on building the system, including a sensitive laser light detector. Although the "laser bug" is patently illegal, it's fun to play around with and to use as a way to test positional or geometrical modulation.

The system, as indicated in the article, is comprised of a laser mounted on a tripod and a receiver mounted on another tripod (you can combine the two on the same tripod but alignment is very difficult). The laser is aimed at a window, and the reflected beam is directed to the receiver. Voices or sound inside a building cause the windows to vibrate slightly, which positionally modulates the window pane. The movement is picked up by the receiver and amplified. An identical system is covered in Chapter 13 using a speaker and Mylar foil stretched over an embroidery hoop.

An interesting story about the laser bug is included in Forrest Mims' *Silliconnections* book (see Appendix B for publishing information). Apparently, Mims was asked by the *National Enquirer* to construct and use a laser bug to intercept the private conversations of the late Howard Hughes. Mims finally declined, worrying about the legality of the system, but later went on to demonstrate the bug on television.

You can conduct your own laser bug experiments using a He-Ne laser and the universal laser light receiver found in Chapter 13. You can make the photosensor more directional by mounting it on the back of a riflescope, as shown in FIG. 22-2. Experiment with the placement of the sensor until the received audio signal is the strongest. When using the bug during the daytime, place two polarizing filters in front of the sensor or scope to prevent swamping from sunlight.

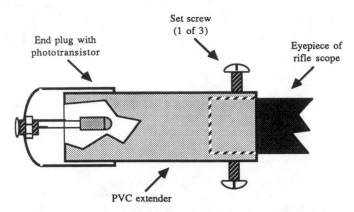

FIG. 22-2. *Use a piece of PVC 1-inch pipe to attach the end plug and phototransistor to the eyepiece of the rifle scope. Three set screws (set in a triangular configuration) clamp the pipe to the eyepiece.*

Depending on the type of window, drapes, and acoustic conditions inside, the sounds you pick up could be faint or overpowering. Strong background noise, like a dishwasher, stereo, or air conditioner, can totally mask any intelligible conversations inside. Of course, if the sound source you want to listen to isn't near a window, you won't hear anything.

Be aware that owning and using a laser bug might be illegal. It's decidedly a bad idea to construct and use a bug to intercept the conversations of others unless you have their permission.

LASER TACHOMETER

Pulses of light can be used to count the rotational speed of just about any object, even when you can't be near that object. The heart of the laser tachometer is the counter circuit shown in FIG. 22-3 (pars A through D). A parts list is provided in TABLE 22-1. In use, shine a helium-neon laser at the rotating object you want to time. If you can, paint a white or reflective strip on the object so the beam is adequately reflected. Place a photosensor and amplifier at the point where the reflected beam lands, and connect the amp to the input of the counter circuit.

At each revolution, the light beam is reflected off the reflective strip on the object and directed into the photosensor, amplifier, and counter. The counter resets itself every second, thereby giving you a readout of the rate of the revolution per second. For example, if a car wheel is turning at 100 revolutions per second, the number 100 appears on the display. To compute revolutions per minute (rpm), multiply the result on the readout by 60.

The maximum count using the three digits of the counter is 999. That equates to 59,940 revolutions per minute, faster than even a jet turbine. You shouldn't run into

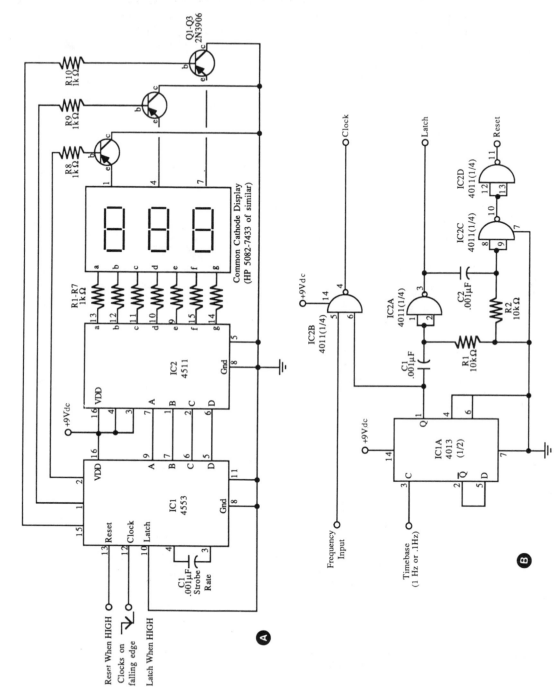

FIG. 22-3. *A schematic diagram for a light-activated tachometer, shown in subsections. (A) Main counter circuit; (B) Trigger logic circuit; (C) Crystal-controlled time base; (D) Phototransistor inputs for trigger reset (optional).*

345

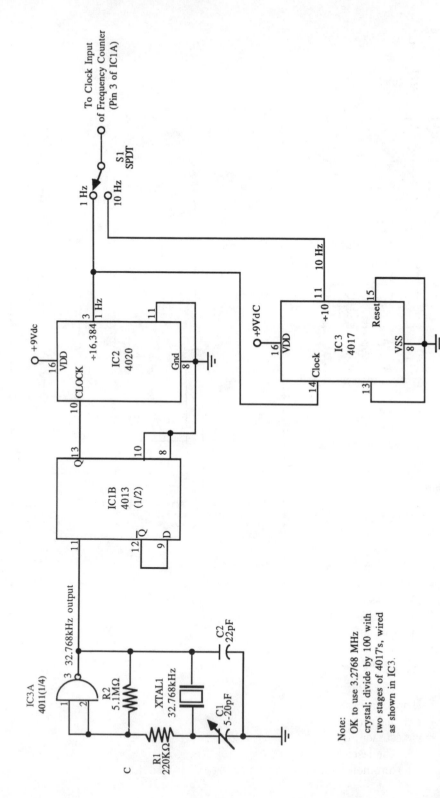

Fig. 22-3. Continued.

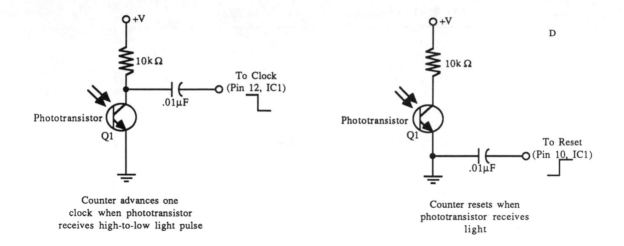

Counter advances one
clock when phototransistor
receives high-to-low light pulse

Counter resets when
phototransistor receives
light

Notes:
Use appropriate filters (red, IR)
depending on the laser used.

Adjust sensitivity by replacing 10kΩ resistor
with 250kΩ potentiometer.

Fig. 22-3. *Continued.*

too many things that outpace the tachometer. If the object you are timing is distant, use the riflescope arrangement presented in the previous section that allows you to aim the sensor directly at the reflective strip.

PERIMETER BURGLAR ALARM

Many stores use infrared break-beam systems to detect when a customer walks through the front door. Each time the beam is broken, a bell in the back rings, telling store personnel that someone has entered. A similar approach can be used in a perimeter burglar alarm system. The narrow divergence of the lasers means you can bounce a single beam around the yard, thus protecting a relatively large area. FIGURE 22-4 shows a few ways to position the laser, mirrors, and receiver around the house.

To actuate an alarm, connect the output of the receiver to a relay and bell. When the beam is broken, the voltage present at the output of the receiver drops, the relay kicks in, and the bell sounds off.

BASICS OF THE LASER GYROSCOPE

The latest commercial jets use a laser-based inertial guidance system. Three ring-shaped lasers detect rate and rotation of the aircraft in all three axes (pitch, yaw, and roll) and provide the data to an on-board computer. The advantage of the laser gyroscope is accuracy, even after many thousands of hours of use.

The laser gyroscope, shown schematically in FIG. 22-5, is modeled after a Michelson interferometer. Two beams are passed around the circumference of the gyro and

Table 22-1. Laser Tachometer Parts List

Counter Block (Fig. 22-3A)
IC1   4553 CMOS counter IC
IC2   4511 CMOS LED driver IC
R1-R10 1 kilohm resistor
C1   0.001 μF disc capacitor
Q1-Q3 2N3906 transistor
LED1-3 Common-cathode seven-segment LED display

Trigger Logic Circuit (Fig. 22-3B)
IC1   4013 CMOS flip-flop IC
IC2   4011 CMOS NAND gate IC
R1,R2 10 kilohm resistor
C1,C2 0.001 μF disc capacitor

Crystal-Controlled Time Base (Fig. 22-3C)
IC1 4013 CMOS flip-flop IC (from trigger logic circuit)
IC2 4020 CMOS counter IC
IC3 4017 CMOS counter IC
IC4 4011 CMOS NAND gate IC
R1   220 kilohm resistor
R2   5.1 megohm resistor
C1   5 to 20 pF miniataure variable capacitor
C2   22 pF disc capacitor
S1   DPDT switch

Phototransistor Inputs (Fig. 22-3D)
Q1   Infrared phototransistor
R1   10 kilohm resistor
C1   0.01 μF disc capacitor

All resistors are 5 to 10 percent tolerance, ¼ watt. All capacitors are 10 to 20 percent tolerance, rated 35 volts or more, unless otherwise indicated.

integrated at one or more photosensors and receivers. When at rest, the two beams travel the same distance and there is no change at the photosensors. But when the gyroscope is set into motion, one beam travels a longer distance than the other, and that results in a Doppler shift that causes beat frequencies or optical heterodyning at the detectors. These beat frequencies, which are like low-frequency audio tones, are correlated by a flight computer.

The Michelson interferometer detailed in Chapter 10 can be modified to work as a laser gyroscope. Just mount the base, with laser, on a ball-bearing turntable (lazy Susan).

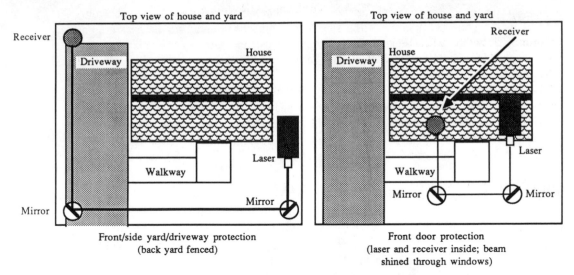

Top view of house and yard
Top view of house and yard

Front/side yard/driveway protection
(back yard fenced)

Front door protection
(laser and receiver inside; beam
shined through windows)

FIG. 22-4. *Two approaches to building a break-beam perimeter laser alarm system. For very long distances, collimate the beam as detailed in Chapter 8.*

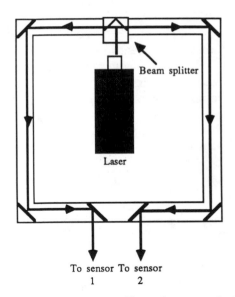

FIG. 22-5. *Basic configuration of the laser gyroscope. The two beams may also be directed to one photosensor.*

Position a photosensor at the spot where the two beams meet and route the signal to an amplifier. You can hear the effect of movement when the interferometer is rotated.

STUDYING FLUID AERODYNAMICS

You can readily see the effects of wind on airfoils by rigging up your own laser smoke chamber. Build an accurate plastic model and make sure that the wings, fuselage, and other parts are adequately sealed. A coat of paint or lacquer will seal the seams and provide better results. Suspend the airplane in a cardboard box that has its top and bottom cut out. Cut a small portion out of the side and fit a sheet of clear acrylic plastic as a window. Fill the box with smoke and use a motor or galvanometer to scan a laser beam over the wing surface of the aircraft (details on these techniques are covered in Chapter 20, ''Advanced Laser Light Shows'').

Direct a fan into the box and watch the effect of the smoke as it streams past the airplane. Point the laser at different parts of the airframe to study the aerodynamics at specific points. With enough smoke, you should clearly see the effects of the wings, the turbulence behind the airplane, drag on structural elements, and more. Load your camera with a fast black-and-white film and photograph the results for later analysis.

CRYOGENIC COOLING OF SEMICONDUCTOR LASERS

All semiconductor lasers become super efficient at low temperatures. The first diode lasers could only be operated at the sub-freezing temperature of liquid nitrogen (minus 197 degrees Celsius). Only by the mid 1970's had they perfected the room-temperature laser diode. By dipping a low-power (1 to 5 mW) double-heterostructure cw laser in a glass filled with liquid nitrogen, you can increase its operating efficiency by several hundred percent.

Try this experiment. Connect a laser diode as shown in FIG. 22-6, and dip it into a glass Pyrex measuring cup. Connect a meter to the monitor photodiode to register light output. Note the reading from the photodiode on the meter. Now slowly fill the cup with liquid nitrogen. The liquid will bubble violently as it boils. Watch the reading on the meter jump as the diode is cooled. In my experiments, the reading on the meter was some 850 times higher at cryogenic temperatures than it was at regular room temperature.

This extra light can be readily seen not only because of the higher output of the laser, but because the laser operates at a lower wavelength when cooled. Instead of operating at the threshold of visible light (about 780 nm), the liquid nitrogen brought the operating wavelength down to perhaps 700 nm, in the far red region of visible light. Use a lab-grade spectroscope to measure the exact wavelength of the emitted light.

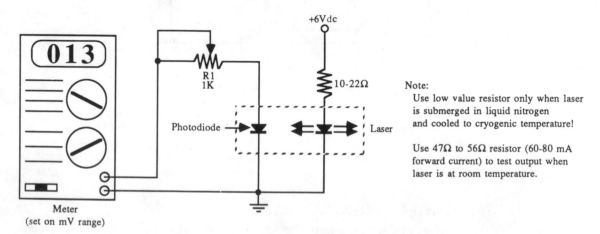

FIG. 22-6. *Use this setup to test the power output of a diode laser in and out of a bath of liquid nitrogen. The laser can be placed directly in the liquid without fear of short circuits because liquid nitrogen is not electrically conductive.*

350

Liquid nitrogen tips and techniques:

★ You can buy liquid nitrogen at welding, hospital, and medical supply outlets. Price is typically between $2 and $3 per liter.

★ Use a stainless steel or glass Thermos bottle to hold the liquid nitrogen (some outlets won't fill these canisters due to breakage and waste; check first). Drill a hole in the top of the Thermos to allow the nitrogen vapor to escape. Without the hole, the Thermos will explode.

★ The liquid nitrogen will last about a day in a Thermos. If you want to keep it longer, use a Dewar's flask or other approved container designed for handling refrigerated liquid gas.

★ Wear safety goggles and waterproof welder's gloves when handling liquid nitrogen. Never allow the liquid to touch your skin or you could get serious frostbite burns.

★ If the liquid touches clothing, immediately grasp the material at a dry spot and pull it away from your body.

★ While experimenting, fill liquid nitrogen only in Pyrex glass or metal containers. Avoid plastic and regular glass containers as they can shatter on contact with the extremely cold temperatures.

ADDITIONAL PROJECTS

There are numerous additional applications of lasers. These include using lasers in surveying as a means to calculate distances, as well as provide straight lines for grading, leveling, and pipe laying. For example, you can use an unexpanded beam to help you dig a straight trench in your backyard for a water pipe. A laser beam can also be used to test for flatness of a foundation or flooring. Place the laser on the ground and either move it manually or scan the beam using one of the techniques detailed in Chapters 19 and 20.

Very small movements in an object can be detected by attaching a mirror to the object and shining a laser on the mirror. Position a card or screen some distance from the object, as shown in FIG. 22-7, and watch the beam scan back and forth as the object is moved.

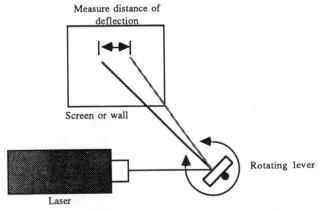

FIG. 22-7. *The basic arrangement for using a laser as a remote lever.*

This chapter has covered only a handful of useful applications for lasers; there are many, many more. Give it some thought, and you can probably come up with dozens of intriguing ways to put lasers to use. A good source for ideas is Metrologic's *101 Ways to Use a Laser*, a short mini-book that is bound into their catalog. In 15 pages, you are provided quick glimpses of ways to put lasers to work and how you can apply laser light to solve even the most demanding problems.

23

Tools and Supplies
for Laser Experimentation

Take a long look at the tools in your garage or workshop. You probably have all the implements necessary to build your own laser systems. Unless your designs require a great deal of precision (and most don't), a common assortment of hand tools are all that's really required to construct all sorts of laser projects.

Most of the hardware, parts, and supplies are things you probably already have that are left over from old projects from around the house. The pieces you don't have can be readily purchased at a hardware store and a few specialty stores around town or through the mail.

This chapter discusses the basic tools and supplies needed for constructing hobby laser systems and how you might use them. You should consider this chapter a guide only; suggestions for tools and supplies are just that—suggestions. By no means should you feel that you must own each tool mentioned in this chapter or have on hand all the parts and supplies.

Some supplies and parts might not be readily available to you, and it's up to you to consider alternatives and how to work these alternatives into the design. Ultimately, it will be your task to take a trip to the hardware store, collect various miscellaneous items, and go home to hammer out a unique creation that's all your own.

CONSTRUCTION TOOLS

Construction tools are the things you use to fashion the frame and other mechanical parts of the laser system. These include hammer, screwdriver, saw, and so forth. Tools for the assembly of the electronic subsystems are discussed later on.

353

Basic Tools

No workshop is complete without the following:

★ **Claw hammer**, used for just about anything you can think of.

★ **Rubber mallet**, for gently bashing pieces together that resist going together; also for forming sheet metal.

★ **Screwdriver assortment**, including various sizes of flat-head and Philips-head screwdrivers. A few long-blade screwdrivers are handy to have, as well as a ratchet driver. Get a screwdriver magnetizer/demagnetizer to magnetize the blade so it attracts and holds screws for easier assembly.

★ **Hacksaw**, to cut anything. The hacksaw is the staple of the laser hobbyist. Get an assortment of blades. Coarse-tooth blades are good for wood and PVC pipe plastic; fine-tooth blades are good for copper, aluminum, and light-gauge steel.

★ **Miter box**, to cut straight lines. Buy a good miter box and attach it to your work table (avoid wood miter boxes; they don't last). You'll also use the box to cut stock at near-perfect 45-degree angles, helpful when building optical benches.

★ **Wrenches**, all types. Adjustable wrenches are helpful additions to the shop but careless use can strip nuts. The same goes for long-nosed pliers, useful for getting at hard-to-reach places. A pair or two vise-grips (indispensable in my workshop) help you hold pieces for cutting and sanding. A set of nut-drivers make it easy to attach nuts to bolts.

★ **Measuring tape**. A six- or eight-foot steel measuring tape is a good choice. Also get a cloth tape at a fabric store for measuring flexible things.

★ **Square**, for making sure that pieces you cut and assemble from wood, plastic, and metal are square.

★ **File assortment**, to smooth the rough edges of cut wood, metal, and plastic (particularly important when working with metal for safety).

★ **Drill motor**. Get one that has a variable speed control (reversing is nice but not absolutely necessary). If the drill you have isn't variable speed, buy a variable-speed control for it. You need to slow the drill when working with metal and plastic. A fast drill motor is good for wood only. The size of the chuck is not important, because most of the drill bits you'll be using will fit a standard ¼-inch chuck.

★ **Drill bit assortment**. Good, sharp ones *only*. If yours are dull, have them sharpened (or do it yourself with a drill-bit sharpening device), or buy a new set. *Never* use dull drill bits or your laser systems won't turn out.

★ **Vise**, for holding parts while you work. A large vise isn't required, but you should get one that's big enough to handle the size of pieces you'll be working with.

★ **Clear safety goggles**. Wear them when hammering, cutting, drilling, and any other time flying debris could get in your eyes.

If you plan on building your laser systems from wood, you might want to consider adding rasps, wood files, coping saws, and other woodworking tools to your toolbox. Working with plastic requires a few extras as well, including a burnishing wheel to smooth the edges of the cut plastic (a flame from a cigarette lighter also works but is harder to control), a strip-heater for bending, and special plastic drill bits. These bits have a modified tip that isn't as likely to rip through the plastic material. Bits for glass can be used as well. Small plastic parts can be cut and scored using a sharp razor knife or razor saw, available at hobby stores.

Optional Tools

There are a number of tools you can use to make your time in the laser shop more productive and less time-consuming. A *drill press* helps you drill better holes, because you have more control over the angle and depth of each hole. Use a drill press vise to hold the pieces; never use your hands.

A *table saw* or *circular* saw makes cutting through large pieces of wood and plastic easier. Use a guidefence, or fashion one out of wood and clamps, to ensure a straight cut. Be sure to use a fine-tooth saw blade if cutting through plastic. Using a saw designed for general wood-cutting will cause the plastic to shatter.

A motorized *hobby tool* is much like a hand-held router. The bit spins very fast (25,000 rpm and up), and you can attach a variety of wood-, plastic-, and metal-working bits to it. The better hobby tools, such as those made by Dremel and Weller, have adjustable speed controls. Use the right bit for the job. For example, don't use a wood rasp bit with metal or plastic, because the flutes of the rasp will too easily fill with metal and plastic debris.

A *nibbling tool* is a fairly inexpensive accessory (under $20) that lets you "nibble" small chunks from metal and plastic pieces. The maximum thickness depends on the bite of the tool, but it's generally about $1/16$ or $1/8$ inch. Use the tool to cut channels, enlarge holes, and so forth. A *tap and die set* lets you thread holes and shafts to accept standard size nuts and bolts. Buy a good set. A cheap assortment of taps and dies is more trouble than its worth.

A *thread size gauge* made of stainless steel might be expensive ($10 to $12), but it helps you determine the size of any standard SAE or metric bolt. It's a great accessory for tapping and dieing. Most gauges can be used when chopping threads off bolts with a hacksaw, providing a cleaner cut.

A *brazing tool* or *small welder* lets you spot-weld two metal pieces together. These tools are designed for small pieces only; they don't provide enough heat to adequately weld pieces larger than a few inches in size. Be sure that extra fuel and/or oxygen cylinders or pellets are readily available for the brazer or welder you buy. There's nothing worse than spending $30 to $40 for a home welding set, only to discover that supplies are not available for it. Be sure to read the instructions that accompany the welder and observe all precautions.

A *caliper* and *micrometer* let you measure small things such as lenses and other optical components. The projects in this book don't call for an extremely accurate caliper or micrometer, but if you're serious about laser work you'll want the best laboratory-grade instruments you can afford. At the very least, the caliper should be accurate to $1/64$ of an inch and the micrometer to 0.001 of an inch.

ELECTRONIC TOOLS

Constructing electronic circuit boards or wiring the power system of your laser requires only a few standard electronic tools. A *soldering iron* leads the list. For maximum flexibility, invest in a modular soldering pencil with a 25- to 30-watt heating element. Anything higher could damage electronic components. (If necessary, a 40- or 50-watt element can be used for wiring switches, relays, and power transistors.) *Stay away from "instant-on" soldering irons.* Supplement your soldering iron with these accessories:

★ **Soldering stand**, for keeping the soldering pencil in a safe, upright position.

★ **Soldering tip assortment**. Get one or two small tips for intricate PCB work and a few larger sizes for routine soldering chores.

★ **Solder**. Resin- or flux-core only. Acid core and silver solder should *never* be used on electronic components.

★ **Sponge**, for cleaning the soldering tip during use. Keep the sponge damp and wipe the tip clean after every few joints.

★ **Heatsink**, for attaching to sensitive electronic components during soldering. The heatsink draws the excess heat away from the component to help prevent damage to it.

★ **Desoldering vacuum tool**, to soak up molten solder. Used to get rid of excess solder, to remove components, or redo a wiring job.

★ **Soldering or "dental" picks**, for scraping, cutting, forming, and gouging into the work.

★ **Resin cleaner**. Apply the cleaner after soldering is complete to remove excess resin.

★ **Solder vise** or "third hand." The vise holds together pieces to be soldered, leaving you free to work the iron and feed the solder.

VOLT-OHMMETER

A *volt-ohmmeter* is used to test voltage levels and the impedance of circuits. This moderately priced electronic tool is the basic requirement for working with electronic circuits of any kind. If you don't already own a volt-ohmmeter, seriously consider buying one. The cost is minimal considering the usefulness of the device.

There are many volt-ohmmeters (or VOMs) on the market today. For work on lasers, you don't want a cheap model, but you don't need an expensive one. A meter of intermediate quality is sufficient and does the job admirably. The price for such a meter is between $30 and $75. Meters are available at Radio Shack and most electronics outlets. Shop around and compare features and prices.

Digital or Analog

There are two general types of VOMs available today: digital and analog. The difference is not that one meter is used on digital circuits and the other on analog circuits. Rather, digital meters employ a numeric display not unlike a digital clock or watch, and analog VOMs use the older fashioned—but still useful—mechanical movement with a needle that points to a set of graduated scales.

Digital VOMs used to cost a great deal more than the analog variety, but the price difference has evened out recently. Digital VOMs, such as the one shown in FIG. 23-1, are fast becoming the standard; in fact, it's becoming difficult to find a decent analog meter anymore.

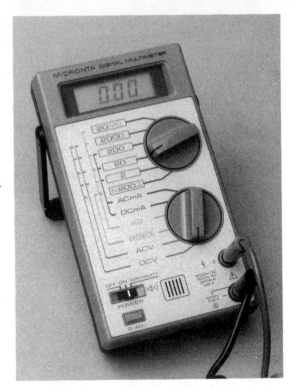

FIG. 23-1. *A typical digital volt-ohmmeter.*

Analog VOMs are traditionally harder to use, because you must select the type and range of voltage you are testing, find the proper scale on the meter face, then estimate the voltage as the needle swings into action. Digital VOMs, on the other hand, display the voltage in clear numerals and with a greater precision than most analog meters.

Automatic Ranging

As with analog meters, some digital meters require you to select the range before it can make an accurate measurement. For example, if you are measuring the voltage of a 9-volt transistor battery, you set the range to the setting closest to, but above, 9 volts (with most meters it is the 20- or 50-volt range). Auto-ranging meters don't require you to do this, so they are inherently easier to use. When you want to measure voltage, you set the meter to volts (either ac or dc) and take the measurement. The meter displays the results in the readout panel.

Accuracy

Little of the work you'll do with laser circuits requires a meter that's super accurate. A VOM with average accuracy is more than enough. The accuracy of a meter is the minimum amount of error that can occur when taking a specific measurement. For example, the meter may be accurate to 2,000 volts, ±0.8 percent. A 0.8-percent error at the kinds of voltages used in most laser experiments—typically 5 to 12 volts dc—is only 0.096 volts!

Digital meters have another kind of accuracy. The number of digits in the display determines the maximum resolution of the measurements. Most digital meters have 3 and one-half digits, so it can display a value as small as .001 (the half digit is a "1" on the left side of the display). Anything less than that is not accurately represented.

Functions

Digital VOMs vary greatly in the number and type of functions they provide. At the very least, all standard VOMs let you measure ac volts, dc volts, milliamps, and ohms. Some also test capacitance and opens or shorts in discrete components like diodes and transistors. These additional functions are not absolutely necessary for building general-purpose laser circuits, but they are handy to have when troubleshooting a circuit that refuses to work.

The maximum ratings of the meter when measuring volts, milliamps, and resistance also varies. For most applications, the following maximum ratings are more than adequate:

dc Volts	1,000 volts
ac Volts	500 volts
dc Current	200 milliamps
Resistance	2 megohms

One exception to this is when testing current draw for motors and other high-demand circuits. All but the smallest dc motors draw an excess of 200 milliamps, and an entire laser system for a light show is likely to draw 2 or more amps. Obviously, this is far out of range of most digital meters. You might need to get a good assessment of current draw, especially if your laser projects are powered by batteries, but to do so, you'll need either a meter with a higher dc current rating (digital or analog) or a special-purpose ac/dc current meter. You can also use a resistor in series with the motor and apply Ohm's Law to calculate the current draw.

Meter Supplies

Meters come with a pair of test leads—one black and one red—each equipped with a needle-like metal probe. The quality of the test leads is usually minimal, so you might want to purchase a better set. The coiled kind are handy. They stretch out to several feet yet recoil to a manageable length when not in use.

Standard leads are fine for most routine testing, but some measurements require the use of a clip lead. These attach to the end of the regular test leads and have a spring-loaded clip on the end. You can clip the lead in place so your hands are free to do other things. The clips are insulated to prevent short circuits.

Meter Safety and Use

Most applications of the meter involve testing low voltages and resistance, both of which are relatively harmless to humans. Sometimes, however, you might need to test high voltages—like the input to a power supply—and careless use of the meter can cause serious bodily harm. Even when you're not actively testing a high-voltage circuit, dangerous currents might still be exposed.

Proper procedure for meter use involves setting the meter beside the unit under test, making sure it is close enough so that the leads reach the circuit. Plug in the leads and test the meter operation by first selecting the resistance function setting (use the smallest scale if the meter is not auto-ranging). Touch the leads together: the meter should read 0 ohms.

If the meter does not respond, check the leads and internal battery and try again. If the display does not read 0 ohms, double-check the range and function settings and adjust the meter to read 0 ohms (not all digital meters have a 0 adjust, but most analog meters do).

Once the meter has checked out, select the desired function and range and apply the leads to the circuit under test. Usually, the black lead is connected to ground, and the red lead is connected to the various test points in the circuit.

When testing high-voltage circuits, make it a habit to place one hand in a pants pocket. With one hand out of the way, you are less likely to accidentally touch a live circuit.

LOGIC PROBE

Meters are typically used for measuring analog signals. *Logic probes* test for the presence or absence of low-voltage dc signals that represent digital data. The 0s and 1s are usually electrically defined as 0 and 5 volts, respectively, with TTL ICs. In practice, the actual voltages of the 0 and 1 bits depend entirely on the circuit. You can use a meter to test a logic circuit, but the results aren't always predictable. Further, many logic circuits change states (pulse) quickly and meters cannot track the voltage switches fast enough.

Logic probes, such as the model in FIG. 23-2, are designed to give a visual and (usually) aural signal of the logic state of a particular circuit line. One LED on the probe

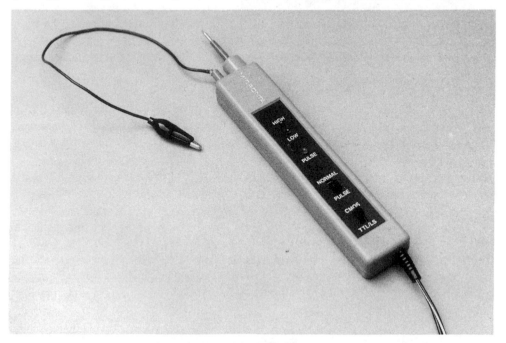

FIG. 23-2. *A logic probe.*

lights up if the logic is 0 (or LOW), another LED lights up if the logic is 1 (or HIGH). Most probes have a built-in buzzer that has a different tone for the two logic levels. That way, you don't need to keep glancing at the probe to see the logic level.

A third LED or tone can indicate a pulsing signal. A good logic probe can detect that a circuit line is pulsing at speeds of up to 10 MHz, which is more than fast enough for laser applications, even when using computer control. The minimum detectable pulse width (the time the pulse remains at one level) is 50 nanoseconds, again more than sufficient.

Although logic probes might sound complex, they are really simple devices and their cost reflects this. You can buy a reasonably good logic probe for under $20. Most probes are not battery operated; rather, they obtain operating voltage from the circuit under test. You can also make a logic probe if you wish. A number of project books provide plans.

Using a Logic Probe

The same safety precautions apply when using a logic probe as they do when using a meter. Be wary when working close to high voltages. Cover them to prevent accidental shock (for obvious reasons, logic probes are not meant for anything but digital circuits, so never apply the leads of the probe to an ac line). Logic probes cannot operate with voltages exceeding about 15 volts dc, so if you are unsure of the voltage level of a particular circuit, test it with a meter first.

Successful use of the logic probe really requires you to have a circuit schematic to refer to. Keep it handy when troubleshooting your projects. It's nearly impossible to blindly use the logic probe on a circuit without knowing what you are testing. And because the probe receives its power from the circuit under test, you need to know where to pick off suitable power. To use the probe, connect the probe's power leads to a voltage source on the board, clip the black ground wire to circuit ground, and touch the tip of the probe against a pin of an integrated circuit or the lead of some other component. For more information on using your probe, consult the manufacturer's instruction sheet.

LOGIC PULSER

A handy troubleshooting accessory when working with digital circuits is the *logic pulser*. This device puts out a timed pulse, letting you see the effect of the pulse on a digital circuit. Normally, you'd use the pulser with a logic probe or an oscilloscope (discussed below). The pulser is switchable between one pulse and continuous pulsing. You can make your own pulser out of a 555 timer IC. FIGURE 23-3 shows a schematic you can use to build your own 555-based pulser; TABLE 23-1 provides a parts list.

Most pulsers obtain their power from the circuit under test. It's important that you remember this. With digital circuits, it's generally a bad idea to present to a device an input signal that is greater than the supply voltage for the device. In other words, if a chip is powered by 5 volts, and you give it a 12-volt pulse, you'll probably ruin the chip. Some circuits work with split (+, −, and ground) power supplies (especially circuits with op amps and digital-to-analog converters). Be sure to connect the leads of the pulser to the correct power points.

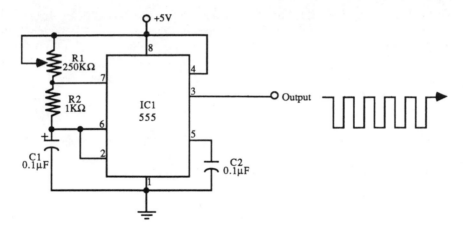

FIG. 23-3. *Schematic diagram for making your own logic pulser. With the components shown, output frequency is approximately 2.5 Hz to 33 Hz.*

Also be sure that you do not pulse a line that has an output but no input. Some integrated circuits are sensitive to unloaded pulses at their output stages, and improper application of the pulse can destroy the chip.

OSCILLOSCOPE

An *oscilloscope* is a pricey tool—good ones start at about $500—and only a small number of electronic and laser hobbyists own one. For really serious work, however, an oscilloscope is an invaluable tool—one that will save you hours of time and frustration.

Things you can do with a scope include some of the things you can do with other test equipment, but oscilloscopes do it all in one box and generally with greater precision. Among the many applications of an oscilloscope, you can:

★ Test dc or ac voltage levels.
★ Analyze the waveforms of digital and analog circuits.
★ Determine the operating frequency of digital, analog, and RF circuits.
★ Test logic levels.
★ Visually check the timing of a circuit to see if things are happening in the correct order and at the prescribed time intervals.

Table 23-1. Logic Pulser Parts List

IC1	LM555 timer IC
R1	250 kilohm potentiometer
R2	10 kilohm resistor
C1	2.2 μF electrolytic capacitor
C2	0.1 μF disc capacitor

The designs provided in this book don't absolutely require the use of an oscilloscope, but you'll probably want one if you design your own circuits or want to develop your electronic skills. A basic, no-nonsense model is enough, but don't settle for the cheap, single-trace units. A dual-trace (two channel) scope with a 20 to 25 MHz maximum input frequency should do the job nicely. The two channels let you monitor two lines at once, so you can easily compare the input signal and output signal at the same time. You do not need a scope with storage or delayed sweep, although if your model has these features, you're sure to find a use for them sooner or later.

Scopes are not particularly easy to use; they have lots of dials and controls that set operation. Thoroughly familiarize yourself with the operation of your oscilloscope before using it for any construction project or for troubleshooting. Knowing how to set the time-per-division knob is as important as knowing how to turn the scope on. As usual, exercise caution when using the scope with or near high voltages.

Lastly, don't rely on just the instruction manual that came with the set to learn how to use your new oscilloscope. Buy (and read!) a good book on how to effectively use your scope. Appendix B, ''Further Reading,'' lists some books on using oscilloscopes.

FREQUENCY METER

A *frequency meter* (or frequency counter) tests the operating frequency of a circuit. Most models can be used on digital, analog, and RF circuits for a variety of testing chores—from making sure the crystal analog-to-digital circuit is working properly to determining the modulation frequency of your laser beam communication system. You need only a basic frequency meter—a $100 or so investment. Or you can save some money by building a frequency meter kit.

Frequency meters have an upward operating limit, but it's generally well within the region applicable to laser experiments. A frequency meter with a maximum range of up to 50 MHz is enough. A couple of meters are available with an optional *prescaler*, a device that extends the useful operating frequency to well over 100 MHz.

WIRE-WRAPPING TOOL

Making a printed-circuit board for a one-shot application is time consuming, though it can be done with the proper kits and supplies. Conventional point-to-point solder wiring is not an acceptable approach when constructing digital and high-gain analog circuits, which represent the lion's share of electronics you'll be building for your lasers.

The preferred construction method is *wire-wrapping*. Wire-wrapping is a point-to-point wiring system that uses a special tool and extra-fine 28- or 30-gauge wrapping wire. When done properly, wire-wrapped circuits are as sturdy as soldered circuits, and you have the added benefit of making modifications and corrections without the hassle of desoldering and resoldering.

A manual wire-wrapping tool is shown in FIG. 23-4. You insert one end of the stripped wire into a slot in the tool, and place the tool over a square-shaped wrapping post. Give the tool five to ten twirls, and the connection is complete. The edges of the post keep the wire anchored in place. To remove the wire, use the other end of the tool and undo the wrapping.

FIG. 23-4. *A wire-wrapping tool in action.*

Wrapping wire comes in many forms, lengths, and colors, and you need to use special wire-wrapping sockets and posts. See the section below on electronic supplies and components for more details.

BREADBOARD

You should test each of the circuits you want to use with your lasers (including the ones in this book) on a *solderless breadboard* before you commit it to wire-wrap or solder. Breadboards consist of a series of holes with internal contacts spaced $\frac{1}{10}$ of an inch apart, which is the most common spacing for ICs. You plug in ICs, resistors, capacitors, transistors, and 20- or 22-gauge wire in the proper contact holes to create your circuit.

Solderless breadboards come in many sizes. For the most flexibility, get a double-width board, one that can accommodate at least 10 ICs. Smaller boards can be used for simple projects; circuits with a high number of components require bigger boards. While you're buying a breadboard, purchase a set of pre-colored wires. The wires come in a variety of lengths and are already stripped and bent for use in breadboards. The set costs $5 to $7, but the price is well worth the time you'll save.

HARDWARE SUPPLIES

A fully functional laser system of just about any description is about 75 percent hardware and 25 percent electronic and electromechanical. Most of your trips to get parts for your laser schemes will be to the local hardware store. Here are some common items you'll want to have around your shop:

Nuts and Bolts

Number 8 and 10 nuts and pan-head stove bolts ($8/32$ and $10/24$, respectively) are good for all-around construction. Get a variety of bolts in $\frac{1}{2}$-, $\frac{3}{4}$-, 1-, $1\frac{1}{4}$, and $1\frac{1}{2}$-inch lengths. You may also want to get some 2-inch and 3-inch-long bolts for special applications.

Motor shafts and other heavy-duty applications require $\frac{1}{4}$-inch 20 or $\frac{5}{16}$-inch hardware. Pan-head stove bolts are the best choice; you don't need hex-head carriage bolts unless you have a specific requirement for them. You can use number 6 ($6/32$) nuts and bolts for small, lightweight applications.

Washers

While you're at the store, stock up on flat washers, fender washers (large washers with small holes), tooth lockwashers and split lockwashers. Get an assortment for the various sizes of nuts and bolts. Split lockwashers are good for heavy-duty applications because they provide more compression locking power. You usually use them with bolt sizes of $\frac{1}{4}$-inch and larger.

All-Thread Rod

All-thread is 2- to 3-foot lengths of threaded rod stock. It comes in standard thread sizes and pitches. All-thread is good for shafts and linear motion actuators. Get one of each in $8/32$, $10/24$, and $\frac{1}{4}$-inch 20 threads to start.

Special Nuts

Coupling nuts are just like regular nuts but have been stretched out. They are designed to couple two bolts or pieces of all-thread together, end to end. In lasers, you might use them for a variety of tasks including linear motion actuators and positioning tables.

Locking nuts have a piece of nylon built into them that provides a locking bite when threaded onto a bolt. Locking nuts are preferred over using two nuts tightened together.

EXTRUDED ALUMINUM

For most of your laser designs, you can take advantage of a rather common hardware item: extruded aluminum stock. This aluminum is designed for such things as building bathtub enclosures, picture frames, and other handyman applications and comes in various sizes, thicknesses, and configurations. Length is usually 6, 8, 10, or 12 feet, but if you need less, most hardware stores will cut to order (you save when you buy it in full lengths). The stock is available in plain (dull silver) anodized aluminum and gold anodized aluminum. Get the plain stuff—it's 10 to 25 percent cheaper.

Two particularly handy stocks are $41/64$-by-$\frac{1}{2}$-by-$\frac{1}{16}$-inch channel and $57/64$-by-$\frac{9}{16}$-by-$\frac{1}{16}$-inch channel (some stores sell similar stuff with slightly different dimensions). I use these extensively to make parts for optical benches, lens holders, and other laser system parts. Angle stock measuring 1-by-1-by-$\frac{1}{16}$-inches is another frequently used item, usually employed for attaching cross bars and other structural components. No matter what size you eventually settle on for your own designs, keep several feet of the stuff handy at all times. You'll use it often.

If extruded aluminum is not available, another approach is to use shelving standards— the bar-like channel stock used for wall shelving. It's most often available in steel, but some hardware stores carry it in aluminum (silver, gold, and black anodized).

The biggest problem with using shelving standards is that the slots can cause problems when drilling holes for hardware. The drill bits can slip into the slots, causing the hole to be off-center. Some standards have an extra lip on the inside of the channel that can interfere with some of the hardware you use to join the pieces together.

ANGLE BRACKETS

You need a good assortment of ⅜-inch and ½-inch galvanized iron brackets to join the extruded stock or shelving standards together. Use 1½-by-⅜-inch flat corner irons when joining pieces cut at 45-degree angles to make a frame. The 1-by-⅜-inch and 1½-by-⅜-inch corner angle irons are helpful when attaching the stock to baseplates and when securing various components.

ELECTRONIC SUPPLIES AND COMPONENTS

Most of the electronic projects in this book and other books with digital and analog circuits depend on a regular stable of common electronic components. If you do any amount of electronic circuit building, you'll want to stock up on the following standard components. Keeping spares handy prevents you from making repeat trips to the electronics store.

Resistors

Get a good assortment of ¼- or ⅛-watt resistors. Make sure the assortment includes a variety of common values and that there are several of each value. Supplement the assortment with individual purchases of the following resistor values: 270 ohm, 330 ohm, 1 kilohm, 3.3 kilohm, 10 kilohm, and 100 kilohm.

The 270 and 330 ohm values are often used with light-emitting diodes (LEDs) and the remaining values are common to TTL and CMOS digital circuits.

Variable Resistors

Variable resistors, or potentiometers (pots), are relatively cheap and are a boon when designing and troubleshooting circuits. Buy an assortment of the small PC-mount pots (about 80 cents each retail) in the 2.5k, 5k, 10k, 50k, 100k, 25 kilohm and 1 megohm values. You'll find 1 megohm pots often used in op amp circuits, so buy a couple extra of these. I also like to have several extra 10k and 100k pots around because these find heavy use in most all types of circuits.

Capacitors

Like resistors, you'll find yourself returning to the same standard capacitor values project after project. For a well-stocked shop, get a dozen or so each of the following inexpensive ceramic disc capacitors: 0.1, 0.01, and 0.001 μF. The 0.1 and 0.01 μF caps are used extensively as *bypass* components and are absolutely essential when building circuits with TTL ICs. You can never have enough of these.

Many circuits use the in-between values of 0.47, 0.047, and 0.022 μF, so you may want to get a couple of these, too. Power supply, timing, and audio circuits often use larger polarized electrolytic or tantalum capacitors. Buy a few each of 1.0, 2.2, 4.7, 10 and 100 μF values. Some projects call for other values (in the picofarad range and the 1000's of microfarad range). You can buy these as needed unless you find yourself returning to standard values repeatedly.

Transistors

There are thousands of transistors available, and each one has slightly different characteristics than the others. However, most applications need nothing more than "generic" transistors for simple switching and amplifying. Common npn signal transistors are the 2N2222 and the 2N3904. Both kinds are available in bulk packages of 10 for about $1. Common pnp signal transistors are the 2N3906 and the 2N2907. Price is the same or a little higher.

I don't discriminate between the plastic and metal can transistors. For example, technically speaking, the plastic 2N2222 are called PN2222 while the metal can version carries the 2N2222 designator. In any case, buy the plastic ones because they're cheaper.

If the circuit you're building specifies another transistor than the generic kind, you might still be able to use one of these if you first look up the specifications of the transistor called for in the schematic. A number of cross-reference guides provide the specifications and replacement-equivalents for popular transistors.

There are common power transistors as well. The npn TIP31 and TIP41 are familiar to most anyone who has dealt with power switching or amplification of up to 1 amp or so. The pnp counterparts are the TIP32 and TIP42. These transistors come in the TO-220 style package.

A common larger capacity npn transistor that can switch 10 amps or more is the 2N3055. It comes in the TO-3 style package and is available everywhere. Price is between 50 cents and $2, depending on the source.

Diodes

Common diodes are the 1N914 for light-duty signal switching applications and the 1N4000 series (1N4001, 1N4002, and so forth). Get several of each and use the proper size to handle the current in the circuit. Refer to a databook on the voltage and power handling capabilities of these diodes.

LEDs

All semiconductors emit light (either visible or infrared), but light-emitting diodes (LEDs) are especially designed for the task. LEDs last longer than regular filament lamps and require less operating current. They are available in a variety of sizes, shapes, and colors. For general applications, the medium-sized red LED is perfect. Buy a few dozen and use them as needed. Some of the projects in this book call for infrared LEDs. These emit no visible light and are used in conjunction with an infrared-sensitive phototransistor or photodiode.

The project in Chapter 4, "Experimenting With Light and Optics," uses a special high-power visible red LED. Refer to that chapter for more information on this LED and where to obtain it.

Integrated Circuits

Integrated circuits let you construct fairly complex circuits from just a couple of components. Although there are literally thousands of different ICs, some with exotic applications, a small handful crops up again and again in hobby projects. You should keep the following ICs in ready stock:

✶ **555 timer**. This is by far the most popular integrated circuit for hobby electronics. With just a couple of resistors and capacitors, the NE555 can be made to act as a pulser, a timer, a time delay, a missing pulse detector, and dozens of other useful things. The chip is usually used as a pulse source for digital circuits. It's available in dual versions as the 556 and quadruple versions as the 558. A special CMOS version lets you increase the pulsing rate to 2 MHz.

✶ **LM741 op amp**. The LM741 comes second in popularity to the 555. The 741 can be used for signal amplification, differentiation, integration, sample-and-hold, and a host of other useful applications. The 741 is available in a dual version—the 1458. The chip comes in different package configurations. The schematics in this book and those usually found elsewhere, specify the pins for the common 8-pin DIP package. If you are using the 14-pin DIP package or the round can package, check the manufacturer's data sheet for the correct pinouts. Note that there are numerous op amps available, and some have design advantages over the 741.

✶ **TTL chips**. TTL ICs are common in computer circuits and other digital applications. There are many types of TTL packages, but you won't use more than 10 or 15 of them unless you're heavily into electronics experimentation. Specifically, the most common and most useful TTL ICs are the 7400, 7401, 7402, 7404, 7407, 7408, 7414, 7430, 7432, 7473, 7474, 74154, 74193, and 74244. All or many of these are available in "TTL chip assortments" through some of the mail-order electronics firms.

✶ **CMOS chips**. Because CMOS ICs require less power to operate than the TTL variety, you'll often find them specified for use with low-power laser and remote-control applications. Like TTL, there is a relatively small number of common packages: 4001, 4011, 4013, 4016, 4017, 4027, 4040, 4041, 4049, 4060, 4066, 4069, 4071, and 4081.

Wire

Solid-conductor, insulated, 22-gauge hookup wire can be used in your finished projects as well as connecting wires in breadboards. Buy a few spools in different colors. Solid-conductor wire can be crimped sharply and can break when excessively twisted and flexed. If you expect that wiring in your project might be flexed repeatedly, use stranded wire instead. Heavier 12- to 18-gauge hookup wire is required for connection to heavy-duty batteries, motors, and circuit-board power supply lines.

Wire-wrap wire is available in spool or pre-cut/pre-stripped packages. For ease of use, buy the more expensive pre-cut stuff unless you have a tool that does it for you. Get several of each length. The wire-wrapping tool has its own stripper built in (which you must use instead of a regular wire stripper), so you can always shorten the precut wires as needed. Some special wire-wrapping tools require their own wrapping wire. Check the instruction that came with the tool for details.

CIRCUIT BOARDS

Simple projects can be built onto solder breadboards. These are modeled after the solderless breadboard, so you simply transfer the tested circuit from the solderless breadboard to the solder board. You can cut the board with a hacksaw or razor saw if you don't need all of it.

Larger projects require perforated boards. Get the kind with solder tabs or solder traces on them. You'll be able to secure the components onto the boards with solder. Most perf boards are designed for wire-wrapping.

IC Sockets

You should use sockets for ICs whenever possible. Sockets come in sizes ranging from 8-pin to 40-pin. The sockets with extra-long square leads are for wire-wrapping.

You can also use wire-wrap IC sockets to hold discrete components like resistors, capacitors, diodes, LEDs, and transistors. You can, if you wish, wire-wrap the leads of these components, but because the leads are not square, the small wire doesn't have anything to bite into, so the connection won't be very strong. After assembly and testing and you are sure the circuit works, apply a dab of solder to the leads to hold the wires in place.

SETTING UP SHOP

You'll need a work table to construct the mechanisms and electronic circuits of your lasers and laser systems. Electronic assembly can be indoors or out, but I've found that when working in a carpeted room, it's best to spread another carpet or some protective cover over the floor. When the throw rug fills with solder bits and little pieces of wire and component leads, I can take it outside, beat it with a broom handle, and it's as good as new.

Unlike the manufacturing process, actual use of your laser system should be done indoors, in a controlled environment. You'll be using precision optics, so you should avoid exposing them to dust, dirt, and temperature extremes often found in garages. If you plan on building a sand box holography system as described in Chapters 17 and 18, you must be sure to keep the table indoors and away from moisture, because sand has a tendency to soak up water that can impede the creation of your holographic masterpieces.

Whatever space you choose for your laser lab, make sure all your tools are within easy reach. Keep special tools and supplies in an inexpensive fishing tackle box. Tackle boxes have lots of small compartments for placing screws and other parts.

For best results, your workspace should be an area where the laser system in progress will not be disturbed if you have to leave it for several hours or days (as will usually be the case). The work table should also be one that is off limits or inaccessible to young children or at least an area that can be easily supervised. This is especially true of helium-neon-based lasers and the high-voltage power supplies used with them.

Good lighting is a must. Both mechanical and electronic assembly require detail work, and you need good lighting to see everything properly. Supplement overhead lights with a 60-watt desk lamp. You'll be crouched over the worktable for hours at a time, so a comfortable chair or stool is a must, and be sure the seat is adjusted for the height of the worktable.

24

Buying Laser Parts

Building a laser system from scratch can be difficult or easy—it's up to you. From experience, I've found that the best way to simplify the construction of a laser system is to use standard, off-the-shelf parts like things you can get at the neighborhood hardware store, auto parts store, and electronics store.

Finding parts for your lasers is routine, all things considered, and little thought goes into it. Be forewarned, however, that there are some tricks of the trade, shortcuts, and tips you should consider before you go on a buying spree and stock up for your next project. By shopping carefully and wisely, you can save both time and money in your laser-building endeavors.

PLACES TO BUY

Building laser systems on a budget means you can't take a quick trip to the local industrial laser supply. Even if there is one in your area, the components will cost you more than most people make in a year. Top-grade optical gear carries stiff pricetags, and only well-endowed universities, corporations, and research firms can afford them.

As a laser hobbyist, you must learn how to find and adapt common hardware and other everyday parts to laser components. An old, discarded spyglass, for example, might make a perfect collimating telescope. You might need to refit some of the lenses in the scope, but to help keep costs down, you might find the required lenses at a surplus store or else rob them from another piece of optical equipment. Depending on the quality of the original components as well as the level of your ingenuity, you might end up with a collimating telescope that's every bit as good as one costing several hundred dollars. If you shop wisely, your collimating telescope might only cost you $10.

There are numerous places to buy parts for your laser projects. You'll find the best deals at:

* ★ hardware stores
* ★ electronics stores
* ★ specialty stores
* ★ surplus stores
* ★ mail order

Buying at Hardware Stores

The small-town neighborhood hardware store is a great place for nails to fix the back porch or a rake to clean up the yard. But on closer inspection, it seems that while the hardware outlet carries thousands of items, it doesn't have the ones you need at that exact moment. More often than not, you'll find it necessary to make trips to a variety of hardware stores. Some stores cater to a specific segment of do-it-yourselfers and professionals. Some stores are designed expressly to please professional painters, while other are for weekend plumbers and electricians. Realize this specialization and you'll have better luck in finding the parts you need.

Warehouse hardware outlets and builder's supply stores (usually open to the public) are the best source for the wide variety of tools and parts you need for laser experimentation. Items like nuts and bolts are generally available in bulk, so you can save a considerable amount of money.

As you tour the hardware stores in your area, keep a notebook handy and jot down the lines each outlet carries. Then when you find yourself needing a specific item, just refer to your notes. On a regular basis, take an idle stroll through your regular hardware store haunts. Unless the store is very small, you'll always find something new and perhaps laughably useful in laser system design each time you visit.

Buying at Electronics Stores

As recent as ten years ago, electronic parts stores used to be in plentiful supply. Even some automotive outlets carried a full range of tubes, specialty transistors, and other electronic gadgets. Now, Radio Shack remains as the only national electronics store chain. In many towns across the country, its the only thing going.

Radio Shack continues to support electronics experimenters, but they stock only the most common components. If your needs extend beyond resistors, capacitors, and a few integrated circuits, you must turn to other sources. Check the local Yellow Pages under *Electronics-Retail* for a list of electronic parts shops near you.

Radio Shack isn't known for the best prices in electronic parts (although sometimes they have really good bargains), yet the neighborhood independent electronics specialty store might not be much better. It's not unusual for pre-packaged resistors and capacitors to sell for 50 cents to $1 each, and few stores carry cost-saving parts assortments. Unless you need a specific component that isn't available anywhere else near you, stay away from the independent electronics outlet. There are independent stores that don't charge outrageously for parts, or course, but these are the exceptions, not the rule.

All is not lost. Mail order provides a welcome relief to overpriced electronic components. You can find ads for these mail-order firms in the various electronics magazines such as Radio-Electronics and Modern Electronics. Both publications are available at newsstands. Also, several mail-order firms are listed in Appendix A.

Specialty Stores

Specialty stores are those outlets open to the general public that sell items that you won't find in a regular hardware or electronic parts store. Specialty stores don't include surplus outlets (discussed later in this chapter).

What specialty stores are of use to laser hobbyists? Consider these:

★ **Sewing machine repair shops**. Ideal for small gears, cams, levers, and other precision parts. Some shops will sell you broken machines—break the machine down and use the parts for your laser projects.

★ **Used battery depot**. A good source for cheap batteries for your portable laser designs. Most of the batteries are used, but reconditioned. The shop takes in old car and motorcycle batteries and refurbishes them. Selling price is usually between $15 and $25, or 50 to 75 percent less than a new battery.

★ **Junkyards**. Old cars are good sources for powerful dc motors used for windshield wipers, electric windows, and automatic adjustable seats. Bring tools to salvage the parts you want.

★ **Bicycle sales/service shop**. Not the department store that sells bikes, but a *real* professional bicycle shop. Items of interest: control cables, chains, and reflectors.

★ **Industrial parts outlet**. Some places sell gears, bearings, shafts, motors, and other industrial hardware on a one-piece-at-a-time basis. The penalty: high prices.

Shopping the Surplus Store

Surplus is a wonderful thing, but most people shy away from it. Why? If its surplus, as the reasoning goes, it must be worthless junk. That's simply not true. Surplus is exactly what its name implies: extra stock. Because the stock is extra, it's generally priced accordingly—to move it out the door.

Surplus stores that specialize in new and used mechanical and electronic parts (not to be confused with surplus clothing, camping, and government equipment stores) are a pleasure to find. Most areas have at least one such surplus store; some as many as three or four. Get to know each and compare prices. Bear in mind that surplus stores don't have mass-market appeal, so finding them is not always easy. Start by looking in the Yellow Pages under *Electronics* and also under *Surplus*.

Mail-Order Surplus

Some surplus is available through the mail. The number of mail-order surplus outfits that cater to the hobbyist is limited, but you can usually find everything you need if you look carefully enough and are patient. See Appendix A for more information.

While surplus is a great way to stock up on lasers, optical components, dc motors, and other odds and ends, you must shop wisely. Just because the company calls the stuff "surplus" doesn't mean that it's cheap. A *popular* item in a catalog might sell for top dollar.

Always compare prices of similar items offered by various surplus outlets before buying. Consider all the variables, such as the added cost of insurance, postage and handling, and COD fees. Also, be sure that the mail-order firm has a lenient return policy. You should always be able to return the goods if they are not satisfactory to you.

BUYING LASERS AND LASER POWER SUPPLIES

You'll obviously need a laser and a power supply in order to do any laser experiments (you can build a power supply and some types of lasers, but at first it's best to buy until you gain more experience). Lasers are available from a variety of sources including mail order, the local electronic specialty store, and lab supply outlets.

Mail order presents perhaps the least expensive route. Most deal with used and surplus components at a cost savings of 25 to 80 percent of retail list price. Here are some typical prices for components pulled from a recent catalog of laser surplus:

Item	List Price	Sale Price
2 to 3 mW helium-neon tube	$160	$75
12 Vdc He-Ne power supply	$127	$75
Constant-wave laser diode	$37	$10
Cube beam splitter	$42	$10

Prices change constantly because they are driven by the economy and supply and demand. By the time you read this, the sale prices listed above could be considerably higher or lower than the current going price. The list was provided simply to give you an idea of the kinds of savings possible from laser mail-order dealers.

As always, you must exercise care when purchasing through the mail. Avoid sending money to unestablished companies. If you have never heard of the firm before, call them and talk to them about their merchandise, service, and returns policy. Many mail-order laser surplus outfits are small, and the owner himself might answer the phone. If possible, place your first order by COD. Subsequent orders can be placed by COD or check.

By its nature, laser surplus is a variable commodity. Most laser surplus companies publish a catalog or flyer, but the stock can change at any time. It's a good idea to call first to be sure that the merchandise you want is still available. While you are on the phone, you can ask if they have received new products not listed in the catalog. You never know when they will hit the jackpot and you can get in on a great purchase.

It's hard to judge the quality of merchandise pictured or listed in a catalog. Be sure that you can return defective components or those that aren't as they are described in the catalog.

If you are new to lasers, you might feel more comfortable buying the components at a local electronics dealer. Not all dealers stock lasers, of course, and those that usually handle only surplus tubes and supplies. Prices can vary considerably, so it's a good idea to check the going rate against mail-order catalogs. If the average cost in a catalog of a 1 mW He-Ne tube is $75, for example, you'll be forewarned from buying one at $150.

The advantage of buying in person is that you can try out the merchandise before you get it home. If the stock is surplus, you might be able to root through the shelves to find the best tube you can. Recently, I found a perfectly good 8 mW He-Ne tube in the bottom of a junk barrel at a local surplus outlet that cost $10. Luck isn't always this gracious, but a find like this is impossible when dealing with mail order.

A number of mail-order laser surplus dealers are listed in Appendix A. Others advertise in the electronics magazines; refer to recent issues for names and addresses. Finding mail-order companies is fairly easy because they often go to great lengths to promote their name by advertising. A local electronics store won't advertise in the national magazines and might have only a one-line listing in the telephone directory. The Yellow Pages are your best bet, but plan to spend a few hours making some calls. Look up suitable outlets under *Electronics—Retail and Surplus*. Phone them and ask if they deal in laser surplus. The answer will usually be no, but every once in a while you'll hit the jackpot.

Electronic flea marts are becoming more and more popular, particularly among computer and amateur radio enthusiasts. If you aren't aware of any flea marts in your area, ask around at the local electronics stores or see the latest issue of Nuts & Volts and Computer Shopper magazines (see Appendix B).

One flea mart in my area is held at the last Saturday of every month in the parking lot of a large electronics firm. Buyers and sellers come free and most of the stuff is sold by electronics hackers and ham radio operators. Occasionally, one or two dealers come loaded with laser stuff. There's always a crowd around them.

Buying at a flea mart is tricky business because most of the sellers aren't in regular business. Most don't offer any type of guarantee so be sure the gear you buy is in proper working condition before you leave. If you can't test the merchandise at the flea mart, get a receipt that has the telephone number and address of the seller. Announce that you plan to get a replacement if the component you buy proves defective. Few people will argue; they'd do the same if they were on the other side of the table.

APPENDIX A

Sources

COMPONENTS, PARTS, AND SYSTEMS

A.C. INTERFACE, INC.
17911 Sampson Lane
Huntington Beach, CA 92647
Representative for Stanley high-output LEDs.

ADVANCED FIBEROPTICS CORP.
7650 East Evans Rd., Ste. B
Scottsdale, AZ 85260
(602) 483-7576
Edu-Kit fiberoptic kit, fiberoptic components, and systems.

ALL ELECTRONICS CORP.
P.O. Box 567
Van Nuys, CA 91408
(800) 826-5432
(818) 904-0524 (in CA)
Retail and surplus components, switches, relays, keyboards, transformers, computer-grade capacitors, cassette player/recorder mechanisms, etc. Mail-order and retail stores in L.A. area. Regular catalog.

ALLEGRO ELECTRONICS SYSTEMS
3E Mine Mountain
Cornwall Bridge, CT 06754
(203) 672-0123
Mail order. Laser equipment. Catalog available.

ALLIED ELECTRONICS
401 E. 8th St.
Ft. Worth, TX 76102
(800) 433-5700
Electronic parts outlet; catalog and regional sales offices. Good source for hard-to-find items.

ALLKIT ELECTRONICS
434 W. 4th St.
West Islip, NY 11795
Electronic components, grab bags, and switches—all at attractive prices.

ALLTRONICS
15460 Union Avenue
San Jose, CA 95124
(408) 371-3053
Mail-order and store in San Jose, CA. New and surplus electronics.

ALPHA PRODUCTS
7904-N Jamaica Ave.
Woodhaven, NY 11421
(800) 221-0916 (orders)
(203) 656-1806 (info)
(718) 296-5916 (NY orders)
Mail-order. Stepper motors and stepper motor controllers (ICs and complete boards), process control devices (relay cards, Touch-Tone decoders, etc.).

AMERICAN DESIGN COMPONENTS
62 Joseph St.
Moonachie, NJ 07074
(201) 939-2710
New and surplus electronics, motors, and computer gear.

AMERICAN SCIENCE CENTER, INC.
601 Linden Place
Evanston, IL 60602
(312) 475-8440
Parent company to surplus outfit Jerryco, American Science Center sells new and surplus lab and optic components. Most of the line is drawn from Edmund Scientific stock at about the same prices. A few interesting buys, such as Ronchi rulings, polarizers, and prisms.

ANALYTIC METHODS
1800 Bloomsbury Ave.
Ocean, NJ 07712
(201) 922-6663
Mail order. Integrated circuits, LEDs, surplus parts, computer cables.

ANCHOR ELECTRONICS
2040 Walsh Ave.
Santa Clara, CA 95050
(408) 727-3693
Electronic components. Catalog available.

BARRETT ELECTRONICS
5312 Buckner Dr.
Lewisville, TX 75028
Mail-order electronic surplus: components, power supplies, computer-grade capacitors.

BCD ELECTRO
P.O. Box 830119
Richardson, TX 75083-0119
Electronic components of all types. Some surplus, including laser systems. Very good prices. Catalog available.

BIGELOW ELECTRONICS
P.O. Box 125
Bluffton, OH 45817-0125
New and surplus electronics, hardware, and HAM gear. Catalog available.

BISHOP GRAPHICS
5388 Sterling Center Dr.
P.O. Box 5007EZ
Westlake Village, CA 91359
(818) 991-2600
EZ Circuit PCB-making supplies.

C & H SALES
2176 E. Colorado Blvd.
Pasadena, CA 91107
(800) 325-9465
Electronic and mechanical surplus including some optics like prisms, mirrors, and lenses. Reasonable prices for most items; regular catalog. Their walk-in store in Pasadena has more items than those listed in the catalog, so if you're in the area, be sure to drop in.

CIRCUIT SPECIALISTS
Box 3047
Scottsdale, AZ 85257
(602) 966-0764
New electronic goodies including hard-to-find Sprague motor control chips (stepper, half-bridge, full-bridge). Also full complement of standard components at good prices.

COMPREHENSIVE GUIDES
7507 Oakdale Ave.
Canoga Park, CA 91306
Laser plans, kits, and supplies.

COMPUTER PARTS MART
3200 Park Blvd.
Palo Alto, CA 94306
(415) 493-5930
Mail-order surplus. Good source for stepper motors, lasers, power supplies, and incremental shaft encoders (pulled from equipment). Regular catalog.

COMPUTER SURPLUS STORE
715 Sycamore Dr.
Milpitas, CA 95035
(408) 434-0168
Surplus electronics. Mostly computers, printers, and power supplies, but also carries components and sometimes even lasers. Walk-in store in Northern California and limited mail order. If you don't see what you want in their flyer, contact them and tell them your needs.

DATAK CORP.
3117 Paterson Plank Rd.
North Bergen, NJ 07047
(201) 863-7667
Supplies for making your own printed-circuit boards including the popular direct-etch dry transfer method.

DIGI-KEY CORP.
701 Brooks Ave. South
P.O. Box 677
Thief River Falls, MN 56701-0677
(800) 344-4539
Mail order. Discount components—everything from crystals to integrated circuits (including 74C926 counter chip) to resistors and capacitors in bulk. Catalog available.

DOKAY COMPUTER PRODUCTS
2100 De la Cruz Blvd.
Santa Clara, CA 95050
(408) 988-0697
(800) 538-8800; (800) 848-8008 (in CA)
Electronic parts (most popular linear, TTL, and CMOS devices) and computer gear (including computer chips). Catalog available.

DOLAN-JENNER INDUSTRIES, INC.
P.O. Box 1020
Woburn, MA 01801
Fiberoptic components.

EDMUND SCIENTIFIC CO.
101 E. Gloucester Pike
Barrington, NJ 08007-1380
(609) 573-6250
Mail order. New and surplus motors, gadgets, and other goodies for laser building. Includes laser tubes, power supplies, complete systems, holography and optics kits, lenses, and much more. Regular catalog (ask for both the Hobby and Industrial versions).

ELECTROVALUE INTERNATIONAL
Box 376
Morris Plains, NJ 07950
(201) 267-1117
Electronics components.

ERAC CO.
8280 Clairemont Mesa Blvd., Suite 117
San Diego, CA 92111
(619) 569-1864
Mail-order and retail store. PC-compatible boards and subsystems, surplus computer boards, computer power supplies and components.

FAIR RADIO SALES
1016 E. Eureka St.
P.O. Box 1105
Lima, OH 45802
(419) 223-9176/(419) 227-6573
An old and established retailer of surplus goods of all types, particularly military communications. A boon to the amateur radio enthusiast and moderately useful to the laser experimenter. Catalog available.

FOBTRON COMPONENTS
21738 S. Avalon Blvd.
Suite #155
Carson, CA 90745
Laser components including tubes and power supplies, optics, and mirrors. Flyer available.

FORDHAM RADIO
260 Motor Parkway
Hauppauge, NY 11788
(800) 645-9518
(516) 435-8080 (in NY)
Electronic test equipment, tools, power supplies. Catalog available.

G.B. MICRO
P.O. Box 280298
Dallas, TX 75228
(214) 271-5546
Mail order. Components, 300 kHz crystal, UARTs. Most popular TTL, CMOS, and linear ICs, construction parts.

GENERAL SCIENCE & ENGINEERING
P.O. Box 447
Rochester, NY 14603
(716) 338-7001
Laser components, power supplies, power supply kits, optics, high-output Stanley LED, surplus goodies of all types.

GIANT ELECTRONICS INC.
19 Freeman St.
Newark, NJ 07105
(800) 645-9060
(201) 344-5700
New and surplus electronics, motors, computer peripherals, and more.

GIL ELECTRONICS
P.O. Box 1628
911 Hidden Valley
Soquel, CA 95073
Electronic parts, books, new and surplus computer components.

H&R CORP.
401 E. Erie Ave.
Philadelphia, PA 19134
(215) 426-1708
Surplus mechanical components. Excellent source for heavy-duty dc gear motors. Regular catalog.

HALTED SPECIALTIES CO.
3060 Copper Rd.
Santa Clara, CA 95051
(408) 732-1573
Mail-order and retail stores. New and surplus components, PC-compatible boards and subsystems, ceramic resonators (surplus item), power supplies, most all popular ICs, transistors, etc.

HAL-TRONIX, INC.
12671 Dix-Toledo Highway
P.O. Box 1101
Southgate, MI 48195
(313) 281-7773
Mail order. Surplus computers, computer components, PC-compatible boards and subsystems.

HEATHKIT
P.O. Box 1288
Benton Harbor, MI 49022
(800) 253-0570
Perhaps the best source of professionally produced electronic kits. Heathkit offers a few laser projects including a laser trainer geared to accept a modulated input. The Fischertechnik engineering kits are ideal for use as building blocks in your own laser designs. Also available are testing gear (assembled and kit form) and computers.

HOSFELT ELECTRONICS, INC.
2700 Sunset Blvd.
Steubenville, OH 43952
(800) 524-6464
New and surplus electronics at attractive prices. Catalog available.

INFORMATION UNLIMITED
Box 716
Amherst, NH 03031
(603) 673-4730
Plans and kits for laser and other high-tech gadgets. Good source for reasonably priced new laser tubes. Among the plans are details for building a wide range of Class IV lasers, including CO_2, argon, and tunable dye systems.

JAMECO ELECTRONICS
1355 Shoreway Rd.
Belmont, CA 94002
(415) 592-8097
Mail order. Components, PC-compatible boards and subsystems. Regular catalog.

JDR MICRODEVICES
1224 S. Bascom Ave.
San Jose, CA 95128
(408) 995-5430
Large selection of new components, wire-wrap supplies, PC-compatible boards and subsystems. Mail-order and retail stores in San Jose area.

JERRYCO INC.
607 Linden Place
Evanston, IL 60202
(312) 475-8440
Regular catalog lists hundreds of surplus mechanical and electronic gadgets for lasers. Good source for motors, rechargeable batteries, switches, solenoids, lots more. Don't build a laser system until you get the Jerryco catalog.

J. I. MORRIS CO.
394 Elm St.
Southbridge, MA 01550
(617) 764-4394
Small components and hardware; miniature screws, taps, and nuts/bolts.

JOHN J. MESHNA, JR. CO.
P.O. Box 62
E. Lynn, MA 01904
(617) 595-2272
New and surplus merchandise. Catalog available.

MARTIN P. JONES & ASSOC.
P.O. Box 12685
Lake Park, FL 33403-0685
(407) 848-8236

All sorts of goodies, including electronic components, (transistors, capacitors, resistors, ICs, etc.), optical stuff, and more. Catalog available.

MCM ELECTRONICS
858 E. Congress Park Dr.
Centerville, OH 45459-4072
(513) 434-0031
Test equipment, tools, and supplies. Catalog available.

MEADOWLAKE
25 Blanchard Dr.
Northport, NY 11768
TEC-200 direct-transfer film for making quick integrated circuits from artwork in magazines and this book. Try this stuff out! All you need is a plain paper copier (or access to one).

MEREDITH INSTRUMENTS
P.O. Box 1724
Glendale, AZ 85311
(602) 934-9387
Laser surplus including tubes, power supply, optics, components, more. Stock comes and goes, so call first to make sure they have what you want. Flyer available; very good prices.

MICRO MART, INC.
508 Central Ave.
Westfield, NJ 07090
(201) 654-6008
Electronic components (ICs, transistors, etc.). Their grab bags are better than average, and prices are low.

MJ NEAL CO.
6672 Mallard Ct.
Orient, OH 43146
(614) 877-3719
Surplus laser gear, including tubes, power supplies, and optical components. Catalog available.

MOUSER ELECTRONICS/TEXAS DISTRIBUTIN CENTER
2401 Hwy 287 North
North Mansfield, TX 76063
(817) 483-4422

MOUSER ELECTRONICS/CALIFORNIA DISTRIBUTION CENTER
11433 Woodside Ave.
Santee, CA 92071
(619) 449-2222
Mail order. Discount electronic components. Catalog available.

OCTE ELECTRONICS
Box 276
Alburg, VT 05440
(514) 739-9328
New and surplus electronic stuff at reasonable prices. OCTE carries a lot of complete components, such as cable converters and power supplies, but individual parts, like batteries and connectors, are also available.

PRECISION ELECTRONICS CORP.
605 Chestnut Street
Union, NJ 07083
(800) 255-8868
(201) 686-4646 (in NJ)
Electronic components such as linear ICs, transistors, and hard-to-find Sanyo and Zenith ICs (mostly for TV).

RADIO SHACK
One Tandy Center
Fort Worth, TX 76102
Nation's largest electronics retailer. Many popular components, though short on ICs. Good source for general electronic needs including some fiberoptic components. Catalog available through store.

R & D ELECTRONICS
1202H Pine Island Rd.
Cape Coral, FL 33909
(813) 772-1441
Mail order. New and surplus electronics (components, switches, ICs).

R & D ELECTRONIC SUPPLY
100 E. Orangethorpe Ave.
Anaheim, CA 92801
(714) 773-0240
Mail order. Power supplies, computer equipment, test equipment.

SHARON INDUSTRIES
1919 Hartog Road
San Jose, CA 95131
(408) 436-0455
Mail-order and retail store. New and surplus electronic components, ICs, computers, PC-compatible boards and subsystems.

SILICON VALLEY SURPLUS
4401 Oakport
Oakland, CA 94601
(415) 261-4506

Surplus electronic, computer, and mechanical goodies. Mail-order and retail store (Oakland, CA).

SMALL PARTS
6901 NE Third Ave.
Miami, FL 33238
(305) 751-0856
A potpourri of small parts, ideally suited for miniature mechanisms. Not cheap but good quality.

SPECTRA LASER SYSTEMS
P.O. Box 6928
Huntington Beach, CA 92615
Laser light-show equipment, components (including laser tubes), and consultation.

STOCK DRIVE PRODUCTS
55 S. Denton Ave.
New Hyde Park
New York, NY 11040
Gears, sprockets, chains, and more. Available through local Stock Drive distributor. Catalog and engineering guide available.

SYNERGETICS
Box 809
Thatcher, AZ 85552
(602) 428-4073
Columnist Don Lancaster's company, with "hacker's help line." Lancaster offers free technical advice (within limits), a collection of his old and new books (his TTL and CMOS cookbooks are classics), and several "info packs" of useful programming, graphics, and technical stuff.

UNICORN ELECTRONICS
10010 Canoga Ave., Unit B-8
Chatsworth, CA 91311
(800) 824-3432
(818) 341-8833
All popular electronic parts including resistors, capacitors, ICs, and components. Some surplus. All at good prices.

UNITED PRODUCTS, INC.
1123 Valley
Seattle, WA 98109
(206) 682-5025
Mail order. Stepper motors, computer components, test equipment.

WINDSOR DISTRIBUTORS
19 Freeman St.
Newark, NJ 07105
(800) 645-9060
Mail order. Surplus electronics.

SEMICONDUCTOR MANUFACTURERS

Most semiconductor manufacturers maintain a network of regional sales and distribution offices. If you would like more information on a particular product or would like to place an order, contact the manufacturer at the address below and ask for a list of dealers, distributors, and representatives in your area. Most firms will work with individuals, but sales might be subject to minimum orders and/or service charges.

ADVANCED MICRO DEVICES
901 Thompson Place
Sunnyvale, CA 94088
(408) 732-2400

ANALOG DEVICES
One Technology Way
Norwood, MA 02062
(617) 329-4700

BURR-BROWN
P.O. Box 11700
Tucson, AZ 85734
(602) 746-1111

CHERRY SEMICONDUCTOR CORP.
2000 South Country Trail
East Greenwich, RI 02818-0031
(401) 885-3600

CYBERNETIC MICRO SYSTEMS
P.O. Box 3000
San Cregorio, CA 94074
(415) 726-3000

DATA GENERAL CORP.
4400 Computer Dr.
Westborough, MA 01581
(617) 366-1970

EG&G RETICON CORP.
345 Potrero Ave.
Sunnyvale, CA 94086
(408) 738-4266

EXAR INTEGRATED SYSTEMS, INC.
750 Palomar Ave.
Sunnyvale, CA 94088-3575
(408) 732-7970

FAIRCHILD
10400 Ridgeview Ct.
Box 1500
Cupertino, CA 95014
(408) 864-6250

FUJITSU MICROELECTRONICS, INC.
3320 Scott Blvd.
Santa Clara, CA 95054-3197
(408) 727-1700

HARRIS SEMICONDUCTOR
P.O. Box 883
Melbourne, FL 32901
(305) 724-7000

HITACHI AMERICA LTD.
2210 O'Toole Ave.
San Jose, CA 95131
(408) 435-8300

HOBBY SHACK
18480 Bandilier Circle
Fountain Valley, CA 92708

INTEL
3065 Bowers Ave.
Santa Clara, CA 95051
(408) 987-8080

INTERSIL
10600 Ridgeview Ct.
Cupertino, CA 95014
(408) 996-5000

ITT SEMICONDUCTORS
7 Lake St.
Lawrence, MA 01841
(617) 688-1881

MAXIM INTEGRATED PRODUCTS
510 N. Pastoria Ave.
Sunnyvale, CA 94086
(408) 737-7600

MICRO SWITCH
11 West Spring Street
Freeport, IL 61032
(815) 235-6600

MITEL SEMICONDUCTOR
P.O. Box 13320,
Kanata, Ontario, K2K 1X5
Canada

MITSUBISHI ELECTRONICS AMERICA
1050 E. Arques Ave.
Sunnyvale, CA 94086
(408) 730-5900

MONOLITHIC MEMORIES
2151 Mission College Blvd.
Santa Clara, CA 95054
(408) 970-9700

MOSTEK
1310 Electronics Ave.
Carrollton, TX 75006
(214) 466-6000

MOTOROLA
5005 E. McDowell Rd.
Phoenix, AZ 85008
(602) 244-7100

NATIONAL SEMICONDUCTOR
2900 Semiconductor Dr.
Santa Clara, CA 95051
(408) 721-5000

NCR
8181 Byers Rd.
Miamisburg, OH 45342
(513) 866-7217

NEC ELECTRONICS, INC.
401 Ellis St.
Mountain View, CA 94039-7241
(415) 960-6000

OKI SEMICONDUCTOR
650 E. Mary Ave.
Sunnyvale, CA 94086
(408) 720-1900

PENWALT PIEZO
Box C
Prussia, PA 19406
(215) 337-6710

PLESSEY SOLID STATE
9 Parker St.
Irvine, CA 92718
(714) 472-0303

PRECISION MONOLITHICS, INC.
1500 Space Park Dr.
Santa Clara, CA 95052-8020
(408) 727-9222

RAYTHEON SEMICONDUCTOR
350 Ellis St.
Mountain View, CA 94039-7016
(415) 968-9211

RETICON
245 Potrero Ave.
Sunnyvale, CA 94086
(408) 738-4266

ROCKWELL INTL.
4311 Jamboree Rd.
P.O. Box C
Newport Beach, 92658-8902
(714) 833-4700

SGS SEMICONDUCTOR
1000 E. Bell Rd.
Phoenix, AZ 85022
(602) 867-6100

SHARP ELECTRONICS CORP.
10 Sharp Plaza
Paramus, NJ 07652

SIGNETICS
811 E. Arques Ave.
Sunnyvale, CA 94088-3409
(408) 991-2000

SILICONIX
2201 Laurelwood Rd.
Santa Clara, CA 95054
(408) 988-8000

SPRAGUE ELECTRIC
115 NE Cutoff
Worcester, MA 01613-2036
(617) 853-5000

SPRAGUE SOLID STATE
3900 Welsh Rd.
Willow Grove, PA 19090
(215) 657-8400

TEXAS INSTRUMENTS
Literature Response Center
P.O. Box 809066
Dallas, TX 75228
(214) 232-3200

3M ELECTRONIC PRODUCTS DIVISION
P.O. Box 2963
Austin, TX 78769
(512) 834-6708

TRW SEMICONDUCTORS
P.O. Box 2472
La Jolla, CA 92038
(619) 457-1000

TOSHIBA AMERICA INC.
2692 Dow Ave.
Tustin, CA 92680
(714) 832-0102

XICOR
851 Buckeye Ct.
Milpitas, CA 95035
(408) 432-8888

ZILOG, INC.
210 Hacienda Ave.
Campbell, CA 95008-6609
(408) 370-8000

LASER AND LASER COMPONENTS MANUFACTURERS AND RETAILERS

ADVANCED CONTROL SYSTEMS CORP.
205 Oak St.
Pembrooke, MA 02359
(617) 826-4477

ADVANCED KINETICS
1231 Victoria St.
Costa Mesa, CA 92627
(714) 646-7165

AG ELECTRO-OPTICS LTD.
Tarporley
Cheshire CW6 0HX
United Kingdom
(08293) 3305/3678

COHERENT INC.
Laser Products Division
3210 Porter Dr.
P.O. Box 10321
Palo Alto, CA 94303
(415) 493-2111

CONTROL TECHNICS CORP.
22600-C Lambert St.
Unit 909
El Toro, CA 92630
(714) 770-9911

COOPER LASERSONICS
Laser Products Division
48503 Millmont Dr.
Fremont, CA 94538
(415) 770-0800

CVI LASER CORP.
P.O. Box 11308
200 Dorado Pl., S.E.
Albuquerque, NM 87192
(505) 296-9541

EASTMAN KODAK COMPANY
Photographic Products Group
Rochester, NY 14650

FAIRLIGHT B.V.
P.O. Box 81037
NL-3009 GA Rotterdam
The Netherlands
(010) 4206444

GLENDALE OPTICAL CO.
130 Crossways Park Dr.
Woodbury, NY 11797

HAMMAMATSU CORP.
360 Foothill Rd.
P.O. Box 6910
Bridgewater, NJ 08807
(201) 231-0960

HARDIN OPTICAL CO.
P.O. Box 219
Bandon, OR 97411
(503) 347-3307

HUGHES AIRCRAFT CO.
P.O. Box 45066
7200 Hughes Terrace
Los Angeles, CA 90045-0066
(213) 568-6838

ISOTECH INC.
3858 Benner Rd.
Miamisburg, OH 45342
(513) 859-1808

LASER APPLICATIONS INC.
Division of Lasermetrics, Inc.
3500 Aloma Ave., Ste. D-9
Winter Park, FL 32792
(305) 678-8995

LASER DEVICES INC.
#5 Hangar Way
Watsonville, CA 95076
(408) 722-8300

LASER DRIVE INC.
5465 William Flynn Hwy.
Gibsonia, PA 15044
(412) 443-7688

LASER LINES LTD.
Beaumont Close
Banbury, Oxon, OX16 7TQ
United Kingdom
(0295) 67755

LASERMETRICS INC.
Electro-Optics Division
196 Coolidge Ave.
Englewood, NJ 07631
(201) 894-0550

LASER POWER OPTICS
12777 High Bluff Dr.
San Diego, CA 92130-2016
(619) 755-0700

LASER SCIENCE INC.
80 Prospect St.
Cambridge, CA 02139
(617) 868-4350

MELLES GRIOT/OPTICS
1770 Kettering St.
Irvine, CA 92714
(714) 261-5600

MELLES GRIOT/GAS LASERS
2251 Rutherford Rd.
Carlsbad, CA 92008
(619) 438-2131

METROLOGIC INSTRUMENTS INC.
Laser Products Division
143 Harding Ave.
Bellmawr, NJ 08031
(609) 933-0100

NEC ELECTRONICS
401 Ellis St.
Mountain View, CA 94039
(415) 960-6000

NEWPORT CORP.
P.O. Box 8020
18235 Mt. Baldy Circle
Fountain Valley, CA 92728-9811
(714) 963-9811

J.A. NOLL CO.
Box 312
Monroeville, PA 15146
(412) 856-7566

NON-LINEAR DEVICES
126 Andrew Ave.
Oakland, NJ 07436
(201) 337-0666

OPTIKON CORP. LTD.
410 Conestogo Rd.
Waterloo, Ontario Canada N2L 4E2
(519) 885-2551

POLYTEK OPTRONICS INC.
3001 Redhill Ave.
Bldg. R, Suite 102
Costa Mesa, CA 92626
(714) 850-1831

PRECISION OPTICAL
869 W. 17th St.
Costa Mesa, CA 92627
(714) 631-6800

QEI
5A2 Damonmill Sq.
Concord, MA 01742
(617) 369-8081

SPECTRA DIODE LABS
3333 N. First St.
San Jose, CA 95134-1995
(408) 432-0203

SPECTRA-PHYSICS INC.
Laser Analytics Division
25 Wiggins Ave.
Bedford, MA 01730
(617) 275-2650

SPEIRS ROBERTSON & CO. LTD.
Laser Division
Moliver House, Oakley Rd.
Bromham, Bedford
United Kingdom
(02302) 3410

OTHER IMPORTANT ADDRESSES

AMERICAN NATIONAL STANDARDS INSTITUTE (ASNI)
1430 Broadway
New York, NY 10018
Sets and maintains standards; useful data on laser practices and specifications.

LASER INSTITUTE OF AMERICA
5151 Monroe St.
Toledo, OH 43623
(419) 882-8706
Provides publications of interest to users, manufacturers, and sellers of lasers. Several good publications included Laser Safety Guide, Laser Safety Reference Book, and Fundamentals of Lasers. Ask for a current price list and availability of titles.

CENTER FOR DEVICES AND RADIOLOGICAL HEALTH
(CDRH)
 (formerly Bureau of Radiological Health)
Optical Radiation Products Section
HF2-312
8757 Georgia Ave.
Silver Springs, MD 20910
(301) 427-8228
A department of the Food and Drug Administration (FDA) that regulates the commercial manufacture and use of lasers. If you manufacture, sell, or demonstrate laser systems, you must comply to minimum standards.

U.S. DEPARTMENT OF COMMERCE
Patent and Trademark Office
Washington, DC 20231
Provides general information on patents. For information on specific patents, it's better to visit a library that offers copies of old patents and patent applications or consult a patent attorney.

APPENDIX B

Further Reading

Here is a selected list of magazines and books that can enrich your understanding and enjoyment of all facets of lasers and laser applications.

MAGAZINES

Computer Shopper
5211 S. Washington Ave.
P.O. Box F
Titusville, FL 32781

Monthly magazine (some call it a bible) for computer enthusiasts. Probably containing more ads than articles, Computer Shopper carries updated listings of swap meets and bulletin boards as well as classified advertising from small surplus dealers.

Electronics Today
1300 Don Mills Rd.
Toronto, Ontario M3B 3M8
Canada

General-interest electronics magazine with emphasis on hobby how-to articles.

Hands-on Electronics
500 Bi-County Blvd.
Farmingdale, NY 11735

Monthly magazine put out by the editors of Radio-Electronics. The articles and construction projects are aimed at beginning electronics enthusiasts. Few articles are specifically on lasers, but some of the circuits can be adapted for laser projects.

Laser Focus
1001 Watertown St.
Newton, MA 02165
A monthly trade magazine for the laser industry. Available by paid or audited (free to qualified readers) subscription. Check a good public library for back issues.

Lightwave
The Journal of Fiber Optics
235 Bear Hill Rd.
Waltham, MA 02154
A monthly trade journal on fiberoptics and its applications.

Modern Electronics
76 North Broadway
Hicksville, NY 11801
Monthly magazine for electronics hobbyists. Don't miss the regular columns by hobby electronic guru Forrest Mims III. Many of the editors used to be involved with Popular Electronics before that magazine changed over to computer-only coverage (and then ceased publication). Check back issues of Modern Electronics for Don Lancaster's fascinating columns (he moved his Hardware Hacker column to Radio-Electronics in late 1987).

Nuts & Volts
P.O. Box 1111
Placeutia, CA 92670
Monthly "magazine" that contains only advertising—both display ads and classifieds. Often carries ads for new and used laser equipment and lists upcoming swap meets (both computer and electronic). Subscription price is fairly low.

Physics Today
335 East 45 St.
New York, NY 10017
Monthly magazine with technical slant; no how-to's but plenty of theory on all subjects of a physical nature. The annual buyer's guide is useful for names and addresses of companies specializing in lasers, optics, and related products.

QST
225 Main St.
Newington, CT 06111
Monthly magazine aimed at the amateur radio enthusiast, but often carries articles of interest to the laser experimenter. Look for stories on electromagnetic spectrum, fiberoptics, project construction, remote control, etc.

Spectra
P.O. Box 1146
Pittsfield, MA 01202
A monthly trade journal that focuses on lasers and other related topics. Available by paid or audited (free to qualified readers) subscription. Check a good public library for back issues.

Radio-Electronics
500 Bi-County Blvd.
Farmingdale, NY 11735
Monthly magazine for electronic hobbyists. Occasional article on lasers. Be sure to read the column by Don Lancaster of Synergetics. Although he seldom addresses lasers in specific, his tips and hands-on help are invaluable for general electronics experimentation. He also provides sources for hard-to-find parts and information.

BOOKS

How to Read Electronic Circuit Diagrams—2nd Edition; Brown, Lawrence, and Whitson
    TAB BOOKS, Catalog #2880
      How to read and interpret schematic diagrams.

Build Your Own Laser, Phaser, Ion Ray Gun, & Other Working Space-Age Projects; Robert E. Iannini
    TAB BOOKS, Catalog #1604
      A guide to making high-tech gadgets, with some insight and designs for laser-based projects. Iannini, who runs a mail-order firm, presents six laser projects plus a few others (such as infrared light detection) that can be used with laser systems. A companion book, Build Your Own Working Fiberoptic and Laser Space-Age Projects *(Catalog #2724) offers more laser-based designs.*

Circuit Scrapbook; Forrest Mims III
    McGraw-Hill
      More of Mims' Popular Electronics columns—these from 1979 to 1981. Several good circuits and designs that can be adapted for laser work. Also check out the sequel, Circuit Scrapbook II *(Howard W. Sams Co.). This volume includes several chapters on experimenting with solid state laser diodes. Be sure to read the sections on laser diode handling precautions.*

CMOS Cookbook; Don Lancaster
    Howard W. Sams Co.
      A classic in its own time, the CMOS Cookbook *presents useful design theory and practical circuits for many popular CMOS chips. The companion book,* TTL Cookbook, *is equally as helpful.*

Computer Peripherals That You Can Build; Gordon W. Wolfe
    TAB BOOKS, Catalog #2749
      Step-by-step instructions for building a variety of functional computer peripherals.

Elementary Plane Surveying; Davis & Kelly
    McGraw-Hill
      Overview of plane surveying, including tools of the trade, taking measurements, and doing the calculations. No specific information on using laser-based surveying equipment, but the information presented can be used as a surveying primer.

Engineer's Mini-Notebook; Forrest Mims III
    Radio Shack book series
      The Engineer's Mini-Notebooks *is a series of small books written by Forrest Mims that cover a wide variety of hobby electronics: using the NE555 timer to optoelectronics circuits to op-amp circuits, and more. The entire set is a must-have, and besides, they're cheap.*

44 Power Supplies for Your Electronic Projects; Traister and Mayo
    TAB BOOKS, Catalog #2922
      Forty-four complete power supplies designed for general electronics projects.

Fundamentals of Optics; Jenkins and White
    McGraw-Hill
      An in-depth and scholarly look at optics. Broken down into logical subjects of geometrical, wave, and quantum optics.

Guide to Practical Holography; Outwater and Hamersueld
    Pentangle Press
      A good, easy-to-understand manual on hologram-making.

Hologram Book, The; Joseph E. Kasper and Steven A. Feller
    Prentice-Hall
      Introduction to lasers and laser light and detailed instructions for making holograms.

Holography Handbook; Unterseher, Hansen, and Schlesinger
Ross Books
Perhaps the best book on amateur holography. It even comes with a white-light reflective rainbow hologram. Although the artwork is too "folksy" for my taste, the designs are technically sound. If you are interested in holography, you need this book.

How to Troubleshoot & Repair Electronic Circuits; Robert L. Goodman
TAB BOOKS, Catalog #1218
General troubleshooters guide, both analog and digital.

IBM PC Connection; James W. Coffron
Sybex Books
A good beginner's guide on connecting the IBM PC (or compatible) to the outside world. Information on circuit-building, programming, and troubleshooting.

Introduction to Lasers and Masers; A. E. Siegman
McGraw-Hill
Although a little old (copyright 1971), this book provides good details of the inner works of all major types of lasers, including crystal, glass, gas, and semiconductor.
Lasers: The Incredible Light Machines; Forrest M. Mims III
Introduction to lasers; includes a short history.

Lasers: The Light Fantastic, Second Edition; Hallmark and Horn
TAB BOOKS, Catalog #2905
A good introduction to the mechanics and applications of lasers. Interesting chapters on laser gyroscopes, quantum mechanics, and lasers in space.

Laser Experimenter's Handbook; Delton T. Horn
TAB BOOKS, Catalog #3115
The hows and whys of lasers. Includes six projects using laser diodes.

Laser and Light; W. H. Freeman
W. H. Freeman
Material drawn from back issues of Scientific American on laser principles.

Magic of Holography; Philip Heckman
Atheneum
A concise and easy-to-understand explanation of holography and its applications. Although the book lacks specific information on how to make your own holograms, there are plenty of setup illustrations you can use as blueprints.

Masers and Lasers; H. Arthur Klein
J.B. Lippincott Company
Although dated (copyright 1963), this book provides some interesting aspects about lasers not found in other books and gives an easy-to-understand overview of lasers, electromagnetic spectrum, and early pioneering work in light physics.

Optical Holography; Robert L. Collier
Academic Press
A technical and engaging text on optical (as opposed to acoustic) holography. A little old (the original copyright is 1971), but most of the information is still valid.

Optics; N. V. Klein
John Wiley & Sons
A highly technical text about optics with lots of formulas and math on optics design.

Practical Interfacing Projects with the Commodore Computers; Robert H. Luetzow
TAB BOOKS, Catalog #1983
How to use a Commodore 64 computer to control appliances, robotic devices, and more.

Principles & Practice of Laser Technology; Hrand M. Mucheryan
TAB BOOKS, Catalog #1529
An introduction to lasers and laser applications. Heavy on the industrial side of laser use.

Programmer's Problem Solver, for the IBM PC, XT, & AT; Robert Jourdain
Brady
A technical book on the inner-working of the IBM PC, with special emphasis on programming in BASIC, assembly, and machine code. Extensive section on parallel ports.

Principles of Holography; Howard M. Smith
John Wiley & Sons
A technical overview of holography, covering its history, application, and setup, written by a research associate at Kodak. Good source for application formulas and information on holographic emulsions.

Robot Builder's Bonanza; Gordon McComb
TAB BOOKS, Catalog #2800
My earlier book on a compendium of projects useful to the robot experimenter. Some of the information, such as dc motor operation and remote control, can be suitably adapted to laser work.

Silliconnection: Coming of Age in the Electronic Era; Forrest M. Mims III
McGraw-Hill
A history and personal autobiography of the electronics revolution. Mims, a writer and inventor, contributed to the development of the first personal computer and was employed at the Air Force Weapons Laboratory in New Mexico where he worked with early solid-state diodes. This book includes the interesting story of how the National Enquirer *offered to pay Mims to build a lightbeam listening device using a laser and phototransistor receiver to tap into the private conversations of the late Howard Hughes.*

Understanding Digital Electronics; R. H. Warring
TAB BOOKS, Catalog #1593
Introduction to the principles of digital theory.

Glossary

aberration—A defect in an optical component that can degrade the purity of the light passing through it.

absolute zero—The lowest "possible" temperature, equal to minus 273.16 degrees C (-459.69 degrees F).

ac—Alternating current. Current that fluctuates to positive and negative values about a zero point. The current available at wall outlets.

access time—The time required to get a piece of information from a memory chip or disk drive.

address—A number that indicates the location of a piece of information in computer memory.

amplitude—The relative strength (usually voltage) of an analog signal. Amplitude can be expressed as either a negative or positive number referenced to a particular standard.

analog—A continuous electrical signal representing a condition (such as temperature or the position of game control paddles). Unlike a digital signal that is discrete and has only two levels, an analog signal can have an infinite number of levels.

analog-to-digital converter (ADC)—An electrical circuit (usually one integrated circuit) that transforms analog signals to their digital equivalents. A digital-to-analog converter performs the reverse function.

angstrom—A unit of measurement used to describe wavelength or size; equals 100 billionths of a meter (10^{-10} meter).

anode—The positive terminal of a laser, light-emitting diode, laser diode, or other electronic component. See also *cathode*.

antihalation backing—A semi-opaque material or coating applied to the back side of photographic film that prevents the spreading (halo) of light during exposure.

ASCII—Acronym for American Standard Code for Information Interchange. Used by all personal computers.

assembler—A program that converts the computer's memory into binary code for execution. Acts as a compiler for assembly language.

assembly language—Machine language codes translated into mnemonic codes that are easier for programmers to remember.

attenuation—The restriction or loss of electrical or optical power through a medium or circuit. Optical attenuation occurs when light passes through a length of optical fiber.

axial ray—A ray of light that travels along the optical axis.

bandwidth—A continuous range of frequencies or wavelengths, defined by an upper and lower limit.

BASIC—Acronym for Beginner's All-purpose Symbolic Instruction Code. Programming language for computers developed as a simplified form of FORTRAN. BASIC is not standard and can vary from computer to computer. The BASIC dialect for IBM PC and compatible computers is Microsoft's GW-BASIC; the dialect for the Commodore 64 is a specialized Commodore BASIC.

baud—A measure of the rate at which digital data is transmitted, in bits per second.

band-pass filter—A filter that blocks both high and low frequencies but passes a middle band. Can pertain to both electrical signals or light. See also *low-pass filter* and *high-pass filter*.

beam—A collection of rays (light waves) moving in one direction.

beam splitter—An optical component that divides a beam two or more different ways. Beam splitters are rated by the ratio of light they reflect and transmit. For example a 50:50 beam splitter splits a beam equally in two directions (usually by reflection and transmission).

beamwidth—The linear width of the beam, usually specified as the region over which the beam intensity falls within predetermined limits.

binary—A numbering system with just two digits: 1 and 0. Computers group these 1s and 0s together to create more complex forms of data.

birefringence—The property of splitting a beam of light in two directions due to double refraction.

bit—Acronym for *bi*nary dig*it*. Represents either of two binary states—1 or 0. Bits are usually grouped in sets of eight (called a *byte*) for easier manipulation.

blackbody—A substance or medium that absorbs light and thermal energy completely. The blackbody is a technical impossibility but is often used as an ideal model for light and temperature studies.

bleeder resistor—A resistor placed across the output of a power supply to drain the current from the filtering capacitors when power is removed.

boot—A program on disk, tape, or in a permanent portion of the computer's memory (ROM), used to start the computer and get it ready for applications or programming software.

Brewster's Angle—The angle at which a transparent material, such as glass or quartz, is placed with respect to the normal of incident light so that both refracted and reflected rays are perpendicular. Brewster's Angle windows placed in gas lasers cause the light output to be polarized in one plane.

bus—A set of electrical contacts that carry a variety of computer or analog signals.

byte—A group of bits, usually eight, universally used to represent a character.

candle—A unit of luminous intensity. Specifically, one candle is equal to $\frac{1}{60}$th of one square centimeter of projected area of a blackbody radiator operating at the temperate of solidification of platinum.

carrier—A radio frequency signal superimposed over another signal.

carrier frequency—The frequency of the carrier signal.

cathode—The negative terminal of a laser, light-emitting diode, laser diode, or other electronic component.

CCD—Short for *c*harge-*c*oupled *d*evice, a type of integrated circuit, that is sensitive to light and used as an imaging device.

chip—An integrated circuit, such as that used for computer memory or the microprocessor.

chopper—A device or electronic circuit that provides a pulsating or on/off characteristic to a beam of light or electric current. A mechanical chopper is an incremental shaft encoder, where the light from an LED or laser to a photodiode is intermittently blocked by slits in a wheel.

chromatic aberration—A type of lens distortion where colors are focused at different points due to refraction.

clad—A refractive coating over the interior core of an optical fiber.

clock—An electronic metronome used for the purpose of timing signals in a circuit. The clock times out signals so that they occur at a steady, predictable rate and maintain the proper sequence of events.

coherence—The property of identical phase and time relationships.

coherence length—The greatest distance that the beam from a laser will remain temporally coherent. Coherency is often related as a percentage of deviation, not an absolute; therefore, the coherence length is subject to the acceptable range of coherency for a given application.

coherent radiation—Electromagnetic radiation where the waves are in phase in both time and space (temporal coherence and spatial coherence); as opposed to non-coherent radiation whose waves are out of phase in space and/or time.

collimate—To make parallel.

collimator—An optical component that forces a diverging or converging light beam, as from a laser, to travel in parallel lines. The collimator lens (sometimes a mirror) is placed at its focal distance from the light source.

common—The ground point of a circuit, or a common path for an electrical signal.

compiler—A program that converts high-level language (like BASIC) into the binary code required by the computer. Compiler instructions are known as "object code." The original high-level language program is known as the "source code."

concave lens—A type with at least one surface that curves inward. Concave lenses include plano-concave and double-concave. A concave lens diverges parallel light rays to a virtual (not real) focal point.

conductivity—The measure of the ability of a material to carry an electric current, expressed as ohms or ohms per meter.

constructive waves—Waves reaching an area in the same phase. Since each wave is in phase with the others, the waves act to constructively add to one another, thereby increasing amplitude. See also *destructive waves*.

continuous wave—A type of laser whose output is continuous as opposed to pulsed; an uninterrupted beam of laser light.

convergence—The bending of light by a lens or mirror to a common point.

converging lens—Generally, a lens that is thicker in the middle than the edges.

convex—A type of lens with at least one surface that curves outward. Convex lenses include plano-convex and double-convex. A convex lens converges parallel light rays to a common real focal point.

corona—The blue glow surrounding a conductor when high voltages are present. The corona is caused by the ionization of the surrounding air and is usually accompanied by a crackling or "spitting" noise.

coupling loss—The loss of light output at the mechanical connections of fiberoptics.

CPU—Acronym for *c*entral *p*rocessing *u*nit. The part of the computer responsible for processing, storing, and retrieving data. The *microprocessor* is often referred to as the CPU, but the term

CPU can also encompass the computer proper minus the keyboard, disk drives, monitor, and so forth.

critical angle—The maximum angle of incidence for which a beam of light will be transmitted from one medium (such as air) to another medium (such as an optical fiber or prism).

cylindrical lens—A lens that expands or reduces an image in one axis only.

dc—Direct current. Current such as that from a battery where the voltage level remains the same (either positive or negative) with respect to ground.

decibel (dB)—A unit of electrical measurement used extensively in audio applications. An increase of 3 dB is a doubling of electrical (or signal) strength; an increase of 10 dB is a doubling of perceived loudness.

default—In computer applications, the normal.

demodulate—The separation of the message signal from a carrier wave.

destructive waves—Waves reaching an area that are not in the same phase. Because the waves are out of phase, they act to partially or completely cancel each other out, thereby diminishing amplitude. See also *constructive waves*.

dichroic filter—An optical filter using organic or chemical dyes that transmits light at selected wavelengths but blocks others.

diffraction—A change in the direction of a beam of light when encountering an edge or opening of an object. For example, diffraction takes place when passing through a small aperture.

diffraction grating—An optical component that splits a light beam into many discrete parts.

digital—Information expressed in binary—ON and OFF—form. The OFF state is usually indicated as a numeral 0; the ONC state is usually indicated as a numeral 1. Many 0s and 1s can be grouped together to represent any other number or value.

digital-to-analog converter (DAC)—An electrical circuit (usually one integrated circuit) that transforms digital signals to their analog equivalents. An analog-to-digital converter performs the reverse function.

diode laser—A solid-state injection laser, similar to a light-emitting diode (LED).

dispersion—Usually applies to the separation of polychromatic light into individual monochromatic frequencies. A prism is often used to disperse white light into the visible spectrum.

divergence—The bending of light rays away from each other; the spreading of light.

diverger—An optical component that spreads light rays.

diverging lens—Generally, a lens that is thinner in the middle than at the edges.

double-concave—A type of negative lens where both faces curve inward. Also called a *double-concave* lens.

duty cycle—In electronics, the ratio of the ON and OFF states of a circuit. The higher the duty cycle (approaching 100 percent), the longer the circuit remains in the ON state.

electroluminescence—In a semiconductor, the direct conversion of current into light.

electromagnetic waves—Transverse (up and down) waves having both an electric and magnetic component. Each component is perpendicular to one another, and both are perpendicular to the direction of propagation.

electro-optic effect—The general change in the refractive index of a material when that material is subjected to an electric field. Also referred to as Pockels and Kerr effects. Similar to acousto-optic and magneto-optic effects, where an acoustic or magnetic pulse changes a material's refractive index.

emulsion—In photography, a chemical coating, usually on clear acetate or glass, that is sensitive to light.

etalon—An extremely flat optical component with parallel surfaces engineered to increase the coherence length of a laser by eliminating modes that are slightly out of phase.

excited state—The state of an atom that occurs when outside energy, such as from an electric field, causes the atom to contain more energy than normal.

f/number—A number that expresses the relative light-gathering power of a lens. The f/number is calculated by dividing the diameter of the lens by the focal length of the lens.

fiberoptic—A solid glass or plastic "tube" that conducts light along its length.

fiber bundle—Many individual strands of optical fibers grouped together. The bundle can be coherent or non-coherent, depending on its ability to transmit an undistorted optical image through the fibers.

filter—1. An electrical circuit designed to prevent the passage of certain frequencies. 2. An optical component designed to block the passage of light at certain frequencies.

focus coil—An electromechanical coil, often used in compact disc and video disc players, that moves an objective lens up and down for proper focus. Surplus coils can often be used in laser experiments.

focal length—The distance from the center of a lens or curved mirror to the point where light converges to a point. Lenses with a positive focal point cause the light rays to form at a specific point; lenses with a negative focal point only appear to focus at an imaginary point.

focal point—That point in space where rays converge to a common point (positive lens system) or from which they appear to diverge (negative lens system).

foot-candle—A unit of illumination. One foot-candle is defined as the amount of light that falls on an area of one square foot on which there is uniform distribution of one lumen.

foot-lambert—A unit of brightness or luminance. One foot-lambert is defined as the uniform distribution of a surface emitting or reflecting light at the rate of one lumen per square foot.

Foucault focusing—A system of focusing whereby the separation of two beams of light changes according to variances in the distance of the focal point.

frequency—The repetition rate of an electromagnetic wave, whether it be light or an electric signal.

fringe—An individual interference band, created by one cycle of waves out of phase (constructive and destructive waves).

front-surface mirror—Also called a *first-surface mirror*. A mirror where the reflective coating is on the front side of the glass. Light rays do not pass through the glass medium before striking the reflective layer, thereby eliminating the ghost image that otherwise appears.

Gabor zone plate—Usually a photographic film made from the pattern formed by a plane wave interfering with a spherical wave. One of many types of holograms.

gain—Amplification, usually expressed in dB.

getter—A supplemental component placed in tubes (including gas laser tubes) that vaporizes any remaining air and gas or that scrubs out impurities after the tube is sealed.

graded index—The design of an optical fiber where the density (and therefore refractive index) of the cladding is graded through its width. Graded indexing is the opposite of step indexing and is said to improve the light-passing capacity of the fiber.

ground—Refers to the point of (usually) zero voltage, and can apply to a power circuit or a signal circuit.

ground state (or level)—The normal unexcited state of an atom.

half wavelength—One half of a wavelength of light; the distance between the crest and trough of a single wave of light.

hertz—Abbreviated Hz. A unit of measurement used for expressing frequency or cycles per second, named after German physicist H.R. Hertz. One hertz is equal to one cycle per second. Also commonly used with the letters "k," "M," and "G" to indicate thousands, millions, and billions, respectively.

He-Ne—Shorthand for helium-neon laser.

hexadecimal—A counting system based on 16 numerals. In computers, hexadecimal counting (or "hex" for short) uses the numerals 0 through 9, plus A through F.

high-pass filter—A filter that passes only high frequencies. Can pertain to both electrical signals or light. See also *low-pass filter* and *band-pass filter*.

holography—A form of photography that uses sound or light waves to record a three-dimensional image of an object. Holography records the instantaneous intensity and phase of reflected and/or transmitted waves onto photographic film.

IC—*I*ntegrated *c*ircuit. Also called a chip. A complete electrical circuit housed in a self-contained package. See also *LSI*.

illumination—Light falling onto a defined area; the photometric counterpart to irradiance. Illumination is commonly expressed in foot-candles.

impedance—The degree of resistance that an alternating current will encounter when passing through a circuit, device, or wire. Impedance is expressed in ohms.

incandescence—Typically, the creation of light by passing an electric current through a wire filament.

incoherent—Lacking the property of coherency.

index of refraction—A relative or absolute ratio of the velocity of a specific wavelength of light within a particular medium and that of air or vacuum.

infrared (IR)—The portion of the electromagnetic spectrum between about 7,800 angstroms (780 nanometers) to about 1,000,000 angstroms (100,000 nanometers or 1 mm). The infrared band is between the visible light spectrum and microwave spectrum. Infrared (or IR) illumination beyond about 880 nm is largely invisible to the human eye.

injection laser—Synonymous with diode laser.

I/O—Short for *i*nput/*o*utput. Refers to the paths by which information enters a system (input) and leaves the system (output).

interference—1. An unwanted signal combining with a desired signal. 2. Light waves out of phase mixing and causing banding or fringing. The superimposing of one light wave on the other, causing the loss of light energy at some points and the reinforcement of light energy at others.

interferometer—An apparatus designed to mix two beams of coherent light (usually from a laser) to study the interference patterns that result. Interferometry is the study of the effects of interference fringes.

irradiance—The amount of light radiating on a defined area; the radiometric counterpart of illumination. Irradiance is usually expressed in watts per square centimeter (watts/cm^2).

kilobyte—Term used to denote "1,000" bytes, or 1K (precisely, 1024 bytes).

kilohertz—A unit of electrical frequency equal to one thousand cycles per second, abbreviated kHz.

laser—A mechanical device that produces intense, coherent radiation (mostly in the visible light and infrared regions). Laser is an acronym for *l*ight *a*mplification by *s*timulated *e*mission of *r*adiation.

lasing—The process of producing laser light.

LED—Short for *l*ight *e*mitting *d*iode, a unique type of semiconductor that is made to emit a bright beam of light. Often used as a panel indicator, but also employed in remote-sensing systems and infrared remote-control devices.

lens—An optical device used to refract (bend) light waves in a specific direction and amount.

lightguide—An optical fiber.

logic—Primarily used to indicate digital circuits or components that accept one or more signals and act on those signals in a predefined, orderly fashion.

longitudinal wave—A wave that oscillates and travels in the same direction, as opposed to *transverse wave*.

low-pass filter—A filter that passes only low frequencies. Can pertain to electrical signals or light. See also *high-pass filter* and *band-pass filter*.

LSI—*L*arge *s*cale *i*ntegration. A complex integrated circuit (IC) that is a combination of many ICs and other electronic components that are normally packaged separately. LSI (and VLSI, for *v*ery *l*arge *s*cale *i*ntegration) chips are used in the latest video equipment and held proprietary by the manufacturer.

megabyte—A term used to indicate millions of bytes; one megabyte (1 Mb) is equal to 1,048,567 bytes, or 1,024 kilobytes.

megahertz—A unit of electrical frequency equal to one million cycles per second; abbreviated MHz.

meridional ray—A light ray that crosses through the optical axis.

micrometer—A unit of metric measurement used to define one millionth of a meter, or 10^{-6} meter. Usually abbreviated as μ.

micron—A unit of metric measurement used to define one millionth of a meter, or 10^{-6} meter. Usually abbreviated as μ. Since about 1965, ''micron'' has fallen into disfavor as a metric term and has been replaced by *micrometer*.

microprocessor—The brain of a computer or computerized system. Performs all of the mathematical and logical operations necessary for the functioning of the system. Sometimes called the *CPU*.

mode—The degree to which the beam of a laser is spatially coherent. Two common modes are TEM_{00}, characterized as spatial coherence across the diameter of a beam and an even spread of light, and *multimode*, where the light appears dark in the center and has rings on the outside edges.

modulation—Altering the characteristic of a wave by imposing another wave on top of it. Often used to carry intelligent communication signals over electromagnetic (radio and light) waves.

monitor photodiode—A special photodiode sandwiched behind the laser diode for the purpose of monitoring the light output of the laser.

monochromatic—Possessing only one color, or more specifically, a specific wavelength (or a very restricted range) in the electromagnetic spectrum.

motherboard—The main printed board in a computer that contains the microprocessor, memory, and support electronics.

negative lens—A lens that has a negative (virtual) focal point. Negative lenses cause light to diverge. See also *positive lens*.

Newton's Rings—A series of rings that appear due to interference caused by two closely spaced parallel surfaces. Newton's Rings occur mainly when sandwiching glass or plastic pieces together.

noise—An undesired signal. In audio circuits, noise is usually hiss and hum; in high-gain amplification circuits, noise is often the result of thermal effects on the junctions of semiconductors. This noise impairs and limits amplification.

normal—In optics, an imaginary line drawn perpendicular to the surface of a lens, mirror, or other optical component. Often referred to as *line normal*.

objective lens—The lens used to focus a beam of light on a subject.

ohm—The unit of measure of impedance or resistance.

optical axis—Basically, the path taken by light rays as it passes through or reflects off the components of an optical system.

optical fiber—The same as *fiberoptic*.

optical filter—Any type of a number of mediums that restrict the passage of light at specific wavelengths.

parallax—The shift in the perspective of an object when the viewing position is slightly changed.

parallel—A type of input/output scheme where data is transferred eight (or more) bits at any time.

paraxial ray—A ray that's close to, and nearly parallel with, the optical axis.

peak wavelength—The wavelength at which the radiant power of a source is at its highest. Peak wavelength is generally expressed in nanometers or angstroms.

perpendicular—At right angles.

phase—The position in time of a sound, electrical, or light wave in relation to another wave. Expressed in degrees. Waves are sinusoidal—with peaks and valleys. Zero degree phase is when the peaks and valleys of both waves are even. A phase of 180 degrees is when the peaks of one wave coincide with the valleys of another.

photodetector—Any of a number of different types of electrical devices that are sensitive to visible light or infrared radiation. The photodiode, phototransistor, silicon solar cell, and cadmium-sulfide cell are common types of photodetectors.

photon—A "packet," or quanta, of light energy, used to describe the particle-like characteristics of light.

piezoelectric effect—An effect inherent in certain substances (mainly crystals and ceramics) where an application of current causes vibrational motion. Conversely, vibrational motion (including stress, bending, and friction) causes an output voltage.

point source—Radiation (usually light) whose maximum width or dispersion is less than ⅒th the distance between the source and the receiver. Generally any source of light that can be considered originating as an infinitely small point.

polarizer—A material that blocks light waves traveling in a particular plane. The material may also alter the polarization characteristics, changing it between plane, elliptical, and circular.

polarized beam splitter (PBS)—An optical component used in some compact disc players that consists of two prisms with a common 45-degree face. Polarizing elements in the beam splitter are oriented so that only properly polarized light passes through.

population inversion—A condition where more atoms are in the abnormal high-energy excited state than those atoms that are in the normal low-energy ground state. Population inversion is a must in order for lasing to occur.

positive lens—A lens that has a positive (real) focal point. Positive lenses cause light to converge. See also *negative lens*.

pps—Short for *pulses per second*, expressed as hertz if the pulses are electrical.

prism—An optical component usually in the form of a wedge that redirects a light beam by diffraction and reflection.

Q-switch—A mechanism that inhibits oscillation within a laser until a certain amount of energy is stored. When the desired energy level is reached, the laser is permitted to output its light as a short, high-output pulse.

quantization—The conversion of the instantaneous amplitude of an instantaneous moment of sound (sample) into its approximate digital equivalent.

quantum—A bundle of energy; photons.

quarter wave plate (QWP)—An optical component that shifts the polarity of light 90 degrees.

RAM—Acronym for *random access memory*. A type of temporary memory used for storing data, either entered by the user or loaded from the software. RAM is volatile (its contents are lost when the power is removed).

real image—Light focused in space.

rectilinear propagation—Radiation traveling in a straight line.

reflection—The "bouncing" of light off the surface of a medium.

refraction—The bending of light as it passes from one medium to another. Refraction occurs because the velocity of light changes depending on the density of the medium it is passing through.

resistance—Opposition to direct electrical current (dc), expressed in ohms.

ROM—Acronym for *r*ead *o*nly *m*emory. A type of permanent memory where program instruction can be stored and accessed any time. Unlike RAM, ROM is not volatile; the contents of ROM are not lost when the power is removed.

sample-and-hold—An electronic circuit used to sample incoming data and hold it momentarily until the next sampling interval. Often used to maintain a voltage level for a period of time for analog-to-digital conversion.

sampling—The measurement of the instantaneous amplitude of a signal, at regular intervals.

serial—A type of input/output scheme where data is transferred one bit at a time.

servo—An electronic circuit that modifies its output in accordance to a constantly varying input signal.

signal—The desired portion of electrical information.

signal-to-noise (S/N)—The relationship, expressed as a ratio in dB, between signal and noise.

skew ray—A light ray that does not cross or come into contact with the optical axis.

spatial coherence—1. The uniform arrangement of electromagnetic waves as they travel through space. 2. Coherence across the diameter of the beam.

spatial filter—A type of optical component used to pass only a small portion of a light beam. The filter, consisting of a pinhole and focusing lens, cleans up the beam by eliminating the effects of dirt, grease, and scratches on lenses and spatial incoherence across the diameter of a laser beam.

speckle—The grainy appearance of reflected laser light, caused by light reflecting off a small area of the object and interfering with itself (also caused by local interference within the eye).

spontaneous emission—Radiation, usually visible light or infrared, which is emitted when atoms at an excited state drop back down to a ground state.

step index—The design of an optical fiber where the density (and therefore refractive index) of the cladding changes abruptly through its width. Step indexing is the opposite of *graded indexing*.

stimulated emission—Radiation emitted when atoms at an excited state drop to a ground state while in the presence of radiant energy at the same frequency.

temporal coherence—The uniformity of electromagnetic waves over time.

transmittance—The ratio, expressed in percentage, of the radiant power emitted from a source to the total radiant power received.

transverse wave—A wave that oscillates at right angles to the path along which the wave travels. Most light waves are transverse, as opposed to *longitudinal*.

ultraviolet—The portion of the electromagnetic spectrum immediately above visible light and below X-rays.

vacuum—The absence of matter, including air.

virtual image—An image formed by diverging light rays that appear to emerge from a point.

waist—The diameter of a laser beam.

wave—In lasers, an oscillation, in the form of a sine wave, of electromagnetic radiation through a medium (or through a vacuum).

wave train—A series of identical waves.

wave front—A shape (either 2D or 3D) formed by wave points of identical phase meeting at some point in space. Also see *wavelet*.

wavelength—The distance between valleys and peaks of an electromagnetic or acoustic wave.

wavelet—The leading edge of a wave that combines with the leading edges of neighboring waves to form a wavefront.

Index

Edited by Lisa A. Doyle

Other Bestsellers From TAB

Other Bestsellers From TAB

☐ **THE ENCYCLOPEDIA OF ELECTRONIC CIRCUITS—Rudolf F. Graf**

Here is every professional's dream treasury of analog and digital circuits—nearly 100 circuit categories . . . over 1,200 individual circuits designed for long-lasting applications potential. Adding even more to the value of this resource is the exhaustively thorough index which gives you instant access to exactly the circuits you need each and every time! 768 pp., 1,762 illus.

Paper $39.95   Hard $60.00
Book No. 1938

☐ **BUILD YOUR OWN LASER, PHASER, ION RAY GUN AND OTHER WORKING SPACE-AGE PROJECTS—Robert E. Iannini**

Here's the highly skilled do-it-yourself guidance that makes it possible for you to build such interesting and useful projects as a burning laser, a high power ruby/YAG, a high-frequency translator, a light beam communications system, a snooper phone listening device, and much more—24 exciting projects in all! 400 pp., 302 illus.

Paper $13.95   Book No. 1604

Send $1 for the new TAB Catalog describing over 1300 titles currently in print and receive a coupon worth $1 off on your next purchase from TAB.

(Pa. residents add 6% sales tax. NY residents add sales tax. Orders outside U.S. must be prepaid with international money orders in U.S. dollars.)

*Prices subject to change without notice.

To purchase these or any other books from TAB, visit your local bookstore, return this coupon, or call toll-free 1-800-233-1128 (In PA and AK call 1-717-794-2191).

Product No.	Hard or Paper	Title	Quantity	Price

☐ Check or money order enclosed made payable to TAB BOOKS Inc.

Charge my   ☐ VISA   ☐ MasterCard   ☐ American Express

Acct. No. _____ Exp. _____

Signature _____

Please Print
Name _____

Company _____

Address _____

City _____

State _____ Zip _____

Subtotal	
Postage/Handling ($5.00 outside U.S.A. and Canada)	$2.50
In PA add 6% sales tax	
TOTAL	

Mail coupon to:

TAB BOOKS Inc.
Blue Ridge Summit
PA 17294-0840   BC

KISSER

BOOKS BY STUART WOODS

FICTION

Hothouse Orchid*
Loitering with Intent[†]
Mounting Fears[‡]
Hot Mahogany[†]
Santa Fe Dead[§]
Beverly Hills Dead
Shoot Him If He Runs[†]
Fresh Disasters[†]
Short Straw[§]
Dark Harbor[†]
Iron Orchid*
Two-Dollar Bill[†]
The Prince of Beverly Hills
Reckless Abandon[†]
Capital Crimes[‡]
Dirty Work[†]
Blood Orchid*
The Short Forever[†]
Orchid Blues*
Cold Paradise[†]

L.A. Dead[†]
The Run[‡]
Worst Fears Realized[†]
Orchid Beach*
Swimming to Catalina[†]
Dead in the Water[†]
Dirt[†]
Choke
Imperfect Strangers
Heat
Dead Eyes
L.A. Times
Santa Fe Rules[§]
New York Dead[†]
Palindrome
Grass Roots[‡]
White Cargo
Deep Lie[‡]
Under the Lake
Run Before the Wind[‡]
Chiefs[‡]

TRAVEL

A Romantic's Guide to the Country Inns of Britain and Ireland (1979)

MEMOIR

Blue Water, Green Skipper (1977)

*A Holly Barker Novel   †A Stone Barrington Novel
‡A Will Lee Novel   §An Ed Eagle Novel

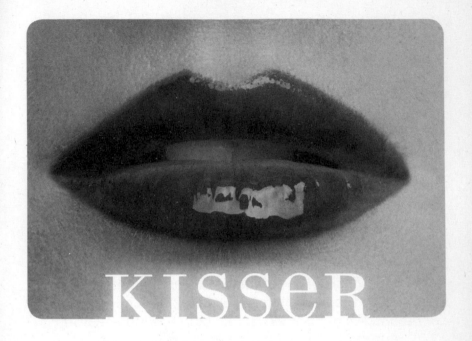

KISSER

STUART WOODS

**Doubleday Large Print
Home Library Edition**

G. P. PUTNAM'S SONS
New York

This Large Print Edition, prepared especially for
Doubleday Large Print Home Library, contains the
complete, unabridged text of the original Publisher's Edition.

PUTNAM

G. P. PUTNAM'S SONS
Publishers Since 1838
Published by the Penguin Group
Penguin Group (USA) Inc., 375 Hudson Street,
New York, New York 10014, USA • Penguin Group
(Canada), 90 Eglinton Avenue East, Suite 700,
Toronto, Ontario M4P 2Y3, Canada (a division of Pearson
Penguin Canada Inc.) • Penguin Books Ltd, 80 Strand,
London WC2R 0RL, England • Penguin Ireland, 25 St
Stephen's Green, Dublin 2, Ireland
(a division of Penguin Books Ltd) • Penguin Group
(Australia), 250 Camberwell Road, Camberwell,
Victoria 3124, Australia (a division of Pearson
Australia Group Pty Ltd) • Penguin Books India Pvt Ltd,
11 Community Centre, Panchsheel Park, New
Delhi–110 017, India • Penguin Group (NZ),
67 Apollo Drive, Rosedale, North Shore 0632,
New Zealand (a division of Pearson New Zealand Ltd) •
Penguin Books (South Africa) (Pty) Ltd, 24 Sturdee
Avenue, Rosebank, Johannesburg 2196, South Africa

Penguin Books Ltd, Registered Offices: 80 Strand, London
WC2R 0RL, England

**This Large Print Book carries the
Seal of Approval of N.A.V.H.**

This book is for Bob and Liz Woodward.

KISSER

1

ELAINE'S, LATE.

Stone Barrington and his former NYPD partner, Dino Bacchetti, were dining in the company of herself, Elaine, who, as usual, was making her rounds. "So?" Elaine asked as she joined them.

"Not much," Dino replied.

Stone was deep into his *spaghetti alla carbonara*.

"Nice, isn't it?" she asked. Elaine had a good opinion of her food.

"Mmmmf," Stone replied, trying to handle what he had stuffed into his mouth and speak at the same time.

"Never mind," Elaine said. "Enjoy."

Stone swallowed hard and nodded. "Thank you, I am."

The waiter came with the wine and poured everybody a glass.

Stone began to take smaller bites, so as to better participate in the conversation. As he took his first sip of wine, he froze.

Dino stared at him. "What's the matter? Am I gonna have to do a Heimlich?"

Stone set down the glass but said nothing. He was following the entrance of a very beautiful woman. She was probably five-eight or -nine, he thought, and closer to six feet in her heels. She was dressed in a classic Little Black Dress that set off a strand of large pearls around her neck. Fake, probably, but who cared? She had honey-blond, shoulder-length hair and a lot of it, cascades of it, big eyes, and plump lips sporting bright red lipstick. Dino and Elaine followed Stone's gaze as the woman turned to her left and sat down at the bar.

"She can't be alone," Dino said.

"Who is she?" Stone asked Elaine.

"Never saw her in here," Elaine replied, "but you'd better hurry; she's not gonna be alone long."

Stone put down his glass, got up, and walked toward the bar, straightening his tie. Normally, the people at the tables didn't have much to do with the people at the bar; they were different crowds. But Stone knew when to make an exception.

"Good evening," he said to her, offering his hand. "My name is Stone Barrington."

She took the hand and offered a shy smile. "Hello, I'm Carrie Cox," she said, and her accent was soft and southern.

Stone indicated his table. "My friends Dino and Elaine agree with me that you are too beautiful to be sitting alone at the bar. Will you join us?"

She looked surprised. "Thank you, yes," she said after a moment's thought.

Stone escorted her back to the table and sat her down. "Carrie Cox, this is Elaine Kaufman, your hostess, and Dino Bacchetti, one of New York's Finest."

"How do you do," Carrie said. "Finest what?"

"It's a designation meant to describe any New York City police officer," Stone said, "without regard for individual quality."

"Stone should know," Dino said. "He used to be one of New York's worst."

Carrie laughed, a low, inviting sound.

"You must be from out of town," Dino said.

"Isn't everybody?" Elaine asked.

"I've only been in New York for three weeks," Carrie said.

"Where you from?" Elaine asked.

"I'm from a little town in Georgia called Delano, but I came here from Atlanta. I lived there for two years."

"And what brought you to our city?" Stone asked.

"I'm an actress, so after a couple of years of training in Atlanta, it was either New York or L.A. Since it's spring, I thought I'd start in New York, and if I hadn't found work by winter, I'd move on to L.A."

Stone was fascinated by her mouth, which moved in an oddly attractive way when she talked.

"And have you found work yet?"

"Almost immediately," she said, "but not as an actress. I've been working as a lip model."

"I'm not surprised," Stone said.

"A *lip* model?" Dino asked.

"I've been modeling lipstick," she explained, "in the mornings. In the afternoons

I've been making the rounds, looking for stage work."

"That's tough," Elaine said.

"Well, I've had one very attractive of-fer," Carrie said, "from a man called Del Wood."

Stone knew him a little, from a couple of dinner parties. Wood was a king of Broad-way, who composed both music and lyrics and who owned his own theater. "The new Irving Berlin," Stone said, "as he's often called."

"Unfortunately," Carrie said, "the offer came with some very unattractive strings."

"Ah," Stone said. "Del Wood has that rep-utation. He is also known as Del Woodie."

Carrie laughed. "I can believe it. Do you know what he said to me?"

"I can't wait to find out," Dino said, lean-ing forward.

"He said—and please pardon the lan-guage; it's his, not mine—'I want to strip off that dress, lay you on your belly, and fuck you in the ass.'"

"Oh," Dino said.

Stone was speechless.

"I was thinking of suing him for sexual harassment," Carrie said.

"Well," Dino said, indicating Stone, "meet your new lawyer."

"Oh, are you a lawyer?" Carrie asked Stone.

"Yes, but I'm not sure you'd have much of a case."

"Why not?"

"Did he force himself on you?"

"No. I got out of there."

"Were there any witnesses?"

"No."

"Then I'm afraid it would be your word against his," Stone said.

"Well," Carrie said, "I did get him on tape."

2

STONE NEARLY CHOKED on his wine. "That was prescient of you," he rasped.

"Well, I had heard a little about him," Carrie replied. "A girl has to protect herself."

"Certainly," Stone replied.

"Too fucking right," Elaine added.

"And by what means did you record him?" Stone asked.

"Small dictator in my open purse on his desk," Carrie replied. "So, shall I retain you as my attorney and sue the son of a bitch?"

"First things first," Stone said. "What may I get you to drink, and will you have some dinner?"

"Thank you, a Knob Creek on the rocks, please, and no, I'm not hungry, having already dined—partially, anyway."

Stone ordered the drink. "And what do you mean by having dined 'partially'?"

"Well, a friend, a stage manager, invited me to a very nice dinner party being given by a well-known actress. We arrived a little late, and to my surprise, I found myself seated next to Mr. Del Wood, who couldn't keep his hands to himself. Having fought that off in the afternoon—something the other diners seemed to be aware of—I tried to make conversation, but then Mr. Woodie interrupted me and announced for all to hear that the offer he had made me that afternoon was still open. He was beginning to explain to everyone what the offer was when I tipped his dinner plate into his lap—we were having *spaghetti Bolognese*—then I got up, offered my thanks to my hostess, and left."

"Wow," Dino said. "I wish I'd been there for that."

"So do I," Stone said. "Perhaps you'd like dessert, Carrie?"

"Thank you. Perhaps I would."

Elaine grabbed a passing waiter and ordered up the dessert tray. Normally, she would have moved to another table by then, but she seemed to be enjoying the conversation.

The waiter appeared, and Carrie chose a crème brûlée.

"How many people were at the dinner party, and were they all theater people?"

"Twelve, and yes, they were actors, composers, producers, the works. I was rather looking forward to doing myself some good there, but Old Woodie spoiled that."

"Well," Stone said, "by lunchtime tomorrow you will be famous among a certain level of the Broadway cognoscenti; people will be dining out on that story for weeks, and I wouldn't be surprised if it made the gossip columns."

"Would that be a good thing?" Carrie asked.

"Good for everybody but Mr. Woodie," Stone replied. "You'll be immediately famous, as long as they spell your name right."

"Oh, good."

"What part did he offer you?"

"The lead in his new musical."

Stone was stunned. "The *lead*? What sort of audition did you do?"

"I sang 'I Loves You Porgy' from *Porgy and Bess* and a Sondheim tune, 'I'm Still Here,' and I danced a little. This was in the theater."

"And he let you get all the way through the two songs?"

"Yes, and there were a dozen or so people sitting in the orchestra seats who all stood up and applauded. That's when Mr. Wood invited me up to his office to talk."

"That sounds like something out of a movie about a Broadway show," Stone said. "Small-town girl shows up in the big city and wows everybody at her first audition."

"Well, it wasn't my first audition," Carrie said. "I had to audition for the lip modeling, too."

"And who did you have to kiss?" Dino asked.

"A mirror. I didn't mind that; a mirror has no hands." Her crème brûlée arrived, and she did it justice.

"Coffee?" Stone asked

"A double espresso, please."

"No trouble sleeping?" Stone asked.

"No trouble at all," she replied, giving him a little smile that made those beautiful lips enchanting again. "The benefit of a clear conscience."

"Always a good thing to have," Stone said. "Tell me, do you remember the names of the people at the dinner party?"

"Most of them. My date, Tony, will know them all."

"And have their addresses?"

"Yes, I think so. They were all his friends."

"First thing tomorrow morning you should write little notes to those people, expressing your regret for having to depart the party and say how sorry you were that you didn't have time to get to know them better. Start with your hostess."

"Just to remind them who I am?"

"Exactly, and please be sure your address, phone number, and cell number are clearly printed on your letterhead. If the letters don't get you other auditions, they will, at least, get you some dinner invitations— dinners Mr. Wood will not be attending."

"What a good idea, Stone," she said. "Now, will you be my attorney so that I can sue Mr. Woodie?"

"I'm afraid I have a serious conflict of interest that would prevent my representing you. However, I'd be happy to give you some free advice and to recommend an appropriate attorney."

"What's the conflict of interest?" Carrie asked.

"I am so impressed with your beauty, your intelligence, and your quick wit that I would much rather take you out to dinner than take you to court."

She laughed. "I think I would like that, too," she said. She opened a tiny purse and gave him a beautifully engraved card, and Stone reciprocated.

"Now, give me the free advice."

"I don't think you should sue Mr. Wood—at least, not right away. I think the dinner party incident will show up in tomorrow's papers, and with nearly all the details. Mr. Wood can't hold you responsible for that; he has only himself to blame. And who knows? You might even end up working for him some day, but under more favorable circumstances. Do you have your Equity card yet?" This referred to Actor's Equity, the union representing stage actors.

"No, but all I need is one job to get it."

"I think you are more likely to get that first job, if you don't have a reputation for suing producers for sexual harassment. Anyway, having drawn a very firm line in the sand with Mr. Wood, you will henceforth have a reputation as an actress who does not brook unwanted advances from potential employers, and you will be treated with some respect."

"A good point," she admitted. "I will take your advice."

"And, should you feel receptive to an advance at some point in the near future," Stone said, "I will be around to fulfill that need in an entirely nontheatrical setting."

She smiled broadly at him. "We'll see," she said.

3

WHEN STONE ARRIVED at his desk the following midmorning, the *New York Post* was lying on his desk, open to the "Page Six" gossip column, which was not on page six. His secretary, Joan Robertson, had left it there and had conveniently highlighted the passage:

> Last night at dinner at the home of theater diva Gwen Asprey, the composer/producer Del Wood, whose reputation as a casting-couch Lothario is richly deserved, was given his comeuppance after having previously made advances on (including, we hear, a

request for anal sex) and been rejected by
a new girl in town, the beautiful and talented
Carrie Cox. When Woodie, as he is known
to some, began to tell the table of his thwarted attempt, Ms. Cox, who had, unaccount-
ably, been seated next to him, dumped his
own plate of red-sauce pasta into his lap
and made a grand exit. The evening was
greatly enjoyed by everyone present, except Mr. Wood. Incidentally, only that afternoon Carrie Cox had performed a brilliant
audition for Mr. Wood and his backers that
resulted in an offer of the lead in his new
musical. Unfortunately, Woodie considered
the transaction a trade instead of an offer, so
the lovely Ms. Cox remains at liberty. (Other
producers, take note!) Later in the evening,
she was seen at Elaine's in the company of
local lawyer Stone Barrington. Out of the
frying pan and into the fire!

Stone thought that the piece was a remarkably accurate account of events, for a
gossip column, and he was surprised to
see a very good photograph of Carrie Cox,
in balletic flight, accompanying it. He wondered where the paper had found it on
such short notice.

His phone buzzed. "Carrie Cox on line one," Joan said.

He picked up the phone. "Is this the beautiful and talented Carrie Cox?" he asked.

"That's what it says in the papers," she replied, giggling. "You were right!"

"I've seen the *Post*," Stone said. "How did they get it so accurately?"

"There was a message from them on my answering machine when I got home," she said, "and I played the tape for them."

"If the tape should ever be mentioned again, deny its existence and tell them you took notes after the conversation."

"All right," she said, "but I made them promise not to mention that, and they didn't."

"You're a lucky woman, as well as a smart one."

"Thank you, kind sir."

"How about dinner this evening?"

"I've been invited to a dinner party," she said. "Another prediction of yours come true. Why don't you come with me?"

"You're on. Where shall I pick you up?"

"I'm downtown, and you're closer to the dinner; why don't I pick you up? You can make me a drink around, say, seven?"

"You're on again. Is this a necktie party?"

"Well, I hope I'm not going to be hanged."

"For me, not you."

"My mother always said a gentleman can't go wrong by wearing a necktie, and tonight you're supposed to wear a black one along with a dinner jacket."

"Then wear one I shall. You have my card; see you at seven."

"Bye-bye." She hung up.

Joan was leaning against his doorjamb. "I don't believe this," she said.

CARRIE ARRIVED at seven on the dot, and Stone met her at the door.

"*Oooh,*" she murmured, looking around the living room. "I want the tour! How many bedrooms?"

"Five, and as many baths, with three powder rooms scattered around the place."

"How long have you owned it?"

"Since I inherited it from my great-aunt. I did most of the renovation myself. Come on. I'll show you this floor." He took her through the living room, the dining room, and a garage. Finally he sat her down in the study and produced a half-bottle of Schramsberg champagne from the wet bar.

"Such wonderful woodwork and book-cases," she said.

"My father built all of them. In fact, you could say that this house saved his career and his marriage. He was going door-to-door in Greenwich Village, doing whatever carpentry work he could find. This house bought him his shop and equipment and made him feel that he could earn a living at what he did best."

"That's a wonderful story," she said.

"I haven't heard your story yet," Stone said, "except the part about Delano and Atlanta."

"Ah, well, there is a bit more," Carrie said. "After Agnes Scott College I went to the Yale Drama School for a master's, then went back to Atlanta and married my college sweetheart instead of going to New York when I should have. That went bad pretty quickly, but I did last a few years before I divorced him."

"How long ago?"

"Three years, when his property development business was at its peak. That improved my settlement. Now he resents me because he's nearly broke."

"Wasn't your fault," Stone pointed out.

"Tell him that!"

"I hope I don't have to."

"Don't worry; he's well in my past."

"So, after the divorce . . ."

"I danced with the Atlanta Ballet and worked in local theater and studied acting. I enjoyed it, but I wanted to try a bigger arena."

"I'm glad you chose New York instead of L.A.," Stone said.

She raised her glass. "So am I."

"Tell me, where did the *Post* get the photograph?"

"I directed them to the *Atlanta Constitution*, which had done a piece on me last year."

"I think you're going to do well in this town."

"From your lips to God's ear," she said. "I Googled you and read some of your old press."

"Not all of it favorable," Stone said.

"Oh, I don't know. Like you say, they spelled your name right. I was confused about your connection to a law firm."

"Woodman & Weld. I'm of counsel to them, which means I handle the cases they don't want to be associated with publicly.

They're far too prestigious to be representing people who are involved in nasty divorces or have been accused of drunk driving or spousal abuse. Once in a while they throw me a nice personal-injury suit to settle, but I also generate a good deal of my own business."

"Well, if I'm ever in terrible trouble, I'll call you," Carrie said.

"Don't wait until then," Stone replied. He looked at his watch. "Perhaps we'd better move along."

"Yes, we're already fashionably late," she said, jumping gracefully to her feet.

They walked out into the spring night, hand in hand.

4

THE PARTY WAS a ten-minute cab ride away, in a large apartment on Central Park South, overlooking the park. A uniformed maid answered the door, and the glitter began.

Stone didn't know anybody there, but he recognized a few faces from the Broadway stage. There were at least forty people for dinner, so he reckoned it would be a buffet, and he was right.

They worked the room slowly, and they could just as well have stood still and let the crowd come to them, such was Carrie's new fame. Stone admired the way

she met people, not as an equal, but as the
new girl. One or two of the young women
seemed to be looking her over enviously,
but most people seemed impressed with
her. Some of them were agents who offered their cards.

"I wish I could recommend somebody,"
Stone said, "but this crowd is not part of
my world. I'm a theatergoer, but I'm no in-
sider."

"I think that's refreshing," Carrie said. "I
love theater people, but it's nice to know
people from other worlds, too."

They sat on the big terrace with the park
views, and a waiter brought them plates.
When they had finished dining and were
on brandy, a middle-aged man pulled up a
chair in front of Carrie, turned and spoke
briefly to Stone, then turned his attention
back to Carrie.

"I'm Mark Goodwin," he said, "and I'm
one of the two or three best theatrical
agents in this town. I'm not going to tell
you who the others are." He gave her the
names of half a dozen clients, and it was
an impressive list. "I want you to talk to everybody you can, then come and see me."
He gave her his card. "You've made a

splash already," he said, "and I'm not talking about the columns, though that doesn't hurt. I heard about your audition for Del Wood less than an hour after you finished it, and so did a lot of other people."

"If I were your client," Carrie asked, "how would you handle me right now?"

"The first thing I would do would be to heal the breach with Del, though not in a way that would put your virtue in jeopardy. Del is an important man in this business, and the part he offered you is the best thing to come along in years. I've read the script and heard the score, and you're perfect for it."

"How are you going to get him to apologize?" Carrie asked.

"Oh, he's never going to apologize," Goodwin said. "The best you can hope for is that he will deign to forget what he did in his office and what you did at the dinner party. If you can forget it, too, he might be willing to call it a draw. I've known him a long time, and I know how to handle him."

"Mr. Goodwin," Carrie said, "I'm well aware of who you are and how good you are. Get me the part, and I'll be your new client the same day."

"It won't be that hard," Goodwin said. "After all, you've already aced the audition. Come see me tomorrow afternoon at three." He shook her hand, then Stone's, and then wandered off into the crowd.

"That sounds promising," Stone said.

"If I could have picked anybody for an agent, it would have been Mark Goodwin," Carrie said. "The day before yesterday, I couldn't have gotten in to see him."

"Your movie continues," Stone said. "Next, we'll have some shots of rehearsals, then a triumphant opening-night scene, then trouble of some sort—alcohol or drugs or an awful man, then recovery and . . . well, you know the rest."

"I'm not inclined toward addictions," Carrie said, "and especially not to bad men. I've had one, and that was enough."

"I'm glad to hear it."

Carrie stood up. "Let's get out of here. I want to show you something."

Stone followed her downstairs and into a cab, and she gave the driver an address in the West Fifties, between Fifth and Sixth avenues. Once there, they got out of the cab in front of an elegant building. Taking

a key from her purse, she led him up the front steps, opened the front door, then another door.

Stone found himself standing in the large room that had, apparently, been the living room when the building had been a single-family house. It was empty of furniture, but it had recently been painted and seemed in very good condition.

"It's a duplex," Carrie said, pointing to a balcony at one end of the room. "The bedrooms are up there, and I signed the lease this afternoon."

"That was quite a leap of faith," Stone said. "Maybe you'd better slow down a little."

"No need; I told you that I got a good divorce settlement and that my ex was a rich man then. I've been living downtown with a friend, and when I've furnished this place, it will be a good leading lady's apartment. The lease is for two years, and after that I'll buy something grander on the East Side."

"A woman with a plan," Stone said.

"I've learned to make my plans happen," Carrie replied. "It's something I'm really good at."

"What other plans do you have?" Stone asked.

"If I had planned better, I would have had a bed delivered this afternoon," she replied, standing on her tiptoes and kissing him. "I guess we'll have to make do with one of your bedrooms." She took his hand and trotted him out to the street and into another cab.

Stone did not offer any resistance.

5

STONE WOKE SLOWLY to the sound of Carrie on the phone, speaking quietly but urgently. She had been a transcendent lover the night before, and in the middle of the night, too, and he felt a little worn out.

Carrie finished her conversation and hung up. "Oh, you're awake. Good morning. Your housekeeper made me tea and toast." She began pulling on clothes. "I've got a dance class in half an hour, then I'm meeting my designer at the apartment. I'd like you to attend my three o'clock meeting with Mark Goodwin, if you're available."

Stone pressed the button on the remote

control that raised his bed to a sitting position. "Good morning, Carrie," he said. "I should tell you that I have no experience with theatrical work, so I'm not sure what use I'd be to you."

"I just want you to represent me in dealing with Goodwin. I'm told he has a boilerplate client contract that isn't entirely client-favorable, and I think I need some help with my negotiations with him."

"Okay. What time?"

She handed him a slip of paper with the address. "Three o'clock. Be five minutes early, will you?" She bent over and kissed him. "You were just great last night; now I've gotta run."

"You're going to a dance class in an LBD?"

"I've got dance clothes in my locker at the studio. Bye-bye." Then, with a wave, she fled downstairs.

Stone shaved and showered, got dressed, had some breakfast, and went down to his office. Once again, "Page Six" in the *Post* awaited him:

Last night at a black-tie dinner for fifty at the home of Broadway angels David and

Shirley Medved, Carrie Cox, the new girl in town, continued her sweep through Broadway circles by signing with superagent Mark Goodwin on a handshake. We hear that, before the day is out, he'll have her signed to her first major role.

My God, Stone thought. How does she do this? His phone rang. "Hello?"

"It's Dino. You seen the *Post*?"

"Yeah, just now."

"How does she do this?"

"I was just wondering the same thing. I was with her continuously from seven last evening until about an hour ago, and I never saw her make a phone call until this morning. She must be communicating psychically with 'Page Six.'"

"Don't get knocked down in the whirl-wind."

"I'll try not to."

"Dinner?"

"See you at eight thirty."

"Are you bringing the girl?"

"I don't know yet." Stone hung up.

MARK GOODWIN'S SUITE of offices was up-stairs over a big Broadway theater and

reached by a tiny elevator. Carrie was sitting in his reception area, flipping through a fashion magazine.

"Oh, hi," she said. She turned to the receptionist. "Now you can tell Mr. Goodwin we're here."

The woman spoke on the phone. "You can go right in," she said.

Stone followed Carrie into a large office overlooking Schubert Alley. Mark Goodwin kissed Carrie, shook Stone's hand, and waved them to a sitting area with a sofa and chairs.

"I had lunch with Del Wood," he said. "My girl is typing up the contract now."

"Contract?" Carrie asked.

"Two contracts, actually," Goodwin replied. "One between you and Del and one between you and me."

"Tell me about the one between Woodie and me."

"Oh, we sorted things out over lunch and worked out what may be the best deal for a first-time starring role in the history of the Broadway theater."

"Tell me about it," Carrie said.

"It's a one-year contract with an option for another three months. He wanted a

run-of-the-play deal, but I nixed that; you
may be getting even better offers after
the West Coast crowd sees you onstage.
Hollywood is going to be interested, I can
promise you." He ran through the salary
and other conditions.

"That does sound good," Carrie said.

"Listen, I already know Del's production
costs, the number of seats in his theater,
and the kind of money he's paying the rest
of the cast, some of whom are my clients;
believe me, this is a good deal."

"Wonderful," she said. "Now tell me
about my deal with you."

A young woman walked into the office
and handed him a file folder. "Here's my
standard client contract," he said, handing
her two sheets of paper, which she turned
over to Stone without looking at them.

Stone read quickly through the agreement while Carrie and Goodwin sat silently,
waiting. "Two things," Stone said. "There's
a paragraph in here that says you take a
commission on anything she ever does involving somebody you introduced her to.
That won't do."

"It's standard," Goodwin said.

"The other thing is, you can fire her as a

client whenever you like, but she has to give you a year's notice. That won't do, either. We want termination on thirty days' written notice by either party, and the other paragraph comes out."

"Can't do it," Goodwin said.

"I'm so sorry we couldn't reach an agreement, Mark," Carrie said, "but I think Stone's points are valid." She got to her feet.

"Sit down, sit down," Goodwin said. "For you, I'll do this." He made some notes on the contract and buzzed for his girl. "Make these changes pronto," he said, and then turned back to Carrie. "Here's your contract with Del Wood." He handed it to her, and she signed it without reading it.

"You don't want your attorney to read it first?"

"Not necessary," Carrie said, handing the contract back to him. "You represent me to others."

The secretary returned with the other contract, and Stone looked it over and handed it to Carrie. "Looks fine with me," he said.

Carrie signed it and handed it to Goodwin. He signed both contracts and handed

copies to Stone, then he handed Carrie a script and another thick booklet. "Carrie, here are your script and score. You start rehearsals Monday morning at Central Plaza, ten o'clock sharp. You should learn the first act by then, and you should run through the score with a pianist, so that you're familiar with it."

"Who's directing?" she asked.

"Jack Wright," he replied.

"Oh, good." She stood up. "Thank you so much, Mark. I look forward to working with you. By the way, I don't need my hand held; I'll call you if I have any problems with Woodie."

Goodwin stood up. "Remember not to call him that," he said. "He doesn't like it."

"I'll be nice to him, if he's nice to me," she said.

"If he gets mad and fires you for any reason, don't worry about it, just call me." He handed her a card. "Here's my BlackBerry number. Memorize it, then eat the card." He offered Stone his hand. "Nice working with you, Stone. I take it you'll be Carrie's personal attorney from here on."

"That's correct," Carrie said, not giving Stone a chance to reply. "Bye-bye, Mark."

They left the office. Stone looked at his watch: They had been there for twenty-seven minutes. "You do business briskly," he said to Carrie.

"You have no idea," she replied. "Please bill me for this and any other work at your usual hourly rate. Now come with me."

They hailed a taxi, and five minutes later they were at Carrie's new address. "I want you to see this," she said, getting out of the cab.

"I saw it last night, remember?"

"No, you didn't," she said. She let them into the building. The double doors to her apartment were already open, and some men were carrying boxes upstairs.

Stone's jaw dropped. The living room was completely furnished, down to small objets d'art on side tables, and there was a Steinway grand piano in a corner. It looked as though Carrie had lived there for a year.

"Like it?" she asked.

"It's gorgeous. How did you do it so fast?"

"A friend of mine is the best theatrical designer in town. I told him to do it fast,

with the best stuff he could find on short notice. I had the pictures and some smaller things in storage."

"It took me two years to get my house to this state," Stone said.

"As you said, I do things briskly. What time is dinner?"

6

STONE AND DINO WERE on their second drink, and Carrie still hadn't arrived. It was nearly nine o'clock.

"She didn't strike me as the late type," Dino said.

"She's had a busy day," Stone replied, "and she's just moved into her new apartment; she probably couldn't find what she wanted to wear in the boxes." Stone told Dino about the instant furnishing and decoration of the new apartment.

"Here we go," Dino said, nodding toward the door.

Carrie, dressed in slacks and a sweater, was walking toward the table, limping.

Stone stood and held a chair for her, and it was not until he sat down and looked at her closely that he realized something was wrong. He waved at a waiter, pointed at his drink, then at Carrie.

"I'm sorry I'm late," Carrie said, trembling.

The drink came, and Stone handed it to her. "Big swig," he said, and she complied.

"Now tell me what's wrong."

She gulped. "I was leaving my building, and as I came down the front steps I saw a man coming down the street from the direction of Fifth Avenue."

Stone waited while she took a couple of deep breaths.

"He was backlit by a streetlight, so his face was in shadow. To get a taxi I had to walk toward Sixth Avenue for a little bit, because the parked cars were so close together that I couldn't squeeze between them without getting my clothes dirty. As I walked I could hear his footsteps getting quicker and realized he was running toward me. I saw a cab coming from up the

street, and without even looking back, I just threw myself over the hood of a parked car and in front of the cab. As soon as I got inside, I screamed at the driver to get out of there, and I locked the door, because I saw the man reaching for the handle. There was a knife in his other hand."

"Did he hurt you?" Stone asked. "You were limping when you came in."

She reached down, took off a shoe, and held it up. The heel was missing. "This was the only wound," she said. Calmer now and breathing more slowly, she took another big swig of the bourbon.

"Describe him," Dino said.

"Tall, over six feet, athletic-looking, wearing a raincoat and a felt hat."

"Any distinguishing features?" Dino asked. He was taking notes now.

"Small scar at the corner of the left eye, another scar on the inside of the right wrist—childhood injury—and a broken nose from football that never healed properly."

"You saw all that?" Stone asked. "How?"

"I've known him since college; he's my ex-husband."

"Did you ever see his face?"

"No, but I know how he walks. I know his fascination with knives; he has a collection. It was Max."

"What's his last name?" Dino asked.

"Long."

"Address?"

"It used to be on Habersham Road in Atlanta, big house. He's living in an apartment now. I don't know where; it's just what I've heard. Maybe one of his own developments."

"But in Atlanta."

"Yes. He wouldn't go any farther from Habersham Road than he had to." She was perfectly collected now.

Dino produced his cell phone. "I'll get the precinct looking for him now."

"No, don't," Carrie said, putting her hand over the cell phone. "I can't have this in the papers."

"Carrie," Stone said, "if you know Max was the guy, then we have to get him off the street. He knows where you live."

"Monday morning I start rehearsals, the biggest break of my life," she said. "I've been all over the papers for two days; they would just love this."

Stone looked at Dino and shook his head. "Do you have an alarm system in your apartment?" he asked Carrie.

"No."

"Is there another entrance besides the front door?"

"Yes. There's a rear door from the kitchen and stairs down to a garden."

"Excuse me for a minute," Stone said. He walked into the empty dining room next door and made a call to Bob Cantor, an ex-cop who did many jobs for him.

"Cantor."

"Bob, it's Stone."

"Hey, Stone. What's up?"

"I need a bodyguard for a woman first thing tomorrow morning at my house. Her name is Carrie Cox; she's at Elaine's with me. Are you free right now?"

"Yeah, but I'll put somebody else on guard duty."

"She needs a security system: double front door, kitchen door leading to a garden, the usual windows, front and rear."

"You got a key?"

"You can pick it up here."

"I'm on it."

"Listen, on the bodyguard, not too much

of a gorilla—she travels in polite circles—but somebody who can handle a man with a knife and deal with an angry ex-husband."

"Gotcha. I'll be there in half an hour." Cantor hung up, and Stone returned to the table.

"What did you do?" she asked.

"Tomorrow morning there will be somebody with you, and they will be until it's no longer necessary. Give me the key to your apartment."

She took a small ring from her purse, took off one of two identical keys, and handed it to him. "What for?"

"My friend is going to install a security system; it's probably going to take all night, because he does these things right, so you should come home with me tonight."

"All right."

Stone handed her a cocktail napkin and his pen. "Make a list of what you need from your apartment for the weekend; my friend will put it together and bring it to you."

Carrie began writing and filled up one side of the napkin, then the other.

Bob Cantor walked into the restaurant and stood at the front, waiting. Stone

waved him over and introduced him to Carrie.

"Hi, Bob," she said. "Let me explain this list to you, where everything is in the apartment." She took him through it, item by item, and told him where to find a suitcase.

"Got it," Cantor said, pocketing the list. "Do you have a photograph of your ex-husband?"

"No, I threw all of them away."

"What's his name and address?"

"Max Long, Atlanta. I don't know his street address."

"Your protection is named Willie Leahy. He'll be at your house with his brother Jimmy at nine tomorrow morning. You want them to rent a car? I think it's best; you can be a target while trying to get a cab."

"They can use my car," Stone said.

"Good idea, with the armor and all."

"You have an armored car?" Carrie asked.

"Lightly armored," Stone said. "It came that way, and it'll stop a bullet."

"You," Carrie said, putting her hand on his and squeezing, "are the second-best thing to happen to me in a long time."

7

CARRIE SLEPT IN STONE'S ARMS for most of the night, and neither of them was much interested in sex. Stone took a handgun out of his safe and kept it in the bedside drawer.

Carrie didn't wake up when he gently disengaged from her. He put on a robe, went down to the kitchen, and made them bacon and scrambled eggs, English muffins, coffee, and orange juice, then sent it upstairs in the dumbwaiter. He got the *Times* and went back upstairs to find Carrie sitting up in bed with a breakfast tray in her lap, barebreasted, which was all right with him.

"Your dumbwaiter woke me," she said. "A little bell went off."

Stone took his own tray from the dumbwaiter and got in bed with it, adjusting the back with the remote control. "I'm glad you're feeling better this morning," he said. She was digging into the breakfast with enthusiasm.

"I am, and I'm starved," she said.

Breakfast finished, he put their trays back into the dumbwaiter and sent it downstairs. He poured them both some more coffee and got back into bed. "I need to know a lot more about your ex-husband," he said, "if I'm going to be able to help."

"What do you want to know?" she asked, sipping her coffee.

"How long were you married?"

"Nine years."

"What was the character of the marriage?"

"At first, okay, then increasingly distant, then finally violent."

"You beat him up?"

She laughed. "I got in a couple of good licks," she said, "but I got the worst of it. I moved in with a girlfriend and got a lawyer."

"Tell me about the settlement."

"He wouldn't settle, so it was really an award by the judge. I got the house on Habersham, which I sold immediately, half his brokerage account, which I put into a municipal bond fund, and one million dollars in cash, most of which I invested conservatively."

"Did the house have a mortgage?"

"No; times were good when he bought it. He paid a million two, and I sold it for four and a half million."

"So, you've got several million dollars squirreled away."

"Winter always comes," she said.

"What is he so mad about?" Stone asked.

"The fact that I left him and the size of the award. It amounted to half of what he had."

"He was surprised that you divorced him after he beat you up?"

"Not surprised, I think, just angry. It made the papers, and that made him look bad. He's angry about the award, because he wouldn't have given me a dime, unless he had been forced to. He's mad, too, because he knows that he could have settled

for less than the judge gave me. That *really* got him angry. That and the fact that, in the real estate crunch, he's lost most of what he had left."

"Does he have anything to gain by killing you? Insurance, maybe?"

"No."

"So, it's just irrational anger?"

"That's what he's good at."

"You said you don't know his address in Atlanta?"

"That's right."

The doorbell rang on his phone, and Stone pressed the speaker button. "Yes?"

"It's Bob. I've got Carrie's luggage, and the Leahys are here."

"Take the Leahys to the kitchen. There's coffee already made and Danish in the fridge. We'll be down in a few minutes." He pressed the button again and turned to Carrie. "We'd better get dressed; Bob is going to want to brief you about your security."

THEY FOUND the three men sitting at the kitchen counter, drinking coffee and eating pastries.

"Morning, Carrie," Cantor said. "This is Willie and Jimmy Leahy."

The two husky men waved.

"Tell her what she needs to know," Stone said, and they both sat down.

Bob handed Carrie his card. "Your security code is written on the back: 1357. I tried to make it easy. You've got a keypad in your living room, next to the front door, another in the kitchen, next to the back door, and another upstairs, next to your bed." He handed her a bunch of keys. "I've changed the locks on your front and rear doors; the old ones were worthless. All the exterior windows are alarmed."

"Got it," she said. "Can I change the code?"

He handed her an instruction book. "Easily. The instructions are in here."

"Thank you, Bob. Send me your bill."

"Will do. Now, let me explain Willie and Jimmy. One of them drives the car; one sits in the back with you. The car doors will be locked at all times. When you get somewhere, say to the theater, one opens the door for you. Don't ever, *ever* open your own door. He comes inside with you

and remains close, while the other deals with the car and then joins you inside or just sits in the car, depending on the circumstances.

"One of them stays in your apartment at night, near the stairs up to your bedroom. They'll take turns. They're both armed, and they're very good at dealing with assaults without killing the perpetrator, but they may have to. You'll have to leave that to their judgment."

"I'm happy to do that," Carrie said.

"If you go to someone's home, say a dinner party, one will stay outside their door; there'll be no intrusion into your privacy unless it's necessary to protect you."

"Thank you."

"Carrie," Stone said, "does your husband own a handgun?"

"Yes, at least a dozen. He collects them, along with knives."

"He's not going to get a handgun from Atlanta to New York on an airplane," Bob said.

"Maybe not," Stone admitted, "but if he's a planner, he could send one to his hotel by an overnight shipper."

"Right," Bob said. "We'll keep that in mind. Any questions, Carrie?"

"No, I don't think so."

Stone spoke up. "Bob, we need to locate Max Long in Atlanta; Carrie doesn't know his address. You know somebody down there?" Cantor had a network of ex-cops who handled this sort of thing.

"Sure thing. Last known address?"

Carrie gave him the Habersham address.

"I want to know if somebody in Atlanta can place him in New York last night, besides Carrie," Stone said. "Could be important later."

"What's wrong with me?" Carrie asked. "I can place him here."

"You said you didn't see his face," Stone replied. "It wouldn't hold up in court. We need copies of a plane ticket or a hotel reservation or a credit card record. Somebody who drove him to the airport would help."

"I'll deal with it," Cantor said. "What's your schedule like today?" he asked Carrie.

"I've got an accompanist coming to my place at one o'clock," Carrie said. "I have a score to learn."

"Willie and Jimmy are ready when you are," Cantor replied.

"Now is good," she said.

Stone put his keys on the counter. "You know how to get into the garage, Bob." He turned to Carrie. "There's a house key there, too. Remember, you're sleeping here tonight," Stone said, "just in case he's still in town."

"Her suitcase is in the living room," Cantor said, tossing the keys to Willie, "and so is a cardboard box she wants to send to her ex-husband."

"Bob, you keep the box for when we find out his address," Stone said. He turned to Carrie. "I think you're in good shape now."

"I feel very safe," Carrie replied. She kissed Stone and followed Cantor and the Leahys to the garage.

8

STONE TOOK CARRIE'S SUITCASE upstairs and put her things in a closet and chest of drawers. As he was about to get into the shower, the phone rang. He noticed that the caller ID showed the call as being from area code 404: Atlanta. He grabbed a pen and wrote down the number, then he pressed a button on the phone to have the conversation recorded.

"Hello?"

"Is this Stone Barrington?" A male voice, deep, the accent southern, the words a little slurred.

"Hello, Max," Stone said.

There was a moment's silence. "So you know who I am?"

"I don't know all that many people in Atlanta. Are you back home now?"

"Maybe."

"I have some things to send you," Stone said. "What's your mailing address?"

Max Long gave him a post office box number.

"No. I'm sending the package FedEx; I need the street address and phone number."

"What are you sending?"

"Some things that Carrie thought you might like to have. She found them when she unpacked."

"What things?"

"I don't know; I haven't opened the package."

"I'm not giving you my address," Long said.

"Whatever. I don't really care whether you get this stuff. I'll put it out with the garbage. Why did you want to speak to me?"

"I want to speak to Carrie."

"She isn't here, and she doesn't want to talk to you. After the encounter last night, she wants nothing further to do with you."

"So you're the new boyfriend, then?"

"I'm her attorney."

"Why does she need an attorney?"

"I'm also a retired police detective with excellent contacts in law enforcement."

"So you're going to protect her?"

"You can count on it, and let me give you some free advice: The New York Police Department takes a very dim view of a person carrying any sort of weapon on the streets of the city, gun or knife. Anyone caught with a weapon can count on jail time, and you wouldn't enjoy our penal system."

"So you're threatening me?"

"Certainly not. I'm just giving you good advice. Here's another good piece: Stay away from Carrie. She's taking out a protection order, barring you from coming within a city block of her. Violate that, and you'll do jail time. You see, there'll be lots of opportunities for you to go to jail."

"Tell her to give me back my money, and I'll leave her alone," Long said.

"Ah, now, that's extortion. Did I mention that I'm recording this conversation?"

"You can't do that."

"It's already done," Stone said. "Now tell

me if you want this package, because I'm tired of talking to you."

"Go fuck yourself," Long said.

"I'll take that as a 'no,'" Stone said. "Tell me, are you always drunk at this hour of the day?"

Long hung up. Stone called Bob Cantor.

"Hello?"

"I've just had a phone call from Max Long. Here's the number." Stone recited it. "He wouldn't give up his address, but if it's his home number you can trace it back. It may be a cell phone, in which case he could still be in the city, and he's drunk."

"That prefix is a cell phone," Cantor said. "If it's not a throwaway I can get an address for it."

"He gave me a P.O. box number," Stone said, giving it to him.

"That's harder, because it's federal, but one of my Atlanta contacts might be able to do something."

"I'll get Dino to trace the location of the cell phone," Stone said.

"Anything else?" Cantor asked.

"Not at the moment." Stone hung up and called Dino.

"Lieutenant Bacchetti."

"I just got a call from Carrie's husband, from a cell phone. He may still be in town; will you run the number for a location?" Stone gave him the number.

"I'll get back to you," Dino said, then hung up.

Stone shaved, showered, and dressed, then he took the *Times* down to his study with a second cup of coffee. He had finished reading the paper and was on the crossword when the phone rang.

"Hello?"

"It's Dino. Your guy was calling from La-Guardia, at a gate that a Delta flight is scheduled to depart from in five minutes. He may have already been on the plane."

"Thanks, Dino."

"Dinner?"

"Sure. See you then." Stone hung up and called Bob Cantor.

"Cantor."

"Bob, Max Long called from LaGuardia, and he's apparently on a Delta flight to Atlanta, leaving now."

"I'll have somebody pick up on him there and follow him home. You want my guy to say anything to him?"

"You might have him give Long the impression that he's under constant police surveillance, without using those words."

"Give me a description."

"Get that from Carrie," Stone said. "I've never seen the man. I just know that he's tall and slim."

"Will do," Cantor said. He hung up.

Stone went back to the crossword. It was a bitch, as it often was on Saturdays. He was still working on it nearly three hours later when Cantor called back.

"Hello?"

"It's Cantor. My guy met your guy and imparted your suggestion to him. He's tailing him now. I ran his license plate, but it's still registered to the Habersham Road address; he didn't bother to change it after moving. I'll call you back when I get an address."

"Good going," Stone said. He went to the kitchen, made a ham and mozzarella sandwich on whole grain, toasted it, and brought it back to the study with a Diet Coke. He finished it and was down to the last couple of impossible words on the crossword when Cantor called again.

"Got a pencil?"

"In my hand."

"Max Long drove to an apartment complex in northeast Atlanta called Cross Creek. Nice place, with a golf course. My guy couldn't follow him past the guard at the gate, but fifty got him the address: 1010 Cantey Place. His phone is unlisted, but I'll have it for you later. You want my guy to surveil?"

"For a couple of days."

"I can put a watch for his name on the Delta reservations computer," Cantor said.

"Great idea. That'll give us some notice if he decides to come back, and we can have him met at LaGuardia."

"Consider it done," Cantor said. "By the way, Max Long is six-three, two hundred pounds, longish dark hair going gray, broken nose. I'll do a search for a photo; shouldn't be hard to come up with one."

"Sounds like we've got the guy just about boxed," Stone said.

"We're getting there."

"Talk to you later." Stone hung up and attacked the last two words on the crossword. They took another half hour.

9

STONE AND DINO HAD BEEN at Elaine's just long enough to order a drink, when Carrie came rushing in, flushed and excited. Stone signaled for a drink for her. "You look happy," he said.

"I feel happy," she said. "I've got two very good solos in the show and one absolute, solid-gold showstopper."

"I look forward to hearing them," Stone said.

"Not until opening night; I want you to get the full effect."

"I'm already getting the full effect," he

replied. Their drinks arrived, and they clinked glasses.

Dino spoke up. "It's nice to see you both so happy."

"If you'd had my day," Carrie said, "you'd be happy, too."

"I *am* happy," Dino said. "Can't you tell?"

"He always looks dour," Stone said. "You could know him for years before seeing him smile."

"Do you have a wife, Dino?" Carrie asked.

"Had. Don't want another."

"A girl?"

"Until recently."

"What happened?"

"I got tired of obeying. Stone and I spent a little time in Key West, and I discovered I didn't miss her."

"He smiled more then," Stone said.

"If I goose him, will he smile?" Carrie asked.

"If you goose me in the right place," Dino said.

Carrie laughed, a healthy, unrestrained sound. Dino smiled a little.

"There, I knew I could do it," she said.

"So, do you know your script and score?" Stone asked.

"I will by Monday morning," she said.

"How'd it go with Bob and the Leahys?"

"Bob showed me how to work the security system, then left with Max's box to take it to FedEx. The Leahys are sweet and made me feel very safe. They dropped me off here, and I've dismissed them until Monday morning."

"I think we've got Max pretty boxed in now," Stone said, "so you shouldn't have to worry. I wouldn't go back to Atlanta any time soon, though, or if you do, don't tell anybody who might tell him."

"How long will we have to deal with this?" she asked.

"It could go two ways: Either he'll mellow with time, like most people, or he'll obsess about it until he can't stand it anymore, and then make a move."

"Knowing Max, it's going to be the latter," she said. "He's the obsessive type, believe me."

"Then we'll just have to be ready for him," Stone said.

"Am I going to have to have bodyguards for long?"

"Hard to say. Cantor and I may feel better about it in a week or ten days, but when the show opens, that's when we'll have to watch ourselves."

"You mean, watch me."

"Well, yes. In the meantime, I'll cultivate his dislike for me. I'm already off to a good start, after only one phone conversation."

"Why?"

"We'll see if we can deflect him from you to me. By the way, on Monday morning we're going to get you a protection order from the court and have it served on him in Atlanta."

"If you say so," Carrie replied, "but I have to warn you, he has a broad antiau-thoritarian streak. I used to have to pay his speeding tickets to keep him from get-ting arrested, and he missed a couple of court appearances during the divorce process."

"Still, if he violates it, it's an excuse to put him behind bars, and that's where I'd like him to be."

"So would I," Carrie said.

"What was in the box you sent him?" Stone asked.

Carrie sighed. "Two guns he gave me,

and some small things of his that somehow got packed with my stuff—neckties, cuff links, socks, things like that."

"Maybe you should have kept the guns," Stone said.

"I still have one."

"Don't take it out of the house; New York City has a very rigid licensing law, and they turn down everybody who applies, unless you're carrying around a briefcase full of diamonds or large sums of cash. The city believes that protecting property is more important than protecting life."

"But you have a gun," she said. "I saw you put it in the bedside table."

"I have several guns, but retired cops get licenses. Dino's packing right now, but he's still on the force, so he has to."

"The one I have is small enough to put in my purse," she said.

"Have you had any firearms training?"

"I fired a .22 rifle at camp when I was twelve."

"Then you're more likely to hurt yourself or an innocent bystander than Max."

"You underestimate me."

"Maybe so, but here's the sort of thing that happens. Maybe you're injured in a

taxi accident, and the EMTs come. At the hospital they go through your purse, looking for ID and an address, and they find your gun and call the cops. Then we're in court, and believe me, you wouldn't want to go through that."

"So I'm vulnerable."

"You have the Leahys, Dino and me, and Cantor. You have your security system and a phone to call 911. If you have to do that, tell the operator that someone has broken into your house and you're hiding. That will get immediate attention."

Dino gave her his card. "Put my cell phone number into your speed-dial list," he said. "You can always get my immediate attention, even though you're not in my precinct."

She took out her cell phone and entered the number. "Thank you, Dino."

The waiter came with menus, and they talked about other things.

10

ON MONDAY MORNING the Leahys picked up Carrie and took her to her first rehearsal, and Stone went to work in his office, as usual. Shortly after ten o'clock, Joan buzzed Stone. "Bob Cantor on one."

Stone pressed the button. "Good morning, Bob. Did you have a nice weekend?"

"I did until a minute ago," Cantor said.

"What's up?"

"I had my people in Atlanta on Max Long all weekend. They found a cooperative guard on the apartment complex gate who let them in for a hundred. He was in and out until yesterday afternoon, and then he

seemed to hunker down for the evening. Then, this morning, FedEx delivered the box I sent him, and nobody answered the door. Since it required a signature, the guy put it back on the truck.

"My guy got suspicious when this happened. He called Long's phone number, but there was no answer. Finally, he looked in some windows, and there's nobody home. His car is still parked outside."

"So, he got past your guy?"

"His place is on the ground floor; he could have left by a back window and called a cab, I guess. This is not good."

"No, it's not. Did the airline's reservation computer alarm go off?"

"Nope."

"If he booked under a false name, he'd have to show ID at the ticket counter, wouldn't he?"

"Yes, but he could have made a reservation under another name and had an e-ticket e-mailed to him."

"Have you warned the Leahys?"

"Yep, and that's about all we can do for the moment. Carrie is rehearsing at the theater, isn't she?"

"Yeah. Since Del Wood owns the theater, they didn't have to go to a studio."

"How many ways in?"

"Front doors are locked, so the stage door is the only way. There's a guard there, and we've alerted him, but he's an old guy, and it might not be too hard to get past him."

"Keep in touch." Stone hung up.

TEN MINUTES LATER, Joan buzzed him. "Carrie Cox on one."

"Hello?"

"What's going on?"

"What do you mean?"

"I mean, the Leahys are all over me."

"That's their job."

"Has something happened?"

"Am I interrupting your rehearsal?"

"No. I'm in the ladies' room on a break."

"Max has disappeared from his apartment, and we don't know where he is."

"Wasn't somebody watching him?"

"Apparently, he went out a back window."

"Is he on his way to New York?"

"There was no Delta reservation in his name, but he could already be here, so listen to the Leahys."

"How's the weather?"

"What?"

"Between here and Atlanta," she said.

"Jesus, I don't know. When I got up this morning the national forecast was for good weather for the entire East Coast."

"Then he's in his airplane."

"He has an airplane?"

"Yes."

"Why didn't you mention that before?"

"It didn't come up."

"What kind of airplane?"

"It's a King something or other."

"A King Air?"

"Yes."

"With two engines?"

"Right."

"What's the tail number?"

"N-something," she said.

"Every airplane in the United States is N-something."

"I don't remember the rest."

"Does he often fly to New York?"

"Sometimes."

"Where does he land?"

"I don't know, exactly."

"Did you ever fly to New York with him?"

"Yes."

"Where did he land?"

"I don't remember."

"How did you get from the airport to New York?"

"In a limo."

"Did you go through a tunnel?"

"No, we went over a bridge, the big one."

"The George Washington Bridge?"

"That's the one."

"Did you land at Teterboro?"

"Yes, that's it!"

"When you got out of the airplane you were at an FBO. Do you remember its name?"

"You mean, like a terminal?"

"Like that, but for private aircraft."

"What are some FBOs?"

"Jet Aviation, Meridian Aviation, Atlantic Aviation, Furst Avia . . ."

"Atlantic, that's it!"

"Is that where he always lands?"

"I guess so."

"Is there anything else you haven't told me about how Max travels?"

"I don't think so."

"How's your rehearsal going?"

"We're just reading through the script right now. Gotta run!" She hung up.

Stone got on his computer and went to the FAA aircraft registry, then typed in "Max Long" in the search engine. Nothing. Must be owned by a corporation. Stone called Cantor.

"Cantor."

"It's Stone. Carrie forgot to mention that Max Long owns an airplane, a King Air."

"I thought he was broke."

"Me, too. He usually lands at Teterboro, at Atlantic Aviation."

"Got a tail number?"

"That would be too easy."

"I'm on it." Cantor hung up.

Stone was left, tapping his foot. Twenty minutes later, Cantor called back.

"I'm here."

"He landed at ten fifteen last night. Teterboro Limousine took him to the Lowell Hotel, on East Sixty-Third Street."

"You may need more than the Leahys," Stone said.

"What, for a guy with a knife?"

"There's nothing to stop him from carrying a gun on a private airplane."

"Oh. Okay, I'll get up to the Lowell now, see what I can see. I don't think we'll need more people. I'll let the Leahys know that

he may be packing, but I think the two of them can handle him."

"If you say so," Stone said.

HALF AN hour later, Bob Cantor walked into the Lowell, a small, elegant Upper East Side hotel, carrying a box from a florist's shop. He approached the front desk. "Good morning," he said.

"Good morning," the desk clerk replied. "May I help you?"

"Do you have a Max Long registered here?" Cantor asked.

The man consulted his computer. "Yes, we do." He reached out for the box. "He's out just now; I'll take the flowers."

"Just tell Mr. Long that Stone Barrington says, 'Hi,'" Cantor said. He turned and walked out of the hotel, dumped the empty box in the trash can on the corner, and called Stone.

"Hello?"

"It's Cantor. Long is registered at the Lowell but on the loose."

"Swell."

11

BOB CANTOR DROVE HIS VAN down to the theater district, parked fifty yards from the Del Wood Theater, and turned down the sun visor with the NYPD badge on it, so as not to be bothered. He sat there through the morning, lunching on a sandwich he had packed before leaving his apartment downtown. In his pocket he had the protection order Stone had obtained over the weekend from a friendly judge.

He opened a book of *New York Times* crossword puzzles and began his routine: read a definition, then look outside while thinking of the answer. This was not his

first stakeout. He had finished two of the puzzles, occasionally peeing into a bag designed for use on small airplanes, and was working on a third puzzle when he saw the tall man approaching the theater from the direction of Eighth Avenue. He popped open his cell phone and pressed a speed-dial button without taking his eyes off the man.

"It's Willie," one of the Leahys said.

"It's Cantor. Guy coming toward the theater, answers the description. He's wearing a raincoat, hands in his pockets, so watch out."

"I'm on it," Willie said, then hung up.

Cantor hopped out of the van and pressed the lock button on his remote key. He had a quarter of a million dollars' worth of electronic equipment in the van, and he was taking no chances. He had to wait for a procession of cars to pass before crossing the street, and he made it to the alley down which lay the stage door just as the man did.

"Mr. Long?" he said. "Is that you?"

The man turned and looked at him. "Do I know you?"

"I've got something for you," Cantor said, handing him the envelope.

The man stared at it but did not take his hands out of his raincoat pockets.

With his left hand, leaving his right in his own coat pocket, Cantor tucked the envelope into the top of the man's raincoat. "You've been served," he said.

"Served with what?"

"A protection order from the Supreme Court of New York State," Cantor said. "It orders you to remain at least a hundred yards away from Ms. Carrie Cox at all times, and you're violating it at this very moment."

"That's ridiculous," Long said, ripping open the envelope and looking at the document.

"I'm afraid it's very serious," Cantor said. "As you can see at the bottom, the penalty for violating the order is thirty days in jail and a thousand-dollar fine. Oh, and did I mention that New York State has a very effective antistalking law? You could get a lot more time by violating that." Cantor reached up and took the taller man's arm, high under the armpit, and gently steered

him down the street toward Broadway. "There will be people watching you every moment you're in New York or Atlanta," he said, "so don't give Stone Barrington an opportunity to put you in jail."

Cantor had not lied about Long's being watched, because as he held his arm, he had attached a tiny bug to the armpit of Long's raincoat that emitted a radio signal. Cantor stopped walking. "Bye-bye," he said. "Enjoy your stay in our city." He turned and walked back toward the theater, then stopped at the entrance to the alley and looked back. Long was moving quickly toward Broadway.

Cantor ducked into the alley and went to the stage door. When he opened it Willie Leahy was standing there. "I served him the order," Cantor said, "and warned him off. I got a bug on him, too, so we'll know if he's within five hundred yards." He handed Willie a small, black object that looked like a pager. "If this beeps, he's around. A distance in yards will appear on the display."

"Gotcha," Willie said, looking at the thing. "He's two fifty and moving away."

"Okay," Cantor said. "You don't need me anymore, so I'm outta here."

"Thanks, Bob," Willie was saying as Cantor closed the stage door.

Cantor went back to his van and called Stone.

"HELLO?"

"I caught up with our friend Max outside the theater. I served him, gave him a little talk about the antistalking law, and attached a bug to his raincoat at the armpit, where he's unlikely to notice it. Willie Leahy has a pager thing that gives him a distance on Max if he's within five hundred yards."

"Good day's work, Bob."

"I mentioned your name, since you apparently want him pissed off at you."

"Better me than Carrie," Stone said. "Let's hope he makes a move, so Dino can fall on him from a great height."

"Yeah," Cantor said. "I'd feel a lot better with him in jail. Oh, I also left him a message from you at the front desk of his hotel. He's gonna feel surrounded by you."

Stone laughed. "I like it."

"Listen, you watch your ass," Cantor said. "It wouldn't do to underestimate his guy. I did a background check, and in his youth

he was a marine. Those guys don't lack confidence."

"I'll keep that in mind," Stone said. "Thanks, Bob." He hung up and called Carrie's cell phone, got voice mail, and left her a message.

She called back an hour later. "What?" she said.

"Max is in town. Bob Cantor served him with the protection order. He's now wearing an electronic bug that will let the Leahys know if he's near."

"Wow, how did you do that?"

"It's the sort of thing, among many other things, that Bob Cantor does."

"Why don't you come over to my place tonight, and we'll order in some Chinese?"

"Sounds good. You're sure you're not going to be too tired?"

"No. I'm wired, but you can give me a back rub."

"I'll rub anything you like," Stone said. "See you at seven."

STONE ARRIVED on Carrie's doorstep at the same time as the deliveryman from the Chinese restaurant. He paid the man and rang the bell.

"Yes?" Carrie said on the intercom.

"Chinese delivery," Stone said, and was buzzed in.

Carrie met him at the door. "Very funny, Chinese guy," she said, laughing and taking the food from him. She went into the kitchen and made a little buffet of the containers, and they served themselves. They had dinner on the floor in front of the living room fireplace and shared a bottle of wine, while a Leahy waited outside her apartment door.

"I'm in love with Bob Cantor," she said. "How do you know him?"

"From when I was on the NYPD. He and Dino and I were in the same detective squad. By the time Bob retired and went into business for himself, I was practicing law, and he's been invaluable to me ever since."

"How come you stopped being a policeman?"

"Because I stopped a bullet with my knee, and when my captain and I had a little disagreement over the conduct of a case, he used that to force me into medical retirement."

"That's shitty," she said.

"Not entirely," Stone replied. "When you retire because of an in-the-line-of-duty disability, you get a pension of seventy-five percent of your pay, tax free. If you've got to be forced out, it's a nice good-bye kiss."

When they finished dinner, she took away their dishes and then came back and sat between his legs.

"I believe you were going to give me a back rub," she said.

"That's how we're going to start," Stone said, starting.

12

WHEN STONE GOT to his desk the following morning, there was a note on his desk from Joan. "Bill Eggers wants to see you ASAP," it read.

Stone walked over to the offices of Woodman & Weld, the law firm to which he was of counsel. Bill Eggers was its senior attorney and managing partner. When Stone had been forced out of the NYPD, Eggers, an old friend from NYU Law School, had taken him to lunch and suggested that Stone put his law degree to work for Woodman & Weld. Stone had taken a cram course for the bar and passed, and Eggers

had started feeding him cases, the sort that the firm didn't want to be seen handling. The work from Woodman & Weld amounted to well over half of Stone's income, and when Eggers called, Stone answered.

Bill Eggers waved him to a chair. "How are you, Stone?"

"Very well, thanks, Bill."

"I had a call this morning from an old friend of mine who's a top guy in the biggest law firm in Atlanta," Eggers said. "It seems you're representing the ex-wife of an important client of his, and I use the word *representing* loosely."

"You would be referring to Carrie Cox, former spouse of the creep Max Long? And I use the word *creep* expansively."

"That I would."

"From what I've heard I'm surprised to hear that Mr. Long can afford to retain an attorney who doesn't advertise on late-night television," Stone said.

"My friend brought me up to date on Mr. Long's affairs, so I'll bring you up to date. After his divorce he went through a bad patch, complicated by the shortage of money from the banks, and he lost a bundle. Shortly after that he acquired copious

financing from a Saudi prince who keeps a
house in Atlanta, and whose poker buddy
he is. He used the money wisely, buying
up prime parcels of land that were going at
foreclosure prices and selling chunks of it
to other investors at a handsome profit. His
company is now earning money, and Mr.
Long's personal fortune has been recov-
ered well into eight figures."

"I'm sorry to hear it," Stone said.

"I wanted you to hear it, because I suspect that you've been operating on the
assumption that Mr. Long did not have the
resources to be much of a problem to you."

"I confess I was operating on that assumption," Stone said. "I'm also operating
on the assumption that Mr. Long is a real
and proximate danger to Ms. Cox and that
he is obsessive about her."

"It's clear," Eggers said, "that you are
relying on the testimony of Ms. Cox."

"I am. She seems a smart and sensible
woman."

"My friend's firm in Atlanta represented
Mr. Long in his divorce, and he formed a
somewhat different opinion of Ms. Cox."

"That's not surprising," Stone said. "Divorce attorneys often adopt the opinions

of their clients; they represent clients better, if they believe them."

"He tells me that, on two occasions, Ms. Cox made attempts on Mr. Long's life, once with a gun and once with a straight razor, which I thought was a quaint choice of weapon."

"Then why isn't she in prison?"

"Because Mr. Long would not bring charges against her and because he managed to keep the police out of it, even to the extent of having his personal physician come to his home and repair the damage from the razor, to the tune of more than a hundred stitches. Mr. Long required a transfusion, as well."

"If that is true, one would think that Mr. Long would be giving Ms. Cox a wide berth, would one not?"

"Apparently," Eggers said, "the man still loves her, and we know how that is. He gave her an inordinately generous divorce settlement without complaint, and if that isn't love, I don't know what is."

"Those things generally arise from necessity, not love," Stone observed. "It's my understanding that a judge allotted the

marital assets. After all, they had been married for nine years."

"It was less than three years," Eggers said. "My friend's view is that his client, besotted, spent a fortune on Ms. Cox's training as an actress and dancer, not to mention her wardrobe and jewelry, before and during the marriage, and that she returned the favor by sleeping with her acting teacher, her dancing coach, and whoever else was handy. My friend described her as sexually wanton."

"A trait I've always admired in a woman," Stone said.

"Though not necessarily in a client," Eggers pointed out.

"Bill, do you have some suggestion about my course of action in this case?"

"I do, though I know you are unlikely to accept any such suggestion."

"I'll try to be broad-minded," Stone said.

"I suggest that you extricate yourself from this woman's clutches as quickly as you can politely do so, because if my friend's opinion is of any consequence, she will eventually turn on you, and she may still own that razor."

"I must say that I hadn't noticed that I was in her, as you put it, 'clutches,'" Stone said.

"Perhaps 'clenches' would have been a better word," Eggers said.

"Perhaps, but that is not a bad place to be."

Eggers sighed. "All right, I suppose the only other thing I can do is to exhort you to be very, very careful in your dealings with her and to keep your physician's number in your pocket."

"All right, I'll do that," Stone said.

"That said, I have something for you."

"Oh, good. Wayward wife? Wayward son?" A good deal of Stone's work for Woodman & Weld had involved one or the other.

"Wayward daughter," Eggers said.

"Uh-oh."

"Exactly." Eggers wrote something on a slip of paper and handed it to Stone. "Her name is Hildy Parsons, and this is her address and phone number."

"What is her particular problem?" Stone asked.

"How much time do you have?"

"I'm at your disposal."

"All right, it began in high school, when she had an affair with one of her teachers that resulted in his firing and her transferring to an institution operated by nuns. Her father managed to keep this business fairly quiet, and the girl is very bright, so she actually got into Harvard and earned her degree in the usual four years, though she formed a number of other inappropriate attachments along the way."

"And what sort of inappropriate attachment has she now formed?" Stone asked.

"An artist," Eggers said, "or so he styles himself. He has a studio downtown somewhere, from which he is alleged to be operating a dealership in drugs. Her father is concerned first that he might persuade her to partake and second that when the authorities finally nail him, she will be charged as an accessory—before, during, and/or after the fact."

"Is her father Philip Parsons, the art dealer on East Fifty-seventh Street?"

"He is, and I think it a good idea if you visit with him." Eggers consulted the eighteenth-century clock in the corner behind his desk. "You won't need an appointment; he's expecting you in ten minutes."

"And what, exactly, does Mr. Parsons expect me to do?"

"I'm sure that will emerge in your chat with him," Eggers said.

Stone got to his feet. "You did tell him that I don't do contract killings, didn't you?"

Eggers shook his hand. "I don't believe I mentioned that," he said. "Good day, Stone, and please, please be careful."

Stone left, still feeling unendangered.

13

STONE WALKED FROM EGGERS'S OFFICE in the Seagram Building, up Park Avenue, and took a left on East Fifty-seventh Street. On the way he pondered his friend's information about Carrie and decided to discount ninety-five percent of it as the rant of a rejected husband, but he was not entirely sure of which five percent to believe.

His reverie was interrupted when he arrived at the Parsons Gallery, a wide building with a gorgeous Greek sculpture of a woman's head spotlighted in the center of the window. Stone approached a very beautiful and impossibly thin young woman

who was seated at a desk thumbing through a catalogue.

"Good morning. Can I help you?" she asked.

"My name is Stone Barrington. I believe Mr. Parsons is expecting me."

She consulted a typed list of names on her desk. "Yes, Mr. Barrington," she said. "Would you take the elevator to the fourth floor?" She pointed. "Someone will meet you."

Because she was so beautiful, Stone thanked her and did as he was told. He was met on the fourth floor by an equally beautiful but less bony woman in her thirties, he judged.

"Mr. Barrington? I'm Rita Gammage. Good morning. Please come this way."

Stone followed her down a hallway to an open door, where she left him. Inside the office a man who was talking on the telephone waved him to a chair on the other side of his desk.

Before sitting down, Stone made a slow, 360-degree swivel to look at the walls. He recognized a Bonnard, a Freud, a Modigliani, and two Picassos among the work

hanging there. He sat down and turned his attention to the man on the phone.

He appeared to be in his early sixties and was handsome in a tweedy sort of way. He was wearing a cashmere cardigan over a Turnbull & Asser shirt, and he needed a haircut, or, perhaps, he had had it cut in such a way as to seem to need a haircut.

The man hung up and stood, extending his hand. "I'm Philip Parsons," he said. "I expect you're Mr. Barrington."

Stone stood and shook the hand, then sat down again. "It's Stone, please." He waved a hand. "I think this is the most extraordinary collection I've seen in someone's office."

"Thank you," Parsons said, seeming pleased with the compliment.

"Are these part of your inventory or your own collection?"

"These are all mine," Parsons said. "Occasionally, I tire of a piece and sell it, but most of these things I bought many years ago, when an ordinary person could still do that."

Stone wondered how Parsons defined *ordinary*. "You're fortunate to have them."

"Yeesss," Parsons drawled, but then went quiet.

"Bill Eggers suggested I come and see you," Stone said unnecessarily, but somebody had to get to the point. "How may I help you?"

Parsons gazed out the window at the facade of the Four Seasons Hotel across the street and finally mustered some words. "I'm sorry if I seem halting," he said, "but I find it difficult to speak about my daughter."

"Tell me a little about her," Stone said.

"She was a beautiful child, looked extraordinarily like her mother, who died when she was six. I'm afraid I may have relied too much on help to raise her."

"I expect being a single father is difficult," Stone said.

"Well, I was building this gallery, and it took nearly all of my waking hours traveling, searching for good work; cultivating artists and buyers; evenings spent at openings, my own and others. You seem to have a good eye. Do you know art?"

"My mother was a painter," Stone said. "I spent a good deal of my youth in museums and galleries."

"What is her name?"

"Matilda Stone."

"My goodness, what a fine painter. She's not still alive, is she?"

"No, she's been gone for many years."

"Twice I've had paintings of hers to sell, and they both went very quickly. I think I must have asked too little." He turned and looked at Stone. "Do you have any of her work?"

"I have four oils—village scenes."

"She was renowned for her Washington Square pieces."

"Yes, we lived near the square."

"I'd love to see them some time."

"I'd be happy to show them to you," Stone said. "You must come for a drink."

"Where do you live?"

"I have a house in Turtle Bay."

"I will make a point of it," Parsons said, then turned to gaze at the hotel. "Hildy's troubles began, I suppose, with the onset of puberty. I don't know if all girls have such a hard time with the transition, but she certainly did. Her grandmother, who never really thought I should have been allowed to raise her, was scandalized, and she found that Catholic school to send her

to. It was far too rigid an environment for a free spirit like Hildy, but I didn't know what else to do."

"How old is Hildy now?" Stone asked, hoping to bring him to the present.

"Twenty-four. She'll be twenty-five in three months, and she will then have free access to her trust, which came to her from her grandmother through her mother. I fear that three months after that, it will all be gone if she continues to see this man."

"What is his name?" Stone asked.

Parsons rummaged in a drawer and came up with a single sheet of paper. "Derek Sharpe, with an *e*," Parsons said, "né Mervin Pyle, in some squalid border town in Texas, forty-six years ago. No education to speak of; four marriages, three of them wealthy, though not when they were divorced. One of society's leeches, born to the task—trailer trash with a thin veneer of sophistication. I was appalled when I met him." He shoved the paper across the desk to Stone.

Stone glanced at it. "May I have this?"

"Yes. It was put together by a fairly seedy private detective for only twelve thousand dollars."

Stone scanned the document. "He got virtually all of it from the Internet; it cost him less than a hundred dollars. Is the man still on the case?"

"No, something about Mr. Derek Sharpe frightened him, I think. He took his money and ran."

"You should know that I'm not a private investigator but an attorney," Stone said. "However, I have access to good people who provide more and better value than this." He held up the paper.

"Yes. Eggers told me that," Parsons said.

"What would you like done?" Stone asked, and he steeled himself for the reply."

"If I could hire you to shoot him in the head, I would," Parsons said. "Forgive me, I know you're not in that business, and I would probably shrink from the task, if I met someone who was."

"Of course."

"I suppose what I want is for him to go away," Parsons said, "out of Hildy's life, never to see her again. But I don't know how to accomplish that. I've thought of try-ing to buy him off."

"I think that effort might be fruitless," Stone said, "unless you offered him a great deal—more than Hildy's trust fund—and maybe not even then. Does he know about her impending wealth?"

"I'm sure he does," Parsons said. "Hildy is not the sort to be closemouthed about anything."

"Perhaps we could begin by my meeting Mr. Sharpe," Stone said.

"Perhaps so," Parsons replied. He pushed a card across his desk. "I have an opening this evening on the second floor for a painter named Squires, who is *very* good. Hildy will be there, and I'm certain Mr. Sharpe will be tagging along."

Stone stood and put the invitation and the information on Sharpe into a pocket. "Then I'll come," he said, "and we'll see where we go from there."

The two men shook hands, and Stone departed the gallery. Why, he wondered as he walked home, had most of the women he knew been abused by men?

14

AS HE ENTERED HIS HOUSE through the office door, Joan waved a message at him. "Carrie Cox called," she said. "She wants you to call while she's on her lunch break."

Stone went into his office, buzzed his housekeeper, Helene, in the kitchen, and asked for a sandwich. Then he sat down at his desk and returned Carrie's call.

"Hello?" she said, and by the sound of her voice she seemed to be eating something.

"Hi, it's Stone."

"Oh, hi."

"How are your rehearsals going?"

"Just great!"

"That sounds delicious."

"It's something called a falafel," she said. "Exotic New York food, not bad. Are we doing something this evening?"

"I have to go to an opening for a painter," Stone replied. "Would you like to come?"

"No, I called to beg off whatever you had in mind; I have to learn the second act. Who's the painter?"

"Someone called Squire. I've never heard of him."

"I have," she said. "He's *very* good."

"That's what the gallery owner says."

"Who is he?"

"Philip Parsons."

"He's *very* big," she said.

"How do you, being from Atlanta, know all this New York stuff?"

"I am conversant with most of the arts," she said. "And besides, I read magazines."

"Aha. Tell me, do you own a straight razor?"

"Aha, yourself. You've been researching me."

"Do you?"

"No, but Max does. We were having an argument in the bathroom once, while he

was shaving, and I threw a bar of soap at him. He ducked, and in the process nearly cut his throat. I had to call the doctor."

"Oh."

"I suppose you've somehow heard Max's version of that story, in which I attacked him with the razor and murderous intentions."

"Something like that."

"Well, believe me, it's a lie."

"I believe you," Stone said, and he meant it. "Things uttered in divorce court sometimes take on too much color."

"You're *very* right," she replied.

"Call me tomorrow, when you get a break," Stone said.

"Wilco," she replied, then hung up.

STONE WALKED into the Parsons Gallery half an hour after the time on the invitation and joined the crowd walking up the stairs to the second floor. He lifted a glass of champagne from the tray of a passing waiter and was surprised at how good it was.

"We don't serve the cheap stuff at openings," said a female voice at his elbow.

He turned to find Rita Gammage standing there. She was really lovely, he thought.

Tall, slim without being skinny, with long, dark hair, and breasts that looked real in spite of her slimness. "You certainly do serve the good stuff," he said. "What is it?"

"Schramsberg. Philip feels it's the best California stuff and the patriotic thing to serve."

"The man is truly a patriot," Stone said. "Can I fetch you a glass?"

"No, thanks; I've already had my single allowable glass at an opening. Come let me show you Squire's work."

"What's his first name?" Stone asked.

"He doesn't use one, just Squire."

"Easier to remember that way, I guess." Stone walked slowly along a wall, taking in the work. "An American impressionist," he said. "I like that."

"So does the market," Rita said. "We sold half the stuff before tonight, and we've already sold half a dozen. There won't be anything left at the end of the evening."

"It's a big show," Stone said, "and I'm glad to hear of an artist getting a big paycheck. What's the price range?"

"Thirty to eighty thousand," Rita replied.

"That makes for a very nice paycheck indeed, even after the gallery's cut."

"A good paycheck for us, too, especially in this economy."

"A lot of people in this city don't have to cut back when the economy goes sour and the market is down."

"I guess half of a hundred-million-dollar portfolio is still fifty million," she said. "A person could scrape by on that."

"Indeed," Stone said, looking around. "Is Hildy Parsons here?"

"Behind you, just getting off the elevator," Rita replied.

Stone turned and looked. Hildy Parsons was an attractive young woman, blond and athletic-looking. The man with her was a different thing entirely.

"Is that Derek Sharpe?" he asked Rita.

"I'm afraid so," she said.

Sharpe was wearing a white suit a size too small for him, white shoes, no socks, and a black T-shirt. His hair was graying, greasy, and down to his shoulders.

"Good God," Stone said.

"My sentiments exactly."

"Grotesque," he said.

"I'm afraid that, in the art world, not everyone dresses as immaculately as you do," Rita said.

"Or gets a haircut," Stone added. "Would you introduce me to them?"

"I will, if you'll take me to dinner when I'm done here," she said.

"You've got a deal."

The couple moved into the room, and Stone followed Rita toward them.

"Hello, Hildy," Rita said, and the two women exchanged air kisses."

"Hi, Rita. You know Derek, don't you?"

"Of course," Hildy said without acknowledging the man. "And this is Stone Barrington."

Stone shook Hildy's hand and looked into her eyes. She seemed smarter than her choice of companion would indicate. "How do you do?" he said.

"This is Derek Sharpe, the painter," Hildy said.

Stone shook his hand and found it soft and damp. "How do you do?"

"I do very well," Sharpe replied.

"I'll bet you do," Stone said tonelessly. He turned back to Hildy. "You're Philip's daughter?"

"Sometimes," she said.

"He speaks fondly of you."

She looked at him in surprise. "When?"

"As recently as this morning."

"Well!" she breathed.

Rita jumped into the conversation. "Stone is a prospective client," she said. "Philip especially wanted him to see Squire's work."

"Oh, you must come downtown and see Derek's paintings," Hildy said.

"I'd like that."

She took a card from her purse and handed it to Stone. "Be sure and call first; he doesn't like to show people around when he's working."

"I'll certainly do that. Will you excuse me, please? I want to see the rest of Squire's pictures."

"Of course," Hildy said.

Stone nodded at Sharpe and peeled off toward another wall of paintings, glad to be increasing his distance from Sharpe. Rita went to greet some new arrivals.

Ten minutes later he heard a hubbub from the other end of the room and turned to see a knot of people gathered around a picture. He wandered over to see what was happening and saw that the picture had been slashed from one corner to another. Apparently, straight razors were coming back into vogue, he thought.

He looked around and saw Hildy Parsons and Derek Sharpe on the other side of the room, studiously looking away from the damaged painting.

15

THEY SAT AT Stone's favorite corner table at La Goulue, on Madison Avenue, sipping their drinks and looking at the menu. The waiter, a young Frenchwoman with a charming accent, came over, told them about the specials, and stood ready to take their order.

Rita ordered sweetbreads and Dover sole, while Stone went for the haricots verts salad and the strip steak. He picked a bottle of Côtes du Rhône, the house red.

"I know you want to know more about Derek Sharpe," Rita said.

"I'd like to hear anything you can tell

me," Stone replied. "I confess I don't understand why women are attracted to him."

Rita sipped her wine while she thought
about that. "I think it's a combination of the
bad-boy thing and the art, and I should
place quotes around that."

"Not good, huh?"

"He's an abstract painter, the sort who
looked at Jackson Pollock's stuff and
thought he could do that. Do you remember a little documentary film called *The
Day of the Painter*?"

"Refresh my memory."

"A fisherman lives in a shack on the
shore. He sees some Pollocks in a magazine, so he buys some buckets of paint
and a big sheet of plywood, puts it on the
foreshore next to his shack, and paints it
white with a roller. Then he stands on his
deck a few feet above the plywood and
spills dollops of paint onto the white surface of the plywood. Finally, he goes down
to the foreshore with a power saw and
cuts the plywood into smaller squares,
then he sells them as abstract paintings."

"That's a funny idea."

"That's the kind of painter Mr. Sharpe is.
If someone criticizes the work, then they

just don't have the artistic taste or mental capacity to appreciate it, and he raises the price."

"He actually gets galleries to show this stuff?"

"No. When everybody turned him down, he hired a publicist to plant stories in the papers about him and then started selling out of his studio. He gets a prospective buyer down there, and he's quite a good salesman, spewing gobbledygook about passion and genius, and people fall for it."

Their dinner arrived, and Stone tasted the wine.

"Tell me about the drug rumors," Stone said. "I suppose that's what they are—rumors."

"Well, yes, but not entirely. I know someone who bought half a kilo of marijuana from him, and I've heard secondhand stories about his dealing in coke: not little bags, nothing smaller than an ounce, but as much as a kilo."

"Why has no one put the police onto him?"

"The buyers are not going to turn him in—he's their connection—and the non-buyers don't know about it, I guess."

Stone found Sharpe's card in his pocket and looked at it. "That's a pretty expensive part of SoHo these days, isn't it?"

"Yes, it is. Since I've been aware of him, he's moved twice, both times to a bigger and better place. He bought the building he's in now; he has a garage on the ground floor, his studio on the second, and his apartment on the third. He rents out the two floors above him."

"How did Hildy become involved with him?"

"I'm not sure, but she probably met him at an opening much like tonight's. That's the sort of event where he does his trolling."

"What can you tell me about Hildy's relationship with her father?"

Rita sighed. "I love Philip, and I wish I could say that he's the sweet, adoring, indulgent father and that Hildy is an ungrateful little shit, but it's not really like that. Philip is an enclosed man, and he doesn't let much into his life that isn't art or people associated with it."

"He told me that he thought he had left too much of her upbringing to help," Stone said.

"That's an understatement. After his wife died, he hardly saw Hildy. I doubt they had a meal together when she was between the ages of six and sixteen. Her grandmother hired the governesses, chose the schools, and complained about his parenting or lack thereof, but she never hauled him into court and tried to take Hildy. I don't know why. By the time Hildy started fucking her teacher it was too late, I guess. She was acting out big-time to get back at Philip for his neglect, and I think she still is, with Sharpe."

"And he has a low opinion of Sharpe?"

"It wouldn't work for Hildy if he didn't. She got him to look at some slides of Sharpe's work once, and he reduced it to the visual drivel it is in a few pointed sentences. Then he pissed off Hildy by refusing to go down to Sharpe's studio and look at his stuff."

"The relationships are circular," Stone said. "Hildy hates her father for ignoring her, so she chooses a man like Sharpe to annoy him, then Philip hates the guy's work to belittle him, and that reinforces Hildy's opinion of her father."

"Neat, isn't it?"

"Yes, except for the drug sales and the fortune at risk. If Sharpe got busted while Hildy was there, she could be charged as an accessory. I mean, she must know what he's doing."

"I don't see how she couldn't, but who knows?"

"Then there's her trust. I suppose Hildy has no regard for money."

"About the same regard as most young people who've never had to give money a thought, because it was readily supplied by parents who used it to keep them from underfoot."

"And Hildy knows about his background, the name change and the four marriages?"

"Oh, yes. Did Philip tell you that Sharpe was trailer trash?"

"Yes."

"He doesn't even know what that means. He says it only because he knows it's contemptuous. Actually, Sharpe's father made a fortune in the scrap metal business, and they lived in a nouveau riche house in one of San Antonio's better neighborhoods. Sharpe's mother, who knew nothing about art, imbued him with artistic pretensions,

even though he exhibited no discernible talent. I hear he can't even draw."

Stone thought about it all for a minute while he finished his steak. "God, what a mess," he said finally.

"I take it Woodman & Weld sent you around to fix it," Rita said.

"Something like that."

"What are you going to do?"

"I don't know. I don't think there's much point in having an avuncular chat with Hildy—older man/young girl."

"Not really. Her only use for older men is to fuck them. Of course, it's a bonus if they annoy Philip."

"What sort of father did you have?" Stone asked.

Rita chuckled. "My father, bless his heart, is everything Philip should have been but isn't."

"Sweet, adoring, and indulgent?"

"Pretty much, and my mother supports him in all those things. They're peaches, both of them."

"You're a lucky woman."

"I am, indeed.

"Dessert?"

"Not on my diet, thanks."

Stone signaled for the check. "Where do you live?" he asked Rita.

"Park and Seventy-first," she said.

Stone signed the credit card slip. "Come on. I'll drop you."

"It's early," she said. "Where are you off to?"

The waiter pulled out the table and freed them. "I'm going to see a man who might be able to do something about Derek Sharpe," Stone replied.

16

STONE GOT TO ELAINE'S by ten o'clock and found Dino having dinner with cop about their age, Brian Doyle, who had served with them in the 19th Precinct detective squad years before. Stone shook his hand and sat down. A waiter appeared with a Knob Creek and a menu.

"I'm not dining," Stone said and then turned to Doyle. "You're looking pretty good for an old fart," he said.

"And you're looking as slick as an otter," Brian replied. "I hear you're making more money than Donald Trump."

"I heard Trump was broke," Stone said.

"Not anymore; he found some more hot air to inflate the balloon," Brian said, laughing.

After Dino and Brian finished their dinner, they ordered brandies. Then the three old buddies sat back and began telling each other stories they'd all heard before, until, finally, Stone got to the point. "I've got a heads-up for you," he said, handing Derek Sharpe's card to Brian.

"I've read about this guy somewhere," Brian said. "I know a lot of what's called art ought to be illegal, but I don't think the city council has gotten around to passing the law yet."

"This guy churns out the kind of art that ought to be illegal and sells it briskly to the artistically clueless."

"I guess you can make a living doing that," Brian said.

"From what I hear, that's not how he makes his living," Stone replied. "If he had to rely on his art for money, he'd be living in a garret in the East Village instead of owning a five-story building downtown and living in three floors of it. He rents the top two."

"So what's his dodge?" Brian asked.

"Pretty simple: He's moving quantities of drugs from his space."

"What kind of quantities are we talking about?" Brian asked.

"I don't know that he's wholesaling, though I've heard he's sold up to a kilo of coke, but it's more likely he's moving larger than usual quantities to individuals for personal use."

"Sounds boring," Brian said. "Can't you give me something sexier?"

"Brian," Stone said, "when this hits the *Post* and the *News* it's going to be sexy enough to knock your eye out. This guy is plugged into the art scene from one end of this town to the other. He's very well-known, and the press is going to love it, if he gets busted."

"Like Julian Schnabel?"

"Yeah, but without the talent, the work to prove it, or his following. Schnabel is the real deal; Sharpe is ersatz."

"And you want me to bust him? Tell me why."

"He's glommed on to a young woman who's about to become wealthy, and if he isn't stopped, he's going to get her hooked on something bad, steal her money, and

throw her into the street if she doesn't actually do time for being close to him."

"About to be wealthy? What's she going to do, win the lottery?"

"She's about to become twenty-five, and when she does, a fat trust is hers to do with whatever she wants, and what she wants is Derek Sharpe. By the way, his real name is Mervin Pyle, and he's from San Antonio, Texas. He's skinned three or four wives already, and it might be interesting to run his names and see if he has a record back home."

"You know anything else about him?"

"His old man made big bucks in the scrap metal business. Anything else you want to know you can learn by just meeting him. He's a real lizard."

"Look," Brian said, "instead of wasting resources on this guy, why don't I just send a couple of people over there who'll beat him to death and throw the corpse in the East River?"

"That's too easy," Stone said. "Be a cop instead."

Brian took a notebook, wrote down Sharpe's particulars, and pushed the card

back to Stone. "Okay, I'll put somebody on him."

"Might be a good idea to insinuate some young detective into his crowd and see what happens."

"How about a girl detective?" Brian said. "I've got a hot one on the squad, young and gorgeous."

"Add rich to that, and she'll attract Sharpe like flies to honey."

"Is he dangerous?" Brian asked.

"He doesn't appear to be but cornered, who knows? That's why I think it would be good to wander around in his background and see what turns up."

Brian looked at him closely. "Come on, Stone, there's more to this than what you're telling me. You got something else against the guy?"

"Brian, I never heard of him until this morning and never met him until this evening at a gallery opening. I've got absolutely nothing against the guy, except for hating him on sight and hearing bad things about him."

"Well, I guess that's enough."

"Who's the lady cop?"

"Her name is Mitzi Reynolds. She's midthirties, been on the squad for two years, and she's from South Carolina—still has the accent."

"She anything to do with the tobacco family?"

"Nah, her father's a shrimper out of Charleston. She went to a nice school, though. I forget what it's called."

"Well, she can use her own name, and I'll bet Sharpe will think she's from cigarette money. Charleston is far enough away that he won't be able to check her out easily. Use some budget to buy her some clothes."

"Yeah, she'd love that, but don't worry; she dresses good, has a real sense of style."

"I might be able to fix her up with a Park Avenue address," Stone said, "on a temporary basis. I'll make a call tomorrow morning and see." The building where he had dropped Rita Gammage was said to be the best address in the city; it would certainly impress Derek Sharpe.

"I'll have Mitzi call you tomorrow morning. You should get together with her and tell her what you know. If you can get her

into this apartment, that'll keep down the budget, which ain't going to be big for a small-timer like this Sharpe guy."

Stone gave him a card. "Tomorrow morning's good."

Brian stood up. "Well, I've got to go out and work for a living tomorrow," he said, "unlike you guys. You buying, Dino?"

"Nah, Stone is," Dino said.

They all shook hands, and Brian left.

"I hope you're not jerking Brian around," Dino said.

"Certainly not. I think this is a bad guy; he'd fit right in at Attica."

"Yeah, Attica is a real artist's colony."

"Don't think artist; think con man, and you'll be closer to the mark," Stone said.

"What's in this for you?" Dino asked.

"Eggers asked me to do what I can; the girl's old man is a client of the firm."

"Who is he?"

"Philip Parsons."

"Gallery on Fifty-seventh?"

"One and the same. How the hell would *you* know?"

"I know a lot of stuff," Dino said.

17

STONE WAS SITTING up in bed the following morning with a cup of coffee and the *Times* crossword when the phone rang.

"Hello?"

"It's Rita Gammage."

"Good morning."

"I just wanted to thank you for dinner last night."

"You're very welcome. Let's do it again."

"Love to. Did you talk to your man last night?"

"Yes, and I've been able to interest the downtown cops in Mr. Sharpe's business dealings. In fact, I'm supposed to have

lunch today with a lady cop who's going to be leading the effort."

"Wonderful!"

"Say, why don't you join us?"

"Sure, where and what time?"

"How about my house at noon?"

"Sounds good. I've got your card, so I'll know where."

"See you then."

Stone had hardly hung up when the phone rang again. "Hello?"

"Mr. Barrington?" spoke a honeyed woman's voice.

"Yes."

"This is Mitzi Reynolds. Brian Doyle asked me to call you."

"Yes, we talked about you last night. Can you come to lunch at my house at noon? A lady with some knowledge of the man in question will be here, too."

"Surely."

Stone gave her the address, then hung up and pressed the page button on the phone. "Helena?" He waited a moment, then she picked up.

"Mr. Stone?"

"I have a couple of people coming for lunch today. Could you fix us something?'

"I will be happy to."

"Will it be warm enough in the garden to sit out there, do you think?"

"Oh, yes. Lots of sun, too. What would you like?"

"You decide. They're invited for twelve, so let's sit down at twelve thirty."

"I will do this." Helene hung up.

Stone went back to the puzzle.

HE WAS WORKING in his office when the upstairs doorbell buzzer rang. He picked up the phone. "Yes?"

"Your luncheon guests," Rita said.

"I'll buzz you in and meet you there in just a moment." He pressed the buzzer and then called Joan.

"Yep?"

"I have guests for lunch, so I'll be a while," he said, and then he hung up and walked upstairs.

Rita Gammage and Mitzi Reynolds were standing in his living room, looking around. Mitzi, in what appeared to be an Armani business suit, was shorter than but just as good-looking as Rita, who was dressed in slacks and a cashmere sweater.

Stone gave Rita a peck on the cheek and introduced himself to Mitzi.

"We've already met each other," Mitzi said. "We arrived simultaneously."

"Follow me," Stone said, then led them through the house and down to the kitchen, where Helene was working away. He introduced her to the two women.

"Anybody for a glass of champagne?" he asked, opening the fridge.

"Why not?" Mitzi said, and Rita nodded.

He took a bottle of Veuve Cliquot from the fridge, picked up three crystal flutes from a cabinet, and then led them outside to a group of chairs around a teak cocktail table. Helene had already set the lunch table with the good china. Stone poured them all a glass, and they sipped. Stone was having the problem he always had when meeting two beautiful women: which one to pursue?

"Rita, why don't you tell Mitzi what you told me about Derek Sharpe last evening?" he said. He sipped his wine while Rita talked.

"That's about all I know," she said, finally.

"You make him sound repellent," Mitzi said.

"Then I've done my work," Rita replied.

Helene bustled out with two platters and set them on the table. "Lunch is served," she said.

They took their seats at the table and served themselves from the Greek salad, *taramasalata*, hummus, and dolmades Helene had made.

"Mitzi," Stone said, "did Brian give you some idea of what you're supposed to do?"

"He pretty much left it up to me," she said, "but I think the idea is that I will appear on his social radar and get him interested in the Reynolds fortune."

"Oh, you're from the Reynolds tobacco family?" Rita asked.

"No, I'm from the Reynolds shrimp family—no relation," Mitzi said.

"Mitzi's father operates a shrimp boat," Stone explained.

"No," Mitzi said, "he operates thirty shrimp boats, up and down the coast, from an office on the Charleston waterfront. Brian tends to get confused about my roots."

"Ah," said Stone, "and how . . ."

"Did a girl like me get to be a New York City cop? It was easy. I had a boyfriend for a couple of years who was a detective. I didn't have any real work, and I was fascinated by his, so he suggested I take the police exam. I did well on that and joined the force. I got my gold shield six years later."

"Brian said you went to a good school down there somewhere."

"Agnes Scott College, in Atlanta."

Stone blinked. "I know someone who went to school there, Carrie Cox—do you know her?"

"She was a year behind me," Mitzi said, "and she was a piece of work."

Stone wanted to ask exactly what she meant by that, but Rita interrupted. "She's the actress with the lead in the new Del Wood musical, isn't she?"

"That's the one."

"Yes, I read about her on 'Page Six.'"

"So did I," Mitzi said, "and I can't say I was surprised. How do you know her, Stone?"

"I've done some legal work for her," Stone replied, and hoped she would leave it at

that. "Tell me," he said, "do you have a regular partner?"

"Tom Rabbit," she said. "He's due back from vacation tomorrow."

"Good, because I think you'll need some backup."

"What's he going to pose as?" Rita asked.

"Not as anything," Mitzi said. "He wouldn't fit into Derek Sharpe's crowd. He'll watch my back; he'll be the cavalry that rides in if something goes wrong."

"You make this sound dangerous," Rita said.

"That's unlikely," Stone said, "but an undercover cop has to operate on the premise that he—or she, in this case—is in danger at all times. These things tend to have a happier ending if you think that way. Shall we have another bottle of champagne?"

They did.

18

THEY HAD FINISHED LUNCH and the second
bottle of champagne and were on coffee.

"Rita," Stone said, "I need your help on
something else."

"What's that?"

"I need to find Mitzi a temporary place
in a good building on the Upper East Side,
somewhere she can operate from. Her address will be the first thing Derek Sharpe
will learn about her, and it has to impress
him."

Rita turned to Mitzi. "Mitzi, why don't you
just bunk with me? I live in my parents'
apartment in a nice building. They spend

most of their time at their house in the Hamptons, and there are comfortable guest rooms."

"Thank you, Rita," Mitzi replied. "That's very kind of you."

Stone relaxed; that had gone just the way he had hoped. He heard the phone ring in the kitchen.

Helene stuck her head out the back door. "Phone for you, Mr. Stone!"

"Will you ladies excuse me?" Stone said. He took the call so they would have an opportunity to get to know each other better in his absence. He went into the kitchen, sat down at the counter, and picked up the phone. "Hello?"

"Stone, it's Brian Doyle."

"Hey, Brian. Thanks for putting Mitzi on this. I've introduced her to a woman who can help her get to know the scene, and she now has the best address on Park Avenue."

"That's good news," Brian said. "I have some of my own."

"Shoot."

"Mr. Mervin Pyle, aka Derek Sharpe, does not have a record under either of those names."

"I'm surprised to hear it," Stone said.

"Don't be too surprised; he has records under three other names. Apparently our boy took to identity change as a way of life in his youth. He lived in Dallas, L.A., and San Francisco, where he managed an art gallery for a while."

"What sort of stuff?"

"Burglary, embezzlement, battery, attempted murder, all under different names."

"Did he do time?"

"Only while awaiting bail. His IDs were so good that, each time he pled out, and as, supposedly, a first offender, he got no jail time."

Rita and Mitzi came into the kitchen, and Stone asked Brian to hang on.

"Do you mind if we have a look around your house?" Rita asked.

"Not at all. Explore to your heart's content."

She handed him a card. "You might have your secretary have some cards like this printed for Mitzi."

Stone took the card: "71 East Seventy-first Street? I thought you lived on Park."

"It's the side-door address for those who want to be discreet. Maybe you should

use 740 Park on her cards for Sharpe's edification."

"Sure." The women wandered off, and Stone went back to his call. "I'm back."

"I was particularly interested in the battery and attempted murder charges," Brian said, resuming. "I got hold of a San Francisco detective who worked the latter case, and he told me that Sharpe has a very bad temper, especially when drinking, and he has a propensity for violence. The attempted murder case arose out of a fight between him and another guy he nearly beat to death. It took four cops to pull him off."

"What was the battery charge about?"

"He beat up a girlfriend, and she called the cops."

"Mitzi tells me her partner is out of town until tomorrow," Stone said.

"And she won't start until then," Brian replied. "Her partner, Tom Rabbit, is a big Irish guy who can handle anything and who is very protective of her."

"Brian, can you get her a car to be driven around in? Rabbit could be the chauffeur."

"Good idea. Let me check the pound and see what we've confiscated lately."

"You were right," Stone said. "She's a very bright lady. Oh, here's her new address: 740 Park Avenue." Then he read out the phone number.

Brian let out a low whistle. "How'd you swing *that* building? I read a book about that place."

"It's where Rita Gammage lives; Rita works for Philip Parsons."

"Then she's a very rich lady."

"Or her parents are."

"Same thing," Brian said. "I gotta run. Tell Mitzi to call me later today, and I'll check on a car."

"Nothing too flashy," Stone said. "Let's not overdo it."

"Gotcha." Brian hung up.

Stone walked to his office, then down the hall to Joan's room. "Can you get some of these printed in the name of Mitzi Reynolds? 740 Park Avenue? Same zip and phone. It's a rush job."

"Sure," Joan said. "I'll run them over to our printer and wait for them." She grabbed her coat.

"On nice stock," Stone said.

"I get it." Joan was gone.

Stone walked back to the kitchen, where

Helene was washing the champagne flutes by hand. "Where are the ladies?"

"Haven't seen them," Helene replied.

"That was a delicious lunch," Stone said, and Helene beamed at him.

He walked up to the living room and had a look there and in his study: no sign of the women. He walked upstairs and looked into a couple of guest rooms, then continued on to the master. As he approached, the door was ajar, and he heard giggling. He opened the door and stood there, transfixed.

The two women were in his bed, and, judging from the pile of clothing on the floor, they weren't wearing any. He didn't know what to say.

Rita took up the slack. "Join us?" she said.

19

STONE WOKE SLOWLY in a champagne-induced haze. He was in the middle of his bed, and the women were nowhere to be seen. Then he heard a laugh from his bathroom and heard the shower go on. He drifted off again.

HE AWOKE to a pair of lips attached to each of his cheeks.

"We're off," Rita said.

"I'm off, too," Stone replied sleepily.

"You were just great, Stone," Mitzi said.

"Yes," Rita said, "but for a moment I

thought you were too shocked to accept our invitation."

"Only for a moment," Stone said

"We'll be in touch," Mitzi said, and the two women moved toward the stairs. Stone drifted off again.

THE PHONE WOKE him a couple of hours later, and he reached for it.

"Hi, it's Carrie."

"Hi, there."

"You sound sleepy."

"Yeah, I had an afternoon nap," he managed to say.

"Will you and Dino be at Elaine's?"

"Sure, eight thirty."

"May I join you?"

"Of course."

"See you then."

Stone hung up, turned on his side, and went back to sleep. He woke in the dark, switched on the bedside lamp, and stood up. He staggered a little before he caught himself; he felt as if he had just run a marathon. Well, he thought, he had, in a way. The bedside clock said almost eight, and he ran for the shower.

———

CARRIE WAS ALREADY at the table with Dino when Stone walked in. He waved for a drink and sat down.

"You look different," Carrie said, kissing him.

"Different?" He didn't know how to respond to that.

"Completely relaxed," she said. "It must have been a good nap."

"It certainly was," Stone replied.

"I talked to Brian," Dino said. "Sounds like you got what you wanted."

"It does, doesn't it?"

"What is he talking about?" Carrie asked.

"Just a little police operation downtown."

"Is it a secret?"

"Yes."

"I hate secrets; tell me."

"Can't. Lives are at stake."

Carrie turned to Dino. "That's a lie, isn't it?"

"Nope," Dino said. "Lives are at stake."

"Oh," Stone said, "I met someone who knew you at Agnes Scott College."

"Who?"

Stone backtracked. "I can't remember her name; she was from Charleston."

"Mitzi somebody?"

"That sounds right."

"She was a year or two ahead of me. She was very pretty."

"She still is."

Carrie's eyes narrowed. "And how did you meet her?"

"I had lunch with a business associate, and she came along."

"I'd love to see her. Did you get her number?"

"She went back to Charleston this afternoon, I believe."

"Good."

So much for changing the subject, Stone thought. He hadn't seen Carrie jealous before, and it was a little scary. He remembered the straight razor. "How are rehearsals going?"

"I had a little contretemps with the choreographer today," she said. "He wanted me to do a move that would have broken my back."

"And how did you handle that?"

"With a flat refusal, a display of temper, and a couple of bad words."

"How did that work out?"

"He removed the move from the routine," she said with some satisfaction. "I mean, I

might have managed it when I was eighteen, but I know my body better than he does."

"I'm glad to hear it."

"*You* know it better than he does," she said with a sly smile.

"*Harrumph*," Dino sputtered. "Too much information."

"Oh, Dino, you're sweet," she said, laughing.

"Was that the only problem?" Stone asked.

"There was an unwelcome twist," she said. "He asked my understudy to demonstrate the move for me. Her name is Melissa Kelley, and she's in the chorus, and if he weren't gay I would suspect something between them."

"And she was able to do the move?" Dino asked, now fascinated.

"Perfectly," Carrie said, "the bitch. I could have throttled her."

"It's probably better if you don't throttle anybody," Dino said. "Then I'd have to get involved."

Carrie laughed. "It's okay, Dino; she tried to apologize after rehearsal, but it came out all wrong. I mean, what was she going

to say—'I'm sorry I could do the move and you can't'?"

"I can see how that could be awkward," Stone said.

"She watches me all the time," Carrie said. "It's unsettling."

"Maybe she's just working very hard to learn your part," Stone offered.

"No, it's more like *All About Eve.* You know the movie? The young actress wants everything the star has, including her lover?"

"I remember it well."

"You'll meet her eventually," Carrie said. "When you do, watch yourself."

"I'll be very careful," Stone said solemnly.

"So, what's Mitzi up to?" Carrie asked.

"She didn't say a lot."

"She has a rich daddy, I recall."

"She said he was in the shrimp business."

"That sounds right. You're sure she went back to Charleston?"

Stone shrugged. "I believe so. She had to leave lunch early to catch her plane."

"What did she say about me?"

"She said you were a piece of work."

"And what did she mean by *that*?"

"I don't know, and somebody changed the subject before I could ask."

"It's just as well," Carrie said.

Stone allowed himself to think, just for a moment, about what Carrie might do if she knew how he had spent the afternoon.

Carrie dabbed at his forehead with a cocktail napkin. "You're perspiring," she said. She put two fingers on his throat. "And your pulse is up."

"Isometric ab exercises," he said. "I do them at dinner sometimes."

"By the way, I think you can send the young Irish gentlemen home. Not a peep out of Max. I think he's been subdued."

"Are you sure?"

"Yes. In fact, I sent them home when they dropped me off here. They said they would return your car tomorrow morning."

Stone signaled for a menu, but he had trouble concentrating on it. He was still thinking of all those limbs.

20

STONE WAS AT HIS DESK the following morning when Willie Leahy rapped on his doorjamb.

"Good morning, Willie," Stone said.

Willie tossed him his car keys. "It's in the garage," he said. "I filled it up with the premium stuff."

"Thanks," Stone said.

"Listen," Willie said, "I don't know if we shouldn't be watching her for a while longer."

"Why do you say that? She's feeling safe now."

"Just a feeling," Willie said. "That and a phone conversation I overheard."

"What was that about?"

"Well, there's a pair of restrooms in the wings of the theater—ladies' and gents'— and there's some sort of vent, and you can hear the girls talking sometimes."

"You been eavesdropping, Willie?"

"Look, I was having a splash, and I heard Carrie on the phone."

"Yes?"

"She was talking to Delta Air Lines."

"Yes?"

"She was making a reservation to Atlanta this weekend."

"*Atlanta?*"

"I kid you not," Willie said, "and I don't know why the fuck she would want to be in the same city as that ex-husband of hers."

"Neither do I," Stone said. "I mean, she lived there a long time, and I suppose she could have some business there."

"On a weekend?"

"You have a point," Stone admitted.

"Well, let us know if we can be of further service," Willie said, and, with a little wave, he left.

Stone was still thinking about this when Joan buzzed him. "Brian Doyle on one."

"Hello, Brian."

"Morning. I found Mitzi a car: a Bentley, would you believe?"

"How did you come to confiscate a Bentley?"

"Drug bust, what else? It's an Arnage, a few years old, but it looks good."

"I guess it would," Stone said.

"Listen, Mitzi's new friend Rita found out there's a party at Derek Sharpe's studio tonight. She wangled Mitzi an invitation, but she doesn't want to go with her, figuring that her connection to Parsons might affect the way Sharpe sees Mitzi. Will you take her to the party?"

"Sure, I guess so."

"Great. A Bentley, chauffeured by a cop, will pick you up at six thirty."

"Sounds good."

"Some guys have all the luck." Brian hung up.

Joan came into his office and put a box on his desk. "Sorry, the printer couldn't get them done yesterday."

Stone opened the box and removed

one of Mitzi's new cards. "Very nice," he said. "That should do the trick."

AT SIX THIRTY sharp Stone's bell rang. When he opened the door, it was filled by about six feet four inches of Irish American, dressed in a black suit with a black tie.

"Evening," he said. "I'm Tom Rabbit."

Stone shook the extended paw. "Good to meet you, Tom."

"You ready?"

"Yep."

"She's in the car already."

Stone set the alarm and locked the door, then walked to the car. Tom had the door open for him. He slid in beside Mitzi and kissed her on the cheek.

"Don't say anything about yesterday afternoon when Tommy is around," she whispered, before the driver could get into the car.

"Right." He handed her the box of cards. "Your credentials."

She opened the box and inspected the contents. "Hey, very good," she said, tucking some of them into her small purse. "Makes me feel like I really live there."

"Is it a nice place?"

"Haven't you seen it?"

"Nope."

"It's a fucking palace," she said. "Sorry, I'm talking like a cop. Got to get over that."

"I'm glad you're comfortable there."

"My room is better than anything at any hotel in this city," she said.

"I wouldn't talk about that tonight," Stone said. "The card will say everything that's necessary to impress Sharpe."

"What's Sharpe like?" she asked.

"Reptilian," Stone replied, "but women seem attracted to him."

"Oh, we love reptiles," Mitzi said, laughing. "They can always be relied on to slap us around and steal our money."

"I'm sure Derek Sharpe won't disappoint," Stone said.

They drove downtown and arrived at Sharpe's building to find half a dozen drivers waiting outside in their cars, mostly black Lincolns, the preferred transport for New York's affluent, who don't like to arrive at a party in a taxi.

The building looked like a factory, except for the huge murals splashed on the outer walls.

"Ugh," Mitzi said.

"Be sure to compliment Sharpe on them," Stone said.

The elevator held a dozen arriving guests without crowding any of them and opened into a huge space filled with big canvases and many people. Some sort of pop music Stone didn't recognize was blaring from a sound system.

"His paintings are worse than I expected," Mitzi said.

"Sharpe may be, too," Stone replied. He steered her to a bar and collected two plastic flutes of champagne. "This is as bad as the paintings," Stone said, sipping his.

"Shall we hunt down Mr. Sharpe and introduce me?"

"No, let's look at the pictures and pretend to appreciate them," Stone replied. "That should bring him to your side."

They walked along a wall, stepping around people and gazing at the big canvases, stopping before a particularly awful one.

"He's looking our way," Stone said. "Nod and smile a lot."

"I'm nodding and smiling," she said,

pointing at a corner of the canvas. "Look, he had the guts to sign it."

"Well, good evening and welcome," a deep, Texan voice said from behind them.

Stone turned and tried to look surprised to see Derek Sharpe accompanied by Hildy Parsons. "Hello, Derek, Hildy," he said. "May I introduce Mitzi Reynolds? She's recently moved to New York from Charleston, South Carolina."

"Well, hey, sugar," Sharpe said, taking her hand, draping an arm over her shoulder and leading her back the way they had come. "Let me show you some of my work."

"I'd love to see more," Mitzi said. "I particularly liked the murals on the building."

"Everybody likes those," Sharpe said. "It's a pity I can't peel 'em off the building and sell 'em."

Mitzi laughed becomingly. "Oh, I like your composition here," she said, framing a canvas with her hands.

Then, from behind them, came a female voice. "Well, hello, Mitzi," it said.

The two couples turned around to find Carrie Cox standing there with a willowy young man.

"Carrie!" Mitzi said, and a big air kiss

was exchanged. "What on earth are you doing here?"

"I live here," Carrie said.

"Isn't that funny!" Mitzi replied. "So do I!"

"That *is* funny," Carrie said. "It was my information that you returned to Charleston yesterday." She glared at Stone.

"Oh, shit," Stone muttered to himself.

21

MITZI LOOKED INQUIRINGLY AT STONE. "Excuse me for a moment," he said, stepping forward, taking Carrie by an elbow and steering her away from Mitzi and the others. She tried to snatch her arm away, but he held on tightly.

"Don't say anything," he said, marching her across the room toward an unoccupied corner.

"I'll say whatever I damn well please," Carrie spat.

"Not until you've heard me out." He stopped and turned her so that her back was toward the group across the room.

"Remember that police operation Dino and I were talking about last night?"

"Sort of," she said petulantly.

"It's happening right now, and Mitzi is a part of it."

Carrie brightened. "Oh, she's going to be arrested? This I want to see." She tried to turn around, but Stone stopped her.

"Mitzi is a New York City police officer," he said.

Carrie screwed her face into an incredulous glare. "*That* is the most preposterous thing I've ever heard! You're going to have to come up with a better story than that."

"No, I don't," Stone said firmly, "and unless you can accept the fact and keep your mouth shut I'm going to throw you out of here right now."

"And how does a shrimper's daughter get to be a New York cop?" Carrie demanded.

"Some years ago, she took the police exam, was accepted, and graduated from the academy. She served as a street cop for several years before she was promoted to detective. That's how it's done."

"I don't believe you."

"I haven't formed the habit of lying to you or anybody else," Stone said, "and if you repeat any of this to anyone, you will put Mitzi's life in danger, and that is no exaggeration."

Carrie stood there smoldering, avoiding Stone's gaze.

"Do you understand me?" Stone demanded.

She wheeled on him. "Yes!" she said. "And now, if you don't mind, I'll be going." She turned and yelled across the room, "Paco!!!"

The willowy young man came trotting across the space.

"We're leaving," she said to him.

"But we just got here," Paco protested.

"I don't care. We're going."

"Well, I'm not," he replied. "There's somebody I want to meet." He gazed across the room at another young man.

Stone guided Carrie toward the elevator. "Downstairs there's a black Bentley Arnage, driven by a very large man. Tell him I said to take you wherever you want to go and he's to be back here in no more than an hour."

"I'll make my own arrangements," she said, then marched into the elevator.

Stone rejoined the others. "I'm sorry about that," he said. "A misunderstanding."

"Not to worry," Mitzi said.

"Do you have a cell number for Tom?"

She pressed a speed-dial number and handed Stone the phone.

"It's Tom," he said.

Stone stepped away. "Tom, it's Stone. There's a beautiful blonde named Carrie on her way down. Put her in the car, take her somewhere else, then come back as soon as you can. Don't be more than an hour."

"I'll call you when I'm back," Tom said. "Here she comes now." He hung up.

Stone handed Mitzi her phone. "That's taken care of." At least for the moment, he thought.

"Oh, good," Mitzi said. "Derek was just telling me about how he does his work. It's fascinating."

"I'll bet," Stone said, trying to keep the irony out of his voice.

AN HOUR LATER, Mitzi answered her phone. She listened, then hung up. "My driver is back," she said.

"The party seems to be winding down,"

Sharpe said. "Why don't we get some dinner?"

"I'd love to," Mitzi said brightly.

"Sure, why not?" Stone said. He noted that Hildy didn't seem to have any objections.

They rode down in the elevator with the last of the celebrants, and Tom was waiting out front with the Bentley.

"We'll take my car," Mitzi said.

"I'll take the front seat," Stone said, and got in while Tom held the door for the others.

"Where to, Ms. Reynolds?" Tom asked when he was in the car.

"Derek," she said, "we're in your hands."

Sharpe gave directions, and soon they were stopping outside a chic-looking restaurant. Stone hardly ever came downtown, so he didn't know it.

They went inside, where Sharpe was fawned over by the manager and the reservations lady before they were shown to a big table in the center of the room. Sharpe ordered a bottle of expensive wine and menus.

"I hope you like sushi," Sharpe said to the group.

"Love it," Mitzi said.

Stone detested sushi but said nothing. The menus came, and he began looking for something cooked. He was relieved to find a shrimp teriyaki and ordered that, while the others chose raw things.

"So, Mitzi," Sharpe said. "How long have you been in town?"

"A few weeks, off and on. I bought an apartment uptown, and I've been seeing to the decorating."

"Oh," Hildy said, "let me have your address and number."

Mitzi fished a card from her purse and handed it to her.

Sharpe took it from her, looked at it, froze for a moment, then handed it back to Hildy. "Nice neighborhood," he said.

"I like it," Mitzi replied.

"How did you ever find it?" Hildy asked. "You never see anything listed in that building."

"It was a private sale," Mitzi said smoothly. "A friend of my family owned it."

"That's the best way," Hildy said. "Did you have any problems with the co-op board? I hear they can be tough."

"None at all," Mitzi said. "In fact, they were rather sweet."

Stone admired how, in a few words, Mitzi had told them that she came from money, serious enough to impress a board made up of people with serious money.

"Are you all settled in now?" Hildy asked.

"Perfectly," Mitzi replied. "My decorator brought over the last pair of lamps today."

"And who is your decorator?" Hildy asked.

"Ralph Lauren," Mitzi replied.

"Who at Ralph Lauren?"

"Ralph."

"Ralph who?"

"Lauren."

Stone nudged her under the table. Ralph Lauren did not deliver lamps. Mitzi was going too far.

"I've never heard of Ralph personally doing decorating jobs," Hildy said.

"He and Daddy are old friends," Mitzi replied. "Daddy was one of Ralph's first backers many years ago, when he was still in the necktie business."

This, Stone thought, was a high-wire performance. He hoped to God that Philip Parsons and Ralph were not old friends.

Hildy answered his question. "How in-

teresting. *My* father and Ralph are old friends, too. Ralph has bought a number of pictures from him."

"Oh, is your daddy in the art business?" Mitzi replied.

"The Parsons Gallery," Hildy said.

"Oh, of course. I didn't make the connection. A lovely gallery it is, too. I bought a Hockney there."

"Oh? Whom did you deal with?"

"Rita Gammage."

"Oh, yes."

"Your father was busy with something else that day."

This was out of control. Stone tried desperately to think of a way to change the subject. Fortunately, dinner arrived.

22

THE TERIYAKI WAS GOOD. Stone tried not to watch the others eating raw animals. As soon as he had finished his main course, Stone asked to be excused and left the table. He found a quiet corner of the restaurant and called Rita Gammage.

"Hello?"

"Rita, it's Stone. We've got problems."

"Did something go wrong?"

"If anything, it's all gone too well," Stone said.

"What do you mean?"

"I mean that Mitzi has gotten a little too

much in the swing of things. She's impressed Sharpe and, incidentally, Hildy, too much. Among other things, she has told them that she bought a Hockney from you, and the way things are going, next she'll be inviting them over for drinks."

"Oh, God."

"Does Philip have a Hockney in the gallery?"

"Yes, he does."

"Borrow it, will you? And will you please call him right now and tell him that Mitzi bought it? I have the feeling Hildy is going to call her father tonight and ask him."

"I'm sure he'll loan it to me for a few days when I explain why," she said. "I'll get right on it."

"Another thing," Stone said. "Mitzi has told them that Ralph Lauren personally decorated her apartment."

"That's outrageous!"

"I know, but she did it."

"Fortunately, most of my upholstered furniture is from Mr. Lauren's store."

"That will be a big help," Stone said, "but there's a further complication."

"Now what?"

"When Hildy questioned whether Lauren personally does decorating jobs, Mitzi told her that Lauren and her father are very old friends and that he was one of Lauren's early investors."

"Oh, shit. If I know Hildy, she'll find a way to track that down."

"That's what I'm afraid of. Do you know Lauren?"

"I've met him a few times, but I don't think he'd recognize my name."

"Does Philip?"

"I think he sold him a picture once, a few years back."

"Do you think Philip would call him and try to get him to back up this story?"

"I'm not at all sure about that," Rita said. "Let me think about how to do this, and in the meantime, I'll call Philip and ask about the Hockney."

"I'm afraid that I don't know Mitzi's father's first name," Stone said.

"It's Mike. She told me."

"Good, I'll leave it with you."

"Are you home? I'll call you back."

"No, we're in a sushi restaurant downtown with Hildy and Sharpe."

"Call me when you get home. I'll be up late."

"Will do." Stone hung up and returned to the table.

"Oh, Stone," Mitzi said, "Derek and Hildy are coming for drinks tomorrow evening."

"How nice," Stone said, very glad that he had called Rita. Then he had a terrifying thought: Had Hildy ever visited Rita's apartment?

THEY FINALLY WRAPPED up dinner, and the check came. It sat there. Stone was damned if he was going to pick it up; this had been at least a seven-hundred-dollar dinner, given the wine Sharpe had ordered, and it wasn't Stone's party. He decided to take the bull by the balls. "Thank you so much for dinner, Derek," Stone said, pushing the check across the table. That was very extravagant of you." He thought he saw Sharpe turn pale. He turned to Mitzi. "Shall we go?"

"Yes, let's do," she replied. "Can we drop you?" she asked Hildy and Sharpe.

"We're going to have an after-dinner drink at the bar," Sharpe said. "We'll make our own way home."

Stone hustled Mitzi out of the restaurant and into the car.

"How'd that go?" Tom Rabbit asked.

"Wonderfully well," Mitzi said.

Stone thought she was a little drunk. "You really threw a monkey wrench into the works," Stone said.

"How's that?" She seemed baffled.

"Well, first of all, that business about the Hockney."

Mitzi giggled. "Oh, yes, I forgot about that."

"I spoke to Rita. She's going to borrow a Hockney from Philip Parsons."

"Well, that's all solved, then, isn't it?"

"Not quite. Now we have to deal with your chummy relationship with America's most famous designer, who has personally decorated your apartment."

"Well, it *looks* as though he decorated it," she said innocently.

"And that stuff about your father investing with Lauren years ago."

"Oh, that's perfectly true," she said.

Stone looked at her skeptically. "Are you sure about that? Because that's a loose end that can't be left untied."

"Of course, I'm sure."

"All right, then we're okay on that story

about your father and Ralph. What are we going to do if Hildy gets to him and asks if he decorated your apartment?"

"Oh, I'll call Ralph in the morning and square that with him." She turned and took him by a lapel. "Did you really think I would spout all that stuff without being able to back it up?"

"Frankly, yes. I had no idea where that was coming from, and it would have been nice if you had tipped me off before you said it."

"Oh, ye of little faith," she said.

"And what about the Hockney? Did you have that all squared, too?"

"Well, Rita took me to the gallery, and I saw a Hockney there. I figured something could be done."

"Mitzi, if you continue this high-wire act, you're going to give me a coronary," Stone said.

"Yeah," Tom echoed from the front seat, "she gives me coronaries all the time. You'd better get used to it."

"Tell me about your own little monkey wrench," Mitzi said.

"What are you talking about?" Stone asked.

"I'm talking about Carrie Cox," she said. "God, what a scene."

"Well, I had no idea she was going to be there," Stone said lamely. "I hustled her out of there as fast as I could."

"And did you tell her I'm a cop?"

"I had to; she would have blown you on the spot."

"Talk about high-wire acts," Mitzi said, laughing. "You know, I think she actually lent some credibility to our little farce. Even her jealous act helped."

"I hope you're right," Stone said.

"So, you and Carrie are an item," Mitzi said.

"I told you, I've done some legal work for her."

"Well, I guess it was legal," Mitzi replied. "I mean, she is of age, isn't she?"

AT 740 PARK, Stone walked Mitzi to her door.

She kissed him on the cheek. "By the way," she said, "you acquitted yourself very well yesterday afternoon."

"I must say, that was a surprise," Stone said.

"Judging from the look on your face, I'd say it was a shock!"

"Well . . ."

"Let's do it again sometime."

"Absolutely," Stone tried to say with confidence. He was still a little rattled by the experience.

"And Rita feels the same way," Mitzi said. "Good night." She gave him a little wave and went into the building.

Stone got into the front seat of the Bentley. "That woman is something," he said to Tom.

"You don't know the half of it," Tom replied.

23

THE FOLLOWING DAY STONE WENT to the stage door of the Del Wood Theater, gave his name to the watchman, introducing himself as Carrie's attorney, and went and stood in the wings.

Carrie was in the middle of what was apparently her big dance number, and Stone was impressed. Paco, from the night before, was her dance partner, and he was trying gamely to keep up and almost making it. The number ended, and the choreographer called Paco over for a chat.

Carrie grabbed a towel and patted her

face. When she saw Stone in the wings she came over. "Visitors aren't allowed at rehearsals," she said. "Wait for me in my dressing room." She pointed the way and then walked back onto the stage.

Stone found a door with a star tacked to it and let himself in. It was fairly large, with a big dressing table, a long couch, and a couple of chairs, as well as an en suite bathroom. The decor wasn't much, he thought, but there were a couple of paint cans and some wallpaper rolls in a corner, so he reckoned that would change soon. He settled on the sofa and leafed through a *Variety* from the coffee table.

Carrie came in after a few minutes and slammed the door behind her.

Stone got up to greet her.

"You were very mean to me last night," she said, pouting.

"You were behaving badly," he said, "so I had to be mean. You could have caused a great deal of damage."

"So she really is a police detective?"

"She is."

"That's what Tom, her driver, said."

"Tom is a cop, too. He's Mitzi's partner."

She pushed him onto the sofa and sat

beside him. "All right, I want to hear the whole story."

"I'll give you the *Reader's Digest* version," he said, and he managed it in a few sentences. "And you should stay away from Derek Sharpe," he told her.

"I can see that," she said. "Anyway, I hate his stuff. I don't know why anyone would buy it."

"You have excellent taste."

"Yes, I do," she said, getting up and stripping off her sweater and tights. "I'm going to take a shower," she said. "You want to buy me dinner later?"

"Sure."

"Can we go to Elaine's and see Dino?"

"I'm fairly certain he'll be there; he always is."

She dropped her clothes into a hamper and took off her bra and panties.

Stone was impressed all over again. She had a dancer's body: slim with long muscles and high breasts. She went into the bathroom and turned on the shower without closing the door. Stone was happy to watch. When she came out, drying herself with a towel, she gave him a long look, then locked the door and sat on his lap, facing him.

"Your lips become fuller when you're turned on," Stone said. "That's some kisser you've got there."

She kissed him. "That's what the lips are for," she said, then slid to the floor, unzipped his fly, and showed him how else the kisser could be used.

Afterward, Stone fell asleep, waiting for her to get dressed.

DINO DIDN'T SEEM surprised to see them. Stone ordered them drinks.

"Dino," Carrie said, "you were very naughty last night not to tell me about Mitzi being a cop and all."

"You aren't supposed to know about that," Dino said, shooting Stone a sharp glance.

"She turned up at Derek Sharpe's studio, unannounced," Stone said in his defense.

"Do I have to tell you everything I do?" Carrie asked, sipping her drink.

"You have to tell me when you decide to go to Atlanta," Stone said.

"I'll do that," she said.

"You didn't do that," he replied.

Her jaw dropped. "How did you find out?"

"Why, it was all over 'Page Six' in the *Post*," Stone said. "'Crazy Dancer/Actress to Visit Her Atlanta Ex-husband, Who Wants to Kill Her.' Didn't you see it?"

She laughed. "It was not."

"Tell me," Stone said, "what was the point of our pulling out all the stops to keep you safe if you're going to go running into his arms at the first opportunity?"

"It's not like that," she said.

"What is it like?"

"A mutual friend has offered to mediate the settlement," Carrie said.

"You told me you already had a settlement."

"There are a few loose ends," she said. "Dear Max has bounced back financially with the help of a Saudi prince, who has a house in Atlanta. I'm told he's actually better off now than he was before."

"I'm told that, too," Stone said. "So you're going to hold him up for more?"

"For more cash. He was strapped a year ago, so I took not very liquid assets."

"There's nothing like cash," Stone said. "It makes a wonderful motive for murder. What makes you so sure Max won't be

meeting your flight and taking you for a little ride?"

"I know what would make you feel better about this," Carrie said. "Come with me."

Stone was brought up short. He had no desire to go to Atlanta, but having made a fuss about it, he could hardly say no. "All right," he said.

"I'll book you on the same flight," she said. "And I've already booked a suite at the Ritz-Carlton Buckhead."

"Who else is going to be at this meeting?" Stone asked.

"Max's lawyer and our mutual friend, a lawyer named Ed Garland."

"I know Ed," Stone said. "Had you planned to do this without an attorney of your own?"

"I was going to ask you," she said, "and I would have last night, if you hadn't marched me out of Derek Sharpe's studio."

"I'm sorry I had to do that," Stone said.

"I'm sorry you had to do that, too," she replied. "I apologize for my behavior."

"No need to apologize."

Dino spoke up. "Does anybody want to order dinner? Or do you two want to get a room?"

"Dinner now, room later," Carrie said, shooting Stone a leer. "You owe me." She picked up a menu.

"I do, and I'll pay," Stone promised.

24

STONE WAS AT HIS DESK the following morning when Bill Eggers called.

"Good morning, Bill," Stone said.

"Can you give me a progress report on the Parsons problem?"

"I can," Stone said. "I've arranged for a female police detective to be dangled before Derek Sharpe, pretending to be an heiress from South Carolina. Actually, she's not pretending, because that's what she is."

"Go on."

"The idea is that, having loosened him up with a displayed interest in buying his

work, she will attempt to buy drugs from him. If that works, he's off the street."

"I like that," Eggers said, sounding surprised."

"Why do you sound surprised?" Stone asked.

"Well, frankly, I hadn't expected such fast action with the promise of such permanent results."

"This hasn't worked yet, Bill," Stone replied. "Things can go wrong, and the detective is placing herself at some risk."

"I'll keep that in mind. Have you spoken with Philip Parsons about this?"

"He's being kept apprised by a staff member of his gallery."

"And he's happy?"

"I've no reason to think that he's not."

"Good work, Stone. I'm proud of you."

"Thanks, Bill, but be proud when it's done."

"I'll be proud then, too. Good-bye." Eggers hung up.

Carrie, holding the straps of her duffel, appeared in his office. "Our flight is in two hours," she said.

"Where'd you get the clothes?"

"From your closet. Didn't you notice they were there?"

"Nope."

"Where are your clothes?" she asked, her head cocked to one side, hand on hip.

"They're in my closet, too," Stone replied.

"Had you planned to take some with you?"

"What will I need?"

"Something to make you look lawyerly at our meeting and whatever else you need. We'll be flying home tomorrow."

"I'll be right back," Stone said, rising from his desk.

JOAN DROVE them to LaGuardia in Stone's car, and their flight was on time. They were on the airplane before Stone realized that he would rather be flying himself. Well, at least they were in first class.

They were met by a car and driver at Hartsfield International and driven to the Ritz-Carlton.

"What time is our meeting?" Stone asked.

"Four o'clock."

"Why aren't we returning to New York tonight?"

"In case we need a second meeting tomorrow."

THEY ARRIVED AT Ed Garland's office on time and were greeted warmly by Garland, with whom Stone had previously worked on a case, and coolly by Max Long and his attorney. The meeting was called to order, and Stone sat silently while Carrie enumerated her demands. He tried not to hold his breath.

Long's attorney opened his mouth to speak, but Max stopped him. "Yes," he said.

"We'll take yes for an answer," Stone said. "Ed, can I borrow a typist for a moment? We'll get this signed now."

"Sure, Stone."

Half an hour later, both parties signed, and Max Long wrote a large check. Everyone shook hands and parted.

On the way back to the hotel, Stone handed Carrie her copy of the agreement. "Tell me again why I was at this meeting?" he asked.

"For bodily protection," Carrie said, "and as a prop."

"A prop? Like a stage prop?"

"Exactly. You were the attorney prop."

"You mean you knew that Max would meet your demands?"

"I did."

"How?"

"He knew that if he didn't, I would make his life miserable until he did. I knew that he knew that it would be a whole lot easier for him if he just caved immediately, before I could think of something else to ask for."

"You should have been a divorce lawyer," Stone said.

"I have been, for the past year or so," she said. "I've learned a lot."

"You're a quick study."

"On stage and off."

After dining at the excellent Ritz-Carlton restaurant, they made love until they were exhausted and then fell asleep.

The following morning they were driven to the airport, and as the airplane lifted off the runway, Stone relaxed. Nobody had tried to kill Carrie, and it appeared that nobody would. He was able to sleep all the way home.

When he got back to the house, there

was a phone message from Mitzi Reynolds, time-stamped the afternoon before.

"Our drinks with Sharpe and Hildy have been postponed until tomorrow night," she said. "My place at seven. We're going to dinner afterward."

Stone breathed a sigh of relief; he had completely forgotten their appointment of the evening before.

"I have plans for this evening," he said to Carrie, "so I'm going to put you in a cab home."

"Plans?" she asked.

"In connection with the police operation."

"You're seeing Mitzi, then?"

"I am."

"Do I have to get used to that?"

"You do," he said, "until we pull this thing off."

"I'm going to pout now," she said, pouting.

He kissed her and put her into a cab.

"Call me tomorrow," she said.

He waved her off and went back inside, still tired from his exertions of the past two nights.

When he walked into his office his phone was ringing. He picked it up. "Stone Barrington."

"It's Willie Leahy."

"Hi, Willie."

"You're lucky you're not dead," Willie said.

"Tell me why you think that."

"You were followed from the lawyer's office in Atlanta."

"By whom?"

"Well, after I tapped him on the back of the neck and went through his pockets, he was identified as an Atlanta P.I. named Wallace Higgs."

"And you think he meant us harm?"

"He was carrying a loaded Glock and a homemade silencer."

"Oh."

"Yeah."

"But we settled everything at the lawyer's office. Max wrote her a check for everything."

"Tell her to cash it quick," Willie said.

"Willie, how was it that you happened to be in Atlanta and happened to be following us?"

"I've been following you since LaGuardia," Willie said. "I was in steerage, while you were drinking champagne up front."

"Why were you doing that?"

"I like the lady. I didn't want her to go to Atlanta, and I didn't want anything to happen to her."

"Willie, you can bill me for that one."

"Don't worry," Willie said, and then hung up.

Stone called Carrie on her cell.

"Hey, Stone. Forget something?"

"Yes. Be sure you deposit that check the moment the bank opens tomorrow and tell them to call the Atlanta bank and ask them to put a hold on the funds."

"Do you know something I don't?"

"Usually," Stone said. "Just do it. Talk to you tomorrow." He hung up and began to go through the mail on his desk.

25

STONE ARRIVED AT Rita's apartment fifteen minutes early. The elevator opened directly onto the foyer, and Mitzi met him at the door with an affectionate kiss on the lips. "Please come in," she said.

Stone followed her into the living room and stopped to have a look around. It was a large room with a seating area that would accommodate a dozen people around the fireplace, another seating area at the west end, and a seven-foot Steinway grand piano at the east end, which wasn't in the least crowded.

"What do you think?" Mitzi asked. "Do I have good taste?"

"Well, Ralph Lauren does," Stone said. He nodded toward the painting over the fireplace. "Love the Hockney."

"Isn't it something?"

"I wish I could afford his work," Stone said.

"There were some very nice New York scenes on your bedroom wall," she said.

"My mother's work."

"They're beautiful."

"She thanks you."

"Can I get anybody a drink before I disappear?"

Stone turned to see Rita entering the room. She gave him the same sort of kiss that Mitzi had, one that caused a stirring.

"Sure," Stone said.

Rita poured the drinks from a wet bar concealed behind some paneling.

"It's a beautiful apartment," Stone said, "but you'd better get rid of the photographs on the piano, the ones of you and your parents."

"Oh, God, I forgot about those," Rita said. She scooped them up and put them in a drawer.

Mitzi ran out of the room and came back with an armful of silver frames. "I brought these from home," she said, arranging them on the piano. "My family."

"Good work," Stone said. The phone rang, and Mitzi picked it up. "Yes? Send them up, please." She hung up. "We're on."

"I'll be in my room," Rita said. "I hope I don't hear any shooting." She left the living room.

"Which lamps did dear old Ralph, the family friend, bring over?" Stone asked.

"The pair at each end of the sofa."

"They're not Lauren's—they're antiques," Stone said.

"Ralph has a wonderful eye for antiques," Mitzi replied. "And I called him yesterday and squared things."

"What was his reaction?"

"He was delighted to hear from me, and amused by my situation and happy to help."

The doorbell rang, and Mitzi went to answer it. She came back with Derek Sharpe and Hildy Parsons and another couple, whom Sharpe introduced as Sig and Patti Larsen. Sig looked Swedish; Patti didn't. Drinks were offered and accepted, and a

uniformed maid appeared with a tray of hors d'oeuvres.

They arranged themselves before the fireplace.

"Sig is my financial manager," Sharpe said, "and he's very good. Mitzi, I thought you might need some New York help in that line."

Here was an interesting move, Stone thought. If Mitzi bit, then Sharpe would, in no time, have a complete picture of what he could steal from her.

"I'm very well taken care of in that respect," Mitzi said. "My father has three people in his office who do nothing but handle our family's money."

"Perhaps I could meet with them sometime," Sig said.

"They're in Charleston, and they hate New York," Mitzi said.

"You know, I'm going to be in Savannah early next week," Sig said. "Perhaps I could pop up to Charleston and see them."

"I'll ask Daddy," Mitzi said.

"I'm at your disposal," Sig said.

"Where are we dining?" Mitzi asked.

"I've booked us at Sette Mezzo," Sharpe replied. "In half an hour."

This was interesting, Stone thought. Sette Mezzo didn't take credit cards, only cash, unless one had a house account.

Mitzi picked up the phone and dialed a number. "Please be downstairs in twenty minutes," she said into the instrument.

"I love your Hockney," Hildy said, speaking for the first time. "I saw it at my father's gallery, of course."

"Yes, I'm very pleased with it," Mitzi said.

"Oh, by the way," Hildy said, "I ran into Ralph Lauren this morning; he sends his regards."

"That's sweet of him," Mitzi said. "Do you like the lamps?"

"Very much," Hildy said, and Sharpe murmured an assent.

"Ralph found them at one of the Paris flea markets," Mitzi said.

"Wonderful places," Patti Larsen interjected.

"Aren't they?" Mitzi said.

Conversation continued along these lines until they finally made their way downstairs. Stone and Mitzi got into the Bentley,

and the other two couples boarded their own black Town Car.

"How did drinks go?" Tom asked from the front seat of the Bentley.

"Just as you'd expect," Mitzi said. "We're all squared away on the Hockney and Ralph Lauren."

"Lexington and Seventy-sixth, please, Tom," Stone said.

SETTE MEZZO WAS, as always, crowded with the voluble, so Stone reckoned their conversation would be subdued at a table for six, since they wouldn't be able to hear each other. They were shown to a corner table, which helped. Sharpe revealed himself as never having been to the restaurant by ordering martinis for everyone. If he had been there before, Stone thought, he would have known that the restaurant served only wine, except for secret bottles of Scotch and vodka kept for more demanding guests. Stone now knew that he would be buying dinner.

Mitzi was seated between Sharpe and Sig Larsen, and Stone between Patti Larsen and Hildy Parsons. This meant that Stone would have difficulty, in the noisy restau-

rant, understanding what Sharpe and Larsen were saying to Mitzi, not that she would have any difficulty handling them.

"So, Stone," Patti Larsen said, "what do you do?" Her hand crept onto his knee.

"I'm an attorney," Stone replied. "I sue people."

She removed her hand. "How nice for you."

"Usually," Stone replied.

"Where is your office?"

"I'm of counsel to Woodman & Weld, but I work from offices in my home."

"That's cozy," she said. Her knee was now rubbing against his.

Stone turned to Hildy and made conversation.

WHEN THE CHECK came, Stone picked it up and signed it, avoiding a scene where Sharpe and Larsen would be short of cash. What the hell, he thought, Bill Eggers would be getting the bill anyway.

BACK IN the Bentley, Stone asked Mitzi how it had gone at dinner.

"They were pressing me about Sig giving me financial advice," Mitzi said.

"Was that true about the financial people in your father's office?"

"Yes, but there's only one; I made up the other two."

"Why don't you call him and ask him to make up a fictitious financial statement and stock portfolio?" Stone suggested. "Something that will water Sharpe's mouth?"

"What a good idea," she said. "I'll do it first thing Monday morning. That should thicken the plot."

"I think that, after they see your statement, you should broach the subject of drugs. I'd advise you to tell them the stuff is for friends, not for you. You don't want to get into a situation where you're pressed to actually use something around witnesses. That could blow your case."

"I'm way ahead of you," Mitzi said.

"Believe her," Tom added.

Stone did.

26

STONE GOT A CALL from Bob Cantor the next morning. "Hey, Bob."

"Hey, Stone. Willie Leahy thinks he and his brother should be back on Carrie's case."

"Yeah, he told me he followed us to Atlanta."

"And he told you about the P.I. with the loaded gun and the silencer?"

"Yes."

"Doesn't that make you think the Leahys should be back on the case?"

"But the P.I. was in Atlanta, not New York."

"Max has already made one stab at her, so to speak, in New York. Why wouldn't he try again?"

"Because Carrie settled everything with him in Atlanta. He even wrote her a check."

"Has the check cleared?"

"We're working on that."

"And why, if it clears, do you think Max would lose interest in hurting her?"

"Well . . ."

"In my experience, guys who hate their ex-wives go right on hating them, even after giving them the money. In fact, they hate them *more* after giving them the money."

"You have a point," Stone admitted.

Joan buzzed him. "Carrie Cox on two."

"Hang on, Bob." Stone put him on hold and pressed the button for line two. "Carrie?"

"Hi. I'm at the bank, and they've put a hold on the funds in Max's account. The check will clear tomorrow."

"That's good news. Hang on a minute, will you?" Stone went back to Cantor. "Bob, let's put them on her for another week."

"It will be done," Cantor said and then hung up.

Stone went back to line two. "I've got some news," he said.

"Good news, I hope."

"No."

"Oh, God, what now?"

"Willie Leahy followed us to Atlanta on Friday, and he caught an Atlanta private investigator following us."

"That doesn't make any sense."

"Bob Cantor makes the point that ex-husbands hate their ex-wives even more after giving them money, and the P.I. was carrying a loaded gun and a homemade silencer."

"And what does that mean?"

"It means that he planned to shoot us—or at least, you—quietly, so nobody would notice."

"That doesn't sound like Max."

"Who else hates you?" Stone asked.

"Nobody—at least not enough to actually have me murdered."

"Are you sure about that?"

"Of course, I'm sure."

"Then it's Max. I've put the Leahys back on you; cooperate with them, will you?"

"Oh, Stone!"

"Do you want to make it to opening

night? Someone who hates you might love to prevent your dream from coming true."

"Oh," she said. "I see your point. All right, I will welcome Willie and Pete back into my life."

"Give them a nice gift, a necktie maybe."

"I'll give them some new cologne—the one they wear is toxic."

"Good idea."

"Gotta run; I'm due at rehearsal. Dinner tonight?"

"Come over here, and I'll cook you something."

"Done. Seven?"

"Good."

She hung up.

FIFTY FEET from Carrie Cox's front stoop, Willie Leahy sat in his car surveying the street. He got out of the car and looked both ways, then crossed the street and looked again.

The speaker/microphone for the radio on his belt popped on. "We're ready. Everything okay?"

"Everything okay," Willie replied. He crossed the street, got into the car, and drove up to Carrie's stoop. Peter hustled

her into the car. "Where we off to?" Willie asked.

"To Stone Barrington's house," she replied.

"Gotcha." Willie headed for Turtle Bay.

As he turned into Stone's block, he slowed. "A guy I don't like, across the street from Stone's," he said. "Black raincoat."

"Drop me here," Peter replied, "and go around the block."

Willie did so. "Carrie, lie down on the backseat," he said.

"Will do. Are there bad guys?"

"Maybe. We'll know soon." Willie drove slowly past the man and made mental notes: five-eleven, two hundred, suit and tie under the raincoat, forty to forty-five. He drove around the block.

PETER LEAHY PUT his hands in his coat pockets and walked down the block at a normal pace. As he came up to the man in the black raincoat he stopped behind him and whispered in his ear, "Don't turn around."

The man froze.

"The guy who lives in that house doesn't like loiterers," he said.

"It's a free country," the man replied, not moving.

Peter flipped up the lapel of his coat and removed a four-inch-long hat pin that had belonged to his grandmother. He gave the loiterer a quick jab in the ass.

The man cried out and spun around. Then, walking backward, he shoved his hand inside his coat and made his way down the block.

"If you pull that thing on me, you better kill me with the first shot," Peter said.

The man kept his hand inside his coat but didn't draw anything. He turned and now began walking fast, hurrying away.

"And don't come back," Peter called after him. He looked over his shoulder, saw Willie coming, and held up a hand for him to stop. He waited until the watcher had turned the corner before he waved Willie on. They hustled Carrie into the house.

STONE MET THEM at the door. "Any problems?"

"Just one," Peter said. "I sent him on his way."

"How'd you do that?" Stone asked.

Willie showed him the hat pin.

Stone laughed. "I haven't seen one of those things since I was a kid."

"You'd be surprised how useful it can be," Peter said. He turned to Carrie. "Are you staying the night?"

"Yep," she replied.

"Then we'll leave you in Stone's capable hands."

The Leahys departed.

27

STONE WALKED CARRIE DOWN to the kitchen, put her duffel on the dumbwaiter, and sent it upstairs. Then he poured them both a Knob Creek, and they sat down on the large kitchen sofa.

Carrie rested her hand lightly on Stone's crotch. "You know what I like about you?"

"I think I'm getting an idea," Stone said.

"Exactly. And it's always ready to go." She began kneading.

"How could it not be, under the circumstances?"

"Until I met you it had been a long time

since I had gotten anywhere near as much sex as I wanted."

"I'm glad to be of service," Stone said.

She unzipped his fly and put her hand inside. "Men don't really understand how much sex women need," she said.

"I'm beginning to get the picture," Stone said.

She pulled him down on the sofa, took down his trousers, shucked off her slacks, and straddled him, taking him inside her. "How's that?"

"*Mmmmm*," Stone replied.

"Oh, I'm going to come," she said.

"Don't wait for me."

She didn't.

"You're so easy," Stone said. "Again."

"Here I come." And she did. "How about you?"

"I'll save myself for later," he said.

She lay down beside him on the sofa and put her head on his shoulder. "I know I can be a pain in the ass," she said, "but I really appreciate the way you've been protecting me."

"You're paying for it," Stone reminded her.

"Yes, but I never would have arranged it for myself. You've thought of everything."

"I've tried to."

She sat up, pulled her sweater over her head, and undid her bra, freeing her breasts. "I'm dining naked tonight," she said, then started on his clothes.

"I hope you don't mind if I wear an apron while I'm cooking," Stone said. "Gotta watch out for those spatters."

"You do that, sweetie. I'll still get to look at your ass, which is very nice, by the way."

"Same to you, kiddo."

"Did you ever take dance?" she asked him.

"Ballroom, when I was twelve—my mother insisted."

"You've got a dancer's ass," she said. "Muscular and tight."

"Maybe I should start wearing leotards," he suggested.

She laughed.

THEY DINED, NAKED, on veal chops and risotto.

"This is wonderful," she said, tasting the risotto. "What do you put in it?"

"You watched me make it."

"I was watching your ass," she said.

"Combine some butter and olive oil in a pan; add twelve ounces of Arborio rice, some salt, and the zest of a lemon; and sauté until the rice turns golden. Start adding small cupfuls of hot chicken stock, stirring until each addition is absorbed before adding the next, and continue until a whole carton has been absorbed. Then stir in the zest of another lemon, a couple of fistfuls of Parmigiano-Reggiano, and half a carton of crème fraîche, and serve. Takes a little less than half an hour."

"That's so simple."

"Why do you think I make it?"

She attacked her veal chop, and Stone poured a good Australian Shiraz into their glasses.

When they had finished she sat back and rubbed her naked belly. "God, that was good; I'm almost too full to make love again."

"Would you like some dessert?" he asked. "There's ice cream."

"I think I'll have you for dessert," she said, taking him by the cock and leading him upstairs.

JOAN BUZZED them at nine, waking them.

Stone picked up the phone. *"Mmmmf."*

"And good morning to you, too," Joan said. "There's a man watching the house."

"Go look out your office window. Do you see the Leahys?"

She put the phone down for a minute, then came back. "They just drove up, and the man ankled it out of here."

"Pete stuck a hat pin in him last night," Stone said. "I guess he didn't want another one."

"And where would Peter Leahy get a hat pin?"

"From his grandmother."

"An heirloom—wonderful."

"Pete's an old-fashioned kind of guy."

"I just thought you'd like to know," Joan said, then hung up.

Carrie was sitting up in bed now. "I've got a rehearsal in half an hour," she said, climbing out of bed. "I wish I had time to fuck you again." She ran into the bathroom and turned on the shower.

Stone drifted off for a few minutes until she woke him with a kiss.

"Tell Willie and Peter the next time they

see that guy, I'd like them to have a chat with him," Stone said. "Find out who he is and see if they can connect him with Max."

"Okay," Carrie replied. "We'll talk later."

"I want the night off," Stone called after her. "I'm exhausted."

"We'll see," she called back over her departing shoulder.

Stone went back to sleep.

28

STONE WAS WAKENED by the phone again a little after eleven. "Hello?"

"Hi, it's Mitzi," she said.

"Good morning."

"You don't sound up yet."

"I'm awake—*up* would be too strong a word."

"Rough night?"

"Not exactly."

She gave a low laugh. "I got my fake financial statement from Daddy's office this morning. You'll be happy to know I'm worth thirty million dollars—on paper, at least."

"Whose letterhead is it on?"

"William H. Barrow, CPA."

"Not your father's. Good.

"Should I just give this to Sharpe?"

"Why don't you call him and tell him you'd like to meet with him and Sig Larsen again?"

"Okay."

"Give him your statement and ask how he would handle it."

"Right."

"Does it have individual stocks listed?"

"Yes, about forty of them."

"Good. Tell him you want his plan in writing."

"Wouldn't that put him off?"

"You don't want to be too easy a mark; *that* would put him off. Con men get special satisfaction from screwing smart marks."

"That wasn't quite what I had in mind."

"All right, *fooling* smart marks."

"Actually, I did have that in mind, but with you, not Sig."

"What a nice idea. What's the setup this time?"

"Not a threesome; I'd rather have you to myself."

"I'm a little under the weather," Stone said. "How about later this week?"

"I'll call you," she said.

"And you can give me a full report then."

"I'll give you more than that."

"Bye-bye." Stone hung up and groaned. "When it rains, it pours," he said aloud to himself.

DINO WAS more cheerful than usual. They had met at P. J. Clarke's for lunch and were having burgers and beers.

"You're in a good mood," Stone said.

"Ben got accepted at Choate," Dino said, speaking of his son.

"Congratulate him for me."

"I will."

"Doesn't this mean you'll see him less often?"

"Well, yeah, but it means I'll have to deal with Mary Ann less often, too. No squabbles about which days I see him or what we do together."

"I'm sure Eduardo will miss him." Eduardo Bianci was Dino's ex-father-in-law, a very rich man who had been—perhaps still was—a major Mafia figure, but who had been very discreet about it, ruling from afar.

"That's true, and I feel for the old man.

I'll make sure Ben sees his grandfather when he's home."

"How is Eduardo?"

"Amazingly well. For a man his age, I'd guess you'd say he's in robust good health. I'm sure he'd appreciate a call from you."

"I'll call him today."

"How's it going with Carrie?"

"She's wearing me down," Stone replied. "Literally."

"You lead such a tough existence," Dino said.

"You don't know the half of it. What are you doing for female company since splitting the blanket with Genevieve?"

"Catch as catch can," Dino replied.

"As long as you catch a few."

"There's the desk sergeant at the 19th," Dino said. "We have a nice evening about once every week or two. Keeps the machinery oiled and working."

"She's the one who ended your marriage, isn't she?"

"No. Mary Ann took care of that; Sarge was just the excuse."

"Is that what you call her?"

"In bed as a joke."

"What's her real name?"

"Madge Petrillo."

"Not married, is she?"

"Nah, divorced. I think she may be banging the captain, too, but if so, they're very, very discreet."

"Busy lady."

"You know it. How's the Derek Sharpe operation going?"

"It's going. Mitzi's a smart cop; she's handling it very well. I'm just trying to stay out of the way."

"That doesn't sound like you."

"Well, I've seen Sharpe with her a couple of times, and I give her advice."

"That's very fatherly of you. What else is going on there?"

"Let's not get into that," Stone said, a little embarrassed.

"Oh, so *that*'s what's going on."

"Don't jump to conclusions."

"What, you think I condemn you for sleeping with more than one woman at a time?"

"It's your Catholic upbringing," Stone said.

"I got over that a long time ago," Dino replied.

"Catholics never get over it. I'll bet you still go to confession."

"Every couple of years, maybe. I love shocking the priest."

"I'll bet you do."

"It's a good thing you're not Catholic," Dino said. "At confession, you'd give a priest a heart attack."

"You're right. It's a good thing I'm not Catholic; I'm not sure I could bear the guilt."

"Guilt is very important," Dino said. "It keeps you on the fairly straight and narrow."

"The *fairly* straight and narrow? I like that."

"So do I," Dino said.

They split the check and walked outside, where Dino's unmarked car with driver awaited him.

"You want a lift?" Dino asked.

"No, thanks. I think I'll walk home, get some exercise."

"I thought you were getting lots of exercise," Dino said, laughing.

"Well, the cardiovascular thing is important," Stone said.

"See you later." Dino got into his car and was driven away.

Stone walked home and entered through the outside door to his office.

Joan flagged him down. "Eduardo Bianci's secretary called. He would like you to come to lunch at his home tomorrow at noon."

Eduardo was a mind reader, Stone thought. "Say that I accept with pleasure."

29

STONE DROVE OUT to the far reaches of Brooklyn to the elegant Palladian house with a view of the water that was the home of Eduardo Bianci.

Stone's relationship with Eduardo went back some years, to a time that predated even his brief marriage to Eduardo's daughter, Dolce. Dolce was an extraordinarily beautiful woman who turned out to be deeply disturbed, with homicidal tendencies, which were directed mostly at Stone and cost him considerable discomfort, including the pain of a bullet wound. Dolce, now safely ensconced in a suite of

rooms in Eduardo's house, was tended by an elderly aunt and professional nursing help. No one but Eduardo had seen her for years.

Stone was admitted to the house by Eduardo's wizened butler, who, according to Dino, previous to—and perhaps after—his employment by Eduardo, had pursued a highly successful career as an assassin, specializing in the Sicilian stiletto. He greeted Stone with a tight smile, or grimace, depending on interpretation, and led him to the rear garden, where Eduardo waited, seated at an umbrella-shaded table near the edge of the pool.

Eduardo, who was unaccustomed to rising for anyone short of the Holy Father, did not rise but extended a slender hand and gave Stone a warm handshake and a broad smile, revealing either amazing teeth or gorgeous dental work, Stone had never figured out which. He was dressed, as usual, in a dark suit, a white silk shirt, and a muted pin-dotted necktie.

"Stone," Eduardo said in his smooth, rich baritone—the voice of a much younger man—"how very good to see you. It has been far too long."

Stone took a seat. "It's good to see you, too, Eduardo. Oddly enough, I was on the point of telephoning you yesterday when I returned from lunch and got your message. You're looking extremely well."

"I am extremely well for a person of my age," Eduardo said, "and I am grateful to my ancestors for the genes passed down to me. My father lived to a hundred and three, and my mother only a year short of that. When she died, my father remarried shortly afterward to a woman of fifty. He told me he had considered a woman of thirty-five but did not wish to be burdened with more children at his age."

Stone laughed. The butler appeared with an ice bucket, opened a bottle of Pinot Grigio, and poured them each a glass. "I hear from Dino that Benito has been accepted to Choate, which is wonderful news."

"Yes, though it means I will see him less often. I think it will be good, though, for him to be out of the city and in the companionship of boys who will grow into leaders in this country."

"I'm sure he will fare well in their midst," Stone replied.

"I have great plans for the boy," Eduardo said.

"Oh? Have you already chosen a profession for him?"

"Not those sorts of plans," Eduardo said, shaking his head. "He will excel at whatever work he chooses. Eventually, he will, with my advice and that of his mother, look after my interests until they become his own."

"What are your interests these days, Eduardo?"

Eduardo permitted himself a small laugh. "You are curious, aren't you, Stone?"

"I confess, I am."

"My interests are broad and deep, ranging from Wall Street, which has been a disappointment lately, to Silicon Valley, with many stops in between."

"Are you still involved in banking?"

Eduardo shook his head slowly. "No. At a board meeting many months ago I heard of this awful bundling of mortgages. I looked into it and immediately resigned from three boards and sold all my bank shares over a period of weeks, well before the crash. A bit later, I moved to cash in the market. Now I have begun to buy again,

companies with futures and at very good prices."

Lunch was served: medallions of pork in a garlicky sauce, with tiny, crisp potatoes and perfectly cooked broccoli.

When the plates were taken away, Eduardo leaned back in his chair. "I am given to understand," he said, "that you are involved with two men called Sharpe and Larsen."

Stone was once again astonished at Eduardo's apparent knowledge of everything about everybody. "I met them both recently," Stone said. "Beyond a couple of dinners I am not directly involved with either."

"I must tell you, Stone, that it is dangerous to invest with Mr. Larsen, as I have reason to believe that he has created a Ponzi scheme along the lines of that perpetrated by Bernard Madoff but on a much smaller scale."

"He will not see any of my money," Stone replied, "such as it is."

"Good. And I must tell you that it is dangerous merely to be in the company of Mr. Sharpe."

"How so?"

"The gentleman has ventured into waters that are rather thickly populated by

others of more experience and cunning. In addition, he has attracted the attention of the police, and when his business associates learn of this, his existence will become uncertain."

"I will certainly heed your warning," Stone said. "And I will tell you, in confidence, that I have had a hand in pointing the police in his direction."

Eduardo looked surprised, an expression Stone had never seen on his face. "Have you, really? That speaks well of you, Stone."

"I'm afraid that Mr. Sharpe has gained some sway over the soon-to-be-wealthy daughter of a client of Woodman & Weld, and I was asked to see what I could do about it."

"Ah, that would be Miss Parsons, would it not?"

"It would."

"I had heard that she had been seen often in Mr. Sharpe's company, and I was concerned. Her father is a friend of mine, and I have bought a number of artworks from him over the years. I hope that your endeavor will be successful soon, for I fear there is not much time."

Dessert was served, a light, Italian cheesecake. Then, over coffee, Eduardo radically changed the subject.

"Dolce has been feeling much better the past few months," he said.

"I'm glad to hear that," Stone said carefully. Not since the divorce Eduardo had effected for him had he mentioned his daughter's name to Stone.

"She has expressed a desire to see you," Eduardo said.

Stone nearly choked on his coffee. "If, in your judgment, that would be a good idea, then I would be happy to see her."

Eduardo laughed his little laugh again. "That was an artful lie, Stone," he said, "but in my judgment, as you put it, I think it would be good for Dolce to speak with you for a short while." Eduardo turned and looked over his shoulder toward the rear terrace of the house.

Stone followed his gaze and saw Dolce, clad in a pretty, summery dress, standing on the terrace. His heart stopped. Then she began walking slowly toward them.

"If you feel that, then I will redouble my efforts."

30

SHE LOOKED YOUNGER, somehow, than when Stone had last seen her, when she was being hustled into a private ambulance, wearing a straitjacket, frothing at the mouth. She now seemed untroubled, at peace, and not in the least dangerous.

Stone got to his feet. "Hello, Dolce," he said, offering his hand. "It's good to see you."

Dolce took his hand then offered a cheek. "And you, Stone," she said.

Stone moved to kiss the cheek, but she turned her head to place his lips at the corner of her mouth and flicked her tongue

snakelike at his. He gave her the chair next to her father, then sat down with her between them. "You're looking very beautiful," he said.

"Thank you, Stone. You were always so gracious."

Why then, he asked himself, did you want so badly to kill me? "Thank you," he said aloud.

"Dolce has taken up painting," Eduardo said, "and she is exhibiting a hitherto unseen talent."

"Oh, I painted as a little girl, Daddy," Dolce replied. "You just don't remember. In those days you were preoccupied with business."

"I suppose I was," Eduardo said. "I was at that time withdrawing from certain activities and moving into others that seemed more . . . inviting."

"You mean more legitimate, don't you?" she asked, giving him a smile.

"If you wish, my dear." Eduardo turned toward Stone. "At that time certain federal agencies were taking too much of an interest in my associates. I had managed never to be in a situation where my conversations might be recorded or my face photographed,

but I believed that it would be impossible to continue that way for long. As it turned out my beliefs were confirmed more quickly than I had imagined, but by that time, I had receded into privacy, and my communications with my former associates had become less frequent and more indirect."

"You have always struck me as the most prudent of men," Stone said.

Eduardo shrugged. "I came to the view, earlier than my partners in . . . such activities, that those activities, as the saying goes, did not pay, at least not for long nor in proportion to the risks required. I judged that it was better to be involved in enterprises where good behavior was enforced by law rather than by vengeance."

Stone smiled. "I have had a number of clients who came late to that realization, to their regret."

"Every one of my associates from those days ended up dead by extraordinary means, deported to birthplaces they did not long for, or permanent guests of the federal government."

"Daddy, on the other hand," Dolce said, "ended up lord of all he surveyed and much more."

"My daughter is too impressed with her father," Eduardo said, shooting her a glance.

"Did you know he was offered the Presidential Medal of Freedom but declined?"

"I have never wished to be famous," Eduardo said, "even for a brief moment at the White House."

"Oh, Daddy, you're too modest," Dolce said. "You've been to the White House many times to visit half a dozen presidents."

"But never with television cameras present," Eduardo pointed out.

"Daddy won't even allow his photograph in the annual reports of the companies and charitable institutions on whose boards he sits," she said.

"I admit it, my dear, I am shy," Eduardo replied. "Now let's turn the conversation back to you." He dusted imaginary crumbs from his suit, a rare gesture of irritation.

Dolce looked over her shoulder, and Stone followed her gaze. A large man in a dark suit stood on the back terrace. He looked at his watch. "Oh," she said, "I'm afraid Alfonzo is becoming impatient. We're going shopping."

Stone was startled to think of Dolce roaming Madison Avenue, a free woman, but perhaps Alfonzo could manage her.

"Dolce needs new clothes," Eduardo explained, "now that she is going out more often."

Dolce stood. "Perhaps Stone would like to tag along with me sometime."

Stone stood, too. "I'm afraid I'm rather occupied with someone who wouldn't understand."

"Yes, I know," she said, leaning forward to kiss him good-bye. This time her tongue momentarily found Stone's ear.

"Good-bye, dear Stone."

"Good-bye, Dolce," Stone managed to say. He watched her walk away, an inviting performance.

"Sit for a moment more," Eduardo said, "until she has made her escape."

Stone sat down, hoping Eduardo did not mean that literally. "She really is looking very well," he said.

"I think her mental state, particularly her anger, made her seem older," Eduardo said. "Now that she has been relieved of those tensions, it shows in her demeanor."

"I suppose so," Stone said. "How long has she been going out?"

"Only for the past ten days or so," Eduardo replied. "I am being very careful with her, following the advice of her psychiatrist, who is a sensible woman."

"I wish I could have helped her," Stone said.

"No one could have helped her in those days, Stone," Eduardo said. "And I would not wish you to feel that you must try again."

"Thank you, Eduardo," Stone said. "I must go now, but it has been a very great pleasure to see you, and I'm glad that Dolce is making such a good recovery." He stood and took Eduardo's hand again.

"I think seeing you was good for her," Eduardo said, "and I'm glad we had an opportunity to talk about Sharpe and Larsen."

"So am I. I will take your advice to heart." Stone walked back to the terrace and through the house. The butler was there to open the front door for him. He got into his car and began the drive back to Manhattan.

He had calls to make now, after Eduardo's warning about Sharpe. Previously, he

had been concerned only about Hildy Parsons with regard to her fortune. Now, it seemed, she was in more immediate danger. So, indeed, was Mitzi Reynolds, above and beyond the call of her duty. Sharpe needed to be shut down quickly and Larsen with him, and not by just a loss of reputation.

Beyond those thoughts, a knot had been forming in Stone's stomach, and he searched for the reason. Then he remembered: Dolce, when told he was seeing someone, had said, "I know."

Stone's heart thudded in his chest, and his hands made the steering wheel slippery.

31

STONE PUT THE CAR in the garage and went quickly to his office. Several message slips were on his desk, among them one from Brian Doyle at the downtown precinct. He called the number.

"Lieutenant Doyle."

"Brian, it's Stone Barrington."

"Hello, Stone."

"I'm returning your call."

"I had a meeting with Mitzi earlier this afternoon, and she told me how well things are going. She said you have been a big help. 'Invaluable,' was how she put it."

"I'm glad to have helped."

"We're getting to the point where we can set up a purchase and a bust," Brian said.

"Brian . . ."

"We don't think it will have to be too big to get a conviction: A pound of grass and half a kilo of coke should do it—plenty to charge him with distributing."

"Brian, listen to me."

"Okay, pal, I'm listening. What's up?"

"I have some new information that you're going to have to take into consideration before you decide whether to continue."

"What sort of information?"

"I have it from a very reliable source that Sharpe has stepped on the toes of some pros who take a very proprietary view of their business operations."

"And which pros are these?"

"I don't know, but they are pissed off at having what they consider to be an amateur dipping into their exclusive territories, and they are planning to do something about it."

"And where does this information come from?"

"I'm sorry, but that's completely confidential."

"That's not good enough, pal."

"Then I'm going to have to invoke attorney-client privilege."

"Stone, if you want me to believe you, you're going to have to give me something more than your word."

"Listen, you started this operation on nothing more than my word."

"That's not quite so," Brian said. "There had been rumblings from other quarters."

"What quarters are those, Brian?"

"Sorry, that's confidential—official police business."

"I'm sorry, Brian, but *that*'s not good enough," Stone said.

"That's how it works, Stone: You have to tell me; I don't have to tell you."

"I'm telling you that very soon somebody is going to remove Derek Sharpe from your precinct in a decisive way, and when that occurs anybody who happens to be standing near him is going to be removed, too. That includes Mitzi and, not least of all, Hildy Parsons, on whose behalf I initiated this whole thing."

"I'll worry about Mitzi," Brian said, "but you're going to have to deal with your little rich bitch who got into the sack with the wrong boyfriend."

"I have a responsibility to Mitzi, too," Stone said, "and I'm telling you she is not well enough protected with just Tom watching her back. He's usually waiting in the car while she's dealing with Sharpe and, incidentally, with somebody called Sig Larsen, a financial advisor who's running a Ponzi scheme."

"Well, Mitzi is going to be wearing a wire from now on, so we'll know who she's talking to and every word they say."

"And you think a wire is going to make her safer? It's more likely to get her killed."

"Stone, a wire these days doesn't mean what it meant back in the olden days, when you were on the force. They're very clever little devices now."

"Brian, if you send Mitzi in there you're going to have to find a way to get her some on-site help. You need somebody at the scene in case things turn bad."

"Well, as it happens, I've got just the guy to go in there with her. He's known to all the participants, and he'll fit right in."

"Good. Who is that?"

"His name is Stone Barrington," Brian said.

"Oh, no you don't," Stone said. "I'm retired, remember?"

"Oh, I think I can get you put on temporary, active status until we're done with this."

"I don't want that, Brian, and in any case, you need a lot more than me. You need guys in black suits and body armor parked in a vegetable truck around the corner, ready to storm the place.

"Speaking of body armor, Mitzi is being fitted out in the latest fashion as we speak. I'm told it will make her even more inviting, that it'll add a couple of inches to her tits."

"Brian, you're not getting this: The biggest threat to Mitzi is not from Sharpe or Larsen, it's from the people who want Sharpe permanently out of business. Mitzi wearing a wire and armor is not going to protect her from a hail of shotgun or automatic weapons fire."

"We do the best we can, Stone," Brian said. "Now, I've already put in an application to the commissioner for your reactivation to the force, and I'm ordering you not to decline any invitations from Sharpe or Mitzi to join them on some occasion."

"*Ordering* me? Where do you come off doing that?"

"Detective Second Grade Barrington, you will comply with the lawful orders of your superiors, including me, Lieutenant Brian Doyle, do you understand me?"

"I'm calling the commissioner myself," Stone said.

"Since when does the commissioner take your phone calls?" Brian asked. "I heard never."

"Then why do you think he would approve active status for me?"

"After speaking with him myself," Brian said, "I think he believes it would be better to have you inside the tent, pissing out, than outside, pissing in. I believe Lyndon Johnson first said that, but it hasn't lost its meaning over the years."

"Oh, God," Stone said.

"By the way, don't leave your house; I've got an officer on the way over there to fit you out with some of today's electronic marvels and your own cute little vest."

"I won't let him in the house," Stone said.

"Oh, yes, you will," Brian said, then hung up.

Stone put down the phone, feeling a

little sick at his stomach. First Dolce and now this.

Joan buzzed him. "Willie Leahy on one," she said.

That had been Stone's next call. "Hello, Willie?"

"Yes, Stone."

"What's up? Is Carrie all right?"

"She's still a pain in the ass, but she's fine."

"What's going on?"

"Carrie said you wanted us to have a conversation with the guy staked outside your house."

"Yes, that's right. Is he Max Long's?"

"Apparently not. Never heard of Max, in fact, and he doesn't even know anybody in Atlanta."

"Then what's he doing out there?"

"Watching you."

"For whom?"

"We couldn't get him to say, not even with Peter's hat pin, but *somebody's* paying him well."

"Oh, shit," Stone said.

"A woman. We got that much out of him."

"Shit again," Stone said. "Thanks, Willie.

Oh, does he have any instructions to hurt me?"

"He wasn't armed, and I don't think he's the hand-to-hand-combat type."

"Thanks, Willie. Good-bye." Stone hung up. His very pleasant day had just gone to hell.

32

THE POLICE OFFICER SET a shirt-sized box on Stone's desk. "Take off your shirt," he commanded.

"Go fuck yourself and Brian Doyle, too," Stone replied politely.

The man fished an envelope from a pocket and handed it to Stone. The return address in the corner belonged to the police commissioner. "Read this," he said.

"I'm not touching that," Stone replied.

The man tore open the envelope and extracted a sheet of paper. "I'll read it to you," he said.

"I'm not listening," Stone replied, placing his fingers in his ears.

"Memo to personnel division!" the officer shouted. "'Detective Second Grade Stone Barrington, retired, is hereby restored to active duty in the First Precinct under the command of Lieutenant Brian Doyle until further notice. Signed, et cetera, et cetera.' Got it?"

"Stop shouting," Stone said, removing his fingers from his ears. "I can hear you."

The officer dug into another pocket and came out with a wallet containing a detective's shield and an ID card with a very old photograph of Stone. "This is for you. Now take off your shirt. Orders from Lieutenant Doyle."

"The police commissioner can't draft somebody into the NYPD," Stone said.

"He can, if you're a retired cop on a pension," the officer said. "Read your retirement papers."

"Do they really say that?" Stone asked.

"Read 'em yourself. Now take off your shirt, or I'll tear it off you."

Stone said a bad word and stood up, unbuttoning his shirt. "What's in the box?" he asked.

"The latest in fashion," the cop said, opening the box and holding up a gray undergarment. "They say it'll stop anything that doesn't have an armor-piercing tip."

Stone fingered the garment. "Feels rough."

"I'll be gentle," the cop said. "Turn around."

Stone turned, and the man slipped the thing on him. "Zip it up," he said.

The garment overlapped, like a double-breasted jacket, giving double protection for most of the important internal organs.

"A perfect fit," the cop said. "You'll take it."

"Gee, thanks," Stone said.

"Now sit down; I've got to fit you with the earpiece."

"The what?"

The cop held out his hand, and a small bit of soft plastic lay in his palm with a wire protruding from it.

"People will be able to see that," Stone said. "Bad people."

"Nah," the cop said. "It fits too far down in your ear canal. The wire has a hook on the end; that's how you get it out: You hook the end of the wire in right here and just pull it out. My advice is, don't lose the

wire." He turned Stone's head to one side, stuck the device into his right ear, removed the hook, and handed it to Stone.

"How do you turn it on?"

"It's on all the time. The battery is good for ten days."

"What do you do after ten days?"

"If you're still alive, I'll bring you a new one."

"Joan!" Stone shouted. "Bring me your makeup mirror!"

Joan came into the room with the mirror and handed it to him. "Cute underwear," she said.

"Oh, shut up." Stone held the mirror in position to look at his ear. "Can you see anything in my ear?"

She took back the mirror. "Yeah, daylight from the other side." She went back to her office.

"Nice lady," the cop said.

"Not always," Stone replied. "Take my advice and stay away from her."

"I heard that!" Joan yelled from her office.

"They heard it downtown," the cop said, tapping his ear. He pulled out a vibrating

cell phone. "Yeah? Good deal." He closed the phone. "Like I said, they heard that downtown."

"How do I get the fucking thing out?" Stone asked.

"Use the little wire with the little hook on the end."

Stone began rooting around in his ear with the wire. "What am I supposed to hook it onto?"

"There's a little plastic loop. I showed you, remember?"

Stone made contact and extracted the earpiece.

"It's a good idea to wear it awhile, get used to it," the cop said. He took the thing from Stone and reinserted it. "By the way, if you put a phone to that ear, downtown can hear both ends of the conversation, and they can speak to you."

"That's just great," Stone said without enthusiasm. "It's time for you to go away now."

"Enjoy your badge, vest, and bug," the man said, and with a little wave, he left.

Joan came back into the office. "What's in your ear?" she asked.

"A bug."

"Put your head on your desk; I'll pour some water into your ear, and it'll float out."

"Not that kind of bug," Stone said.

"Oh, you're wired?"

"In a manner of speaking."

"What's the badge?" She picked up the commissioner's letter and read it, then giggled. "You're a cop again? How can you afford to pay me?"

"It isn't funny," Stone said. "Brian Doyle is trying to get me killed."

"What did you do to Brian Doyle?"

"Nothing much. I just handed him a very nice bust on a platter, and now he's pissed off because I made more work for him, so he did this to me."

"This is so much more fun than working in an actual law firm," Joan said.

"This *is* an actual law firm," Stone replied.

"If you say so," Joan said, flouncing back to her office.

"Don't flounce," Stone called down the hall after her.

"I'll flounce if I want to," she called back. "It's not like this is an actual law firm."

Stone tidied his desk, took off the vest,

and put his shirt on. The phone rang. He didn't wait for Joan to answer it; he just picked the phone up. "Hello?"

"It's Dino. Dinner?"

"Sure. See you there."

Another voice spoke on the line. "You boys have a nice evening, now."

"What was that?" Dino asked.

"I'll explain later. Good-bye—and go fuck yourself."

"What?" Dino said.

"That last part was for the other guy on the line."

"Oh."

Stone hung up and started looking for the little wire with the hook.

33

STONE ARRIVED AT ELAINE'S shortly after Dino, and they both ordered drinks.

"What was all that about on the phone earlier today?" Dino asked.

"It's too embarrassing to tell you about."

"Oh, good. Tell me about it."

"Well, first of all, I'm back on the force."

"What?"

"No kidding. The commissioner has re-activated me and assigned me to Brian Doyle. I've been drafted."

Dino began to laugh.

"You think this is funny?"

Dino tried to answer but couldn't. He was laughing too hard.

Elaine came over and sat down. "So, what's funny?"

Dino couldn't stop laughing but pointed at Stone.

"Yeah?" Elaine asked. "What about him?"

Stone produced his new badge and ID and showed them to her.

"You gotta be kidding," she said.

"It's only temporary."

"I'm amazed they'd have you back," she said.

"They insisted," Stone replied.

Dino continued to laugh.

"All right," Stone said, "you can shut up now."

Dino gradually got control of himself.

Stone stuck a finger in his right ear. "And they bugged me, too."

"You mean you're wearing a wire?" Dino asked, wiping tears away with his napkin.

"Right this minute."

"Where is it, in your crotch? And why do you have your finger in your ear?"

"It's not in my crotch—it's deep down in

my ear, and I've got my finger in it so they can't hear us downtown."

"Why don't you just remove the thing?" Elaine asked.

"Because you need this little wire with a hook on it to get it out, and I lost the wire."

Dino began to laugh again.

"You look kind of silly with your finger in your ear," Elaine said.

"Do you want to be recorded downtown?" Stone asked.

"Not particularly."

"Well, if I take out my finger, they can hear everything you say."

"Okay," she said, "keep your finger in your ear. It's starting to look attractive that way."

Stone took a big slug of his drink. "God, I needed that."

"You know," Dino said, "this is the funniest evening I've ever spent in this joint. I've never laughed so much."

"It's good for you," Elaine said.

Stone looked up to see Mitzi Reynolds walk into the restaurant, and she headed for his table.

She gave him a kiss. "Don't tell me, you've lost the little wire, and you've got

your finger in your ear so they can't hear you downtown."

"Drop it," Stone said.

She leaned over and whispered in his left ear. "Rita Gammage is outside in a limo; why don't you and I join her, and we'll go down to your house and have some fun."

"What, with this thing in my ear?"

"I'll show you how to get it out without the wire," she said.

"You're on," Stone replied. "Will you excuse us?" he said to Elaine and Dino before tossing back his drink.

"What, you're not eating?" Elaine said, looking shocked. "You took up a whole table, and you're not eating?"

"Dino's the one taking up the table," Stone said, "and he's eating. Maybe I'll eat later."

"What's going on?" Dino asked.

"Something's come up," Stone replied.

Mitzi leaned over and whispered, "Something's *going* to come up."

They left the restaurant and got into the rear seat of the limo. Rita was there, and she kissed Stone and continued to kiss him as they rode downtown, while Mitzi unzipped his fly and got a hand inside.

"This is working," she said.

Stone still had a finger in his ear. They got to his house and upstairs. "How do I get this thing out?" he asked. Rita was working on his buttons.

"Stand over the bedside table," she said, "with the right side of your head down. Stick your finger in your left ear, hold your nose with your right hand, take a deep breath and blow, but hold your breath in."

Stone followed the instructions and the bug popped out onto the table. "Thank God," he said.

Rita had his shirt off, and Mitzi was getting his trousers down. After another few seconds of the frantic shedding of clothes, the lights were turned off, and they were all naked in bed.

Stone lay on his back while somebody kissed him and somebody else had his penis in her mouth. He couldn't tell which was which in the dark, but it hardly mattered. He did what he could with his hands, then somebody mounted him and somebody else sat on his face. He could not remember such a medley of sensations.

AFTER A WHILE, they all lay in a heap, panting and sweating.

"So, Stone," somebody asked, "how was that?"

Stone was panting too hard to reply.

"Again?" the other voice said.

"You'd better start without me," Stone said, and they did, while he explored their bodies with his fingers, entering here and there. The two girls were talking to each other and to him, issuing instructions while they played, then they both seemed to come again, nearly simultaneously.

"Let's order a pizza," someone, perhaps Mitzi, said.

"What kind?" Rita asked.

"Domino's—Extravaganza, hold the green peppers," Stone said. But nobody could move, and they dozed off.

STONE WAS JERKED awake by the noise the front door bell was making on the telephone. He picked it up. "Yes?"

"Pizza delivery," a voice said.

"Hang on," Stone replied. He found a robe and some money, then went down to

the front door and brought the pizza upstairs. The girls were sitting up in bed, and
the light was on.

He handed them the box and got some
beer out of the little bar fridge.

Mitzi was looking at him oddly. "I remember talking about pizza," she said,
"but I don't remember anybody actually
ordering it."

Rita opened the box and held up a slip
of paper. "What is this?"

Stone took it and read it aloud. "'From
the guys at the First Precinct. Bravo!'"

"Uh-oh," Mitzi said, pointing at the bedside table.

The little bug sat there where Stone had
dropped it, pointing toward the bed.

This time they rested and dozed a little.

34

STONE HAD NEVER EXPERIENCED a night quite like it. The pizza had revived them, and after having stuffed the ear bug into his sock drawer, they began again.

Now, at ten in the morning, they were having breakfast in Stone's garden, snug behind the ivy-covered brick walls on either side of them and facing the Turtle Bay Common Garden at the end.

The girls seemed fresh as a daisy—showered, shampooed, coifed, and made up, their clothes freshly pressed with Helene's iron. Stone was freshly showered, shaved, and dressed, too, but despite his

having drunk a cup of strong Italian coffee—
and he was now drinking his second—he
felt tired, sore, and sleepy.

"Do you have any important work to do
today, Stone?" Rita asked.

"Nothing that can't wait until tomorrow,"
he mumbled.

"Then maybe you should go back to
bed," she said.

"And maybe we could join you!" Mitzi
offered.

Stone held up his hands in a gesture of
pleading. "Not today; maybe never again."

"We'll see about that," Mitzi said.

"What I need is a massage," Stone replied.

"I'd love to do that, but I've got a meeting at the precinct."

"Thank God," Stone said.

"And I have to go to work," Rita added.

"And good luck to you."

Mitzi spoke again. "The meeting downtown is about our next step with Derek
Sharpe."

"What about Sig Larsen?" Stone asked.

"The feds have taken an interest in him.
We're going to give them the recordings
that you and I make."

"That you and I make when?" Stone asked.

"Perhaps as early as this evening," Mitzi said, "so you'd better get some rest."

"Has Brian Doyle explained to you how dangerous this is, and why?"

"You mean from Derek's rivals in the drug game?"

"I do."

"I'm not particularly worried about that; we'll be well protected. Still, I'm going to armor up, and you should, too."

Stone nodded.

The girls got up and took turns kissing him.

"And don't forget your ear bug," Mitzi said.

"I think you're going to get a hard time from the guys at your meeting," Stone said.

"Oh, no; they'll save that for you, and it will be mostly admiration. They have no idea who you were with last night."

"I hope not," Stone said, waving good-bye to them.

LATER, STONE WAS so zonked out on the massage table that the masseuse had to turn him over when the time came. He had no memory of it when she finished. She

helped him to the bed, and he fell into it, his body an oily overcooked noodle.

IT WAS a little after five when Mitzi called. "We're on for tonight," she said.

"Do we have to go to Sharpe's studio? It's dangerous there."

"No, this is about Sig and my so-called money, so we're meeting at 740 Park at seven. After Sig makes his pitch and we've recorded that for the benefit of the feds, I'll take Derek aside and tell him I need some drugs for a friend."

"Good. Don't tell him you're a user, or he'll make you use some with witnesses around."

"My story is that I use only booze, which is all he's seen me use."

"What are you going to ask him for?"

"Half a pound of marijuana and five ounces of coke."

"Are you going to have cash?"

"I've already signed for it."

"You're not going to get a receipt for the drugs, you know."

"Don't worry, we have a bookkeeping way of keeping track of that."

"You should insist that he give you the

drugs in the apartment, too, not at his place and especially not in a car."

"Yeah, yeah, Stone, I know. We've worked all that out. Can you be at the apartment at six thirty?"

"Yes, I guess so."

"We can have dinner afterward," she said.

"Okay. See you then." He hung up.

He had just gotten out of the shower when the phone rang. "Hello?"

"Hey, it's Carrie."

"Good afternoon."

"Dinner tonight?"

"I can't; business."

"Cop business?"

"If I told you, I'd have to kill you."

"How much longer is this going to go on?"

"I hope not much longer."

"Me, too. I've been working hard, and I miss you."

"Same here," he said, but he didn't sound very convincing.

"You sound funny."

"I just had a massage, and I'm half asleep."

"Oh."

"Any movement from Max?"

"Not a peep out of him. Tomorrow's the last day I'm using the Leahys. I really don't feel threatened."

"I would advise you to keep them on for another week, at least."

"They're expensive!"

"You can afford it. Max's check cleared, didn't it?"

"It's already in T-bills," she said.

"Keep them on for another week."

"We'll see. Bye-bye, sweetie." She hung up.

Stone struggled out of bed and into some clothes. He was about to leave his bedroom, but he remembered something. He went to his sock drawer, retrieved the ear bug, and slipped it into the ticket pocket of his jacket.

He arrived at Rita's apartment on time, and Mitzi greeted him with a big kiss. She leaned into his left ear. "You were sensational last night."

"So were you," he said, "but you don't have to whisper; the bug's in my pocket."

"Mine's in my ear," she whispered, "so be careful."

Stone nodded.

Mitzi held out her hand. "Give it to me," she mouthed.

He dug out the bug and handed it to her, and she stuffed it into his right ear and pushed it home with the tip of her little fingernail.

"All set, guys," she said. "They should be along in about twenty minutes," she said to the air. "In the meantime, all you're going to hear is the clink of ice cubes." She went to the bar and poured them each a Knob Creek.

Stone accepted it gratefully, then sat down to rest and wait.

35

AT FIVE MINUTES after the appointed time the phone in Rita's flat rang, and Mitzi picked it up. "Yes, please send them up," she said, then hung up.

"They're not going to like having a lawyer here," Stone said.

"I'll handle it," Mitzi replied. She went to the door and let in Derek Sharpe, Sig Larsen, and Sig's wife, Patti. This time there was no maid to serve, so Mitzi trotted out some pre-prepared hors d'oeuvres from the bar fridge, then handed Stone a bottle of vintage Krug champagne to open.

Stone was stunned that Mitzi would

waste such a fine bottle on these people, but he uncorked it and filled their thin crystal flutes.

After some small talk Sig placed his briefcase on the coffee table, snapped it open, and lifted the lid. "Mitzi, we have some very exciting things to talk with you about," he said, "but do you always have your attorney present at financial meetings?"

"Stone is not my attorney," Mitzi said. "He's just a friend I've been seeing a lot of who happens to be an attorney."

"Still," Larsen said, "I'd be grateful if we could meet alone with you. We'll be discussing some highly confidential information."

"Perhaps a good investment would interest me," Stone said.

"With respect, Stone," Larsen replied smoothly, "I think we're out of your league here."

"Stone," Mitzi said, "would you mind?"

"Not at all," Stone said, rising.

"Patti," Larsen said, "why don't you keep Stone company?"

Stone walked off down a hallway, having no idea where he was going, and Patti trotted along behind him. After a short

walk, he emerged into a kitchen, a large room filled with the latest in appliances but decorated as though it were a part of someone's comfortable home. Stone opened a refrigerator door. "Can I get you something, Patti?" he asked.

Patti came over and looked into the fridge, placing her hand on his ass and squeezing. "*Mmmm*. Why don't you open that half bottle of champagne?" she asked.

Stone brought it out then searched the cabinets until he came up with a pair of flutes. He opened the half bottle and poured. There was a sofa in the room, but sexually sated as he was, he didn't want to share it with Patti, who, on their previous evening together, had been very seductive, so he took a kitchen stool at a counter in the center of the room.

Patti used a stool as a ladder that allowed her to sit on the butcher-block countertop beside him. "I'm glad we have a little time together," she said. "Last time we met I didn't see enough of you, so to speak."

Stone glanced at her hiked-up skirt, which hadn't been long to begin with and was now near crotch level. "Well, I'm seeing a lot of you now," he replied.

"Would you like to see more?" she asked playfully, hiking up the skirt until there was nothing between the countertop and her ass. She was not wearing panties, and her wax job was Brazilian.

"Is that the new fashion?" Stone asked. "No underwear?"

"Like it?" she asked.

"What's not to like?" Stone asked. "I'm sure it attracts a lot of attention."

"It attracts the attention of only those I'm attracted to," Patti replied.

"That's very flattering," Stone said. He couldn't think of anything else to say. Clearly, Patti had been sent by her husband to keep him out of the living room, and she was using every technique at her disposal. "I hope no one suddenly walks in here," he said.

"Oh, no one will," Patti said. "It's obviously the maid's night off, and the others are talking about money, which will hold their attention for some time. I'd say we have at least an hour alone before someone invites us back to the living room."

"Perhaps you're right," Stone said, becoming aroused in spite of himself. He sipped his champagne. "Are you always so free with your favors?"

"When I feel like it," Patti replied, "and I feel like it tonight. In fact, I'm getting wet just thinking about it."

"Then I don't think you need me for a satisfactory resolution to your, ah, condition."

"Oh, I never need a man for that," she said, "but there are times when I'd like one, and this is one of those times."

Stone was short of words again.

"In fact," she said, "all you have to do is stand up. This counter is exactly the right height for you to just sort of walk into me."

"I suppose it is," Stone said.

She reached over and stroked his crotch. "And I can tell you're ready." She squeezed.

Stone twitched involuntarily. God knows, I'm ready, he thought. He looked for a way out of this without insulting her. "Actually, I was quite active last night, and I'm pretty sore."

"I'll be gentle," she said. She took his arm, pulled him off the stool onto his feet, and kicked the stool away. She put a hand inside his belt and pulled him toward her.

"I really am very uncomfortable with this," Stone said, removing her hand from his belt.

"Then let's free things up," she said, reaching for his zipper.

"Let's not," Stone said, removing her hand again.

"Stone!" a male voice called from the hallway.

Stone turned. "Yes?" he called, trying not to sound relieved. When he turned back, Patti had hopped off the counter and returned her skirt to its full length.

Derek Sharpe walked into the kitchen. "Sig would like you back," he said.

"Sure," Stone replied, and followed Patti, who was following Derek.

She reached back for his crotch, but he evaded her by sidestepping.

Stone concentrated on reducing the bulge in his trousers, but it was difficult. He took a seat. "How can I help?"

"Derek," Mitzi said, "may I speak to you privately for a moment while Stone chats with Sig?"

"Of course," Sharpe replied. He got up and followed Mitzi from the room.

"I've been explaining to Mitzi how profitable it can be to invest in emerging technology," Larsen said.

"What sort of emerging technology did you have in mind?" Stone asked.

"A new software company that's developing software for the iPhone," Larsen replied.

"Lots of people are developing software for the iPhone," Stone said. "What's so different about this one?"

"It's very, very different," Larsen said, "but I'm afraid I can't go into that."

"Did you go into it with Mitzi?" he asked.

"In broad terms. I'm prepared to give her a prospectus, if she's interested, but she wanted your opinion."

"It's hard to have an opinion," Stone said, "when you're talking in generalities." He really wanted to be listening to the conversation between Sharpe and Mitzi, but at least downtown was listening.

"I'll make sure that you see the prospectus," Larsen said.

"Do you have a copy with you?"

"Yes, but that's Mitzi's; I'll send someone to you tomorrow with a copy that you can peruse, then return to me."

"You're being very cautious," Stone said.

"The opportunity is large; I don't want word to get around until I have my investors in this company."

"Good thinking," Stone said. Then it got very quiet. He caught Patti looking at his crotch and involuntarily crossed his legs.

36

MITZI LED DEREK SHARPE into the study off the living room, and they sat down on a sofa. She turned to face him. "This is awkward," she said.

Derek placed a hand on her knee. "I don't want you ever to feel awkward with me."

She shifted her position to dislodge the hand. "I have some friends in Charleston who want something that I can't supply them," she said.

"And what would that be?" Sharpe asked.

"Something that I have no experience in

obtaining," she said, "since I have no personal need for it."

"Well, if we were in the nineteen-twenties I'd think you were going to ask me where you could buy a case of Scotch."

"That's not a bad analogy," Mitzi said, trying to seem more nervous than she felt. "It's just that I've been in New York for such a short time that my circle of acquaintance doesn't extend to people who . . . have a wider circle of acquaintance."

"Now it sounds as if you want me to provide you with a porno star for your personal use. Or that of your friends."

"That's not a good analogy," she said. "What they want is unavailable over the counter, so to speak."

"Are we talking about illegal recreational drugs?" Sharpe asked.

Mitzi heaved a big sign of apparent relief. "Yes," she said.

"In what sort of quantity?" he asked.

"Oh, just small stuff," she replied. "They asked me if I could find them half a pound each of marijuana and cocaine."

"Half a pound of either of those is not small stuff," Sharpe replied. "Together, they

make a quantity that ordinary dealers might be reluctant to sell you."

"Oh?" Mitzi asked innocently. "Why? Don't they want to sell as much as possible?"

"Yes, but they become uncomfortable when someone asks for a quantity that could subject them to arrest for dealing."

"But that's what they do, isn't it?"

"They do, but the penalties for simple possession of a small amount of drugs for personal use and for possession in sufficient quantity to suggest intent to sell are very different, so they become cautious when such a request is made."

"If it's about money, that's not a problem," Mitzi said.

"It's not about money, Mitzi; it's more about discretion."

"Am I being indiscreet?" she asked, widening her eyes.

"Just a little."

"I'm sorry. I have no experience at this sort of thing," she said. "I apologize. Please forget I asked." She began to rise, but he stopped her.

"It's for that reason that I want to advise you," Sharpe said.

"All right, what is your advice?"

"First, we need to find some place to receive the package," Sharpe said.

"How about right here?" Mitzi asked, waving an arm. "This is not exactly a street corner."

"No, it's not," Sharpe admitted, "and this apartment would be a discreet place for you to accept delivery."

"Oh, good," she said, brightening.

"You understand that you must pay in cash?"

"I wasn't planning to write a check or use my American Express card," she said.

"Good, because you're talking about quite a lot of cash." He quoted a number.

"Goodness, that much?"

"That much."

"Well, it's not my money," she said. "I guess if that's the going rate, they'll have to pay it."

"Do you think they might object to that amount?" Sharpe asked.

"They left it entirely to my discretion, and I leave it entirely to yours, Derek."

"All right. How soon can you have the cash?"

"I already have it," Mitzi said. "I always

keep some cash in the safe. I hate ATMs—such small bills!"

"I agree entirely," Sharpe said. "Would you like to give me the money now?"

"I believe I'd prefer cash on delivery," Mitzi said. "That's how my daddy brought me up."

"Well . . ."

"I'm good for it, Derek. I hope you know that."

"Of course I know that, Mitzi. I'll send the man over with it tomorrow morning, if that's all right."

Mitzi shook her head. "I'm perfectly happy to receive the package here," she said, "but I won't have some drug dealer in this apartment. I'd be scared to death."

"Well, suppose I send Hildy Parsons over with it."

Mitzi shook her head again. "I wouldn't ask Hildy to do that," she said. "I hardly know her."

"Oh, she won't know what's she's delivering," Sharpe said.

"I don't care about that. I mean, if she had some sort of accident and got caught with it I'd never forgive myself. I'm surprised you'd let her do such a thing, Derek."

"You want me to deliver it myself?" he asked.

She put her hand on his. "Oh, Derek, would you?"

"Well . . ."

"I'd be your friend forever," she said, squeezing his hand. "I might even buy a picture . . . or two."

Sharpe smiled broadly. "I'd be very happy to help you out," Derek said.

"And if my friends are happy with what they get, could you get them more in the future?"

"I'm sure I could," Derek said. "Tell me, how are they going to get the package back to Charleston?"

"They have their own jet," she said.

"Perfect," Sharpe said. "And you'll have the money ready?"

"Of course. I'll find something to put it in for you."

"That won't be necessary; I'll bring a briefcase."

"Oh, good," Mitzi said, standing up.

Sharpe stood up, too, and made a move toward her.

Mitzi hadn't been expecting it, and suddenly she found his lips on hers. It was a

struggle not to grab a letter opener from the desk next to her and plunge it into his neck, but she stood still and let him put his tongue in her mouth for a moment, before pushing him gently away.

"Oh, Derek, you're so impulsive."

"I'll be more deliberate next time," he said.

"What would Hildy say?"

"I think Hildy might find it exciting," he said.

"Please don't bring her with you tomorrow," she said. "I would be embarrassed if she found out what we're doing."

"I'll come alone," he said, rubbing the back of his fingers across her right breast.

"Oh, good," Mitzi said, taking his arm and leading him back into the living room. "Did you say ten tomorrow morning?"

"That's good for me," he replied.

She squeezed his arm. "That's good for me, too."

37

STONE AND MITZI SAT sipping bourbon at a front room table at the Park Avenue Café.

"So, it went well?"

"So well I can't believe it," Mitzi said. "Downtown was thrilled with what they got on tape." She smiled. "They enjoyed your tape, too."

"I'm afraid Patti had been given the task of keeping me out of the living room, and she was enjoying her work a little too much." He gave her an account.

Mitzi nearly choked on her Knob Creek. "I'm surprised you didn't succumb!"

"If you and Rita hadn't worn me out last night, I might well have."

"Men have no stamina," Mitzi said.

"I didn't know we were so weak."

She nodded. "One orgasm and you're done."

"Well, with a little time out in between I can sometimes manage a second round."

"Sex renders men unconscious," she said. "Whereas Rita and I could have gone on all night. In fact, we nearly did!"

"But I was unconscious."

"Well, yes."

"Maybe we had the wrong kind of three-some," she said.

"You mean . . ."

"Yes, you and another guy and me, lest you mistake my meaning."

"I have no interest in guys."

"Doesn't matter, as long as you're both interested in me."

"You're a glutton," Stone said.

"Sometimes. I've never seen the harm in getting everything you want."

"Hard to argue with that," Stone agreed.

"I mean, Rita and I gave you everything you wanted, didn't we?"

"Everything my heart desired."

"I rest my case."

Stone took a sip of his drink and tried to think of something to say.

"So," she said, "do you know another guy?"

"Dino is the only single man I know, and as much as I love him, I don't think I'd like to get into bed with him."

"I take your point. I guess I'll have to do my own hunting."

"I'm afraid so." Stone finally thought of something else to say. "By the way, tomorrow morning, you should have your people in place a couple of hours before you expect Derek Sharpe with the goods."

"Good idea."

"You could put one of them in a doorman's uniform."

She shook her head. "The co-op board would be outraged if they thought the NYPD was staging a drug bust in the building."

"Come to think of it, you're not going to need a lot of help to take Derek. You and Tom should be able to handle him; then you can walk him out, and the board will be none the wiser."

"I think that's best," Mitzi said. "I'd hate

to get Rita thrown out of the building, especially when she's asked me to move in with her."

Stone almost choked on his bourbon. "You two are getting very chummy, aren't you?"

"Well, you're a witness to that, aren't you?"

"I know you like men, Mitzi, but does Rita?"

"You have to ask? She enjoyed you as much as I did."

"I suppose."

"Women are not embarrassed about being attracted to other women. Men, on the other hand, are worried that someone will think they're gay."

"That's perfectly true," Stone admitted, "but I wouldn't have thought you and Rita . . ."

"Rita and me *sometimes*," Mitzi said. "Anyway, it's nice for a girl to have a roommate, somebody to sit around in pajamas with, eating chocolates."

"And each other."

"That, too. Nothing wrong with a full life."

Stone had nothing further to contribute on the subject. "I suppose Brian is pleased

with the way your case is going," he said lamely.

"He'd sure better be," Mitzi said. "When we tag Derek, the tabloids are going to go nuts, and he'll be the guy standing in front of the cameras. He'll get noticed at One Police Plaza."

"I guess he'll enjoy that," Stone said. "Is he bucking for captain?"

"You bet your ass he is," Mitzi said, laughing. "And if this case puts him over the top, I'm never going to let him forget it!"

"What about Sig Larsen?" Stone asked.

"I told you, Brian isn't interested in him. He's got the U.S. Attorney's office on pins and needles, though. After Bernie Madoff they think it's fashionable to bring in financial scam artists."

"Tell Brian I don't think he should mention my name to the U.S. Attorney."

"The beautiful blonde? Why not?"

"Well, a couple of years ago, right after she got the job, we had a little thing that ended up getting us into the papers."

Mitzi looked shocked. "That was *you*? You actually got videotaped in bed with her?"

"Fortunately, my face was out of the frame, but she got recognized. She was the one on top at the time."

Mitzi hooted. "Brian is going to love this!"

"Just tell him it's in his interests not to bring my name into it. By the way, did you keep a copy of Sig's prospectus?"

"No, he wouldn't let me. I read most of it, and it sounds very appetizing, if you've got a lot of money to throw around."

"He said he would send someone to my office with a copy that I could read but not keep."

"I know Brian would love it if you found a way to make a copy," Mitzi said.

"I don't live to make Brian Doyle happy," Stone said.

"He loved it that he got you put back on active duty."

Stone winced. "He loves it that he can use that to give me orders."

"Exactly."

"Don't worry; when he starts doing that, I'll ignore them."

"Don't piss him off, Stone; I've still got to live with him."

"Do you and Brian have something going on?"

"A long time ago," she said, "before he made lieutenant. He was my first partner, assigned to break me in."

"And he did?"

"In a manner of speaking," she said with a sly smile.

38

STONE WOKE UP, exhausted again. He was going to have to get some real rest, he thought, as he swung his legs over the side of the well-mussed bed. He could smell bacon frying.

Mitzi had left him a razor and toothbrush in her bathroom. He shaved, showered, and then looked for his clothes. Nowhere in sight. He found a robe in a closet and walked down to the kitchen. Rita was cooking, and Mitzi was ironing. A woman he didn't know was sitting at the counter having coffee.

"You're up!" Mitzi said.

"Sort of. I'm pretty tired."

Rita laughed. "You'd be even more tired if I'd known you were in the apartment."

"Good morning," Stone said to the attractive young woman at the counter.

"Oh, Stone," Rita said. "This is my friend Emma Suess. She served you canapés the first time you were here, in the maid's uniform?"

"How do you do," Emma said, extending a hand. "I'm not really a maid; I'm an actress. I was playing the role of maid that night."

"I'm pleased to meet you, Emma," Stone said. He wondered what other roles she played around the house.

Mitzi handed him his freshly ironed shorts and shirt. "I'll be done with your suit in a minute."

Stone got into them, then his pants, when she had finished.

"Now don't you feel all fresh and new?" Mitzi asked.

"Fresh, maybe, but not new."

"Tom will be here around nine."

Rita put eggs and bacon on the counter, and they all ate with gusto.

"So," Rita said, "you're going to put away Mr. Derek Sharpe this morning."

"We hope," Stone said.

"For sure," Mitzi interjected.

"Let's not get ahead of ourselves," Stone said.

"We've got the guy boxed, Stone. Why do you sound so discouraged?"

"I'm not discouraged. I just don't know what you and Sharpe said to each other last night and if it's going to translate into a successful prosecution. One thing drug dealers always have is plenty of cash for the best lawyers."

"Once we nail him with the goods, he'll cop a plea, and we'll put him away for ten years."

"The Rockefeller laws have been repealed," Stone said, "or hadn't you heard about that? A conviction doesn't mean an automatic ten-year sentence anymore; the judge is going to have discretion."

"Are you saying a judge can be bought?"

"That, too," Stone replied.

"I talked to Brian this morning," Mitzi said. "The minute we've got the cuffs on Sharpe they'll be in his building with a search warrant, and we'll find his stash. I'll bet it's a lot."

"I'll bet it's not in the building," Stone said. "Sharpe is not stupid. I think you'd do better to let this morning's arrest slide, then set up another one in a few days and nail him then."

"So why didn't you mention this last night?"

"I was thinking about other things last night."

"That's sweet of you, but since you didn't get your two cents in, we'll have to go with it as it is."

"You can call Brian and suggest a new plan."

"He wouldn't go for it."

"At least you'd have your ass covered if this goes wrong."

"Well," she said, "there's a lot to be said for having your ass covered."

"Call him," Stone said.

Mitzi took her plate and went into another room.

Rita took a sip of her coffee and looked at Stone over the brim of the cup. "Now she's going to be all pissed off," she said. "You're spoiling her party."

"I'm trying to protect her from Brian Doyle," Stone said.

"You think she needs protecting from her boss?"

"Brian is a . . . mercurial guy, and if this goes wrong, he's not going to take the blame."

"And if it goes wrong, what happens to Hildy Parsons?"

"There's that, too," Stone said. "And that's my principal interest in all this."

"Mine, too."

Mitzi came back into the room. "Brian says to go ahead with the buy but not to bust Sharpe, just let him walk out with the money."

"Are the bills marked?"

"If they are, Brian didn't tell me."

"I wouldn't be surprised if Sharpe owns an ultraviolet light," Stone said. "He'll be looking for marks."

"Too late to change plans now," Mitzi said. She went to the big Sub-Zero fridge, opened the freezer, and took out a large plastic bag.

"That's your safe?" Stone asked.

"I've got a real safe," Rita said. "My jewelry's in it, but there's room for that, too."

Stone took the bag and fished out a

bundle of hundred-dollar bills. He flipped through them like a deck of cards. "I can't see anything. I don't suppose you have an ultraviolet light?"

"Nope," Rita said.

"Where's the safe?"

"In the study," Rita replied.

"Why don't you put this in the safe and let Sharpe see you take it out? It'll be good for his morale."

"What would be good for his morale is for me to fuck him," Mitzi said. "He's already made a big pass at me, and I'm expecting more of the same this morning."

"Slap him hard across the chops," Stone said.

"I think that would just make him mad."

"Rita, does the phone system in the apartment allow you to call between extensions?"

"Yes."

"What's the extension number for the study?"

"Eleven."

"Okay, Mitzi," Stone said, "I'm going to give you three minutes with Sharpe, then call that extension. Answer it, say, 'Send

him up,' and tell Sharpe your driver is on the way up."

"Okay."

"What if she's unable to answer the phone?" Rita asked.

"Then I'll interrupt you," Stone said. "By that time you should have completed the deal. Make sure you do that immediately after he arrives. Tell him you have to be somewhere. Make up something."

"What if Sharpe wants to meet your friends from Charleston?" Rita asked.

"I'll tell him they're just in town for the day and have a full schedule," Mitzi replied.

"I'm sure you can handle anything he throws at you," Stone said.

"I'm moved by your confidence in me, sir," Mitzi said, curtseying.

Rita spoke up. "If he throws his dick at you, there's a large pair of scissors on the desk in the study."

"Always use the right tools," Mitzi said. "That's what my daddy always told me."

The phone rang, and Rita answered. "Send him up," she said.

Stone looked at his watch. "Already?"

"It's Tom," Rita said. "Don't have a heart attack."

"What do you want me to do?" Emma asked.

"Put on your maid's uniform, just in case Sharpe comes to the kitchen."

Emma put down her coffee cup and left the room. "Be right back," she said.

Mitzi looked at Stone. "You're more nervous than I am," she said.

"I have a better imagination than you do," Stone replied. "I can think of a dozen things that can go wrong."

39

TOM ARRIVED AND WAS GIVEN a croissant and some coffee. "Are you playing in this game?" he asked Stone.

"Only if I'm needed from the bench," Stone replied.

Emma returned to the kitchen wearing a maid's uniform, but not the one she had worn when she served canapés. The skirt was short, the stockings were black fishnet, and the bodice was tight and featured lots of cleavage.

Stone burst out laughing. "Can you come and play maid at my house?" he asked.

"Emma," Rita said, pointing at the door, "you get out of that garb right now and put on the uniform I gave you. This is not a French farce."

"I don't know about that," Stone said, watching her go.

The phone rang, and Mitzi picked it up. "Send him up," she said, then hung up. "It's Sharpe. He's half an hour early."

"Rita," Stone said, "get that money into the safe and make sure that Mitzi knows how to open it—then get to your room." The two women ran out of the kitchen.

Emma came back wearing a more prosaic maid's uniform.

"Emma," Stone said, "as soon as Rita is back in her room, let Sharpe in, show him to the study, and get back here. You, Tom, and I will be drinking coffee together, should he decide to have a look around."

"Got it," Emma said.

"Okay!" Rita yelled from down the hall just as the doorbell rang.

"You're on," Stone said to Emma, and she started down the hall.

MITZI SAT DOWN at the desk in the study and began writing a letter to her father on

Rita's creamy stationery. She heard Emma go to the front door, and a moment later there was a knock on the study door. "Come in," Mitzi said.

Emma opened the door and stepped inside. "Miss Reynolds, Mr. Sharpe is here." She let him in, backed out, and closed the door.

Sharpe stood by the door holding a large briefcase and looking nervous. "You didn't tell me the maid would be here."

"She's here every day," Mitzi said.

"Who else is in the apartment?"

"Just the maid and Stone. He's down the hall in the kitchen having breakfast."

"I don't think you understand how sensitive this transaction is," Sharpe said.

"I don't think you understand that nobody in the kitchen cares what you and I are doing in here," Mitzi said. She stood, slid back a shelf of fake book spines, and started opening the safe. "I'm glad you're early," she said. "I've got things to do this morning. Did you bring the drugs?"

"Do you have the money?"

Mitzi opened the safe, removed a brown envelope, and took out several bundles of bills. "There you are," she said. "Count it,

and let's get this done." She left the safe open and kept the desk between them.

Sharpe set his briefcase on the desk, picked up some bills, and began counting them. "It's not that I don't trust you," he said, "but my supplier would take offense if I didn't show up with the correct amount."

"I understand," Mitzi said, sitting down again.

Sharpe continued to count. "So you and Stone are an item, huh?"

"You've seen us together before. I like him a lot."

"Didn't he used to be a cop?"

"He retired years ago, I believe; now he's a lawyer."

"So he's not going to come in here and bust me?"

Mitzi laughed. "No, he is not."

Sharpe finished counting the money. He opened his briefcase and put the bills inside, then closed it.

"And where are the goods?" Mitzi asked.

"You'll get them as soon as I deliver the money," Sharpe said.

"Our deal was cash on delivery," Mitzi said. "You've got the cash, now deliver."

"I'll be back in an hour."

"I won't be here in an hour," Mitzi said. "The deal's off; leave the money on the desk and go."

"Now you listen to me . . ." Sharpe began.

The phone rang, and Mitzi picked it up. "Hello?"

"Everything all right?" Stone asked.

"Yes," she replied. "Send him up, please." She hung up. "My driver is on the way up," she said to Sharpe. "And you're not leaving here with my money."

Sharpe opened the briefcase again and extracted two packages wrapped in opaque plastic and sealed with tape. "I was only joking," he said. "Here are your goods. I'll be going."

"Just a minute," Mitzi said, picking up the large pair of brass scissors on the desk. She began working on the tape of the larger package.

"I thought you were in a hurry," Sharpe said nervously.

"I am, but I just want to see this stuff." She got the package open and smelled it. "That smells like marijuana," she said.

"The finest stuff, I promise you," Sharpe said.

Mitzi began working on the other package.

There was a knock on the door. "Ms. Reynolds?"

Sharpe looked like a trapped rabbit.

"Tom, please wait in the kitchen," Mitzi called back. "I'll be ready in a minute." She continued to work on the smaller package and finally got it open. "You're supposed to taste this, aren't you?"

"Lick your finger, dip it in, and taste."

Mitzi did so. "What's it supposed to taste like?"

"Exactly what it tastes like."

"Is it pure?"

"Of course not. It would take your head off if it were pure. It's been cut; all cocaine is cut. Don't worry, your friends will love it."

"Okay, if you say so," Mitzi said. She put the two packages in the safe, closed it, and turned the handle. "Thank you very much, Derek," she said. "I believe that concludes our business."

"I believe it does," Sharpe said, still looking as though he might be arrested.

"If you'll excuse me, I have an appointment."

"Sure, let me know if you want more."

"I'll see what my friends think," she said. "Come, I'll show you out." She walked him through the living room and to the front door. "See you soon," she said, giving him a kiss on the cheek.

Sharpe seemed too nervous to kiss her back or grope her. "Bye-bye," he said.

Mitzi closed the door behind him, leaned on it, and heaved a big sigh. Then she walked down the hall to the kitchen, where Tom, Emma, and Stone were waiting.

"He was as nervous as a cat," she said, "and he tried to hold out on me, but we got it done."

"He won't be so nervous next time," Stone said.

40

DEREK SHARP STARTED sweating in the elevator, and when he hit the lobby he had to will himself not to run. His car was waiting where he had left it, guarded by the doorman to whom he had given a hundred-dollar bill.

He looked up and down Park Avenue for something that could be an unmarked police car. Across the avenue a garbage truck was loading the trash from another building, and one of the sanitation workers seemed to look at him for a long time. The man wiped his face with his sleeve and seemed to pause for a moment with his

wrist to his lips. Was he speaking into a microphone?

Sharpe's hands were shaking, and he had trouble getting the key into the ignition, but he finally got the Mercedes started. He pulled into traffic, and, looking more into the rearview mirror than ahead, he made it down Park a couple of blocks to where the light was just turning red. He floored the car and, tires squealing, made a hard left turn before the uptown traffic could block his progress. Anybody following him would have to wait for the light to change to make that turn.

He drove across town to Second Avenue and turned downtown just as the light changed, still watching his rearview mirror. It seemed safe, but that was what they wanted him to think, wasn't it? Now he would have a ten-block head start, chasing green lights, which were set to a thirty-mile-an-hour speed. He was feeling very pleased with himself until he finally had to stop for a light, and a blue Crown Victoria with two men dressed in business suits in the front seat pulled up beside him. It was an unmarked police car, no doubt about it.

Sharpe contemplated making a left and

running, but he was frozen with fear. Then the light changed, and the blue car pulled away from him and continued down Second Avenue. He was startled by a horn from behind him and got the car moving again. He cut across three lanes of traffic and made a right. When he got to Lexington Avenue, he turned downtown again. The cops in that car had probably not been looking for him, he thought, then he started looking down Lex for the car, wondering if they were going to drive across town and cut in front of him.

When he finally got downtown to his building, after suspecting a dozen other vehicles along the way, he drove around the block twice before using the remote control to open the garage door on the ground floor of his building. Only when the steel door had closed behind him did he feel safe.

He took the big lift up to his studio and let himself in. Hildy was stretched out on a sofa at the end of the big room, which covered the width of the building.

"How did your business go?" she asked, yawning.

"Very well," he replied. "Has anyone come to the door?"

"No, it's been very quiet."

"Any phone calls, especially with the caller hanging up?"

"The answering machine took a couple of calls," she said. "Messages were left."

Sharpe went to the machine and re-played the messages, both routine calls from an arts material supplier and a sta-tioner. He walked from the studio into the office, where two middle-aged women worked keeping books and paying bills, then on to the lower level of his apart-ment.

He went into the kitchen, opened the refrigerator door, grabbed a handle inside, and rolled the big unit away from the wall. Behind it was a cutout in the Sheetrock, with the cutout replaced. He took a small knife from his pocket and pried out the loose area, revealing a large Fort Knox safe. He entered the code into the key-pad, spun the wheel, and swung open the double doors. Inside were stacks of tightly packed plastic bags in the lower half and papers and stacks of cash above. He opened his briefcase, removed the brown envelope, and stacked the newly earned money on a shelf. Then he took a ledger

from the safe and made a coded entry.
He closed the door, replaced the Sheetrock, wheeled the big refrigerator back
into its place, and then leaned against it
and mopped his brow.

He was getting paranoid, he thought.
He had never made such a large delivery
so far from his base, and the experience
had wrecked him. The thought of the
money in the safe made him feel better,
though. How could he have thought that
Mitzi Reynolds could be a cop?

Sharpe went upstairs and changed into
paint-stained work clothes, then he went
back to the studio, where he found Sig
Larsen seated next to Hildy on the old
sofa waiting for him. "Hildy, make yourself
scarce," he said to her. "Sig and I have to
talk."

Hildy left the room without a word.

Sharpe collapsed on the sofa. "Jesus,"
he said, mopping his brow again. "I must
be getting old."

"What's wrong?" Larsen asked.

"I made that delivery to Mitzi uptown,"
he said, "and every cell in my body was in
alarm mode. Once I was there I thought
I'd be busted with all that product. For a

minute, I even thought that Mitzi might be a cop."

"That's called paranoia," Larsen said. "If Mitzi is a cop, then I'm Warren Buffett."

"Or maybe Stone, who used to be a cop," Sharpe said. "He was there for the buy, but he was in the kitchen. He must have stayed the night."

"But you got out okay?"

"Yeah, but then I thought every car I saw was the cops."

"Derek, you need to take some time off," Larsen said. "Why don't you take Patti to a hotel and fuck her for a couple of days? She could use it and, apparently, so could you."

"So could Hildy, but it's so boring with her, why bother?"

"When does she come into the money?"

"In a few weeks. She's cagey about when her birthday is, so I don't know exactly."

"I can't wait," Larsen said. "I want her out of our lives."

"So do I," Sharpe replied. "You can't imagine."

"I can imagine. Patti's got to go, too; she's beginning to take being called my

wife seriously. If we can scam both Hildy and Mitzi we'll have enough to get out of this town to some place with nice weather and no extradition treaty with the United States."

"And where is that going to be?"

"How does Brazil strike you?"

"I could never learn to speak Portuguese," Sharpe replied.

"How about Spanish?"

"I've got my Tex-Mex from back home; I could get by on that."

"Let me do some research."

"You'd better research some passports for us, too."

"The trick is to leave legally, with our own passports, before the Feds or the cops shut us down."

"We've got to move some cash soon," Sharpe said. "The safe is full."

"Sell the product that's in there, and I'll take a couple of suitcases down to the Bahamas and make the hop to the Caymans."

"Not without me, you won't," Sharpe said. "Anyway, the jet charter is cheaper per person, if you have a few people aboard."

"You don't think like an accountant, Derek."

"Have you sent that prospectus to Stone Barrington?" Sharpe asked.

"It's on the way uptown as we speak."

"You think he has any money?"

"Not enough for us to bother with," Larsen said.

41

STONE HAD MADE IT HOME and was at his desk when Joan buzzed him.

"A man to see you. He says he's from Sig Larsen," Joan said on the intercom.

"Send him in," Stone replied.

The man did not look like someone from a messenger service; he looked like someone from the Russian mob, tall and thick. "Good morning," he said in unaccented English. He handed Stone an envelope. "Mr. Larsen says you can read this, but you can't copy it; I have to take it back with me."

"Would you like some coffee?" Stone asked.

"Yes, thank you." The man took the offered chair. "Black, please."

Stone buzzed Joan and asked for a large coffee, and she brought it in.

The proposal was forty-one pages long, and Stone began to read every line.

The man finished his coffee and began to look restless.

Stone was on page eight.

"Could I use a restroom?" the man asked.

"Right over there," Stone said, pointing to a door.

The man got up, went to the toilet, and closed the door.

Stone picked up the proposal and ran down the hall to Joan's office. She watched incredulously while he shoved the stack of papers into the Xerox machine and pressed the button. "How many pages a minute does this thing copy?"

"I don't know, maybe twenty-five."

Stone tapped his foot impatiently, and when the last copy came out he grabbed the original and ran back to his office. He had just sat down when the man let himself out of the toilet.

"Sorry this is taking so long," Stone said.

"Take your time," the man replied.

Stone began reading faster, then scanning. Finally, he restacked the sheets and handed them to the man. "Tell Sig thanks," he said.

The man returned the pages to their envelope and left.

Stone called Mitzi.

"Hello?"

"Hi, it's Stone. Sig sent over his proposal, and I read it."

"What was it like?"

"Too good to be true. There is no corporation or company mentioned, no names of the principals, and no audited balance sheet."

"A scam, then?"

"Of course, what did you expect?"

"And you weren't allowed to copy it?"

"I wasn't allowed, but I copied it anyway, while the messenger was in the john."

"Oh, good. Will you fax it to the U.S. Attorney's office?"

"No, but I'll give it to you, and you can fax it to her without mentioning my name in any context."

"Is it really that bad between you and her?"

"I don't know, and I don't want to find out."

"Okay, here's the fax number at the apartment." She gave it to him. "Dinner tonight?"

"Can't tonight."

"Tomorrow?"

"Let me call you; I'm still in recovery."

She laughed. "Poor baby."

"Bye-bye," Stone said. He hung up, gave Joan the fax number, and asked her to send the document to Mitzi.

"Sure," Joan said. "Oh, a delivery arrived for you."

"Bring it in."

Joan came in holding a crystal vase containing at least two dozen red roses. "Here's the card," she said, then stood waiting while he read it.

With fond memories and anticipation

The card didn't need a signature; Stone immediately recognized Dolce's bold, slanted handwriting.

"Who?" Joan asked.

"Will you kindly send these to the nearest hospital or old folks' home?" Stone said.

"I thought so," Joan said. "I saw her across the street yesterday afternoon, looking as if she was trying to decide whether to come over here."

Stone was further alarmed. "Was she alone?"

"There was a large man with her."

"Her keeper," Stone said. "Eduardo is allowing her out of the house for shopping trips."

"Oh, then she must be a lot better," Joan said.

"Don't you believe it," Stone replied. "I saw the look in her eyes: She's still mad dog crazy."

Joan looked worried. "Oh, God, what should I do if I see her out there again?"

Stone thought about that. "I don't know."

"Well, thanks, that's very helpful. Should I call the cops or just shoot her?"

"Neither of those options works for me," Stone said. "Are you on friendly terms with Eduardo's secretary?"

"Well, I imagine her as some sort of Sicilian bat, hanging upside down in his house, but she's civil, in an abrupt sort of way."

"Call her and tell her you didn't want to

mention this to me, but Dolce is hanging around my house."

"That's taking yourself out of it very nicely," she said.

"Look, I do *not* want to call Eduardo and tell him his lunatic daughter is stalking me."

"No, you want me to do it."

"No, just mention it to his secretary in the terms I outlined, and I'm sure word will get to Eduardo in the proper manner."

"You know I have a .45 in my desk drawer, don't you?"

"Yes, of course I know it. Have I ever mentioned to you the amount of paperwork and the number of court appearances required to deal with charges of murder and possessing an illegal weapon?"

"It's not illegal; you got me a license, remember? I can even carry it around."

"Getting you that license the way I got it is almost as difficult to deal with as a murder charge," Stone said. "So for God's sake, don't shoot Dolce—or anybody else."

"I'll try not to," Joan said, and flounced out.

"And don't flounce!" Stone called after her.

Joan buzzed again. "Bob Cantor on one."

"Hello, Bob, what's up?"

"I'll tell you what's down," Bob said, "the spirits of the Leahy boys."

"What's the problem?"

"They're bored stiff. They're saying I promised they could shoot somebody, but there's nobody there."

"Gee, I'm sorry they're not being entertained by shooting people. You'd think they would be happy they're not being shot *at*."

"What are you gonna do?"

"All right, tell them to drop the surveillance on Carrie, and tell them to explain carefully to her that they think there's no longer any danger."

"Oh, thank you!" Bob said with a faked sob. "Bye-bye." He hung up.

Stone tried to think of something to do.

42

STONE WAS HAVING A SANDWICH in the kitchen when the phone rang. Joan was at lunch, so he picked it up. "Stone Barrington."

"It's Tiffany Baldwin, Stone," said the U.S. Attorney for the Southern District of New York.

"Hello, Tiff," he said warily. "I didn't know you were speaking to me."

"Well, you made up for everything by sending me this very nice fax this morning."

How the hell did she know it came from him? "Which fax was that?"

"The one about this character, Sig Larsen."

"Oh, that one."

"I know you sent it to the NYPD first, but when I got it, it still had your imprint at the top from your fax machine."

"Oh."

"This is a very interesting situation," she said.

"Is it?"

"Yes, it's the first I've heard of it."

"I thought the NYPD had mentioned Larsen's name to you."

"Maybe to a minion, but it didn't float up to my desk until your fax came in."

"I'm happy to be of help."

"Have you actually met this Larsen?"

"Yes, I have."

"What did you think of him?"

"A very slick con man, I thought."

"And he's trying to fleece your client?"

Stone didn't want to pour out everything about Mitzi's undercover work; he didn't know if she had heard about that. "In a manner of speaking," he said.

"I assume it's a she."

"I don't know why you assume that, but she is a she."

"It's always a she with you, isn't it, Stone?"

"Sig Larsen isn't a she."

"And how did you happen across Mr. Larsen?"

"I was looking into an associate of his for a client, when he turned up."

"And who is his associate?"

"A so-called artist named Derek Sharpe."

"I've heard of him. Is he complicit in this scam?"

"He introduced me to Larsen, and he was present when Larsen first mentioned this investment."

"You think Sharpe knows it's a scam?"

"Based on what I've seen and heard of him, I'm prepared to believe the worst about Mr. Sharpe."

"So, I should investigate them both?"

"Tiff, I can't tell you what to investigate; if you like Larsen and Sharpe, go get 'em. I'd be happy to see them both off the street for an extended period."

"You mean your client would be happy?"

"Him, too."

"I thought it was a she."

"There's a he and a she; I don't believe they've met."

"Tell me about the she."

"She's from the south, new in the city, wealthy, and Larsen and Sharpe must think she's vulnerable."

"Is she?"

"Not really."

"Then you're giving her good advice."

"I try."

"What is her name?"

"I can't divulge that without her permission."

"Then get her permission."

"Next time I speak to her I'll ask her if she'd like to be an undercover agent for the federal government."

"You can be smoother than that, Stone."

"I find that when someone wants to embroil my client in what might be a dangerous situation it's better to be blunt about what's wanted of her."

"All right, be blunt with her, but do it quick, all right?"

"I'll do my best."

"Dinner sometime, Stone? Without the cameras, I mean."

"Tiff, I tried to explain that the presence of cameras in my bedroom was unknown to me, but you wouldn't listen."

"My investigation of the event confirmed your claim of innocence, if not *total* innocence."

"I'm relieved to hear it."

"We had some good times," she said. "It might be fun to revisit them."

"Right now, Tiff, I'm embroiled in a number of things that are creating great pressures on my time. Maybe in a few weeks." She might forget about it in a few weeks.

"I'll look forward to it," Tiffany said. "Good-bye."

Stone hung up and dialed Mitzi's cell phone.

"Hello?"

"I've just had a phone call from the U.S. Attorney," he said.

"Oh?"

"Don't play innocent with me. You failed to remove my name from that prospectus before you faxed it to her."

"I asked Brian to do that," she said. "I'm sorry, if he didn't."

"I might have known," Stone said. "Ms. Baldwin would like you to be an undercover agent for her in the pursuit of Sig Larsen. What shall I tell her?"

"Does she know I'm a cop?"

"No."

"I'd better speak to Brian about this, then."

"Do it now; Tiffany is an impatient woman."

"You should know," Mitzi said, with a vocal leer. "I'll get back to you." She hung up.

Stone went back to his sandwich, which had grown cold. He nuked it for a few seconds, then started to eat again. The phone rang.

"Stone Barrington."

"It's Brian Doyle, your commanding officer."

"Go fuck yourself, commander."

"I hear you've got the U.S. Attorney trying to poach one of my people."

"You sent her the fucking prospectus without taking my name off it, as requested. That's why she called me."

"What did you tell her?"

"Nothing. I refused her to give her my client's—Mitzi's—name. She wants to use her to get at Larsen."

"I'm using her to get at Sharpe."

"Look, if you'd shown some interest in busting Larsen, this wouldn't have happened. Trust me, Tiffany Baldwin is going

to gnaw away at this case until she knows everything, so my advice to you is to call her right now and offer to share the fruits of your investigation and the use of your undercover officer in making a federal case against Larsen. Maybe Sharpe, too. It's an easier way for you to get him off the street."

"But without the credit."

"So work out a credit-sharing plan with Tiff. She'll keep her word if you get it in writing."

"Why did you get me into this shit, Stone?"

"*You* got you into this shit, Brian, and unless you call Ms. Baldwin right now, she's liable to approach you through the commissioner. It would be a lot better if you could tell the commissioner you got the Feds involved and worked out a deal with them."

Doyle didn't say anything for a moment.

"Look," Stone said, "if she calls me back, I'm going to have to tell her more."

"Don't threaten me, Stone."

"It's how it is, Brian. Now go deal with it." Stone hung up. His sandwich was cold again.

43

STONE SAT AT ELAINE'S with Dino, gulping bourbon.

"What's the matter?" Dino asked.

"What's the matter?" Stone made a moue. "Well, let's see: I've been assigned by Eggers to save a fair damsel from the clutches of an evil fortune plunderer, as a result of which I've become embroiled in an NYPD undercover drug operation; I've been shanghaied back into the department, reporting to Brian Doyle, of all people; I've been fucking his undercover detective and her girlfriend at the same time, all the while trying to protect Carrie Cox from her

evil ex-husband while fucking her; Tiffany Baldwin has reared her beautiful but addled head again and wants me to fuck her, and she's going to try to shanghai me into working on *her* undercover operation to bust Sig Larsen. Let's see, did I leave out anything?"

"Well, mostly, it sounds as if you're fucking every woman in sight. What else is new?"

"Two undercover operations."

"They don't sound all that daunting."

"They're plenty daunting, believe me; multiple opportunities to get one or more of these women killed along with myself."

"Wear armor."

"Brian Doyle has thoughtfully provided that along with an ear bug that's hell to get out once it's in. Did I mention that?"

"I don't remember," Dino said. "Have another drink." He waved at a waiter.

"You talked me into it," Stone said, draining his glass and setting it aside to make room for another, which arrived with lightning speed. "It's hot in here," he said to the waiter. "Please make it cooler." He patted his forehead with his napkin. "It's always too hot in here."

"It's the bourbon," Dino said, "and all this talk about sex."

"I used to enjoy sex," Stone said disconsolately.

"Don't you still?"

"There are too many demands being made on me."

"Most guys would be very happy to have those demands made on them."

"Maybe I'll just go up to the Maine house for a while," Stone said. "Nobody would think of looking for me there this time of year."

"That's because you'd freeze your ass off this time of year," Dino pointed out. "You wouldn't enjoy it; you don't like extremes of temperature."

"It seems a small price to pay for a little peace."

Eggers came through the front door and headed for their table.

Stone looked up. "Oh, shit."

Eggers hung up his coat and sat down. "Evening, gentlemen."

"Evening," Dino said.

Stone just stared into his drink.

"What's wrong with him?" Eggers asked Dino.

"He feels put upon," Dino replied.

"Put upon?"

"That's it, put upon."

"I suppose I'm the putter-upon?"

"One of several, I believe," Dino said.

Stone took a gulp of his Knob Creek.

"Has he been drinking like that all evening?" Eggers asked.

"No," Dino replied, "just for the last half hour, but the night is young."

"You didn't return my phone call, Stone," Eggers said.

"What phone call?"

"Don't you ever get your messages? I sent you an e-mail, too."

"I forgot to look at my e-mail."

"What's wrong with you, boy?"

"Too much sex from too many women," Dino offered.

"Good God!" Eggers said. "You haven't been fucking our client's daughter, have you?"

"No!" Stone said. "I haven't laid a hand on her."

"She's the exception to the rule," Dino said.

"Because I don't know how I would explain that to Philip Parsons," Eggers said.

"Since it's not happening, you won't have to explain it," Stone said, looking up from his glass.

"Well, it's a relief to hear that you make an exception now and then. Or is Hildy the first?"

"Hildy is *not* the first," Stone said emphatically. "I have a normal sex life. Normally."

Dino burst out laughing, and so did Eggers.

"Are you people here just to torment me?" Stone asked. "Can't you see I'm in pain?"

"Oh?" Eggers said. "Where does it hurt?"

Dino started laughing again.

"I withdraw the question," Eggers said. "Can we have some menus?" he said to a passing waiter. "You'll feel better, Stone, when you get some food into your stomach to keep the bourbon company."

"I'm not hungry," Stone said.

"We're going to have to force-feed him," Dino said, trying not to laugh.

"Well," Eggers said, "I didn't come here to put any pressure on you."

"Thank you, Bill," Stone said gratefully.

"Now what the hell is going on with Philip's daughter and that so-called artist?"

"Gee, thanks for not putting any pressure on me," Stone said.

"Come on, give me the lowdown."

"An undercover cop has made a buy from Sharpe, and it's on tape," Stone said.

"So he's in jail?"

"No, not yet."

"Why the hell not?"

"They want him to do it again, so it'll be a bigger bust. If he does it twice, maybe he'll get a longer stretch."

"How much did he sell the cop?"

"Half a kilo of coke and a pound of grass."

"Shit, that'll get him at least ten years, no parole."

"The legislature repealed the Rockefeller laws, haven't you heard?"

"Now that you mention it," Eggers said. "What would he get now?"

"Who knows? There's a lot of money at stake; somebody might get to a judge."

"Well, they haven't repealed greedy judges," Eggers said. "When is this business going to get wrapped up, so I can return Hildy Parsons to her father intact?"

"Who knows?" Stone said. "But I wouldn't count on her being intact."

The waiter came, and they ordered. Stone ordered another bourbon. "Did I mention that Dolce is stalking me?" he asked Dino.

"What?"

"Don't make me repeat myself."

"Wait a minute," Eggers said, "you're fucking Eduardo Bianci's crazy daughter?"

"No, but she wants me to. She sent me two dozen roses, and she's hanging around outside my house."

"I thought she was locked in a rubber room in Eduardo's house," Dino said.

"Not anymore. She goes out shopping with a minder."

"Now *this* is dangerous," Dino said.

44

STONE OPENED HIS EYES and gazed at the ceiling. It was moving around. He held on to the mattress to steady himself and got his feet on the floor. He barely made it to the bathroom before he knelt at the throne and emptied his stomach.

He lay down on the bathroom floor, pressing his hot cheek against the cool marble. From the bedroom came the sound of Joan buzzing him. He struggled to his feet, splashed cold water on his face, staggered back, sat on the bed, and picked up the phone. "What?"

"You sound awful."

"What is it?"

"Shall I call an ambulance?"

"Just skip a step and call an undertaker."

"You're hungover, aren't you?"

"The word doesn't cover it."

"This ought to help: Tiffany Baldwin is on the phone."

"Tell her I'm ill and can't talk."

"That won't work; I've been on the phone with you for too long."

Stone pressed the button. "Hello?"

"Did I wake you?" Tiffany asked.

"No. You can't wake the dead."

She laughed. "You have to be in my office in an hour for a meeting."

"I'm sorry," Stone said. "I thought you said I have to be in your office in an hour."

"You have to be in my office in an hour," she said, "for a meeting."

"Tiffany, I don't have any current business with your office. What is this about?"

"We're all meeting in an hour," she said. "It's a strategy session."

"Can you hold on for just a minute," he said. He pressed the hold button, ran into the bathroom, and threw up again. He ran some cold water on a facecloth and went back to the phone, swabbing his face. "I'm

sorry, I don't know what you're talking about, and if I did, I wouldn't come."

"Your Lieutenant Doyle requested the meeting," she said.

"He's not *my* Lieutenant Doyle; he's just a cop I know."

"It's my understanding that the commissioner has placed you under his command."

"That's a lie."

"That's not what the commissioner says; I called him."

"Okay, it's not a lie; it's just a perversion of justice."

"Once again, Stone, be in my office in an hour for this meeting. The commissioner will be here, and if you're not, he'll notice." She hung up.

Stone wanted to collapse into bed again, but he got to his feet and threw himself into a cold shower, regretting it immediately. He shaved, cutting himself twice, struggled into some clothes, and went downstairs. He went into Joan's office, poured himself a cup of coffee, and began sipping it.

"You were right," Joan said. "I should have called an undertaker."

"Too late," Stone said. "I have to go downtown to the Federal Building."

"To see Tiffany Baldwin?"

"Among others. She said the commissioner is going to be there, too, but that may have been just to scare me."

"Did it work?"

"Sure did. I don't want him messing with my retirement pay."

"I'm sure that's beneath him."

"It's not beneath Brian Doyle, who hates me because I make more money than he does."

"I'm sure that's not the only reason."

"If I talk about this anymore, I'm going to throw up," he said. "Again. Will you drive me downtown? It seems to be raining outside."

"Oh, all right," she said, putting on her raincoat.

Stone found his trench coat and an umbrella and followed her to the garage.

MORE THAN slightly damp, Stone stood in the line at the metal detector and waited while a woman emptied her handbag onto a steel table and then put everything back, one item at a time. He was cold from the

heavy rain, and his trench coat was soaked, being very old and no longer waterproof.

He emptied his pockets into the tray, put his umbrella on the conveyer belt into the X-ray machine, and passed through the metal detector. *Beep.* He took off his belt; the large silver buckle must have set it off. *Beep.*

"Take off your shoes," the uniformed woman said. "Sometimes it picks up the nails in the heels."

Stone took off his shoes, put them on the conveyer belt, and stepped through the metal detector again. No beep.

The guard at the X-ray machine pushed his shoes toward him with the back of his hand. "You always wear two different shoes?" he asked.

Stone stared at his shoes. The man was right: one black and one brown. "Only when it's raining," he said.

He got his shoes back on over socks that were wet from treading in the pool of water that other people had left behind and went upstairs in the elevator. He found the office and presented himself to a receptionist who reported his presence.

"You may go in," she said.

Stone opened one of the double doors that led into a large corner office, furnished in the federal government's best taste plus a few personal touches from Tiffany. She sat with her long legs propped on her huge desk, reading glasses poised on her nose, a thick document in her lap.

"You're ten minutes early," she said.

Stone looked at his wrist, but there was nothing there. "I seem to have forgotten to wear a watch."

She peered at him over her glasses. "What?"

"The phrase 'death warmed over' comes to mind."

Tiffany got up and led him to a sofa at the other end of the room. "Let's sit here for our meeting." She sat down, crossed her legs, and leaned into him.

The phone on the coffee table buzzed. Saved, Stone thought. He got up and moved to a chair beside the sofa.

"Send them in," Tiffany said into the phone.

The door opened and Brian Doyle

entered, accompanied by Mitzi and the loyal Tom.

Tiffany got up and greeted them. "I suppose you all know Stone," she said.

"Yeah, sure," Doyle replied, and Mitzi gave Stone a big smile. They sat down and looked at each other.

"I think we should wait for the commissioner to arrive before we start," she said.

There was a knock at the door, and a secretary opened it and stepped back. "The commissioner," she said.

The commissioner, a fireplug of a man, marched into the office and took a seat at the end of the sofa nearest Stone. He looked at Stone's feet.

"Barrington," he said, "do you always wear two different shoes?"

45

STONE LOOKED AT THE COMMISSIONER. "Only when it rains."

The commissioner didn't laugh, which was like him.

"Let's get this show on the road," he said to Stone.

Stone blinked. "It's not my show."

"Commissioner," Tiffany said smoothly, "we're here to coordinate the investigations into Derek Sharpe and Sig Larsen."

"Who's Larsen?" the commissioner asked, frowning.

"Short for Sigmund, presumably. He's

the man who's running some sort of Ponzi scheme."

"Be nice to catch one of these guys *before* he steals everybody's money," the commissioner said.

A secretary came into the room with a tray of Danish pastries and set them on the coffee table in front of Stone, who became ravenous at the sight of them. Desperately in need of something to get his blood sugar up, he grabbed a cheese Danish and took a big bite of it.

"Barrington," the commissioner said, "as I understand it, you initiated these investigations, so give us a rundown."

Stone, whose mouth had been dry to begin with, chewed faster and tried to swallow some of the cream cheese. He looked desperately for coffee, but none had been brought. He made a shrugging motion to gain time.

"Barrington, are you hearing me?"

Stone nodded and chewed faster. "It's like this," he managed to say, then chewed and swallowed some more. The secretary returned with a coffee jug and cups, and Stone poured himself some. He scalded his tongue taking a big swallow, but most

of the Danish went down with it. "It began as a private thing," he said. "A client of the law firm to which I am of counsel asked me to investigate Derek Sharpe, fearing for his daughter's trust fund, which she was about to come into."

Brian Doyle interrupted him. "That's when we got involved," Brian said.

Stone fought back. "Yes, that's when I called Lieutenant Doyle and suggested he might be interested in Sharpe. I don't believe he had heard of him until then."

Doyle turned red. "Sharpe was already on my radar, but we hadn't yet had cause to move." He explained in some detail the involvement of Mitzi and Tom, leaving out Stone whenever possible.

Stone used the opportunity to take a smaller bite of the Danish, which helped cool his tongue. "Then Sig Larsen entered the picture," he said. "I can understand why Lieutenant Doyle wasn't interested in him, and I wasn't surprised to hear that the U.S. Attorney became involved."

"And that's why we're here," the commissioner said. "To coordinate the two investigations."

"Actually," Tiffany said, "I don't want to

assign investigative personnel to this matter at this point. Lieutenant Doyle seems to have the situation well in hand."

"Thank you, Ms. Baldwin," Doyle said.

"Then there's nothing to coordinate?" the commissioner asked.

"All we need is your go-ahead to proceed, sir," Doyle said.

"I would have given that on the phone," the commissioner said, rising to his feet and snagging a Danish. He wrapped it in a napkin and put it in his jacket pocket. "Good day to you all," he said, and marched toward the door. But before reaching it he stopped and said, "Barrington, step outside with me."

Stone reluctantly set down his Danish and followed. The sugar was making its way to his brain now, and he was thinking more clearly. He followed the commissioner out of the office and through the reception area into the hallway outside.

"Listen," the commissioner said to Stone. "Has Doyle really got this thing in hand?"

"I'm afraid I don't know," Stone said truthfully. "So far, I've been used as a beard for Detective Reynolds for the most part."

"Not a bad place to be," the commissioner said with a little smirk.

"She's a very competent detective," Stone said, not wishing to mention her other area of expertise.

"I'm going uptown," the commissioner said. "Can I give you a lift?"

"Thank you, sir, yes," Stone said. A detective came out of the office with Stone's coat and umbrella. They took the elevator to the basement garage and got into the commissioner's black Lincoln, which followed a black SUV and led another, and shortly they were motoring through driving rain. Stone kept quiet, knowing that the commissioner didn't like small talk.

"How come you never made detective first grade?" the commissioner asked suddenly.

Stone was surprised he knew that. "I was due for promotion at the time I was retired for medical reasons," Stone said.

"Bullet to the knee, wasn't it?"

"That and a lot of precinct politics," Stone said. "I disagreed with the direction an investigation was taking, and somebody wanted me out. The knee was an excuse."

"Ah, yes, the Nijinsky investigation. I

heard some stuff about it at the time," the commissioner said. "I was captain of the First Precinct, and shortly after that I got moved up the ladder. I reread the file when Doyle wanted you reactivated. I know how to read between the lines. If it's any consolation, I added an addendum, correcting the impression your captain left in it."

"Thank you, sir," Stone said, surprised. "That was very kind of you."

"I hear you've done all right since leaving the department," the commissioner said.

"I can't complain," Stone said.

"You might have done better, if you'd had Brian Doyle's political instincts."

Stone said nothing.

"Doyle will go far," the commissioner said, "but only so far. Somebody will cut him off at the knees before he gets to my office."

"There's usually somebody willing to do that," Stone agreed.

The car came to a halt in front of Stone's house. He had forgotten how fast a police motorcade could move through traffic.

The commissioner shook Stone's hand. "Try not to let anybody get hurt in this in-

vestigation," he said, holding on to Stone's hand. "That's not the sort of thing Doyle thinks about."

"I'll do my best," Stone said. "Thank you for the lift."

Stone opened the car door, got his umbrella outside first, and ran for his office door.

Joan looked surprised to see him back. "How'd it go?" she asked.

Stone hung up his wet coat. "Better than I could have hoped," he said. "The commissioner is a better guy than I had thought."

The phone began ringing.

46

JOAN HANDED THE CALL OFF to Stone. "Hello?"

"It's Mitzi."

"Hi."

"Where did you go?"

"The commissioner wanted to talk to me, and he offered me a ride uptown."

"Brian is livid."

"Because I left his meeting?"

"Because you left with the commissioner."

"Oh."

"Tiffany Baldwin was a little upset, too, but she hid it better. I think she didn't want to share you with the commissioner."

"If you say so," Stone said.

"What did you and the commissioner talk about?"

"He wanted to talk about old times," Stone said.

"You had old times *together*?"

"Not exactly. He apparently followed a case I worked right before I left the department."

"Tell me about it."

"It's a long story."

"Does that mean I'm not supposed to ask?"

"I'll tell you about it when we have more time."

"And when is that going to be?"

"I'm at your beck and call," Stone said. "You tell me."

"I'll have to place another order with Derek Sharpe first," she said.

"And when is that going to happen?"

"We're letting him stew a bit; besides, I don't want to appear too eager."

"If it's any help, I think Sharpe and Larsen are going to decamp."

"Why do you think that?"

"Because they're both involved in enterprises that can't continue forever without

their getting caught, and I think they're too smart to wait too long. I think you should see Sharpe for coffee and place a really big order."

"How big?"

"Forget the marijuana. Ask him for ten kilos of cocaine, and imply that the orders could grow. You want to order enough to appeal to his greed; he'll hang around a little longer for a big sale."

"Good idea," she said. "I'll run it by Brian."

"Don't tell him it was my idea; he'll screw it up just to spite me."

"So I get all the credit?"

"And all the blame if it spooks Sharpe."

"You said have coffee with him?"

"Don't go to his studio; he'll rape you."

"Yuck. Coffee it is."

"Some place where Tom can see you from the street."

"Okay."

"When you've got the buy set up, tell Sharpe you want the delivery at your apartment. He ought to be comfortable there now."

"All right. Then after we bust him, you and I will celebrate."

"You're on," Stone said. He hung up, and the phone rang immediately.

"It's Tiffany Baldwin," Joan said.

"Hello?"

"What did you do to get the commissioner to get you out of my meeting?" she asked.

"I think he thought that if I kept eating Danish, he might have to perform the Heimlich maneuver," Stone replied. "Did anything happen after I left?"

"Not a hell of a lot. I don't think I trust Lieutenant Doyle," she said.

"You have good instincts," Stone said. Line two began flashing on his phone. "I've got another call coming in," he said, "so I'm going to have to go."

"Let's get together."

"Maybe after this is over. Bye." Stone hung up and waited for Joan's voice.

"Brian Doyle on two," she said.

"Hello?"

"It's Brian."

"Hi, there."

"What was that you pulled with the commissioner?"

"He offered me a ride home, and it was raining like hell."

"If you think you can pull something behind my back, Stone . . ."

"Didn't you notice that he asked me to step outside? It wasn't my idea."

"All the same . . ."

"What happened at the meeting?"

"We just got our priorities straight with the U.S. Attorney."

"And how do you intend to proceed?"

"I've been thinking about it, and I believe Derek Sharpe and Sig Larson are going to run for it soon."

"Oh? Why do you think that?"

"I think they're too smart to think they can get away with what they're doing forever."

"That's very insightful of you, Brian," Stone said. "You might very well be right."

"Here's what we're going to do," Doyle said. "Mitzi is going to ask Sharpe for ten kilos of coke and forget about the grass. I think he's greedy enough to hang around until the big deal gets done."

"And what do you want me to do?"

"I want you to try to bring the thing with Larsen to a head; get him to commit an actual crime."

"And what would that consist of?"

"It would consist of Mitzi giving him a ten-million-dollar check to invest."

"Like a fake check?"

"No, like a real one?"

"Whose money are we playing with?"

"I've got a banking connection who will issue the check and then put a hold on paying it."

"You mean a delay at the bank to keep Larsen in town a little longer?"

"Exactly. I can tell we're on the same page."

"I think you might put somebody on checking out the jet charter services at Teterboro and White Plains airports," Stone said, "because when they run, I think that's how they'll do it."

"Good idea," Doyle said. "I'll get that started today."

"They've probably used the same service before to move money. And I'd send your guys to the airports to do the inquiry in person. I think that might encourage the charter service to play straight with you."

"I'll keep that in mind," Doyle said. "See ya." He hung up.

The phone rang again immediately.

"Mitzi on line one," Joan said.

"Hello?"

"Are you and Brian on the same page now?" she asked.

"Oh, sure. He told me *his* big idea, and I loved it."

"Brian thinks you're fucking me."

"Now where would he get that idea?" Stone asked.

She was laughing when she hung up.

47

STONE DUG OUT Sig Larsen's card and called the number.

"Larsen Enterprises," a British-accented woman's voice said.

"Sig Larsen, please. It's Stone Barrington calling."

"One moment, please, Mr. Barrington. I'll see if I can find him."

This was apparently designed to create the impression of a large office, Stone thought.

"Just one moment, please, Mr. Barrington. I'm getting him out of the conference room."

Yeah, I'll bet, Stone thought.

"Stone? It's Sig. How are you?"

"Very well, Sig, and you?"

"Just great. What did you think of my prospectus?"

"Well, I had a look at it, and I thought it was a little skimpy on information." Best not to overenthuse, Stone thought.

"Stone, I hope you appreciate the need for absolute secrecy in this matter; I'm the only person outside the company itself who is privy to this new product, and I've given my word not to disclose the kind of information I think you're talking about. Now if either you or Mitzi isn't comfortable with that level of confidentiality, I'll understand if you don't want to participate."

"Mitzi is more comfortable with it than I am," Stone said, "and she's the boss. She should be in touch with you today about her investment."

"Great, Stone. I'll look forward to hearing from her. Thanks for your help." He hung up.

Stone called Mitzi's cell. "Okay, I've baited the hook with Larsen."

"Terrific."

"How big a bad check are you going to give him?"

"Ten million dollars."

"Whoa! Way too much. Your bogus net worth is only $39,000,000, remember? You'll scare him off."

"How much, then?"

"Five million, tops. What bank will it be on?"

"My Charleston bank, the real one. I've already talked with my guy there, and he understands and will not pay the check."

"Suppose Larsen has his bank call and put a hold on the funds?"

"I thought of that. My guy will tell them it's against bank policy; they'll have to present the actual check."

"That could work. When are you going to give Larsen the check?"

"Tomorrow morning; we're meeting for coffee at the Carlyle Hotel at ten a.m."

"Will Tom be able to see you?"

"Yes. I'd like it if you could be there, too."

"Participating or just watching?"

"Participating."

"I made a point of sounding as if I have reservations about the investment, and I'll

continue that pose at the meeting. The enthusiasm will have to come from you."

"I'll be enthusiastic," Mitzi said.

"All right, I'll meet you there at ten."

"See you then. Dinner tomorrow night?"

"Just the two of us?"

"If you like."

"I think that's best for now."

"I'll try to make up for Rita's absence."
She hung up.

STONE MET DINO for lunch at P. J. Clarke's,
and they both ordered a rare bacon cheeseburger and fries.

"I hear you and the commissioner are
getting chummy," Dino said.

"Where the hell did you hear that?"

"You can't keep anything from me."

"No, seriously, how did you know about
it?"

"His driver is a buddy of my driver. What
did the old man say to you?"

"He asked me why I never made detective first grade."

"And what did you tell him?"

"The truth, what else?"

"You told him it was politics?"

"I did."

"That sounds really lame, you know."

"The commissioner didn't think so. He said that he'd read my file and that he could read between the lines."

"Why the hell would he read your file?"

"He said he read it when Brian asked to have me put on active status."

"Why the hell should the commissioner be interested in you, Stone?"

"I guess he just likes the cut of my jib," Stone said with a smirk.

"Horseshit. He was a captain downtown when all that went down."

"He said he heard about it at the time," Stone replied. "You're beginning to sound jealous of my new relationship with the commissioner, Dino. You want me to put in a good word for you?"

"Yeah, sure," Dino said. "Don't you dare mention my name; I don't want to be associated with you in the commissioner's eyes."

"And why the hell not? What's wrong with being associated with me?"

"Because you're a well-known pain in the ass in the department and a self-important fuckup."

"I am not," Stone said. "I have the reputation of a cop who did his job until he was

wounded in the line of duty and given a medical retirement."

"If that's the way you want to think about it, go ahead. Still being in the department, I have a different viewpoint."

"Who the hell said that about me, anyway?"

"Guys who served with us in the squad."

"That crowd? Who gives a shit what they think? They're a bunch of bums. Anyway, most of them are tending bar in Queens by now. I guess the commissioner bases his opinions on better information than squad room gossip."

"You know, there are a lot of guys serving time in uncomfortable precincts who once thought the commissioner had a high opinion of them. He's like that; you can't read him."

"I'm not reading him," Stone said. "I was just telling you what he said. If you think he's a liar, fine. Anyway, I'm not subject to a transfer to an uncomfortable place. This active crap is just a paperwork thing to make Brian Doyle think he's my boss."

"If you say so."

"I say so," Stone said. Then he looked

across the room and saw Hildy Parsons being seated at a table alone.

"Excuse me," Stone said. "Somebody I've got to talk to." He got up and headed toward Hildy.

48

STONE WALKED UP to her table and held out his hand. "Hello, Hildy," he said.

Hildy took his hand. "Oh, hello, Stone."

"May I speak with you for a moment?"

"Sure, please sit down. I'm expecting a friend, but I'm a little early."

"Hildy, I have some information for you, but I'm going to have to ask you to give me your word that you will not discuss this with *any other person.*"

"All right."

"I mean, not with your father, not with Derek Sharpe, and not with anyone else."

She looked at him suspiciously. "Are

you going to try to talk me out of seeing Derek?"

"I'm not going to try to talk you out of anything. I just have important but highly confidential information to give you."

"All right, I promise I won't discuss it with anyone else."

"I'll trust you to do that."

"Well, what is it?

"How much do you know about Derek?"

"I know that he's from Texas and that he had a hardscrabble childhood."

"Wrong. He's the son of a prosperous junk dealer, and he grew up with money."

"Look, I don't need this from you, Stone. This smacks of something my father would do. Are you working for him?"

"I'm telling you this of my own knowledge," Stone said.

"I don't care whose knowledge it is—I don't want to hear about it. I'm a grown woman, and I can judge people for myself."

"All right, then let me tell you something you don't know that might help you form your own judgment."

She sighed. "All right, and then this conversation will be over."

"If you continue to be close to Derek for so much as another day, it is likely that you will be arrested." That seemed to register with her, so he continued. "And it is very likely that you will end up in prison."

She stared at him wide-eyed but said nothing.

"That's all I have to tell you," Stone said. "If you pass that on to Derek, someone could get killed. I would advise you to absent yourself from Derek for a few days—a death in the family, a sick friend, any excuse."

"Derek and I are about to take a vacation," she said. "Out of the country."

"If you go with him, you will find yourself a fugitive from justice," Stone said. "I tell you this only because I don't want anything bad to happen to you. I hope you understand that."

He started to rise, but she put her hand on his arm, and he sat down again.

"You seem like a trustworthy person," she said, "but so does Derek."

"One of us has ulterior motives," Stone said. "One of us is lying to you. One of us wants your money. If you need a place to go for a few days I have a house in Turtle

Bay with guest rooms." He took a card from his coat pocket and handed it to her. "My secretary is there all day. May I tell her to expect you?"

"No, I don't need a place to hide," she replied, but she put the card in her bag.

"My cell phone number is on the back of the card," Stone said. "Call me day or night, but whatever you do, don't go back to Derek's place and don't see him for a few days." He took a key from his pocket. "This will let you into my house." He wrote the security code on another card and gave it to her. "Please, please, make yourself safe by being alone for a few days."

"I'll think about what you've said," Hildy replied, then looked up and waved. "My friend is here."

Stone got up and went back to his table, where Dino had started without him.

"Your cheeseburger is getting cold," Dino said. "Who was that?"

"Her name is Hildy Parsons. She's the reason I got mixed up in this thing with Brian Doyle."

"That looked like a pretty earnest conversation," Dino said.

"I hope she heard me." Stone's cell phone rang. "Hello?"

"It's Mitzi. I wanted you to know that we hit pay dirt at Teterboro," she said. "Larsen and Sharpe have chartered half a dozen times from the same company, every time to the Bahamas or some other island."

"Have they been to the Cayman Islands?" he asked.

"I'm not sure if that's one of them."

"It's probably where they're banking," Stone said. "They would probably go to some other island first and then change planes if they're carrying cash."

"Got it," she said.

Stone wanted to tell her about Hildy Parsons, but he decided not to. "See you tomorrow morning at the Carlyle," he said.

"Sure," she said. "Gotta run." She hung up.

49

STONE ARRIVED at the Carlyle Hotel at Madison and Seventy-sixth at the stroke of ten. He didn't see Mitzi or Tom, but Derek Sharpe and Sig Larsen were sitting at a corner table in the dining room, so he joined them.

"Good morning, gentlemen," Stone said, and hands were shaken. He sat down and looked at his watch.

"Women!" Sharpe said.

"What's that about women?" Mitzi asked, and they all turned to look at her. She was wearing a flaming red suit and carrying a handbag to match. Every head in the dining room had turned to follow her.

Everybody stood up, Larsen held a chair for her. "Would you like something, Mitzi?"

"Yes. I'll order breakfast." A waiter appeared, and she ordered scrambled eggs, bacon, and toast.

"I'll have the same," Stone said, "with orange juice, coffee later."

The two men seemed surprised that Stone and Mitzi were ordering food.

"Derek and I had breakfast earlier," Larsen said, pouring himself and Derek another cup of coffee from the pot on the table.

There was idle chat for a moment, then Larsen said, "So, Mitzi, what did you think of our investment opportunity?"

"I think it's very exciting," she replied. "Stone is slightly less enthusiastic."

"Not at all," Stone said. "I'm just accustomed to having more information before I advise a client to make an investment."

"As I told Stone," Larsen said, "I am the only person outside the company who has all the facts, and since it's crucial to keep the news of this software a secret until the company is ready to announce it, I simply can't tell anyone anything that isn't in the

prospectus, and I promise you, very few people have seen that."

"I understand completely," Mitzi said. "And when do you think the announcement will be made?"

"In no more than ninety days," Larsen said.

"And what would you anticipate the stock price will do at that time?"

"That's when the initial public offering would be made," Larsen said, "and I believe it will at least triple on the first day of the offering. It's going to be the hottest thing since Google."

"Is the software in beta yet?" Stone asked.

"It finished beta testing yesterday," Larsen said, "and the results were fantastic—very few bugs for a brilliant new program. The next three months will be devoted to organizing the IPO and slipping subtle hints to the trade and business press to create a high level of buzz."

"And at what level will the stock be offered?" Stone asked. He turned his head slightly so that his earbug would capture their voices clearly.

"Somewhere in the fifty to seventy-five

range, probably," Larsen replied. "You could make a bundle, Mitzi, by selling on the first day."

"That's what I wanted to hear," Mitzi said.

"And at what level would you like to participate?" Larsen asked.

"I'll take a hundred thousand shares," she replied, removing an alligator checkbook from her handbag and opening it. "At fifty dollars a share. Do you have a pen, Sig?"

Larsen nearly broke an arm extracting a pen from his jacket pocket and handing it to her. "I will get you that price," he said. "I must say, I had expected a cashier's check."

"You think my personal check isn't good, Sig?" Mitzi asked, gazing at him across the table.

"Of course I don't think that, Mitzi; I'll just have to wait until the check clears before having the stock issued to you."

"Well, that will take only a few days," Mitzi said. "To whom shall I make the check?"

"Larsen Enterprises," Sig replied.

"Not directly to the company?"

"I'll have to move your money through my firm and issue my own check to the company, since its name must remain secret. I shouldn't think it would be more than four or five days before I can issue the stock."

Mitzi wrote a check for five million dollars and noted "100,000 shares" on it. "Let's be clear," she said. "This is for shares in the company that you described in the prospectus, not in Larsen Enterprises."

"Of course it is," Sig said, looking at the check. "A Charleston bank?"

"I don't have a New York account yet," Mitzi said. "Perhaps you could suggest a bank here?"

"I work with half a dozen," Larsen said, "mostly small, privately owned banks. I should think that for your purposes one of the big banks, Morgan Chase, perhaps, would be fine. Just pick a branch near your home."

"Thank you. I may do just that," Mitzi replied.

Their eggs arrived, and Mitzi and Stone began to eat.

Conversation seemed to pall, and Larsen and Sharpe seemed a bit antsy.

Larsen consulted his wristwatch. "Oh, Derek and I have another appointment downtown in half an hour," he said. "I hope you don't mind if we leave you to your breakfast." They stood up and hands were shaken. "You're going to be a very happy woman in three months," Larsen said. "Bye, now. Bye, Stone."

"Derek, could I speak to you for a moment before you leave?" Mitzi asked.

Stone put down his fork. "Please excuse me for a moment." He went looking for the men's room.

SHARPE TOOK Stone's seat. "How can I help you, Mitzi?"

"Well, Derek," she said, "my friends from Charleston were very pleased with the quality of the, ah, 'art,' you sold them, and they'd like to make another purchase."

"The same again?"

"No. This time they're less interested in the grassy picture and more interested in the powdery ones."

"All right. How much would they like?"

She leaned forward and whispered, "Ten kilos."

"My goodness," Sharpe said. "Your

friends have become more . . . commercial, shall we say!"

"Perhaps. I'm not familiar with their business arrangements."

"Of course not."

"And how soon could you deliver?"

"Two, three days," Sharpe said. "And at the same price per."

"Oh, I should think a volume discount would be in order," Mitzi said.

"I might be able to get you five percent off," Sharp replied.

"Oh, I think ten percent would be more acceptable to my friends," Mitzi said, giving him a brilliant smile.

"Given the quantity, I can do that," Sharpe said.

"We'll do it the same way as last time," Mitzi said. "I'm more comfortable with this sort of transaction in my own home."

"I don't know about that, Mitzi," Sharpe said. "My sources don't like to repeat themselves geographically. I'm sure you understand."

"No, I don't," Mitzi said firmly. "And I'm not going to do this on some street corner. Anywhere else but my home would be a deal breaker."

Sharpe shrugged. "All I can do is try," he said.

"Try hard," Mitzi replied. She shook his hand, and he went to join Larsen in the lobby, just as Stone was returning.

"How'd it go?" Stone asked.

"I got ten percent off!" Mitzi squealed. "He bridled at doing it in the apartment again, but I put my foot down." She looked around. "This is an awfully nice hotel; why don't we get a room?"

Stone looked at his watch. "I'm afraid you'll have to wait until tonight before I can jump you. Eight thirty at Elaine's?"

"Oh, all right," she said, giving him a luscious kiss.

50

STONE WALKED HOME, and as he came through the front door, Joan flagged him down.

"A Brian Doyle is waiting in your office," she said. "He insisted; he showed me a badge."

"Right," Stone said. He tiptoed down the hall to his closed door and put his ear to it. He could hear the sound of drawers being opened and closed. Silently he turned the knob, then threw open the door.

Brian Doyle was caught with a handful of cancelled checks. "What do *you* want?"

he demanded, as if Stone had entered his office unannounced.

"I think that's *my* question," Stone replied, "since you're rifling my desk."

"Oh, this?" Doyle tossed the bundle of checks onto the desk. "They were just lying here."

"No. They were at the back of my center drawer," Stone replied. "You're the one doing the lying."

"I have a perfect right to search your desk," Doyle said, as if he really did.

"I think that's called breaking and entering," Stone said.

"Not if you're my subordinate."

Stone came around the desk, grabbed Doyle's necktie, dragged him to a chair, and pushed him into it. "Let's get something straight, Brian," he said, "once and for all: I am not your subordinate in any sense of the word—intellectually, morally, or sartorially. I am your superior in every department, and if you think your little prank with the badge makes any fucking difference, I'll stick it up your ass sideways."

Doyle held up his hands in a gesture of surrender. "All right, all right, just calm down."

"State your business, then get out," Stone said, glaring down at him.

"I just want to talk about the Sharpe and Larsen bust," he said.

"So, talk."

"I'm concerned about Mitzi's safety," Doyle said.

"So soon? I've been concerned about it from day one."

"Well, me, too. Why do you think I put Tom there to take care of her?"

"Because he's her partner, and it's his responsibility, perhaps?"

"Well, sure, but he's the right guy for the job."

"So, why aren't you talking to Tom instead of me?"

"Because since we have him set up as her driver, he's not going to be welcome at the buy. You will be, though."

"I'm aware of that," Stone said. "I've just come from a meeting with Sharpe and Larsen where Mitzi proposed the big buy, and Sharpe agreed to the terms."

"I heard that from Mitzi's earpiece," Doyle said. "And why weren't you wearing yours?"

"Because it's a pain in the ass and

because I don't want you listening to every word I say," Stone replied. "I'll wear it when it's necessary."

"It's necessary every time you have a meet like that," Doyle said. He was beginning to recover his composure and adopt his superior attitude again. "We've got to have yours as a backup, in case Mitzi's goes on the fritz."

"I'll wear it when it's necessary," Stone repeated.

"I want us to have another meeting with Tiffany Baldwin about the bust," Doyle said, changing the subject.

"You have another meeting with her, not I."

"What, are you afraid of her?"

"If you knew her better," Stone said, "*you'd* be afraid of her. You'd better watch your ass, Brian, because I think even the commissioner is a little afraid of her. Otherwise, he wouldn't have been at the last meeting."

"Why should I be afraid of that bitch?" Doyle asked.

"Because she could destroy you in a heartbeat if she felt like it," Stone explained.

"And how would she do that?"

"Oh, I don't know, how about a federal grand jury indictment?"

"Indictment? For what?"

"Don't you think that if she chose to put a couple of investigators on you she wouldn't find something? You're not exactly squeaky clean; you never have been."

Doyle reddened. "I have nothing to fear from her."

"No? Well, you'd better not screw up the Larsen part of the bust, because if you do she'll come down on you like an Amazon goddess, and she'll hand you your balls."

Doyle pushed his chair back and stood up. "I can see I'm not going to get any-where with you," he said.

"Finally," Stone said. "Now let me tell you how this bust is going to go down. Mitzi has set it up at the apartment, but you're not going to have anybody in the building except me."

"Why the hell not?"

"Because Mitzi is borrowing the place from a friend of mine, and her neighbors would not take kindly to having a SWAT team in their lobby and elevators. And you can't grab him when he comes out of the building, either. You'll have to put four cars

on him and wait until he's well away from there."

"At his place? Why?"

"Probably not at his place."

"Then where?"

"If you want Sharpe and Larsen together, you'd better do it at Teterboro Airport, because they're ready to run."

Doyle shook his head. "I don't want to pull any Jersey cops in on this."

"Then you'd better have some FBI there, hadn't you?"

"That's what I want to talk to Tiffany about," Doyle said. "I don't want them there. This is our bust."

"It's yours because Tiffany allowed you to do it, and she said so in the presence of the commissioner," Stone said. "So you'd better not fuck it up, and that means having a federal presence there."

"I hate the FBI," Doyle said sullenly.

"What cop doesn't?" Stone asked. "You think you've got a monopoly?"

"I don't want to ask her for help."

"She's waiting for you to do just that, and if you don't, then this case is going to fall on you from a great height."

Doyle thought this over. "Teterboro, huh?"

"That's where Sharpe and Larsen have chartered in the past," Stone said, "but you'd better have enough people to cover Westchester Airport if they decide to go there instead."

"You think they might do that?"

"If they have the slightest inkling that you're on to them, they could do anything."

"How many people do you think we'll need?"

"An army," Stone replied. "Go put it together, and ask Tiffany for help."

Doyle got up and left, muttering under his breath.

51

MITZI LOOKED AT STONE over the rim of her glass of Knob Creek. "You seem a little down," she said. "What's wrong?"

"I'm worried about the bust," he said.

Mitzi adjusted her push-up bra. "I thought you liked it."

"Not that bust," Stone said, laughing in spite of himself. "Sharpe and Larsen."

"Sounds like a Dickensian accounting firm, doesn't it?" Mitzi said.

"I wish it were," Stone replied.

"Oh, come on, Stone. It's pretty straight-forward, once we cover all our bases."

"We don't even know where all the bases are," Stone said.

"Brian and Tom had a meeting with the U.S. Attorney this afternoon and asked for some of her people. That should help."

Stone admired her bust again. "Do you have a vest that will protect those?"

"Without looking overweight and dowdy? No."

"Just this once?"

"Maybe, after we make the buy."

"Wear it during the buy."

"You think Derek is going to shoot me in the apartment?"

"I don't know what to think. How are you going to pay for the drugs?"

"I already have, remember?"

"Sharpe is going to want real money, not a bad check."

"Tiffany had a word with Sharpe's bank."

"How do you know which bank he uses?"

"By the deposit stamp on the back of the check."

"You're not going to get a New York banker to tell Sharpe that your check has cleared and the funds are available."

"No. An FBI agent on the banker's phone line will confirm that. The bank isn't liable for what an FBI agent says to Sharpe, especially since they won't know what the agent is telling him."

Stone nodded. "I like that. Whose idea was it?"

"Mine, but I let Brian propose it to Tiffany."

"You shouldn't be so self-effacing," Stone said. "It won't do you any good. Brian will get all the kudos from the bust, and he'll leave you high and dry."

"Can I trust you with a secret?"

"Sure."

"I passed the lieutenant's exam last week."

"So you think you'll get Brian's job?"

"Only if he gets kicked upstairs," she said. "Otherwise, they'll give me a squad in Staten Island or someplace way out in Queens. But if Brian does get kicked upstairs I'll have a shot, mostly because there's not much competition at the precinct."

"They'll transfer you either way; they're not going to put a woman in charge of a squad of guys she's been working with. Never happen."

"We'll see," Mitzi said.

"Good luck to you," Stone said, raising his glass.

Dino came through the door and shot Stone a questioning glance.

"You mind if Dino joins us?" Stone asked Mitzi.

"You think I didn't expect to have dinner with Dino, too?" she asked.

Stone waved him over.

Dino sat down and ordered a Scotch. "You two still drinking that Kentucky swill?" he asked by way of a greeting.

"I don't trust any booze that has to take a boat here," Mitzi said. "Also, my daddy once told me he'd disinherit me if I drank un-American."

Dino looked at Stone, then at Mitzi. "What's the matter with him?" he asked her.

"He's worried about the bust," she replied.

"What have you got to be worried about?" he asked Stone. "Let the cops take care of it."

"By 'the cops' you mean Brian Doyle?"

"Oh," Dino said. "I get your point."

Mitzi looked at both of them askance.

"What is it with you guys? Brian's not so bad."

"We've known him longer than you have," Dino said. "He's the kind of guy who'll take credit for your work."

"It isn't enough for Brian to take the credit," Stone explained. "For him to feel good about himself, he has to make everybody else look bad."

"Oh, really!" Mitzi laughed. "Why don't you two get him in here, then put 'em on the table and we'll measure."

Dino looked at Stone and shrugged.

"Mitzi," Stone said, "has Brian ever complimented you on your work?"

"Many times," she replied.

"Has he ever said anything good about you to your captain?"

"Well," she said, "I assume he passed it up the line; he said he would."

"Have you ever read your file after a performance review?" Dino asked.

"Yes, I have."

"Has he ever given you a positive review that didn't make it sound like he was responsible for your success?"

Mitzi thought that over.

"Let me guess what he had to say," Dino

said. "He said something like, 'This officer has responded well to the training and advice of her commander.'"

Mitzi's brow furrowed, a strange sight. "I think I see what you mean," she said softly.

"Who's your rabbi?" Stone asked. "Not Brian, I trust."

"Not exactly," Mitzi said.

"You don't have a rabbi, do you?" Dino asked.

"Not exactly."

"All you've got is Brian."

"I have other friends in the department," she said uncertainly.

"I'm really glad to hear that," Dino said, as if he didn't entirely believe her.

Nobody spoke again until a waiter came to take their orders.

52

THEY STARTED FOOLING around in the cab on the way home, and by the time they had made it upstairs they were leaving a trail of clothing across the bedroom.

Mitzi undid her bra and threw it as far as she could. "Free at last!" she half-shouted. She tackled Stone, and they fell onto the bed, writhing in the mutual pleasure of their naked bodies. In a moment they were conjoined.

"I think this is what they mean by 'one flesh,'" Stone said.

"I like it," Mitzi said, sticking her tongue in his ear.

It was, perhaps, her tongue that kept him from properly hearing the first outburst.

"What?" Stone asked.

Mitzi froze. "That wasn't me," she whispered.

"What was it?"

"Lying scum!" a female voice said.

"You promised not to bring your roommate," Stone said to Mitzi.

"I didn't."

Stone sat up and looked around the darkened room, lit only by a few shafts of moonlight cutting through the venetian blinds. As he squinted, a naked female stepped out of his dressing room.

"Miserable son of a bitch," Carrie Cox said. "And with *her*." She pointed at Mitzi.

"Oh, come on, Carrie," Mitzi said, sitting up on one elbow. "You've got to get over high school."

"Carrie," Stone said. "What are you doing here?" He realized that sounded hollow, but he couldn't think of anything else to say.

"What am *I* doing here? What is *she* doing here?" Carrie pointed again.

"You want to join us, Carrie?" Mitzi asked.

"What?"

"Stone's pretty good at threesomes," Mitzi said. "Come to think of it, so am I. And I like your dancer's body."

"Mitzi, please," Stone said. "Let me handle this."

"Okay, handle it," Mitzi replied. "I'll wait here."

"Carrie," Stone said, getting to his feet, "let me get you a cab home."

"Why should *I* leave?" she demanded.

"Carrie," Mitzi said, "I'm trying to make the best of this. Either get into bed or get out of here."

Carrie seemed to be thinking it over, and Stone found himself speechless. Then Carrie disappeared into his dressing room, and a moment later she came out, holding her clothes in her arms.

"I'll get my own cab," she said, stalking out of the room.

Stone made to follow her but found his wrist locked in Mitzi's iron grip.

"She's an actress," Mitzi said. "Don't spoil her exit."

Stone sat down on the bed, and a moment later he heard the front door slam. "I hope she got her clothes on before going outside," he said.

53

CARRIE SAT, SEETHING, between Stone and Willie Leahy in the back of the cab.

"Carrie," Stone said, "I . . ."

"I'm not speaking to you," she said.

"Now wait a minute . . ."

"And I'm not listening, either."

Willie wisely kept his mouth shut.

"Willie," Stone said, "did you get a look at him?"

"At his back," Willie said. "Tall, slim, black raincoat."

"It was Max," Carrie said.

"Did you see him?"

"I didn't need to see him," she replied. "It was Max."

"Carrie, during rehearsals has anyone shown any animosity toward you?" Stone asked.

"Everyone," she replied.

"Beg pardon?"

"I'm the star; nobody likes the star."

"And you've been behaving like the star?"

"It's my right."

Stone looked at Willie. "I think the list of suspects is growing."

"Yeah," Willie said. "Anybody in the show could have done it; she's been a perfect bitch."

"What?" Carrie screamed. "You're fired!"

"I don't work for you, remember?" Willie seemed to have had enough.

"Stone, fire him this minute."

"He doesn't work for me," Stone said, "and I don't doubt for a minute that Willie is right."

Carrie started to get out of the moving cab, but Stone and Willie held her down.

"You're hurting me!" she shouted.

"No, you're hurting you," Stone said. "Stop it."

Amazingly, she went both limp and silent. The cab arrived, and the three got out.

"I want to go to bed," Carrie said. "I've got a rehearsal at ten."

"You're going to be late," Stone said. "You've got to talk to the police before you can go anywhere."

"The police? Why?"

"Because they take gunshot wounds seriously, and Lenox Hill Hospital has already reported this one to the police. We just happened to get out of the ER before they arrived."

As they reached the top of the steps an unmarked police car pulled up, and two detectives got out. Stone didn't know them.

"Carrie Cox?" one of them asked.

"Come on in, fellas," Stone said, flashing the Brian Doyle badge. "Let's get this done."

Stone left the four of them in the living room and used the kitchen phone.

"Bacchetti."

"It's Stone. Can you get over to Carrie's house?" He gave Dino the address.

"What for?"

"Somebody took a shot at her, only a graze. Probably her ex-husband. She's

supposed to open in the big show next week, and we don't want it in the papers."

"Any of our people there?"

"Two. I didn't get their names."

"Gimme fifteen minutes."

Stone went back to the living room and sat down, knowing that Willie would have steered the conversation in his absence.

"You got anything to add?" one of the detectives asked Stone.

"Nope. I wasn't here. I went to the hospital as soon as I heard."

"Why didn't you report this to the police?"

"I am the police," Stone said. "You want to see my badge again?"

"What precinct?"

"The First."

"Who's your boss?"

Stone gritted his teeth. "Lieutenant Doyle. I'm on special assignment."

"What kind of special assignment?"

"If I was allowed to tell you that it wouldn't be special," Stone explained. It went on like this until Dino arrived.

Dino showed his ID. "You two," he said, pointing two fingers at the detectives, "listen up."

The detectives tried to look attentive.

"I'm taking care of this," Dino said. "There's no report to make."

"We gotta make a report, Lieutenant," one of them said softly. Dino was well-known in the department, and they were being appropriately deferential.

"You don't gotta do nothing," Dino said, "except forget this. Mention it to nobody, and if anybody mentions it to you, refer them to me at the Nineteenth. Believe me, you don't want to be involved in this one."

The two detectives looked at each other, then back at Dino. They nodded simultaneously, got up, and left the house.

"Thank you, Dino," Carrie said. "That was sweet of you."

Dino patted her on the head. "Don't you worry about it, sweetheart." He looked at Stone. "You want a lift?"

"Please," Stone said, getting up.

"You're leaving?" Carrie asked, looking surprised.

"There's nothing more for me to do here," Stone said.

"But plenty for you to do in your bedroom," she said, pouting.

"My bedroom is none of your business,"

Stone said. "Now shut up and let Dino do his work."

Stone and Dino left the house and walked down the front steps.

"You're sure it's the ex-husband?" Dino asked Stone.

"No. Apparently, Carrie has treated the entire cast of her show like shit. It could be anybody."

"I'll have the airports watched."

"Just Teterboro," Stone said. "The guy flies himself."

"That makes it easier."

"He's off the ground by now, but the tower will have a record of his departure."

"Where does he land in Atlanta?"

"Probably Peachtree DeKalb," Stone replied.

"I'll pull a favor and get him talked to. How long would his flight take?"

"He flies a King Air. Say, three hours. All this happened between five thirty and six. If he went straight to Teterboro, he'd be in the air by seven. You've got a shot at having him met."

"But no evidence."

"Well, there is that."

"What about a bullet?"

"Passed through," Stone said, but he turned and looked at the front of the house. "There," he said, pointing at a brick with a missing chunk. "Ricocheted from there."

They both looked around for the bullet but couldn't find it.

"It'll be distorted anyway," Dino said. "Wouldn't provide any ballistics to check."

They got into Dino's car and left.

54

STONE FOUND MITZI in the garden, dunking a croissant into her coffee.

"Charleston manners?" Stone asked.

"My mother would turn over in her grave," Mitzi replied, "but I love it this way."

Stone asked Helene for some breakfast and sat down at the garden table.

"So, what was the emergency?" Mitzi asked.

"Somebody took a shot at Carrie," Stone said.

"Hit her?"

"Yes."

"Oh, good."

"Don't gloat; it wasn't that bad. She's going to rehearsal later this morning."

"I'll bet the list of suspects is a long one," Mitzi said.

"How'd you guess?"

Mitzi made a snorting sound. "You could include all the members of her high school class."

"And the cast of her show, apparently, but it was probably her ex-husband. He's been stalking her."

"You think he meant to kill her? I mean, he missed."

"Most people are lousy shots," Stone said. "The untrained just point in the general direction and yank the trigger."

"More people should train," Mitzi said.

"If they did, we'd just have a lot more successful shootings."

"Good point. Do you suppose we could persuade the NRA to support training shooters badly?"

Stone laughed. "Probably not."

"You were good last night," Mitzi said. "There are times when I'm so discouraged with men that I think about becoming a card-carrying lesbian. You've restored my faith in men."

"Really?"

"Well, mostly; a lot of them are still shits. Women are more empathetic."

"Am I a shit?"

"Never," Mitzi said, "at least, not on purpose."

"Well, I guess that's a compliment."

"A higher one than you might think."

"You said you took the lieutenant's exam?"

"Right."

"I thought you were a detective first grade."

"I made sergeant two years ago. I don't talk about it much; three members of my squad flunked the sergeant's exam."

"All the more reason for the brass to transfer you if you get the promotion."

"I have other things going for me," she said. "Some of them might offset male cop jealousy."

"Has the department come that far since I retired?"

"Ask me after a few dozen more cops retire or die."

"You think Brian will get bumped upstairs?" Stone asked.

"I don't think he'll be where he is much longer," she replied.

"Not even if this bust is a big success?"

"If it is, it won't be Brian's fault. I think enough people in the department know that."

"I hope you're right," Stone said.

Helene came into the garden from the kitchen, carrying Stone's breakfast and the cordless phone. She handed it to Stone. "For you." She went back to the kitchen.

"Hello?"

"It's Tiffany."

"Good morning."

"Are you alone?"

Stone thought about this before he answered. "Yes," he said finally.

"Let's have dinner tonight."

Stone didn't hesitate. "I don't think that's a good idea until this bust is over. Let's not get talked about right now."

Mitzi's eyebrows went up. She mouthed, "Tiffany?"

Stone nodded. "There's something else I want to talk to you about, though."

"What's that?" Tiffany asked.

"I think we need a chopper to cover this bust."

"Why?"

"We're dealing with two experienced and very tricky con men, and I'm worried about being thin on the ground."

"Why can't the NYPD furnish the chopper?"

"The demand for their air fleet is heavy; yours is lighter."

"Should I speak to the commissioner about this?"

"I don't think that's necessary," Stone replied. "All I want is to be able to make a cell phone call and get something in the air instantly."

"You worry too much."

"I think it's best to worry too much before the bust than afterward."

"Oh, all right, I'll make the call, but you owe me for this one."

"Yes, I owe you."

Tiffany hung up without saying goodbye.

"That's interesting," Mitzi said.

"Asking for a helicopter?"

"Yes, that, too, but more that Tiffany is calling you."

"You know we have some history."

"Everybody who reads 'Page Six' in the *Post* knows you have some history."

"That was speculation; I didn't appear in the photographs, and they couldn't prove that the woman was Tiffany."

"Sorry, I should have Mirandized you before I asked about that. But why is Tiffany calling you?"

"She wants to have dinner."

"She wants a second chance to become infamous?"

"That's an interesting way to put it," Stone said. "I never considered that dining with me carried the risk of infamy."

"I shouldn't think it would do either of you any good. It's obviously a toxic relationship."

"Mitzi, you don't have to talk me out of it; I don't want to have dinner with her."

"Well, you did put her off, didn't you?"

"I thought it best."

"I'm glad," she said, leaning over and kissing him on the forehead.

Stone rolled his eyes upward. "Do I have lipstick on my forehead now?"

"It's very becoming," Mitzi said, patting his cheek.

Stone resisted the urge to wipe it off with his napkin.

Mitzi put down her napkin and stood up. "Well, I have to go to work."

Stone stood, too. "Have you heard anything from Derek about the buy?"

"Not yet. Don't worry; he'll call. He's on the hook."

"I hope we can keep him there," Stone said. He walked her to the front door and let her out, then went down to his office.

Joan walked in with the mail, took one look at him, and burst out laughing.

"What?" Stone asked, mystified.

She put the mail on his desk. "Oh, nothing," she said, then she went back to her office, chortling.

55

Dino was uncharacteristically late for dinner at Elaine's. Stone and Elaine were sitting together, chatting, waiting for him to show. Stone ordered a second Knob Creek.

"You're looking better," Elaine said. "You didn't look so hot last night."

"I'm feeling better," Stone admitted.

"You got laid last night, huh?"

"In a manner of speaking. You know Carrie, the actress?"

"Sure. From what I hear on the grapevine, everybody's going to know her next week."

"Right."

"You weren't with her last night, were with Mitzi."

"Right again. I had to go to the hospital very early this morning, because Carrie's ex took a shot at her."

"She's dead?"

Stone shook his head. "Barely wounded. She'll make opening night."

"Somebody ought to lock that guy up."

"Dino's working on it."

At the mention of his name, Dino walked through the front door and headed for his table. A waiter saw him and ordered his usual Scotch. He sat down at the table, and Elaine pinched his cheek.

"Aw, come on, Elaine," Dino said. "Everybody's watching."

"You two enjoy," Elaine said and moved to another table.

"Yeah, I know," Dino said to Stone. "I'm late."

"What happened in Atlanta?" Stone asked.

"You mind if I get a drink first?" A drink appeared before him, and he took a tug at it.

"So?"

"Don't rush me."

"Me rush you?"

"All the time."

Stone sighed, sat back, sipped his bourbon, and waited for Dino to speak.

Dino took another tug at his Scotch. "Okay," he said, "two Atlanta PD detectives met your man at the airport. He denied being in New York and showed them a flight plan from Charleston."

"Anybody can run off a flight plan on a computer," Stone said. "That doesn't mean he flew it."

"They called the FAA, but there was some screwup. Apparently, he did fly from Charleston, but they weren't able to figure out when he got there."

"And I'll bet he has a Charleston alibi."

"You got it," Dino said. "And since we don't have any evidence against the guy—no ID, no bullet—he can't be touched."

"So that's why you were late?"

"No. I was at a meeting with Brian Doyle and the commissioner."

"Subject?"

"Your pending bust."

"It's not *my* pending bust. It's Brian's; he owns it."

"Yeah, I know, and that's what worries

me. I hear you got Tiffany to give you a chopper."

"Shit! Was that mentioned at the meeting?"

"No, but I have other sources."

"I think we need it."

"I think you're right," Dino replied. "If there's a way to fuck this up, Brian will find it. He's a walking, framed copy of Murphy's Law."

"How did he ever make lieutenant?" Stone asked.

"You mean, whose cock was he . . .?"

"Exactly."

"I think he did whatever was necessary."

"It doesn't speak well of the NYPD that they would promote the guy."

"Look, you and I could name a dozen guys who got promoted above their level of competence," Dino said.

"Yeah, we could. I just wish we didn't have one of them running this bust."

"All right, tell me who you're worried about," Dino said.

"Mitzi," Stone replied, "and Hildy Parsons."

"Oh, that's right. Hildy is why you're in this."

"Exactly. But I've come to feel a lot for Mitzi, and she could get hurt."

"You want me to be around when it goes down?"

"Yes, please. I'd like you at Rita Gammage's apartment when the buy is made, and we'll take it from there."

"When?"

"I don't know yet; we're waiting for a call from Derek Sharpe to tell us he has the goods. Mitzi will see that we have some notice, though."

"Okay, I'm available."

"Do me a favor?"

"What is it this time?"

"I need you to call the NYPD flight department and inquire about a helicopter pad somewhere in the vicinity of Park and Seventy-second Street."

"Okay, I can do that."

"I think that's all I need until the bust goes down," Stone said. His cell phone vibrated on his belt, and he dug it out of its holster. "Hello?"

"It's Mitzi."

"Hello, there."

"The buy is tomorrow morning, eleven a.m., at the apartment."

"Gotcha. Dino and I will be there early."

"Great."

"Something I'd like to know about the apartment."

"What?"

"The windows, the ones overlooking Park Avenue, do they open?"

"You mean, are they not sealed shut?"

"Exactly."

"Hang on."

Stone waited until she came back.

"Yes, they open," she said.

"Thanks. See you tomorrow." He hung up. "We're on," he said to Dino. "Eleven a.m. tomorrow."

"Good."

"You still have your old .22 target pistol?" Stone asked.

"Yeah, it's in my safe."

"Bring it."

"Why?"

"Just bring it."

Dinner arrived, and they dug in.

In spite of the bourbon and the good food, Stone was nervous again. He didn't like being nervous; something bad usually happened when he was nervous.

56

STONE WOKE EARLY, shaved, showered, and got to Rita's apartment at eight. Dino met him on the sidewalk.

"I didn't get breakfast," Dino said.

"Neither did I," Stone replied, ushering him into the building, "but we will." He gave the doorman their names and waited until they were allowed upstairs. Before they went to the elevator, Stone pulled the door-man to the front door and pointed. "See that parking space?"

"Yes, sir."

Stone put a hundred-dollar bill in his

hand. "Please make sure no one parks there but a Mr. Sharpe. He drives a black Mercedes, and he'll be here around eleven. Tell him that Miss Mitzi reserved it for him."

"I'll put a couple of cones out and watch for him," the doorman said.

Mitzi answered the door in a silk dressing gown, and it looked as though she was wearing nothing under it. The sight stirred Stone, but there wasn't time.

"You want some breakfast?" she asked.

"You betcha," Stone said.

She led Dino down the hall toward the kitchen, but Stone went to a front window and made sure it would open, then he went to the kitchen and sat down at the table with Mitzi, Rita, and Dino. Moments later they were eating omelets and croissants, Mitzi dunking hers.

They lingered at the table, chatting, until after ten, then the women went to dress. Stone walked to the big stainless-steel refrigerator, took two eggs from the door shelf, and slipped them into his jacket pocket. Then he went into the living room and began reading the *Times*.

Dino joined him and took the Business section.

"Since when did you start reading about business?" Stone asked, surprised.

"When I got my hands on some money." Dino had received a generous settlement when he was divorced.

"So now you're a capitalist?"

"You bet your ass."

"You brought the .22 pistol?" Dino had won a department championship with that pistol.

"It's on my belt," Dino said, not bothering to show him. "Are you armed?"

"I am," Stone said.

"Not that you could hit anything."

"Why do you think I asked you to bring the target pistol?" Stone said. He didn't argue with Dino's opinion of his marksmanship.

At ten thirty Dino used his cell phone to check on the status of the bust, then he hung up.

"Everything set?" Stone asked.

"Yep."

"Oh, what did you find out about a helicopter pad?"

"There's a tennis club a couple of doors from the corner of Seventy-ninth that's being renovated. They're taking down the nets and posts on the rooftop courts. My car is parked a block from here; my driver will run us there."

"How many courts on the roof?"

"Four, stacked."

Stone called the number Tiffany had given him for the helicopter pilot.

"Hello."

"This is Stone Barrington."

"Right, Mr. Barrington. We're all set."

"How long a flight from your position to the corner of Seventy-second and Park?"

"Two minutes."

"At eleven a.m. sharp, start your engines and be ready." He explained about the tennis club.

"I know the place; I've seen it from the air. The space is plenty big."

"See you there," Stone said.

At ten minutes to eleven the buzzer rang from the doorman, and Mitzi answered it. "Send Mr. Sharpe up," she said, then hung up. "He's on his way; you two had better get into the kitchen."

Stone went to the window and opened

it. The black Mercedes was parked, nine stories down. He leaned out the window, aimed carefully, and dropped an egg. "Bull's-eye!" he said.

"What the fuck are you doing?" Dino asked.

Stone didn't reply but aimed the second egg. "Hah!" he shouted. "Let's get to the kitchen."

They ran down the hallway just as the doorbell rang.

Mitzi opened the door and let Sharpe in. He was carrying two catalogue cases.

"Who else is here?" he asked.

"Just the maid," Mitzi said. "You're not going to get all paranoid on me again, are you?"

"Let's get this done," Sharpe said. He knew the way to the study.

Mitzi sat him down, and he opened both catalogue cases and began removing one-kilo bricks of cocaine.

"Do you promise me that this cocaine is just as good as the first shipment you sold me?"

"If anything, it's better," Sharpe said.

"Okay, put the bricks back into the cases," she said, and Sharpe did so.

"I assume my check cleared or you wouldn't be here," Mitzi said.

"You're absolutely right," Sharpe replied. "I've already wire-transferred it out of the country."

"We're done, then?"

Sharpe stood up. "We are. Take care of yourself, Mitzi."

"You sound like you're going somewhere."

"Just a little vacation. I'll be back in a couple of weeks to supply your friends again, if they're still in business."

"They'll still be in business," she said. She showed him to the door and let him out. Then she turned, leaned against the door, and heaved a great sigh. She went to the phone and pressed the Page button. "He's gone," she said. "Let's get moving."

Stone and Dino ran down the hall and into the living room, and Stone continued to the window. "Any problems?"

"Not a one," Mitzi said.

Stone looked out the window. "There he goes."

Dino called for his car, while Stone called his helicopter, and then they both ran to the elevator.

When they emerged from the apartment

building they found Dino's car waiting for them at the curb. They hopped in and, after making a quick U-turn, raced up Park Avenue and around the corner of Seventy-ninth Street.

As they turned the corner, Stone saw the helicopter approaching the building and inside a cop who was holding an elevator that would take them up. They emerged from the top floor fire door onto the roof just as the aircraft landed on the tennis courts, jumped in, and buckled their seat belts.

Stone took the left seat, next to the pilot, and put on his headset. "Okay," he said, "we're looking for a black sedan that's been marked with two raw eggs."

"How'd you do that?" the pilot asked.

"From a great height," Stone replied.

57

STONE SPOKE INTO the headset microphone. "Let's stay as low as possible, until we spot the car. When we do, let's go higher, so as not to worry our man."

"Shall we try Park Avenue first?" the pilot asked.

"Affirmative," Stone said.

The helicopter rose vertically from the tennis courts for a couple of hundred feet, then the pilot executed a ninety-degree turn toward Park Avenue and pointed the machine downtown. They had moved only a few blocks when Stone looked down and saw the egg-decorated Mercedes.

The pilot made the turn north. "Well," he said, "I hope it's the right helicopter."

"So do I," Stone said.

"Is the airplane going to be waiting?" Sharpe asked Larsen.

"It's already there," Larsen replied. "I'll call him when we're five minutes out and tell him to start the engines."

"Man, oh, man," Larsen said. "This is really happening."

"What's happening?" Hildy asked. "We're just going to the Bahamas, right?"

"You'll see when we get there," Sharpe said.

Dino tapped Stone on the shoulder and spoke through his headset from the rear seat. "What the fuck is happening?"

Stone turned toward the rear seats. "They took a helicopter from the West Side Heliport," Stone replied, "and they're headed for Westchester. Just enjoy the view of the Hudson."

Mitzi spoke up. "Should I call Brian?"

"I guess you'd better," Stone said. "Tell him to alert the team at Westchester that

Sharpe and Larsen are headed there in a helicopter and to arrest them on sight."

"Will do," Mimi said.

Stone turned back and looked north. "I don't see the chopper," he said.

"I was just about to mention that," the pilot replied. "I don't see him, either. He was there; then I looked at my chart for a couple of seconds and when I looked up, he was gone."

"I heard that," Dino said. "Now what?"

58

STONE WAS ANXIOUSLY LOOKING UP and down both shores of the Hudson River. The George Washington Bridge was coming up and the pilot climbed another hundred feet to clear it.

"I don't get it," Stone said. "How could a helicopter just vanish?"

"He's low over land somewhere," the pilot replied. "It's hard to spot a helicopter from above when it's flying low.

Stone began concentrating on looking down. "There . . . No, that's a car."

"See what I mean?"

"Well, it doesn't matter how low he flies

if he's going to Westchester," Stone said. "We've got that covered, and they'll see the chopper when it lands."

"What if he's not going to Westchester?" the pilot asked.

"What are the alternatives?" Stone asked.

"I don't know—Albany? Hartford? Bridge-port?"

Stone remembered something. "When I was getting my instrument rating, I flew some approaches at Oxford, Connecti-cut."

"That's worth a try," the pilot said, flipping through his airport guide. "Five-thousand-foot runway—that's plenty for a corporate jet. If you've got Westchester covered, they won't miss us."

"It's on the way to Hartford," Stone said. "Let's at least take a look at it."

The pilot put the airport's identifier, OXC, into his GPS and swung right, following the needle.

"How long?" Stone asked.

"Twelve minutes," the pilot replied.

IN THE other helicopter the pilot turned and addressed Larsen. "Five minutes," he said.

"I'll call the airplane," Larsen said to Sharpe. He tapped a speed-dial key on his cell phone and listened. "I'm not getting through," he said.

"We may be moving too fast for the cell phone to capture a tower," Sharpe said. "It doesn't matter, we'll be there in five minutes."

"SIX MINUTES," Stone's pilot said.

"Has this thing got any more speed?" Stone asked.

"I'll push it," the pilot said. Then, a moment later, "Four minutes." He looked up. "Can you see the airport?" he asked.

Stone looked hard. "No. We're too low; it just looks like countryside."

The pilot climbed another two hundred feet. "There," he said. "Twelve o'clock and five miles."

"There's the other chopper," Stone said, "setting down now, and I can see what looks like a Citation on the ramp." He turned toward the rear. "Looks like we've got 'em, Dino," he said.

Dino reached into his jacket and produced a Colt .45, 1911 model, and checked it. Mitzi was checking her weapon, too.

"You are wearing your vest, aren't you?"

She pretended not to be able to hear him.

Stone turned back to the pilot. "Set this thing down right in front of the jet, and keep the rotor turning. He won't be able to taxi."

"Got it," the pilot said, and started to descend fast. He called Oxford tower and announced his intentions.

Stone watched as people began to get out of the helicopter and hand baggage to a uniformed pilot. He turned back to Mitzi. "As soon as your cell phone works, get hold of Brian and tell him we're at Oxford, Connecticut." He made cell phone motions.

Mitzi nodded and began trying her cell.

"What's your plan?" Dino asked. "As if you had one."

"We're going to set down in front of the Citation so that he can't taxi, jump out, arrest anybody who moves, shoot anybody who produces a gun."

They were half a mile out now.

"Why did you want me to bring the .22 target pistol?"

Stone looked at him. "I want you to shoot Hildy Parsons."

"*What*?"

"Don't kill her, but make sure she's not able to run for the jet."

"You're crazy. I'm not shooting her!"

"Don't let her get on that airplane, Dino!" Stone turned back just in time to see them set down twenty yards from the Citation. Dino was already getting out of the copter, followed by Mitzi.

Stone unbuckled his belt and started moving toward the door. "Oh, shit," he said aloud, "we're not close enough to the jet."

By the time he made it onto the tarmac everybody on the other copter was running toward the Citation. Sig Larsen produced a pistol and got off a couple rounds. Somebody—Dino or Mitzi—shot him, and he fell to one knee. Derek Sharpe grabbed his arm and started pulling him toward the Citation. Hildy had gone back to the other helicopter for her purse and was not yet running toward the Citation, which had its engines running and was making a sharp turn to the right to clear the helicopter's blades.

"Shoot Hildy!" Stone shouted to Dino, who was closer to the airplane, then pulled

his own gun and began firing at the nose-wheel of the Citation, missing on the first two shots.

Out of the corner of his eye, he saw Hildy go down. Then he aimed again at the Citation's nosewheel and saw it go flat. Sharpe had dragged Larsen aboard the airplane and was trying to close the door. Hildy was screaming at him from the tar-mac and trying to drag herself toward the airplane, which was still moving, even with the flattened nosewheel.

Stone ran to the airplane, jerked the half-closed door open, got hold of Sharpe's jacket lapel, and jerked him off the airplane, spilling Larsen out as well. The airplane stopped moving, and the engines began to spool down. Dino produced handcuffs and went to work. Stone looked around. Where was Mitzi?

Stone turned and looked back. Mitzi was lying on her back, propped up on one elbow. "Oh, God!" he shouted and began to run toward her. He got a glimpse of Hildy and saw blood on her skirt. Dino had put a .22 slug into her ass.

Stone reached Mitzi, got an arm around her, and pulled her into a sitting position.

He realized immediately that she wasn't wearing a vest. "Where are you hit?" he shouted over the noise of the helicopter, whose rotor was still turning.

"I'm not hit!" she cried. "I broke a heel and fell!"

Stone looked at her feet and saw the shoe with the missing heel. He helped her to her feet. "Call 911 and get an ambulance; we've got two down, Larsen and Hildy. Then call Brian again."

She grabbed her phone and began dialing while Stone ran to help Dino.

"Well, you finally hit the nosewheel," Dino said, snapping cuffs onto Sharpe. "How many rounds did that take?"

"One," Stone replied. "The first two were practice."

59

STONE WAS BACK at his desk late that afternoon when the phone buzzed.

"Bill Eggers on one," Joan said.

"Hello, Bill?"

"You *shot* Hildy Parsons?" Eggers said with outrage in his voice.

"Certainly not," Stone said. "There were bullets flying everywhere, and if you'd like to check the bullet that struck her against my gun, you're welcome to."

"Were you carrying a .22?"

"Of course not. You're not going to stop anybody with a .22. I was carrying a 9mm."

"Hildy Parsons was shot with a .22. Cops don't carry .22s."

"My point exactly," Stone replied.

"Then who shot her?"

"Maybe some hunter in the woods. It's a rural area, you know; lots of hunters up there."

"What would a hunter shoot with a .22?"

"Squirrels? Rabbits? Probably some kid."

"Philip Parsons is livid."

"Hildy Parsons is alive."

"But wounded."

"If she hadn't been wounded she might have made it to that jet, and Philip Parsons wouldn't have a daughter anymore. You might explain to Parsons that Sharpe and Larsen were carrying a couple of million in drugs and that much more in cash, and if they had made it, his daughter would have been a fugitive from justice, and he would be spending millions fighting her extradition. As it is, she was just an innocent bystander. I've seen to that."

Eggers thought that over. "Did you hear that, Philip?"

"Yes, Bill, I did."

"I didn't know I was on a conference call, Philip," Stone said, "or I would have been more politic in my statements. Maybe."

"I'm glad you were blunt, Stone," Parsons said.

"How is Hildy?"

"They're keeping her in the hospital tonight for observation. She'll be home tomorrow."

"Have the police questioned her yet?"

"No, it was smart of you to have her taken to New York Hospital."

"It might be a good idea if I have a conversation with her before she goes home," Stone said.

"Now would be a good time," Larkin said. "I'm with her."

"I'll be right there," Stone said.

STONE TOOK a cab to the hospital and found the room. There were two bored-looking detectives sitting in the waiting room.

"Come in, Stone," Philip Larkin said.

Hildy was propped up in bed in a large, sunny room overlooking the East River, and there were flowers everywhere.

"I don't want to speak to him," she said to her father, pointing at Stone.

"Shut up, Hildy," Philip replied.

Stone stood by the bed. "You don't have to talk to me," he said. "In fact, it's better if you don't. You just have to listen." He dragged up a chair and sat down. "You're up to your neck in this, Hildy, and the only way you can get out of it is if you do exactly as I say. There are two police detectives waiting outside to see you . . ."

"I'm *not* going to talk to the police."

"Shut up, Hildy," her father said, "and listen."

Stone continued. "You're going to tell them that you've been seeing Derek Sharpe socially and that you hardly know Sig Larsen. You're going to tell them that you have no idea what happened earlier today, that you had been invited to go to the Bahamas for a few days, and then people started shooting."

"That is exactly what I thought," Hildy said.

"Good, then you won't have to remember a story. You believed Derek Sharpe to be an artist and nothing more. You had no

idea that he might be involved in any sort of illegal activity, and you are shocked at the allegations. Got that?"

Hildy folded her arms and looked down at her knees. "Yes," she said softly.

"As soon as the police have finished questioning you, you are going on a vacation, somewhere out of the country. You will not return for Sharpe's trial, and you will not speak of him to any person in this country or abroad. You will carry a cell phone, so that the authorities will be able to reach you if necessary. If you have told them what I asked you to they will not call you as a witness, since you have no knowledge of Sharpe's extralegal activities. Is all that perfectly clear?"

"Yes," she said. "But, Daddy, I don't want to go on a vacation."

"You will go to the house in Tuscany as soon as your doctor says you're well enough to travel," Philip Parsons said. "Once there, you may invite friends to join you. You will not come back until Derek Sharpe has been tried and convicted, no matter how long that takes."

"Well," she said sheepishly, "Italy is very nice this time of year."

WHEN STONE RETURNED home there was a hand-delivered envelope on his desk. He ripped it open and found a single ticket to the opening night of Carrie's show. There was no note.

60

STONE MET DINO at Elaine's at eight thirty. "You're off the hook for shooting Hildy," he said.

"What do you mean, 'off the hook'?" Dino said. "I was never on the hook."

"You're just lucky no one searched you and found the .22."

"There was no luck involved. The Connecticut State Police were not going to search an NYPD lieutenant."

"That's why you're off the hook. I spoke with her father this afternoon, and he's good with it, too. I think he suspects some-

thing, but he got his daughter back, so he's not going to make a fuss."

"Is Hildy going to get nailed for her part in this thing?" Dino asked.

"No. I sat in on her questioning this afternoon. She played dumb and innocent, too."

"But she had to know something about what Sharpe was doing."

"Maybe, but she doesn't now, so she's not going to have to testify against him." Stone picked up a menu. "You ready to order?"

"I'm expecting a guest," Dino said. "Let's wait."

The waiter brought them both another drink, and Dino kept checking his wristwatch.

Finally, the door opened, and the commissioner entered, preceded by Mitzi, who looked smashing in a red dress.

Stone stood up, shook her hand, then the commissioner's. "Good evening, sir," he said. "I didn't know you frequented Elaine's."

"I have been coming here since Giuliani was mayor," the commissioner replied,

looking around. He turned to the waiter. "You got any single malts?"

The waiter recited the list, and the commissioner chose one. "The lady will have a Beefeater's martini with a twist, not too dry," he said.

Stone shot a glance at Mitzi, but she was not looking at him. However, she delivered a sharp kick to his ankle under the table.

The drinks came, and the commissioner raised his glass. "To successful operations," he said, "and to those who carry them out, even when unexpected circumstances occur."

They all drank, and then they ordered dinner.

"Aren't we missing the, ah, leader of the operation?" Stone asked.

"Oh, Lieutenant Doyle is home studying, I expect," the commissioner said.

"Studying?" Stone asked, puzzled.

"He has been promoted to inspector, and tomorrow he starts his new job as lecturer on tactics at the police academy, his reward for a job well done."

Stone nearly choked on his Knob Creek.

"That said, I think we should raise our

glasses to Mitzi," the commissioner said.
"This afternoon she was promoted to
lieutenant, and tomorrow she will command the detective squad at the First Precinct."

Stone's mouth dropped open, and Mitzi
reached over, placed a finger under his
chin, and closed it. "Congratulations," he
managed to say.

Dino spoke up. "I heard there were
some transfers from that squad," he said,
"to new assignments in Brooklyn."

"Yes," the commissioner replied, "all pro-
motions. Mitzi will pick her own people."

"All of them women," Mitzi said.

The commissioner looked at her. "*All* of
them women?"

She regarded him evenly. "Yes, *sir.*"

Dinner was served. When they were
done, the commissioner stood up, followed
by Mitzi. "We have to be going," he said.
"Barrington, give me your badge," he said.

Stone fished out his Doyle-provided
badge and handed it over.

The commissioner placed a small velvet
box on the table. "Open it," he said.

Stone picked up the box and opened
it. Inside was a retirement badge for a

Detective First Grade. From its weight, he judged it to be not plated but solid gold.

The commissioner handed him an envelope. "Here are your retirement papers," he said, "at your new grade." He shook everyone's hand and left, taking Mitzi with him.

Stone sat down.

"You look stunned," Dino said.

"I am."

"You should be. By the way, I'm your date for the theater tomorrow night."

Stone looked at him. "You?"

"You were hoping Mitzi? Not going to happen. Carrie sent me a single ticket, too, for the seat next to yours. In fact, I don't think you're going to be seeing as much of Mitzi in the future."

"What's going on, Dino?"

"Word is, the commissioner is retiring."

"What's that got to do with Mitzi?"

"Word is, he's getting married, too."

Stone stared at him. "You wouldn't kid me?"

"I kid you not."

"I need another drink," Stone said.

61

Dino picked up Stone in his department car and drove him to the theater.

"Is this a kosher use of the car?" Stone asked as they got out.

"I'm on duty," Dino said.

"What are you talking about?"

Dino saw someone he knew and turned to shake hands. The lights were flashing, and they hurried inside to take their seats, which were fourth row on the center aisle.

"Not bad seats, huh?" Dino said.

"What was that about being on duty?" Stone asked, but his question was drowned

out by a flood of music from the orchestra pit.

Stone and Dino watched as the curtain went up on a nearly bare stage—only a park bench and a lamppost. The backdrop was an autumnal view of Central Park.

Carrie moved onstage, holding the hand of a young man, and they began to dance. After a moment Carrie began to sing.

Stone relaxed and enjoyed it.

WHEN THE FIRST-ACT curtain came down, the audience roared and wouldn't stop until Carrie and other members of the cast came back for a curtain call. Stone had never seen a first-act curtain call, and the critics sitting near him were on their feet, too.

"Have you ever seen anything like this?" Stone asked.

"Nope," Dino said. Then, as the curtain was being slowly lowered for the intermission, a single gunshot rang out.

Stone and Dino turned and looked toward the rear of the theater, where they saw a scuffle going on in the dress circle. A woman screamed, and a second shot was fired, bringing down a drizzle of plaster from above.

"Stay here," Dino said, and he ran up the aisle, pushing people out of his way.

As Stone stood watching the scuffle in the dress circle, he thought he saw Willie Leahy there. Dino joined the group, and someone was dragged up the stairs and out of the theater. The crowd now moved toward the lobby for intermission.

Stone was sipping a glass of champagne at the bar when Dino returned.

"There appears to be something you didn't tell me," Stone said to him.

"I told you I was on duty," Dino said.

"Was that Max Long doing the shooting?"

"Carrie's ex? One and the same."

"How did this come about?"

"I had a tip from Atlanta. Max took off in his King Air this afternoon and, surprise, surprise, turned up at Teterboro. He's been followed ever since by my guys."

"And how did Willie Leahy get involved?"

"Willie took a personal interest in the events," Dino replied. "We got him a seat behind Max."

"And you didn't tell me any of this?"

"I didn't want to concern you," Dino said. "Now let's go enjoy the rest of the show."

Before the curtain went up, Del Wood walked to center stage and held up his hands for silence. "Ladies and gentlemen," he said, "I wish to apologize for the small disturbance at the end of the first act. It appears that someone wasn't enjoying my show as much as you were and wished to register a protest. He has been relocated and will not disturb us further. Please enjoy the rest of the show. Thank you." He walked off the stage to a rousing hand.

AND ENJOY the rest of the show Stone and Dino did, along with the rest of the audience. There were eighteen curtain calls, and the stage was flooded with flowers. The critics rushed up the aisle while the audience was still standing and beating their hands together.

"I'd say it's going to run," Dino said.

AFTERWARD, Stone and Dino went to Sardi's for the opening night party to wait for the reviews with the other invited guests.

Somebody rushed in with stacks of the papers around midnight, and someone else stood on a table and read them aloud, a series of raves, particularly for the show's star.

Stone stood with Dino at the edge of the crowd, watching Carrie accept the congratulations of everyone. At no time did she let go of the hand of her handsome young costar, who was wearing almost as much of her lipstick as she was.

There was a tiny moment when Carrie spotted Stone and gave him a small wave, as if to say good-bye.

Stone and Dino walked into the cool night air and got into Dino's car.

"Elaine's," Dino said to his driver.

"Right," Stone said.

LATER, STONE RETURNED HOME, let himself in, and went upstairs to his bedroom. There was a note on his pillow from Joan.

Stone, I haven't wanted to mention this but something strange has been going on. I've noticed from my office window that a woman has been standing across the street from the house for periods of two hours or more for the past three days. She is accompanied by a large man who seems concerned for her welfare, but she does nothing but stare at the house. Finally, the man seems to persuade her to leave, but

she always returns. I thought you should know about this.

Stone sat down on the bed, put his face in his hands, and made a low, moaning noise.

AUTHOR'S NOTE

I am happy to hear from readers, but you should know that if you write to me in care of my publisher, three to six months will pass before I receive your letter, and when it finally arrives it will be one among many, and I will not be able to reply.

However, if you have access to the Internet, you may visit my website at www.stuartwoods.com, where there is a button for sending me e-mail. So far, I have been able to reply to all my e-mail, and I will continue to try to do so.

If you send me an e-mail and do not receive a reply, it is probably because you

are among an alarming number of people who have entered their e-mail address incorrectly in their mail software. I have many of my replies returned as undeliverable.

Remember: e-mail, reply; snail mail, no reply.

When you e-mail, please do not send attachments, as I *never* open these. They can take twenty minutes to download, and they often contain viruses.

Please do not place me on your mailing lists for funny stories, prayers, political causes, charitable fund-raising, petitions or sentimental claptrap. I get enough of that from people I already know. Generally speaking, when I get e-mail addressed to a large number of people, I immediately delete it without reading it.

Please do not send me your ideas for a book, as I have a policy of writing only what I myself invent. If you send me story ideas, I will immediately delete them without reading them. If you have a good idea for a book, write it yourself, but I will not be able to advise you on how to get it published. Buy a copy of *Writer's Market* at any bookstore; that will tell you how.

Anyone with a request concerning events